BAR, CLUB & LOUNGE GUIDE

2006 NEW YORK

A SHECKY'S MEDIA, INC. PUBLICATION

NEW YORK • NEW YORK

FINLANDIA®
MANGO FUSION
VODKA.

purely refreshing.

Published by
Shecky's Publishing, Inc.
678 Broadway, 4th Fl.
New York, NY 10012

T: 212.242.2566
F: 212.242.3704
E: info@sheckys.com
www.sheckys.com

CEO and Founder: Chris Hoffman
President: Claudia Chan
Art Director: Pas Niratbhand
Senior Editor: Erin Donnelly
Assistant Editor: Brianne Disylvester
Contributing Editors: Brian Niemietz, Kerry Smith
Photographers: Ginelle Ligon, Alecia Reddick, Patrik Rytikangas, Supong Aroonpattanachai
Editorial Assistants: Donitra Clemons, Chris Egan, Rebecca Krause, Monica Perry, David Ragen,
Alecia Reddick, Zoe Swartz
Design Assistants: Ginelle Ligon, Tony Moussa
Ad Sales Associates: Anthony Santorelli, Elizabeth Scherle
Distribution Manager: Kevin Walter
Advertising Coordinators: Jack Posniak, Sara Motejl
Marketing Coordinator: Rashida Boyd
Operations Coordinator: Tamara Rudorfer

Contributing Writers: Diana Adams, Catherine Adcock, Melanie Ahlf, Mae Anderson, Alec Appelbaum, Krista Apple, Stefanie
Arck, Cindy Augustine, Amanda Becker, Michelle Blackley, Jason Boehm, Wynne Boelt, David Botti, Amy Braunschwieger,
Ji Chong, Donitra Clemons, Jessica Cogan, Jo-Anne Costanzo, Brandy Crawford, Daniel Cumberland, Aimee Deeken, Ken
Derry, Fernando DiNino, Brianne Disylvester, Erin Donnelly, Katherine Downs, Clayton Dowty, Mike Dressel, Tanya Dukes,
David Ewalt, Paige Ferrari, Meredith Fisher, McCord Fitzsimmons, Brian Freedman, Angela Gaimari, Matthew Goldberg,
Sharon Gorgiiss, Meredith Grant, Lain Hart, Corinne Iozzio, Reed Jackson, Neil Janowitz, Russ Josephs, Rosa Jurjevics,
Jacqueline Kabat, Jackie Kane, Erin Kandel, Larry Koestler, Rebecca Krause, Nancy Lambert, Kendra Levin, Vadim
Liberman, Becky Lucas, Daniel Maurer, Erika Mayo, Johnny Mays, Clare McCarthy, Emily McCombs, Stasha Mills,
Christopher Moloney, Ken Mondschein, Ali Morra, Ellen Moynihan, Brian Niemietz, Michelle Oberfell, Kevin O'Donoghue,
Sharon Pacuk, Claire Marie Pastre, Meredith Quinn, Adam Rathe, Alecia Reddick, Denise Rehrig, Amanda Reid, Katy Resch,
Kimberly Reyes, Christine Richmond, Benjamin Rippey, Andrea Rizzo, Carlos Rountree, Hugh Ryan, Christina Schoen, Amy
Shearn, Hunter Slaton, Jordan Smedberg, Daniel Hightower Smith, Kerry Smith, AnneLise Sorenson, Carla Sosenko,
Corynne Steindler, Cullen Thomas, Justin Tomsovic, Pauls Toutonghi, Matt Ufford, Teresa Von Fuchs, Michelle Waleck,
Callie Watts, Kristina Weise, Sarah White, Stephanie Woods, Carlyn Worstell, Emily Zdyrko

Publishers note: No fees or services were rendered in exchange for inclusion in this book.

Please note that while every effort was made to ensure the accuracy of phone numbers, addresses, hours, policies,
prices, and details at the time of publication, any of the criteria is subject to change so please call ahead.

All of the editorial in this guide is the sole opinion of Shecky's and our writing staff.

Printed in China

ESTABLISHED
1882

MÉTHODE CHAMPENOISE

KORBEL®

CALIFORNIA CHAMPAGNE

Brut

12% ALC. BY VOL.

America's Champagne Since 1882.

KORBEL®

CALIFORNIA CHAMPAGNE

CONTENTS

TABLE OF CONTENTS

LISTINGS BY NEIGHBORHOOD

LISTINGS BY CATEGORY

Bourbon
IN A WHOLE NEW LIGHT.

HANDCRAFTED IN SMALL BATCHES. WOODFORD RESERVE® BOURBON HAS ARRIVED.

Enjoy your bourbon responsibly.

ICON TABLE

 Shecky's Pick

 Dancing/Club

 Dive Bar/No Frills/Inexpensive

 Food

 Frat/College Scene

 Gay

 Live Music

 Lesbian

 Lounge/Swanky/Upscale

 Neighborhood Bar

 Outdoor Space

 Sports Bar

SHECKY'S TOP 5 LISTS

AFTER WORK
Absolutely 4th
Gaslight
The Ginger Man
Latitude
Puck Fair

BACHELOR PARTIES
Buster's Garage
Chelsea Brewing Company
40/40
Sutton Place
Red Rock West

BACHELORETTE PARTIES
Lucky Cheng's
Nerveana
Show
Spirit
Stir

BEER SELECTION
Blind Tiger Ale House
Croxley Ales
d.b.a.
Ginger Man
Peculier Pub

BROOKLYN BARS
Barcade
Barbes
Floyd, NY
Savalas
Soda Bar

COCKTAILS
Absolutely 4th
Angel's Share
The Dove
Little Branch
Olives

COMEDY
Carolines on Broadway
Comedy Cellar
Comic Strip Live
Laugh Lounge NYC
New York Comedy Club

DANCING/CLUBS
Aer
Crobar
Marquee
Quo
Rock Candy

DATE SPOTS
Angel's Share
5 Ninth
Ludo
Megu
Sapa

DIVE BARS
Cherry Tavern
Duff's
Manitoba's
Mars Bar
Welcome to the Johnsons

GAMES
Ace Bar
Amsterdam Billiards Club
Barcade
Bowlmor Lanes
Slate Plus

GAY/LESBIAN
The Eagle
G Lounge
Girlsroom
Henrietta Hudson's
Metropolitan

KARAOKE
Arlene Grocery
Iggy's
Lucky Cheng's
LuLu Lounge
Winnie's

LIVE MUSIC
Bowery Ballroom
Knitting Factory
Rothko
Scenic
Southpaw

NEIGHBORHOOD
Bar 288 (aka Tom & Jerry's)
Brass Monkey
Farrell's
Good World
Newgate Bar & Grill

NEW
Aer
Frederick's Madison
The Garden of Ono
Groovedeck
Scenic

OUTDOOR
The Garden of Ono
The Gate
One91
The Park
SouthWest NY

PICK-UP SPOTS
Bar None
Bembe
Church Lounge @ TriBeCa Grand
Home
Movida

ROOFTOP BARS
AVA Lounge
Cabanas @ the Maritime Hotel
Rare View @ the Shelbourne Hotel
Red Sky
13

THE SCENE
Bungalow 8
Cain
Hiro Lounge
Level V
Marquee

SHECKY'S PICKS
AVA Lounge
Cain
The Dove
Freemans
Xicala

SPORTS BARS
Back Page
Blondies
Bounce
40/40
Ship of Fools

SWANKY LOUNGES
Brandy Library
Earth NYC
Kimono Lounge
One
PM

WINE BARS
Ara Wine Bar
Bar Veloce
Namia
Morrells Wine Bar & Café
Punch & Judy's

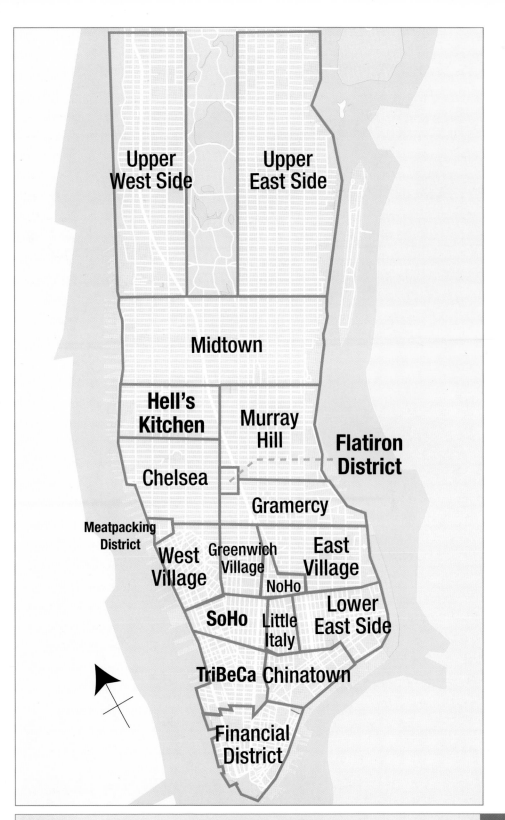

IT'S NOT OFTEN NATURE UNVEILS A NEW TASTE.

Introducing Finlandia® Wild Berries Fusion, vodka featuring the natural flavors of raspberry, black raspberry, strawberry, boysenberry and wild mountain berry. It's a fresh taste made fresher by the pure glacial spring water that goes into every bottle.

FINLANDIA®
WILD BERRIES
FUSION

Please drink responsibly.

www.finlandia.com

Dear Nightlife Lovers,

14,000 beers. 7,000 apple martinis. 9,000 shots. 600 dances to Usher's "Yeah!" And too many hangovers to count. Nobody said reviewing bars and clubs for nine years was easy, but it sure is fun.

For our latest cocktail-soaked edition of Shecky's Bar, Club & Lounge Guide, we sent a staff of over 100 writers to drink their way through over 1,500 bars in Manhattan and Brooklyn. And like an inebriated sorority girl about to drunk-dial, the resulting reviews are brutally honest—which is in keeping with our reputation as New York City's ONLY truly objective, call-'em-like-we-see-'em nightlife guide. You can count on us to tell you which club's bouncers should be sent back to the prison from which they came, which dive bar has smoking-hot bartenders, and which pub is a glorified frat house.

We'd like to thank you, our nightlife-loving readers, for supporting us over the years. In turn, we hope you find some laughs, some undiscovered favorites, and some places to avoid like the plague.

So pull up a stool, pour yourself a beer, and tear into this, our ninth Shecky's Bar, Club & Lounge Guide. It could mean the difference between partying with horny supermodels from Sweden and partying with hornier senior citizens from Schenectady.

Bottoms up!

Sheckys

LEAVE BEHIND YOUR STINKIN' HANG-UPS.

The guilt of paying $4.50 every day for a latte

The fact that you were always picked last for dodgeball

The skinny jeans from '85 that still won't button

The fear that someone will find out you listen to Britney

At Crunch Fitness we love you no matter what. No judgements.

crunch.com • 888.2.crunch

**Unique Classes • Nice People • Shiny Machines • Heavy Objects • Rub-Downs
High-Energy Music • Personal Trainers • Refreshing Beverages • Threads**

A 60

A 60 (@ 60 Thompson)
60 Thompson St. (Spring & Broome Sts.)
SoHo 212.431.0400

What tops a posh boutique SoHo hotel? In this case, it's quite literally A 60—the rooftop lounge that crowns the 60 Thompson hotel. For the most part, visitors wanting to catch a glimpse of the downtown skyline need to be on the hotel registry or possess a membership card. As with most outdoor spaces, sangria *and* margaritas are in high demand, but at A 60, they come with a little something special: The plum sangria is quite a treat. A lot of these folks are of the high-rolling variety, which means tables topped with champagne, men topped with receding hairlines, and attractive ladies who understand the connection between the two. Matching the ground floor's Asian-influenced entrance, which also fronts the fantastic Kittichai restaurant, Pan-Asian appetizers are served.

The A&M Roadhouse
57 Murray St. (Chambers St. & W. Broadway)
TriBeCa 212.385.9005

If you're in the mood to eat mediocre ribs, listen to Def Leppard, and party with people who were born in the '80s, head to the A&M Roadhouse. The décor looks like Daisy Duke's quaint country home—at first, she was excited to decorate, but then she had a few Alabama Slammers and gave up. The bar service is consistently slow and the beer could be much colder; but you won't complain long once you discover that domestics are $2.50 and imported beers are just $3. Heck, there's even the "big game" every night, live music, interactive trivia competitions, darts, and a pool table. So if your idea of heaven looks like a scene from the Patrick Swayze movie of the same name, burn some rubber to this strangely located roadhouse.

The Abbey
536 Driggs Ave. (N. 7th & N. 8th Sts.)
Williamsburg 718.599.4400

The carved wood and stained glass signage, paired with the fact that everyone knows each other, gives this neighborhood institution a divey, Dublin pub feel. On the homey bulletin board by the door hang community announcements, event listings, and snapshots of regulars, but newbies are more than welcome to join the party; there's plenty of room for everyone, especially in the backroom where booths, videogames, a jukebox, and a pool table are found. And for a treat that rivals the greasiest McDonald's burger, ask for a "Happy Meal," a pint of Guinness and a whiskey shot for $7. That leads to Hungover Sundays, which may be frittered away watching classic and cult movies throughout the day.

Absolutely 4th

Absolutely 4th
228 W. 4th St. (@ 7th Ave. S.)
West Village 212.989.9444

If you thought apple martinis were cutting-edge, head to this West Village favorite and sample some of their truly one-of-a-kind flavored cocktails ($10 a pop). Got a sweet tooth? Go for the Cotton Candy Cosmo. Harboring a secret crush on your sister? The White Trash Blue Tease has your name written all over it. Feeling dirty? Down a few Thai-Me-Upaladas and make your move. Sexy dim lighting and a curvy bar provide a chic atmosphere where DJs spin pop tunes four days a week and a mixed crowd gets absolutely smashed during the daily happy hour, which includes 2-for-1 martinis from 4pm-8pm. Absolutely perfect, is what it is.

Ace Bar
531 E. 5th St. (Aves. A & B)
East Village 212.979.8476

So maybe Ace Bar is the embodiment of East Village gentrification, but we're guessing that you weren't here when Avenues A, B, C, and D stood for Assault, Battery, Concussions, and Death. So tell your tattooed pals that Ace is still a good place to rock out, shoot pool, play darts, and throw back tasty pints. They have 12 drafts ($3-$5), all of which are just $2 on Thursdays from 4pm-10pm. On Sundays, there's free pool until 6pm and happy hour from 4pm-7pm. Sure, the kitschy lunch box display might be too cutesy for its own good and the Nickelodeon-tuned TVs in back can make one beg for a crack pipe, but this one-time ruffian haunt is only rolling with the punches, and if you can do the same, you may dig the place.

Ace of Clubs
9 Great Jones St. (Broadway & Lafayette St.)
NoHo 212.677.6963

Because nothing goes better with collard greens and barbecue than a helping of live music and a bottle of Tums, deal yourself into the Ace of Clubs (formerly known as Acme Underground), the spacious bar and performance space underneath Acme Bar & Grill. With a decent-sized stage, a sound booth, and a full PA system, national and local musicians of the rock variety are begging their "managers" (i.e., friends who can't play instruments, but want to be with the band) to get

Ace of Clubs

them booked here. Comedians and theater productions are also welcome, though not necessarily by the regular crowd of humorless indie hipsters. A cover charge is usually in effect, so pass on the pecan pie and check out some sweet tunes instead.

Acme Bar and Grill
9 Great Jones St. (Broadway & Lafayette St.)
NoHo 212.420.1934

This is a product line that never really works out for Wile E. Coyote, but if you're hungry for anything but roadrunner, Acme is a nice choice. Whether it's catfish, jambalaya, hush puppies, or plain ol' burgers, you'll find it at this themey, N'awlins, faux roadhouse. Feeling a need for speed? Slow down with a Turbo Dog beer and look about the darkened orange room, which is lined with hot sauce containers and a smattering of kitschy signage. This place serves lunch and dinner; neither of which brings to mind "light and sexy." Though well-handled, the small bar is an afterthought. Downstairs is another matter entirely—the Ace of Clubs lounge is one of the city's most underrated live music venues, and though small, it rocks in a manner befitting the Big Easy.

Acqua
718 Amsterdam Ave. (@ 95th St.)
Upper West Side 212.222.2752

Everything here is pretty: the servers, the lighting, even the grain of the wood on the backs of the chairs. But there's not much energy in this place: The music, when it's audible, is pleasant enough, but too much time is spent drinking or dining amid the tuneless hum of surrounding conversation. The menu, however, which is well-constructed and primarily Italian, offers solid renditions of the classics, and often with an unexpected and welcome twist. The wine selection is solid, too, so not all is lost. And if your parents are in town, visiting from somewhere greener and quieter, this is the perfect place to take them for their first night in the city. Call it Manhattan 101: A Not-So-Overwhelming Introduction. They'll love it and you'll score a solid A-.

Adä
208 E. 58th St. (2nd & 3rd Aves.)
Midtown 212.371.6060

Far away—literally and figuratively—from the curry-in-a-hurry madness of Sixth Street, Adä is schooling gourmands on the art of authentic Indian cuisine. Offering the only Indian tapas menu in the city, Adä's menu steers clear of the conventional spicy curry dishes in favor of gems like chicken parchey and mini chaat. Novices might be surprised to see Chilean sea bass being enjoyed in the elegant, all-white dining room; here it's accented with a shrimp bell pepper sauce and mint cilantro-marinated prawns to give it a little flair. For dessert, the caramelized banana praline (featuring chocolate chips) is another pleasant surprise. Adä's servers are more than happy to give you a brief history of Indian cuisine, and can help you select the perfect wine to accompany your dish. You'll never look twice at curry again.

Aer
409 W. 13th St. (9th Ave. & Washington St.)
Meatpacking District 212.989.0100

This big new club is on pace to keep its nightlife amusement park of a neighborhood going—or to bring it back, depending on your scene-o-meter. Also designed by ICRAVE, Aer will look familiar to those who dug Rumor, Deep, etc. Upstairs, lighting tricks and mirrors make the main space appear larger than it is, which isn't to say it's not big. But Aer isn't all about size, which is reflected by its light tapas menu and subtle nuances like a wall full of butterflies that are preserved in translucent mountings. The real find here is a small, lightly colored secondary lounge where everything from Blondie to the Doobie Brothers plays in a less cliché setting. There are no real surprises here, which works well for the straightforward crowd.

Agave
140 7th Ave. S. (Charles & 10th Sts.)
West Village 212.989.2100

While cacti and cattle skulls adorn the adobe walls, Agave doesn't overdose on Southwestern kitsch, instead favoring a hip, New Yorkified version of the arid desert. The packed bar buzzes with energy, and the bright, spacious dining area offers a laidback eating environment. A gregarious, model-cute staff adds to the atmosphere, and if you're parched, potent cocktails like the prickly pear ($9) or eponymous Agave margaritas ($8) are a personal oasis. There are dozens of top-shelf tequilas to choose from, offering customers mirages that go away when the night ends, and headaches that don't. Though not necessary, reservations are a good idea for those in need of something more than chips and salsa at the bar.

Agozar
324 Bowery (@ Bleecker St.)
NoHo 212.677.6773

It could be the to-die-for mojitos and phenomenal sangria, the succulent *churrasco* skirt steak and the mouthwatering roast pork loin in a *mojo criolla* sauce, or maybe the bright yellow walls fronted by green palms, but this sassy Cuban hotspot is a hit with the ladies—especially on the weekends, when simultaneous birthday and bachelorette parties steam up the place and provide plenty of eye candy. (If you can't get lucky here, well…) It must be the Latin flavor, because this old Havana-meets-NoHo restaurant draws a late-night crowd, and once the dinner plates are whisked off, tables are pushed together and a lounge vibe pervades. Brother-and-sister co-owners, Gerardo and Diana, along with the dark and handsome staff, ensure that this is the spot "a gozar!" (to enjoy!).

AIX
2398 Broadway (@ 88th St.)
Upper West Side 212.874.7400

If you're a wine connoisseur or avid Francophile, this swanky Upper West Side café is AIX-actly your destination. Their wine selection is one of the most extensive (boasting nearly 500 labels)…and their prices are some of the most expensive. So bring your matron or your sugar daddy along, or find one at the central bar where an after-work set sidles to the bar or cuddles along tiny lounge tables sampling the menu, whispering, and clinking their dearly-paid-for glasses. If you're adventurous enough to stay for dinner, you can dine in the spacious split-level dining area and sample the rich and ample Provençal menu. If you're up for some sampling that won't demolish your 401K, take a chance on one of their tempting signature cocktails—the white strawberry cosmo alone is almost worth the trip north. Almost.

Aja
1068 1st Ave. (@ 58th St.)
Midtown 212.888.8008

If MTV's *Wildboyz* can travel halfway around the world to immerse themselves in far-away cultures, you can certainly drag yourself up to Sutton Place near the base of the 59th Street Bridge to partake in Aja's unique pleasures. This incredibly stylish Pan-Asian restaurant, bar, and sushi joint looks like a Buddhist temple from the outside, all done up in imposing white brick, but inside it's warm and loungey, decorated with colored lights, bamboo, and giant Buddha statues. The décor is dramatic but calming (how many places can you watch koi fish swim underfoot through the clear floor?) and the bar, while small, has a relaxed and quiet vibe. Try a blended green tea margarita or the sliced conch and you'll feel like you've been whisked away on a rickshaw.

Alamo
304 E. 48th St. (1st & 2nd Aves.)
Midtown 212.759.0590

You may remember that this location was the Caribbean-themed C not too long ago. Chances are you probably don't, which is why it closed. Since C isn't a passing grade in this town these owners said "si" to tastefully festive Mexican ornaments, and reopened as Alamo. Though a Mexican restaurant/bar in Midtown is just begging for trouble, this spacious newcomer avoids all cheesiness with a solid menu of chicken- and cheese-filled empanadas, fajitas, enchiladas, and various types of ceviche. The margaritas are strong and flavorful, and they provide a brain freezingly fun way of watching, or ignoring, the Yankee game. Surviving in this location is an uphill battle, but what says resilience more than a place called Alamo?

Aleo Restaurant
7 W. 20th St. (5th & 6th Aves.)
Flatiron 212.691.8286

With a great Flatiron location, Aleo's cozy confines and quiet outdoor garden make for a neighborly restaurant and bar. If you're looking for a place to pick-up, shake your bootie, or be seen, this isn't it. If you're hosting a business lunch or the 'rents are in town, take them here. The Italian/Mediterranean menu features reasonably priced and tasty items like the $9 mussels in tomato broth, and meaty entrées, along with pastas and a choose-your-own antipasto platter. A place for all seasons, Aleo encourages patrons to sit out back in the garden, which is complete with fauna, a retractable cover, and heat lamps. Aleo also offers complimentary popcorn and gourmet snack mix at the bar, which whet the whistle for specialty cocktails like the espresso martini and kumquat mojito. The wine list is also serviceable.

Alfama
551 Hudson St. (@ Perry St.)
West Village 212.645.2500

Alfama offers a highly enticing reason to immerse oneself in Portuguese cuisine and culture for a night. A sprawling menu of national specialties is on display, with fish entrées ranging from $19-$32 a plate. Fado, the nostalgic, longing native music of Portugal, is performed live every Wednesday night, and live jazz is featured on Thursdays. The weekend brunch is steadily getting more and more popular, too. If nothing else, cozy up to the dark wooden bar for a casual round of drinks before starting out—a fully knowledgeable Portuguese wine specialist is there to help you sort it out. Tiles featuring intricately portrayed nature landscapes line the walls. Face it...you moved to New York for just this kind of cultural education. What's your excuse for missing out on Iberia this long?

Alibi
116 MacDougal St. (Bleecker & 3rd Sts.)
Greenwich Village 212.254.9996

The anticipation built up during your descent down the stairs into this candlelit lounge quickly subsides upon the realization that there are five other people in the room, including the DJ and the bartender. The plush brown-leather ottomans surrounding stainless-steel round tables are tempting places to try to wait out the lull in business. Classic, easy-going tunes, combined with the exposed brick and the stone façade behind the bar, create a chill vibe. Sipping on an $8 specialty drink like Liquid Ecstasy, Vanilla Fudge, or Perfect Alibi will help to ease the awkwardness of having all eyes on you. This sleek-looking cocktail lounge is the perfect spot to spend a chill night amidst the usual din of downtown NYC, but if you're involved in a secret tryst you'll certainly be spotted here…but not by many people.

All State Café
250 W. 72nd St. (Broadway & West End Ave.)
Upper West Side 212.874.1883

You'd be hard-pressed to find someone under the age of 40 in this basement bar and grill. What the regulars permanently stationed at the counter might call "character" can easily come off as "dumpy" to the casual visitor. The room is dark and dingy, the floorboards creak—allowing the chairs to rock back and forth with the jukebox—and the scrawls of guests from keggers past are etched into the tables. On the bright side, the burgers are juicy, the service is friendly, and the room maintains a tolerable decibel level. Driving home the overall feel of a suburban barroom, plaques from the café's Little League team, the All State Bobcats, line the walls.

Alligator Lounge
600 Metropolitan Ave. (Leonard & Lorimer Sts.)
Williamsburg 718.599.4440

No question, the draw here is the free pizza that accompanies each drink, and we ain't talking 'bout DiGiorno: these are real deal, brick-oven pies, piping-hot and made-to-order with topping options available for a little extra dough. The vaguely nautical theme is thoughtful enough, but no one comes here for plastic sharks or ropes: They come to get a cheap dinner, to watch the game, and to soak up a night's worth of booze and eschew a hangover. The clipper ship cabin of a backroom plays host to karaoke on Thursdays and to private parties on occasion, too. The constituency is a rowdy neighborhood crowd that feels distinctly collegiate, unlike Alligator's punky counterpart, Capone's, where the pizza's the same, but the crowd is hipper.

Alphabet Lounge
104 Ave. C (@ 7th St.)
East Village 212.780.0202

Tattoos, faux-hawks, and designer jeans are the order at Alphabet Lounge. This large space is filled with wild dancers who dig this spot's live bands and DJs, both of which tend to be rock-oriented. ("Extended East Village" nuthin'—when live rock is playing, this is still Alphabet City.) Those who'd rather tap their sneaker-covered feet in privacy can sink into one of these massive booths, which are fit for rock stars, groupies, and one or two roadies. A large tile mosaic behind the bar serves as "décor," and though the place opened in 1999, the hardened bartenders look like they're ready for tenure. Still, the laidback, come-as-you-are vibe spells a good time for all.

Amarachi Lounge
325 Franklin Ave. (Clifton & Greene Sts.)
Clinton Hill 646.641.4510

Located in the heart of Clinton Hill, this swanky lounge/club and performance space celebrates the music and moves of its African-Caribbean-Latino melting pot community. There's a rotating list of events, with salsa, karaoke, and designated

"sexy" nights, when sultry soul and reggae oozes out of the speakers. Amarachi Lounge offers moderately priced drinks and appetizers, and, if you're feeling tense, loosen up with either a hand or shoulder massage (available upon request) or "Laugh Out Loud" Thursdays, when the latest comedians showcase their talents. During Saturday's Caribbean party, you'll barely be able to find a space on the dance floor, which may prompt you to ask, "Is it getting hot in herre?" You'd better believe it.

Amber

Amber
1406 3rd Ave. (@ 80th St.)
Upper East Side 212.249.5020

Cook the fish. Will someone please cook the fish? While the city may not need another sushi restaurant, this self-proclaimed Asian eatery from the owners of Aja is a welcome addition. A bustling, crowded front room gives way to a more spacious, low-key dining area in back, perfect for dates. Creative sushi and a mix of Japanese, Malaysian, and Thai entrées are priced on the moderate-to-high side, as are drinks: A green tea margarita runs $9, while wine starts at $7/glass and beer at $5/bottle. Walls lined with basket-like straw and a soundtrack of techno-leaning tunes set the tone of modern-day Zen. A TV at the small bar up front detracts a bit from the cool vibe, but good service and fresh sushi help patrons get over it.

American Spirits
1744 2nd Ave. (90th & 91st Sts.)
Upper East Side 212.289.7510

The best part about American Spirits is its full acceptance of being a dive bar, and there ain't nothin' you or your khakis can do about it. Cheap $8 pitchers, billiard greens, and a Beirut table all but condemn this place to frat-dom, but nobody's complaining. (Did we mention the $8 pitchers?) The bar is horribly laid out; it's as if someone lost a bet and was forced to design the most awkwardly shaped bar in history. There's a crappy elevated "stage" near the front, a staircase leading to nowhere in the middle of the bar, an empty, loungey-type area in the back that might as well have tumbleweeds blowing through, and a very old ATM that once dispensed beads and pelts. Like we said, it's a dive, and a good one at that.

American Trash
1471 1st Ave. (76th & 77th Sts.)
Upper East Side 212.988.9008

Just what you'd expect from a neighborhood bar on the Upper East Side: Comfortably worn-in but non-threatening, and peopled with disheveled customers who could use a visit from the *Queer Eye* crew. Tough day on Wall Street? Madison Avenue got you down? There cannot be more effective therapy than a Corona and a game of pool in this unpretentious hideout. The party music is perfect, running the gamut from "No Sleep Till Brooklyn" to "School's Out for Summer." There's a bumper sticker behind the bar, below the flat-screen TV, that says something like, "Get Too Close and I'll Kill You." Don't believe it for a second—the only danger here is that you'll never want to leave. The place is "decorated" with a roadhouse-meets-garage-sale motif that sort of parodies a white trash haunt, but without any contrived kitsch.

Amsterdam Billiards Club
344 Amsterdam Ave. (76th & 77th Sts.)
Upper West Side 212.496.8180

Yes, this is a pool party. And it's also one of the last nightlife spots in town where people openly revel over an eight-ball. But don't get us wrong—we're talking billiards. Billed as New York City's oldest pool hall, Amsterdam Billiards Club is in a league of its own. With 31 tables and darts and decently priced drinks, they definitely rack up business. All skill levels are welcome here, from amateurs to serious pool sharks. If your game's out of sync, you can pull up a stool and watch ESPN at the bar, or sink into one of the cozy couches near the fireplace. The décor is drab but clean, with dark maroon walls and exposed brick, but anyone who comes to a pool hall for the ambiance is about to get hustled.

Amuse
108 W. 18th St. (6th & 7th Aves.)
Chelsea 212.929.9755

Amuse's chic décor of cubes, clean lines, and pastels does a good job of making you feel cool even if you're one of the few patrons without a date at this swanky lounge/restaurant. If you're coupled up, share some of the reasonably priced, protein-

Amuse

heavy American brasserie-style dishes while leaning in close on the banquette seating. Otherwise, keep a low profile at the bar, where complimentary olives and $5 French fries with chipotle dipping sauce help take the edge off. Take advantage of the happy hour beer ($3) and wine ($5) prices, or splurge on yummy specialty drinks like the $11 Dragon Tail. (Lychee and pineapple vodka together at last!). After a couple of those, just about anything will seem amusing.

Andavi

91 Christopher St. (@ Bleecker St.)
West Village 212.604.9696

Just off the busy bustle of Bleecker Street, this Northern Italian oasis lures West Village visitors with an impressive vino list (70 by the bottle, 11 by the glass) that's abundant enough to impress any sommelier. And if the wine alone doesn't do it, the rustic décor and candle sconces studding the exposed-brick walls are sure to evoke that same warm and fuzzy feeling you get from a perfectly aged, full-bodied red. The main dishes on Anadavi's menu aren't exactly a Tuscan picnic (dishes average $30), but the lush back patio, accented by waves of curling ivy, feels like something out of *A Room with a View*. Those with a more rustic budget can snag a spot at the bar and nibble on smaller plates to sufficiently soak up the scene.

Angelo & Maxie's

233 Park Ave. S. (@ 19th St.)
Gramercy 212.220.9200

Thinking about moving to the Midwest? First, come here and meet your future neighbors. This steakhouse is popular with tourists who leave their extra-stuffed fanny packs in the hotel just before dragging their extra-large fannies to Angelo & Maxie's. There are certainly plenty of high-rolling Wall Streeters in the house as well, as this handsome, super-old-school meatery isn't without its decadence. Strong martinis are served at a crowded bar where the scene is decidedly more "local." The throwback cigar lounge in back is a nice respite from the modern world city, not to

mention the lumberjacks in town for the 32nd Annual Logging Convention. This is the kind of place where food is ordered in accordance to its size: Try the 24-oz. T-bone or the 28-oz. prime rib.

Angel's Share

8 Stuyvesant St. (3rd Ave. & 9th St.)
East Village 212.777.5415

This little angel of a lounge has fallen from the heavens to bring New Yorkers intimacy, seduction, and most importantly, booze. Angel's Share's private backroom is one of the city's best-kept secrets, so don't tell anyone…oh, wait. Anyway, this candlelit date spot with its gorgeous picture windows and incredible drinks infused with violet liquor and plum wine does have some rules. For starters, don't bring your posse with you—parties larger than four aren't allowed and if you and your terrible trio of trouble get too loud, you'll be asked to leave. But seeing how this seductive joint is a slam-dunk for romance, you'd be silly to bring anyone other than your date…unless you're Hugh Hefner. The cocktails here are easily some of the best in the city.

Angry Wade's

222 Smith St. (@ Butler St.)
Carroll Gardens 718.488.7253

Shockingly, there was a time not long ago when this Smith Street bar was the only game in town, which is probably why it offers a little of everything: darts, a pool table, six TVs, a Jersey-rock-to-Detroit-funk jukebox, videogames, a laidback, pub-style décor, and, last but certainly not least, unlimited free popcorn. But with the hyperactive youngster bars sprouting up like wildflowers around it, Angry Wade's has gone down a few ranks on the Smith Street trend chart. What's left is a strange brew—part 20-something diehards, part tough-guy locals, and part, well, empty space. This is the kind of space that could fall back into favor with the "in" set soon, or just might disappear as rent prices skyrocket.

Annie Moore's

50 E. 43rd St. (Vanderbilt & Madison Aves.)
Midtown 212.986.7826

Bars lurking in the shadow of train stations and airports are rarely distinctive, since customers only go there because they're on the way home (or if you're in need of a loo that's not overcrowded with stressed-out commuters). And Annie Moore's—located not 50 feet from Grand Central—is no exception. She's a perfectly serviceable Irish pub, with dark wood paneling and a lovely long bar that stretches back to a rear dining room. Plus, there's plenty of room to stand amidst the commuting crowds, and if you're lucky enough to get a seat at the bar, there are plasma-screen TVs every few feet, making it a great place to watch a game. But friendly staff and a decently poured pint don't do much to make this spot stand out.

Anotheroom

249 W. Broadway (N. Moore & Beach Sts.)
TriBeCa 212.226.1418

Barely lit, featuring an array of cheap foreign beer and a stereo that plays the latest in modern rock, Anotheroom clearly aspires to be a down-market outpost in the upscale playground of TriBeCa. Though the suds may be as dark as the room, the suede banquettes lethally comfortable, and the music agreeably loud, this would-be bohemian nerve center can't quite pull it off. The crowd tends to be genteel 30ish types who, one suspects, have not received the promotion necessary to afford them the neighborhood's greater luxuries. Artwork and candles steal the show in this minimalist art gallery/bar space. But if you don't mind a staff that obviously wishes they worked in Williamsburg, Anotheroom can be an affordable, unpretentiously hip antidote to its swank downtown surroundings. Otherwise, go find another room—you know what we mean.

Antarctica

287 Hudson St. (@ Spring St.)
SoHo 212.627.5923

Hey baby, what's your name? Jane? Ezra? Demetrius? Well, if yours is the name of the day at Antarctica, you'll be drinking for free all night (5pm-11pm, Sunday-Friday; 7pm-1am, Saturdays)—so see, being named Ernest only sucks 364 days out of the year. That's one of the many fun quirks found at what would otherwise just be a spacious, well-maintained dive bar in the middle of Manhattan. Quotes of the day written on slabs of chalkboard in this older-than-dirt establishment offer proverbial wisdom from the likes of such greats as Ralph Waldo Emerson and Barry White. The crowd's a mixed bag—some afterwork, some preppy, some punky, some elder, some younger, some who just showed because their name is Gladys and it's their lucky day. And just in case you were planning on doing your homework here on one of the red barstools, a paper sign lets you know, "We have wireless Internet. You're bathing in it."

Anyway Café

34 E. 2nd St. (@ 2nd Ave.)
East Village 212.533.3412

Descending the steps into Anyway Café's dining area is like entering a French bistro in old Russia, with some palm fronds thrown in for good measure. "A French Place with a Russian Soul" is the motto of this shabby-chic hole in the Earth where it seems that Tolstoy and Hugo would've hung out and played chess. Caviar and cheese feature prominently on the appetizer-heavy menu, which spans from crepes to ravioli-like pelmeni. Among Anyway Café's liquor libations, the Russian-inspired vodka infusions are guaranteed to make you "strong like bear." Stop by mid-week to seal the deal on that all-telling third date or come in alone to finish writing your first novel.

Apartment 138

138 Smith St. (Dean & Bergen Sts.)
Carroll Gardens 718.491.0248

Apartment 138 draws Brooklyn's late-night munchers away from the local delis with a full menu available until 3am. With dishes that run the foodie gamut from gourmet specials to bar food (with a couple of paninis thrown in for good measure), Apartment 138 is as much a restaurant as it is a bar. Dinner times and late nights promise the most crowd-watching action, but don't walk in without your sweetie in tow—singles head elsewhere for late-night hookups. Stick around after dinner for cocktails and music served up by DJs on weekend nights. If that's not your bag, check the basement, where an adult playground of vintage arcade games, foosball, and pool tables fill the open space.

Apocalypse Lounge
189 E. 3rd St. (Aves. A & B)
East Village No Phone

Apocalypse Lounge

Earnestly trying to keep a pulse going in the NYC art scene, this creative dive bar is a true-blue East Village staple that exists if for no other reason than to shelter and nurture local artists. A stomping ground for local bands, solo acoustic performers, and a showcase spot for film screenings, literature readings, mural displays, and open mic try-outs, there's no other place to be if the world should come to an end. The décor is just as eclectic—a mishmash of scrappy furniture, odd artwork, and one-of-a-kind jigsaw-puzzle tables. Step right up for some $3 Rheingolds and, most nights, a DJ provides a soundtrack for your evening of artsy immersion. It's the end of the world as we know it, but we feel fine.

Apple Restaurant & BomBar
17 Waverly Pl. (Mercer & Greene Sts.)
Greenwich Village 212.473.8888

With ironically titled drinks like the F.V.C.K. and the Pulp Fiction and prices just right for the girl down the hall's birthday, it's no wonder that the college kids seem to love this Vietnamese/French restaurant/lounge. Boasting the same name as Gwyneth's baby, Apple's food is tasty, if not inventive—duck, tofu lunch boxes—and they offer vegetarian options for vegans-in-training. If you've got a test the next day, you can surf the Net via free wireless access in between karaoke performances in one of the private rooms—or order in; Apple delivers (you'll have to leave the dorms to taste their sake samplers though). The pseudo-swank BomBar lounge is the bomb…for sipping cocktails when you should be in class.

APT
419 W. 13th St. (9th Ave. & Washington St.)
Meatpacking District 212.414.4245

APT

The t-shirt-wearing bartenders at this bi-level lounge/club would put a *Cocktail*-era Tom Cruise to shame, and not even Scientology can save the most-hardened drinkers from their "house punch's" potent knockout blow. Though APT's air of anonymity has waned since its opening a half-decade ago, it's still a safe bet when showing out-of-towners a New York hotspot sans the potentially sticky velvet rope situation. The balcony upstairs offers a respite for smokers, and the downstairs area hosts DJs every night. The chalkboards on the bathroom walls offer visitors a place to post their phone numbers or espouse their views on anything that comes to mind while their pants are down and blood-alcohol level is up; don't expect greatness.

Aquagrill

210 Spring St. (@ 6th Ave.)
SoHo 212.274.0505

This popular oyster bar with an award-winning brunch that earned Aquagrill a 2005 AAA Five Diamond Award attracts a mostly middle-aged crowd and Japanese tourists who likely heard about it from, well, AAA. If you're craving Imperial Iranian caviar or oysters from as far as Washington State and Baja and want to top them off with a nice white wine, such as the hit vintages from the South African–based Neil Ellis Winery, this is your place. And forget the aqua—go straight for cocktails like the Glacier and the Aquabite and watch the shuckers shuck from the bar.

Aquavit

65 E. 55th St. (Madison & Park Aves.)
Midtown 212.307.7311

Marcus Samuelsson has done for Swedish food what Demi Moore has done for woman over 40: given hope. Aquavit goes way beyond herring and meatballs, though both are on the menu. Put your trust in Marcus and ask questions, otherwise you might be alarmed that your lobster roll is actually encased by paper-thin apple slices. Other surprises include a brioche-wrapped salmon with porcini mushroom ketchup and an Arctic Circle dessert that you have to taste to believe. This is not your Grandma Olga's smorgasbord, but what else would you expect for $75 a person? Sample the signature aquavit drinks, which come in flavors like cucumber, horseradish, saffron, and roasted pumpkin and espresso, and you might find yourself digging out your old Ace of Base and ABBA CDs to keep the party going into the night.

Aquavit

Ara Wine Bar

24 9th Ave. (13th & 14th Sts.)
Meatpacking District 212.242.8642.

The Meatpacking District may be past its "prime," but this quaint little wine bar is a choice cut of NYC nightlife. Ara's a cozy nook for sampling wonderful wines, which range from cheap to considerably less cheap. Though there's a whiff of pretension in the presentation, you're guaranteed to find a vintage that suits you; if not, opt for one of the bar's specialty cocktails. The wine list is French, Californian, and occasionally Aussie, but there's a slight Indian influence to the décor. The main room is one large, cushy U-shaped banquette and seating at the bar is limited. Don't come hungry, as it's more wine than dine here, with only small morsels to sate the appetite. You can't really stretch out here, but you can get *Sideways*.

Archer's
1643 1st Ave. (85th & 86th Sts.)
Upper East Side 212.628.6266

The only thing that beats an uninspired hole-in-the-wall Upper East Side bar is a hole in the head. The poorly located Archer's really misses its mark in the already overpopulated Upper East Side bar scene, yet shares the same vicious malady that haunts every other joint in the neighborhood: a dearth of patrons. And that's on a good night. The space itself is fairly small, and while topping the tables with drawing paper and crayons shows low expectations of those who do come, the three or four pudgy guys in Dockers who may stop by to get nutty on a Friday probably aren't into "art." Don't even think about telling your tales of woe to the bartenders; they'll merely shoot you a dirty look and a shifty eye as you realize that, unlike them, you can leave.

Arlene's Grocery
95 Stanton St. (Orchard & Ludlow Sts.)
Lower East Side 212.358.1633

Plan to get a buzz from this live music hotspot's fierce lineup of up-and-coming bands and the fumes emitting from the indie crowd, because the weak drinks don't pack much punch. Actually, the

problem is too much punch, and not enough liquor—at least not enough to inspire the head-banging that comes with a rock 'n' roll joint like this former grocery store. The fireplace gives the bar a nice ambiance, and the front area has somewhat spiffy seating. In the back, where the stage is, it's divier. The spirited operators here probably don't think of their hotspot as a dive, but Mick Jagger also probably thinks he's traditionally handsome. In the tipsy-topsy world of rock 'n' roll, it all works out.

Aroma

Aroma
36 E. 4th St. (Bowery & Lafayette St.)
NoHo 212.375.0100

This cozy wine bar has 90 wines by the bottle and 20 by the glass. Aside from the selection, what sets Aroma apart from neighboring bars is that it smells like hearty Italian food, and not like a frat house the day after a toga party. And while there's a chandelier hanging in the dining room, don't be put off—Aroma isn't pretentious or high-brow; it's just trying to class up a Eurotrash- and NYU-heavy area, and it succeeds. Touches like this match the creativity of Aroma's menu items, like the braised duck salad with walnut oil and the polenta waffles with Amaretto syrup. Enjoy light bites like tasty paninis and sandwiches while you wine and dine your date—they're perfect for soaking up the bottles of wine you just polished off.

Arlene's Grocery

Arriba Arriba Mexican Restaurant

762 9th Ave. (@ 51st St.)
Hell's Kitchen 212.489.0810

Over-the-top campiness in some Mexican restaurants (ahem, Tortilla Flats) can be fun, but for *mas* maturity, hurry to Arriba Arriba. Tucked away on a busy corner in Hell's Kitchen, the restaurant offers satisfying standard Mexican fare, yummy margaritas, and sangria, all with little pretense. The mostly local 30-something crowd packs the dining area even on sleepy Mondays, while a slightly cramped but lively bar in the front offers a street view, loud music, and three sizes of margaritas in all manner of fruity flavors. Patrons get half-off their second margarita during the bar-only happy hour every day from 4pm-7pm. And outside seating on the sidewalk, where the quick, friendly wait staff chats with customers, offers prime people-watching real estate.

Art Bar

52 8th Ave. (Jane & Horatio Sts.)
West Village 212.727.0244

There's some art hanging on the walls here, but if ever there were a misnomer for a bar, it would be Art Bar. Frequented by post-modernist theory-spewing West Villagers, Art Bar also tends to pack in post-college cliques every Friday and Saturday night. Like the neighborhood it has occupied for 20 years, Art Bar is not what it used to be. Still, the devil-may-care downtown attitude of the Village is kept alive by the thrown-together décor—second-hand couches, an old fireplace, and comfy booths—but now the place is filled wall-to-wall with khakis and Polo shirt-wearing wannabes. Art Bar does paint a picture of a laidback local hangout; be sure to make a beeline for the cozy backroom, where there's plenty of nooks for conducting frisky business.

Arté

21 E. 9th St. (University Pl. & 5th Ave.)
Greenwich Village 212.473.0077

If your idea of preparing an Italian meal is opening a can of Chef Boyardee, then you need to haul your culture-less rump to this upscale, (read: pricey, but it's worth saving up for if you have someone you want to impress) Italian eatery. Arté features a fairly standard menu, but the portions are large, the wine flows freely, and the staff and service have an impeccable reputation (maybe it's because the owner is on-site every night). Arté is one of those quiet, beautiful secrets with a comfortable, homey ambiance. The fireplace, outside garden, and romantic atmosphere inspires most of its guests to get all gussied-up before they come here to dine. Just don't let your grandmother pick out your tie, *capice*?

Arthur's Tavern

57 Grove St. (7th Ave. S. & Bleecker St.)
West Village 212.675.6879

If you roll into Arthur's Tavern around 1am, the house band is likely to be hitting off its second set, featuring Johnny "Tasty" Parker, a trumpet player so hot he has to sit down for fear of lighting the roof on fire (or maybe it's because he's pushing 80 and needs to nap occasionally). Either way, this old-school jazz and blues joint is a delightful blast from the past. Arthur's legendary late-night scene is banging with all the breath it has left, as everyone from middle-aged music lovers to young hellions pack this tiny club. Arthur's prides itself on the ancient holiday decorations covering the place from floor to ceiling. Merry Christmas, Happy Halloween; whatever, admission is yours with a one-drink minimum and the jazz is smokin'.

Artisanal

2 Park Ave. S. (@ 32nd St.)
Murray Hill 212.725.8585

This huge, elaborate French bistro caters to the area's after-work professionals and business types looking to impress their clients with a dazzling wine selection (around 300 options) and several varieties of cheese fondue. The place has a

Asia de Cuba

genuinely French atmosphere of decadence, pretension, and chaos. Well-dressed waiters whiz around dangerously, and added to the high ceilings, give a feeling of a busy European train station at the turn of the century. Spacious, elegant, and expensive, Artisanal is not for amateurs, but it's a great place for the pros to wine, dine, and impress each other and admire the view of 32nd Street through the huge plate-glass windows.

Artland

609 Grand St. (Leonard & Lorimer Sts.)
Williamsburg 718.599.9706

The stained-glass doors to this dive bar lead to a pleasantly artsy room—and by artsy, we mean crafts class at camp and not MoMA. Glass grape chandeliers, a hodgepodge of ratty tables and chairs, a vintage wooden DJ booth, rotating art by local artists, Christmas ornaments, and other glittery accoutrements decorate the place. From behind the S-shaped bar, bubbly bartenders pull slushy beers from a claw-foot tub full of ice, before pouring great Manhattans, martinis, and cosmos for their family-like patrons. Artland is borderline kitsch in that shabby hipster kind of way; it could easily be located off Bedford Avenue, but Artland's more East Williamsburg location keeps the booze cheap and the kids cool (and coming back for the purple-felt billiards table and the perennial $5 PBR-and-well-liquor-shot special).

Asia de Cuba

237 Madison Ave. (37th & 38th Sts.)
Murray Hill 212.726.7755

Alas, no longer trendy, Asia de Cuba (the first of several worldwide), which has famed restaurateur Jeffrey Chodorow and designer Philippe Starck behind it, is however still lively and cool and simply beautiful with its flowing white fabrics and see-and-be-seen bi-level seating. The mojitos and caipirinhas are still excellent, the Asian-Latin fusion menu's still worthwhile, and the bar seating areas are still filled with patrons waiting for tables as well as local businesspeople here for an after-work cocktail. (Downstairs is a cozy living room-like space and upstairs, there's a pretty but narrow area with wait service as well as some high stools and tables by the bar.) On the other hand, it's hard to get hipsters to Murray Hill, so you'll probably be sitting next to Texan businessmen or a nice New Jersey couple.

Asia Roma

40 Mulberry St. (Worth & Bayard Sts.)
Little Italy 212.385.1133

Asia Roma is the answer to the age-old nightlife quandary of where to find an Asian-Italian restaurant/karaoke bar. Appropriately nestled near Little Italy and Chinatown, Asia Roma serves as a sketchy nexus for its surrounding neighborhoods. The real charm of this restaurant isn't in its seemingly eclectic cuisine, but rather its basement karaoke lair. You'll feel right at home there—especially if you live in a creepy, wood-paneled, remodeled basement. (The weathered upstairs space is considerably more mainstream.) The unpretentious atmosphere does however lend for even the most intimidated performer to belt it like Tina Turner…or Ike Turner, depending on your mood. Either way, Asia Roma will put a song in your heart and a pasta dish or teriyaki chicken in your belly.

Asylum

149 Bleecker St. (Thompson St. &
LaGuardia Pl.)
Greenwich Village 212.254.8492

It's been said that insanity is repeatedly doing the same thing and expecting different results. Lock this place up! Please. A strange and seedy mix of NYU students and those who come in from towns and boroughs we didn't even know were out there congregate here, where cheesy radio-friendly hip-hop provides a soundtrack for predictability. In Asylum's defense, nothing cool could survive on this street. The room, a long storefront with a bar on one side and banquettes on the other, is dark and a bit creepy with a mental institution theme about as wild and fun as the Insane Clown Posse. (That's not a good thing.) The crowd and staff are a little thugged-out, but who else would pay a cover on Bleecker Street? The guy collecting money at the door seemed to work here, but on second thought...

Atrium Lounge (@ the Marquis)

1535 Broadway, 8th Fl. (45th & 46th Sts.)
Midtown 212.704.8900

Lacking the eye-to-eye Times Square view of its neighbor, the Broadway Lounge, but sharing many of the same specialty cocktails and snack options as its other neighbor, Katen Sushi, the Atrium Lounge is little more than a fancy, Vegas-style food court. Fancy not just because you're sipping an $11.25 pomegranate mojito and ordering appetizers like beef Wellington served in a puff pastry, but because you're sitting at a bar underneath the open dome of 37 floors of chain-hotel glory. The three-year-old remodeled design gives this hotel-bar-of-hotel-bars an updated feeling, and when the Broadway Lounge is closed for private parties and you're waiting for your wife to finish up her yoga DVD in your hotel suite, the Atrium is open and ready for you.

Aubette

119 E. 27th St. (Lexington & Park Aves.)
Murray Hill 212.686.5500

This ostentatious wine bar looks like someone's idea of romantic—someone like Fabio, or Donald Trump perhaps. The heavy leather curtains, the granite slab inscribed with a Latin quotation over the bar, and the inconsistent doorman all say that "Aubettes" are off. However, the professional crowd who frequents this Murray Hill spot seems to feel at home in its bogus-loungey interior that's begging for a piece of corporate art. Perhaps a painting of mating unicorns? The wait staff is friendly and knowledgeable, and can easily talk you into dropping $10 on a decent glass of wine. The Black Diamond Party on Tuesdays is geared toward "professionals" looking to network, but it's largely an excuse to overcharge for a menu of bite-sized snacks with fancy names.

Auction House

300 E. 89th St. (1st & 2nd Aves.)
Upper East Side 212.427.4458

Remember that scene in *Cruel Intentions* where Sarah Michelle Gellar makes out with Selma Blair? You're not going to see much girl-on-girl action here, but now that we have your attention, you have an idea of the vibe at this bar, where 20-somethings make out in a parlor-like room. Many a trashed bar-hopper trolling the UES crashes at this huge, two-room, "old saloon"-themed bar that's fully decorated with plush red sofas and velvet curtains. If your date isn't going so well, lead her into a dimly lit corner, where the preppy couples groping in the semi-private corners will stir memories (and hopefully, fire in the loins) of her skeevy 8th-grade boyfriend. The other option is to order a few drinks and pretend that you'll have your butler escort her to the sidewalk.

Automatic Slims

733 Washington St. (@ Bank St.)
West Village 212.645.8660

A truly cute neighborhood corner bar, Automatic Slims has the attitude of a Southern-style juke joint, but with contemporary patrons. It's easy to get snake eyes upon rolling into this place, as there's a subtle dice theme going on. This point is made via a tiled entrance, as well as the tables

AVA Lounge's outdoor space

made of blocks of die. This intimate space holds a booth and a narrow bar with '50s chrome-style stools while pictures of old soul and jazz legends adorn the walls. The not-so-"slim" food menu is an inventive departure for us Northeast folk—an extensive selection of seafood, po' boys, steaks, and bar grub hit the palate like a runaway pickup truck. Automatic Slims reaches top gear in the late afternoon and on weekends.

AVA Lounge (@ the Dream Hotel)
210 W. 55th St. (Broadway & 8th Ave.)
Midtown 212.956.7020

Located in the penthouse of the swank, sexy Dream Hotel, this retro Rat Pack-inspired lounge offers a stunning view of the city in a setting that'll make you feel like a king of the hill, top of the heap. The pinstriped walls and matte metal décor, dim lighting, and hot clientele set the scene for meeting with your very own Ava Gardner (for whom the bar was named) arm candy for a secret tryst. Cocktails are on the pricey side (the signature Gin and Sin is $9), but the view is unparalleled. If things go well—or a little too drunkenly— there are plenty of luxurious rooms below for sleep and other nocturnal activities.

Avalon
47 W. 20th St. (@ 6th Ave.)
Chelsea 212.807.7780

It'll be a long time before Avalon stops getting mentioned in the same breath as Limelight, the club that occupied its space first. The truth is that this club, housed in a former church, is grand enough to break free of most of the stereotypes. In other words, even if you're not usually into swanky lounges, it's worth suffering through the line to check out. Much of the original church layout is preserved and embellished, mixing heavy stone walls with specially lit plexiglass floors. There's an outdoor area for smokers, too. But giving the whole thing its occasion is the massive dance floor, with one of Avalon's three state-of-the-art sound systems. International celebrity DJs are business as usual in this absolute work of nightlife art. One word of warning, er, actually, make that two letters: B&T.

Avenue A Sushi
103 Ave. A (6th & 7th Sts.)
East Village 212.982.8109

Have you had enough of fly-by-night hipster sushi joints where the scene is lively and the food is mediocre? Imagine how this place must feel. At 17 years old, Avenue A Sushi is practically a landmark in this neighborhood. And while the scene is hip, the commendable old-world/new-world Japanese cuisine isn't just pre-drinking filler. Nightly DJs, a hip staff, and funky décor shift customers into party gear and drinks like the lychee martinis and sake concoctions provide the fuel. Imagine Sushi Samba as built by shabby-chic Lower East Side artists who consulted with their Japanese exchange student, and you've got the look and feel of this place down.

Azaza

891 1st Ave. (@ 50th St.)
Midtown 212.751.0700

Were it displaced to the Meatpacking District, Azaza would surely command a velvet rope and eye-gouging prices. Instead, this sexy red lounge is located in way-east Midtown and only livens up on the weekends—apparently the UN crowd is too busy solving world problems to…ha ha, can't even finish that joke. Azaza boasts dim lighting, an upstairs lounge with flat-screen TVs, and decorative attention to detail like beaded throw pillows. The music, an eclectic, lively jazz-house-Bollywood-salsa-funk mix, is just loud enough to make you lean close to your date, and the smell of the Asian fusion food will make you hungry even if you're not. The drinks aren't anything to write home about, but you probably shouldn't be writing home about your drinking anyway. This bar deserves your business.

B Bar (aka Bowery Bar)

40 E. 4th St. (Lafayette St. & Bowery)
NoHo 212.475.2220

B Bar's 15 minutes are up, and the celebrity clientele seems to have moved on to the next big thing, but the bar still wins brownie points for its half-off beverages during happy hour and all-you-can-drink-mimosas during Sunday brunch. B Bar's inviting 4,000-square-foot patio and Beige, Tuesday's popular A-list gay party, keep this for-

mer Gulf gas station pumping past its prime. Come early to enjoy quiet dining of classic American eats and cocktails like the ginger kamikaze. Later in the night, expect to see Bridge and Tunnel types unsubtly perusing the spaciously sleek dining area in search of members of the opposite sex.

The Back Fence

155 Bleecker St. (@ Thompson St.)
Greenwich Village 212.475.9221

The Back Fence has achieved a certain degree of notoriety for its peanut shell-covered floors and venerable Polish staff. Grouchy geezers who apparently have no interest in being tipped serve your two mandatory drinks. The stuffy character of this place holds a certain appeal, though, and bands like the Blue Collars rattle the place with their multi-hour sets of classic rock hits that are more tired than the waiters. The young, chuckling crowd keeps this "world-famous" 60-year-old corner bar going through the night, but thanks to its induction as a destination on the annual Greenwich Village bar tour, the Back Fence may have finally jumped the shark.

Back Page

1472 3rd Ave. (83rd & 84th Sts.)
Upper East Side 212.570.5800

You know that a sports bar is serious when it shuts off the music so visiting Yankees fans can hear the play-by-play. Since this place sports more than a dozen TVs, seeing the game isn't a problem either. Once this neighborly haunt finishes with the sports section, the tubes are turned down, and in come Frank, Smokie, and similar crooners who fill the jukebox. If you want to rock, there's plenty of classic stuff, but don't expect to hear the latest Williamsburg sensation. It's all fun and games downstairs. When it's open, the lower level sports a second bar where air hockey and darts are played in a setting reminiscent of a 13-year-old boy's room. Calm down, Michael Jackson—we're referring to the pennants and posters.

Baggot Inn
82 W. 3rd St. (Thompson & Sullivan Sts.)
Greenwich Village 212.477.0622

The Irish ownership behind Slainte and Dempsey's Pub begot Baggot Inn, and it echoes the folksy sentiments of its brothers—albeit with a country (or more accurately, honky-tonk) twist. There's an occasional $5 cover, but it's justified when bands such as Jack Grace or Van Hayride (a countrified Van Halen cover band) rock the stage. On Wednesday nights, bluegrass performances draw red-eyed Irishmen and Greenwich Village old-timers, while Tuesday's "Quiz with Fizz" appeals to NYU students who come with the hopes of winning the $25 bar credit prize. In case math isn't your strong suit, that's five pints of Guinness (they're $5 each!). The Baggot Inn promises live music seven days a week, including an open mic and bluegrass jams. BYOG (bring your own guitar) and rock out.

Bailey's Corner Pub
1607 York Ave. (@ 85th St.)
Upper East Side 212.650.1341

Welcome to the no-man's land that is the bar scene east of Second Avenue on the Upper East Side. While you can find a drinking establishment seemingly every three feet on the aforementioned avenue, venturing east can be a complete crap-shoot. Which is why Bailey's is something of an enigma; it's actually a solid bar unfortunately situated in a diarrheic location. These bartenders are friendly and though people do show up, the place never feels overly crowded. As far as neighborhood pubs with an Irish namesake go, this one has pretty much everything one might expect: dim lighting, relatively uncomfortable-looking couches strewn about, loyal patrons, a bunch of TVs, the requisite dart trophies, an Internet jukebox, and a fish tank. Wait…a fish tank? Woo-hoo! We have a winner for Most Exciting Bar on sleepy York Avenue.

Baker Street
1152 1st Ave. (@ 63rd St.)
Upper East Side 212.688.9663

Anyone coming for the raucous showmanship Tom Cruise gave this place in *Cocktail* will surely be disappointed. What you will find in this Sherlock-themed corner bar and restaurant (you can't miss the black awning that runs down the side of the building) is a well-spaced, yet hard-backed seating area where burgers and pints can be enjoyed. The pub quiz every Wednesday (9pm-11pm) is popular with the regular crowd, which includes local folks and those working at the nearby hospital. Sports fans will be happy to know that Baker Street carries the Setanta channel—so you don't have to miss South Africa's Currie Cup.

Balanza Bar
426 Lorimer St. (Ten Eyck & Stagg Sts.)
Williamsburg 718.302.5055

Located on a seemingly desolate strip in Williamsburg, Balanza looks like a bodega storefront that you might pass by and never think twice about. And sometimes people don't, but that's their loss, because Balanza's a gem. Reminiscent of a basement rec room and complete with all the forgotten toys that ferment down there, this bar's outfitted with a long-neglected piano, a pool table (play for free on Sundays), and a stage that hosts everything from traveling plays to burlesque shows on Amateur Night. The liquor selection is as sparse as what's left over from mom and dad's last BBQ, but it's served up with all the familiar friendliness of home. Sunday is "fun day," since happy hour lasts all day long ($1 off all beers, wine, and well drinks).

Balthazar
80 Spring St. (Broadway & Crosby St.)
SoHo 212.965.1785

Like moths to a flame, New Yorkers swarm to the French-drenched Balthazar, whose perennial popularity is richly deserved. Known for its superb

Balthazar

Shake your "bann bann" over to the newest Korean restaurant to hit Midtown. Bann, which opened in mid-August, is Woo Lae Oak's new restaurant and infuses traditional Korean food with Western dining. House specials include beef short ribs simmered in a sake ginger soy glaze with daikon, shitake, and Chinese broccoli ($24) and fresh lobster sautéed in a chili clam reduction served over a seafood croquette ($28). The restaurant even comes equipped with a self-barbecue built into the tables and the menu boasts a long list of fresh marinated meat, fish, and vegetables for you to grill right there on the spot. Try their specialty drinks such as the lychee martini ($8) for a sweet treat or the soju cocktail ($7). The décor is serene with pebbles lining the walkway, gauze curtains with Korean script, and large windows providing a bright and relaxing atmosphere.

brunches, Balthazar is also an ideal spot for a tête-à-tête at the long bar or leather banquettes, where you can nuzzle under lazily spinning fans, fresh-cut flowers in enormous vases, and aged mirrors reflecting rows of wine. Over 300 bottles of *vin* are on offer, from Bordeaux to Burgundy, both of which pair well with the delicious $14 bar steak. The extensive champagne selection ranges from affordable to Chapter 11; there's a $700 Dom Perignon for those trying to impress their dates and themselves. Balthazar's infectious atmosphere is hard to resist, especially once you've caught a voyeuristic glimpse of it through the soaring windows overlooking Spring Street.

BAMcafé
30 Lafayette Ave. (Ashland Pl. & St. Felix St.)
Fort Greene 718.636.4100

Care for a little jazz with that cocktail? Housed in the upstairs portion of the Brooklyn Academy of Music, BAMcafé offers a dining/bar/performance space that matches the glamour of the downstairs theater. With huge vaulted ceilings and enormous tiered windows, the space is roomy yet personal, sparing visitors the feeling of having drinks in a museum. The live performers are top-notch, and the dining area is separated between those having full dinners and those partaking of the light and limited menu. (This dynamic spares loungers the inconvenience of bustling waiters and related intrusions.) Seeing a movie at the accompanying BAM cinema? The café's a good all-in-one after-film choice.

Bann
350 W. 50th St. (8th & 9th Aves.)
Hell's Kitchen 212.582.4446

Banshee Pub
1373 1st Ave. (73rd & 74th Sts.)
Upper East Side 212.717.8177

From the burgundy barstools to the perfectly shabby walls, much of the Banshee looks as if it came from the Dublin edition of the Restoration Hardware catalog, and we mean that in the best of ways. There are some days when you simply need a drink at the local pub, and neither scruffy nor upscale will do. That's where the Banshee comes in. Most everyone's welcoming and gregarious, which has as much to do with the constant flow of beer as it does the warm atmosphere. And the red-headed Medusa-looking banshee mural that's been hand-painted behind the bar is far from the harbinger of death we've all read about—she's just there to make sure Thursday's guest bartenders keep things rolling.

Bao 111
111 Ave. C (7th & 8th Sts.)
East Village 212.254.7773

Going to war in Vietnam was probably a mistake. Bringing fantastic Vietnamese dishes like those at

Bao 111

Bao 111 to the East Village was a very good move. Unfussy, deceptively charming, semi-minimalist, and very popular, this date destination is refreshingly calm. True, tattooed punksters can be found at the teeny bar, which extends along the neatly curtained front window, but harmony is found in these authentic Vietnamese dishes, some of which were inspired by the chef's Vietnamese mother. That inner peace continues with infused hot sake, saketinis, and specialty drinks; we like the Mekong Fizz. Still not feeling relaxed? Swing by on Sundays, when a jazz trio plays until late. It's not the most economical place to have a drink, but it's definitely a pleasant and sophisticated choice.

Bar Americain
152 W. 52nd St. (6th & 7th Aves.)
Midtown 212.265.9700

Bar Americain

Bobby Flay and Lawrence Kretchmer's two-story, American-style brasserie will transform you into the sophisticate you were born to be. Boasting high ceilings, warm earth tones, floor-to-ceiling windows, and a bar that's nicely overshadowed by a slightly tilted aged mirror, you'll feel simultaneously welcomed and overwhelmed. Dim lighting and secluded clusters of tables on each side of the room will have you whispering sweet nothings to your date as you share a lemon meringue crème brulee, sample the raw bar, or dine on entrées such as the smoked chicken pot pie. Sojourn to the second floor for even more privacy, where you can watch revelers below or slink away to the elevated backroom replete with sliding doors (reminiscent of a geisha house). No pesky passport application or lengthy flight necessary.

Bar Below
209 Smith St. (@ Baltic St.)
Carroll Gardens 718.694.2277

There's a "no dancing" sign on the wall at Bar Below, but we can't say how strictly enforced the cabaret laws are when the sign is upside-down. Part lounge with a makeshift after-hours dance floor, part bathhouse with its blue-tinted steam-room-tile décor, the basement space under Middle Eastern restaurant Faan hosts weekly parties with an impressive rotating list of DJs. On any other night, you'll hear DJs spinning Afro-Cuban beats or straight-up hip hop with live drumming thrown into the mix. Brooklyn clubbers rejoice—it's like you've died and gone to Manhattan without even taking the F train…or actually dying for that matter.

Bar Bleu @ Café Deville
103 3rd Ave. (13th & 14th Sts.)
East Village 212.477.4500

Surely you've peeked through Café Deville's big bay windows on your way into and out of the East Village. What you might not have seen is Bar Bleu, which is the space downstairs. With its exposed brick walls and a wooden dance floor tucked snugly against the DJ booth, a cozier, homier spot for private events is scarcely found downtown. Bar Bleu features the same menu as Café Deville, whose $13.95 express lunch is a steal. More importantly, Bar Bleu has its own bar. Recognizing the strength of this space, ownership here is happy to work with those planning an event, often offering assistance from the kitchen. It turns out that the staff here is like a good watch—they look good and they work.

Bar East

1733 1st Ave. (@ 90th St.)
Upper East Side 212.876.0203

Just when you were all set to give up on the Upper East Side, along comes Bar East to inject some life into the scene and save the day. Bar East's a sizeable joint that has everything a patron could ask for—two pool tables, a jukebox, videogames, darts, and Sunday-night bingo. The friendly staff at this up-and-coming hangout is top-notch, and the prices won't make you groan in agony upon inspecting the contents of your wallet the next morning. The owners recently renovated the downstairs space and opened it up as a musical venue called the Underscore with its own bar, great sound system, and terrific acoustics. On Sunday nights they have karaoke with a live backing band, Wednesday nights are host to open mics, and bands play every Thursday, Friday, and Saturday night. An Upper East Side bar that doesn't suck? What's next—a tolerable Ben Affleck movie?

Bar 89

89 Mercer St. (Broome & Spring Sts.)
SoHo 212.274.0989

Voyeurs beware: Despite what you've heard, you can't watch hot strangers using the loo at Bar 89, which is praised for its unique WCs. (The gorgeous glass stall doors turn opaque when closed.) However, you can actually see a very diverse crowd in this refreshingly well-lit, airy space that's sleek and sophisticated, sans pretense. Fresh-scrubbed, chirpy waiters are helpful, suggesting snacks from a menu that's surprisingly down-to-

Bar 89

earth, and explaining just what's in the creative cocktails. Drinks are large and potent, so after a couple of caipirinhas you'll find the cojones to chat up that table of cuties, or dance around with a lampshade on your head, which might actually energize Bar 89's relaxed vibe…as will your being forcefully and justifiably removed.

Bar @ Etats-Unis

247 E. 81st St. (2nd & 3rd Aves.)
Upper East Side 212.396.9928

The first thing one might hear upon entering this tiny bar/restaurant might be "Yeah, Triscuits!" The bartender serves them with the spicy guacamole when Etats-Unis runs out of homemade tortilla chips. Yes, chips are in high demand at this attractive little gem across the street from its older, more conservative parent, the restaurant Etats-Unis. On its own slimmed-down menu, the bar offers some of the same delicious dishes as the restaurant. Its ripe red shelves seem to be bursting with bottles and avocados, lemons, and limes. Wine fans will be happy to find quality bottles in the mid-$20s range and they pair nicely with this French-influenced small-plates menu. This neighborhood has some growing up to do, and this handsome cherry wood-lined bar is ready and waiting for the day that happens.

Bar 515
515 3rd Ave. (34th & 35th Sts.)
Murray Hill 212.532.3300

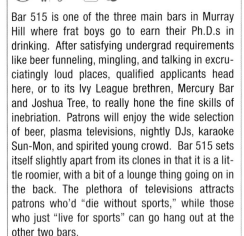

Bar 515 is one of the three main bars in Murray Hill where frat boys go to earn their Ph.D.s in drinking. After satisfying undergrad requirements like beer funneling, mingling, and talking in excruciatingly loud places, qualified applicants head here, or to its Ivy League brethren, Mercury Bar and Joshua Tree, to really hone the fine skills of inebriation. Patrons will enjoy the wide selection of beer, plasma televisions, nightly DJs, karaoke Sun-Mon, and spirited young crowd. Bar 515 sets itself slightly apart from its clones in that it is a little roomier, with a bit of a lounge thing going on in the back. The plethora of televisions attracts patrons who'd "die without sports," while those who just "live for sports" can go hang out at the other two bars.

Bar 4
444 7th Ave. (14th & 15th Sts.)
Park Slope 718.832.9800

Park Slope's Bar 4 doesn't want to be your neighborhood destination lounge. It does, however, want to be your neighborhood martini lounge, and that, the veteran owners swear, makes all the difference. For those who simply yawn at the sight of another lager flowing from the tap, Bar 4 breaks the monotony with a list of 20ish martinis, a Salvation-Army-chic décor, neighborhood-artist-adorned walls, and local DJs spinning three to four nights a week. Monday nights have $3 tap and well drinks, and Tuesday boasts an open mic. This isn't to say that Bar 4 has no love for beer drinkers—Wednesday hosts an all-you-can-drink $15 PBR extravaganza. The inevitable crowd cramp that happens every weekend encourages a "come in alone, but leave together" mentality.

Bar Minnow
444 9th St. (@ 7th Ave.)
Park Slope 718.832.5500

If Coney Island is the closest to the seaside you usually get, save yourself a longer F train ride and hop off at Bar Minnow, an enclave of New England ocean fare. With a host of over 40 wines, Bar Minnow will satiate both the booze-hound and the foodie inside you. The dishes range from burgers to lobster rolls, making up in quality what it lacks in quantity. The dark-toned wood and tin roof mix well with the marble bar top, creating an atmosphere that's both casual and luxurious, hitting the right tone for young and old Park Slope types that frequent this abode. Dock here for a late-night snack or pre-show drink with your catch of the day before you head off into the sunset (or the subway).

Bar 9
807 9th Ave. (53rd & 54th Sts.)
Hell's Kitchen 212.399.9336

A wave of cultural identity crisis hits you just inside Bar 9 in the form of an "Aloha" sign, a patio umbrella, 21 Club jockey statues surrounded by antique red-velvet sofas, chairs scattered in candlelit corners, and a projection TV hanging in the middle of the expansive room showing a sports game or film. Clearly the biggest draw for this aesthetically confused lounge is the cheap alcohol (which you are advised to drink slowly, lest you feel lost in the throes of interior-décor hell). Bar 9 offers good deals on beer and cocktails served in beer brand-emblazoned plastic cups. It's standing-room-only in Bar 9, where you'll find yourself immersed in a pick-up-friendly crowd who should have grown out of the Spring Break milieu by now.

Bar None
98 3rd Ave. (12th & 13th Sts.)
East Village 212.777.6663

What is essentially a laidback, non-offensive bar in the early evening transforms under cover of darkness into a breeding ground for backwards-hatted boys and bottle-tanned girls in micro-minis at this pick-up spot for the undiscerning. On the plus side, Bar None works double-time to make up for its annoying clientele, with what's probably the longest happy hour in the city (noon-11pm). The

$2 draft and well drink "power hour" (11pm-midnight) and specialty nights like Wednesday's ladies' night ($1 dollar drinks for not having a Y chromosome) and rotating Monday night events help matters too. On the weekends, the pool table is cleared out of the back to uncover a dance floor, and the multiple TVs show most major football games. Hit it up early for cheap drinks and get out before the frat attack.

Bar on A (BOA)
170 Ave. A (@ 11th St.)
East Village 212.353.8231

So BOA, as this place is nicknamed, is the abbreviation for "Bar on (Ave.) A." However, "BOA" takes on a different meaning when considering the snakeskin décor that abounds, including a cool serpentine bar. (There's also a subtle Asian thing going on, as evidenced by hidden Buddha statuettes and hanging lamps.) This used to be a tiny, low-key lounge that was good for brief dates and small groups with broad musical interests. Now, despite its recent expansion, BOA has maintained its chill atmosphere while adding live music and a little room to move…or at least to sit. The international "tapas-style" menu also offers plenty of wiggle room, offering calamari, Asian dumplings, edamame, and nachos for starters. With 25+ beers to wash it all down, there's nothing constricting about BOA.

Bar Reis
375 5th Ave. (5th & 6th Sts.)
Park Slope 718.832.5716

Despite this arty Park Slope favorite's excellent local buzz, it's very much hit or miss. On busy nights, the place is packed with a solid mix of locals and all-borough visitors. But on slower weeknights, you can almost hear the crickets chirping. Bar Reis' small entrance is deceiving, as the area unfurls into several connected rooms—an inside balcony reached by a winding staircase, the downstairs lounge with its own bar, and a back garden with the only outdoor pool table for miles around. The trendy bartenders are chatty and knowledgeable about alcohol, and aren't afraid to show off their booze IQ. When this place is hot it's hot, and when it's not, it's still a bit warm.

Bar Seine (@ the Hôtel Plaza Athénée)
37 E. 64th St. (Madison & Park Aves.)
Upper East Side 212.734.9100

Every New York hotspot needs something to set it apart from the droves of other bars who hope to satisfy 8 million New Yorkers' alcoholic needs. The brown-leather floor at this quiet lounge is one of Bar Seine's many eccentric touches. Most of the continents are represented (OK, there aren't any stuffed Antarctic penguins, but they wouldn't exactly look amiss here) in the décor, which mixes leather and animal-print upholstery with an Indonesian mirror, Turkish vases, European paintings, and a Persian rug. Separate seating areas in different rooms, big, leafy potted plants, and dark velvet curtains allow for privacy. A varied menu from the hotel's French Arabelle restaurant is available during bar hours.

Bar Seine

Bar 6
502 6th Ave. (12th & 13th Sts.)
Greenwich Village 212.691.1363

Whether celebrating with friends or trying to

Bar 6

impress a date, toast a glass of Veuve Clicquot Yellow Label at Bar 6. Then show off your perfect pronunciation of "croque monsieur," one of the many affordable culinary delights served until late at this Euro-style bistro. Mirrors reflect a warm glow, causing visitors to melt into these red leather banquettes for a while. Despite all Francophiliac appearances, the wine list spans the globe; the bar also stocks a small but exotic selection of beers, as well as grappa, port, and a good pick of Highland single malts. Pre-smoking ban, this place was perfect for lighting up and embracing the European atmosphere. Now you'll just have to make do by breathing in the smoking-hot staff that's also capable of damaging one's heart.

Bar Toto
411 11th St. (6th & 7th Aves.)
Park Slope 718.768.4698

Formerly the less successful Lulu, this place seems determined to find success, and to find it while using a dog's name. A reasonably priced neighborhood spot thriving on a quiet corner between the slightly different scenes of Seventh and Fifth Avenues, Toto might be on to something. Catering equally to families and barflies, Bar Toto offers a unique and delicious weekend brunch, affordable lunch and dinner menus, and enough outdoor patio seating, indoor booths, and stools to accommodate strollers and beer guts. The rusty, neon beer sign-laden exterior hides a classic, attractive décor with well-placed mirrors and huge windows overlooking 11th Street. The gregarious owner and manager, who ambles around dispensing hugs to friends and greetings to newcomers, is always eager to chat and do whatever it takes to make you feel at home. Because, as we know, there's no place like home.

Bar XII
206 E. 34th St. (@ 3rd Ave.)
Murray Hill 212.545.9912

Featuring the world's only draught-mounted 5-inch plasma TVs, and a bathroom hand dryer that blows wet hands clean in seconds, Bar XII (aka Bar 12) seems as though it was underwritten by Sharper Image. A sleek long counter points customers to a wall lined with flat-panel TVs showing music video mixes and local sports. Bar XII also offers one of the greatest meal bargains in town: the Monday night Angry Lobster special. Every Monday, a Cajun-spiced lobster can be had for $11.95, and a second one for a mere $6.95. Brunch is served Saturday and Sunday, and there's enough of a lounge vibe for this place to be a late-night destination, as well. For a back-to-the-future night out in a part of town that's more chic than shabby, Bar XII isn't a bad option.

Bar XII

Bar 288 (aka Tom & Jerry's)
288 Elizabeth St. (Houston & Bleecker Sts.)
NoHo 212.260.5045

Lots of bars need shtick to attract customers. This friendly joint doesn't need help from a kitschy theme, but it's here nonetheless. Wooden shelves

Bar 288

behind the bar are lined with the owners' impressive collection of vintage punch bowls and china cups—some painted with apple-cheeked youngsters sledding through a winter wonderland, others gilded and patterned with boughs of holly; all are inscribed with "Tom & Jerry" (yes, the cat-and-mouse duo who would break all of this fine teaware in one short cartoon skit). The retro dish collection might be a draw, but really it's the attitude-less, hang-out-as-long-as-you-want vibe and eclectic crowd of NoHo locals, paper-reading gents, and slackers playing chess that makes Bar 288 the perfect spot to start or end your bar crawl.

Bar Veloce Chelsea
176 7th Ave. (20th & 21st Sts.)
Chelsea 212.629.5300

Italian vineyard meets New York at Bar Veloce where there are 22 wines by the glass and 41 by the bottle. Sake, grappa, and other dessert wines are also offered up in this warm, intimate trendster wine bar. Soft jazz plays in the background as a 9-5 crowd in its late 20s and early 30s gathers in the candlelight for some laidback conversation. Parties of more than two might have a problem grabbing a table or spot at the bar, but the whitewashed brick interior is a perfect place for a first or second date. Light Italian fare (gelato, sandwiches, and appetizers like prosciutto and bruschetta, and of course cheese) is moderately priced, as are the wines. There's also a much smaller Bar Veloce in the East Village.

Bar Veloce East Village
175 2nd Ave. (11th & 12th Sts.)
East Village 212.260.3200

If you're wondering where that cute bartender who served you the other night can be found for round two of your discussion of Cubism and the history of Italian silent films, try Bar Veloce. A longtime stronghold for downtown's service-industry employees, Bar Veloce's understated glassy décor, soft music, and the black-and-white films screened back-to-back soothe the weariest drink slinger in its itsy-bitsy confines. Of course it's great for the rank-and-file wine drinker, too. A large range of wine, including the hard-to-find Fernet, is offered alongside a long list of Italian dishes. The cheese plates are very popular here, and so are the panini sandwiches. If you're so inclined, there's even a panini made with Nutella. Try splitting one with that cute bartender from Pianos sitting next to you...

bar.vetro
222 E. 58th St. (2nd & 3rd Aves.)
Midtown 212.308.0112

This modern Italian restaurant balances sexy sleekness and a cool décor with genuine friendliness and comfort. Inside, the first thing you'll notice is the small, glowing glass bar ("vetro" is Italian for glass) and calm, lavender lighting. Vivolo next door serves a hearty Italian meal, but the real draw is the ambiance and the welcoming feel at bar.vetro; the staff is extremely friendly and the owner himself is often on hand to greet customers. At night, half of the restaurant turns into a lounge space, and the bar becomes a hidden favorite for cool kids otherwise stranded in Midtown. Impress your date by claiming to know Italian (the menu offers quick crib note-like headings to get you started) and order her a Fragolini (a martini with fresh strawberries). Mangia!

Baraza
133 Ave. C (8th & 9th Sts.)
East Village 212.539.0811

When you don't have *el dinero* for a trip to Latin America, grab your life raft and head to sea—Avenue C, that is. The pulsing Cubano beats can be heard a block away from the unmarked blue wood and frosted glass façade of Baraza. Tread your way through waves of people packed between the exposed-brick walls and long bar to get to the dancing area in back and shake your hips to hot Latin-inspired songs. Take a break on the black leather banquettes and try to count the dolls and doll heads that spy on you from cubby holes carved into the wooden walls. This fiesta of fun has its risks, though; bouncers warn you to watch your personal belongings and a small plaque reads "No cocaine peddling."

Barbalùc
135 E. 65th St. (Lexington & Park Aves.)
Upper East Side 212.774.1999

Most patrons are probably unaware of the derivation of this fresh and modern restaurant's name and of the whereabouts of Friuli, the region that inspires its menu (for the record, a barbalùc is a wine elf and Friuli is northeast of Venice). They're most likely just attracted to this small, stylish, lively wine bar and restaurant, first noticing its elegant yet simple white façade and then drawn in by its soft lighting and clean interior design. The bar only has eight seats plus a couple of tables by the front windows; opposite the bar is the main part of the restaurant. (A private dining space is downstairs.) The food here is somewhere between very good and breathtaking, but nearly three years after opening, the place hasn't quite found consistency in its presentation or its following. Your gain—claim a table now.

Barbes
376 9th St. (@ 6th Ave.)
Park Slope 718.965.9177

Don't expect any *Moulin Rouge* action at this cozy, French-inspired watering hole. Named after a Parisian commune and owned by two French musicians, Barbes may put on the red light in its front bar, but this tavern is better suited for friends and couples than those looking to pick up any Satine types. Young Brooklynites dig Barbes' laid-back, neighborly vibe and Hotel D'Orsay, the bar's performance space that's booked every night of the week with live bands (often playing world music, ragtime, or rumba) and various literary

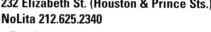
Barbes

events. Behind the well-stocked bar, traditional French liquor like Pernod and absente is available, as well as a long list of bourbons and single-malts, including the rare Johnny Walker Green. The only thing missing is the Djarm vending machine.

BarBossa
232 Elizabeth St. (Houston & Prince Sts.)
NoLita 212.625.2340

Who's the Bossa? This newly opened restaurant in NoLita, which features moderately priced Brazilian-inspired food served by a very friendly wait staff, that's who. Like a NY real estate agent would say, the restaurant is "cozy," which actually means it's small and has fewer than 10 tables. But unlike that cramped hole-in-the-wall apartment, the size here actually does help to create a comfortable, warm atmosphere. While the emphasis is definitely on dinner (the hours are 5:30pm-11:30pm, plus a weekend brunch), a small bar occupies a prominent place in the restaurant, although BarBossa does not yet have a full liquor license (boo!). But wait—to compensate, the drink menu features sake-based cocktails such as saketinis, sakeritas, and sake mojitos in addition to beer and wine. All is forgiven.

Barbuto
775 Washington St. (Jane & 12th Sts.)
West Village 212.924.9700

Chef Jonathan Waxman has made his career of simple cooking a gluttonous experience despite Barbuto's small dishes and limited ingredients. An earthy and organic take on Italian Mediterranean, Barbuto favors seasonal salads and wood oven-cooked dishes like pollo al forno ($17) which, when paired with any of their 100 wines, can only be enhanced. Located on the semi-outskirts of the Meatpacking District, Barbuto's laidback vibe provides cover to the area's trendier counterparts, especially when you're not feeling so *Sex and the City*-ish. Not your typical tucked-away café, Barbuto can be seen from a distance with its unusual, garage-style doors. Like Barbuto's main dishes, the understated décor parallels Waxman's rustic vision with an exposed kitchen and white-painted brick walls. The service may be dry, but with dishes $20 and under, you can put up with a little 'tude.

Barcade
388 Union Ave. (Ainslie & Powers Sts.)
Williamsburg 718.302.6464

'Fess up—your cell phone ring tone is the Super Mario Bros. theme, you own a copy of "Pac-Man Fever," and you had carpal tunnel at age eight. Do we have the bar for you: Williamsburg's Barcade is just that—a bar and arcade in one, where the impressive selection of American brews average $4-$5, but the games are just 25 cents a play. The collection of over 20 videogames includes such retro stalwarts as Ms. Pac-Man, Tetris, Super Mario, Galaga, Rampage, and Tapper, and the crowd varies in age from Atari to Playstation 2. A pool table rests at the end of this very long, spacious bar, with a small area for lounging, a change machine that spits out quarters, and an outdoor smoking area out front. High scores are scrawled on a chalkboard overhead in this bar where one hand holds a joystick and the other a mug of beer.

The Barclay Bar and Grill (@ Intercontinental Barclay)
111 E. 48th St. (Park & Lexington Aves.)
Midtown 212.906.3130

The Ian Schrager era made hotel lounges synonymous with moneyed glamour, but in the bar of the Intercontinental Barclay, they've either taken the young model thing way too far or this is a serious family joint. (We know where Michael Jackson's release party is going to be.) Despite the strollers, hotel guests seem to have no problem unwinding in this wood-paneled, dimly lit space. Businessmen and tourists linger on barstools, tipping back nightcaps of bourbon and cognac before turning in for the evening. A light menu is also available for those returning from late business meetings or unsuccessful dates. While the setting is old-world, the prices are not. The $21 Barclay burger and $66 tumbler of Johnnie Walker Blue can leave patrons crying like a baby. Well, that and dropping their pacifiers.

Bar-Coastal
1495 1st Ave. (@ 78th St.)
Upper East Side 212.288.6635

This neighborhood spot is chock-full of locals seeking familiar bartenders and steady sports coverage. Beach bums of the Upper East Side will

Bar-Coastal

appreciate the "Cali" aura with a sporty twist. (Think surfboards and flat-screens.) The outdoor bench is a good spot to chat up the friendly bar staff away from the action or bask in the comfort of the after-work crowd. Try a frozen raspberry margarita for a taste of the beach or let the area jocks wow you with wing-eating ability from noon-6pm on "Sports Saturday." While the jukebox may well have been stocked with CDs from your fresh-man year of college, patrons from surfers to suit-clad men find themselves glued to the stools at this comfort zone.

Barfly
244 3rd Ave. (@ 20th St.)
Gramercy 212.473.9660

It's unlikely that Bukowski would've hung out amidst these neon Bud Light signs and 12 TVs, while classic rock blares from the jukebox, but $6 mixed drinks like the Flyjuice speak to a wide range of alcoholics. Just because there are 10 beers on tap doesn't mean this is a place for drunks only—winos have 20 vinos by the glass from which to choose. There's no need to worry about finding a place to sit—the bar, booths, tables, and outdoor area are usually vacant and the line for the pool table runs one- or two-people deep. The friendly bartender relaxes behind a long, beautiful wooden bar while patrons gamble at the "Touch Machine." One could easily do the late shift here thanks to comfort food that provides more than ample sustenance.

Barmarche
14 Spring St. (@ Elizabeth St.)
NoLita 212.219.2399

Located on one of the quaintest, prettiest blocks in downtown Manhattan, Barmarche is a sunny little café with just enough panache to fit in, but not as much pomp as most of its neighbors. Opened by two former Bungalow 8 employees, Barmarche features a top-notch beverage selection (sample the Brazilian sangria—fresh lime juice, sugarcane rum, and red wine—or the lemonade du jour), a pleasantly light lunch and dinner menu prepared by former Spice Market chef Angel Andrade, and a

tasteful décor (French door windows, intricate tin ceiling). Frequented by a young, sprightly (and pretty) crowd, this corner spot is also great for brunch. Barmache is a breath of fresh air for the neighborhood—it's like a drop-dead gorgeous model-type who has it all—beauty, brains, AND belching skills.

Barna (@ Hotel Giraffe)
365 Park Ave. S. (@ 26th St.)
Murray Hill 212.532.8300

Hotel bars can be hit or miss depending on how "out of town" the guests are. But with its simple, stylish décor and Catalonian-leaning menu, Barna is a daily circus of semi-foodies and cocktailers. Located below street level in Murray Hill's Hotel Giraffe and outfitted with lime-green banquettes and striped columns and arches, Barna gives diners a contemporary Latin experience with dishes like paella ($22), grilled pork chops ($27), and patatas fritas ($7). A slightly elevated bar area with more banquettes is stocked with a strong selection of Spanish wines ($26-$135 a bottle), and seems to be the center of activity once 10pm hits. Once it warms up, outdoor seating attracts native and tourists alike.

Barracuda
275 W. 22nd St. (7th & 8th Aves.)
Chelsea 212.645.8613

This bar is a joke—and that's a good thing. Nightly drag shows here ensure that there's never any shortage of raunchy humor. Whether it's drag queen Candis Cayne detailing her glamorous life on Mondays or Shequida imparting the news on Tuesday's "Gayly Show," you're sure to leave here with a smile on your face. Of course, super-strong drinks served by cute waiters and bartenders probably contribute to that outcome as well. Barracuda also attracts some of the city's friendliest 20- to 30-something dudes, who manage to be outgoing without going out of their way. So pick up a drink, pick up a guy, or just sit back, relax, and enjoy the show. It's a gay old time.

Barrage

401 W. 47th St. (9th & 10th Aves.)
Hell's Kitchen 212.586.9390

An eclectic mix of men mingle at this joint—from theater queens to twinks with drinks, to Chelsea boys who've ventured far north. Regardless of the night, you're sure to find someone interesting to chat up at this recently renovated lounge. The miniature chandeliers dangling from the ceiling, comfy couches, and red walls (which are plastered with nude portraits) make you feel as though you're hanging out in some swanky bordello. And indeed, as the night progresses, it often feels like mating season is every season as neighborhood men drop by to see which intoxicated patron they can bring home. Regardless of whether you come here after work or later in the night, you'll definitely discover a barrage of booze and boys at this oddly placed den of debauchery.

Barramundi

67 Clinton St. (Stanton & Rivington Sts.)
Lower East Side 212.529.6900

If you're looking for a little taste of "Down Under" downtown, hike to Barramundi. And no, you won't see any croc hunters or Aborigines here. Barramundi's set off from the surrounding bars for two reasons—the crowd here is a little older and more buttoned-down than the normal LES neighborhood crowd, and they serve a selection of Australian beers. Tree-trunk tables contrast nicely with lamps constructed out of old beer bottles. Even though the recent move forced Barramundi to leave their outdoor garden behind, this place is still full-fledged outback. Barramundi may be named after an Australian fish, but there is nothing fishy about this place. G'day, mate; drink up.

Barrio Chino

253 Broome St. (Orchard & Ludlow Sts.)
Lower East Side 212.228.6710

If you're trying to grab a cocktail here, you'd better roll with the early-bird crowd because this place is definitely more of a restaurant than a bar. A Mexican eatery with a Chinese theme is as frightening as a taco stand that sells lo mien; the only thing more troubling than a fish taco is a Szechwan chicken taco. Luckily, the Chinese influence has not crept into the menu at all. There is no sake, but they do have tequila, mojitos, and margaritas. The bay windows open up to the street, giving this closet of a restaurant a little more elbowroom. Barrio Chino is a little confused and you will be too after a couple of throat-burning tequila shots.

Barrow Street Ale House

15 Barrow St. (7th Ave. S. & 4th St.)
Greenwich Village 212.691.6127

It's billed as an "ale house" but a sports bar by any other name is still a sports bar, as indicated by the enthusiastic yelps of fans watching any number of the games broadcast on the bar's satellite TVs. The décor is pseudo-rustic lodge, with stuffed deer heads on the wall. It's a bit of a sausage-fest here, attracting mostly young college types. Downstairs you can get your game on with darts and a pool table. There's a good bourbon selection, and happy hour runs Monday through Friday from noon-7pm, with $1 off all drinks and $2.50 Bud and Bud Lights. The above-average menu means you can sate your need for food, drink, and sport in one fell swoop.

Barrymore's

267 W. 45th St. (@ 8th Ave.)
Hell's Kitchen 212.391.8400

Don't expect to see Drew here, but you will see the likenesses of Barrymores past in the form of Broadway memorabilia. Tucked away in the Theater District, this neighborhood haunt is a quiet and cozy, old-style hangout. The décor of this restaurant row establishment embraces the golden age of cinema and the spectacle of Broadway. Barrymore's functions as a restaurant, too; it caters to the locals as well as the theater crowd who crave comfort food and a stiff drink after being subjected to over two hours of people singing about raised rents. Marked by a humble awning, Barrymore's is filled with the sounds of an excited crowd, soft jazz, and chatty bartenders; it's a tried-and-true oasis in the sea of tourists, overpriced restaurants, and tacky bars overcrowding Times Square.

Basso Est
198 Orchard St. (Houston & Stanton Sts.)
Lower East Side 212.358.9569

In Italian basso means "lower east" and while this Lower East Side place is on the small side, it's still stately—white tablecloths, white napkins, and white collars fill this bar. And though this Italian bar/restaurant looks high-brow in comparison to the dive bars the neighborhood is known for, Basso Est is still affordable. Don't even bother coming here if you're not intending on dining, though. The aroma inside is divine, the setting is romantic, and the Abruzzi Italian cuisine (homemade spaghetti with lamb ragout and percorino cheese, $12.50), desserts (tiramisu, $8), and homemade sangria are delicious. Chief Paulo Catini makes it so when you want Italian, Little Italy never even crosses your mind. Now, how about some more of that sangria?

Bayard's Blue Bar
1 Hanover Sq. (Pearl & Stone Sts.)
Financial District 212.514.9454

Bayard's is like a Jekyll and Hyde of classy establishments. In the daytime it's the India House, one of the oldest private clubs in the country. Come nightfall Bayard's opens its doors to people who actually work during the day. With the classic maritime styling, a comfortably elegant atmosphere, and on most nights a piano player in the corner, Bayard's offers one of the most unique and classy experiences in New York. Stepping into Bayard's is like looking way back into America's colonial, er, past. (No political debates please—this may not be a bar, but it is a bar guide!) Anyway, all that culture will cost you, but with an enticing menu, and a wine list with nearly 1,500 choices, chances are you'll find something you won't mind paying for.

B.B. King's Blues Club & Grill
237 W. 42nd St. (7th & 8th Aves.)
Midtown 212.997.4144

Uninformed tourists would usually be barking up the wrong tree if they were seeking good music above 14th Street, but in the case of B.B. King's Blues Club & Grill, Times Square is the place to be for soul food and down-home blues. Named for the legendary axe man (and opened by the owners of the Blue Note), B.B.'s boasts the biggest blues, R&B, and soul artists this side of the Mississippi—Etta James, Cody Chestnutt, Maxi Priest, Al Green (the list is unbelievable). Come by on Sundays from 12:30pm-2:30pm for the Gospel Brunch featuring the Harlem Gospel Choir and sinful soul food. On the occasional Saturday, the Strawberry Fields band plays during Beatles Brunch. Visit Lucille's Bar & Grill downstairs (it's named after B.B.'s beloved guitar) for even more jams.

Beast
638 Bergen St. (@ Vanderbilt Ave.)
Prospect Heights 718.399.6855

Beast

It didn't take long for Brooklyn hipsters to sink their claws into Beast, one of the cool new bar/restaurants to join the Prospect Heights pack. Depictions of mythological beings adorn the walls and windows of this medieval-looking tavern where, on weekdays, mellow, yuppyish couples pass around plates of tapas and sip sherry. The daily "reverse" happy hour (11pm-1am; 4pm-7pm) is enough to awaken one's inner animal, with $3 draughts and two-for-$5 well drinks. On weekends, when neighborhood party monsters and ravenous singles are on the prowl, the front

B.E.D. NYC

room gets so packed you can hardly see the gold-enameled bar, let alone squeeze into a wooden banquette and order a meal. When the weather's nice, the party spills onto an outdoor patio.

Beauty Bar
231 E. 14th St. (@ 3rd Ave.)
East Village 212.539.1389

Here lies yet another hipster hive that's themed after its former working-stiff tenants. At Beauty Bar, makeup products are displayed above the liquor bottles and vintage hair-dryers line the walls, reminding you that people once came here to get beautiful; now beautiful people just show up to get drunk, or to partake in the $10 manicure-and-drink special. After you study the classic vogue furnishings, try and slide past the bottle-necked crowd to the "Blue Rinse Lounge" in back. Here you'll find a décor of Euro-trash minimalism, where the ever-played-out disco ball twirls and a second bar services thirsty drinkers. Add a DJ and walls sprinkled with glitter, and you get the pic-ture. And girls, ask your "manicurist" how many drinks they've had before asking for bright-red nails. It's dark in here.

Becky's
1156 1st Ave. (63rd & 64th Sts.)
Upper East Side 212.317.8929

Stop in this friendly, multitasking pub for the Tunisia vs. Germany match, a Hawaiian pizza, karaoke, 25-cent wings (all day on Monday), live music, comedy, DJs, and varying drink specials (weekdays, 11:30am-7pm)—phew! The menu boasts a heartburn-inducing selection of pizzas, fried chicken, and tacos—bring your own Tums. The usual flags and mirrored bar decorations line not only the walls but are hung from the ceiling as well. And if you want to see the bar's namesake, look on the floor around 1am. No, she's not the blonde who just passed out. She's the friendly black-and-white cat underfoot.

B.E.D. New York
530 W. 27th St. (10th & 11th Aves.)
Chelsea 212.594.4109

After much anticipation and many imitations, B.E.D. NYC has finally arrived and anxious scen-esters who knew the Miami locale are lining up to get three sheets to the wind. The journey to this gorgeous two-story restaurant and club starts with a rather crummy freight elevator ride that climbs up the side of Spirit, which occupies the bottom portion of the building. When that elevator opens, a ubiquitous, top-notch staff welcomes guests to a plush décor of subtle pinks, purples, and whites. On the main floor, three walls of connected bed-like sofas surround one big round table, which eats up the center of the room. The fourth wall houses a big bar where Dale DeGroff's exceptional specialty cocktails are served in often cramped confines. B.E.D.'s upstairs club, which could be called "Hammock," is much better executed: The sweeping panoramic view makes it an after-work and brunch destination.

The Beekman

15 Beekman St. (Nassau & William Sts.)
Financial District 212.732.7333

When the market is a bit bearish, the Beekman is a wonderful place to hibernate. This Irish pub-ish establishment has been a Wall Street landmark for over 70 years, from back when angry grizzlies ruled the earth. The inexpensively priced beers ($4-$6) and very sensible entrées ($8-$15) are priced low enough for underachieving traders who can't discuss swapping natural gasses without giggling. And with frequent live entertainment and occasional karaoke, the Beekman is a nice departure from the Financial District's standard no-frills "scene." The beer selection includes more than 20 picks from the tap and wines by the glass hit the dozen mark. You wouldn't know it by walking in here after work, but jackets and ties are not required.

Beer Bar @ Café Centro

200 Park Ave. (@ 45th St.)
Midtown 212.818.1333

A beer bar for not-so-serious aficionados, Café Centro's Beer Bar offers several bottled imports and up to 10 drafts, which helps to justify the name. Jutting off the northwest end of Grand Central Terminal, this spot attracts a gaggle of thirsty white-collar workers stopping by for a round or three of afternoon and pre-commute brews. Businessmen hold late lunch meetings in

the large, art-deco-inspired dining room, while younger desk jockeys take to the outdoor area to "network" with interoffice hotties. The cross-cubicle pick-up scene lasts until about 8, when folks can no longer put off catching their trains back to the 'burbs. In fact, Beer Bar is such a lunch and after-work spot, it isn't even open on weekends.

Believe Lounge

1 E. 36th St. (@ 5th Ave.)
Murray Hill 212.481.4955

Believe Lounge

What was once fantasy has become reality. Recently opened to the public (it was a private establishment for the past seven years), Believe Lounge is so eclectic, you'd swear it was ripped from the pages of *Harry Potter*. The atmosphere is pure chimera à la *The Twilight Zone*—featuring everything from decapitated mannequins to an Everlast punching bag. Believe's owner, Chynna Soul, adds the finishing touch with her unique brand of philosophy and mixology (try the "Your Majesty"). Making out is encouraged on the fluffy chairs (or the full-sized bed, take your pick). This spellbound lounge should be visited at least once—if not for the service, drinks, or ambiance, then for the occasional belly dancers, reflexologists, and bewitching bartenders dressed up as angels, or just for a story to tell your friends.

Belly

155 Rivington St. (Clinton & Suffolk Sts.)
Lower East Side 212.533.1810

Hiding deep within the belly of the beast that is the LES, this cozy lounge is a frugal bar-hopper's dream—from the $2 shots to the menu of $4 munchies (chips, nuts, olives, and cheese). Belly's menu of specialty cocktails are just waiting to splash into your, you guessed it—belly. Drinks like the Belly-ni, sparkling white wine, tangerine juice, and raspberry essence; the Wicked Lychee, lychee and whiskey; the Sake-To Me, sake and plum wine; and Cuban iced teas are real tummy-rumblers, so remember your drinking mantra: "Beer before liquor..." They're generously sized too; and the bartenders are as sweet as the concoctions they shake. If you're lucky, they'll even let you pick the jams.

Belmont Lounge

Belmont Lounge
117 E. 15th St. (Park Ave. S. & Irving Pl.)
Gramercy 212.533.0009

Thanks to post-concert spillover from Irving Plaza and beer-gut spillover during the 2-for-1 happy hour Monday-Friday, this trusty standby has been going strong since...aw, who knows? Let's just say "a while." Thirty-somethings in suits come here after work for the specials, and are herded out around 9pm to make way for 20-somethings dressed to the nines and looking to pick up rock stars, but usually leaving with scruffy roadies. The backroom booths are prime real estate and offer great people-watching, especially once the DJ begins. A small but decent menu of finger foods, salads, and sandwiches will help absorb any of the 11 specialty cocktails that are as tasty in a quiet corner as they are outside.

Bembe
81 S. 6th St. (@ Berry St.)
Williamsburg 718.387.5389

Candles flickering from tiny nooks in the exposed-brick wall make the already sexy clientele, bar staff, and resident drum-bangers all the more alluring at this hidden den. A low hipster quotient means lots of straight men—some nice (they'll buy you a drink), some naughty (they'll buy you four), and some who will dance up such a storm you'll be doing a tequila shot between every song. Refreshing watermelon mojitos and mango guava margaritas fuel the salsa-driven dance floor madness here. If you aren't coordinated enough to step to blaring bolero at this house party-type den of iniquity, don't worry; this is a place where gringos dance with reckless abandon and no shame.

Bemelmans Bar (@ the Carlyle)
35 E. 76th St. (@ Madison Ave.)
Upper East Side 212.744.1600

Brown leather, mahogany, and candlelit lamps play grown-up to the playful, bucolic murals by Ludwig Bemelman—artist and creator of the *Madeline* children's books—that adorn the walls in this upscale bar. Piano-centric live entertainment is provided six nights a week, for which $20 is charged after 9:30pm. Add this to your double-digit cocktail and choice snack of mini lamb chops, foie gras, or cheese gourgères in the shape of Madeline, and the evening quickly adds up. This charming hideaway located inside the Carlyle Hotel has served presidents, celebrities, and society's movers and shakers for more than 50 years. The old-time bartenders mix cocktails like the Bemelmans Barter—cognac, caraçao, pineapple juice, Angostura bitters, and nutmeg. Put on your top hat and take a slug.

Beppe
45 E. 22nd St. (Broadway & Park Ave. S.)
Flatiron 212.982.8422

The orange hues of this fawning tribute to Italy's Tuscan region are warm and inviting, like sitting in the sun. The wine list rotates frequently but sticks strictly to formula, a lock-step fit with the food on the menu. A bit heavier on seafood than most Italian fare, this western seaside region's specialties range from pastas to a wide range of fish entrées like sautéed salmon and roasted monkfish. Salads and familiar Italian soups go on the side. With such a discriminating selection, the prices are a little high: Entrées range from $26 to $30. But if Tuscany's your thing, Beppe's for you. Book the upstairs dining room for a private get-together. There are but seven seats at the bar, but one can still get lucky there, thanks to a nonstop pouring of fine vino.

Bette
461 W. 23rd St. (9th & 10th Aves.)
Chelsea 212.366.0404

Can Amy Sacco make the leap from club queen to restaurant royalty? You Bette. Think of Bungalow 8 with food, and you've got the crowd figured out at Sacco's hot new restaurant. Though the chef at this culinary hotspot is a Jean-Georges's protégé, this stylized room speaks more to a younger, more informal set that wears jeans to everything but weddings. The floors are made of dark wood and the ceiling is carpeted, which seems to keep noise levels down in the apartment building where the owner lives. The menu is a safe mix of upscale surf and turf with $20-something entrées including lamb, lobster, and short ribs. As with any Sacco venue, getting in won't be easy, but book now and you will someday be dining in the crossfire of air kisses that start at the teeny bar and continue to the elevated tables in the back of the earth-toned space.

Bice
7 E. 54th St. (5th & Madison Aves.)
Midtown 212.688.1999

Thankfully not named for any long-haired *American Idol* runner-ups, this art-deco institution has all the ingredients of greatness—good Italian food, a classy atmosphere, talented waiters, a beautiful dining room, and even a few sidewalk tables. But it all adds up to more flash than substance. Better Italian fare is to be had downtown (and certainly at better prices, unless you savor the more-for-your-money $35 prix fixe menu). The staff is knowledgeable, but they can also be intimidating. Out front, there's a small bar, which mostly serves as a crowded waiting room for diners and genuine Italian types sucking on stogies before they get to their tables. If your idea of fun is hanging out with upper-management types in suits, this is your place, but otherwise, don't add Bice as a vice.

Biddy Early's
43 Murray St. (@ Church St.)
TriBeCa 212.732.2873

We've always thought that beer pong should be indoctrinated as an Olympic sport. Biddy Early's is a traditional after-work Irish pub where, on most nights, patrons drink, chatter, and splurge on timely buy-backs. But when the room gets going, the beer pong tables fill up and affordable pitchers of good beer disappear faster than a freshman's boxers at the first frat party of the semester. Thus, Biddy's attracts a certain kind of crowd—one that never hesitates to guzzle plastic cups of beer in which dirty ping-pong balls have fallen. Still, Biddy's is a great place to have a Guinness (to be even more authentic, ask for a "Smif-ick's") and sharpen your beer sports skills. A word to the wise: Don't fake a brogue; that's just not cool.

Biddy's Pub
301 E. 91st St. (1st & 2nd Aves.)
Upper East Side 212.534.4785

Just what Manhattan needs—another no-name Irish pub. Granted, Biddy's has established a niche for itself as a neighborhood go-to place for its fiercely loyal patrons, but those just stopping by will feel quickly alienated. Biddy's may be the tiniest bar in the city and the poor lighting only adds insult to injury. The regulars that do show up will make you long for the ugly booty call you swore you were going to cut yourself off from. And given Biddy's far-away address, you'll be "biddy" hailing a cab for the long ride home. Given the dearth of customers at most UES locations, we're not sure how a place like Biddy's continues to stay open, but the alcoholic in us certainly isn't complaining.

Big Bar
75 E. 7th St. (1st & 2nd Aves.)
East Village 212.777.6969

Like a guy who stuffs his shorts, this "Big Bar" is actually more of a wee wonder. The regulars perched on the six barstools turn their heads and give a suspicious eye to any unfamiliar face that passes through the door of what appears to be a converted '50s diner. Black pleather booths line the wall, and the art-deco mirrors and tile floors will make you regret leaving your poodle skirt and leather jacket at home. The red lighting and iridescent tabletops add to the casual, intimate atmosphere, but order a drink quick or you'll be kicked out for sucking up too much oxygen in these claustrophobic surroundings.

Big Cheech
21 1st Ave. (1st & 2nd Sts.)
East Village 212.420.4900

In this annex to the popular Lil' Frankie's Pizzeria, homey charm oozes as thick as olive oil. With black-and-white Italian wedding photos punctuating the old-fashioned wallpaper and wine lists scribbled on chalkboards, it's like your Neapolitan grandmother moved into the neighborhood and you're invited over for a plate of wood-roasted garlic bread and a glass of grappa anytime. With wines by the bottle in every price range, this bar somehow manages to be casual, yet sophisticated, while still retaining a sense of humor. Pull up a seat to the L-shaped bar when waiting for a table at Lil' Frankie's, or pop by after work and join the other young professionals gathered under elegant

chandeliers for happy hour, dinner, and evening drinks all under one embossed-tin ceiling. East Village Radio also broadcasts from here.

Big City Bar & Grill
1600 3rd Ave. (@ 90th St.)
Upper East Side 212.369.0808

Formerly Carnegie Hill Brewing Co., Big City still hasn't quite figured out its niche. Is it a neighborhood bar? Is it a sports bar? Is it a restaurant? The atmosphere tends to blend all three, which isn't necessarily a bad thing, although it can make for an uneven night on the town. The Big City foray begins with a large bar area on the right, a separate dining area to the left, and the requisite outdoor seating for the easy warm weather draw. Those who live in this area will find this a great place to watch the game, but when that final whistle sounds, so much for the Big City. Fortunately, BCBG's food and drink prices are more Weehawken than Manhattan.

Big Easy

Big Easy
1768 2nd Ave. (@ 92nd St.)
Upper East Side 212.348.0879

Did you spend the majority of your days in college throwing ping-pong balls into beer-filled plastic cups? Did you then go on to become president? No? Well, Manhattan's most popular Beirut bar provides frat types another shot at those college days, but it's unlikely Poli-Sci 101 is part of the offerings. The staff sets up mini Beirut tournaments every Monday night, and holds monthly big money tournaments on Saturday afternoons. The bar also has nightly specials, generally consisting of girls drinking for free (Thursday is ladies' night), as well as Wednesday night karaoke and $2 Buds and Bud Lights from 11pm-12am. They're not exactly splitting atoms in here, but those things are neither Big nor Easy. Now show us your tits.

Bill's Gay Nineties
57th E. 54th St. (Madison & Park Aves.)
Midtown 212.355.0243

Travel the few steps down from the street into this tongue-in-cheek tavern, and you'll feel like you're taking a trip back in time. In the 1920s, Bill's was one of the area's swingingest speakeasies, and not much has changed in the interim. You can still chill with some of Manhattan's coolest seniors and sample from the fairly standard bar menu in the dark and ancient-feeling downstairs bar area. Old portraits of forgotten pugilists and long-since put-down race horses dot the walls. At night, a piano player takes over the joint and regales diners with old-school melodies. Upstairs, there's more of a cabaret feel, and a more extensive menu to choose from while you listen to the tunes. Classy, moody, and unique, Bill's is a real character for those who can't get enough of their *Golden Girls*.

Billy Mark's West
332 9th Ave. (@ 29th St.)
Chelsea 212.629.0118

Where did this place come from? Seriously. Billy Mark's West is amazingly un-Manhattany and not even in an ironic way like other so-called "dives" where art-school dropouts feel at home. How this place stays in business is a mystery of Agatha Christie proportions. That said, these customers may get a little edgy if investigators started poking around for any reason. Billy Mark's cocktails are cheap, the beer is cheaper, and nobody who hangs out here seems to mind the odd smell, creepy bathrooms, grimy barflies, occasional flies, and surly service. So you think that Manhattan has become too gentrified in recent years? Come spend an hour here and you'll soon be looking for apartments in the Meatpacking District and collecting *Sex and the City* DVDs.

Biltmore Room

Biltmore Room
290 8th Ave. (24th & 25th Sts.)
Chelsea 212.807.0111

If you didn't think there was a way to effortlessly incorporate things like chocolate and watermelon into Asian fusion-inspired cuisine, you haven't had a chance to dine like the other half does at this upscale Chelsea bar/restaurant. Although trendy, reservations aren't always necessary during the week and the comfy lounge area opens just in time for those looking to pop in for a quick champagne mojito after work. The swanky décor, in all of its enveloping marble and wood glory, does a good job of warning/preparing visitors for the bill. Many of these ornaments were from the burned-down Biltmore Hotel, even the "cell phone booth," which was once a regular phone booth. In case you hadn't heard, Chef Gary Robbin's Asian fusion cuisine is some of the best on the planet.

BINY
8 Thompson St., 2nd Fl. (Canal & Grand Sts.)
SoHo 212.334.5490

Karaoke anyone? Take a stroll down to 8 Thompson St., pop on up to the second floor, and discover BINY—a sushi bar where you can have a bite to eat and awaken your inner Bon Jovi. There's something about sake that lends itself to sing-alongs and this place's big selection makes many a crooner out of average folks. If you get tired of playing larger venues, as rock stars are wont to do, bring three friends and get a private room for smaller, more intimate appearances that will only offend your closest pals. The modern-chic interior makes you feel like a real star, and there's just the right element of shabby to make things accessible. BINY's friendly staff treats everyone like a Sinatra.

Birdland
315 W. 44th St. (8th & 9th Aves.)
Hell's Kitchen 212.581.3080

You don't just stumble into Birdland for the Creole food (although the Southern fried chicken and waffles are sinfully addictive). Cats come here to see world-class jazz performed live. Unlike other clubs, Birdland is not a standing-room-only joint. Here at what Charlie Parker called "the jazz center of the world," crowds witness musical magic from the comfort of barstools or candlelit tables forming a semicircle around the performance stage. There's generally a $20-$40 door charge and a $10 drink minimum at the tables (this is why you don't just come in for the food); at the bar, though, that includes a complimentary Pale Ale. But you won't be whining about the cost once you know that you can get a load of greats like Chick Corea or Roy Haynes doing their thing here. If the original Bird approves, it must be cool.

The Bitter End
147 Bleecker St. (Thompson St. &
LaGuardia Pl.)
Greenwich Village 212.673.7030

Late on Friday nights, the Bitter End is a funky free-for-all. All they've got on tap is Bass, so if you're looking for a variety of drink selections, you'll just have to stop being so damn picky. But you'll soon forget that once you get into the groove of the band playing on the huge stage dominating the center of the room. The Bitter End's "music first, talk later" mantra is echoed by the walls, which are covered with vintage concert posters boasting a famous artist roster at this New York City classic (past performers include Bob Dylan, Patti Smith, and Les Paul). Founded in 1961, the Bitter End is NYC's oldest rock club; it's not unlikely for a soul-packed funk band to rock the hell out of the place at 2am. Never bitter, always sweet.

Bivio
637 Hudson St. (@ Horatio St.)
West Village 212.206.0601

This horseshoe-shaped restaurant appears to be little more than a service bar; the main event here is the food. The classic Italian menu boasts an unforgettably delicious lobster pappardelle and pear carpaccio, but you get the feeling that your money is really covering the steep rent of this joint's Hudson Street location than the price of the ingredients. At around $20 an entrée, the prices here certainly weed out any local students looking for a healthy meal, and the drinks aren't much better. Nevertheless, the atmosphere is charming and much more relaxed than many of the area's high-volume, high-pretense options, giving Bivio something of an edge in the neighborhood. Lots of windows and close, bistro-style tables are lovely in the spring and summer, and Bivio gets crowded early, so make reservations.

Black & White
86 E. 10th St. (3rd & 4th Aves.)
East Village 212.253.0246

If not for the pesky patrons, Black & White could be the perfect bar. The striped walls, awesome DJ (expect anything from the Smiths to Bjork to Bowie), and generally cozy atmosphere have made this little nook a favorite among Village hipsters, carefully managing to be cool without crossing over into sceney or obnoxious. Too bad the not-far-enough Murray Hill crowd got wind of it. While you and your much cooler friends are chatting, be prepared to be jostled by former frat boys and *Sex and the City* wannabes who decided to brave the world below 14th Street. If you're lucky enough to come on an "on" night and forgive the lack of drink specials, you just might enjoy Black & White's colorful ambiance.

The Black Bear Lodge
274 3rd Ave. (21st & 22nd Sts.)
Gramercy 212.253.2178

"Bear Crossing" signs aren't a common occurrence in Manhattan (well, outside the Chelsea leather bars), but at the Black Bear Lodge it makes sense. This unpretentious bar with a cozy log-cabin vibe welcomes regulars and newcomers with open paws. Patrons can enjoy libations at either the front bar or backrooms that are packed with picnic tables, dartboards, videogames (Big Buck Hunter, MegaTouch, Golden Tee 2004), TVs, and a working fireplace. The Lodge serves up draft beers in chilled mugs and carries a variety of liquors and wine. During happy hour, draughts and frozen margaritas are just $3 and well drinks are $4; test your manhood with the Lodge's Cherry Bomb and Pepper F*cker shots—either will put hair on your chest.

Black Betty
366 Metropolitan Ave. (@ Havemeyer St.)
Williamsburg 718.599.0243

Dancing fools pack it into this smallish venue to unabashedly groove to soul and funk classics. (Whether or not they can actually dance is not for us to say, but we will state that there are other things which hipsters do well.) The candlelit sconces and adobe-rounded doorways give Black Betty's dark room a Spanish-haunted-castle-meets-Aladdin feel where every patron can shake his or her groove thing without fear of hard looks from too-cool-for-school Billyburg scenesters. The ladies tend to be hotter than the dudes, which gives a regular average Joe a chance with a sexy Stella, if only by default. Fuel up on Middle Eastern tapas at the adjoining restaurant, and sample a few Black Betty margaritas if you're feeling shy.

Black Door
127 W. 26th St. (6th & 7th Aves.)
Chelsea 212.645.0215

While some black holes will lead you into deep

Black Door

space and endless nothingness, the black door to this bar will lead you to a hangout that has "good nightlife" written all over it. Though strikingly similar to its sister bar, Union Square's Park Bar, Black Door is nearly twice the size, but with a more subdued social ladder-climbing sophistication. Soft techno music is drowned out by loud, friendly conversations exchanged by the mixed crowd of young pre-professionals. The huge wooden bar offers a congenial contrast to the gold-tinted tin ceiling, and the backroom decorated with twinkling white lights offers a romantic atmosphere to the mostly non-singles crowd, while candles provide a warm ambiance that's not intimidating—even if the good-looking people surrounding you are.

Black Duck (@ Park South Hotel)
122 E. 28th St. (Park & Lexington Aves.)
Murray Hill 212.204.5240

The Black Duck in the Park South Hotel is named after a Prohibition-era rum-running ship. Ya gotta respect that. Despite its seemingly dubious inspiration, it's a fine choice for a sophisticated cocktail in the Murray Hill area. This is the personification of an old boys' club, with merlot-colored velvet club chairs situated around the fireplace in the front lounge, and portraits above the wooden tables in the dining room. Blue-bloods and out-of-towners mix at the large bar while they watch the Yankees over specialty martinis. And if you get there early, you might be able to snag one of three sidewalk tables. The American menu features dishes like fried calamari, Caesar salad, and, of course, crispy duck. There's a lot of buzz about Black Duck and it's all it's quacked up to be.

Black Finn
218 E. 53rd St. (2nd & 3rd Aves.)
Midtown 212.355.6607

This Cajun-flavored bar and restaurant will make sports fans say, "Lord have mercy!" when they get a glimpse of the 20+ plasma-screen TVs and individual tubes at each booth. Granted, fellow spectators include a heavy frat pack and their older yuppie bros, but if you frequent sports bars that's probably a moot point. The downstairs bar looks like somebody's mom's kitchen, with bright yellow walls and ceiling fans overhead; a more loungey space upstairs feels more like a living room (but without the frilly handmade pillows). The best reason to stop by is a happy hour where you'll pass out from $20 all-you-can-drink wine, beer, and well liquor from 5pm-7pm, Wednesday-Saturday. On Monday nights during basketball season (when isn't it basketball season?) $20 covers all-you-can-eat wings and Buds during the game. $20 hasn't given you so much pleasure since that hooker in Tijuana.

Black Sheep
583 3rd Ave. (38th & 39th Sts.)
Murray Hill 212.599.3476

The only thing that seems out of sorts about this Murray Hill haunt is that unlike its neighbors, the patrons at Black Sheep appear to be locals looking for respite from the stereotypical neighborhood meat market. Ah, a black sheep indeed. So if you're craving a laidback atmosphere, friendly staff, a subdued crowd, and pub food priced far below the neighborhood standard, you'll fit right in at this Irish-American bar. But if you keep your frat house paddle under your bed for safe-keeping, then you might be well-advised to hawk your Chris Farley movie quotes elsewhere. The Black Sheep offers over 35 types of imported beers and ales and 100 different frozen drinks. If that doesn't entice you, come watch drunk patrons trying to count the pennies decorating the bar top (shh! there are over 25,000).

Blaggard's Pub (35th St.)
210 W. 35th St. (7th & 8th Aves.)
Midtown 212.564.8221

This Irish haunt is as nondescript as it is unremarkable. It's hard to explain the need for one Blaggard's Pub, let alone the two that exist within a five-block radius of each other. The décor is uninspired and predictable (cityscapes and architecture shots), as is the beer selection and clientele. As soon as the neighboring stores and offices go "lights out," there's little to attract a sizable gang for a pint besides the congenial bartender and no-fuss, no-muss trappings. If sedate and utterly ordinary is what you crave, it's arguable that you could end up at worse places to drink yourself into a solitary stupor. On the bright side, though, Blaggard's Pub 35th Street is a step above drinking alone in your studio.

Blaggard's Pub (39th St.)
45 W. 39th St. (5th & 6th Aves.)
Midtown 212.997.3595

The big brother to the 35th Street Blaggard's incarnation may be as close to a monument of cheese as you'll find in New York City. Filled with overdone city nostalgia—right down to the artwork—this pub is an everyman's bar…provided that man does not have sophisticated tastes. Regulars should not be surprised when they're greeted raucously by the always-obliging barkeeps on their stopovers after work. Although the bulk of business comes before 8 or 9pm with the after-work crowd monopolizing the most space, the room is always abuzz (albeit a quiet buzz). Unlike the Armani-laden bars that surround Bryant Park, it's OK to let yourself relax at Blaggard's; take your time with that beer and enjoy an audible conversation rather than struggling to hear your friends in an overcrowded hotspot.

Blarney Cove Inc.
510 E. 14th St. (Aves. A & B)
East Village 212.473.9284

In the same way that hipsters don't actually call themselves "hipsters," NYC's best dive bars don't actually aspire to be the best, well, of anything. Take the Blarney Cove, an Irish spot wedged among the jewelry repair joints and bodegas on a particularly ungentrified stretch of lower 14th Street. This is a true boozer's bar where the drinks are cheap (we're talking $1.25 Bud drafts here), the lights are low, and the décor is definitely not a priority. You'll find few ironic T-shirts and pretty poseurs here, but true dive denizens will enjoy inhaling the Blarney Cove's stale, beer-scented air and Colin Farrell brand of Irish patriotism.

Blarney Rock
137 W. 33rd St. (6th & 7th Aves.)
Chelsea 212.947.0825

There is a magical Blarney Rock somewhere in Ireland, where it has been said that those who visit on the first day of spring will live to be more than a hundred years old. It's highly unlikely that frequent visits to this blue-collar, green-themed pub will increase anyone's lifespan, but it may make those years on Earth a bit more livable. This Blarney is the motherland for sports fans, working-class folk, and Irish ex-patriots alike. The 14 TVs broadcast all of the sports one could imagine and during Rangers games, free wings and fries are served. After all, what's more Irish than…ice hockey? The friendly bartenders pour a strong drink, but beer is the standard here. They're not reinventing the wheel here, but the place is worth a spin.

Blarney Stone
11 Trinity Pl. (@ Edgar St.)
TriBeCa 212.269.4988

Good luck telling the Blarney Stone downtown apart from the Blarney Stone in Chelsea. Or any other Blarney Stone, presumably. About as glamorous as a high-school cafeteria, the downtown installation of this chain gets around the neighborhood's nighttime traffic by doing a brisk business at lunch. The mainly construction worker crowd constantly "fixing" Manhattan's southern tip flocks here so the TriBeCa Grand needn't fear competi-

tion. Sandwiches run between $5 and $8, and the price range on beer is working man-friendly—$1.50-$4.75. The help is also quite friendly and the bartender recommends the brisket. Places this rough don't stay open because of their incompetence…heck, why not tuck into a burger for a quiet evening of watching baseball, shooting pool, and realizing life could be worse. Here's wagering the coast'll be clear.

Blarney Stone
340 9th Ave. (29th & 30th Sts.)
Chelsea 212.502.4656

Imagine an elegant and alluring space of pleasant fragrances, exquisite libations, a good-looking crowd, and that certain "je ne sais quoi." Nice, huh? Now, imagine the complete opposite and you have the Blarney Stone—a real dump on the dark and scary losing side of Madison Square Garden. Dingy, dank, and damp, this haven for middle-aged drunks which abuts a Halal takeout joint (anyone feel like elbowing past some cabbies for creepy late-night nosh?) will leave you feeling a little gross and a lot relieved that this is a city full of better options…like the nearby Port Authority, for example. Legend states that the real Blarney Stone has magical powers, but this place's only trick is making one's will to drink disappear rather quickly.

Bleecker Street Bar
58 Bleecker St. (Broadway & Lafayette St.)
NoHo 212.334.0244

This is the place to go if you want to blow some doe—to "Kingdom Come," that is. Save your quar-

Bleecker Street Bar

ters and play Big Buck Hunter right by the bar, where TVs and local sports fans are never far away. If you're a lefty pacifist and the only thing you shoot is pool, there are three tables in the back of this joint. Those with an edge might opt for one of the dartboards that also hang around in back. Boss driving you to drink? Skip the three-martini lunch and get sloshed the old-fashioned way: From noon-8pm every day happy hour offers $3.50 super-sized mugs and $6 pitchers of 17 beers from the tap. There's no kitchen, but bartenders have a stash of local takeout menus.

Blind Tiger Ale House
518 Hudson St. (@ 10th St.)
West Village 212.675.3848

For the crème of the hops, keep your eye on the Tiger and its 26 brews on tap. Regular beer buffs know exactly what nip to sip; novice drinkers play "eeny meany miney moe" with the bar's detailed drink menu, where samples are available. Despite the noisy after-work crowd, literary types sidle up in wooden booths reading by candlelight and devouring free cheese on Wednesdays and complimentary bagels for Sunday brunch. At night, the vibe takes a turn for the fraternal, with rowdy NYUers pushing their way to the front of the bar, and seconds later, the front of the line leading to graffiti-strewn bathrooms. But don't let the crowds deter you—this New York institution is well worth a little innocent elbow-throwing among drunks.

Bliss Bar and Lounge
256 E. 49th St. (2nd & 3rd Aves.)
Midtown 212.644.8750

Bliss's electric-blue sign that's cast onto the sidewalk makes it easily spotted from afar, like your very own hip bar-tracking GPS system. Two floors encase three bars that are usually packed with a fun-seeking, tie-loosening professional after-work crowd who enjoys a generous happy hour and decent Polynesian-leaning food. The crowd and staff are as hip and good-looking as the interior layout. The street-level lounge is home to space-age-type silver barstools; for a cozier vibe, the lounge area is conducive to good conversation and comfort with its red velvet banquettes and brick walls. The upstairs bar has a cabana feel to it. The best spot, however, is the open-air patio. This little slice of heaven snuggled within the embassies of the East Side will show you what Bliss really is.

Blondies
212 W. 79th St. (Broadway & Amsterdam Ave.)
Upper West Side 212.362.4360

If television is the opiate of the masses, then Blondies is the crack house where sports junkies score all of the sports bar fixings with greater frequency than the Knicks score points. With TV sets lining the walls, this uptown standard is a haven for sports fans, fanatics, and passing enthusiasts alike. "Yankees" might be the only two syllable word spoken at Blondies, but if you're coming here to discuss Kafka, guess who's the dumbest person in the room? The bar has a soft spot for our hometown heroes, as there are NYPD and FDNY t-shirts displayed on the ceiling, but it has an even softer spot for testosterone-fueled antics, which makes it an ideal hangout for those wanting to get a little loud and a lot drunk.

Blondies
1770 2nd Ave. (92nd & 93rd Sts.)
Upper East Side 212.410.3300

With more television sets than an NBA locker room and all the baseball, basketball, and football you can shake a locked-out hockey player at, Blondies definitely has more fun. Their wings are legendary and have made an appearance at many a Super Bowl party, and while some may question the legitimacy of a bar with multiple locations, Blondies is a good enough time to turn that corporate-hating frown upside down. There's nothing terribly earth-shattering about the layout of the place, but that's partly what gives Blondies its charm—it's a no-frills sports bar that does its damnedest to make sure you get your money's worth.

Blu Lounge
197 N. 8th St. (@ Driggs Ave.)
Williamsburg 718.782.8005

Blu Lounge

Blu Lounge has the makings of a hipster hangout: shabby curbside furniture, red walls, a friendly goth barmaid, and a digital jukebox playing songs you think you know, but probably don't. But don't expect art-school grads with designer haircuts—sensitive ponytail types and townies converge at this populist hangout, and most of them are dudes. Due to its proximity to the Bedford stop, stragglers vainly in search of Williamsburg hip are likely to be the majority. Take your gratis grilled cheese (from 7pm-11pm) to the backroom, a place where kitschy couches go to die: Note the '80s high heel chairs, a crushed velvet number from the '70s, and an orange monstrosity from the '60s. A dartboard and TVs keep patrons from feeling Blu.

Blue & Gold Tavern
79 E. 7th St. (1st & 2nd Aves.)
East Village 212.473.8918

East Village old-timers, NYU students, international backpackers, and recent graduates all converge on Blue & Gold for one reason: cheap drinks. Named for the national Ukrainian colors and not for the patrons' hair and teeth, this no-frills tavern has been thrilling New Yorkers for years. Maybe it's the pool table, maybe it's the rowdy patrons, or perhaps it's the selection of over 15 beers and well drinks for under $5 that makes Blue & Gold a dark, cramped, riotous good time. Use the tight quarters as an excuse to slide into a booth and introduce yourself to that cute British student on holiday, but with a night this fun there's always a

price—you'll be paying for it in the morning when your new snaggle-toothed honey wakes you up.

Blue Fin (@ the W Hotel-Times Square)
1567 Broadway (46th & 47th Sts.)
Midtown 212.918.1400

With some of the best seats in Times Square, Blue Fin is the bar du jour for street-level gawking at tourists without actually having to join them. With floor-to-ceiling windows, the bar at Blue Fin is more about seeing than being seen. And for a Times Square hotel, the scene actually isn't too bad either. Enjoying the signature Blue Fin cocktail ($11; citrus vodka, Alize Blue, and white cranberry juice garnished with a Swedish fish) and the ample raw bar offerings sure beats the meat carts on Broadway. Often harried, it's easy to understand how the wait staff is affected by the pace in and around their restaurant, but the semi-swanky jazz club upstairs is a nice and easy place to unwind from "city mode."

Blue Lady Lounge (@ Shelly's)
104 W. 57th St. (6th & 7th Aves.)
Midtown 212.245.2422

Shelly's is a classic, upscale restaurant with delicious, fresh seafood and multiple enclaves that serve many purposes. The second-floor Blue Lady Lounge overlooks 57th Street through wide windows, where patrons can lounge on comfy couches, sit at tiny tables, or perch at the bar, closer to the non-intrusive live jazz but further from the view. The classy, creative interior creates a confident, attractive ambiance, and the friendly, seasoned wait staff treats each night as though they understand it's all brand-new to somebody. It's not cheap, but for a swanky evening, it's well worth the cost. Don't forget to gargle with the mouthwash provided in the bathroom and snag a couple complimentary chocolate truffles on your way out. This is a very good date spot for locals and tourists alike.

The Blue Mahoe

243 E. 14th St. (2nd & 3rd Aves.)
East Village 212.505.1180

Despite a garish front window display that confuses and astonishes potential diners, the Blue Mahoe (named for the national tree of Jamaica) is quite a classy joint. Billed as "Elegant Caribbean Splendor" and decorated with excessive candles and plants, the restaurant formerly known as Bambou is a bit out of place on this fast-food-and-booze-soaked stretch of 14th Street. Far from a nightlife destination, the bar is merely a waiting area reminiscent of the *Golden Girls*' living room. So if you're looking for an island feast at a pretty penny, the Blue Mahoe is the place for you. Otherwise, attempt to avoid staring directly into the front window and walk on by.

The Blue Mill Tavern

50 Commerce St. (7th Ave. S. & Hudson St.)
West Village 212.352.0009

A nostalgic nook tucked within the West Village's maze of tricky twists and turns, the Blue Mill Tavern (back in its original 1926 glory after Grange Hall snagged the space in 1992) is a jazzy jaunt back to a bygone era. Trendy types jonesin' for Red Bull shooters and the latest club hits need not embark upon this sentimental journey because this hip joint serves retro cocktails (Singapore Sling or a sidecar, anyone?) to the tune of yesteryear's crooners, jazz cats, and big bands, and the hearty, all-American menu offers up classic comfort food in an art-deco dining room that's pure sepia-toned chic. Ladies, wear your red lipstick and fishnets; gents, don that vintage fedora—and don't be surprised if the urge to jitterbug strikes!

Blue Note

131 W. 3rd St. (6th Ave. & MacDougal St.)
Greenwich Village 212.475.8592

Historically, Blue Note is THE place for jazz in New York, and many famous artists still perform exclusively at this Greenwich Village institution. Legendary performers past and present, such as Tony Bennett, George Benson, Ray Charles, Natalie Cole, Sarah Vaughan, Dizzy Gillespie, and Chris Botti have all been on the bill. But despite the joint's reputation, a visit can sometimes end on a sad note. Each act requires a separate cover charge ($8 and up) along with a $5 drink minimum; sometimes when you're worrying about the escalating tab, it's hard to enjoy the music. A better bet is to stop by on Sundays for brunch, when

The Blue Mill Tavern

$19.50 covers the show and 2-for-1 drinks and food. Like you need an excuse to drink before noon.

The Blue Room
1140 2nd Ave. (@ 60th St.)
Upper East Side 212.688.4344

Lurking in the shadow of the Queensboro Bridge, this aptly named, no-frills bar will remind you of your college hangout, with its Jäger machine at the ready, pool table, dartboard, jukebox, and food choices from the Atomic Wings outpost in the back. Happy hour is nearly every hour here; from 12pm-8pm Monday-Friday domestic beers are $3, imported beers and micro-brews are $4, and well drinks top out at $5. Catch the NFL, MLB, and other sportsy acronyms on the plasma-screen TVs, and, if you get here when the bar opens early for certain international matches, make friends with the Brits cursing out the refs. If you need more enticement than sporty Scots, Tuesday is karaoke, Thursday a lounge singer croons, and a DJ spins on Friday.

Blue Smoke
116 E. 27th St. (Lexington & Park Aves.)
Murray Hill 212.447.7733

From the mouthwatering aroma of barbecue that greets you at the door to the friendly, down-to-earth wait staff, this bar/restaurant invites informality and indulgence, and they're not just blowing smoke. Out of place in a neighborhood full of precious wine bars and themed pubs, Blue Smoke is refreshingly relaxing, unpretentious, and, above all, thirst-quenching. With 34 varieties of bourbon and whiskey, the appealing Blue Smoke Original Ale, and intriguing cocktails like Coltrane's Resolution, one could get lost upstairs and miss the live jazz downstairs. Definitely don't miss the Southern-style ribs, noteworthy barbecue, and of course, mac and cheese. Jazz and Murray Hill may seem an odd pairing, but the $15-$30 downstairs cover is justified by what's on the stage, more so than what's in the neighborhood.

BLVD
199 Bowery (@ Spring St.)
Lower East Side 212.982.7821

BLVD is the kind of place you want to hate, in large part because of their famously finicky door staff. But truth be told, BLVD has a gorgeous interior, a fun set-list of dance tunes, and the people aren't so bad-looking, either. The best way to finagle your non-VIP self into BLVD is to RSVP online. At least then you'll have some credibility (we didn't specify how much cred, though, so be sure you have tons of sexy female friends in tow as back-up). Otherwise, you could stand outside all night trying to figure out how to penetrate these defenses. A word of advice: Head downstairs to Crash Mansion and enter BLVD from inside after midnight—and dance, dance, dance with the LES hotties.

Boat
175 Smith St. (Warren & Wyckoff Sts.)
Boerum Hill 718.254.0607

The jukebox at Boat is legendary. If indie rock floats your boat, drift into this dimly lit space on Smith Street, order a margarita, and give into some real Brooklyn charm. Soon you will be unobtrusively nodding your head to your favorite song by Broken Social Scene or Telefon Tel Aviv. The margaritas here are tremendous; they seem to have an addictive secret ingredient that parallels that of the Colonel's chicken recipe. Décor is minimally nautical, though not in such a way that it strikes you as a gimmick. There's something indefinably interesting about Boat; it feels like the building, itself, has life to it. A variety of board games are available and the crowd that frequently plays them at the bar doesn't have much regard for the "hip factor."

Boat Basin Café
79th St. (@ Hudson River)
Upper West Side 212.496.5542

Need a break from the asphalt jungle, but can't afford a house in the Hamptons? At least you can escape for a little al fresco dining at the Boat Basin Café. The open-air patio overlooks the marina, where you can watch the sun set over the Hudson or you can opt to eat under the covered rotunda. Sadly, this oasis is far from a secret so you very well may find yourself next to a loud-mouthed lout representing the first generation of his family to have actually lived indoors. Wine and beer are served in plastic cups, and the plastic lawn furniture adds to the picnic-y feel. This family-friendly spot is the perfect port to drop anchor and enjoy the great outdoors—weather permitting.

The Boathouse
Central Park Dr. N. (@ 72nd St.)
Upper West Side 212.517.3623

Can't decide how to spend your sunny Saturday afternoon? You'll never have to choose between drinking your hangover away and enjoying Central Park again because at the Boathouse, you can do both. At this famous lakeside spot—a major attraction for tourists and the Upper West upper-crust—you can tuck some New York swank under your belt without taking out a second loan to pay the tab. "How," you ask? Skip the $18 omelets and enjoy a liquid brunch of mimosas from the bar. After getting good and tipsy, feel free to pass out on the grass for a nap and a suntan. Just don't get too drunk and decide to take a bath in Bethesda Fountain.

bOb
235 Eldridge St. (Stanton & Houston Sts.)
Lower East Side 212.529.1807

bOb

Been bobbing around for a bar that is hot every day of the week? Catch the Moroccan vibe and get your head bobbin' at bOb. There are a lot of Bobs out there—Bob Villa, Bob Dole, Bobby Brown—but none mix a lounge atmosphere with a hip-hop vibe quite so well. (Except for that Villa guy—he knows how to throw it down.) bOb's size is best suited for Oompa Loompa reunions, so expect to be grooving shoulder-to-shoulder and ass-to-groin on the dance floor…but isn't that how you're supposed to dance to hip-hop anyway? If you bump into something hard, it could be the bathroom sink, which has been relocated. *Could* be.

Boca Chica
13 1st Ave. (@ 1st Ave.)
East Village 212.473.0108

When Boca Chica, a Latin libation-serving lounge in the East Village, opened 15 years ago, the owners figured that even if people didn't stay to sample the South American food, the strong, fruity margaritas would win them over. With a little help from its friends the mojito and sangria, this semi-kitschy drink menu has proven sufficient cover for a less-than-authentic, but still serviceable menu. Boca Chica's a destination spot for large groups, including bachelorette parties and uptown couples in search of a downtown night out. Service here is a bit rushed, so scarf down the fried plantain chips and dip before they're taken away. The bright colors and kitschy décor add an element of fun at the full-contact bar where a Santeria-like décor seems to keep it all safe.

Bogart's
99 Park Ave. (@ 39th St.)
Murray Hill 212.922.9244

With its glowing counters, massive windows, and private booths, Bogart's emits a club-lite atmosphere. But with their loose neckties, business cards, and harried expressions, Bogart's clientele seems to betray the aesthetics, instead creating an after-work scene. Hey, yuppies can have fun

Bogart's

too—that's where expense accounts help. The drinks are pricey, the bartenders are perpetually busy, and the crowd skews heavily male. Of all the gin joints in town, you don't have to walk into Bogart's, but if you do, definitely stick around until the downstairs club scene picks up, complete with hip-hop DJs and hip-shaking dancers. It's hard to say what they're going for in this hybrid, but for better or worse, they're getting a little of everything.

Bolo

23 E. 22nd St. (Broadway & Park Ave. S.)
Flatiron 212.228.2200

Being the "restaurant of the moment" is great. Being a really good restaurant is better. Bobby Flay's 12-year-old Spanish treasure is considerably more subtle than its owner, not to mention his Mesa Grill, which is nearby. Rivaling its neighbor's long list of tequilas, Bolo boasts a formidable collection of 30 sherries. Hold the extensive wine list open for more than three minutes and the house sommelier is standing next to you asking if she can help. When your chic aunt comes to visit, take her to the bar for a drink and some tapas. Sure, you'll have to fight off Food Network groupies with a stick, but at least the stick will have a succulent piece of pork tenderloin on the other end.

Bond 45

154 W. 45th St. (6th & 7th Aves.)
Midtown 212.869.4545

Even with the lights of Times Square still in your eyes, to miss this monstrosity of a restaurant and the giant red neon lights that spell out its name could mean you're legally blind. But inside this former Broadway theater, restaurateur Shelly Fireman has transformed a sprawling expanse into a cozy trattoria designed to bring to mind days past on the Great White Way. A bustling Italian kitchen is complemented by a plethora of food bars devoted to shellfish, meats, and cheeses, while a dark wood Prohibition-era bar invites onlookers to have a drink while waiting for a table. Go ahead, it's legal now. In an area where cuisine rarely justifies costs, this off-Broadway showstopper gives customers a good run for their money.

Bond Street Lounge

6 Bond St. (Broadway & Lafayette St.)
NoHo 212.777.2500

You may have to elbow a celeb or two to get to your table, but that's Uma and Bobby DeNiro's problem, isn't it? Better yet, whip out your Prada shades and your Blackberry and pretend you're one of them in this slightly dated, but still happening, Japanese restaurant and lounge. From the sheer curtains down to the orgasmic slivers of raw fish—and with a wait staff as sleek as the furniture—Bond Street has deservedly achieved its steady über-trendy status. The cool crowd swells with models, their friends, and their friends' friends, along with hip downtowners and more than just the occasional B&T with money to burn. If you don't want to spring for dinner, then kick it in the sexy downstairs lounge, where $8-$11 drinks don't come cheap, but the looking's free.

B1 Drink Club

139 E. 45th St., 2nd Fl. (Lexington & 3rd Aves.)
Midtown 212.370.0080

Blink and you'll miss the entrance to this Pan-Asian lounge that's hidden between noodle shops on the pedestrian-packed Midtown streets near the insanity that is Grand Central Station. B1 feels like it should be located downtown, or maybe on top of some high-rise hotel in Tokyo; inside, Japanese lanterns illuminate a varied crowd that has gathered to listen to DJs spin hip-hop, reggae, and R&B while munching on pork and shrimp mini egg rolls. Want to commune with nature or sneak a cigarette? Check out the backyard bamboo garden. You don't have to be famous to get into this Drink Club; you do, however, have to "B(some)1" to get inside the VIP section.

B1 Drink Club

Bongo
299 10th Ave. (27th & 28th Sts.)
Chelsea 212.947.3654

Attention all claustrophobes: Stay far, far away from Bongo. This admittedly modest space is so customarily jam-packed with faithful followers that one could more easily negotiate a path to the rear reaches of this trendier-than-trendy oyster lounge by springing into the air and swinging from light fixtures than by attempting to traverse the 30-foot journey on foot. Do you enjoy a cozy social atmosphere or incomparably impressive personal service? Do you have an ominously overstated passion for seafood—particularly oysters? Then, make haste, my friend, to Bongo. With drinks so fine they'll numb your mind, and one of the most entertainingly informative menus—including "Little Known Facts About Oysters" and "Reasons to Celebrate at Bongo's" sections—you'll feel right at home.

Boogaloo
168 Marcy Ave. (S. 5th St. & Broadway)
Williamsburg 718.599.8900

On the fringe of the up-and-coming south side of Williamsburg and the less desirable enclave below the Broadway train tracks, Boogaloo is one of those places that attracts the cool, the edgy, and the looking-over-the-shoulder-while-pretending-the-neighborhood-isn't-making-anyone-nervous types. Resting in the basement of a brownstone, this locale further adds to the people-under-the-stairs feeling that haunts its block. The upside of the neighborhood is its ability to scare away suburban joy-riders who don't want to park their SUVs on the street. Ultra-hip, modern, and very cool, Boogaloo merits braving boogie men and other things that go bump in the Brooklyn night. A total scene for good-looking dudes and dudettes who want the feel of a house party without actually opening their houses to anyone, and who aren't afraid to board the J train, this is a find.

Boom
152 Spring St. (W. Broadway & Wooster St.)
SoHo 212.431.3663

You'll hear a lot of sexy foreign accents at this SoHo lunch and dinner spot; the best are sure to come from the cute Italian girls who dine here. At this Italian restaurant (though you wouldn't guess it from the name), the accommodating waiters' black t-shirts declare, "Make Food Not War," and the menu boasts an array of weapons like bruschettas, creative pizzas, and homemade pastas (main courses cost $14 to $25). When the weather is right, Boom's wide doors are thrown open to Spring Street and the sunlight and fresh air sweep over the rustic décor—worn, wooden floors, antique chandeliers, candlelight, and colorful walls—while trance music plays overhead and you plot a way to strike up a conversation with the lovely bambinas chatting over a bottle of wine—all in the name of peace, of course.

Boots & Saddle
76 Christopher St. (7th Ave. S. & Bleecker St.)
West Village 212.929.9684

This West Village bar is like home for many small-town dudes who are weary of big-city attitude. Though this 33-year-old gay bar never seems to get crowded, a 2-for-1 happy hour (weekdays, 3pm-9pm) lures enough cowboys that you're bound to find someone to chat with (but not if you want to discuss Cher, the gym, or Prada; this isn't that kind of gay bar). The patrons here are older everyday guys looking to relax with a bottle of beer. And though it may seem like they want to be left alone with their Budweisers, once you approach them, you'll discover they're friendly and eager to talk. Just don't ask what protein supplements they take or you'll be hung by your bootstraps from the ox harness hanging from the ceiling.

Boss Tweed's Saloon
115 Essex St. (Rivington & Delancey Sts.)
Lower East Side 212.614.0473

Boss Tweed's is a manly man's bar. And all the primal needs are here—suds, babes, an outdoor beer garden, and live Irish music (plus weekly karaoke so dudes can sing all the Johnny Cash, Garth Brooks, or AC/DC they want). In other words, Boss Tweed's tries really hard to be the kind of place that has something to offer besides just booze. It works, too; with $8 pitchers of Bud, pool table, dartboard, TVs, drink specials ($5 for a can of Bud and a shot of Jim Beam or a can of Rheingold with a shot of Jack Daniel's), and spe-

cial events, this gritty bar (named for the swindling Tammany Hall politician) stands out as a fun, fratilicious frenzy of suburban goodness.

Boston (212) Café
79 Madison Ave. (@ 28th St.)
Murray Hill 212.686.8787

If you're a diehard Yankees fan, hated *Good Will Hunting*, and cringe whenever you hear someone say "wicked pissah," stop reading now. Though it has only been open a few months, owner Charlie Garland has transformed this basement space into a friendly, congenial haven for transplanted Massholes and their friends to meet, greet, and go on a "bendah." Virulent Yankees loyalists may prefer to avoid this cheerful dive's in-your-face Boston pride, but the patrons don't "hahbah" any resentment toward New Yohkahs. So whether you're a Sox sympathizer, a fan of classic rock, or you just want to meet cute bartenders sporting that oh-so-sexy Boston accent, there's a place for you here. Just don't come expecting to find Jimmy Fallon practicing his "Boston teens" skit.

Botanica
47 E. Houston St. (Mott & Mulberry Sts.)
NoLita 212.343.7251

True to its namesake, Botanica peddles voodoo-influenced wares in its dark and dank environs. Flickering votive candles and religious iconography behind the bar bring a little Santeria to the scene and the cheap bottled spirits work their magic too. At this basement dive in NoLita, people exorcise their demons with pints of Bud and $2.50 cans of PBR. For the munchies, there are hot dogs and fries. With its mismatched linoleum tables and back lounge of lumpy sofas, Botanica's prime territory for NYU students and thrift store-wearing, sideburned 20-somethings whose second-hand wallets appreciate the late-night happy hours (Friday and Saturdays 2am-4am, and the rest of the week 1am-3am). DJs spin most nights of the week: Saturday is reggae, Wednesday old 45s, and Friday hip-hop.

Bottino

246 10th Ave. (24th & 25th Sts.)
Chelsea 212.206.6766

Mangia, mangia! This Italian food tastes so authentic you'll think your Nonna made it. Old favorites like Bocconcini of Mozeralla ($8), Spaghettini ai Sapori di Mare ($16), and Gemellia al Pesto ($15) are sure to quench the appetites of the largest Italian men. Wash it all down with the mile-long wine list but for true Italians, whet your whistle with the crisp and fizzy Prosecco or the authentic Italian Negroni. Stake out a spot and soak up some sun in the back garden beautifully lined with white-washed walls and wild orchids. In true European style, cap off your meal with a cup of Illy Espresso ($2)—so good you'll be saying "grazie" the whole way home.

Bouche Bar

540 E. 5th St. (Aves. A & B)
East Village 212.420.9265

Bouche Bar literally translates to "mouth bar" in French, which is apropos for the sexy make-out spot. The intimate boîte has exposed bricks, candles, and mirrors, making the tiny space seem bigger than it is, which is unnecessary as most folks here are focused on the person right next to them. Unlike other bars on this block that cater to the punk-'n'-metal-loving sort, Bouche attracts lots of locals on dates and those looking to score, whether or not they brought their own score. Bouche offers generous drink specials such as a daily happy hour that runs until 9pm.

Bounce

1403 2nd Ave. (@ 73rd St.)
Upper East Side 212.535.2183

DJs, plasma screens, belly-button rings, and the UES's more dressed-up crowd come together at this sports-geared lounge where cocktails with names like "Steinbrenner" are served by waitresses sharing cleavage and an occasional smile. Elegant lighting makes this a relaxed spot despite the modern, upscale interior. You'll drop a pretty penny on the top-shelf, but specialty cocktails can be had at a reasonable price while you relax on leather sofas in the back of the railroad layout. Communal sinks ensure that employees and dates wash their hands before returning to check the scores or partake in the fancy bar menu. Bounce is an uppity addition to this pub-heavy neighborhood, but offers a retreat from which to watch the revelers stumble by.

Bourbon Street

407 Amsterdam Ave. (79th & 80th Sts.)
Upper West Side 212.721.1332

Bourbon Street

It's not quite *Girls Gone Wild* at Bourbon Street, which attempts to approximate the debauchery of the Big Easy…but it is close, thanks to a 2-for-1 happy hour from 4pm-8pm daily (noon-8pm on Sundays). Appropriately, beads and bras decorate the bar, and the disco ball and strobe lights add to the dizzying effects of the alcohol. There's darts, videogames, a pool table, live music on Wednesdays, 50-cent drafts on Tuesdays, and even karaoke (shudder!) on Mondays and Tuesdays. Mardi Gras comes just once a year to New Orleans, but its spirit is alive and well 365 days a year on the Upper West Side. Have two of the frozen hurricanes ($6) and you will be flashing your breasts, beads or not—male or female.

Boutique del Vino

200 Spring St. (@ Sullivan St.)
SoHo 212.431.1212

Do you want to whine (and wine) over how SoHo has changed over the past 20 years? Here's a good place to start. In the back of the Savore Restaurant, which bears the same exact awning of the restaurant across the street and another 20 or so in the neighborhood, this perfectly manicured corner spot is almost too smooth. The airy restaurant, where French doors open onto the street and outdoor tables cover the perimeter, leads to this spiffy-looking wine bar where vino is considerably less expensive than the glisteningly polished wood bar and floors would imply. Tourists and locals wine on nearly 50 bottles of reds and whites and dine on small apps and pastas. Like the music, the older crowd is relatively innocuous, making this a great place to take your parents or your kids, so long as they're out of college.

Bowery Ballroom
6 Delancey St. (Bowery & Chrystie St.)
Lower East Side 212.533.2111

Three full bars operate at this art-deco music venue. Downstairs, couches line stone walls under gilt-framed mirrors, as lamps shaped like maces hover delicately over the subterranean-level U-shaped bar. The Bowery isn't a place you'd just drop into for a drink; it's THE music venue for up-and-coming indie rock bands (Our Lady Peace, Yeah Yeah Yeahs, Modest Mouse). The changing lineup provides a new crowd every night, but there's never a shortage of the stock-in-trade patron—youngish hipster boys and girls in all their horn-rimmed, Converse-wearing glory. The upstairs bar in the main space serves beer and wine, and as you ascend even further into rock 'n' roll heaven, you'll find a third bar, a VIP section, and private booths in the rear flanking the stained-glass window overlooking Bowery.

Bowlmor Lanes
110 University Pl. (13th & 14th Sts.)
Greenwich Village 212.255.8188

The good times have been rolling at Bowlmor Lanes since just after the end of Prohibition, but as with everything else, the '60s changed everything. Now, there's a decidedly psychedelic spin on New York City's hippest bowling institution. The price for hanging out between gutters here certainly

Bowlmor Lanes

reflects the modern age—$8.95 per game per person, plus $5 for shoes. However, on Mondays, it's $20 for all-you-can-bowl. A range of delectable finger foods are at the ready and these house sliders are the perfect lubricant for sliding those digits into a 12-lb. ball. The whole Day-Glo hyper-stimulation of this spot can be a bit overwhelming and it does draw heavily from nearby NYU, but by bowling alley standards, this is pretty damn sexy, not to mention fun. (Always phone first to reserve a lane here!)

Boxcar Lounge
168 Ave. B (10th & 11th Sts.)
East Village 212.473.2830

Never mind hobos—this boxcar comes complete with a cheery bartender and a heated outdoor rear garden. The list of specialty martinis is a mile long and with each one priced at under $10, the price is right on track. The interior is dark and casual and reminiscent of simpler times—the narrow space and corrugated tin wall add to the old-timey theme (but without too much kitsch). Mojitos and their regular reading series make recent memories of work fade like long-forgotten dreams. The Boxcar spills over with so much personality and eclecticism, you'll feel cozy any night of the week. All that's missing is the ladies—for some reason the crowd here is primarily made up of the XY sex chromosome set.

Boxer's
190 W. 4th St. (6th & 7th Aves.)
West Village 212.206.7526

Brother Jimmy's BBQ™

www.brotherjimmys.com

serving carolina style BBQ with southern hospitality service

daily southern specials and discounts

we do private parties and corporate events

check out all the ACC football and basketball games on our new flat screens!

try some of our savory pork ribs smoked for 6 hours in our own hickory wood smoker

FREE DELIVERY SERVICE

1485 Second Ave 212.288.0999
(btwn 77&78 sts)

428 Amsterdam Ave 212.501.7515
(btwn 80&81 sts)

1644 Third Ave 212.426.2020
(corner of 92 st)

Grand Central 212.661.4022
(lower level dining concourse)

Cross a T.G.I. Fridays with a recently closed bordello of pink Tiffany lamps hanging from the ceiling and you've just gone toe-to-toe with Boxer's. There's no *Antiques Roadshow* reject junk stuck to the walls, but the glow of a sports-oriented TV illuminates the old black-and-white photos covering these gloomy wood walls. For food and drink take a trip to the Deep South with $3.50 Mississippi Mud Pie and $8.50 mint juleps. Real country folk can catch a $6 Bass. Tourists find this place rather easily and frequently and the after-work crowd has their reasons for coming here: Monday to Friday, starting at 4pm, happy hour has them seeing double with 2-for-1 drinks until 7pm.

Boysroom
9 Ave. A (1st & 2nd Sts.)
East Village 212.995.8684

Standing inside this super-small, bi-level gay bar on a weekend night is a lot like riding the subway during rush hour—whether you're packed like a sardine or pressed against a cute guy's shirtless body, you can't wait to get off. One of the East Village's popular havens for debauchery, Boysroom never fails to entertain. Some choose to come on Thursdays to dance in their undies, while others gather for the Friday night "Boys Gone Wild" party. But the most popular night is Saturday, when scenesters Amanda Lepore and Cazwell host "Go-Go Idol," during which hot guys will do almost anything to win $300. The only thing both harder and easier than the contest at this sexy bar (where you can't stop staring at the X-rated wall collage) are the patrons.

Brady's Bar
1583 2nd Ave. (@ 82nd St.)
Upper East Side 212.650.0567

Brady's is a comfortable Irish pub with all the standard fixins'—five TVs, Yankee schedules and trophies posted on the walls, an arcade game, a pool table (free pool on Sundays), and a dartboard. Requisite crusty regulars and salty dogs are on hand, but so are younger Upper East Side residents who come in to rock out and have their fill of Guinness. Handed down through generations of

Bradys, this well-aged pub has been servicing the neighborhood for over 40 years, but she looks no worse for the wear. Happy hour is Monday to Friday, 4pm-7pm, with $2.50 Bud and Bud Light bottles and $3.50 bottled imports. Join one of Brady's two sponsored softball teams or a pool league and try and balance a pint with your pool stick.

Brady's Tavern
67 Murray St. (Greenwich St. & W. Broadway)
TriBeCa 212.732.1592

Brady's is as local as local gets in TriBeCa. Some friendly lass fresh from Cork will promptly pull you a pint and then leave you to your sorrows, or newspaper, or to watch another disappointing New York baseball season on one of the tellies, reminding you non-verbally that it ain't so bad. Brady's keeps it real with whiskey and Scotch "on tap" along with moderately priced Irish imports and domestics as cheap as you will find downtown. (Pints of Bud and Bud Light are $2.50.) The pub grub is pretty decent and the backroom is often full of older guys talking trash between burgers and mash. Weekday happy hours are the best bet for Brady's—there's no jiggy-getting into the wee hours here.

Branch
226 E. 54th St. (2nd & 3rd Aves.)
Midtown 212.688.5577

If you manage to get past the unnecessarily obnoxious men in black manning the door, you'll be impressed with Branch. The interior is a sleek and sexy blend of natural hues, from the wave-like railing to the round brick columns and earth-toned furniture. But this club is all show. The overpriced drinks come in plastic cups, the DJs are purely pedestrian, and the crowd is so B&T that you'll want to make like a tree and leave. Branch wants badly to be a top-tier club, but they're forgetting that you can't treat customers like dirt until *after* you've got celebs swigging Cristal in the back.

Brandy Library

Brandy Library
25 N. Moore St. (W. Broadway & Hudson St.)
TriBeCa 212.226.5545

In under a year, the Brandy Library has warmed up a formerly cold West Side storage space with high-society opulence that's still quite accessible. Inner-lit walls covered with shelves of brown spirits make the room look like a very slightly labored museum exhibit of booze. The brassy light suffuses the broad room in sepia. Cocktail waitresses dodge the velvet couches where the young and restless kibitz about their portfolios. Surely those portfolios are impressive...drinks price out at $300, but one can drink here without going anywhere near that mark. Come Monday nights to hear the house pianist make the vibe almost gratuitous...you might lose yourself in all this class and just start toasting perfect strangers until they throw you out.

Brandy's Piano Bar
235 E. 84th St. (2nd & 3rd Aves.)
Upper East Side 212.650.1944

The Upper East Side is generally associated with white-bread post-collegiate trust-funders with considerably more attitude than personality. The fact that Brandy's predominantly gay and otherwise open-minded patrons have been braving these streets for 20+ years is pretty surprising. A genuine piano bar frequented by real talent that commands the mic and belts out whatever comes to mind, Brandy's is full of folks who like to have fun, but they have little patience for drunken karaoke buffs who want to, "Give it a try." The long bar holds about two-dozen seated and standing combined, but mostly, these folks opt for the tables in the middle of the room or the long banquette along the wall opposite the bar. Monday nights here can be pretty lively.

Brass Monkey
55 Little W. 12th St. (Washington St. & 10th Ave.)
Meatpacking District 212.675.6686

This funky monkey/Irish pub has all of the youthful exuberance of that seminal Beastie Boys track,

Brass Monkey

with a seemingly endless long bar you can step up to and girls to put down. You can take big gulps and pass beer around. Brass Monkey is as cavernous as a castle in Brooklyn, but it fills up fast on weekends. The crowd is more hipster than frat boy but the fellas here are fighting for their right to pah-tay with sporadic sing-alongs and impromptu dancing (shh!). Nestled nearby high-brow designers like Stella McCartney, the Brass Monkey brings the Meatpacking District down a few necessary social-status notches with its relaxed atmosphere, finger-licking-good tavern food, and non-pretentious vibe. With 20 beers on tap, if you don't have a good time here, it's time to stop going out.

Brasserie
100 E. 53rd St. (Park & Lexington Aves.)
Midtown 212.751.4840

This futuristic bar and restaurant looks like something out of a Stanley Kubrick movie, and we don't mean that crappy one with Tom and Nicole. Despite its sleek trappings, Brasserie keeps an old-fashioned French café vibe going. A bar runs down one wall of the cavernous space, offering a wide variety of drinks and specialty cocktails like the Brasserie Bellini, made with fresh white peaches and champagne. But the real draw is the food, which is excellent—Brasserie's crab bisque is good enough to place a long-distance call to Paris about. The sub-level dining room can only be accessed by descending a glass staircase, but the elite clientele—which tends towards the young and cosmopolitan—seems to relish this catwalk-like entrance; you will too once you taste the Bouillabaisse Royale.

Brasserie 8 1/2
9 W. 57th St. (5th & 6th Aves.)
Midtown 212.245.2422

The Bank of America building, a giant stone slab that dominates the block it squats on, houses this icy and lonely glorified basement restaurant/bar. Brasserie 8 1/2 serves as the building's business lunchroom, catering to the power lunches and the corporate post-work thirst. The dining room is majestic and elegant, and the French-American

fusion food suits the business crowd's somewhat discerning appetite, but the bar itself lacks an identity of its own. The muted lounge area is filled with brown leather couches that look like someone's ailing dad picked them out, and the barstools are fixed in the floor with strangely large gaps in between, as if to discourage social interaction instead of encouraging it. This feels like the setting for a dissolute bank exec with a failing marriage to drown his sorrows in an elegant five o'clock cocktail.

The Brazen Head
228 Atlantic Ave. (Court St. & Boerum Pl.)
Boerum Hill 718.488.0430

If you're one of the few actors in town that hasn't made at least one guest appearance on *Law & Order*, then pull up a stool and prep for upcoming auditions at the Brazen Head. (The outside patio isn't so bad either.) Choose between an impressive rotation of 15 draft beers, and mingle among the law students, public defenders, and judges that fill the bar after a long day at the nearby courthouse. The Brooklyn beer pub has much to offer those not legally inclined as well, with darts and complimentary wings on Mondays, Tuesday's pint night (read: good beer on the cheap), Wednesday's ladies' all-night happy hour of complimentary wine and cheese, Thursday's themed beer spectacular, Friday's Scotch specials, Saturday's "martini madness," and Sunday's bagels and Bloody Marys.

Bread Bar @ Tabla
11 Madison Ave. (@ 25th St.)
Murray Hill 212.889.0667

From its location in the Met Life building, you'd think that this exotic Indian restaurant appeals to the hoity-toity foreign dignitary type. But they do have a beer called Smuttynose India Pale Ale ($8), which sounds silly enough. Versus Eleven Madison Park, its neighbor and sister restaurant, Bread Bar at Tabla is equally impressive to look at, but much more inviting, with warm tones and homey touches. Hungry? The lounge is hidden under the stairs, so it offers a bit of privacy for nibbling...on your date. If you're hungry for food, snack on plates of Indian-inspired tapas. In the summer, sit outdoors with a specialty drink like the Ginger Citrus Snap ($12), and remember to bring some bread, or better still, the company credit card—you'll want to try all of the 30+ small plates.

Bridge Café
279 Water St. (@ Dover St.)
Financial District 212.227.3344

A stunningly well-kept secret even to longtime downtown dwellers, the Bridge Café is worth the necessary search. Tucked in that little quiet corner waaaay down under the Brooklyn Bridge, its front doors open onto a 1920s-esque dining room decked out in candlelit place-settings on flawless white tablecloths. One wall is set off with a bar where a laundry list of fine Scotches ($7-$33) is on offer, some of them all the way from Japan. Find out which one goes best with fresh softshell crab ($28), because that's the house specialty. Dinner ranges in price from $18 to about $30, anything from seafood to chicken. It'll all be worth it, if only for that feeling of satisfaction you'll get while walking home. A place like Bridge Café is a little slice of delicious New York obscurity.

Brite Bar
297 10th Ave. (@ 27th St.)
Chelsea 212.279.9706

Brite Bar

Being the only bar in this area without a tough velvet rope is a Brite idea indeed. Tables are small, the bar is long, and there's even a huge window where passersby can peek in and see the welcom-

ing minimalist space. When the Clubland rejects and pre-clubbers gather, the tile floor can get a bit dirty with panini. But the meal isn't the appeal here; it's the über-friendly service and accessibility of the people and place alike. Light up the night with one of several house-special margaritas, grab a seat, then think long and hard about whether you want to tolerate nearby Marquee's long line.

Broadway Bar & Terrace (@ the Novotel Hotel)
226 W. 52nd St. (Broadway & 8th Ave.)
Midtown 646.459.5820

It isn't a good sign when the security guards at your hotel aren't quite sure if there's a bar upstairs when the concierge raved about it when you checked in. The Broadway Bar does in fact exist, but you can forgive people for forgetting it, because, except for the great view of the city, this could be just about any bar in any hotel in Anywhere, U.S.A. The patrons here tend to be your average jovial tourist types (stereotypically so, right down to their novelty clothing) and despite the bar's efforts at swank, everything here is a passing thought. The family from Michigan probably think it's swell, but unless it's New Year's and there's nowhere else to pee or get out of the cold, the rest of us aren't biting.

Broadway Dive
2662 Broadway (101st & 102nd Sts.)
Upper West Side 212.865.2662

If the definition of a true dive is one that smells of spilled alcohol, has no solid identity, and carries a music selection as random as its patrons, then Broadway Dive is the Platonic ideal. The wall adjacent to the dartboard here is plastered with plaques commemorating years of bull's-eyes. In one corner, a group of drunk Columbia-types can be found singing along to "Disco Inferno" (though the jukebox display is stuck, oddly enough, between Ray Charles and Neil Diamond), and in the other, a well-scrubbed girl and her whipped beau sip pink cocktails. The seven TVs show dizzying combinations like ESPN, WB melodramas, and between-channels snow. The beautiful fish swimming behind the bar seem blissfully unaware of how out-of-place they really are. This is a dive bar par excellence—for better or worse.

Broadway Lounge (@ the Marriott Marquis)
1535 Broadway, 8th Fl. (45th & 46th Sts.)
Midtown 212.398.1900

One of the first upscale hotel chains in Times Square, the Marriot Marquis set the standard for what luxury hotel bars should be. Located on the eighth floor, the Broadway Lounge used to revolve like its upstairs neighbor the View, but after serious renovations and updates a few years ago this swanky (if slightly mall-like) lounge has eye-level views of Times Square instead—so make your New Year's reservations a year in advance to avoid standing nose-to-nose with thousands of other frozen out-of-towners. The Broadway Lounge's 20-year veteran bartender makes a decadent Almond Joy Martini, the perfect liquid dessert. And when it's not closed for a private party, this upscale lounge can be a surprisingly quiet, serene place to watch the bustle of New York City—in peace.

Brooklyn Ale House
103 Berry St. (@ N. 8th St.)
Williamsburg 718.302.9811

Featuring more white dudes than the Stanley Cup Finals, Brooklyn Ale House offers ample seating around its main bar area where the men can scrutinize, albeit not too critically, the few females that wander in. True to Williamsburg, the clientele is geek-chic with a touch of funk. Microbrews prevail and the jukebox has the floor as would-be hustlers cue up at the little pool table in the back, while those who've had too many ales queue up for the graffiti-riddled john, which, not surprisingly, is sans mirror. When you're sick, the Brooklyn Ale House's laidback style is the cure for what ails you.

Brooklyn Brewery

Brooklyn Brewery
79 N. 11th St. (Berry St. & Wythe Ave.)
Williamsburg 718.486.7422

Did you ever wonder what happened to the normal folks in Willy-B after the hipsters invaded? Believe or not, there is a demographic of 30- to 40-something professionals who prefer the Rolling Stones to the Bedford-Avenue-Band-of-the-Month and the Gap to the Salvation Army, and you can spy on them Friday nights at the Brooklyn Brewery, an indoor beer garden on Williamsburg's north side that makes and serves up its own beer. Yes, this is the birthplace of the Brooklyn Lager found everywhere in the city. Friendly and boisterous, the crowd here is not about the scene, but about pure beer-swillage. Also, this is a great place to take out-of-towners as it's easily penetrable and they sell souvenirs!

Brooklyn Inn
148 Hoyt St. (@ Bergen St.)
Boerum Hill 718.625.9741

This beautiful old building on the corner of a quiet, tree-lined street in Boerum Hill draws the local 30-something post-brunch crowd thirsty for a mean Bloody Mary made from scratch but not yet ready to stumble to the Boat around the corner to try and get laid. This neighborhoody bunch all knows each other and feels right at home in the Brooklyn Inn's classic structure with its long bar, stained glass windows, and high ceilings—but they welcome strangers. The room in the back is just big enough for a game of pool, but gets crowded with too many elbows on busy nights. The clientele know the bartenders by name, and bartenders from other local bars enjoy a beer here before heading off to work. Ahh, doesn't that make you feel all warm and fuzzy?

Brooklyn Social Club
335 Smith St. (Carroll & President Sts.)
Carroll Gardens 718.858.7758

The clientele may have changed a bit from back when this classy Carroll Gardens joint was an actual members-only (and male-only, of course) Italian social club, but the décor—and the Rat Pack-era atmosphere—remains. Sure, you may have to elbow your way through a crowd of local hipsters to order up your Old Fashioned at the bar, but these days, where isn't that the case? At least at Brooklyn Social you'll have the smiling faces of old club members looking down at you from their sepia-toned stasis on the wall of photographs. Put a little jazz on the juke, even order up a grilled cheese if you like (they serve them well into the night), and try to relive the days when being "hip" wasn't ironic.

Brother Jimmy's
428 Amsterdam Ave. (80th & 81st Sts.)
Upper West Side 212.501.7515

There's a BBQ bonanza happening in Manhattan lately, with new rib joints springing up left and right. As such, it's easy to forget Brother Jimmy's, one of the first to set up shop in the city with a simple mission, to "put some South in yo' mouth." (Isn't that how Brooks met Dunn?) Bringing their Carolinian pride and some serious smoked flavor, they've been delighting pork enthusiasts for years with an ever-evolving selection of savory dishes. And sports fans flock to the bar for the cheap drinks while they watch the game. In keeping with its down-home charm, there are Christmas lights strung along clapboards, and corrugated tin for decoration. At Brother Jimmy's, the beer comes in cans, the liquor in mason jars and fishbowls. Patrons wouldn't have it any other way.

Brother Jimmy's

Brother Jimmy's Bait Shack
1644 3rd Ave. (@ 92nd St.)
Upper East Side 212.426.2020

Arguably the most well-known family of bars in the city, Brother Jimmy's brings a down-home Southern spirit to the big bad city and manages to succeed despite the fact that they really have no business doing so. The 92nd Street Brother Jimmy's is the smallest of the three, which is to its detriment because the seating area takes up the majority of the bar, and it becomes an incredibly uncomfortable place to be when the crowds start pouring in—and during the daily happy hour, pour in they do. Even if the Southern style-menu isn't your cup of tea, Brother Jimmy's still offers down home hospitality with karaoke Thursdays, and even the fastest-talking city-slicker can appreciate $1 after-work beers.

Brother Jimmy's BBQ
1485 2nd Ave. (78th & 79th Sts.)
Upper East Side 212.288.0999

Don't be fooled by the gritty backwoods décor—this Upper East Side ode to the Carolinas is a local hangout for the Polo set seeking home-style cooking and a lively bar. A flirty bar staff pours from a well-stocked shelf that doesn't rely on huge flatscreens for entertainment. For the Ritalin-dependent there are retro amusements wedged into the scene, including an unlikely skee ball table. Kosher gets the kibosh here, with a pork-heavy menu of Carolina ribs and barbecue, while preppie 30-somethings leer at tight-shirted waitresses. On the subject of annoying, please leave the cowboy hat at home, buckaroo.

Bryant Park Grill
25 W. 40th St. (5th & 6th Aves.)
Midtown 212.840.6500

The idyllic location of this classy spot, sandwiched between the main branch of the NY Public Library and Bryant Park, ensures a certain level of sophistication. The Grill features three primary spots to fulfill drinking and dining needs: an upscale restaurant with an elegant menu, and two outdoor cafés—one located on the roof of the restaurant, the other closer to the park and offering more casual fare. Though the beer selection is somewhat limited, the wine offerings are bountiful and generous. But beware, the crowd that festers here throughout the week is mostly corporate lackey types loudly blowing off steam after work while the weekend crowd is mostly comprised of tourists. But since this isn't a residential area, the only real "locals" sleep on benches and wear tin-foil hats.

B-Side
204 Ave. B (12th & 13th Sts.)
East Village 212.475.4600

"Trendy dive" isn't often an oxymoron that works, but for B-Side, the moniker fits. This Alphabet City hangout has a little something for everyone. Who wouldn't want to wile away the hours here? A well-stocked jukebox, a pool table, and a hearty selection of board games behind the bar all add to the attraction of this otherwise inconspicuous former laundromat. On slow days ask the affable bartender to pop in a movie (selections range from teeny-bopper to horror flick) or plug in your Powerbook and hunker down for an afternoon of "work" interspersed with mini-cans of Budweiser. $5 buys a shot of whiskey and a Rheingold chaser. Friends who deem themselves too sophisticated for such potables can order the Lemondroptini.

B61 @ Alma
187 Columbia St. (@ Degraw St.)
Carroll Gardens 718.643.5400

There is a part of Carroll Gardens that actually has a 6:1 bar to Starbucks ratio, and there sits B61, the bar below Alma restaurant. By no coincidence, B61's also the name of the bus line that takes you to West Carroll Gardens, Upper Red Hook, Outer Cobble Hill, the Waterfront District, or whatever this new 'hood is being called this week. The place packs in laidback young locals on the weekend, and it has ample space to house them. A long bar stretches farther back than the eye can see, ending in a couch-filled space for those wanting to canoodle or shoot pool. And with only a handful of bars to choose from between the East River and crazy, crazy Smith Street, the local single set is in full force every Friday night.

Bua
126 St. Marks Pl. (Ave. A & 1st Ave.)
East Village 212.979.6276

St. Marks Place can be a discouraging strip for anyone over 21—crappy fast food and grungy college pubs set the tone. Thankfully, there's Bua, a bar for those grown-up enough to actually hold their liquor and a conversation at the same time. The upwardly mobile hipster clientele bend their elbows to alt-rock tunes out on the sidewalk patio or in the low-key, candlelit lounge; another downstairs room has vintage sofas and is a good spot for private parties. Friendly, experienced bartenders cook up suitably stiff drinks; you'll stay on their good side by avoiding the overwrought apple martini variety (go for sangria instead). And, if the neighborhood leaves you with a hankering for salty snacks, you can bring your own grub to accompany your booze.

Bubble Lounge
228 W. Broadway (Franklin & White Sts.)
TriBeCa 212.431.3433

Built for those who long for the days when expensive champagne was more than a prop in rap videos, Bubble Lounge is an homage to old-school, upper-class New York. Filled with meticulous 19th-century furniture, a mosaic tile floor, and cavernous ceilings, this shrine to the vine revels in aristocratic ritziness, providing the perfect back-

Bubble Lounge

drop in which to pop a vintage bottle of bubbly (the shelves are overflowing with over 300 varieties of the stuff) or snack on caviar, oysters, desserts, and cheese platters. Fortunately for the average quaffer, there's a fine selection of wine too, including many reasonably priced workaday glasses. Patrons can be a bit smug about the specifics of their sophistication and the size of their yearly bonuses, but the classy ambience here makes all your troubles float away.

Buddha Lounge
29 E. 3rd St. (2nd Ave. & Bowery)
East Village 212.505.7344

Making the daring leap from beige to brown, the Opium Den has become the Buddha Lounge, and aside from some furniture shopping, not much has changed. Is it a bar? Mmmm, not organic enough. Is it a club? Not ambitious enough. Is it a standard East Village lounge that does its thing hoping those possessing the same inner peace stop by to meditate over relatively inexpensive cocktails? Yes, Grasshopper, that is the way of the Buddha Lounge. This brick exterior, darkened interior, and egalitarian scene is easy enough on the eyes and ears, and the crowd isn't so bad either. Buddha Lounge isn't going to change the world, but it is a corner of serenity that isn't afraid to rock.

The Bull and Bear
540 Lexington Ave. (@ 49th St.)
Midtown 212.872.4606

Sometimes you've got to pull out the stops and go fancy. No, not leaving-Williamsburg-for-the-Lower-East-Side-fancy, but old New York, top-hat-and-tie kind of fancy. The Bull and Bear has been a knickerbockers (as well as tourist) destination since the Waldorf-Astoria opened in 1893. Known for its generous helpings of Angus beef and its excellent martinis, the Bull has not lost an ounce of class. And even though this place still holds its head high, many of the blue-shirted business travelers and ritzy families from Kansas who stay at the Waldorf (now a Hilton hotel) snarf a little too loudly about "good ol' New York City" as they order another cosmo and a well-done Porterhouse. So New Yorkers, get out there and show 'em how it's done.

Bull McCabe's
29 St. Marks Pl. (2nd & 3rd Aves.)
East Village 212.982.9895

A frat bar on St. Marks? Sure, just put it next to the Quizno's. That's pretty much what's happened here. It's kind of McCabe and it's a bunch of Bull, but what can you do? Neighborhoods gentrify and the more they change the more they become the same—as each other. With 10 draughts at $5 a pop and 16 bottles ranging from $4-$5 this dive has something to offer, though. After-work and weekend afternoons are pretty chill, with ample outdoor seating in front and out back, but as that sun sets, the Greek letters spell d-u-m-b. The crowd's not all frat, but with a pool table, darts, jukebox, and even pinball, the nights are, if nothing else, lively.

Bull Moose Saloon
354 W. 44th St. (8th & 9th Aves.)
Hell's Kitchen 212.956.5625

If you're a cowboy looking for a showdown at sundown, don't come shaking your chaps here. But if you're a sports fan looking for a place to be with your kin at game time, then come on over with your guns drawn. A standard sports bar, Bull Moose has a pool table, multiple TVs, and a solid, well-stocked bar. The friendly staff is glad to pour you anything you want and the kitchen staff works hard until 2am, bringing you traditional bar food while you cheer on your favorite team. Tiffany lamps class the place up a bit, but the neon beer signs scattered around remind you of why you're here in the first place. Every cowboy will have his day, and Bull Moose can help the sports fan have his.

Bull Run
52 William St. (@ Pine St.)
Financial District 212.859.2200

Bull Run is the frat bar for cultured Wall Street fat cats. But instead of dartboards and white baseball caps, it's mahogany counter tops and power suits. The upbeat atmosphere keeps traders stopping in for quick after-work drinks and eats, and many a $20+ red meat entrée is consumed. (The continental cuisine also includes pastas and salads.) Bull Run's bright lighting and less than intimate surroundings make it a poor choice for a date, but a rather blushed and soothing interior provides a post-work decompression zone. Whether for dessert or by itself, the $10 key lime martini is a popular choice here.

Bull's Head Tavern
295 3rd Ave. (22nd & 23rd Sts.)
Gramercy 212.685.2589

Once you squeeze past the post-fraternity guys crowded at Bull's Head's electronic gambling machines, you're greeted by a long bar, two pool tables, a dartboard, and girls who never got a sorority bid. An Internet jukebox plays classic rock that can barely be heard over the obnoxious patrons; a cover band plays Thursday nights. The dark-reddish lighting counters a wall mural and three TVs. Booths run along the brick walls where bulls' heads and horses' asses would look better than this crowd. This is a place to go to get wasted and let loose, indulging in the 18 beers on draft. Good for you if you get banished. The liveliest thing at Bull's Head is the man at the end of the tables pounding out a beat on makeshift drums—and even he needs work.

Bungalow 8
515 W. 27th St. (10th & 11th Aves.)
Chelsea 212.629.3333

To call this place "amazing" is like saying Jaws was an angry fish. After two years of insider-status success, Bungalow 8 is still NYC's house of hotness. Celebrities are a constant in this Beverly Hills-influenced space where palm trees rest under skylights and a DJ spins rock and funk from an overhead area that offers standing and gawking room for the plebeians who are lucky enough to have made the cut. No flash photography is allowed here, and that's a big part of why "Page Six" regulars like Mary-Kate Olsen feel free to do as they please in the green leather booths. Why don't we hear lascivious stories of what goes on inside? Because nobody wants to get scratched off of club queen Amy Sacco's guest list.

Burp Castle
41 E. 7th St. (2nd & 3rd Aves.)
East Village 212.982.4576

Conjuring pubescent memories of summer camp,

CHERRY TAVERN

212.777.1448
441 E. 6th St. (1st Ave. & Ave. A)
New York, NY 10009

Voted 1392nd
Best Sports Bar
in the World.

(But we're #1 in Hell's Kitchen)

COPPERSMITHS
A Bar's Bar

793 9th Ave. (@ 53rd St.), NYC; 212.957.2994
www.coppersmithsbar.com

Burp Castle is not what you'd expect, albeit Homer Simpson's wet dream. Devotion to the beer gods is the name of the game here—nothing else is served. The "Brewist Monks" worship their nectar seriously, and the atmosphere is part urbane and part medieval orgy (just look at the murals). Yes, the music is always chant, and for those pagans who don't accept good beer as the Truth and the Way, they have Budweiser, but it comes with condemnation to an eternity of soulless McPubs. These gourmands serve from a list of 12 draughts ($2-$6), with more choices downstairs ($4-$40). The monk outfits and "shushing" gets old in a hurry, and the whole thing comes off a bit nerdy, but ah, that beer selection.

Bushwick Country Club
618 Grand St. (Leonard & Lorimer Sts.)
Williamsburg 718.388.2114

The flowing beer, the grace. Bald. Striking. Paying homage to the ultimate golf movie, *Caddyshack*, this bar is the real-world version of the Bushwood Country Club (albeit a bit tweaked so as to avoid a lawsuit). The vibe is more East Williamsburg than suburb, so it's got that going for it, which is nice: lots of beer and booze (and hot dogs), thrift-store nostalgia tchotchkes (Smurf-stuffed toys, an Elvis tapestry, and metal lunchboxes), flickering chandeliers and sconces, and last but not least, six holes of DIY miniature golf featuring a PBR windmill, a passed-out hobo, and a robot made from a massive ice bin, all encased in industrial refrigerators. And that's all she wrote.

Buster's Garage
180 W. Broadway (@ Leonard St.)
TriBeCa 212.226.6811

Much in the same way goldfish are welcomed to a piranha tank, women are more than welcome to this frat party. Boys will be boys in this former auto garage that turned the testosterone level up another notch before opening this sports bar. There is literally and figuratively wood everywhere at Buster's, minus the spaces where big flat-screen TVs cover the walls. There are a few bras behind the bar, a couple of videogames, lots of hot

barbecue, and even more cold beer that can be enjoyed indoors or outside on the wood deck. The very rural feel to this rather isolated sports bar is like that of a college town and the clientele often looks the state school part, except for the happy hour, which draws local Wall Streeters and Jersey folk looking for a quick one before hitting the Holland Tunnel. This is a big favorite for University of Georgia fans.

Butter
415 Lafayette St. (Astor Pl. & 4th St.)
East Village 212.253.2828

Welcome to the well-lit, trendy forest known as Butter. Enhanced by vaulted ceilings and an arched promenade carved in Western red cedar, dark-red leather banquettes, and an abundance of wood paneling, NoHo's sleek, upscale restaurant/lounge ambitiously puts out quite a spread for the hippest of woodsmen. A Hamptons-ready crowd enjoys tasty, innovative meals and designer cocktails in an atmosphere oozing with mohair, trees, and yes, even bark. A giant 3D photographic mural of a forest illuminates the main dining room's back wall, while the darker lounge area downstairs welcomes pretty urbanites to sit and schmooze on cedar-carved love seats as they tune into DJ-spun soul, funk, R&B, hip-hop, disco, and classic rock. Come dressed to kill and beware of splinters.

Buttermilk
577 5th Ave. (@ 16th St.)
Park Slope 718.788.6297

As young and shaggy as its hipster clientele, Buttermilk baits your inner college freshman with cheap beer, good tunes, and board games. Behind the bar's Venetian blind-covered windows, you'll find young South Slopers packed into jumbled tables and steel chairs sharing rounds of $3 brews and playing rainy-day classics like checkers, backgammon, and Connect Four. A well-stocked jukebox blasting obscure indie rock and alternative hits adds to the loud and grungy appeal, as do the drunk Atari competitors who end up making out on the couches in the back after getting their high scores; games are available on Sundays only. On Wednesday evenings, soak up the booze with the free pizza that's served after 10pm.

Buzz Bar @ Pershing Square
90 E. 42nd St. (Lexington & Park Aves.)
Midtown 212.286.9600

Pershing Square tries to do it all: coffee shop, breakfast diner, upscale restaurant, and bar. But more isn't always…more. Plus, being on the periphery of Grand Central can really kill a Buzz… or a Buzz Bar, as this place is so unfittingly named. Sandwiched between the bakery and the dining room, there isn't much happening in this place's drinking area. If a hot scene isn't what you're after, there are definitely worse places to grab a glass of wine before hopping onto or in front of that train to Westchester. With over 30 bottles under $30, these warm and well-lit booths serve as a serviceable spot for plotting a good after-work buzz. (Oh, now we get it.) Better yet, stop in for a muffin on your way to work, or linger over coffee and a newspaper.

Cabana
89 South St., 3rd Fl. (@ Fulton St.)
Financial District 212.406.1155

How long does a girl have to wait for a beer? At Cabana, specializing in Spanish and Mexican cuisine, the answer might be *por eternamente*. One wall of this long, narrow bar/restaurant is floor-to-ceiling windows, all the better to gaze down upon the clueless tourists. Otherwise, the view of the docked ships, Brooklyn Bridge. and East River are beautiful. The bulk of the clientele is from out of town; yuppies and couples pepper the sizable dining area. True to the name, all the barstools and booths are upholstered in fabric printed with a jaunty, pastel sea motif. Large plastic tropical-looking plants loom everywhere, completing the theme, while a soundtrack of salsa, meringue, and, curiously, zydeco rounds out the experience. Like its customers, Cabana seems to sometimes wish it were elsewhere.

Cabanas (@ the Maritime Hotel)
363 W. 16th St. (@ 9th Ave.)
Chelsea 212.242.4300

When the temperature rises, it doesn't get any hotter than Cabanas, the Maritime Hotel's rooftop see-and-be-seen bar. Cabanas is actually two separate bars connected by a long, breezy outdoor walkway. The greenery is lush and rampant, giving

Cabanas

it the feeling of a European outdoor café (sans food). Don't expect a scenic view of the city or even the Hudson, though—the top of the hotel consumes a lot of view, but you will see stars (celestial and otherwise). Cabanas has one section covered with a colorful awning and boasts loud tunes for a mobile crowd, while the other is open-air, catering to revelers leaning towards smoking and chatting. Overall, the crowd and vibe at this beachy hotel bar (an Amy Sacco creation) is classy. Sit back, drink a Sea Breeze, and pretend you have your very own cabana boy.

Cabin
234 W. 14th St. (7th & 8th Aves.)
West Village 212.206.0430

Think of an upscale, Euro-influenced Lincoln Log house that's built for mature adults and you've got Cabin. One of the owners is a carpenter, so he designed it himself and gave it some special touches, like antique scales on the service window and hanging copper lanterns filled with candles. Ring the triangle for dinner time, which features a menu of "Cabin Classics" and comfort food like a $6.95 Cobb salad and $5.95 turkey chili. There are many specials here, from lunch to happy hour and freshly ground coffee, which caffeine addicts would call special. Slightly off the beaten path, Cabin is a welcome retreat from those who've stumbled off the Meatpacking District's beaten path. Of course, that's not to say visitors can't still get a watermelon martini here.

Café Andalucia
533 9th Ave. (39th & 40th Sts.)
Hell's Kitchen 212.736.9411

We're confused. Is Café Andalucia a tapas bar? A greasy spoon? A coffee shop? This tiny Spanish café is also a Wi-Fi hotspot with a jukebox; but then again, it looks like a local sports bar and has the same ambiance (cheap domestic beers during happy hour, for example) as a pub. If you want to be seen, Andalucia isn't for you; but if you crave tasty tapas at prices slightly less insane than downtown, Andalucia is worth the trip. Be sure to check out the extensive selection of Argentinian

and Spanish wines, and keep a watchful eye out for the sketchy characters who congregate under the bus trestle just a half-block north of Andalucia. *Disfruta*!

Café Carlyle (@ the Carlyle)
35 E. 76th St. (@ Madison Ave.)
Upper East Side 212.744.1600

This celebrated epitome of an urbane supper club has remained a classic for decades. The biggest names in cabaret, formerly including the recently deceased Bobby Short, take center stage in this intimate venue featuring pastel murals from the Oscar-winning art director for 1952's *Moulin Rouge* (no showy Baz Luhrmann colors here). Café Carlyle serves a full dinner, has an enormous wine list, and the bar is under the watch of Audrey Saunders, the mixologist and former protégé of Dale de Groff. To enjoy all this, you'll have to fork over a dollar for every year the club's been in business—that's $50. Fans of both Woody Allen and Dixieland jazz come on select Mondays to hear the man better known for his films and his taste in women play the clarinet. Now if all this isn't true New York, what is?

Café del Bar
945 Columbus Ave. (@ 106th St.)
Upper West Side 212.749.3313

Café del Bar is an oasis of intimacy in an often overwhelming city—the atmosphere is unpretentiously hip, and the owner/bartender, Baba Tunde, is funny and welcoming. Tucked in a space that's certainly smaller than some closets 20 blocks south, the seductive red walls at Café del Bar are covered with a rotating selection of artwork by both local and international artists. The world music is just loud enough to get your body moving, but not so much as to prevent conversation. Share a large bottle of Star beer from Ghana, lay back on one of the couches, and feel much cooler than you probably have in a very long time.

Café Deville
103 3rd Ave. (@ 13th St.)
East Village 212.477.4500

Ooh la la—this Parisian-style bistro teems with young, attractive East Villagers. The large, high-ceilinged space accommodates big groups in the huge dining room and at the oversized bar. Good thing too, because it gets crowded in here with after-work neighborhood folk. With outdoor tables, complete with heat lamps blazing on colder days, and prime viewing of the metrosexuals leaving Kiehl's across the street, Café Deville serves up tasty bistro bites and 15 wines by the glass. Stop by for a free one with your $13.95 brunch, or opt for a hair of the chien mimosa.

Café Gitane
242 Mott St. (Houston & Prince Sts.)
NoLita 212.334.9552

A petite slice of French Morocco in the heart of NoLita, this is the kind of casual little café where you could see Graham Greene kicking back, stiff drink in hand. Café Gitane's ongoing appeal might well be that behind many a New Yorker, there's a Francophile who just wants to smoke Gitanes and slouch around in a beret. The itty-bitty outdoor cocktail tables are "parfait" for channeling your inner European and ogling the passing trendsters. Or, stake out a cozy nook in the small, eavesdrop-friendly dining room with a smattering of tables and a counter with a few stools. Tuck into Moroccan-influenced nibbles, like spicy olives ($5) or a terrific combo of gorgonzola, walnut, and honey ($5), and wash it all down with a French red ($6.50-$9 a glass) or an imported beer ($5-$7)—the Belgian Leffe Blonde and Bavarian Ayinger are tasty, sudsy bets.

Café Luxembourg
200 W. 70th St. (Amsterdam & West End Aves.)
Upper West Side 212.873.7411

When you step into Café Lux, you might think one of two things: One, you're not uptown anymore, and two, the steak frites is how much? (For the record, it's $32.) The art-deco flair and French bistro nuances of the walls, bar, and floors to this Upper West Side mainstay feel more than out of place in such a non-hip neighborhood. On the whole, the French food is above par, and the wine list will not disappoint, but it will send your wallet running for the nearest bank vault. If you've got a date to impress, or your mom is coming into town, this is a fine choice for a cozy atmosphere and rumored glitterati-spotting opportunities.

Café Ma
428 Bergen St. (@ 5th Ave.)
Park Slope 718.638.0645

Ah, bubble tea. With your space-age tapioca floaters and your tasty exotic flavors, it's hard to think that you could ever be made better. Miraculously, the folks at Park Slope's Café Ma have found a way: just add alcohol. Brilliant! Here you can have your kumquat tea (you may not be able to pick it out of a fruit lineup, but it sure tastes good) spiked or un-spiked for prices that will make you remember why you moved to Brooklyn. Sushi is served for anyone with an appetite. Add cushiony sofa seating and you'll want to stay forever.

Café Noir
32 Grand St. (Thompson St. & 6th Ave.)
SoHo 212.431.7910

Follow your inner Ernest Hemingway to Café Noir, where the moody, dark atmosphere is that of a Parisian ex-pat café circa 1920. On busy weekend nights, the service is ditzy bordering on indifferent and the food (French, Moroccan, and tapas) is equally effortless and exciting. Further attempting to be fashionably difficult, Café Noir only takes cash and Amex, "keeping it real" in a very French sense. But Café Noir's intoxicating bohemian vibe, electronica-spinning DJ, and front windows all open up to a certain charm, especially when the weather warms. If you're in the mood to explore the far reaches of SoHo for some fashionable people-watching and good sangria, this is the place for you—just grab something to eat beforehand.

Café Pierre (@ the Pierre Hotel)
2 E. 61st St. (@ 5th Ave.)
Upper East Side 212.940.8195

Long and narrow and sadly with no views of Central Park, Café Pierre looks like your grandmother's living room—if your grandmother has a Fifth Avenue apartment with a pianist. The small bar area, with friendly bartenders and several formal sitting areas as well as barstools, serves food such as a seafood plateau and mini burgers from 6pm-11pm; entertainment starts at 8:30 nightly. Past the piano is the grander still restaurant, with white tablecloths and enormous floral arrangements. The Rotunda—one of the more beautiful small public spaces in the city, with sky blue hand-painted trompe l'oeil murals and ceiling—is another good choice for a cocktail, tea, or mature snack of caviar. These guys actually have a Grasshopper on the cocktail menu. Wouldn't that make Grandma dance a jig?

Café Ronda
249 Columbus Ave. (71st & 72nd Sts.)
Upper West Side 212.579.9929

Complete with dark tiled floors and soft Latin music, the atmosphere at this youthful bistro transports visitors from Columbus Avenue to Mexico—well, maybe not completely, but the tapas and near-perfect chicken soup sure come close. Surely regulars don't frequent this spot for the artwork or green wall ambiance, but rather for the friendly staff and lively din, especially when the late weekend hours roll in and the crowd is more fascinated with drinking Coronas on the sidewalk café than eating empanadas. The bar's specialties like mojitos and tangy treats like the Valencia Swing (champagne, Stoli orange, and passion fruit puree) might appear a bit girly to the *senoras*, but they're worth a taste. After all, you don't go to Cancun to drink Budweiser.

Café Wha?
115 MacDougal St. (3rd & Bleecker Sts.)
Greenwich Village 212.254.3706

The drinks and food are mediocre at best at this café, so what really packs in the late-night crowd is the eclectic music selection that ranges from rock to funk and even stand-up comics. Café Wha? is to music what *Rolling Stone* is to magazines—it has no resemblance today to the revolutionary forum it once was (Allen Ginsberg and Bob Dylan once performed here), but it's still undeniably entertaining. Located on a lively—though some would say tacky—strip of MacDougal Street in Greenwich Village, a very mixed crowd descends downstairs to succumb to the groove. Expect a cover charge if you stay to see the bands, and expect to see more than a few middle-aged ladies clapping their hands and singing along to the oldies faves; culture doesn't come cheap these days.

Cafeteria
119 7th Ave. (@ 17th St.)
Chelsea 212.414.1717

For late-night noshers, this swanky eatery is tummy-grumbling heaven. Featuring a young, urbane crowd most any time of day (it's open 24 hours), Cafeteria serves a range of carefully prepared American fare, seafood, and the kind of comfort food that will put those tater tots you munched on in high school to shame. There's also a full-service bar, and if you're more concerned about seeing your meatloaf than being seen, head downstairs to one of the cozy booths in the lounge. The cooler-than-thou, yet attentive staff serves up cocktails like the Million Dollar Mojito (made with Starr rum, it's a twist on the original) and an extensive wine list. When its garage door-like front windows are thrown open, Cafeteria displays some of the prettiest dishes—and people—in Chelsea.

Cain
544 W. 27th St. (10th & 11th Aves.)
Chelsea 212.947.8000

This is the hottest club to have opened since you bought your last Shecky's guide. Unfortunately, it's going to take most people a while to see it first-hand—the door is strict, demand is high, and the staff won't over-pack the room. No worries, though: Cain will be here for a while. At the entrance, two ornate faux-elephant-trunk door handles prepare a very in-the-know crowd for the South African game lodge experience that awaits them. Inside, a glass-enclosed zebra hide lines the bar top and imported African beads wrap around wood pillars. Thin sheets of canvas line the wall and they're backlit by soft orange tones that imply a safari sunset. A DJ booth carved from a 12-ton, hand-hewn boulder spins a mix of hip-hop and '80s tunes to a crowd that dances wherever they please. Sure, $15 cocktails are steep, but Cain is the big prize of the nightlife hunt.

The Cajun
129 8th Ave. (16th & 17th Sts.)
Chelsea 212.691.6174

The Cajun's traditional New Orleans cuisine, night-ly live jazz, and well-poured Dirty Turtles and Hurricanes keep Chelsea residents bendin' over and squealin' like pigs. (Well, that and the rampant gay sex, which abounds.) Glowing red lamps, shrunken heads, and feathered Mardi Gras masks decorate the walls and add an authentic touch of the Big Easy to this surprisingly mature restau-rant/bar; the behavior that will earn you beads in N'awlins will get you thrown out of here. A busi-ness-casual crowd fills the main dining room and bar area, ready to dig into spicy seafood jambalaya and top-notch blackened catfish. The roomy dining area is ideal for large parties, but call ahead for a table if you want to sit and eat during a live set.

Cake Shop
152 Ludlow St. (Stanton & Rivington Sts.)
Lower East Side 212.253.0036

Apparently you can have your cake, eat it, and wash it all down with a beer too. This new two-

Cake Shop

level space aims to keep the local self-employed crowd buzzing throughout the day: They start slinging espresso and Balthazar goodies at 7:30am, open a used-record store at noon, and unlock a downstairs beer-and-wine bar at 5pm. Live music four nights a week is the icing on this very sweet cake. Between rocker hangouts and the velvet-rope pretense of Ludlow Street's new "lounges," Cake Shop strikes a balance as artful as the LPs in its window. Don't miss the 2-for-1 happy hour from 5pm-8pm daily. Come on in for a sweet slice of Lower East Side life.

Caliban
360 3rd Ave. (26th & 27th Sts.)
Murray Hill 212.686.5155

This artsy cavern boasts a large plate-glass win-dow facing Third Avenue, which is an excellent spot from which to secretly mock people on the street. The vine-lined secret garden in back is per-fect for smoking, chatting, and enjoying warm weather. The bar selection is average, but Caliban is less about drinks than it is atmosphere. With art-covered walls, bowls of fresh begonias, and attractive wooden tables lining the room, the bar's owners make wise use of a narrow space, turning it into a welcoming, cozy place with a creative yet familiar feel. Bring your date on a warm evening for a view of the stars, which you probably won't be able to see. This place may be an oasis, but it's still in Manhattan.

Caliente Cab Co.
21 Waverly Pl. (@ Greene St.)
Greenwich Village 212.529.1500

Caliente Cab Co.

Sure, it's not Puerto Escondido, but the last time we checked, there were plenty of great places to get a margarita and relax in this city—so why are all of these people packing Caliente Cab Co. on weekends? New Yorkers in-the-know know that this Tex-Mex eatery/bar is just Chevy's after the *Queer Eye* boys gave it a makeover. And beneath the tacky décor, the Caliente restaurant chain is about as hot as a food court. Apparently, the super-sized Texas/Vegas/Bourbon Street cocktails served in souvenir cups are a real draw for a crowd that probably spends all of their vacation days in Texas/Vegas/Bourbon Street. Walk a block in any direction and you're sure to find more potent drinks, authentic food, and clientele who wouldn't be caught dead speaking incorrect Spanglish.

Caliente Cab Co.
61 7th Ave. S. (@ Bleecker St.)
West Village 212.243.8517

Look for the checked Studebaker out front, then park yourself south of the border for some "margarita magic!" "Caliente" may mean hot, but the best drinks are served ice-cold, especially the frozen margarita, which comes in a 24-oz. souvenir glass, $13. The predictable Tex-Mex-Manhattan food at this corporate Mexican café is serviceable at best, but no one really seems sober enough to notice; the touristy crowd comes down for a festive yet not surprising atmosphere. Drink too many of their cocktails and you'll definitely need a cab to get you home, but at least it's cheaper than a trip to Cancun.

The Call Box Lounge
148 Kingsland Ave. (Lombardy & Beadel Sts.)
Greenpoint 718.384.0179

With a scenic view of the BQE and a friendly, if occasionally foul-mouthed staff, the Call Box is a taste of vintage Brooklyn with a kitsch factor that's through the roof. Unintentional as it may be, the bar's specialty nights and shabby design are sure to be embraced by the trucker hat set should they ever venture beneath the expressway. Wednesday is Karaoke Night, and Friday is Ladies' Night, but anytime is fine to slide into a chair (regular or barbershop, both are available) and kick back. Take note of the specials: a six-pack of 8-oz. beers is only $7 during the day, and condoms in the men's room are always 75 cents. In Middle America, this is a nightclub. Here, it's a novelty dive.

Calle Ocho
446 Columbus Ave. (81st & 82nd Sts.)
Upper West Side 212.873.5025

This lively Latin restaurant/lounge, named for a bustling thoroughfare in Miami's Little Havana, brings some much-needed tropical heat to the Upper West Side. There are plush banquettes around the bar and a large, bustling dining area in the back. The menu ranges from tapas to tradiional pork and shrimp dishes, which are all mouthwatering. Sultry samba music drifts over the speakers and if you close your eyes, you can imagine feisty bikini-clad ladies and old men in panama hats playing dominoes. Unfortunately, the crowd is mostly the buttoned-up preppy type. The *baños* are designated by pictures of Lucy and Ricky Ricardo, a cutesy touch. A visitor here could make the most debonair, homesick Cuban band leader proclaim, "Honey, I'm home."

Camaje
85 MacDougal St. (Houston & Bleecker Sts.)
West Village 212.673.8184

French-heavy, Pan-European cuisine sans attitude provides the ideal ingredients for a relaxed Sunday brunch. Often featuring live jazz during that time, Camaje fills up quickly as it only seats about 30 at its tables and couches. Dishes range from the $7.50 BLT to the $8 Polish kielbasa, but Franco dishes like $24 filet mignon in a puffy pastry steal the show. The make-your-own crepe option really rounds out a menu that has something for everyone. The bar itself doesn't stay open late, but it does possess an unusually large array of wines along with a few beers that are worth sampling if you've just stopped in to wet your beak while people-watching from one of these coveted outdoor tables.

The Campbell Apartment
15 Vanderbilt Ave. (@ Grand Central Station)
Midtown 212.953.0409

Almost as famous as Grand Central itself is the Campbell Apartment. Once the office of famed industrialist John W. Campbell, this classically elegant haunt still harbors the ghosts and overall spirit of the Roaring '20s. Live jazz bands play on Saturday nights and "gentlemen" in jeans or sneakers will be politely advised to take advantage of that comfort-wear and walk elsewhere. Several tables overlook the great train terminal below. As expected, there is an emphasis on classic cocktails here and the 125-person capacity is obeyed to the highest degree imaginable when after-work crowds pour in to have one for the road…or the tracks as may be the case. This bar is best enjoyed at 3pm when it opens. At night, things die down pretty quickly in these parts.

Canal Room
285 W. Broadway (@ Canal St.)
TriBeCa 212.941.8100

The Canal Room caters to New Yorkers who think that a night out isn't complete without the coveted velvet rope, a bouncer, costly drinks, and a few B-list celebrities. The good news, though, is that the bouncer at this super-sleek-looking club/restaurant/lounge is fairly tolerant and celebrities do occasionally appear to briefly mingle with the masses, unfailingly creating an entertaining stir on the dance floor. Black and white leather couches abound in each spotless, minimalist room, offering a seductive respite. What saves this club from upper-crust irrelevance are an ace music selection, cutting-edge dance music acts, and a refreshingly down-and-dirty aesthetic. As long as you're ready to be sexy and party down, the Canal Room has the berth for you.

Canapa
245 E. Houston St. (@ Norfolk St.)
Lower East Side 212.673.5351

There's no bar at Canapa, but there's plenty of booze. Confused? This Italian restaurant serves 40 wines by the bottle ($60 and under) and nearly 30 by the glass in an, open airy room filled with family-style dining tables. Wine dunce? Relax; on a quiet night, the owner/chef will gladly explain Southern Italian wines to uncouth LES-rs. Canapa's pizzas have been a hit since it opened three years ago, and anything else you order promises to be authentic and delicious. If you tend to feel awkward unless you have a sleek wooden bar top to lean against (or pass out on), pop next door, where sister-restaurant Petrosino features a polished concrete cement bar complete with floating flowers, a Zen atmosphere, and upscale Italian eats.

Candela
116 E. 16th St. (Irving Pl. & Park Ave. S.)
Gramercy 212.254.1600

Candela, as you might expect, is dripping with wax. This is an ideal date spot and the romance starts with a happy hour featuring 2-for-1 well drinks, $3 drafts, and specials on select martinis. For a nooner, check out Candela for their $12.95 brunch that includes an entrée and drink. Should you snag an outside table, bring sunscreen, because the painfully slow service guarantees a long stay. Candela's dinner offerings are a mix of classic American and Asian, and it offers several items taken from Nobu's menu, and while it's less expensive it's not, well, Nobu. Thanks to a good wine selection, this is also a good place to stop by when trying to "wow" out-of-towners, but only if you're not in a hurry.

Cantinella
23 Ave. A (Houston & 2nd Sts.)
East Village 212.505.2550

Only steps away from the raucous downtown nightlife scene, Cantinella is a culinary oasis in a section of the East Village better known for tattoo shops and dive bars than fine cuisine. Keeping with the neighborhood vibe, Cantinella offers up refined Italian dining at Ragu prices. Heavy on delectable antipasti plates featuring plenty of prosciutto and olive oil, appetizers may leave you feeling too full to attempt a main course; those that save room can sample the large selection of pastas and main plates that Cantinella offers, along with a healthy array of daily specials. If there isn't an open spot to sip wine while you wait for a table, never fear: Free delivery is here.

The Cantor Roof Garden (@ the Met)
1000 5th Ave. (@ 82nd St.)
Upper East Side 212.535.7710

After dealing with all the tourists crammed into the Metropolitan Museum of Art, no one will blame you for needing a drink. Snagging a glass of sangria "up on the roof" is also a fab way to get in your culture quota without giving up precious cocktail time. Surprisingly less packed than one would expect, the Cantor Roof Garden offers a view of Central Park that even Pale Male or Lola would covet (you can spot the Dakota, where John Lennon lived). Take a cue from the starving artists downstairs though—forgo the $8 airport-style sandwiches, and stick with the New York-style hot dog stand across the street, then wash it down with an overpriced plastic cup of wine while you pose near the strange life-sized artwork attached to the floor.

Canyon Road
1470 1st Ave. (76th & 77th Sts.)
Upper East Side 212.734.1600

Drink up before you sit down. The frozen parties in a glass—piña coladas, margaritas, and the rest of the usual fruity suspects—are *excellente*, striking the perfect balance between sweet and boozy. Canyon Road's menu offers classic concoctions kicked up just enough notches to be interesting. Quesadillas, for example, come in a number of inventive guises—try the ones with shredded duck and red onions or goat cheese and poblano chile. The homemade guacamole is *muy bueno*;

it's studded with just the right amount of diced onion. The service can be a bit inattentive here, but once you've worked your way through that second piña colada, and the movie-set south-of-the-border décor begins to swirl around you, the wait won't seem to matter much at all.

Capone's
221 N. 9th St. (Roebling St. & Driggs Ave.)
Williamsburg 718.599.4044

Capone's

You may have passed Capone's a number of times mistakenly thinking it was closed due to the ominous industrial warehouse door. Perhaps that's their idea of gate-keeping: The Alligator Lounge's offshoot offers the same crowd-pleasing free brick-oven pizza without the "crowd." The scene is sparse, with punky bike-courier types instead of its predecessor's preppies. Outfitted with backlit stained-glass cathedral panels and a long, dark wood bar, the big, airy warehouse space offers sunken and elevated seating as well as a smoking porch so you can keep an eye on your pie and your date while you puff away. DJs and karaoke spice up this modern pizza parlor throughout the week. In theory, this sounds like a mess. In practice it works well.

The Carnegie Club
156 W. 56th St. (6th & 7th Aves.)
Midtown 212.957.9676

So it's a winter evening and you've been riding in a horse-drawn carriage through Central Park. Now you need to warm up with a stiff drink and a fine cigar—where to? Why, you well-dressed knickerbockers, go to the Carnegie Club, where the air is smoky, the whiskey's neat, and the shrimp cocktail's jumbo. It's an older crowd—men in suits and ladies in pearls—and there's a $10 charge per person at the smoker-friendly tables and cushy sofas. That's a small price to pay for a Sinatra impersonator crooning between oak floor-to-ceiling bookcases. Arrive early or call ahead for the Monday and Friday jazz shows, or "Sinatra" on Saturdays ($30 cover plus a two-drink minimum). Sit back, adjust your monocle, and warm your martini near the fireplace while waiting for your chauffeur.

Carolines on Broadway
1626 Broadway (49th & 50th Sts.)
Midtown 212.757.4100

The jury's still out on whether average Joes who are actually funny get laid more often than good-looking rich men recycling bad knock-knock jokes—so you can decide for yourself after you've heard one of the side-splitting comedians at this top-notch, festively decorated comedy club. Boasting an impressive calendar of talent for 24 years, Carolines has featured funny men (and women) like Dave Chappelle, Dave Attell, and Janeane Garofalo. So when your job's got you down and you need to laugh off some NYC street rage (or you've just run out of good Michael Jackson jokes), head to Carolines and order up the Tower of Onion Rings or an apple martini or two; you'll be laughing so hard you'll forget you're in Times Square.

Carriage House
219 E. 59th St. (2nd & 3rd Aves.)
Midtown 212.838.9464

For those who can't decide whether they want a bar with an Irish, Native American, or a stable-and-carriage theme, there's the Carriage House, which jarringly combines all three. If that isn't enough for your ADD-addled attention span, Carriage House has a myriad of diversions—old-fashioned videogames, two jukeboxes (one digital and one regular), a pool table, darts, and bar food including buffalo wings covered in sauce brought in straight from Buffalo, New York. During the weekday happy hour from 2pm-7pm, regulars enjoy $1 off all drinks. There's so much to do at this neighborhood bar, it's no wonder the Carriage House is a favorite among people who work in the area. Just be sure to pack your Ritalin.

The Carriage Inn
312 7th Ave. (@ 8th St.)
Park Slope 718.788.7747

This never-crowded yet always noisy lump of Americana is the last remnant of skeeziness on Park Slope's yuppified Seventh Avenue. Despite the location, you'll never see a latte drinker or baby carriage in this establishment—their clientele consists mostly of old guys with tenting pants and a sad story. Though the space is large and includes a whole section of booths on the perimeter, it's never fully utilized, although you'd never know it from the hoarse and raucous voices that clamor perpetually on the sidewalk outside. Each table has its own TV, the jukebox is geared toward rock fans, and the mostly fried bar food is a good way to stave off a hangover, but that's not reason enough to visit this misplaced dive.

Casa La Femme North
1076 1st Ave. (58th & 59th Sts.)
Midtown 212.505.0005

If you think a place called Casa La Femme sounds like a strip club, you're not entirely off-base, since this Egyptian restaurant boasts belly-dancing on the weekends and plenty of hookahs. Fortunately, the similarities end there; Casa La Femme North is a civilized, stylish spot that's great for a culture-filled date. Pick up a hookah and rent a tent for two in this Middle Eastern delight, where the atmosphere feels thousands of miles removed from its base-of-the-Queensboro Bridge reality. The lounge smells like lilies and sandalwood, and a small bar off to the side is the next best thing to drinking gin and tonics in the Kasbah. Menu items are a bit difficult to pronounce, but the taste isn't lost in translation. Service can be slow, but the staff is friendly and the atmosphere will be a cool distraction.

Casimir

103-105 Ave. B (6th & 7th Sts.)
East Village 212.358.9683

Slightly out of place in the East Village, this French restaurant is refreshingly hipster-free and is an ideal date spot for late-night romancing. Trays of favorably fragrant food pouring out of the kitchen upstage the itty-bitty, marble-topped bar often being tended by dashing men with indiscernible accents. This makes wine inquiries futile, but at $6-$8 a glass one can afford to experiment. Background jazz makes for a moody backdrop that adds to the classy vibe—think Paris circa 1920. Walking in the door is a little intimidating, but it takes just a few minutes to slip into the scene, which is more of an opportunity for intimate conversation than a social op.

Cassis

52 Stone St. (Pearl & William Sts.)
Financial District 212.425.3663

After a day of "buy, sell, oh shit, sell, sell, sell!" Wall Streeters gather here for a tipple and a taste of French-Mediterranean fusion. Tucked away on the aptly named Stone Street, a cute, cobblestoned alley, Cassis feels worlds away from the concrete jungle looming over it. While the creative offerings are worth trying—Asian sea bass, mussels, grilled steak, asparagus, and pomme frites, to name a few—it's the extensive wine list of over 60 vintages that sets this cozy restaurant apart from the glut of pubs in the area. Sample your way through a varied selection of excellent French and Italian reds—then consider calling in and canceling your morning meetings. Judging from the lively revelers enjoying happy hour, they'll be doing the same.

Cattyshack

249 4th Ave. (President & Carroll Sts.)
Carroll Gardens 718.230.5740

Call off the psychotic groundskeeper and his plastic explosives, because Cattyshack is more about beavers than gophers. Brought to us by the founder of now-defunct Meow Mix, Cattyshack is a deliberately shabby bi-level space accepting of heteros, but catering to lesbians, trannies, and boyz of the more adventuresome variety. A jukebox rocks the concrete floors when DJs aren't spinning. (Expect a $10 cover on those weekend nights.) There's plenty of dancing going on, as well as occasional karaoke, and lots of cruising. Chicks with sticks rule the pool table and there's even an outdoor smoking and chillin' space for those who want to keep Kool. On occasion, these girrrrls even barbecue on the deck and package the fixin's with generous margarita and mojito drink specials of the $10 all-you-can-ingest variety.

Caviar and Banana Braserio

12 E. 22nd St. (Park Ave. S. & Broadway)
Flatiron 212.353.0500

Brazilian cooking show fans will remember *Caviar and Bananas* as the program hosted by this restaurant's chef, Claude Troigrosís. To them, Shecky's sends a heartfelt, "boa vinda." Once home to reality show gimmick/restaurant Rocco's, Jeffrey Chodorow's large, light, and thoughtfully hip room is as energized as its pricey sugar-coated steak, seafood, chicken, and crustacean menu. Fusing the richness of French cuisine with festive Brazilian fare, Caviar and Banana feels like a

Caviar and Banana Braserio

Carnival on your table. The absence of marching bands, fire eaters, and general high-energy cheesiness is appreciated here as that's a direction in which places like this can go wrong. Enthusiastic if not sometimes hurried servers somewhat fill their shoes, but they're altogether necessary for explaining culinary combos that might not occur to non-Sao Paoloans. Caviar and Banana's rum-based tropical cocktails are rich with fruits and they're fittingly creative for this group- and couple-friendly fiesta; have three or four.

CBGB's & OMFUG
315 Bowery (@ Bleecker St.)
East Village 212.982.4052

This historic institution is so punk rock you can smell it—we mean that quite literally. Like the safety pin-wearing artists it's launched, CBGB's is always rumored to be on the verge of dying. With a longtime lease ending in fall 2005, its nearing demise is more than a possibility. Talks of a Las Vegas CBGB's are well under way and surely there will someday be a Broadway musical about the filthy venue that launched the Ramones, Blondie, Talking Heads, and a million other bands you've never heard of. While it's still around, crouch through the graffiti-riddled doorway and step into history—or whatever that is on the floor. A stage occupies the far end of the mid-sized room, a bar lines the wall to the right, and don't even ask about the bathrooms—they're disgusting. God bless this dump.

CBGB's Gallery
313 Bowery (@ Bleecker St.)
East Village 212.677.0455

Separated from the CBGB concert venue only by a single wall, this studio space is essentially an homage to the room next door. There is a long bar here and it doubles as a punk rock museum gift shop, selling the CBGB's t-shirts that essentially keep this storefront in business. The high-ceilinged room is deep and bare-boned with a few tables and benches for the weary, but for the most part, visitors stand and gawk at the photos and paintings on the walls, which change with each

new show. There is generally a minimal cover in place ($5-$10), and who knows where that money goes? But hey, this is part of CBGB's—so long as the doors stay open, a couple bucks is a small price to pay.

Cecil's Bar (@ the Crowne Plaza Hotel)
304 E. 42nd St. (1st & 2nd Aves.)
Midtown 212.986.8800

Cecil's Bar is for anyone who ever tried to order a Metropolitan and was met with a blank gaze by a hipster bartender. The bartenders here know their Metropolitans, and their Lemon Drops, and probably most other drinks that have fallen out of fashion (or aged gracefully, depending on your outlook). While Cecil's, located inside the Crowne Plaza Hotel, will never be a scene, its charm (read: the old lady drinking a martini and watching *Wheel of Fortune* seated at the bar next to framed pictures of 1940s Broadway stars) is rather timeless. However, doomed by its location, Cecil's is more than likely to attract out-of-towners looking for directions to Times Square or 9-5ers whose idea of "letting loose" is taking off their ties.

Cedar Tavern
82 University Pl. (11th & 12th Sts.)
Greenwich Village 212.929.9089

The pleasant ka-ching of an old-fashioned cash register can be heard upon entering this hallowed bohemian haunt, where spirited conversation carries above the din of the digital jukebox, which is kept at a low volume for precisely that reason. There's a TV set playing sports at the far corner of the bar, but no one's paying it much mind. Perhaps it's because people come to this 60-year-old bar for the old-world charm that chain restaurant/bars desperately try to emulate. The amicable and efficient staff adds to the ambiance, while the patronage is mostly actor types, locals, and a smattering of NYU kids who venture in looking for antiques. This former meeting place of great literary and artistic drunks, er, minds, has slowly mellowed over time, but it's still a great neighborhood find.

Cedar Tavern

Cellar Bar

Cellar Bar (@ Bryant Park Hotel)

40 W. 40th St. (5th & 6th Aves.)
Midtown 212.642.2211

With fruity drinks called "Porn Starr," "Thai Me Up," and "Vixen," dancing girls, and waitresses clad in Vegas-chic bustiers and miniskirts, one gets the sense that the Cellar Bar isn't playing hard to get. The waitresses seethe with hostility, but who wouldn't in such an outfit? The bar's backdrop changes color alongside the loungey house soundtrack, and candlelight flickers beneath a vaulted white brick ceiling. Splurge on a $14 single-malt Scotch or an $8 bottled beer, and munch on wasabi peas, edamame, and bread crisps; if you linger long enough, you may even spot a celebrity. Meanwhile, groups of fun-loving city girls wearing sexy stilettos order rounds of "New York Flings." Flirting has never felt so naughty (or nice).

Cellar Bar & Café

325 E. 14th St. (1st & 2nd Aves.)
East Village 212.477.7747

Among Cellar's tasteful novelties are an unofficial make-out nook and faux hunter's den complete with woodland wallpaper and couches straight out of Elmer Fudd's basement. Patrons here show little interest in being seen, choosing instead to find their own way whether in a modest-sized lounge or duking it out over the Missile Command retro arcade console. Touch-screen computer games round out the list of pleasures for the ADD in us all. The real gem lies on the secluded back patio, where lawn chairs invite you to settle in and forget there's an actual city going on outside. Take advantage early because the patio is cleared out around midnight. Of course, you can try again in the morning because Cellar opens at 7am, offering fresh Seattle coffee.

Cendrillon

45 Mercer St. (Grand & Broome Sts.)
SoHo 212.343.9012

This decade-old Pan-Asian SoHo restaurant mixes Asian flavors like so much kinky fetish spam. With an inventive menu, matched by an exotic décor, Cendrillon has something for everyone. The beef salad and slow-cooked spareribs sate the carnivores, and the black rice paella is a treat for seafood fans. Looking to score a nickel's worth of pot? Well, Cendrillon offers $4.95 pots of tea. Disappointed? They do come in far-out flavors including "Monkey Picked" and "Green Sea Anemone." For something a bit more potent, order a Buko coconut martini ($9.50) or mango margarita ($9.50). The exposed kitchen, custom light fixtures, and floral photographs won't let you forget that this is an upscale dining experience, and neither will the prices. Cendrillon's long layout makes service a little sluggish, but the experience should give you plenty to talk about while awaiting your check.

Central Bar

109 E. 9th St. (3rd & 4th Aves.)
East Village 212.529.5333

Friendly neighborhood barflies, NYU students, and a boisterous after-work crowd mix at this Irish-leaning sports bar, which offers standard pub fare like bangers and mash and a decent selection of sports broadcasts from around the world. While the bar has a lounge-like feel in the front with leather couches and low tables, darkness descends in the back where drinkers sit on tottering stools around high tables (the dim lighting is good for couples seeking privacy, not so good for those trying to read a menu). The music, ranging from '80s classics to more modern fare, depends on the bartenders, as do the drink specials, so be a good tipper and they might take your request. Stairs in the back lead to another bar upstairs, but that room is rarely open.

'Cesca

164 W. 75th St. (Columbus & Amsterdam Aves.)
Upper West Side 212.787.6300

The mellow warmth of 'Cesca's décor reflects the richness of its robust Southern Italian cuisine. The young sister restaurant to Ouest, 'Cesca boasts an elegant front lounge that's surrounded by oak walls, tasteful art, and candlelight; it's perfect for a romantic tête-à-tête. Beyond, the cozy dining area encourages boisterous, familial, cheerful gatherings. Straddling all of this is an open kitchen where you can watch your seafood or mushroom risotto (highly recommended) be prepared fresh before your eyes. Or, use your time more wisely by dipping into the endless wine list. The wait staff is friendly and subdued, making 'Cesca a delicious social treat for any night, whether you're on the town *tutto solo* or with 20 of your closest friends and neighbors.

Chai Home Kitchen
124 N. 6th St (@ Berry St.)
Williamsburg 718.599.5889

So, you couldn't get a table at Sea or Planet Thai, decided to try the closest Asian food-serving joint, and ended up at Chai Home Kitchen, huh? Well, as it turns out, this sake bar and Pan-Asian eatery isn't so bad after all. The combined effort of a Japanese architect and his French culinary-trained Thai wife, Chai is a bit of a spillover joint, but it's not without its charm. Small and romantic with just the right amount of hipster ilk to give it Williamsburg cred, Chai Home Kitchen's beers and wines can be counted on two hands, probably because there's such a premium on space here. The $7 vegetarian duck is…well, we don't know what it really is, but it ain't bad.

Chance
223 Smith St. (@ Butler St.)
Boerum Hill 718.242.1515

Chances are you'll fall for the intimate atmosphere of this Brooklyn find. Chance revels in the fusion of dissimilar influences—namely French and Chinese—and everything in the bar/restaurant's sleek space reflects this aesthetic. Red Hong

Kong-style lamps illuminate the bar's bubbly steel surface, while long, modern light strips line the walls of the dining area. Complimentary wasabi peas hold you over at the bar while you sip your merlot. For dinner, try one of the dim sum boxes ($10-$12) for a light meal, or splurge on a first date in the swanky dining area—there's a good chance you'll get lucky.

Channel 4
58 W. 48th St. (5th & 6th Aves.)
Midtown 212.819.0095

Channel 4

This may be the only bar in New York that can boast that its patrons have chug-a-lugged with America's sweethearts of morning television, Katie and Matt. Royal family-style paintings of the *Today Show* casters, along with other NBC stars, adorn the walls of this after-work meeting place located just a commercial break away from NBC's studios. The dress code: "no T-shirts, no tanks, no cut-offs" may sound about as fun as a *Joey* marathon to some, but it works for the 9-5ers who don't mind bobbing their heads to 50 Cent while dining on bacon-wrapped sea scallops ($9.95) or General Tso's pot stickers ($7.95). For a business-casual peacock party you won't forget, tune into Channel 4.

The Charleston
174 Bedford Ave. (N. 7th & N. 8th Sts.)
Williamsburg 718.782.8717

The Charleston is a remarkably malleable institution that has long provided cheap drinks to Williamsburg's residents while adapting to the neighborhood's ever-changing landscape, and

that includes having survived Prohibition. Live rockers take the stage, providing entertainment for a mere one-drink minimum as youngish-looking folks fraternize with the older, more permanent human fixtures at the bar. Connected to a pizza joint, the Charleston serves good, cheap eats and if you're lucky, you'll be served by the kindly owner who also does the "light show" for performances. (See randomly flicking switches and using a laser pointer.) If you're heading out in the 'Burg, this is a great place to start the evening. Let's hope it can hang on for a while longer.

Charley O's Skybox American Bar and Grill
416 8th Ave. (@ 31st St.)
Chelsea 917.351.0607

Keeping a light on for the post-show Theater District refugees, Charley O's décor is a cut above your average sports bar. Exhibit A: They serve up live jazz and cocktails. It's also a bit more dramatic; take for example the big, flowery band stage and long, mirrored bar, handy for indirectly "making eyes" at a special someone. The service behind it is exceedingly friendly, too, just like in the gaping dining room on the other side of the stage. Buffalo wings get mixed reviews, so try the BBQ pork ribs for about $25. On the whole, prices match up fairly closely with other casual dining chains around the city. Beers, in fact, run about $5. Just don't expect the cost-cutting hipster crowd...they're back downtown already.

Charlotte (@ Millennium Broadway Hotel)
145 W. 44th St. (Broadway & 6th Ave.)
Midtown 212.789.7508

Another bar in the long list of Midtown spots that tries to pass itself off as a hip, downtown restaurant or lounge, Charlotte's high-gloss exterior fails to mask its true self: a tourist trap. Popular with theater-goers and out-of-towners who are trying to get a taste of New York chic, the elegant dining room behind the front bar echoes with a retro vibe reminiscent of the *Great Gatsby* and offers tasty—

if not overpriced—New American cuisine and cocktails. Odds are, after one visit, natives will steer clear of this spot, finding it often overpopulated with tourists sporting Sixth Avenue Fendi knock-offs and scrunchies. Those going to see *Rent* might want to keep Charlotte in mind. After all, if you're going to see *Rent*, we can assume that good taste isn't your strong suit.

Cheap Shots
140 1st Ave. (St. Marks Pl. & 9th St.)
East Village 212.254.6631

Ladies, tell that sucker that he can't play games with you. Instead, he can play them at Cheap Shots: chess, checkers, and Monopoly, to name a few, and, oh yeah, the drinks are cheap, too. Every Monday is BYO PlayStation Game night, enabling videogame junkies. The jukebox is loud and holds 200,000 songs, and on a good night, it drowns out the slapping at the air hockey table. Cheap Shots has free drinks for the birthday girl or boy, and the eight drafts and 12 bottles go for around $3 AND there's a happy hour. Cheap shots like Coco Puffs, Road Runner, and Lollipop are $2. As advertised behind the bar, drinking won't solve your problems, but passing out will.

Chelsea Bistro & Bar
358 W. 23rd St. (8th & 9th Aves.)
Chelsea 212.727.2026

Not just for the bitchy and famous, this delightful and romantic French bistro caters to Chelsea's fabulously gay and blandly married couples as well. With a killer menu of savory appetizers, entrées and desserts, you'll drop a pretty euro for a three-course meal here, but Chelsea Bistro doesn't disappoint. The bar is an ante-chamber to the restaurant and it pretty much caters to would-be diners who patiently wait for their table's lagging inhabitants to finish chewing meat from bones and licking their plates. Local celebs come here to dine and they do so because they think it's off the record and on the down-low. *Au contraire*! And while that fireplace crackling in the corner is a worthwhile distraction, looking around this room often nets an eyeful of hipness.

Chelsea Brewing Company
59 Chelsea Piers (@ 18th St.)
Chelsea 212.336.6440

Foretelling a day when we'll all be ruled by giant beer vats, the Chelsea Brewing Company gives you precious little opportunity to forget that, yes, they brew their own suds. And did they mention they brew their own suds, too? Enormous copper tanks loom around the bar and dining rooms...and that tells you how gigantic the place is. Two levels of booths and dining rooms await, bathed in sunlight from the windows facing the Hudson. For non-beer drinkers, CBC offers a serviceable menu of summer drinks. And then there's the food. Pizzas, many o' sandwich, salads, and seafood are all on offer. The prices are a little high (burgers are $11), but, hey, you're going to need something to distract you from that pilsner tank that...just...keeps...STARING.

The Chemist Club (@ the Dylan Hotel)
52 E. 41st St. (Park & Madison Aves.)
Midtown 212.297.9177

In high school, being in the Chemist Club would have gotten you daily wedgies. Now, being in the Chemist Club means you have good taste. But you can leave the Bunsen burners and safety goggles at home—despite its name (which is in honor of an actual chemist club still in existence) and the glass beakers lining the marble atrium, this warm, stylish restaurant/lounge/event space isn't just for the periodic table set. Downstairs, a large ballroom-like space boasts a mahogany parquet floor, a working fireplace, a bar, and cozy leather and wood furnishings where well-to-do diners feast on caviar and crispy battered lobster tail. Upstairs is a second bar and lounge area overlooking the grandeur below. Order up the signature Alchemist cocktail, scope out the good-looking crowd, and do some chemistry experiments of your own.

Cherry Lounge
454 W. 128th St. (Amsterdam & Convent Aves.)
Harlem 212.662.0900

Cousins with Missy Elliot? Timbaland's roadie? Lil' Kim's cellmate? You probably stand a better chance than most at getting into this ultra-exclusive hip-hop club, located a loooooooong subway ride away in Harlem. Unless you're an impresario, glitterati, or you have uptown connections, the doorman follows the strictly selective velvet-rope policy created by the hip-hop star owners (including producer Timbaland). Should you make the cut—or pass a striking resemblance to Queen Latifah—you'll be rewarded with a massive dance floor, swank VIP booths, leather banquettes, and a stylish red-tinted décor. If not, cue 50 Cent on the iPod and jam on the long ride home.

Cherry Tavern
441 E. 6th St. (Ave. A & 1st Ave.)
East Village 212.777.1448

Had Eugene O'Neill written an episode of *Cheers*, Cherry Tavern would have been the set: dark, active, chill, with a clientele that is as fun and conflicted as you. No doubt there will be a run-in, provoking one to ask, "Dude, do you ever leave?" Sometimes you just want a stool, a beer and a cheap shot, and some good tunes in a place where getting sloshed is expected. A pool table and framed art of dogs playing pool ties the room together. Weeknights cater to the regulars while the weekend crowd stops in before turning the East Village into East Newark, but when this place is good, it's quite good.

Chez Oskar
211 DeKalb Ave. (@ Adelphi St.)
Fort Greene 718.852.6250

Maybe it's because the servers speak French, but this place feels like the real deal. With its giltframed mirrors, dark-finished bar, and hazy din of jazz music, Chez Oskar captures the spirit of an authentic bohemian Paris bistro. Join Pratt students and arty folk for the reasonably priced (entrées start at $16) standard bistro fare, like the citrus salad, lamb shank, or steak frites, and a nice glass of wine. Don't roll your eyes when you see flourless chocolate cake on the dessert menu; Chez Oskar does this decadent delicacy right. If chocolate's not your thing, perhaps the brandied pear will settle nicely after a meal of hearty mustard rabbit (it tastes nothing like chicken!). If you can't find this place (that would be difficult given the blazing red façade), just call in your order; they deliver.

Chi Chiz
135 Christopher St. (Greenwich & Hudson Sts.)
West Village 212.462.0027

Beef. It's what's for dinner at this late-night West Village hotspot. And we're not just talking about the food (Chicken fingers, wings) that Chi Chiz serves up—there's also a tantalizing selection of tougher meat at this predominantly African-American gay bar, where there's always a good time to be had. Think you sound just as good as Aretha? Stop by on Mondays for karaoke. If you prefer to handle some balls instead, drop in on Thursdays to compete in the pool tournament. Show off your smarts on Tuesdays during Bingo. Of course, if all you want to do is get trashed, come by on Sundays, when happy hour lasts all day long. And if you're lucky, you'll end up taking home one of the many fine dishes you'll find at Chi Chiz.

Chibi's Bar
238 Mott St. (Prince & Spring Sts.)
NoLita 212.274.0054

Chibi herself greets you at the door of this tiny bar, and may even lick your hand if you stroke her nicely. This is clearly her bar, judging from the framed photo above the bar and the proprietary way she waddles about. Steeped in an aged Japanese aesthetic, incense wafts past yellow walls hung with unfurled Asian fans, and sake bot-

tles with paper umbrellas line the windows. The glasses look awfully tiny, but after a potent sip or two, you'll realize it's really just to keep you from running down the street with your pants wrapped around your head. You can graze on eclectic appetizers like fragrant tofu and chrysanthemum dumplings ($10.50), best washed down with a couple more shots of sake. Just don't offer to buy Chibi a drink—she's a French bulldog.

Chibi's Bar

Chibitini
63 Clinton St. (Rivington & Stanton Sts.)
Lower East Side 212.674.7300

Here' a sake bar that is so lovely and cheeky even people who don't like sake will be content. And for the ones that do, there's an extensive menu of hot and cold sakes and the house's four specialty drinks infused with sake. Chibitini is a small little nook that's full of personality; like its sister bar, Chibi's, Chibitini successfully blends a trendy modern art décor with a simplistic Japanese-meets-French vibe. It's intimate enough for a date, but the friendly wait staff makes it ideal for a sit-down drink with anyone you please. Dumplings, box dinners, and inventive salads are delish and won't bog you down for the rest of the evening's festivities. And the small bar in back is conducive to some serious sake sampling.

Chikalicious Dessert Bar
203 E. 10th St. (@ 2nd Ave.)
East Village 212.995.9511

Seating at this pantry-sized "dessert bar" is severely limited, but it's worth the wait; this place is so sweet, even the names of the chic menu items are enough to make your teeth fall out (try the warm chocolate tart with pink peppercorn ice cream and red wine sauce). Don't go looking for a heaping bowl of banana split, though; the treats here are prim and proper, most of which can fit in the palm of your hand. For $12 you can get your Oompa Loompa-loving self the three-course prix fixe; just make sure your taste buds are on overdrive because each spoonful could buy your subway fare home. Serious sugar connoisseurs will find blends of exotic delicacies, the likes of which are made before your very eyes. This place is to diabetics what kryptonite is to Superman.

China Club
268 W. 47th St. (Broadway & 8th Ave.)
Midtown 212.398.3800

What do hip-hop impresarios, young executives, B-list celebs, sports stars, and the people that love them have in common? They all flock to the China Club, one of New York's premier mega-clubs. (Just ask J.Lo and P. Diddy, who spent a night in jail after a night here got out of hand). Looking like a combination between the Playboy Mansion and a casino, the lounges are complete with large, red couches and gigantic chandeliers. The dance floor has enough beams and strobes to make you feel like you're at a planetarium laser light show. For a little al fresco action, make your way to the Jade Terrace. Note: Even if you can afford the $20 cover charge and steep drinks, don't even try getting in if you're underdressed or a dude without a date. This China girl's not that easy.

Chorus Karaoke
25 W. 32nd St., 2nd Fl. (5th Ave. & Broadway)
Murray Hill 212.967.2244

How can a bar located on the second floor of an office building be anything but stale and cubicle-like? Karaoke!!! An exception to the rule, Chorus Karaoke is nothing like *Office Space*. This futuristic "music room and karaoke bar" is lined with silver portholes featuring portraits of the greatest singers of all time—no, not Clay Aiken. They offer a fantastic selection of music, multiple flat-screen TVs, a giant movie screen at the glowing main bar,

and nine party rooms for private rental. The party rooms feature DIY karaoke and you get your very own cocktail waitress so ordering your drink won't interrupt any crooning (prep your vocal chords with the "Flaming Dr Pepper"). Chorus Karaoke is open until 5 or 6am daily, so get your pipes ready and take the elevator upstairs to join the Chorus.

Chow Bar
230 W. 4th St. (@ 10th St.)
West Village 212.633.2212

Remember when Pottery Barn was the purveyor of style, and Kanji tattoos were sweeping the nation like SARS? Contentious as the full passing of this groovy Pan-Asian fad may be, it's in full flower at Chow Bar. Skip the Green Dragon Martini (a $10 appletini) and try something from the sake list. Otherwise the wines on offer are well-matched to the food menu, which is heavy on tart little bits of seafood arrayed on your plate like so many lotus blossoms. The atmosphere is spa-like—there are Zen garden stones in the bathroom sinks, and Japanese good luck happy cat statues overlook the bar. The tables by the window provide people-watching, but sit anywhere near the spirited bar and you're going to hear lots of people-shouting.

Chubo
6 Clinton St. (Houston & Stanton Sts.)
Lower East Side 212.674.6300

As adorable as its name, Chubo is a cozy little nook catering to those with sensitive and sophisticated palates. First and foremost a French-Asian fusion restaurant, Chubo has an itty-bitty bar in the back, with a maximum seating capacity of four. Here, the polite wait staff doubles as bartenders; they'll walk you through the menu, suggesting you sample their fine wines, sakes, drinks like the Sakura (plum wine, cranberry juice, and champagne), and short list of beers, but most likely you'll want to savor some of the delectable—if dizzying—creations of Chef Claude Chassagne. Ah, Claude…guide us to your gastronomic nirvana.

Chumley's
86 Bedford St. (Barrow & Grove Sts.)
West Village 212.675.4449

Unmarked and sitting alone on a quiet West Village block, Chumley's upholds the tradition of the illegal speakeasy it once was by providing a rugged, comfortable atmosphere where you can still get tanked on homemade booze. It's no bathtub gin, but the arsenal of house brews at Chumley's are tasty and priced to move. The floors are covered in sawdust, and the walls are plastered with framed tributes to a range of literary heroes, which makes sense, given that drunks like Fitzgerald and Faulkner have kept this place in business through the hardest times in American history. Artists, yuppies, transvestites, and just old guys with liver spots—this place has it all and everyone fits in; a true New York staple. Cozy up to the fireplace where blacksmiths worked (and drank) during Prohibition.

Church Lounge (@ TriBeCa Grand)
2 6th Ave. (Walker & White Sts.)
TriBeCa 212.519.6600

Church Lounge is the holiest shrine in TriBeCa's nightlife scene. Without being exclusive, it manages to appear that way anyway, drawing a crowd of New York's most urbane young people and world-class jetsetters. The bar sits in the TriBeCa Grand's cavernous lobby, beneath a sweeping awning with lighting that still manages to seem understated. Sample one of the house's signature entrées, all of which are carefully prepared. (The lobster is $26, and the big bug is served in sweet sauce over noodles.) Drinks are not cheap, but at $8-$14 still below the market rate for such opulence. Topping things off is an adjoining dance space that features some cutting-edge acoustic performances or international DJ shows. On those nights, things get a little more exclusive.

Cibar
56 Irving Pl. (17th & 18th Sts.)
Gramercy 212.460.5656

Just two steps down from Irving Place you'll find yourself in a plush, sexy world miles away from the city. Cibar is the embodiment of a mature date spot, with its velvet sofas, candle-lined shelves, fireplace, and a good-looking mix of 30- to 50-year-olds. Get in the mood with seasonal elixirs mixed by the talented Cibar staff, like a lychee martini ($10) or apple sangria ($9). Wine, dine, and do whatever the hell else you like in this dark space: Feed your date pigs in a blanket, cheese, edamame, or chicken skewers, and keep his or her wine glass full with one of almost 30 bottles. Just a lucky few can squeeze into the back patio for a little PDA, but that doesn't stop the couples inside from giving it a go anyway.

Cielo
18 Little W. 12th St. (9th Ave. & Washington St.)
Meatpacking District 212.645.5700

Everything in this brightly hued club is futuristic and silvery, including the fashionable and mon-eyed clientele. They need to be, though, because the drinks here are steep. The next thing you'll notice is the sunken dance floor; centered in the middle of the room, it's the main attraction where booty-shakers groove to beats spun by resident DJs. Booths surrounding the dance floor are comfy, but they're empty whenever music is play-ing. Smokers love the cigarette-friendly back gar-den and scenesters dig the Monday "Deep Space" party. The music is pretty standard Meatpacking fare—bass-heavy house, soul, techno, and trance. If you're a clubber looking to elevate your taste, come here to move from mega to micro and skanky to swanky.

Cipriani's
376 W. Broadway (Spring & Broome Sts.)
SoHo 212.343.0999

Cipriani's is so timelessly tasteful and intensely cool that P. Diddy had one of his gala birthday par-ties here—okay, bad example. Bask in the reflect-ed glory of any number of SoHo celebrity icons and fashion dignitaries while you recline outside and watch the passersby watch you, or settle down indoors underneath what can only be described as one of the most breathtakingly grandiose chandeliers west of Broadway. Noted as much for its expansive wine list and gourmet Italian menu (both of which are beyond reproach by any sane standard), this is THE place to be seen below Houston. However, greatness has its price; expect to burn some serious bucks if you want to be privy to this party. If your cash stash is lacking, settle for being one of the passersby.

Circa Tabac
32 Watts St. (Thompson St. & 6th Ave.)
SoHo 212.941.1781

At Circa Tabac, you're not only allowed to smoke, you're encouraged! Don't worry, it's legal. Yes, tobacco lovers, there is a God, and he tokes up

Circa Tabac

regularly right here. Light one up worry-free, and check out the amazingly diverse, surprisingly affordable array of appetizers with a Japanese, Italian, French, American, Chinese, or Polish flair. Wash it down with one of the house's eight cham-pagne mixes. Don't dare miss the equally appeal-ing cigar menu with lots of best-loved traditional and eclectic selections (try the Kahlua Corona sto-gie; it's a true taster's choice). Slathered in time-lessly stylish brushed suede, steel, and camel leather tones, this former book store is the quin-tessential embodiment of relaxation for nicotine fiends of every stripe. Cough.

Citrus Bar & Grill
320 Amsterdam Ave. (@ 75th St.)
Upper West Side 212.595.0500

It's not hard to see the appeal of Citrus, a zesty restaurant/lounge that advertises "Latin fare with an Asian flair" (which is basically a green light for people craving quesadillas with a side of sushi). Add top-shelf tequilas to the mix, along with sig-nature cocktails like the key lime pie and the rasp-berry mojito, and Citrus is a refreshing spot. Even the descriptions will make you salivate—take the pomegranate-ancho chile-glazed salmon or the cinnamon ice cream, for instance. The décor is bright and modern, and, in keeping with the Far-East-meets-south-of-the-border theme, boasts splashes of festive colors and Asian touches. The open-air feel of the room is accentuated by ceil-ing-high windows and a running waterfall. Squeeze Citrus onto your list of restaurants to visit.

The City Grill
269 Columbus Ave. (72nd & 73rd Sts.)
Upper West Side 212.873.9400

This classy uptown spot is probably more famous for its impeccable Sunday brunch than it is for its bar scene. A world of white cotton tablecloths and chilled martini glasses, the City Grill has no room for any barroom antics, drunken karaoke, or getting out-right sloshed. Very rarely does the party here run until the wee hours—or even past midnight—as the Grill is more of a restaurant with a bar than a bar with a restaurant. The wine list at this Upper West Side mainstay has something for every palate, and the martinis and margaritas are superb—if not a little on the expensive side. The clientele, usually young professionals and local families around brunch and dinnertime, maintains a casual decorum chatting with the friendly staff while the restaurant still moves like a well-oiled machine.

City Hall
131 Duane St. (Church St. & W. Broadway)
TriBeCa 212.227.7777

Expansive and multileveled, City Hall has the masculine and powerful feel of a steamboat. White pillars around its sidewalk seating set the tone for the sweep of wood and maroon patterns that lead to the sunny main dining room. The darker adjoining bar is embellished with fountains and there's an upper floor for private dining and drinking, as well as private rooms downstairs for events. Try the cucumber martini, a house recipe, with Atlantic salmon for a feast totaling $34. Or, go with the strawberry cosmo with tuna steak for a dollar more. This opulent spectacle is indeed a treat to the eyes and palate so make sure your wardrobe reflects that you're visiting such a place.

Clancy's
978 2nd Ave. (51st & 52nd Sts.)
Midtown 212.755.8383

Clancy's caters mostly to the European sporting crowd, and it gets quite packed when there's a football or rugby game going on overseas. (Don't call it soccer here.) A quaint Irish setting that exudes more character than most other spots on the block, Clancy's has a vast and well-priced Irish-American menu including French fries with curry sauce; they also offer delectably tempting burgers, steaks, and other meaty goodness. A dining room in the rear with a functioning fireplace provides a quieter and more relaxed time than the front area, which can get rowdy when there's a game playing. Though these guys open early for lunch, the bar operates until 4am, and they also feature a pleasant brunch on the weekends.

Clem's
264 Grand St. (@ Roebling St.)
Williamsburg 718.387.9617

Williamsburg's indie filmmakers need look no further than Clem's for a film noir barroom set. The décor is all black, the Venetian blinds that surround the place cast sultry shadows on the clientele, and steam fogs up the windows. Luckily this doesn't mean you have to wear a trenchcoat or call women dames. The social atmosphere is pretty chill, and Clem's is a nice place to settle down and enjoy a drink with friends as the clock ticks away the hours. Happy hour runs from 2pm-8pm, meeting the needs of those creatively employed, alcoholic, or independently wealthy.

Cleopatra's Needle
2485 Broadway (92nd & 93rd Sts.)
Upper West Side 212.769.6969

From the sexy lighting to the groove-inducing jazz, not only is this one of the ultimate date spots for Columbia students, but Cleopatra's Needle is also the shot in the arm tired Upper West Side parents need from time to time. The conversation flows as easily as the up-market Scotch and vodka, as couples hold hands across their tiny tables. Small groups crowd the bar to watch muted games on the TV, but even their Yankees-induced groans of agony don't detract from the overall atmosphere of unpretentious sophistication. The stage area is in a backdrop of exposed brick: It's quintessential

New York cool. The only thing missing is Meg Ryan at a corner table, bantering with either Tom Hanks or Billy Crystal.

Climax
14 Ave. B (1st & 2nd Sts.)
East Village 212.260.7100

The name of this East Village lounge may or may not make people want to come, but the cool international vibe draws a crowd that's a bit Euro, a bit uptown, and a bit Alphabet City too. Plus, what's in a name? This dark, bi-level make-out spot was a big hit in its past life as Delft, where it was a hipster haunt of a different vibe. Upstairs, exotic statuettes are tucked into these brick walls, which surround a civilian-sans-celebrity crowd of singles and groups. Downstairs, the small, less-posh, secondary lounge with a cool mirror mosaic provides an excellent space for private parties. This quintessential East Village haunt gets rocking…er, more accurately house-ing pretty late at night, because no one wants to reach Climax too soon. Think Le Souk lite.

Cloister Café
238 E. 9th St. (2nd & 3rd Aves.)
East Village 212.777.9128

On sunny days in the East Village, Manhattanites head to the Cloister Café for a relaxing brunch in the vine-covered garden. Though the menu is all over the place, from $9 burgers to $16 duck filet, the reasonably priced food is good. But most people don't know that the Cloister is much more than a brunch spot; with a huge wine list, cocktails, draft beer, sangria, champagne, and food that is served until midnight, Cloister Café is a great place to hang out on a starry night. While the rest of the world is lined up outside of trendier local spots, one could do a lot worse than passing time with this friendly staff.

Club Macanudo
26 E. 63rd St. (Park & Madison Aves.)
Upper East Side 212.752.8200

Cigar-chomping men (and a few women) brave the dense air to order single malts and discuss the day's deals in this handsome cigar lounge/bar/restaurant that feels like a private club. In between puffs, you'll discover that there's a full dinner menu (sandwiches, sirloin, salads) and live Latin music every Wednesday. Bring your own cigars, take yours from your private humidor, or pick from the 130 premium brands on offer. The bar requires a one drink, one cigar minimum. Since there are very few places where stogie fans can light up in this city (and even fewer of this caliber), advance table reservations are advised. Otherwise, find a spot at the bar and make some friends. If you feel the need to impress your guests further, order the $63 63rd Street Martini…then duck out quietly so they're left with the bill.

Club Shelter
20 W. 39th St. (5th & 6th Aves.)
Midtown 212.719.4479

It's difficult to tell where the Shelter (from discerning doormen—is that too much to ask for?) begins and the faux exclusivity (i.e., their "membership card") ends with a place like this. Driven by promoters and anyone foolhardy enough to lease this space out, Shelter is yet another soulless chameleon of New York nightlife. Expect grandstanding from the door people (if you can find the hidden "mystery door," that is), and pure anticlimax on entry. What does manage to drive traffic is the occasional name-brand DJ and the rooftop deck area. Otherwise, your hard-earned cover charge gets you a room full of anonymous dancers in a dark, stuffy atmosphere, and an impersonal staff. Keep yourself informed about forthcoming events, if you dare entertain the idea of a visit.

Clubhouse
700 E. 9th St. (@ Ave. C)
East Village 212.260.7970

Don't look for a sign out front—black stairs that lead inside a red wooden building wordlessly proclaim this bar's name. The low-key if lackluster Clubhouse draws Starlight's spillover crowd of mostly gay 20- and 30-something Alphabet City dwellers who relax on unimaginative, uninviting couches and burgundy vinyl barstools. Martini specials and specialty drinks like Apple Berry Fizz and the Japanese Cocktail run a pricey $10, though beer and wine snobs will appreciate the eclectic, well-chosen imports. Candlelight and Bose speakers provide thoughtful touches—the latter no doubt enhance the DJs who regularly perform. Stroll through nearby Tompkins Square Park and have a leisurely dinner and maybe a few drinks beforehand; Clubhouse doesn't start hopping until around midnight, though the area's more creative haunts may inspire you to hop right past it.

The C-Note
157 Ave. C (@ 10th St.)
East Village 212.677.8142

You won't have to drop a C-Note to hear live music in this out-of-the-way venue (sometimes there's a $5 cover, other nights it's free). Jazz, acoustic, rock, country, and singer/songwriters make up the majority of acts that play live seven nights a week, with a few variations during open mic and the Saturday jazz jam (4pm–7pm). This tiny space draws a lively crowd of youngsters decked out in their best thrift-store finds. Besides engaging in some friendly banter with the lead singer between songs, it's too loud to talk to anyone and the crowd's attention is often so focused on the band that they forget to order drinks. The décor earns a "C" but extra credit should be given for the Ms. Pac-Man videogame table and selection of flavored martinis.

The Cock
29 2nd Ave. (1st & 2nd Sts.)
East Village 212.473.9406

Let's face it: We could all use a lot more Cock in our lives. And this East Village dive ensures that there's no shortage of it. Popular any night of the week, the Cock attracts a slew of men who enjoy rubbing up against each other while getting down to some great music. Monday's "Homeskool" party

remains the bar's most popular weeknight, as DJ JonJon spins everything from '80s to hard rock to keep the young crowd rocking hard. But if real sleaze is what you crave, then come here on weekends, when a varying cover buys you a hot night of debauchery; the action gets more intense as the night wanes on.

Cody's Bar & Grill
282 Hudson St. (@ Dominick St.)
SoHo 212.924.5853

Cody's Bar & Grill

This building used to tremble with disco fever when John Belushi opened a nightclub here in the '70s, but the vibe couldn't be more different now. Cody's is a down-home neighborhood bar that also provides a spot right by the Holland Tunnel to grab a pulled pork sandwich, catch the score, and down a Red Bull for the ride home. Like many bars of its kind, it's a little crowded by the five TVs, and has an American flag big enough to fly over the Capitol. But it's comfortable and clean and—most importantly—Hoegaarden and Sierra Nevada Pale Ale are on tap. Not to mention the fact that the potato salad is just about the best to be found at this end of I-95.

Coldwaters
988 2nd Ave. (52nd & 53rd Sts.)
Midtown 212.888.2122

Don't let the $3 happy hour watered-down apple martinis lure you into this fourth-rate Midtown catastrophe. With its pseudo-nautical Red Lobster-goes-hotel-bar ambiance, Coldwaters leaves visitors with a sinking feeling. A cutesy whale motif greets incomers belying a surly, charmless bartender and depressed clientele that just blows on the whole. The family-friendly seafood restaurant wisely separates itself from the adjacent bar room, where classic digs include a few oddly placed chairs in back, aforementioned nautical motifs, a poker machine that sits near a CD jukebox, and for unlucky "happy" hour patrons, a pan containing overcooked chicken wings. Suddenly those watered-down martinis look pretty good, huh? So does finding another neighborhood bar. Ships ahoy!

The Collins Bar
735 8th Ave. (@ 46th St.)
Hell's Kitchen 212.541.4206

This drinking man's (or woman's) bar is a perfect hangout for the young and the restless. Unfortunately, the restless have no room to move in the Collins Bar's space-challenged confines. The often-used dartboard certainly cuts down on usable space too. The bar makes up for its tight quarters with a warm, relaxed atmosphere that befits its same-owned sisters Blind Tiger Ale House and Spring Lounge. It also offers seriously strong, cheap mixed drinks, though you'd better order beer if you plan to mingle…or get out alive. (The pint of the day is just $3.50.) A lively little spot for after-work drinks or weekend pre-gaming, the Collins Bar is best visited in the small groups for which the seating was designed.

Comedy Cellar
117 MacDougal St. (Bleecker & W. 3rd Sts.)
Greenwich Village 212.254.3480

Although Jerry Seinfeld no longer lends any new chuckles to your nightly TV lineup, he does occasionally drop in at the Comedy Cellar. And so do Dave Chappelle, Caroline Rhea, Robin Williams, and the Wayans brothers, with additional laugh-yourself-to-urination routines providing the ultimate comedic variety. Brimming with only the biggest laughs, this basement space beneath Greenwich Village's Olive Tree restaurant also hosts smaller-name comedians—unless you watch *Best Week Ever* and *Tough Crowd*—who can crack you up just as easily. And for those tri-state high-school kids looking for the non-traditional post-prom experience, the Comedy Cellar also offers a Party after Prom Comedy Showcase ($25 per person, including unlimited munchies and soda). Please note that nightly reservations are required, which only makes sense for a lineup packed with America's sharpest stand-ups.

Comedy Village
82 W. 3rd St. (Sullivan & Thompson Sts.)
Greenwich Village 212.477.0130

Comedy still seems to be the realm of the dorky male—at least onstage, that is. But their loss of dignity is your gain at this Greenwich Village laugh factory. The unembellished simplicity of the Comedy Village's interior may scream Elk Lodge to you, but the décor, $5-$10 cover charge, and two-drink minimum are a tiny price to pay (especially when you consider the $5 apple martinis) for the unique talent (usually mainstays of late-night talk shows and Comedy Central) who appear here. The house will bring out pizza if you hang around long enough, too. Here's guessing this is a great date spot; very few guys seem to show up without their favorite shoulder to laugh on. It's a new place, but the owners will surely have the last laugh.

Comic Strip Live
1568 2nd Ave. (81st & 82nd Sts.)
Upper East Side 212.861.9386

Jerry Seinfeld, Eddie Murphy, Adam Sandler, Chris Rock, Ray Romano, Paul Reiser, Damon Wayans, Dave Attell…is this the first ballot for the Comedy Hall of Fame induction? Actually, it's a listing of just some of the comedians who've started out in this fabled institution over the past 28 years. So you think you're worthy of the prime 9pm Saturday slot, class clown? Stop by between 6pm-8pm Thursday for "New Talent Night" and see if others agree. Comedy club prices are never a laughing matter—in addition to a $12 two-drink minimum, a single ticket, which is good for two shows, prices at $38. This place also offers comedy classes so those hoping to add some real punch to the office water-cooler sessions may want to consider that option.

Company
242 E. 10th St. (1st & 2nd Aves.)
East Village 212 420 7101

Located in the increasingly flashy East Village, this neighborhood bar is a humble alternative where you can rest your feet and grab a drink. Sure there's a DJ, but she's playing Van Halen and James Brown instead of English house music, and she's playing it at a fairly low volume to boot. With checkered floors and a tin ceiling, Company seems like a neighborhood relic in the best kind of way, acting as a throwback to the unaffected days of the neighborhood's seedy past. The crowd is made up of laidback punk rockers and aging record store clerks quietly nursing their brews over *High Fidelity*-ish conversations (but without the high-falutin' 'tude). Company isn't a place to score some digits, but for a night of old friends and drunken memories, there's nothing better.

 Company

Compass
208 W. 70th St. (Amsterdam & West End Aves.)
Upper West Side 212.875.8600

If you're searching for a night of upscale drinking and decadent dining, all signs point in the direction of Compass. Wine is the focus here, and the knowledgeable, if slightly pushy, staff can guide you toward a good bottle, though it might not hurt to bone up on your pronunciation should you want to impress a date when perusing this 250+ list.

The sleek, chilly Euro lounge atmosphere is unremarkable, but the savory Creative American menu ($21-$38) is anything but; though the cost-conscious might opt to take advantage of the pre-theater or brunch offerings. If wine isn't your thing, there's a healthy selection of imported beers and cocktails. Just don't blow your cork when the bill comes.

Connie O's
158 Norman Ave. (@ Newell St.)
Greenpoint 718.383.9789

A hip Greenpoint bar on industrial ol' Norman Avenue? Uh…no. Connie O's has nothing in common with the achingly trendy bars nearer the Williamsburg border, but, then again, you probably didn't expect to stumble upon an authentic Irish pub in the middle of a predominately Polish neighborhood, either. But that's exactly what you get at Connie O's: an unassuming neighborhood pub where the patrons care more about community than cool. The average age at Connie's, which displays its Irish pride on the painted green bricks on the bar's exterior walls, is pushing middle-aged, but they don't much mind when good-looking young'uns stop in for a beverage. In fact, there are even videogames and a pool table to keep the kids busy while the "adults" go about their business.

Connolly's 45th St.
121 W. 45th St. (6th Ave. & Broadway)
Midtown 212.597.5126

Colorful stained glass and a brass- and dark wood-infused décor create a certain churchy kind of feel at Connolly's 45th Street, but the efficient barmen don't exactly want to hear your confessions. This location is one of four Connolly's in the Midtown area, so you have a 25% chance of finding your friends if you tell them, "Meet me at Connolly's"…or less if one of your pals' last names happens to be Connolly. Once you find each other, this well-kept and well-stocked Irish pub is a good place to confess your sins over a few drinks. There are 20 beers on tap, solid, late-night pub grub, and every Saturday, the Black 47 play a live set of Irish tunes. So go have a couple pints, say a few Hail Marys, and all will be forgotten.

Connolly's 47th St.
150 E. 47th St. (3rd & Lexington Aves.)
Midtown 212.692.9342

John and Mary Connolly, while strolling through Midtown six years ago, felt something was missing—something they could remedy. That something was a clean, respectable place where all those suits and ties could go after work to meet regular guys and gals, catch up over a pint, and eat some simple, filling pub food. That missing something is missing no longer, with Connolly's on the scene. Midtownies now pack 'em in at this location as well as the other three Midtown Connolly's. New York can never have too many pubs and Connolly's knows this at its very core. Fulfilling the simple maxim, if you build it, stock it with 30 beers on tap, serve food 'til midnight and drinks 'til 4am, they will come—early, often, and to the closest location.

Continental
25 3rd Ave. (St. Marks Pl. & 9th St.)
East Village 212.529.6924

Think of every cliché persona you've ever associated with "punk" culture over the years. Now imagine all of these people in a dark, musty, punk venue and you are entering the Continental. Is this a dream? Your sticky-bottomed shoes say it isn't. This is a genuine punk/hard rock dive for more than the casual joyriding hipster. A nightly parade of raucous local bands brings the noise, and Monday night's Punk Rock Heavy Metal Karaoke is a blast. And hey, you don't have to pretend that you're trying to hide your tattoo here. Should the novelty of head-banging and sweat wear off you can always sidle up to the bar and ask for a chocolate martini…just to see what happens.

Coogan's Parrot Bay
1668 3rd Ave. (93rd & 94th Sts.)
Upper East Side 212.426.1416

More isn't always more, as demonstrated by the oversaturated bar scene on the Upper East Side. If bars were bears up here, they'd declare a 6-month hunting season to thin the population so that some of them might survive the winter. There seems to be no shortage of recent college grads stumbling about drunk on Third Avenue, but still, this poor joint is almost always empty despite a number of reinventions; its previous incarnation was as Lounge 68. The owners have ditched the "lounge vibe" for a tropical-themed décor, but a bad paint job can't mask the lack of UES crackers in Coogan's Parrot Bay. It's a shame, because the bar has a great outdoor seating deck, but fresh air is no replacement for cool.

Continental

Coppersmith's

Copacabana

560 W. 34th St. (@ 11th Ave.)
Hell's Kitchen 212.582.2672

Have you ever been on the subway and heard a group of kids talking about going to "the club" and found yourself wondering, "What is this club that needs no name?" Far less Barry Manilow than Desi Arnaz, the "Copa" is a Latin club run by Latin folks that is mostly attended by Latin people who like to dance to Latin music. *Comprende*? Downstairs they play mainstream music, but the real action happens on the main floor, where live salsa, meringue, bachata, and reggaeton music is played (come for "Tropical Thursdays"). The Copa is literally "the" Latin club in New York and the strict dress code and door policy reinforce the upscale ambiance. For *los jovenes*, check out the Thursday night college dance party and bikini contest. *Muy caliente*!

Copper Door Tavern

272 3rd Ave. (21st & 22nd Sts.)
Gramercy 212.254.3870

With its tin ceilings and mahogany bar, the Copper Door Tavern has an old New York feel, and that's a good thing. Rather than make this former bakery yet another über-sports bar on the Third Avenue strip, the Copper Door entices patrons with a relaxed vibe, a few flat-screen TVs, and daily specials like Tuesday twofers of burgers and Buds. The crowd is a mixed bag of locals fleeing the frat scene and Upper Eastsiders who stop in while bar-crawling (and yes, we know that sounds like a paradox). With reasonable prices and good food, this hangout is one pretty penny.

Coppersmith's

793 9th Ave. (52nd & 53rd Sts.)
Hell's Kitchen 212.957.2994

It seems that single, all-American guys bar-hopping in groups start their evening here, and end up settling in. Maybe it's the speedy female servers bringing serviceable bar fare (wings, nachos, burgers) that draws them. But it's probably the 10 TV screens that line the walls but are high enough so as not to distract from scoping out the other gender's ahem, assets. The scene at Coppersmith's becomes lively (and standing-room-only) around the few high wooden tables and their uncomfortable barstools during college and pro games, but daily drink specials and $8 burger-and-beer deals reinforce a college stadium illusion. Coppersmith's opens the downstairs for private parties, alumni events, or the neighborhood softball team, and the occasional acoustic rock requires a $5 cover.

Cornelia St. Café
29 Cornelia St. (4th & Bleecker Sts.)
West Village 212.989.9319

This classic has the artsy-but-safe café shtick down. Cornelia St. Café is so traditional that the only surprise on the brunch menu is the order in which French toast, eggs, etc. will appear. Healthy stuff like Portobello mushroom sandwiches are always in demand here. The food is surprisingly good and the wine list is rather substantial. If you venture out of the elegant upstairs dining area to the pastel blue room downstairs, you'll find a stage set for nightly performances of music, poetry, or comedy. This probably won't be the site of any groundbreaking art, but Cornelia St. Café doesn't pretend to be any such venue. It's a friendly place to have a tasteful, old-school café time.

Corner Bistro
331 W. 4th St. (@ Jane St.)
West Village 212.242.9502

For a bar perched on a corner, Corner Bistro is a little hard to find, but that doesn't detract from this West Village gem. Stocked nightly with surprisingly down-to-earth locals waiting on line for their favorite well-priced burger, the Corner Bistro is a great spot to cram into with a few friends for cheap drinks and a bustling atmosphere. Wear comfortable shoes because barstools are scarce and the few tables are always full. An owlish bartender directs the scene in this woodsy old spot and busboys fetch empty pint glasses all night long. A lot of people will tell you that these are the best burgers in NYC and we'd be hard-pressed to say otherwise.

Cosmo
359 W. 54th St. (@ 9th Ave.)
Hell's Kitchen 212.582.2200

This groovy little bar features mod blue lighting and a wall of mirrors, which effectively combine for optical singles scoping—that is, if you can get inside the place. Don't even think about coming here without calling first. Since Cosmo often rents out its entire space for private parties (at $200 for three hours), it's not uncommon to unknowingly arrive and see a "Closed" sign. But if the door's open, you'll discover a hip mix of gays and straights clustered around the bar sipping $4 martinis during the 6pm-9pm daily happy hour (all night on Sunday). Unlike most bars, Cosmo encourages you to bring your own food. Forgot your sushi at home? No problem. The bar offers takeout menus from nearby restaurants.

Cotton
105 W. 27th St. (6th & 7th Aves.)
Chelsea 212.627.1444

These guys are either onto something we don't yet get, or they're behind on something we already got—like high school. Flowing, semi-braided fabric is strewn about the former Wye Bar's ceiling, giving the impression of a well-financed senior prom with hints of influences like Dorsia and similar nightclubs past. (The fabric-covered walls are a nice touch.) A poppy house/hip-hop mix of old and new attempts an all-things-to-all-people vibe that searches for the line between retro and hip. Cotton attracts a healthily blended racially and socially diverse clientele, and they cater to VIPs with an in-house limo that can be booked to transport big spenders. The two bars upstairs stay busy while downstairs things are considerably easier thanks to a series of beds and a cotton candy machine.

Counter
105 1st Ave. (6th & 7th Sts.)
East Village 212.982.5870

Millet. Seitan. Lentil. Do these words warm your heart? Make your mouth water? If so, head directly for Counter. A small First Avenue storefront belies a spacious diner-style vegan restaurant with a menu of organic-only food. Don't worry—there's alcohol. Die-hard meat-eaters with visions of rabbit food dancing in their heads will be shocked (and maybe converted) by heaping, delicious servings of pastas and sandwiches, as well as the innumerable culinary possibilities of everyone's favorite soy product—tofu. The crowd includes everyone from stroller-pushing East Village parents who come for the weekend brunch to black-clad nouveau punks who swig biodynamic wine and beer into the night. A knowledgeable and borderline overly friendly staff keeps the mood upbeat. It's enough to make a carnivore think those loopy vegetarians are on to something. Or maybe that's the biodynamic wine talking.

Cowgirl
519 Hudson St. (@ 10th St.)
West Village 212.633.1133

Better than your average campy, Old West watering hole, Cowgirl ropes in West Villagers with its cheap drinks and stick-to-yer-ribs comfort food. Pull up a cowhide stool and kick your boots off at the bar, decked out with real-deal cowgirl kitsch and some awesome antler chandeliers. When the weather heats up, you can slip into a table outside and enjoy fattening Tex-Mex classics like chicken-fried chicken, chili-smothered Frito pie, and the best sweet potato fries (ever). Shots of bourbon or tequila sate the outlaws, but might we suggest one of Cowgirl's creatively flavored margaritas, served in glass Ball jars? Don't miss the country store on your way out for necessities like t-shirts, shot glasses, and a D.I.Y. Frito pie kit, so you can keep clogging your arteries at home.

Coyote Ugly
153 1st Ave. (9th & 10th Sts.)
East Village 212.477.4431

If you're not dancing on the bar at Coyote Ugly, you'd better be chugging beer straight from the pitcher. With free t-shirts for gals who dare to bare it topside (shh! Management doesn't "endorse" that behavior) and pitchers costing $7 on Tuesdays, you'll get your money's worth (and

rocks off) here. Immortalized by Hollywood, the real stars of this saloon are the Daisy Duke-wearing female bartenders (aka "Coyotes"). Don't wear your pricey La Perla bra on a night out here, ladies, as you'll likely be cajoled into adding it to the hundreds draped above the bar. A couple of dartboards grace the back wall, but who's paying attention to those? Certainly not the Japanese tourists who pop in for a photo of this NYC landmark—try not to spill any beer on them.

Cozy Café
43 E. 1st St. (1st & 2nd Aves.)
East Village 212.475.0177

Arabian nights have never been cozier at this tiny nook—it's filled to the brim with oversized cushions that beg to be lounged on. Nestle around one of the undersized tables and share a hookah (over 25 flavors) in what feels like your aunt's living room (assuming your aunt hails from Fez). A garden offers larger tables for dining on Moroccan-inspired salads, meat-heavy entrées, and nutty desserts from Cozy's limited menu, while a guitar and drum in the backroom encourage spontaneous dancing. If you sing or smoke yourself to a sore throat, don't despair—just order a cup of anis tea. The waiters can tell you about the healing properties of each of their exotic teas. If it's more than caffeine you're after, you'll have to BYOB. Always a catch, huh?

Craftbar
47 E. 19th St. (Broadway & Park Ave. S.)
Flatiron 212.780.0880

Craftbar's relocation is a new addition to Flatiron nightlife, though one name will be familiar to area fans. Chef Tom Colicchio, chef and part-owner of the Gramercy Tavern, oversees a Craftbar menu ranging from roast duck, to skate, to rabbit...seemingly Noah's entire ark cooked to taste for $17-$30. But enough about the food. The racks of vino towering over this bar speak to one of the house's strongest suits. Specialty cocktails are served as well, including the namesake drink, a combination of rhubarb and sparkling Italian wine. Craftbar occupies a big bi-level space, stylish and modern in every way. Spots like this serve for anything from an after-work drink to a wedding proposal over dinner. Drop in and see for yourself.

Crash Mansion
199 Bowery (@ Spring St.)
Lower East Side 212.982.7821

Live bands + the Lower East Side = grungy, loud CBGB's rip-offs with gross bathrooms (more often than not). Crash Mansion, on the other hand, is a comfortable, nice-looking alternative. First of all, the vamped-out basement has a hip and modern décor, and secondly, the sound is clean and sharp. With everybody boo-hoo-ing over punk rock venues losing their leases, it's time to suck it up and get to know newer venues for musical acts. Norah Jones has played here on Crash Mansion's stage, and the place is on a collision course to booking more big-time acts. The bar, which occupies the downstairs space of the building that houses the upscale club BLVD, also hosts special nightly events, bump-and-grind-ensuring DJs, and the occasional jam band. And you thought patchouli oil was out.

Crime Scene
310 Bowery (Bleecker & Houston Sts.)
NoHo 212.477.1166

A few years ago, the Bowery was one big chalk outline. Now, the only Crime Scene you'll find down here is this gimmicky working-class bar where a blue siren flashes in the window and big handcuffs are painted onto the walls. In the back of this deep room is a black felt-covered pool table where locals and the occasional off-duty officers shoot billiards while an online jukebox plays mainstream stuff with pop and rock inclinations. The front room is occupied by a conversation-friendly, 50-ft. bar and a few tables. Both rooms have their own movie screens where sports and special events play, but *Starsky and Hutch* reruns wouldn't be inappropriate. Crime Scene's most arresting offering is its hours: 11am-4am daily!

Crispo
240 W. 14th St. (7th & 8th Aves.)
West Village 212.229.1818

A big, airy Italian restaurant with the feel of an Olde English mead hall, Crispo remains an underappreciated culinary experience. The atmosphere is rustic, with lots of exposed brick and wood surfaces, and a long bar you'd sooner recognize in your favorite Irish pub. But don't come for beers—it's the grub you want. The rotating specials include unique prosciutto dishes, salads, and vegetable dishes, alongside a wide-ranging menu of carnivorous delights (veal medaglione, lamb chops). Most entrées are entrenched in the $18-$25 range. And the special $10 martinis feature every fruity flavor under the sun (even pomegranate), which should begin a trend of matching martinis with dishes instead of wine. Don't forget the wine list—it runs longer than the walk home after you've gorged yourself silly. Use caution.

Crobar
530 W. 28th St. (10th & 11th Aves.)
Chelsea 212.629.9000

This is one of the city's worst clubs for doing lines—as in waiting on them. Unless you get here super-early, be prepared to queue up with all the other B&T commoners before paying up to $30 for entry on most nights. Once you do step inside this multilevel club, you'll find great lighting that changes radically depending on where you are in the super-sized warehouse space. Despite the gigantism, there's a surprisingly good vibe among the crowd. Crobar hosts all sorts of parties and performances, so definitely call in advance to get an idea of what kind of crowd to anticipate. One thing you can always expect are pricey drinks (vodka shots, $9). But hey, if big crowds mean big fun for you, then you can't go wrong inside Manhattan's sixth borough.

Crossroads

480 Amsterdam Ave. (@ 83rd St.)
Upper West Side 212.874.9984

For anyone feeling nostalgic about that first drink with Dad at the Knights of Columbus, this friendly little neighborhood haunt will put you right at home. Formerly the Raccoon Lodge (the entire place, complete with Ralph and Norton's ersatz club mementoes, was an ode to *The Honeymooners*), Crossroads retains its predecessor's wood bar, tin ceiling, and homey atmosphere. The beer selection is decent (specializing in bottled imports and single-malt Scotch), the service is friendly (and cute), and the crowd, while not composed of the most attractive people on the Upper West Side, is unprepossessing—heck, it actually feels like the K.O.C. back in the old neighborhood. We're eager to see how the new management develops the place into a blues bar; meanwhile, we think we've found our new local watering hole…even if it does share a name with a Britney Spears movie.

Croxley Ales

28 Ave. B (2nd & 3rd Aves.)
East Village 212.253.6140

Croxley Ales

What's the quickest way to alienate yourself at Croxley Ales? Order a generic beer like Bud, Miller, or Coors. This sports bar doesn't serve them, and they don't need to, thanks to an eclectic mix of 30 international beers on tap and 75 bottles ($5-$16), as well as beer cocktails like the Black Widow and the Royal Crown ($5-$6). When it comes to generic food, however, Croxley isn't as picky—they'll feed you with Euro/bar food, and your nostrils will sting with hot sauce on Mondays, Wednesdays, and Sundays, thanks to 10-cent wing nights. The frat boy contingent is a big, red pimple on Croxley's nose, but the staff and decent outdoor area make for a beautiful cover-up.

Cru

24 5th Ave. (@ 9th St.)
Greenwich Village 212.529.1700

From Cru's 6,400-bottle "wine portfolio," hundreds make the menu every night, and the staff is well-versed in their restaurant's leather-bound, Tolstoy-esque "lists." Cru's restaurant and lounge is covered in beautiful hard wood, and the tasteful décor is matched by tasty dishes. Sound pricey? Then you heard it right. With entrées in the $20-$50 range, and the better wines pushing a couple Franklins, you might have to take out a small loan to do this place right. The pastas are inventive, but the fish is where it's at. Try the sturgeon or the grouper, or if you're a landlubber, go hog wild for a seasonal "Roasted Berkshire Pig." There is a slightly lighter menu available in the small lounge area, but those cramped window seats are best for wine-sipping.

Crudo

54 Clinton St. (Stanton & Rivington Sts.)
Lower East Side 646.654.0116

Italian Crudo is the not-yet-trendy raw bar. But times, they are a changin'. A long railroad bar that opens up to a graffiti-covered garden, Crudo is the perfect spot for a low-key night with a small circle of friends. Crudo's décor is quirky and raw—exposed brick, cinder blocks, and a random log hanging outside the bathroom. The bar area is pretty thin, so grab the right vino to go with your seafaring meal (sushi, oysters, carpaccio) and head to the "Back Lot." A few bricks shy of full-scale hip, Crudo is one of those places best kept to yourself before your Hoboken-based cousins catch wind of it.

Cub Room
131 Sullivan St. (@ Prince St.)
SoHo 212.677.4100

Claiming the former glory of the Stork Club as its own, the Cub Room was built in the image of its namesake, which was the inner sanctum of the high-falutin' club to the stars. This version's a two-part show—one side has a relaxed feel with exposed brick, pub tables, and after-work chatter brewing at the bar. The other side's all glamour and luxe leather lounge chairs. Either room's gonna have the audacity to charge $8 for a pint of Amstel. The $12-$15 cocktail menu alludes to the grandeur of yore: order a Clark Gable, Bette Davis, or the Knickerbocker, the Stork's notorious take on the Manhattan.

Cuba
222 Thompson St. (3rd & Bleecker Sts.)
Greenwich Village 212.420.7878

Cuba closes a little on the early side (11pm on weekdays), but this place crams a full day's party into a rather short amount of time. Upstairs, this quirky, Havana-themed restaurant and lounge serves up authentic Cuban shredded skirt steak, pulled pork, and fresh-rolled cigars. The live music upstairs is a delight, but too loud for intimate dining, so be prepared to listen more than you talk. Additional seating in the back and a handful of cozy corners downstairs fill out this small, old-world hacienda of high spirits. Cuba is ideal for private soirees, and with a dozen traditional Cuban beers by the bottle, everyone leaves feeling like a dictator. There aren't a lot of good drinking options in this neighborhood, but Thompson Street has a nice little thing going.

Cuba Café
200 8th Ave. (20th & 21st Sts.)
Chelsea 212.633.1570

The Latin beats are pumping, the crowd isn't above primping, and the Latin island décor says, "Milonga, milonga, milonga!" Plants adorn the inside of this place, which initially comes across as over-the-top and themey, but eventually makes sense as the vibe takes hold. Could it be the fantastic mojitos pulling the whole ordeal together? *Si*. The mid-priced pollo- and pork-heavy dishes aren't always authentic Cubana in the most conventional sense, as Cuba Café hints of a slightly Americanized Miami-esque look at Castro

Cuba Café

Cupping Room Café

Country. The fusion doesn't end there—Dominican and Spanish dishes make appearances as well. Weekend brunch is a good time to get the food without the scene, which is often heavy with well-toned Chelsea boys. The $12.95 Havana Benedict justifies getting up before noon.

Culture Club
179 Varick St. (King & Charlton Sts.)
SoHo 212.243.1999

NOW are we finished with the '80s? After all, we've pretty much done them twice. In a culture so starved for substance that we start retro movements five minutes after the actual era of choice has passed, Culture Club is a museum, a theme park, and a nightclub all rolled into one tired entity. Duran Duran, Def Leppard, Madonna…you'll hear it all at Culture Club, which sits under the same-owned, '90s-themed club, Nerveana. Granted, Culture Club can be a fun bachelorette spot as the only requirement for entry is meeting the $20 cover. This is where you come if you still associate having fun with Wang Chung. Kitsch only goes so far, folks. If you dig this place please don't vote or reproduce.

Cupping Room Café
359 W. Broadway (Broome & Grand Sts.)
SoHo 212.925.2898

The ideal place to take your Midwestern relatives who swear that the city is filled with tough-talking would-be muggers, this restaurant screams "ye olde New York"—exposed brick, lazily turning ceiling fans, a quaint old-fashioned bar, home-made breads, and friendly waiters (though sometimes they're agreeable in a faux, tip-getting way). Sunday brunch offers the standard fixin's and is always packed to the gills with pancake-munching locals and tourists alike. On weekdays, the place empties out to become a good destination for a quiet dinner (the $16.95 three-course prix fixe dinner menu on Mondays and Tuesdays is a bargain no matter where you're from), and the giant portions should go over big with out-of-towners. Your best bet—the 2-for-1 happy hour. Just be careful the cozy atmosphere doesn't encourage the folks to visit too often.

The Cutting Room
19 W. 24th St. (Broadway & 6th Ave.)
Flatiron 212.691.1900

Co-owned by Sex and the City's "Mr. Big," Chris Noth, the Cutting Room is a restaurant/bar/lounge/live music venue and occasional celebrity hangout. Equipped with a small stage, the back-room provides some respite from the madness with an eclectic gathering of entertainers, comedians, burlesque, jazz and blues grooves, and more.

Cover charges are par for the course at this Flatiron hotspot, but on the whole the bands here merit the cost (with the exception of Jimmy Fallon and Horatio Sanz, who have taken the stage before). Though the service can be inconsistent, the food is better than average and the $11 martinis are tasty if not pricey. Keep this one in mind when you want to hear live music without ending up in a mosh pit.

Daddy-O
44 Bedford St. (@ Leroy St.)
West Village 212.414.8884

You won't find any pompadours or Bettie Page look-alikes at this neighborhood corner bar. What you will find is straight-shooting West Villagers dressed-down in their Polos and wearing oversized diving watches that have never seen the ocean, chumming it up with their buddies or chatting up their dates. That said, Daddy-O is the perfect destination for those who prefer their West Village bar-going experience not too gay (or too far left of center). If you could turn a banker's lamp into a bar, Daddy-O would be it; forest green walls framed with stained wood add to the Ralph Lauren clothing store vibe. Not surprisingly, the affable bartenders serve appropriately run-of-the-mill drinks. But Daddy-O isn't entirely square; the kitchen turns out exceptional versions of standard pub fare until 4am every night.

Daddy's
437 Graham Ave. (Frost & Richardson Sts.)
Williamsburg 718.609.6388

With all the moaning about hipster overload in Williamsburg, sometimes those crazy kids get the balance right. Daddy's is a scenester hang in the least cloyingly way possible—regulars who actually read books and have things going on in their lives beyond wild haircuts and outfits. It's the perfect blend of all things discerning 'Burgers want—a mod rock jukebox sans Bon Jovi, vintagey, antique wallpaper and light fixtures, and a fully functioning fireplace. Hot dogs, tofu pups, and potato chips are served; and there are a couple of pinball games, a sweet outside patio, a frozen

Daddy's

margarita machine, and drinks like the Mermaid (tequila, grapefruit, and grenadine). Plus, it's so perfectly dim in Daddy's that everyone looks totally doable. Now, who's your Daddy?

Dakota Roadhouse
43 Park Pl. (Church St. & W. Broadway)
TriBeCa 212.962.9800

This watering hole has just slightly less "flash" on its walls than your average Applebee's, but you shouldn't judge a book by its cover, right? Weekdays, domestic bottles are on special at $2 each and part of the flash includes neon lighting, two pool tables, and a foosball table. Dakota also has plenty of room, good music, and more than a few bikers (don't ask why) to chat with (though you might only get the urge after you've had more booze). This place doesn't have a velvet rope and they don't want one, ya hear? It's casual, rollicking, and they serve exactly the kind of plain, greasy fuel that you need to go a few more rounds (plus free coffee for lightweights).

Dangerfield's
1118 1st Ave. (61st & 62nd Sts.)
Upper East Side 212.593.1650

The show must go on. Rodney Dangerfield, who died in 2004, owned this joint and it's still full of life. Sunday through Thursday, the laughing (and audience teasing) starts at 8:45pm; Fridays and Saturdays there's a double bill of back-to-back standup. There are no food or drink minimums, but admission can be steep, rising up to $20 on Saturday (2-for-1 coupons are available on their website). The longest-running comedy club—open since 1969—Dangerfield's doesn't have an amateur night, which is good news if you're an audience member and bad news if you wanted to try your shtick. Sit back and show some respect for the progeny of the former New-Jersey-aluminum-siding-salesman-turned-comedy-icon.

Danube
30 Hudson St. (Duane & Reade Sts.)
TriBeCa 212.791.3771

Throughout the '90s, Chef David Bouley was possibly the most celebrated of NYC's celebrity chefs. His famed restaurant of the eponymous name has closed, but his other TriBeCa masterpiece, Danube, has been going strong since 1999. The small and romantic Austrian-leaning restaurant sets aside a quarter of its space for a cozy lounge, and combined, the two rooms hold fewer than a hundred people. Entrées in the $30 range include veal wiener schnitzel, port wine glazed venison with Brussels sprouts, and slight deviations like Japanese yellowtail, that's reeled back into theme with Austrian crescent potato leaf spinach. This is no longer the "must see" spot it was five years ago, but the food is still excellent and the scene is dressed-up and beautiful. Sound expensive? Ya got that right, high roller.

The Dark Room
165 Ludlow St. (Houston & Stanton Sts.)
Lower East Side 212.353.0536

If you're a scenester looking for a good nightspot, then you probably already know about the Dark Room, and wish we'd stop telling people about it. Possibly named after the dress of the indie clientele—true to the LES, everyone in here is either in a band or sleeping with someone in a band—Dark Room predictably doesn't have much in the way of color, except for the occasional white belt and red bulbs that fit with the photo lab theme. There are two bars, which is good news for those who don't want to elbow their way through the often-heavy crowd just to get a gin and tonic. And with hot bartenders, we say the more the merrier. Flirt with one, and see if anything develops.

Dave's Tavern
574 9th Ave. (41st & 42nd Sts.)
Hell's Kitchen 212.244.4408

The gritty pre-Disneyfication of Times Square and Hell's Kitchen is alive and well in this stripped-down dive bar around the corner from the Port Authority Bus Terminal. This bare-bones joint may as well be IN the Port Authority, as its offerings of domestic beer, two old TV screens, and a pool table appear to draw a middle-aged transient crowd looking to knock back a few beers before heading…wherever it is people go when they leave Manhattan. The TVs will only show sports, the online jukebox might read "country or bust," and the barmaid is the only one doing much of anything. Get there before 10:30 if you want your beer in a pint glass; when they run out, they start pouring in plastic cups.

David Copperfield's House of Beer
1394 York Ave. (@ 74th St.)
Upper East Side 212.734.6152

Unlike the magical romance that fizzled between the illusionist of the same name and Claudia Schiffer, this neighborhood bar is working its way into the hearts of Upper East Siders and Sotheby's staffers. The after-work crowd is greeted by a friendly staff and wooed with specials like 25-cent wings on Mondays and "Kill the Keg" Wednesdays

($3 select pints "'til the deed is done"). Similar to its newly opened, downtown sister Hop Devil Grill, Copperfield's is all about the beer; so with two happy hours, 30 drafts, and 100 types of bottled beer, it's easy to make brewskies vanish. It's a tough break for the real David Copperfield, though; it seems like this bar is having better luck with the ladies, and it didn't even have to walk through the Great Wall of China.

Day-O
103 Greenwich Ave. (Jane & 12th Sts.)
West Village 212.924.3160

Southern and Caribbean cuisine may seem like strange bedfellows, but then again, so were Sonny and Cher. This West Village stalwart pulls off that unique combination magically, and the result is spicy, finger-lickin'-good grub. The main attraction is the all-you-can-eat weekend brunch. Jerk chicken draws rave reviews from regulars, but there's an abundance of satisfying dishes like the catfish. The lengthy list of rum cocktails the house serves up (try a little of the knock-your-socks-off rum punch) is nothing to balk at, either. The atmosphere at Day-O might just help to establish a new design genre—palm tree-chic. Call on Day-O the next time you're having a rainy day...you won't want to go home.

d.b.a.
41 1st Ave. (2nd & 3rd Sts.)
East Village 212.475.5097

Thirsty, fella? d.b.a.'s booze list is written on blackboards spanning the bar, and the etchings are reminiscent of your afternoons in detention. With sophisticated beer comes a somewhat sophisticated crowd, and the music therefore steers clear of Top 40 as much as possible. Happy hour is from 1pm until 7:30pm (seven days a week), at which time drinks are a dollar off the normal $5-$6 range. Pick from 18 draughts and a gazillion bottles. Gold-diggers are welcome, as you're likely to see more bald spots than trucker hats in the bar's popular outdoor garden. And bring your appetite, because Sunday is brunch (free bagels) and Monday is dinner (cheese). The

drinking end of the bar is much friendlier than the business end, where the bartenders are somehow cliquey.

Deacon Brodie's
370 W. 46th St. (8th & 9th Aves.)
Hell's Kitchen 212.262.1452

Deacon Brodie's feels like a Killarney pub cross-bred with a small Boise conference center. The lighting flatters the pizza slice you can lug in from the shop on the corner, but try not to drip tomato sauce on the russet cushions. Should you decide to get sloppy, classy but cheery bartenders will mix your drinks and stay out of your business. Yes, drinks come quickly, the game is on the telly, and the Internet jukebox generally plays neighborhood-requisite rock and reggae, yet somehow it doesn't get boring here. There are only six beers on tap, but throw in the 20 by the bottle and it all works out. The location, at the top of an old brownstone's stoop, makes this joint a destination rather than a pub-crawl stumbling stop.

The Dead Poet
450 Amsterdam Ave. (81st & 82nd Sts.)
Upper West Side 212.595.5670

No one knows alcoholic excess quite like writers, and the clever folks at the Dead Poet create an environment where the literati and the lay-drinker can come together and imbibe as one. Lines of verse decorate the walls, and several specialty drinks named for renowned authors abound, like the $8 Walt Whitman (their version of the Long Island Iced Tea). You may even feel inspired to compose an ode of your own after sampling the signature "Dead Poet" cocktail, which is also $8. (It's comprised of seven different liquors.) If writing rhyming couplets isn't your thing, there's a pool table and well-stocked jukebox to inspire greatness. Whether you leave touched by the muse, or just the Frost-y drinks, you'll have a wild time.

Danube

The Dead Poet

Dekk

The Delancey

Decibel
240 E. 9th St. (2nd & 3rd Aves.)
East Village 212.979.2733

An underground secret society of sake, Decibel is authentic Japan—right down to the Tokyo-esque cramped quarters. Stroll down the narrow steps leading from the sidewalk into this dim sake bar, where you'll be policed across the line separating the tiny bar from the dining room. Rustic and cozy, with lots of exposed wood and bamboo, this stage of the house tells you you're in good hands. Devour colorful appetizers for a mere $3-$8; desserts top out at $4. And then there's the sake: $6-$32 gets you a small carafe, and for $16-$145 you can purchase a whole bottle. Pretend you're about to smash it over some Yakusa's head in a breakout karate fight...such is the inspirational atmosphere of this magical little nook.

Deep
16 W. 22nd St. (5th & 6th Aves.)
Flatiron 212.229.2000

The ego-crushing velvet rope is king at this exclusive-feeling club, where UES-type dancing queens donning fake tans and blinding white smiles steal jealous looks at the go-go dancers while ogling Bridge & Tunnelers in Brooks Brothers button-downs ordering bottle service. In a previous life, this bi-level club was known as Ohm; designed by the gang responsible for Lotus and the former Dorsia, Deep has that same muted, polished look but with more of what could be a hipster's idea of an opera house, with the curving balcony and one-way VIP mirror. The first floor proudly boasts a "dancing only" vibe, thanks to a massive wall of speakers and DJs that spin high-octane house music. Upstairs, singles scour for sexy company in between orders of Sex on the Beaches and Long Island Iced Teas.

Dekk
134 Reade St. (Hudson & Greenwich Sts.)
TriBeCa 212.941.9401

Are you a Godard mind in a Schwarzenegger world? Then hit the Dekk and let this chic nightlife multiplex's low lamps, Parisian metro benches, and *cinema fantastique* atmosphere leave you *Breathless*. A new TriBeCa wine bar opened by German filmmakers, Dekk offers a cinema space that screens blockbusters and indie films, as well as a basement lounge and a kitchen of contemporary Italian and Mediterranean cuisine. And if that's not enough, this extensive wine list takes the Prix du Jury. Don't get any of these references? That's fine—*Rocky VI* should be coming out soon. Still following the plot? Great, but get here fast because the bar only stays open until midnight Sun-Tues, 2:30am Wed-Sat. *Fin.*

Del Frisco's Double Eagle Steakhouse
1221 6th Ave. (@ 49th St.)
Midtown 212.575.5129

Smack-dab in the middle of Midtown lies one of the city's most talked-about meateries. Del Frisco's, part of a chain with several Southwestern outposts, has made the leap to the Big City and landed in the good graces of even the most discerning carnivores. Elegant, covered in wood and leather, Del Frisco's emits that top-of-the-food-chain air that one expects of such places, and the just-fewer-than-500 customers who pack this place leave bigger than they entered. The Double Eagle Strip steak prices just pennies under $50. A large bar up front plays host to white-collared stockbrokers toasting another victory in the market. Since steakhouse waiters are a very specific breed, service is always the last thing to catch on in places like this one. Given time, Double Eagle could join the ranks of the steakhouse elite.

The Delancey
168 Delancey St. (Clinton & Attorney Sts.)
Lower East Side 212.254.9920

Whether it's *Sweet Action*'s Porn for the Girls issue release party or a 21st anniversary party for the *Toxic Avenger* thrown by Troma Films, this bar is a special event hotspot. The Delancey is a bar for all seasons with a fireplace on the main floor, a rooftop bar upstairs, and a performance space in the basement. Head downstairs to catch some rock and roll, carry that momentum to the main level's dance floor, then unwind on the roof sipping huge margaritas and gazing at the Williamsburg Bridge while puffing on a Marlboro. Keep your eye on the bridge, because this place is owned by the team behind Billyburg's Red and Black, which means that lots of Brooklyn hipsters make the trip here.

The Delta Grill
700 9th Ave. (@ 48th St.)
Hell's Kitchen 212.956.0934

This Southern outpost in the middle of Hell's Kitchen calls, hoots, and hollers out to those hankerin' for a New Orleans motif, some Cajun victuals, and a gen-u-ine hurricane to wash it all down. Too bad the full-service bar area is mostly empty floor space with the exception of a few tables. Groups looking to sit down may fare better elsewhere, but with lots of standing room and barstools, guests can sit at the counter and order up some jambalaya, fried okra with Creole sauce, and Turbo Dog beer from the attentive staff. The house also offers frozen pina coladas and strawberry daiquiris and mini, pink happy-hour margaritas. Occasional live bands play jazz, bluegrass, and Zydeco, further adding to the Big Easy vibe. Flash the crowd your breasts if you'd like, but it may seem a bit inappropriate.

Dempsey's Pub
61 2nd Ave. (3rd & 4th Sts.)
East Village 212.388.0662

What's friendly, 15 years of age but looks older, and won't get you arrested? Dempsey's Pub in the East Village. Owned by the same management team behind Irish pubs Slainte and Baggot Inn, Dempsey's has everything you're looking for in a local bar, including a genial staff, nightly specials, a pool table, and delivery menus for several nearby restaurants—a welcomed respite from wings and chicken fingers. Ken Jennings wannabes can join in a competitive round of trivia on Wednesday nights, and speaking of which, here's a Double

Jeopardy question: Getting sloshed on 2-for-1 drinks. Answer: What is Friday night happy hour?

Desmond's Tavern
433 Park Ave. S. (29th & 30th Sts.)
Murray Hill 212.684.9472

When's the last time you had Blue Balls? This mix of Malibu, Curacao, and pineapple is the specialty cocktail at Desmond's, a schizo bar if ever there was one. By day, Desmond's resembles a VFW with wood-paneled walls, an older male clientele, and bright lighting. By night live music acts, which have included Sean Lennon and Mott the Hopple, turn the place into a college party with 20- to 30-year-olds swilling beer, eating bar food, and bathing in the glow of neon lights. As the fourth-oldest Irish bar in Manhattan (the bar dates back to 1936 and the current owners have run it since 1968), Desmond's has a long, drunken history, which you can help prolong by enjoying one of 23 bottled beers for breakfast—the bar opens at 10am.

Detour
349 E. 13th St. (@ 1st Ave.)
East Village 212.533.6212

Without a cover charge most nights (it's $5 on Fridays and Saturdays) and any East Village pretensions, this dedicated jazz spot is bare-bones bebop. Aficionados near the stage personally laud their favorite soloists, while casual music fans in the back can chat it up without feeling impolite. Seating in front of the band is limited so if you roll in late, plan on standing or craning your neck from the tables along the side wall. If you simply can't get a sightline, kick back modestly priced drinks until you don't care. For good karma toss a couple of bills into the tip jar and support the arts at your own discretion. The $3 happy hour, which runs seven days a week (4pm-7pm), is perfect for weekend pre-gaming when other bars are still wiping down their tables from the night before.

Dewey's Flatiron
210 5th Ave. (25th & 26th Sts.)
Flatiron 212.696.2337

We hear that Admiral Dewey was a naval officer, and from the selection of beers offered here, it seems he was a drinking man, too. With 20 beers on tap and 10 bottles, you can drink your way across the Caribbean, with Jamaican Red Stripe and good ol' American Bud as your vessels. With a beer selection this big it's easy to see other countries as well, but as with most seaward expositions, there are going to be a lot of males on board. Dewey's also serves food, including pastas and salads, but most of these mates prefer wings and fingers to stave off scurvy. Upstairs, there's a small bar and pool table, but if you plan to drink up there, beware: The steps are high and narrow, and after a few $3.50 happy hour pints, those planks can be treacherous.

Dick's Bar
192 2nd Ave. (@ 12th St.)
East Village 212.475.2071

The East Village gay scene loves Dick's. At this neighborhoody favorite, the drinks are super-strong and super-cheap ($5 for a screwdriver, for instance), which makes it a terrific place to get wasted. Dick's has an '80s, divas, and semi-modern pop jukebox, a shark-free pool table, and even a shopping cart dangling from the ceiling… just in case. The clientele here won't be appearing in any sexy calendars anytime soon, but they're almost endearing in comparison to the rambunctious crowds at other gay pick-up scenes. Those looking for old-school East Village ease and cheap drinks in the semi-swanky hotspots that keep popping up at a breakneck pace in this neighborhood obviously don't know Dick's.

Diner
85 Broadway (@ Berry St.)
Williamsburg 718.486.3077

Things have changed since a mustached waitress named Flo served up grub in this old-school dining car. First and foremost, the staff is hot, in that scruffy, lightly tattooed Williamsburg way. The greasy-spoon fare has been replaced with the best creative comfort food in Brooklyn, and the cocktails rival any swanky Midtown lounge in potency, flavor, and innovation, for about half the price, and this all comes without tourists. The blackcurrant cosmo ($7.50) is a tart purple paradise, and the blood orange margaritas ($7.50) make reading the menu, or anything else, quite the challenge. (Teetotalers will love the freshly brewed coffee, and so will anyone who's had a few-too-many margaritas.) The one thing that's stayed basically the same since the olden days is this train car's charmingly tiled interior dimly lit by soft candlelight, which puts dates on the fast track to Bedroomville.

Diner 24
102 8th Ave. (@ 15th St.)
Chelsea 212.242.7773

It's 3am in Chelsea. You're starving. Hell, you could use a drink, too. Do you go to Cafeteria for the millionth time? Miraculously, a blinking light promises 24-hour eating and drinking salvation. When your usual late-night snack of Slim Jims and Cheetos isn't cutting it, head to this trendy 'round-the-clock spot for meatloaf and disco fries. Blending fine dining with cafeteria kitsch, Diner 24 features a hip crowd that still looks hot in the wee hours of the morning, and you can keep your intoxication going with top-notch tequilas and cocktails like the Money Martini. The relaxed, airy space is just as nice in the daytime, too, when the menu changes and mango mimosas share tables with grilled cheese sandwiches.

The Ding Dong Lounge
929 Columbus Ave. (105th & 106th Sts.)
Upper West Side 212.663.2600

Because of 85-plus-decibel punk bars like this, rock 'n' roll will never die (no matter how many times the Pope declares it an "instrument of the devil"). Owner Bill Noland left his Motor City digs to open the Ding Dong Lounge; part rock bar, part neighborhood beer joint, the DDL is liable to win any bar contest hands-down with the multitude of underground bands that grace its stage (think Boston's legendary Lyres, California's Lazy Cowgirls, and newbies Mr. Airplane Man). DDL hosts anybody-spins DJ nights, when you can bring your favorite records and have your own 15 minutes of fame. And fans of the brew, don't miss Tipsy Tuesdays, when happy hour starts at 4pm and lasts until close at 4am (or until you fall off your barstool).

Dip
416 3rd Ave. (29th & 30th Sts.)
Murray Hill 212.481.1712

Walk through the door and let the melting begin. The dimly lit, chill atmosphere lures in trendsters in their late 20s for a relaxing post-work, pre-weekend celebration. Come with a small group of friends or with that special someone and share some Brownie Fondue S'mores (Dip, get it?) and drinks. Mirrors, potted orchids and bamboo plants, a curvy bar, soft hip-hop and R&B, and smooth upstairs billiards add to the euphoric atmosphere. Increase your sugar high with a White Velvet Martini of Godiva white liqueur, Bailey's, and Chambord. Stick a fork—er, skewer—in us…we're done.

Discotheque
17 W. 19th St. (5th & 6th Aves.)
Flatiron 212.352.9999

For one of New York's last remaining genuine after-hours spots, dodge those early-morning joggers and get yourself to Discotheque. Graciously opening its doors Sunday mornings at 5:30am, the house offers Red Bull, Latin/Asian fusion dishes, and a safe crash pad until the sun hits one o'clock high. The DJs guarantee a sweaty crowd, too. As for the décor, though, it's minimal—two large bars stand ready to serve you, and the atmosphere is dark and understated. So if you've been wondering where all the exotic dancers go after work (every Sunday morning during "Stripper Mania," all dancers from NY/NJ/CT get in free), or you're just looking to get your groove on at a place where

you won't want to sit out a song, get to Discotheque.

'disiac Lounge
402 W. 54th St. (9th & 10th Aves.)
Hell's Kitchen 212.586.9880

This Hell's Kitchen hotspot derives its name from love spells induced by an aphrodisiac, but there's nothing particularly amorous about the place, except maybe for the fact that the quarters are so close you might as well be bumpin' and grindin' at a club. You may have to fake a headache and leave work early to grab a table during happy hour, because by 6pm it's standing-room-only at this chick-magnet bar. Their notable sangria or lychee or chocolate martinis may be just the mojo you need to strike up a conversation with that Aphrodite in the corner. And if you do luck out on a table, especially one of the coveted patio ones, invite her to share your cheese platter or hummus plate. Spread the love.

The Distinguished Wakamba
543 8th Ave. (37th & 38th Sts.)
Hell's Kitchen 212.239.1343

This 20-year-old dive bar should come with a warning: "Disappointment Lies Within." Thanks to the hanging fishnets and ornaments, this place looks like a party waiting to happen. Instead, the Dominican-themed bar's most exotic drink is Presidenté beer. You'd think that with its exotic relations, this place might feature something more fun, like a tamarind cocktail. While the bartenders are polite and happy to switch beers upon request, they can't do anything about the '80s décor or the loud salsa music blaring from the jukebox. The regulars seem to like it; just watch out for the drunken guy dancing around uncontrollably.

Diva
341 W. Broadway (Broome & Grand Sts.)
SoHo 212.941.9024

Some divas are known for their graceful and timely exits from the stage; others stick around much longer than they should. Diva falls into the latter category. The blood-red and yellow walls, rainbow of fruity $9 cocktails, and purple cushions at this teeny Italian restaurant/club/bar create the air of a low-rent brothel. There's no cover charge, but you'll pay the price of seeing sweaty Europeans gyrate to loud thumps of soulless techno. You can retreat to one of a handful of plush banquettes or small wooden tables, but avoid the unappetizing portion of limp menu items that hits a decidedly flat note. On the whole, Diva is one of downtown's least appealing options; this diva should be given the hook.

The Dive Bar
732 Amsterdam Ave. (95th & 96th Sts.)
Upper West Side 212.749.4358

The hardened regular at the bar complains about the frattiness, the frat boys think the local drunk is enjoying their exhibitionism. There are currently three of these charming simulacra of Dive Bars in New York, and while the result is decidedly middlebrow, it works in a harmless though slightly labored sense. The Jacques Cousteau bit comes off as a cute excuse to use the word "dive," but the too-cool-to-work barmaids do little more than complement the décor. When it finally comes, the food's pretty good, and it adds to a decent beer selection, two boards of single-malt Scotch, and the occasional drink special. Still, neither here nor there, Dive Bar comes off as the urban equivalent of Hooters, but scaled-down far enough to work on most nights.

Dive 75
101 W. 75th St. (Columbus & Amsterdam Aves.)
Upper West Side 212.362.7518

Upon seeing the large fish tank, you get the sense that this bar is not the kind of "dive" where your shoes stick to the floor, but rather, one filled with seamen on shore leave. Dive 75 offers board games where wagering is not permitted and Wi-Fi access, which allows visitors to get really drunk

and fire off a tell-it-like-it-is e-mail to the boss. The conscientious staff requests that visitors respect the neighbors and take cell phone conversations and cigarettes to the corner. What kind of dive is this? Bowls of candy on the bar add to the offbeat charm, and parched patrons will find an extensive beer selection and sake served chilled with a cucumber slice in this wonky but well-meaning Upper West Side watering hole.

Divine Bar East
244 E. 51st St. (2nd & 3rd Aves.)
Midtown 212.319.9463

Buried amidst the bright lights of Broadway's theaters and the dim bulbs of the tourist traps that dominate Midtown is this Mediterranean tapas bar, a spot that comes close to earning its name. A huge selection of exotic wines and beers attracts oenophiles and gutter drunks alike for after-work or before-show drinks. Take a "flight" of wine and try some of the different vintages, and once you've got a buzz going the international cheese platter will lift you up with a wide array of exotic treats. Sadly you'll have to hit Divine Bar West if you want unusual cocktails like the "Stinkin' Dirty Whore-Tini," garnished with a blue cheese-stuffed red pepper and a rim of celery salt. But remember—you are what you drink!

Divine Bar West
236 W. 54th St. (Broadway & 8th Ave.)
Midtown 212.265.9463

The '80s music that fills Divine Bar West's semi-sceney restaurant is older than many of these well-manicured clients. Not quite as lively as its East Side cousin, the Divine Bar West's cuisine is top-notch, especially when served in the upper-level seating area, which in warm weather features a balcony. Don't get too excited, smokers—entrance to this balcony requires table service. The endless menu of international "tapas" (read: well-traveled appetizers) provides very good reason for investing in table space. Reservations aren't accommodated, but dates are: The small tables offer the perfect setting for intimate conversations over a glass of one of their many fine wines and a plate of sweet baked brie. After work, before a Broadway show, or simply "just because" are all good reasons to take part in the divinity.

D.J. Reynolds
351 W. 57th St. (8th & 9th Aves.)
Hell's Kitchen 212.245.2912

This small, neighborhood bar is not a hotspot by any estimation, but a steady flow of local regulars keep the atmosphere lively. As a refreshing change of pace to trendier bars, D.J.'s (as regulars call it) is a place where you can have a conversation without having to yell over a loud Britney-pumping jukebox or a pack of co-eds looking for a hook-up. The small restaurant in the back offers fine bar food and ample room for post-theater get-togethers and mingling with larger groups of friends. Like its neighbors, D.J.'s is most often frequented by the older, after-work crowds, but on weekend nights it can become packed with students from the nearby Fordham University celebrating the opening of a new play, the end of class, or a Rams victory. (Yes, Fordham has sports.)

Django
480 Lexington Ave. (@ 46th St.)
Midtown 212.871.6600

When nothing will satisfy your appetite for summering Europeans and old-money snobbery, Django is waiting for you after work or even during lunch—there's nothing like a champagne cocktail at noon. Warm up with a Djangito (what, you've never heard of Zuzu juice before?), buy that perfectly tanned blonde at the other end of the bar a Flirtini, and gamble on that city sun. Inspired by the jazz guitarist Django Rheinhart, this upscale restaurant/lounge sweeps you away to the Riviera faster than you can say, "Mais non!" Dine on succulent dishes like monkfish, skate, duck, or lamb in the immense outdoor seating area or stay inside and sink into the plush seats while you sample the five-course ($75) tasting menu.

Do Hwa
55 Carmine St. (@ Bedford St.)
West Village 212.414.1224

If you're tired of questionable takeout, but can't afford Nobu, have no fear—Do Hwa is here. Get cozy with your date at this Korean restaurant/lounge with "BBQ for Two," where you can cook your meals at your very own grilling table. And if DIY barbecuing brings to mind first-degree burns and Ace bandages, let Do Hwa's capable chefs take care of the cooking for you. There are plenty of options if your date has been vegan since she saw *Bambi*, too. Order her a glass of ginger cinnamon champagne and sample the codfish and fried oysters while she tears into a kimchi and tofu stir-fry. Hunker down at Do Hwa for a classy evening of exotic dining. The helpful staff will take you baby-step style through all the basics of Korean cuisine.

Doc Holliday's
141 Ave. A (@ 9th St.)
East Village 212.979.0312

Ted Nugent wannabes and thirsty college kids find common ground at this East Village haunt. It's a dive, but in the best possible sense: The jukebox blares country tunes, the patrons and bartenders are having a great time, and the booze is cheap—at least during the weekday happy hours with their 2-for-1 drinks and $2 Pabst Blue Ribbons. The honkytonk vibe extends to the Big Buck Hunter II videogame and the cowboy boots that dangle precariously overhead. Those who have enough coordination after downing a few beers can try their hand at a round of pool; those who don't will be in good company.

Doc Watson's
1490 2nd Ave. (77th & 78th Sts.)
Upper East Side 212.988.5300

You've got to love a bar that has all the right moves. Doc hosts a happy hour from 11am-7pm Monday through Friday, invites musicians with fiddles and accordions for an Irish music jam session on Sundays and Wednesdays, airs major sporting events on several TVs, and gives two free cocktails with the $10.95 weekend brunch. In fact, Doc has

Don Hill's

the remedy for just about every ailment—be it hunger (lunch and dinner is served daily with well-priced entrées like the Irish Mixed Grill—Irish sausage, bacon, lamb chop, egg, grilled tomato, and fries), a broken heart (friendly bartenders, a well-stocked jukebox), voyeurism (the sidewalk tables offer ample views of passersby), claustrophobia (there's a lovely backyard patio), and "Bad night last night?" BO (large windows on both ends offer a cross breeze).

D.O.C. Wine Bar
83 N. 7th St. (@ Wythe Ave.)
Williamsburg 718.963.1925

It's safe to believe rumors that Marisa Tomei has been spotted at this smallish, rustic Sardinian wine bar. In fact, D.O.C. Wine Bar has steadily drawn a posh and, at times, celebrity crowd, who appreciate the vast selection of fermented grapes and authentic Italian cuisine. In the summertime, the sidewalk café is a great place to chill with a cool glass of Riesling or a crisp Pinot Grigio (and with bottles ranging from $20-$35, you won't walk away empty-handed). But never fear—if your knowledge of wine is limited to the pink box or the white box, D.O.C.'s staff can help. They know their stuff at this non-intimidating hangout. Savor the flavor of the cheese, bread, and antipasti plates at D.O.C.'s, where it feels good (but doesn't cost much) to feel fancy.

Docks Oyster Bar
633 3rd Ave. (@ 40th St.)
Midtown 212.986.8080

2427 Broadway (89th & 90th Sts.)
Upper West Side 212.724.5588

Break out the corporate credit card because Docks is perfect expense account fodder; it's upscale and enjoyable enough to make you feel good about sticking the bill to The Man, but not so extravagant that the boss will have your head. A classic American seafood restaurant, Docks is home to fresh surf and solid turf. If you're not in the mood for snapper, there's a busy bar where you can set down your anchor for an after-work tipple. This place can get flooded with young professionals, and the Midtown location's proximity to Grand Central lends itself to commuters, so there's not much of a neighborhood feel. But if you can stand feeling landlocked shoulder-to-shoulder when the 5pm whistle blows, navigate your way to Docks, which also hosts a New England clambake on Sundays and Mondays.

Don Hill's
511 Greenwich St. (@ Spring St.)
SoHo 212.219.2850

If you're into leather, eyeliner, and hairspray, you'll

relish this playground for New York's rock 'n' roll players. If not, you might feel a little out of place. It's often hard to tell the difference between the patrons and the staff at this divey rock bar. The main draw, of course, is the music; nearly every night there's either a DJ or bands or both. Wednesday's "Rock Candy" night showcases some of New York's best hard rock and metal bands, but the main attraction is Saturday's infamous Tiswas party (keep your eyes on the stripper poles). Here you'll find eclectic DJs and bands playing everything from Brit pop to garage to post-punk. It's a crazy scene, and lots of fun (particularly if you're brave enough to enter the seedy bathrooms).

Donald Sacks
220 Vesey St. (@ West St.)
TriBeCa 212.619.4600

Located in the (way) out-of-the-way World Financial Center, which is basically a glorified mall with post-9/11 security guards posted everywhere, Donald Sacks isn't exactly a relaxed neighborhood spot. It's located on the first floor, which is reminiscent of an upscale food court, with about as much character. There are several "outdoor" tables, which means they're away from the bar proper, and sort of under a tent-like structure that's clearly all indoors. At the late hour of 9pm, only a few suits generally remain "inside," much like an airport bar but without the promise that you'll soon be far away. For a sanitized, insulated night out you can't do much better (or worse) than this place.

The Door Lounge
508 9th Ave. (38th & 39th Sts.)
Hell's Kitchen 212.594.6095

Hell's Kitchen is becoming a *trés* happening part of town. The Door Lounge is a perfect representation of its neighborhood—a bit unsure of its identity, but aching to find its inner cool. On one of the lonelier stretches of Ninth Avenue, the Door Lounge is marked by a pretty tiled doorway, which is sometimes obscured by a bulky bouncer. Inside is a Marrekeshian paradise complete with cushy

pillows, Moroccan lamps, and hookahs. Homemade hummus and such is available, as is a full bar, a serviceable wine and beer list, and flavored tobaccos. Inexplicably, they also specialize in Brazilian caipirinhas. Depending on when you walk through the Door, you'll catch live jazz, hip-hop, or Latin DJs—and the crowds range accordingly. Be sure to give a call before you go so your night doesn't souk.

Dorian's
226 W. 79th St. (Broadway & Amsterdam Ave.)
Upper West Side 212.595.4350

Whether you're a homesick Southerner or just sick of standard Yankee fare, Dorian's is the place to be for a heapin' helpin' of comfort food. The restaurant/bar, formerly Miss Elle's, doesn't stray far from its roots, and that's a good thing. Though moonshine would have been more appropriate, the bar serves mouthwatering Manhattans and masterful martinis, but the real draw is the menu, chock-full of down-home favorites like meatloaf, pork chops, and macaroni 'n' cheese. The exposed brick walls, mismatched barstools, and lace curtains add to the quaint charm, and there are three separate dining rooms. There's even (strangely) an in-house notary public, and the Bloody Marys at brunch are mighty tasty—can we get a witness?

Dorrian's Red Hand
1616 2nd Ave. (@ 84th St.)
Upper East Side 212.772.6660

We're hard-pressed to explain the popularity of this neighborhood sports bar—that there's a Dorrian's in Jersey City should tell you everything you need to know. Dorrian's is everything a Manhattan bar shouldn't be: trendy, gaudy, loud, and obnoxious. It is considerably sizable, but despite the fact that on the weekends this is one of the few joints on the Upper East Side that really packs 'em in, that still doesn't excuse arriving at 2am and being told you have to wait 15 minutes. This isn't Cain, fellas. Clearly Dorrian's isn't going to mess with its formula—yuppies, ball games, and bar food—but that doesn't mean you'll like it.

Dos Caminos

trunks that act as chandeliers, because after starting on this list of 150+ tequilas, the room will soon be swirling around you. A bit more Tex-Mex, or even Manhattan-Mex, than authentic, the Mexican munchies are top-notch, as are the desserts. Those who are simply cocktailing will want to try the passion fruit margarita or the blueberry pomegranate margarita—though we've got nothing against the five chili-infused vodka margaritas. Though not the super-hotspot is was a couple of years ago, trendsters and celebs still make Dos Caminos a regular stop, so if you want to get a table, dress to impress. Why "Dos" Caminos? There's also a SoHo version of this Steve Hanson/BR Guest restaurant.

Dos Caminos
475 W. Broadway (@ Houston St.)
SoHo 212.277.4300

Situated in prime SoHo real estate along Houston Street, this cantina is a popular spot that attracts the hoards that invade the neighborhood to get their shop on. The nuevo-Mexicano cuisine is reliably tasty but offers no great surprises, though the fresh, made-to-order guacamole is top-notch. Count yourself lucky if you snag one of the tables on the outdoor patio or be prepared to spend an irreplaceable hour of your life waiting for one. Indoors, low, amber-colored lighting and Mexican-themed partitions create a sultry, south-of-the-border atmosphere. Tequila snobs will swoon at the super-sized list of 150-plus tequilas, while the rest will enjoy slurping potent frozen prickly pear margaritas. Prices seem slightly higher than they should be ($14-$16 for a quesadilla?!), but after you've shopped at Prada, who cares?

Dos Caminos
373 Park Ave. S. (26th & 27th Sts.)
Murray Hill 212.294.1000

Don't bother looking around at this lively design of cacti, inlaid glass walls, and hollowed-out tree

Double Happiness
173 Mott St. (@ Broome St.)
Chinatown 212.941.1282

Before its recent incarnation as a hot basement nightspot, Double Happiness was a speakeasy and a Mafia-run gay bar (we're serious). The whackings (heh, heh) have ended and you can now come to Double Happiness to shake it with a hip young crowd. Serving yummy green tea martinis, the bartenders make revelers an offer they can't refuse. Though stylish, this twice-the-fun hangout isn't overly "sceney"—this ain't Marquee. And though you're no longer in danger of waking up with a horse's head on your pillow the next morning, you may find one of these good-looking strangers sleeping next to you.

Double Seven
418 W. 14th St. (9th Ave. & Washington St.)
Meatpacking District 212.981.9099

Someday, someone's going to open a lounge so exclusive that no one will be allowed to enter. In fact, it won't even have a door. Double Seven is practically there. From the people who brought us the loathsome Lotus, this long and semi-narrow lounge seems to be reserved, basically, for those who are too A-list for the area's other A-list clubs. The bar up front has $9 bottled beer and it leads to an earth-toned, Japanese-ish backroom where bottle service is literally provided by waitresses who drop to their knees when pouring vodka into glasses containing one huge ice cube, which stops drinks from watering down. But sorry, you're not on the list.

The Dove
228 Thompson St. (Bleecker & 3rd Sts.)
Greenwich Village 212.254.1435

The Dove just might be the only bar within half a mile of NYU where anyone who doesn't have to use a fake ID can actually leave with their self-respect and eardrums intact. An unpretentiously hip, 25-45-year-old crowd squeezes in between the ornate, velvet red walls, dark brown bar, and white pillars that complete the faux-Victorian décor of this cool, classy joint. Jazz standards play in the late afternoon, and once the frat boys have passed en route to Assy McScratchy's, Billie and Ella give way to Bowie and Jagger. The specialty cocktails here are to die for (try the Cherry Tart or French Lavender), the wine list is surprisingly deep, and snack mix overflows from dainty tea cups. The Dove exudes downtown chic.

Down the Hatch
179 W. 4th St. (6th & 7th Aves.)
West Village 212.627.9747

Entering this subterranean belly of the beast is akin to stumbling into a frat boy's basement. Twinkling Christmas lights line the ceiling of this divey cellar and a foosball table has prominence. One can choose to watch sports on the multiple TVs, play videogames, or compete in a rousing round of beer pong while Top 40 blares from the speakers, adding to the chaotic atmosphere. Buxom bartenders and a chummy atmosphere appeal to an after-work or, more likely, after-class, crowd eager to relive their halcyon days. Wednesday specials include half-priced pints, $6 pitchers, and drink deals spun on the "wheel of alcohol" located behind the bar, while weekends boast all-you-can-eat wings with three pitchers for $19. Throw in the Atomic wings, and it all adds up to a non-stop carnival of consumption.

Dragonfly
47-49 7th Ave. S. (@ Morton St.)
West Village 212.255.2848

Maybe it's the DJ spinning thumping hip-hop, *Kill Bill* playing on the TV, or the Asian décor, but there's a feeling that this is a place where The RZA might kick back on weekends, when the mood is hi-yah meets boo-yah! The menu offers an affordable selection of Pan-Asian goodies, and the bar serves an array of creative cocktails. There are several variations on the passé cosmo, as well as dessert drinks and potent (if fruity) concoctions like the $9 Che Guava and the Jet Li. You can also taste the rainbow, and that's not a Skittles reference—there's a whole selection of rainbow-colored shots to order. A bartender who could be Ashton Kutcher's doppelganger hosts happy hour from 3pm-8pm daily, making this a fun place to get crunk.

Dream Lounge (@ the Dream Hotel)
210 W. 55th St. (Broadway & 7th Ave.)
Midtown 212.246.2211

This just might be the chicest new lounge you'll enter without having to pass a velvet rope test. Situated at the base of the Dream Hotel, Dream Lounge's walls and floors are wrapped in Technicolor carpeting that looks like a cross between a TV test pattern and a Paul Smith dress shirt. While the bartenders in this room can mix some mean cocktails, the $7 pints are a steal here. The music overhead is more pop and rock than one might expect from this conversation-friendly space that seems to be built for picking up among non-scenesters. A cool tube-shaped aquarium filled with trippy Chinese fish is in place in the hotel; take the bait and check this place out after-work or late at night.

Driftwood Inn
114 Nassau Ave. (@ Eckford St.)
Greenpoint 718.383.9427

Dream Lounge

Located in the predominately Polish neighborhood of Greenpoint, this dive bar par excellence is a local delight. Old Polish men and the hipsters that love them fight for space underneath neon Coors signs and near the grandfather clock and wooden phone booth, listening to cheesy American and Polish Top 40 and sipping cheap mixed drinks and dirt-cheap drafts (Coors cost only $1.50). While other bars in the area are more popular (the Turkey's Nest), interesting (Enid's), or rowdy (Tommy's Tavern), if you like your dives historical (read: old), simple (read: no-frills), and full of character, you'll be right at home here. The 70-year-old Driftwood Inn catches locals that are blowing in the wind as early at 8am, which gives these old-timers plenty of time to drink before retiring to bed at 4pm.

Druids

736 10th Ave. (@ 50th St.)
Hell's Kitchen 212.307.6410

Across the street from a windowless, so-called "adult establishment" that resembles an interstate weigh station, Druids truly is a place for grown-ups. The menu's stiffer than vellum, but the pours

and lilting chatter from the bartenders comes fast and loose. Out back, one of Manhattan's mellowest gardens mixes covered and uncovered tables. Forget popcorn shrimp: Meals here deliver hand-picked ingredients, spices, and all that stuff. Your tab runs higher than it would at Scurvy McFaddenglen O'Learybragh up the block, but your buzz will follow a smoother course. Theater types, regular guys from the walkups on Tenth, and sophisticated smokers all share space without talking trash. We're told that these proprietors had nothing to do with Stonehenge, but who believes a druid?

DT/UT

1626 2nd Ave. (84th & 85th Sts.)
Upper East Side 212.327.1327

There comes that time, at the end of every work-day, when office slaves are forced to decide between pushing through the night with a strong cup of coffee or throwing in the towel and having a drink. Serving Amstel and mocha frappacino, DTUT keeps both options open. There's a blurry line between being an alcoholic and a workaholic, and this non-corporate-feeling coffee bar walks it, jittery and stumbling all the way, thanks to super-comfortable couches, bohemian drapery, and a mellow and earthy vibe. Sure, you'll find plenty of horn-rimmed glasses-wearing freelancers toiling away, but while they may think that this is their office, you'll know that it's your after-work bar.

Dublin 6
575 Hudson St. (Bank & 11th Sts.)
West Village 646.638.2900

Dublin 6 is as Irish as Shaquille O'Neal. Wait…we can do better than that; it's as Irish as a freckled leprechaun. Not only is the beer well-poured, but the authentic Irish dishes are a homecoming on a plate for homesick ex-pats. The décor is delightfully new and the atmosphere is classy yet relaxed. With custom-made mirrors and brew-specific beer glasses, Dublin 6 has gone to considerable expenses to offer the complete package. A DJ spins whatever you want to hear in the front, but if you want some peace and quiet (or some make-out time), head to the dark backroom and get comfortable. In the summer, the front windows open up, allowing sunbathers to lean on the windowsill and tan their beer-holding arm.

Due South
399 Greenwich St. (@ Beach St.)
TriBeCa 212.431.3318

A self-described "little universe" of (mostly male) regulars, Due South enjoys a quiet symbiosis with the financial worker bees of the area. Closed on nights and weekends, the house makes its daily bread by serving yours to you. And it's lunch that brings the folks back, with the $9 sirloin beef burgers and boneless chicken wings being the most popular selections. That might sound more like the menu at your favorite dive, but Due South's décor doesn't fit that description at all. In fact, this place looks like a page out of *House and Garden* magazine, and the help is as friendly and unassuming as Martha Stewart at her telegenic best. Likewise, these prices are more "Martha" than divey, but surely you have some insider trading tips to exploit.

Duff's
N. 3rd St. (@ Kent Ave.)
Williamsburg 718.302.0411

A hard rock bar in Williamsburg all but begs for hipsters in trucker caps shouting "Love Sabbath, man!" Inexplicably, however, Duff's clientele is the real deal. Haggard roadies and college-aged dirt-bags yell along to hair metal obscurities while watching Judas Priest videos and swigging PBR. The décor implies owner Jimmy Duff, of the late Bellevue Bar, maxed out his credit card at Spencer Gifts: cliché Bettie Page, *The Shining*, Iron Maiden, and John Belushi "College" posters line the walls and ceilings, and are punctuated by decapitated doll heads and street signs. (Most of the contents are from Bellevue, as are the bartenders and patrons.) The crown jewel is the coffin in the front window, inhabited by a Krueger-esque monster mannequin. The space is small, but there's a large outdoor smoking section where black lungs meet black metal.

Duff's

The Dugout
185 Christopher St. (Washington & Weehawken Sts.)
West Village 212.242.9113

It's the bottom of the night, you've struck out twice, and you're battling your way out of a major-league slump. Actually, you're more likely to see big gay bears than the Chicago Cubs at this bar, which is full of pitchers and catchers, most of whom are hoping to make it to third base before going home. Cruising for older, hairy, full-bellied men is the main sport at this Dugout. Of course, any pastime would be incomplete without food and alcohol. For $10 the Dugout serves up hot dogs and unlimited draft beer every Saturday starting at 8pm. Sunday's 4pm-midnight Beer Bust draws huge crowds and while these boys of summer can play it safe, the Dugout's also a sure place to be called "out!"

Duke's
129 Ave. C (8th & 9th Sts.)
East Village 212.982.5563

Dark, divey, and downtown. Duke's is exactly what you want from a bar—that is, if your low-maintenance needs consist of beer, babes, and rock anthems like "Back in Black." A quintessential East Village drinking hole, Duke's is the antithesis of the overcrowded Alphabet City lounge scene. Drinkers here sit on ratty couches or linger on warmer evenings in the tiny backyard beer garden. Food isn't served here, but a pile of takeout menus is available and you might find someone to split a pizza with. There's no sign outside the front door, but being pretentious (or overtly polite) isn't in vogue here. So as the other spots on Avenue C are scrambling to one-up each other, Duke's remains a low-key spot to be real.

Duke's
99 E. 19th St. (Park Ave. S. & Irving Pl.)
Gramercy 212.260.2922

Longing for a replica of that tried-and-true college hangout you left behind? You know the one—greasy barstools and the BEST chicken wings ever? Duke's offers a cleaner version of your old University of Whatever stomping grounds, com-

plete with freshly graduated frat boys and mounds of onion rings. A great place for after-work congregations to either watch the game or play one, there's Trivial Pursuit cards on every table and it's unlikely any of these guys are going to run the board. Duke's offers a kickback atmosphere with a menu of savory BBQ served in generous portions. Former sorority sisters should beware the occasional predatory professor type who's read Lolita one too many times.

DuMont
432 Union Ave. (Metropolitan Ave. & Devoe St.)
Williamsburg 718.486.7717

With the basic but solid brunch and dinner menus and no-reservations policy, you can expect to wait for a table any time you drop by DuMont. Flying solo is daunting, as patrons generally travel in happy, glamorous packs, with a hot date, or when Mom visits from out of town. There are some seats at the bar in the front dining room, catering to solo stragglers in need of a gourmet mac-n-cheese fix. Boozebags can escape the elbow-to-elbow dining room in favor of the lovely small barroom behind it, replete with antique etched mirrors, a dark mahogany bar, a brass chandelier, and tin ceilings. Check the chalkboard for daily special cocktails ranging from the predictable pomegranate martini to the provocative Between-the-Sheets. Don't miss the charming garden.

The Duplex
61 Christopher St. (@ 7th Ave. S.)
West Village 212.255.5438

So you're the best singer in your shower? Kudos to you. Now it's time to take that act on the road. The Duplex is one of the city's best piano bars and it's also one of its friendliest, complete with singing waiters and bartenders. Downstairs, a skilled pianist and a zany host join forces to make everyone croon like a fool. They generally succeed. Upstairs is the darker and more intimate cabaret room, where major Broadway stars drop by from time to time. And if that still doesn't have you belt-

Duvet

ing out Cher tunes then take a seat in the outdoor area, where you can not only smoke but also try turning back time and serenading hotties at one of the city's cruisiest street intersections.

Dusk
147 W. 24th St. (6th & 7th Aves.)
Chelsea 212.924.4490

A bar/lounge bar hybrid that works well, this place mixes more than just watering hole genres. Gay and straight patrons co-exist peacefully, even shooting pool together in these dark and themey confines, which go from a little kitschy to pretty comfortable just in time for rookie visitors to order that second specialty cocktail. The jukebox provides a pop and classic indie selection so neither Scissor Sisters nor Elvis Costello should come as a surprise. The crowd, a mix of semi-hipsters and semi-corporates, is more likely to don sneakers than wingtips. Despite clubby sofas, a fancy mosaic, and loungey sofas, say goodnight to Dusk if you're looking for bottle service and promoters...though they do offer "Napkin Idol," a doodling contest.

Duvet
45 W. 21st St. (5th & 6th Aves.)
Flatiron 212.989.2121

Going to bed on the first date isn't such a shameful thing anymore—unless you spill your wine all over the sheets. Duvet isn't the first lounge/restaurant to feature beds—and it won't be the last—but there is a certain charm to watching lounging couples awkwardly try to sip $12 Pillow Talk cocktails and munch on Three Way Lamb without falling over onto large mattresses swathed in white curtains and muted gold pillows. (Sheets and pillow cases are changed after each seating.) If you'd like to take things slow, sit at the banquettes in the back or at the multicolored-lit bar, where jellyfish watch you decide between the crispy eel and the oysters. Three-bottle minimums for the beds can put a damper on your one-night stand, but if you're game you'll be in for sweet dreams.

Dylan Prime
62 Laight St. (Greenwich & Hudson Sts.)
TriBeCa 212.334.4783

An upscale fortress tucked away on unassuming Laight Street, this hip spot splits off from the front door into an enormous candlelit dining room and a darker lounge. The crowd is a bit schizophrenic, too, with locals coming in for lunch and a decidedly different crowd streaming in over the bridges at night. Popular with everyone is the listing of $10 specialty drinks; try the Makers Mark Manhattan with bitters and the namesake whiskey, or a pear martini. The appetizer list is a vast array of goodies—prices range from $9-$19 and include everything from seafood to foie gras. Entrées are more strictly steak and pork dishes. The filet mignon goes for $39, and even a rack of pork ribs goes for $28, but eating quality meat in a non-boys' club setting is priceless.

The Eagle
554 W. 28th St. (10th & 11th Aves.)
Chelsea 646.473.1866

The Eagle

The Eagle in Chelsea isn't your ordinary bird. In fact, this West Side Highway establishment is more bear-friendly than your average aviary. The patrons that come here enjoy pawing each other while they guzzle their beers. And for the hungry bear, this two-story club/bar serves up supersized burgers on Sundays in the summer. But for those that prefer to nuzzle up to cows, there's Thursday's "Code" night, when the bar insists that you wear leather. Indeed, The Eagle becomes Leather Central when it hosts the annual "Mr. Eagle" competition. Yet perhaps the best part of all of this is the outdoor roof deck that opens in warm weather.

Eamonn's
174 Montague St. (Court & Clinton Sts.)
Brooklyn Heights 718.596.4969

This Brooklyn Heights establishment has the feel of just that: An establishment. The décor is spacious and mirrored, even including a beautiful chandelier. And who goes to a bar for the chandelier? Apparently this older, semi-moneyed crowd does. Drinks are expensive; even a seltzer sets you back four dollars. Offering serviceable and derivative Italian cuisine with some contemporary American flair, the menu relies heavily on mozzarella and tomato sauce. The booths are spacious and made from traditional red leather; the jukebox is almost entirely classic rock. Compared to the other options in this part of the Heights, Eamonn's glitters with urban style and sophistication, but this may be a reflection on the sparse cultural life of Montague Street as much as it is a credit to the bar.

Ear Inn
326 Spring St. (Greenwich & Washington Sts.)
SoHo 212.226.9060

So close to SoHo yet so far, this pub remains refreshingly removed from the boutiques and bustle and was, in fact, established long, long before SoHo was even a twinkle in the eye of real estate developers. Occupying the ground floor of an 1817 brick-and-wooden three-story house, Ear Inn's storied past is palpable from the moment you open its ancient front door: Low Federal-style ceilings, uneven floors, nautical memorabilia that evokes its seafaring past, and a lovingly worn wooden bar invite you to pull up a seat and have a cold one, or two, or three. Mere paces from the Hudson, this has long been the neighborhood watering hole for everyone from sailors to scribes, and continues to host readings by established and emerging writers on Saturday afternoons, a beloved tradition that dates back to the 1970s.

Earl's
560 3rd Ave. (@ 37th St.)
Murray Hill 212.949.5400

Duke's uptown cousin, Earl, moved into Murray

Hill last year and proved that you can take the trailer out of the park...but it's still a trailer. Sit outside and watch the world go by as you wait and wait and wait for someone to take your order. The staff is young and what they lack in knowledge ("vodka soda" is not vodka with Coke), they make up for in enthusiasm. It's a shame the place is often server-challenged because Earl's is adorable, with crazy kitsch on the walls, a comfort food menu of solid eats, good tunes, and great sidewalk seating. For a quick PBR at the bar when you're in no rush, stop on by.

Earl's

Earth NYC
116 10th Ave. (17th & 18th Sts.)
Chelsea 212.337.0016

Safely off the Meatpacking District's unworldly parameters, Earth NYC combines a little of the erotic with a touch of the exotic and *voila!*—it's a sexy Kama Sutra-flavored club/lounge that's truly da Bombay. Located right between the Park and Red Rock West, this soon-to-be "big deal" won't be stealing any business from the local honky tonk, but it would love to see more scenesters. Earth's doors open at 9pm, at which time tapas are served to the late-night crowd that's getting a jump on the evening. Rows of low-sitting red sofas fill this posh space's two floors, which share a giant wall lined with 132 candles that contain teeny fiber-optic bulbs. (Everyone asks how the staff lights them.) An elevated DJ booth spins international house to a crowd that sometimes dances, and sometimes chills, and while bottle service is recommended, it's not required.

East of Eighth
254 W. 23rd St. (7th & 8th Aves.)
Chelsea 212.352.0075

The quiet babble of the fountain in the garden out back is the only counterpoint to what the bartender describes as "at times, a pretty wild scene." East of Eighth is a multilevel bar/restaurant serving a diverse, gay-friendly clientele with some of the biggest bargains in the city. Above the dark but cheerful barroom is a giant, almost stately dining room, and some of the city's greenest outdoor seating awaits right out the back door. The menu includes some high-end seafood dishes and plenty of vegetarian offerings, and it's stunningly cheap. Try the leg of lamb with goat cheese and mashed potatoes, or the chicken and shrimp over beans and rice for $15-$16. Summer drinks, including mint lemonade and sangria, make for a nice wrap-up.

East River
97 S. 6th St. (Berry St. & Bedford Ave.)
Williamsburg 718.302.0511

Though rather dead on weeknights, Friday and Saturday nights bring stragglers from neighboring (and often overcrowded) Diner and Bembe to East River. True to its 'hood, this Williamsburg bar boasts a jukebox with an esoteric mix of tunes, while the elevated backroom has a pool table to liven up quiet nights. Early birds, take note: Come in for happy hour (5pm-8pm), and you'll get to enjoy your discounted drinks for the rest of the night—it's like staying still in time when in fact you're wasting your life away thanks to cheap booze. The staff aims to please, drinks are served up promptly, and a backyard BBQ pit guarantees some summer lovin'.

East Side Company Bar
49 Essex St. (@ Grand St.)
Lower East Side 212.614.7408

The windowless exterior of this swank speakeasy

is marked only by a tiny brass name plate. Once you gather the courage to open the door, you'll enter a narrow room lit by candlelight and framed by a round tin ceiling. Sit at one of the intimate benches by the bar (snugly sized for two), or join the laidback downtown types in the backrooms. Owner Sasha Petraske has stirred up another successful concoction with this drinkery; beer and wine are available, but go for a blended specialty fresh fruit cocktail, like a Strawberry Capiroska (fresh strawberries, lime, vodka, and sugar) or a Gold Rush made with lemons and bourbon. An odd mix of '70s rock and instrumental funk might be playing, but you'll be too anesthetized by the drinks to notice.

East Side Steak & Ale
1134 1st Ave. (62nd & 63rd Sts.)
Upper East Side 212.223.5800

A lot of people like steakhouses. Most people don't like steakhouse prices. Everybody likes East Side Steak and Ale. (Hey, shut up, you skinny vegans!) The dark wood bar area provides a masculine-looking but female-friendly setting for watching the Yankees devour opponents. The main dining room is a little more elegant, even providing un-steakhouse-like brunch offerings including an $8.95 eggstravaganza, or for the same price a vegetarian-friendly "perfect pancakes" plate. (Are you happy now, non-carnivores?) With white tablecloths, hardwood floors, and big bay windows, the upstairs dining area is perfect for a power dinner that might make potential partners think you're a bigger player than you really are. (A 12-oz. NY Strip is $18.95.) Go ahead and get the check, hotshot. Let the other guys pay when you hit the Palm for your next big deal.

Eatery/Bar E
798 9th Ave. (52nd & 53rd Sts.)
Hell's Kitchen 212.765.7080

Though primarily known for its expansive brunch menu and outdoor seating, the Eatery's bar—Bar E—should not be overlooked. Young, hip bartenders are on hand to offer 40+ wines, specialty cocktails with watermelon flavoring, and home-

made sangria from giant jars resting on the bar counter—hmmm, maybe they should call this place "Drinkery." When the kitchen is open, bar patrons can order anything on the menu of New American food with a twist. (NY strip steak comes with Szechuan steak sauce, $20.95.) The venue, with its minimalist, mostly white décor, is a touch pretentious, but it's a less divey Hell's Kitchen option for a date, a pre- or post-theater drink, or a chance to scope out the attractive waiters, all while avoiding the barrage of tourists east of Eighth Avenue.

Edessa
430 5th Ave. (8th & 9th Sts.)
Park Slope 718.369.1140

Park Slope's Fifth Avenue is undergoing a new kind of gentrification. Once known as a beacon for the dive bar aficionados of the 'hood and beyond, a string of newish bars and lounges are popping up along the avenue that aim for class rather than cheap beer. Edessa, which opened in April '04 and still packs itself with bar-goers, is striving for what they call a "village feel." Plasma-screen TVs, a jukebox, and a 4pm-8pm daily happy hour fill the space between exposed brick walls and a bar that's stocked from top to bottom shelf. Edessa's a good pick for those wishing Fifth Avenue were actually Avenue A, but for those who want to pretend they're right here, but a few years ago, there are still a few dive bars just around the corner.

The Edge
95 E. 3rd St. (1st & 2nd Aves.)
East Village 212.477.2940

Like your favorite pair of broken-in jeans, it's easy to slip into this well-scrubbed dive that's been around since many of us were drinking Hi-C and playing Yahtzee in our friends' basements. Now that you're older, think of the Edge as your personal rec room. With three dartboards, a pool table, and a respectable selection of board games, you need only upgrade from juice to hops to feel the stress of "adult" life melting away. Rock music plays quietly enough that it doesn't obscure the clack of breaking pool balls or the squeaking of sneakers on the abused wood floor. Sunday is trivia night, but the Edge draws a curious mix of NYU students, refreshingly un-hip locals, East Village old-timers, and Hells Angels from the headquarters right next door.

Edward's
136 W. Broadway (Duane & Thomas Sts.)
TriBeCa 212.233.6436

This is not the kind of greasy only-eat-it-while-drunk menu we generally associate with late dinners in the city that invented late-night. Was Edward's the dining car in a former passenger train? That's how it appears, but *au contraire*. Not that this isn't a cool place; Edward's is that kind of "eatery" Americans build in Europe or Europeans build in America: cute and classy but casual. The food is American with an Italian influence and they serve breakfast, brunch, lunch, and dinner all the way until midnight. Prices are reasonable, with the most expensive entrée being $18; there are worthwhile beers on tap, and whether dining inside or outdoors, the service here is pretty decent.

Eight Mile Creek
240 Mulberry St. (Spring & Prince Sts.)
NoLita 212.431.4635

The shrimp's on the barbie and the Coopers is flowing at Eight Mile Creek's Sunday BBQ in the NoLita outback. In the front bar, chatty bartenders trade friendly barbs with the beer-fueled crowd of Aussies and those who love them, while rugby and soccer matches play out on the overhead TV. The BBQ patio is vintage slacker NoLita (brick walls, an old bicycle, a propped-up surfboard) and it's the chillest spot in town to nurse a Sunday hangover. Aussie nibbles include kanga skewers with mountain berry ketchup, best enjoyed in the cool-toned restaurant. Later in the evening, the merriment heats up in the dim downstairs lounge, where after a few Fosters, you'll probably be forgiven for slurring, "That's not a knoyfe. This is a knoyfe."

Eight of Clubs
230 W. 75th St. (Broadway & Amsterdam Ave.)
Upper West Side 212.580.7389

Unless you're looking, you won't notice this dingy gay dive that's tucked away like an ace under a dark awning. Catering to a mostly older clientele, the bar doesn't offer much besides a pool table, a jukebox, and some phallic charcoal drawings on the wall. But wander out back to the lounge, and you suddenly feel as though you're stranded on *Gilligan's Island* with a head full of strong acid. The awe-inspiring art garden resembles a whacked-out wharf; it's decorated with found objects such as traffic cones, twinkle lights, and ironing boards, proving the puzzling adage that "One man's trash is another man's treasure." Sit back on one of the many benches and take in all the kitsch-tastic opulence assembled here. It's a buried treasure in an otherwise staid neighborhood.

85 West Cocktail Bar
85 West St. (West Side Hwy. & Albany St.)
TriBeCa 212.266.6128

Have you ever found yourself downtown longing for the refined corpo-comfort of the Upper East Side? Of course you haven't. No one has. However, 85 West Cocktail Bar in the Marriott Financial Center sands down this area's "downtown edge" with a polished-until-it's-flat approach that conventioneers and burned-out businessmen find comfortable. A dark-wood bar, leather furnishings, and attentive service complete the formula, and the "Sass in the City" cocktail, which they're proud to tell you was in an '05 *Vogue*, actually reeks of 2002 to Manhattanites or anyone with HBO. Wednesday and Thursday nights bring live music from 7pm-10pm. This serviceable bar has its place, but it seems that focus groups were used where personality would've been nice.

El Cantinero
86 University Pl. (11th & 12th Sts.)
Greenwich Village 212.255.9378

If your only experience with Mexican food is Taco Bell or one of the many Tex-Mex chain restaurants polluting the city, do yourself a favor and make a run for El Cantinero. Dining hall-weary NYU and New School students looking for an authentic Mexican restaurant, complete with tasty, affordable food, potent margaritas, and south-of-the-border décor (requisite sombreros on the walls) congregate here to get a quick, spicy bite (tacos, enchiladas, burritos, chimichangas) or to have a drink or two (a favorite is the Cucaracha, made with tequila, Kahlua, and Sprite) in the upstairs bar. So bond with a few co-eds over a huge bowl of the out-of-this-world guacamole or share a pitcher of sangria. You know what they say about sorority girls and sangria…

El Faro

823 Greenwich St. (@ Horatio St.)
West Village 212.929.8210

El Faro

With neighbors like Marc Jacobs and Paris Commune, it's refreshing to see that the hip police haven't kicked the 78-year-old El Faro—the oldest Spanish restaurant in the city—out of its trendy West Village location. This low-key spot's dark décor, diner-style booths, and older clientele don't exactly scream "festive," but go ahead and order a margarita on the rocks anyway. With dishes like paella and even lobster served in what looks like the pot they were cooked in, El Faro isn't exactly big on frills, but the service is friendly and the subdued atmosphere makes for a nice refuge from the hipper-than-thou attitude outside its doors.

El Parador Café

325 E. 34th St. (1st & 2nd Aves.)
Murray Hill 212.679.6812

Ay carumba! El Parador Café has one of the biggest tequila selections north of Tijuana. With over 70 types of tequila and 100 bottles of wine in the offerings, it's a good thing that this place offers outstanding Mexican fare to absorb the toxins. While the enchiladas are great, the steaks here are quite fantastic. El Parador's dark-wood upstairs dining room is typically packed with dates and mates enjoying pitchers of sangria, but downstairs, you'll find a lounge with younger singles drinking copious amounts of margaritas and lounging—and later passing out—on the comfy banquettes that line the space. This is the oldest Mexican restaurant in the city, and it looks and tastes great for 46. *Vamanos*!

El Poblano Sports Grill

593 3rd Ave. (16th St. & Prospect Ave.)
Park Slope 718.788.1331

El Poblano Sports Grill

Dwarfed by a bigger bar next door, this tiny neighborhood establishment feels like it's at the end of the world, overlooking a massive bridge and two huge smokestacks from the scenic crag of Third Avenue. Barely in Park Slope, El Poblano caters to the local, mainly Latino crowd that drops in to enjoy a cold cerveza, watch the game, and maybe have a bite of Mexican food, all to a jukebox of Latin classics. On Friday and Saturday this is one happening hacienda, but on weeknights El Poblano is one lonely hombre. Still, its diner-style booths are inviting, and the well-stocked bar doesn't disappoint. This pleasant little nightspot has avoided the hipster morass of Fifth Avenue, and odds are good that trend will continue.

El Quijote
226 W. 23rd St. (7th & 8th Aves.)
Chelsea 212.929.1855

You have to wonder if Sid and Nancy got to try the lobster before it was too late. (We're guessing there wasn't a whole lot of eating going on in the Chelsea Hotel's infamous room #100.) El Quijote, as much a Chelsea institution as the glorified hospice under which it's tucked, is a big, bustling, yelling international tribute to Spanish food and atmosphere. Yack at the bar with some thrill-seeking tourists, or shuffle past the weary staff into the white noise of one of these giant dining rooms. Everyone...no, really, EVERYONE...swears by the lobster, so get that (always market-priced). Your server will recommend some sangria to go with it, or you can simply ask the French tourists at the next table over for a wine pick.

El Rey Del Sol
232 W. 14th St. (7th & 8th Aves.)
West Village 212.229.0733

This subterranean dive serves up Mexican cuisine at its simplest. Quesadillas, fajitas, burritos, and bean dip come in plentiful portions in their kitschy dining room and garden. Fortunately, El Rey Del Sol serves up pitchers of sangria and margaritas to match their cuisine. And what margaritas they are—they come in varieties including watermelon, cantaloupe, orange, or grapefruit along with alternating daily specials. If "fruity" isn't your thing, your waitress can tell you about their serviceable selection of Mexican beer, which includes 24-oz. Coronas. She'll also tell you that you're in the wrong neighborhood. Should you find yourself settling into one of the garden tables, it just might be time to order all three—sangria, margaritas, and beer—and bid your evening plans a fond *adios*.

El Rio Grande Restaurant
160 E. 38th St. (Lexington & 3rd Aves.)
Murray Hill 212.867.0922

Put on your "training wheels" (aka, the salt and the lime) when you're drinking one of the 10 varieties of tequila at this Tex-Mex restaurant. Arguably boasting "the best margaritas in town," El Rio Grande also serves up free chips and salsa—though you might want to eat a 10-gallon hat's worth to soak up that liquor, otherwise you might end up looking like a beat-up piñata. The menu features standard south-of-the-border fare—enchiladas, "Wild Bill" buffalo wings, tacos, nachos, chuletas (pork chops), and more. Still, unless your favorite spice is of the frat boy and tacky decorations variety, you might want to mosey on past this run-of-the-mill cucina.

Elaine's
1703 2nd Ave. (88th & 89th Sts.)
Upper East Side 212.534.8103

What is it about this by-the-numbers pub that serves mediocre food in a boring neighborhood that draws in the New York celebrity elite? Some credit the eponymous owner, but frankly, there's plenty of other interesting old broads running gin joints in this town, and you don't see Barbra Streisand hanging out in those other places. That said, Elaine's must have something going for it, and even if it is just surviving off the fumes of its own fame, it's worth stopping by at least once. Pull up a stool at the small bar (forget about getting a table), try to avoid making eye contact with the fabulous people who do show up, and enjoy the fact that you and Woody Allen's butts have probably shared the same stool leather.

The Elephant
58 E. 1st St. (1st & 2nd Aves.)
East Village 212.505.7739

If your bank account still hasn't allowed for that trip to the Far East, this crown jewel of East Village Thai establishments offers the next best thing.

The Elephant

Sipping a Singha amongst beaded curtains, signs written in Thai script, and bunches of green bananas hung from the ceiling will make you wonder whether you're on First Street or Bangkok's Ko San Road. On weekends, don't expect much privacy in this far-from-elephantine room, where strangers sit elbow-to-elbow. On weekdays, however, it might be possible to snag one of two mosaic-topped tables in the back, perfect for you and a date to munch on exquisite Thai food or simply knock back a cocktail prepared by friendly bartenders who have learned to deal with the weekend's largely Upper East Side and Euro-trash clientele.

Eleven Madison Park
11 Madison Ave. (@ 24th St.)
Murray Hill 212.889.0905

Beloved by foodies, rich men, and the gold diggers who love them, this French restaurant (located in the Met Life building) is one of the jewels in Danny Meyers' restaurateur crown...and not for those without wads of cash. It's an impressive space even to the most jaded New Yorker with its high ceilings and marble floors, and a plum locale overlooking the recently gentrified Madison Square Park. It's the perfect spot for people (preferably those with expense accounts) to take future in-laws to score some points. And if you can't convince your fiancé's folks you're good enough, ply

them (or just numb yourself) with one of 300 bottles of wine. There's no Bud here, though, so don't order one, or risk being snickered at ever-so-politely by the jovial staff.

11th Street Bar
510 11th St. (Aves. A & B)
East Village 212.982.3929

Great, another Irish pub. No, really. The unmarked 11th Street Bar is easy to miss, but it'll be around long after its hipper neighbors shut down. Exposed brick, polished wood, and soft lighting create a warm, cozy feel. The Irish and English ex-pats here are beyond laidback and this is the NYC home of the world-champion Liverpool Football Club. TVs hang above the main bar, and there's a big-screener in the backroom, where there's also a piano and multiple tables. Somehow, none of the stimulants are overbearing. Traditional Irish music on Sunday nights blends in just as well—picture a scenario where a six-piece acoustic ensemble fits in smoothly. Cheers, 11th Street Bar!

Elmo
156 7th Ave. (19th & 20th Sts.)
Chelsea 212.337.8000

Upscale diner food dominates this friendly Chelsea spot that offers a 10-seater bar and plenty of standing space allowing patrons a glass-enclosed view of Seventh Avenue. Pithy sayings along the wall ("Eschew obfuscation") blend nicely with the restaurant's cherubic kitschy vibe, and the crowd—mostly Chelsea hotties and hipper-than-thou types—isn't above batting their eyelashes at the similarly hot cookie-cutter bartenders. Besides a modest liquor display, Elmo offers five bottled and four tap beers as well as reasonably priced reds and whites. But cocktails are the thing, with 10 standard (watermelon martini, frozen margarita) and signature (pomegranate mojito, vodka basil lemonade) picks priced at $10 each.

Emerald Inn
205 Columbus (@ 69th St.)
Upper West Side 212.874.8840

A group of bachelors keep up a raucous card game in one corner, and an older scene of nice folks who are in good with the owner Charlie (whose pops started the place) cover the barstools. This Upper West Side favorite seems like it should have membership cards—no, not like the SoHo House, more like a get 10-stamps-your-11th-beer-is-free card. It's a welcoming, comfy neighborhood haunt that may not remember names, but definitely remembers the faces of regulars that come every week for pub grub specials. And the food is good…really good. Try the traditional Irish fare of corned beef and cabbage (available Thursdays only). It's magically delicious and it puts the Emerald Isle into an Upper West Side corner of our island that could really use some color.

Emerald Pub
308 Spring St. (Hudson & Greenwich Sts.)
SoHo 212.226.8512

The antithesis to SoHo, this low-frills watering hole sits in that murky, no-name territory just west of Hudson, a pretension-free zone refreshingly devoid of velvet ropes and bouncers with over-inflated…everything. Instead, there's cold Guinness (go for a $5 20-oz.-er, because size does matter), local working folks, crusty regulars trading tall tales 'bout the good old days, and decent pub grub like beer-battered fish and chips, hefty burgers, spaghetti and meatballs, and jalapeño poppers with ranch sauce. Get sloshed for half-price at the daily happy hour, and then wail along with Madonna and Whitney at Thursday's karaoke night. On Fridays and Saturdays, live music—mostly of the "Oh my God, this was, like, my favorite song!" variety—keeps the crowd going until the wee hours.

Employees Only
510 Hudson St. (@ Christopher St.)
West Village 212.242.3021

It's hard to tell where you're allowed to be when the front door's labeled "Employees Only." That may be why this place has a palm reader at the entrance offering direction to wayward drinkers and diners. Cozy and crowded, Employees Only has a woody, neighborhoody, fireplacey olde West Villagey thing going on, while the bright orange lights on the ceiling give it a touch of the new. The front room offers a well-managed bar where meticulously mustached men mix mean martinis and more. The backroom, which sits under a big skylight, is where diners sit elbow-to-elbow noshing on rustic European cuisine. Employees Only is clearly going for a classic cocktails throwback vibe, but what they get is a mix of cool old souls and obnoxious text-messaging trendsters. Fortunately, the latter crowd will soon be on to the next big thing. Warning: Reservations are very hard to come by, and are only taken during the day, so if you don't feel like waiting for hours for a table, this isn't your place.

Enid's
560 Manhattan Ave. (@ Driggs Ave.)
Greenpoint 718.349.3859

At the corner of McCarren Park, Enid's feels like a neighborhood institution even though it's only been around for six years (compare to the venerable Turkey's Nest, across the park at over a century). A friendly, laidback place with crowded weekends, Enid's recently added a full menu of tempting American-leaning-toward-Southern food. (Cornmeal-crusted catfish with two sides for $11.) Picture windows look into a big front space where hipsters bop to DJs. Enid's $3-$5 beers start the party, and the Harrison, a formidable tequila, grapefruit, cranberry, lime, and triple sec affair, served in a pint glass for just $6, sometimes ends it. The nice, low lights, pressed-tin ceilings, and good-looking crowd of smartly dressed too-cool-for-Bedford-Avenue types make Enid's shimmer.

Epstein's Bar
82 Stanton St. (@ Allen St.)
Lower East Side 212.477.2232

It's hard to believe that this cozy bar hosted live music in its former incarnation as the Living Room, but now that Epstein's is here, this space has found its calling as a neighborhood joint. (The new Living Room is only a block away.) While the traffic flow down Allen Street demonstrates that a wall of windows isn't always a plus, everything else in this thoughtful tavern works nicely. A long, well-handled bar stands between friendly barkeeps and a plasma TV that shows sports and movies while providing a "non-TV bar" vibe. There are clearly signs that the Lower East Side is suffering from a too-many-bars syndrome, so there will be nights when Epstein's is empty, but the Sweathogs they do draw tend to be of a kindly neighborhood variety and they take full advantage of the MP3 jukebox.

Esperanto
145 Ave. C (@ 9th St.)
East Village 212.505.6559

In the heart of Loisaida is a Latin paradise where during the summer the doors swing open onto sidewalk seating and live Brazilian and Cuban music pours into the street. The fern trees across the way might as well be palm trees as you sip an exotic, potent pisco sour (Chilean grape liquor with egg whites), a capirinha, guava and passion fruit drinks, or a fluffy coco punch (rum, Brazilian cachaca, ginger, and coconut)—each for $6. The reasonably priced food menu showcases the best of Latin America: Brazilian mocqueca (a savory stew of shrimp, red snapper, coconut milk, and spices), Chilean ceviches, Spanish tapas, and even a Cuban sandwich, with wines from Chile, Argentina, and Spain to match. Inside, the corrugated steel, ship doors, and bright, Caribbean color scheme completes the illusion that this corner of Avenue C is actually the shore of a breezy tropical island.

ESPN Zone
1472 Broadway (@ 42nd St.)
Midtown 212.921.3776

This might be the only bar in the city—if not the world—that actually hinders drinking. With the steady gleam of television sets, the incessant noise from the videogames upstairs, and the pricey taps at the bar, it's virtually impossible to get a good buzz going. Of course, if you're the kind of person who can't decide which team to support—let alone which sport—and you prefer wearing a $25 ESPN Zone t-shirt to a well-worn replica jersey, this is likely the place for you. If not, you're better off heading to the local sports bar on the corner, and leaving this Chuck E. Cheese-y family fun center to the tourists and the kids. It's strange, but this multimillion-dollar corner seemed less cheap and icky when it was occupied by hookers.

Essex Restaurant
120 Essex St. (@ Rivington St.)
Lower East Side 212.533.9616

Liquid brunch. Need we say more? This friendly neighborhood joint distinguishes itself from other hipster depots by offering—you guessed it—a unique morning alternative for those who like their morning carbs in liquid form. For a cool 15 bucks, you can have the true breakfast of champions— brunch and your choice of three hair-of-the-dog drinks. Even if drinking before noon isn't your thing, this bar, which is a little Murray Hill-ish by LES standards (not as divey as neighbor Welcome to the Johnsons, but not as hipper-than-thou as every other bar nearby), is a solid, run-of-the-mill place to hit if you have the urge to grab some drinks or get some late-night potato pancakes, just like your grandparents did when they used to party on Rivington.

Eugene
27 W. 24th St. (Broadway & 6th Ave.)
Flatiron 212.462.0999

For a place with such a dorky name, Eugene gets around. Less a club than a train station for weekly promoters, this Flatiron haunt is alternately small and huge. Come on a night with the Motherfucker crew, and thousands seem packed around the makeshift stage. On off-nights (not too often), you're looking at an overfull furniture store. Actually, the décor is a cut above, with plenty of stylish velvet seating for tipsy movers and shakers. Currently, the rotating promoters celebrate with Latin hip-hop and carefully curated dance nights. But beware the velvet rope when a hot DJ comes around. Those bouncers look like refugees from the WWF for a reason, you know (and you thought the $10 drinks would keep out the commoners…).

Evelyn Lounge
380 Columbus Ave. (@ 78th St.)
Upper West Side 212.724.9888

This Upper West Side haunt is rather staid. Dark maroon walls, red velvet curtains, exposed brick, and borderline candelabra lighting all set an intimate mood at this bar. But while the atmosphere feels antiquated, the crowd is decidedly not. In another era, Evelyn Lounge—composed of the Burton Lounge and Comma Lounge—might have been a classy gin joint or a locale for a late-night rendezvous. Now, it pretty much caters to young professionals with disposable income. A steady soundtrack of adult contemporary music floats through the air, and that pretty much sums up the mood of this bar/lounge. Plentiful, ornate couches and chaise lounges are perfect to loll on, and there's a decent selection of drinks (mmm…mochatinis) to keep you sedate for hours. What's missing here, though, is a sense of real energy.

Euzkadi
108 E. 4th St. (1st & 2nd Aves.)
East Village 212.982.9788

Euzkadi, meaning "Basque Country," is an apropos name for this cozy East Villager serving Basque cuisine. The kitchen serves all of the Spanish favorites like croquettes, paella, and ham and cheese platters, and it's reasonably priced considering the large portions and high quality. Not to be outdone, the bar serves up a large selection of Spanish wines and specialty drinks. There are over 50 bottles of Spanish wine, red and white sangria, and six champagne cocktails, including the Euzkadi with papxaran juice ($8). The décor is artsy and authentic, with Spanish posters on the walls and hieroglyphics of bulls, hands, and hunters on the ceilings. Don't miss the live flamenco dancers on Tuesdays or the pre-theater menu from 5:30pm-7pm. The staff is friendly and welcoming, the crowd is local, and the vibe is ideal.

Excelsior
390 5th Ave. (6th & 7th Sts.)
Park Slope 718.832.1599

In a neighborhood peppered with very few distinctly gay bars, Excelsior is a haven for the Chelsea refugees who fled Manhattan to navigate the brownstones and baby carriages of Park Slope. Laidback yet classy, this loungey neighborhood spot is friendly and welcoming to gays and non-gays alike (i.e., gay boys, feel free to bring your straight girlfriends, and straight girlfriends don't worry, you'll feel right at home). The austere décor makes you feel like you're bathing inside a crisp martini, while the porch and back garden are as homey (and, of course, smoker-compatible) as a friend's backyard. Themed drinks appear seasonally, and a variety of cocktails are available year-round. When it comes to Brooklyn's gay scene, Excelsior ranks among the best.

Exit
610 W. 56th St. (11th & 12th Aves.)
Hell's Kitchen 212.582.8282

A super-club by any other name would smell as sweet: In addition to Exit, this party central has gone by Black and Ikon. We can't keep track of the names or the beats, which have always rocked; the four themed rooms are usually filled to capacity. Some nights, club kids and ravers get busy while on other nights, the Bridge & Tunnel crowd throws down on the dance floor. The cover is at least $20 whether it's trance, house, hip-hop, or reggae. Sweaty dancing queens can cool off on the outdoor deck. Check out their 18+ parties on Thursdays and Saturdays; the door policy is relaxed and the bar seems to sell more water than beer. Go figure. (All other nightts are 21+.)

Faces and Names
159 W. 54th St. (6th & 7th Aves.)
Midtown 212.586.9311

Ironically, Faces and Names is hard to recognize as it doesn't quite fit into any of the regular bar categories; it's neither a dive, nor pub, nor swanky lounge. However, it is an awfully nice, low-key sort of place to relax, chat, and have a few drinks. Sports lovers will be pleased to see several television sets broadcasting games, while their friends can inspect the wide array of caricatures and portraits lining the walls (hence the name). In addition, Faces and Names occasionally has live music and the food is consistently satisfying. All in all, it's a crowd-pleaser. Keep this place in mind for parties and gatherings as well—they're very accommodating when it comes to the after-work birthday celebration thing.

Failte Irish Whiskey Bar
531 2nd Ave. (29th & 30th Sts.)
Murray Hill 212.725.9440

There's something warm and inviting about Failte Irish Whiskey Bar, and it's not the fireplace. (The name is pronounced "FALL-cha.") More than your run-of-the-mill Murray Hill McFrat hangout, this authentic bar's stone walls and unfinished wood bar invoke the Irish countryside…until Wednesday through Saturday nights, when a DJ plays predominantly '80s tunes (unless you consider Dexy's Midnight Runners a genuine taste of the homeland). Failte has a good beer selection and friendly bartenders, but if you feel like being alone, you can take your Guinness to the poolroom and play Golden Tee or poker solo. Alternatively, there's a lounge upstairs that can be booked for private parties.

The Falls
218 Lafayette St. (Spring & Broome Sts.)
SoHo 212.226.5233

Imagine an episode of *Queer Eye for the Straight Guy* featuring the remodeling of a frat house— that's pretty much what you have with the Falls. With an atmosphere of college boys all grown up, the interior of this neighborhood hangout features such Pottery Barn delights as walnut-stained wood paneling and frosted-glass wall sconces (aka fancy lamps). Dudes can be found trying to show their sensitive sides as they sweet-talk the ladies, but easily flattered women who think they're being "checked out" might want to keep in mind that they're probably standing under an HDTV unit. Still, the scene does allow for a surprising amount of diversity, especially in the lounge area in back. A fully stocked bar, including a range of wine selections—and hey, Dom Perignon, if that's your bag—offers the chance to make the night what you wish.

Fanelli's
94 Prince St. (@ Mercer St.)
SoHo 212.226.9412

From the moment you walk into Fanelli's, the red-checkered tablecloths and dark wood décor let you know this ain't just another sleek SoHo contrivance. One of the oldest remaining bars in the area (est. 1847), Fanelli's has hosted such notable characters as Jackson Pollack and Willem de Kooning, and we wouldn't be surprised if Lincoln had been at the opening. The ambiance is hearty and filling, as is the menu—something about the wood molding and etched glass doors make you want to order a burger and a pint. Not necessarily cheap, the prices are still a scaled-down relief from what's charged at surrounding hotspots that haven't yet earned the right. Feeling bold? Try the bison burger with a side of crispy fries.

Farrell's
215 Prospect Park W. (@ 16th St.)
Park Slope 646.644.1039

No sissies, no stools, no service. Got that, kid? Better learn fast at Farrell's. You don't come to this 72-year-old South Slope dive for niceties, just ice-cold beer and the ball game. Stone-faced bartenders serve Budweiser in Styrofoam quarts for $4.25, an unbeatable deal if you can tolerate the trash-talking, blue-collar dudes who know your kind. There's a lot of arm-wrestling, and conversation doesn't stray beyond the game on TV. Most ladies find this bar less than charming, and Farrell's makes no apologies: When crowded, huddles of construction workers prop their chairs against the ladies' room door as if it were a storage closet. Old-school artifacts like the tin ceiling and wooden phone booth show off Farrell's lesser-known sentimental side. Now don't go getting all mushy.

Fashion 40
202 W. 40th St. (7th & 8th Aves.)
Midtown 212.221.3628

Take away the taps at Fashion 40 Lounge, and those churlish beer guzzlers leave. Instead, attract the sophisticated crowd with top-shelf liquor, decorate the lounge with mirrors and diamonds-in-the-sky lighting, and guess who shows up? Women. And this being a Garment District joint, everyone poses from the balcony like they're on an episode of *America's Next Top Model*. Who needs beer? The kitchen serves a Northern Italian menu with prices ranging from the floor to the ceiling, aimed at a 20-something crowd too hip for the casual bar scene, but too nonchalant for fine dining. Now, if you could only get her attention away from those mirrors...

Fat Black Pussycat
130 W. 3rd St. (6th Ave. & MacDougal St.)
Greenwich Village 212.533.4790

A black cat must've crossed the path of this bar a

Fat Black Pussycat

long time ago, as it's shocking to see such a faceless venue still limping along. Dark lighting isn't enough to distract visitors from the Pussycat's basic interior—a pool table, some booths, and a couple of TVs round out the main room. Be assured the long front bar won't feature much more than after-work drifters and oldsters dropping by for half-price drinks Monday through Friday, 4pm-8pm. For something fancier, though, you might try the adjoining underground space (mind the "no casual" dress code), which is loungier.

Fez North (@ Time Café)
2330 Broadway (@ 85th St.)
Upper West Side 212.579.5100

Finding your way here is reminiscent of bygone speakeasy days—travel through the populous but bland Time Café downstairs, go through the back door, up the stairs, and around the corner to find a luxurious enclave replete with cavernous walls, a bar suffused in dim light, and languidly churning ceiling fans. Be sure not to confuse Fez North with its sister restaurant, the now-closed Fez Under Time Café; the downtown Fez was known for its music and live reading scene. And the new Fez—

well, this joint ain't entirely jumpin'. Live music and performance didn't travel north with Fez, and the crowd, while young and hip, is also subdued. Come if you want to escape the hustle and bustle, lounge on pillowy sofas, and sip sangria to your own tune. No goofy hat required.

Fiamma Osteria
206 Spring St. (@ 6th Ave.)
SoHo 212.653.0100

Sometimes, it's all about how you get there. A ride in the glass elevator at Fiamma Osteria takes all of about five seconds, but still, ascending in purring comfort to the third-story bar lends a certain cachet to the evening. The professionally fawning staff also helps, as does the womb-like lounge, in warm reds and oranges, with flickering candles and orchids submerged in crystal vases of water. Fiamma Osteria is a swank Italian restaurant, but you won't have to endure withering looks if you just saunter in for a drink—excuse us—a cocktail. The signature $12 Fiamma will do you right, a sweet-meets-tart concoction of raspberry Stoli, white cranberry, and lime. If you're having any thoughts about joining the mini-mile-high elevator club, just remember—you have about five seconds…tiger.

Fiddlesticks
56 Greenwich Ave. (6th & 7th Aves.)
West Village 212.463.0516

We know what you're thinking—another Irish pub in New York? But Fiddlesticks manages to capture a bit of the magic of the Emerald Isle with charming touches of authenticity in the décor and a menu of stomach-lining staples like fish and chips, shepherd's pie, and an Irish breakfast, which turns out not to be Lucky Charms, but rather bacon, sausage, grilled tomato, and black and white pudding. On weekends the place is packed, and the music can be deafening, so you'll want to take your pint to an outdoor table for a little people-watching. When in doubt, just close your eyes and pretend the yuppies are soccer hooligans, then relax and enjoy this fine Irish establishment.

58
41 E. 58th St. (Madison & Park Aves.)
Midtown 212.308.9455

The space that used to house Au Bar has gone Banana Republic, and we don't mean they're selling cheap linen jackets for $400 a pop. 58 looks like the boudoir of some rich, slightly mad African dictator's wife, with its safari prints and furniture that's off-set by sultry red walls, vibrant, sweeping ceiling-hung drapes, and plush round banquettes. You can still lounge and catch jazz or salsa music during the week, but on weekends, relaxed elegance gives way to dance music and a high-end club crowd. The joint's still serviceable, albeit a bit pretentious, particularly if you're not into the whole P. Diddy gestalt; Lizzie Grubman hosts a weekly party, and that should tell you all you need to know. Try the house drink, the 58 (frozen grapes, grape juice, and vodka).

55 Bar
55 Christopher St. (@ 7th Ave.)
West Village 212.477.0007

Older than your parents, but way hipper, 55 Bar is your cool Uncle Milton's basement made available to the masses. Paneled walls, twinkle lights, and more black-and-white photos of jazz greats than you can count set the stage for nightly live (and often cover-free) jazz and blues acts—the only thing missing from this laidback scene is a haze of cigar smoke. At $4-$7, drinks are basic and cheap, and while a sign recommends you enjoy two per set, that law's enforced in the when-in-the-mood fashion of jaywalking patrol. A mostly older crowd navigates the labyrinth of café tables in the cozy basement space. Now go home and don't tell your mother Uncle Milt gave you beer.

5757 (@ the Four Seasons Hotel)
57 E. 57th St. (Madison & Park Aves.)
Midtown 212.758.5757

5757 is the house bar of the Four Seasons Hotel, and it's as classy and intimidating as the locale suggests. The space—a bright, airy cavern with high ceilings, a baby grand, and vases that probably cost more than all of your furniture put together—was designed by none other than I.M. Pei (and you'll be acutely aware of the money that went into it—and passes through it—during your visit). Much of the space is dedicated to a restaurant, but don't neglect the bar, where some of the most polite and knowledgeable barkeepers in the city serve up perfect cocktails, and some surprisingly dismal bar snacks. Only the Kobe beef mini-burgers are worth your time; but who the hell wants to pay $28 for three White Castle-style sliders?

Figa
281 Bleecker St. (@ Jones St.)
West Village 212.633.2941

With fans like Paris Hilton, Nicole Richie, and P. Diddy, Figa sounds like a hotspot you'd read about in *Us Weekly*. Which is why you'll be pleasantly surprised when you walk in and embrace the warm atmosphere, bolstered by dim lighting and a roaring fireplace. Black-and-white photographs of legends like Sophia Loren overlook a smallish room with a bar on one end while couples tear into hefty portions of pasta and dishes like the mouthwatering filet mignon and red snapper. This being an Italian restaurant, you'll definitely want to order something from the wine list as you admire the quiet streets of West Village through the large windows. Friday nights see live Brazilian music. Maybe we should start giving Paris and Diddy more credit.

Film Center Café
635 9th Ave. (44th & 45th Sts.)
Hell's Kitchen 212.262.2525

It ain't *Breakfast at Tiffany's,* but on weekends, the Film Center Café offers the perfect opening act if you've got tickets to a matinee screening across the street—a $10.95 unlimited champagne brunch. Play a game of "name that movie star" posing in the film stills adorning the walls. Inside, the café, which is really more of a dark lounge

space with sleek, shiny black surfaces and blue lighting, is reminiscent of a movie theater—but there's more than just popcorn and nachos served here. The fare is solidly American (fried chicken, burgers, wraps, and pastas), but the quality is more bistro than diner. The bar scene is good during happy hour, too, and the large booths stay packed pretty late on weekends. Here's lookin' at you, kid.

Finnegan's Wake
1361 1st Ave. (@ 73rd St.)
Upper East Side 212.737.3664

The self-described "James Joyce pub in the heart of the city" caters to an older, rough-around-the-edges crowd. So put away those tasteless Irish jokes, because Finnegan's Wake is the real deal; many of their patrons have been coming here for over 10 years to enjoy the live music, karaoke, a Sunday night table quiz, and the tasty pub food (try their famous shepherd's pie). Finnegan's also offers an assortment of Irish and non-alcoholic beers and draughts, including their own brew, Finnegan's Lager, and 15 types of Irish whiskey. If you think that Finnegan's Wake refers to an Irish water-skiing tournament, get yer foolish arse out!

Finnerty's
108 3rd Ave. (13th & 14th Sts.)
East Village 212.777.3363

If there's a fraternity paddle on your NYC scavenger hunt list, then you'll probably find it hidden behind the bar at this East Village bar. At Finnerty's, you'll also discover that cheap beer makes the casual game of darts more entertaining, er, hazardous. Ladies can usually proffer free pitchers from the overeager male patrons, but it would make more sense to do so in a place where the drinks are more expensive, the Greek quotient isn't so high, and the men are better-looking. Still, if you're nostalgic for those "swooshee" jogging pants you used to wear to your 8am Friday class in college, Finnerty's is the perfect bar for you to meet friends for a casual, just-rolled-out-of-bed pick-me-up pitcher. Finnerty's features delivery menus and Wednesday night Bingo.

Fino
1 Wall St. (Pearl & Beaver Sts.)
Financial District 212.825.1924

Choose from over 150 selections of Fino vinos—from aged Italian to Chilean and Australian vintages—at this very proper, below-street-level restaurant with lots of hushed, private corners that scream post-work "just between you and me" deals, not to mention romantic trysts. Linen tablecloths, beige walls, dim lighting, and attentive waiters who appear out of nowhere all contribute to the discreet ambiance. Tuck into hearty Northern Italian fare like Capellini Frutti Di Mare, angel hair pasta with seafood, or the velvety ravioli stuffed with lobster (all $18) and wash it down with Chianti. Thick carpets that seem to mute all sound surround the long, quiet bar where you can share another bottle, kiss, fondle, break up, scream, whatever—it's all good because nobody's watching.

Fiona's
1664 1st Ave. (86th & 87th Sts.)
Upper East Side 212.348.3783

Fiona's is about as classic an Irish restaurant as it gets, right down to the Irish bartenders who go for brogue. Not particularly large, this place's giant projection-screen TV, which dominates the back of the room, implies they might be going for a sports bar scene more so than the family-style restaurant thing they've got going on. It often works—everyone from hot 24-year-olds to your Grandma Edna will be hanging out here at any given time. The menu lists fairly standard bar fare that gets the job done, and tastes considerably better when washed down with a $3.50 bottle of Bud Light. Wait…did we just say "Bud Light" while praising an Irish joint? The world is getting stranger all the time.

Firebird
365 W. 46th St. (8th & 9th Aves.)
Hell's Kitchen 212.586.0244

If you're curious to know what would happen if a czar married a debutante and opened a country club restaurant, you'll find the answer at Firebird. How the Firebird manages not to scare away business with their strict dress code, though, is beyond us. If you get past the gates and shabby red carpeting, expect an equally high-brow experience at this traditional Russian eatery, where fastidious waiters in white gloves serve Russian-influenced food in near silence. The Firebird is an elegant spot to enjoy borscht, oxtail, chicken Kiev, and dessert wines. The stuffiness and upper-crust prices of this restaurant row establishment is one-upped by the likes of more rustic (and welcoming) downtown Ruskie joints like Odessa.

Firehouse
522 Columbus Ave. (85th & 86th Sts.)
Upper West Side 212.595.3139

If your fire station fantasy involves sliding down the fireman's pole à la Bridget Jones, being one of the firefighters to see her panties, or any other vision of a disco inferno blazin' good time, this is not the place for you. This is the Upper West Side, people. During the purgatory between the end of happy hour and the beginning of real bar hours, there is often a child in the joint, making siren noises with his toy fire engine. The only thing especially hot about this joint is the food. These proprietors claim the $7.50 steakadilla is famous, the $7.95 chili is special, and the $2.95 fries are sexy. While we agree they are pretty awesome, it's the spiced-up wings and solid beer selection that keep locals loyal as Dalmatians.

Fish
280 Bleecker St. (@ Jones St.)
West Village 212.727.2879

Starting with an $8 special that includes half a dozen oysters and a glass of wine, Fish has a few enduring hits on its hands. This restaurant and retail fish market boasts some of the city's freshest seafood at some of its most reasonable prices, along with drink specials that will sweep drinkers off their sea legs. The chalkboard menus, nautical décor, and friendly staff help give Fish an unpretentious atmosphere, and the cold, draught beer is great for washing down a couple dozen oysters. For your cheap friends, Pabst Blue Ribbon is only $1.50 and house wines are only $2 during happy hour, which lasts all day from 12pm-7pm. If you don't feel like you've been out at sea long enough after the Pot o' Bass, keep fishing until you get a bite.

Fish Bar
237 E. 5th St. (2nd & 3rd Aves.)
East Village 212.475.4949

Fish Bar

Folks are hooked on this minnow-sized watering hole that sports more fish in its décor than it does drinks on its menu. A board outside advertises the daily 2-for-1 happy hour (5pm-7pm), tempting bait that reels in passersby who might otherwise miss the hard-to-spot façade. The kitschy interior, reminiscent of an English fish-n-chips shop, is small but never crowded, so a table is usually available for a couple of leisurely rounds amid blue walls that can cause sea sickness. Young hipsters, older neighborhood folks, and chatty bartenders strike up conversation with one another over the catch of the day, which is always $3 cans of PBR. Splashed in candlelight at night, this place could also make for a swimmingly nice end to a date.

Fitzer's
687 Lexington Ave. (56th & 57th Sts.)
Midtown 212.784.2570

Manhattan needs another Irish pub like Pamela Anderson needs another breast implant. From the slightly curt barmaid and drab décor to the out-of-

date music, Fitzer's is not the most appealing place to mull over the meaning of life. That said, they do stock a range of Irish beer, including a decently pulled pint of the classic Guinness, which goes nicely with the hearty and wholesome menu items like shepherd's pie, stuffed potato skins, and the less traditional Cajun chicken. Attached to the Fitzpatrick Manhattan Hotel, this neighborhood bar is a little lacking in Irish charm—but hey, this is Midtown.

Fitzgerald's Pub
336 3rd Ave. (@ 25th St.)
Murray Hill 212.679.6931

It's always happy hour at Fitzgerald's—literally. Daily, they offer a noon-7pm happy hour with various specials, and it's happy hour again from 11pm-1am. What could possibly go wrong? This local Irish pub has its share of older regulars who seek out a barstool when the workday ends at 5pm, but later at night, younger, non-frat postgrads take in the relaxed atmosphere and low prices. Unlike other bars in the area, Fitzgerald's isn't overcrowded during the game, as they don't have satellite TV, so come in for darts and good Irish pub grub without having to elbow your way through a pack of jersey-clad Sigma Thetas. This is such a simple formula that one has to wonder how so many places do it wrong.

5 Ninth
5 9th Ave. (Gansevoort & Little W. 12th Sts.)
Meatpacking District 212.929.9460

5 Ninth is the perfect double agent. At first glance it appears as just another exclusive, stuffy-looking brownstone you could never hope to afford, or for that matter, even enter. But behind this renovated landmark's unmarked exterior hides an intimate bar and restaurant that, with its three stories of exposed beams and bricks, six fireplaces, and lush open garden area, oozes coziness and romance. Behind black-and-white rocker (as in musicians, not chairs) photos, this haunt strikes a chord between hip and classy that's perfect for wining and dining a special date or a potential client. Despite a well-suited and apparently well-

connected crowd, the atmosphere remains comfortable and relaxed. However, like all good double agents, 5 Ninth is not for the faint of wallet: Drinks start around $12 and bottles of wine at about $80.

Five Points
31 Great Jones St. (Bowery & Lafayette St.)
NoHo 212.253.5700

Despite being named after the notorious area that housed 19th-century street criminals, Five Points is anything but seedy. This unpretentiously stylish New American/Mediterranean favorite gushes with Zen and tranquil elements like a tree trunk fountain in the middle of its romantically lit dining room. Downtown hipsters and smartly dressed business types come in for the half-off happy hour martinis and $1 oysters from 5pm-7pm daily. The weekend brunch is a local fave that includes crunchy ricotta fritters ($8), bourbon and vanilla bean French toast ($10), and the highly recommended wood-oven baked eggs rancheros ($12). Bill the Butcher would roll over in his grave, but foodies like Five Points just fine.

Flannery's Bar
205 W. 14th St. (7th & 8th Aves.)
West Village 212.229.2122

Order a Guinness in this authentic Irish bar and you'll receive a customary shamrock, which the bartender etches into the foam. That's just part of Flannery's charm, where a low-key atmosphere, decent jukebox, and spacious layout add to an easy vibe. The five dartboards are a draw, along with televised sporting events including soc..., er, "football." The noise level never interferes with conversation, though a sign advertising sing-along karaoke on Thursdays implies there may be exceptions. Flannery's proximity to the subway and the PATH trains makes it a prime spot for an after-work drink before the ride back to Jersey. For average folks, Flannery's will be the closest they get to drinking in the Meatpacking District. Just don't come hungry, because free pretzels and a peanut machine are the only items on the menu.

Flatiron Lounge
37 W. 19th St. (5th & 6th Aves.)
Flatiron 212.727.7741

The spirit of the speakeasy is alive and well at this chic spot that's chock-full of history—from the vintage bar and art-deco décor to the lounge's original cocktails. The popular "flights" consist of three mini-martinis with similar themes (like the "Flight Back In Time," which "celebrates the Rat Pack's favorites, the Sazarac, Sidecar, and the Aviation Cocktail"), while other expertly crafted drinks include seasonal ingredients and specialty-infused spirits. The bartenders here go beyond just slinging bottles with their knowledgeable suggestions to serious drinkers and newcomers to this bourgeois booze scene. Paying no heed to the bustle of nearby Union Square, the Flatiron Lounge is a cool, calm spot that flawlessly channels the allure of classic New York so precisely you can almost picture ol' Frank at the bar.

Flight 151
151 8th Ave. (17th & 18th Sts.)
Chelsea 212.229.1868

This laidback Chelsea locale takes its aeronautical theme very seriously—and not much else. Salvaged airplane parts hang from the walls, cockpit recordings play in the bathroom, and a suspended model airplane looms overhead. Grown men and women (mostly men) play videogames and mark their tables with crayon, which is sanctioned by the establishment. Midweek drink specials draw an after-work crowd that's decidedly earthbound: Monday is $4 "Margarita Madness;" Tuesday's "Flip Night" offers free drinks for correctly guessing the result of a coin toss; Wednesday's "Spin the Wheel" offers $2 shots of whatever the wheel lands on; and on Thursday answering trivia questions earns free drinks. As with most aerial excursions, the drinks on this flight seem especially effective, but the food is unimpressive.

Everyone's favorite shopaholic, Becky Bloomwood, is back—and she's on a spree in NYC! From the bestselling author of *The Undomestic Goddess.*

A mythic Manhattan apartment building sets the stage for this "delightfully twisted ... divine comedy," (*San Francisco Chronicle*) as exuberant, dark, and dazzling as the city itself.

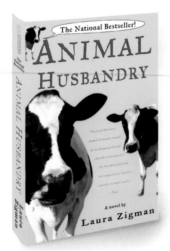

When a New York talk show producer takes her Old-Cow-New-Cow theory of dating and the sexes public, it will change her career and her life. Unless, of course, she's got it all wrong.

CITY that never sleeps.

A great Manhattan apartment . . . a soulless job. An A-list fiancée . . . a secret crush. He's got it all in perfect balance . . . until EVERYTHING CHANGES.

The year is 1896. The city is New York and the hunt is on for a baffling new kind of criminal—a serial killer. "Gripping, atmospheric, intelligent, and entertaining." —*USA Today*

Flor de Sol
361 Greenwich St. (Franklin & Harrison Sts.)
TriBeCa 212.366.1640

This sexy Spanish restaurant is a candlelit, medieval den of decadence. Think pretty girls in dresses, pretty boys in blazers, pillars wrapped with rich red tapestries, and crosses and torches mounted to red brick walls. There are masculine two-handed swords behind the long bar, which sits under a palatial, high ceiling. It's the Inquisition and you're here to feast and drink blood, while committing acts of gluttony and lust. Does that mean there's no happy hour? No, sir. From 5pm-7pm taps are half-priced at the bar and sangria is $4. In addition to delicious tapas, the kitchen churns out noteworthy traditional Spanish dishes. This place definitely has class, but it's also the perfect set-up for that third date where you lean in and ask when you're going to "consummate" this relationship.

Florent
69 Gansevoort St. (Washington & Greenwich Sts.)
Meatpacking District 212.989.5779

Do you remember when the Meatpacking District had a bit of an edge? Florent's still got it—sharp corners and all. Right in the heart of Nightclub Central lies this 1950s gone sci-fi, retro meets post-apocalyptic diner, which is as charming for an onion soup lunch as it is cool for post-clubbing black sausage. Open 24 hours, Florent gives the impression that time has forgotten it and it has forgotten about time. The food is a lite French/progressive American mix of low- to mid-priced greasy treats that are served and prepared with minimum effort, but to satisfactory results. They're just cool like that at Florent, and they couldn't care less. Don't spend all of your dough while clubbing into the wee hours—as you might've guessed they only take cash.

Florio's Grill & Cigar Bar
192 Grand St. (Mott & Mulberry Sts.)
Little Italy 212.226.7610

Florio's is located in the heart of Little Italy. Does that mean it's full of fresh-off-the-boat immigrants from Sicily and Tuscany? Mmmm…Akron and Des Moines perhaps. Still, it's a worthwhile place to order a reasonably priced, heavy, traditional Italian dish and smoke like a Frenchman. That's right—indoor smoking. The owner of this place also owns a nearby cigar store so whether they skirt the laws that way or use old-fashioned, Little Italy-style "persuasion" we don't know, but there aren't many places like this in the city these days. The no-frills décor is simply one of wooden walls and square tables where they'd probably prefer that customers wear suits, but what can ya do when a hungry fanny-pack clan wanders in?

Flow
150 Varick St. (@ Vandam St.)
SoHo 212.929.9444

The constant flow of A-list celebs is now a trickle at this SoHo club, which means good-looking people without a SAG card now come pouring in to party without pretension. There's plenty of bump-'n'-grind booty-grabbin' at this palace of pop and R&B. Avid club-goers won't hear a lot of music here they haven't heard before, which makes dancing easier. The famous lighted fountain still makes a splash and 11 types of bubbly flow for those with dough. (The wine list is limited and servings come at $12 per plastic cup. In case you don't know, ordering wine in a club results in creepy red teeth and stained party clothes.) The guys here are playing that trial-and-error game, so as long as everyone knows the rules, all bets are on.

Floyd, NY
131 Atlantic Ave. (Henry & Clinton Sts.)
Cobble Hill 718.858.5810

Let's hear it for bad beer: For $12 you can get an ice-filled bucket labeled "Crapacopia," which includes one can each of Pabst, Schlitz, Ballantine, Piels, Genny Cream Ale, and Miller High Life. (Beers are subject to change.) It's that sort of egalitarian spirit that has made this newish bar a favorite with the locals. Floyd sprawls off of Atlantic with a light-filled front room and an array of couches that exemplify threadbare-chic, with a fake fireplace and a couple of bookshelves adding to the kitsch. The bar's centerpiece, however, is the clay-and-wood bocce ball court, which is home to year-round bocce ball tournaments. You don't know how to play bocce ball? No one here does, and that's half the fun.

Flute
40 E. 20th St. (Broadway & Park Ave. S.)
Flatiron 212.529.7870

Bottoms up! And after sampling one of over 120 types of champagne at Flute, that expression may refer to your glass...or your ass. Variety doesn't come cheap at the Flatiron location of this champagne bar: The average price of a glass of champagne is $15, and you could spend hundreds on a bottle. Single and looking for a sugar daddy? There are a lot of big spenders in this crowd. If you just want a glimpse at how the other half lives, settle into a plush banquette, order a bottled beer

and some inexpensive tasty treats like specialty chocolates to complement your drink, and you might be able to keep things under $20.

Flute
205 W. 54th St. (Broadway & 7th Ave.)
Midtown 212.265.5169

Despite a more upscale Flute location now operating in Flatiron, the original bubbly bar still dazzles with its simple and unpretentious elegance. Although a popular late-night oasis in the heart of Midtown, this ultra-comfy champagne lounge always has an available sofa waiting to envelope tipsy couples. Try a glass of Francis Ford Coppola's yummy red wine or let the super-patient hostesses recommend a few of their favorites from the large and entertaining selection. Flute is best as either the first or last stop on a long night out, but remember that champagne packs quite a punch and rarely plays well with others, namely, the four tequila shots you downed back at the apartment. As far as date spots go, Flute is the best set-up partner since Ed McMahon.

Floyd, NY

40/40 Club

Food Bar

149 8th Ave. (17th & 18th Sts.)
Chelsea 212.691.0695

Food Bar's name withstands the burden of truth in advertising by offering a big, inviting menu to Chelsea locals. But perhaps they should've chosen the moniker "Food and Dudes" instead...every last foodie in sight looks like they've stepped out of an issue of *Men's Health*. The Cobb salad is popular, but anything from seafood to sandwiches and omelets is available under one roof. Friendly prices (ranging $7-$19; recommendations from the pretty people in the room are free) and a delightful atmosphere make this spot a real "catch" in the area. Big, cheerful paper lamps light up the dining room and the front bar is bright and airy. Enjoy a 2-for-1 happy hour daily; after all, man cannot live on food alone.

Forbidden City

212 Ave. A (13th & 14th Sts.)
East Village 212.598.0500

Like chocolate and peanut butter, classy and inclusive are two tasty ingredients that go great together. Slightly upscale, though sans VIP shtick and ridiculous prices, Forbidden City is the Reese's Peanut Butter Cup of East Village bars. The horseshoe bar and red, candlelit interior lead back to a dining room where Pan-Asian treats like sushi, tempura, and the age-old Asian delicacy of shrimp-wrapped bacon accompany sipping creatively named sake drinks like One Inch Punch or The Drunken Master. If you're lucky there might be a blaxploitation or kung fu movie playing on the backroom projector, or a DJ spinning jazz or hip-hop; Sunday is Afro-Cuban night. The only thing forbidden in this city is having a bad time.

40/40 Club

6 W. 25th St. (@ Broadway)
Flatiron 212.832.4040

Jay-Z's 40/40 Club is a deft combination of New York lounge and high-tech sports bar. Game noise pours from innumerable plasma TVs. It's a fitting volume—one expects cheerleaders to burst out and lead a chant. The décor, all polished chrome and buffed suede, is deliberate and sleek. Even the bathrooms sport the latest in faucet design. The schedule of televised events is available online, as is the menu. (Think skewers, pizzas, and well-manicured finger food.) You won't see hipster haircuts in here as this crowd is closely cropped and dressed up for a night out, but not without representin' a bit of thug life. There are posh private rooms (including a cigar room) upstairs, but unless you've got a Topps trading card as your ID, forget about it, junior.

44 (@ the Royalton Hotel)
44 W. 44th St. (5th & 6th Aves.)
Midtown 212.944.8844

In the fast-beating heart of manic Midtown Manhattan, this trendy little bar is a lifesaver. Saunter through the lobby of the boutiquey Royalton Hotel and you'll find what used to be one of the publishing world's best-kept secret meeting places. The secret's out, but 44 is still worth writing home about. Whether you choose table service or a seat at the bar, this is one of those places that makes everyone feel semi-important. (The champagne and oysters make sure that dipping the pen in the company ink is always an option.) Expect to pay for this classic and masculine décor, but if you snag a cozy couch or club chair, you'll find yourself feeling rich in no time at all.

44&X
622 10th Ave. (44th & 45th Sts.)
Hell's Kitchen 212.977.1170

With a moniker that also serves as directions (yeah, we just got it, too), 44&X is for the unabashedly hip if not the mildly pretentious. This place is the Fashion District crowd's version of heaven: a sparkly, white, European-esque interior with enough alcohol to light ice queen Anna Wintour's night on fire. Our advice? Sip on a Broadway-based cocktail like Stoli Magnolia (Stoli peach, plum sake, cranberry, fresh lemon juice, simple syrup) on the canopied patio. For those who aren't models or modelizers, an order of the crab fritter appetizers, short ribs, mac 'n' cheese, or the award-worthy burgers will make them envy you for a change. 44&X isn't anything to write *Vogue* about, but if you're already in the area it's a pretty place to eat, drink, and be devilish.

49 Grove
49 Grove St. (Bleecker St. & 7th Ave. S.)
West Village 212.727.1100

This low-ceilinged, subterranean space makes for a nice lounging venue, and every year or so, someone new makes a run at it. Maybe it's hard to move walls and bars in lower-level spaces, but the more this space changes, the more it stays the same. Following the haute monde reign of Halo, and the fun days of Play, 49 Grove is attempting a posh look at the four rooms that make up this small space. A big, medieval, tough-to-enter door welcomes those who find themselves immediately descending a candle-lined staircase leading right to a bar area where the traffic flow gets a bit hairy. Past that tough area, which also plagued this space's previous incarnations, an upscale rec room setting caters to a bottle-service crowd while non-intrusive hip-hop plays. If you can grab a curtain-shielded booth in one of the backrooms, a leisurely evening awaits.

46 Grand
46 Grand St. (W. Broadway & Thompson St.)
SoHo 212.219.9311

If 46 Grand's velvet rope and $5 cover charge don't put you off, the fact that there's only one beer on tap and one available wine might. On the other hand, what this itty-bitty bar does right is serve up good (though loud) hip-hop-oriented music to a diverse crowd—and if you're in the mood to groove, you'll be putting up with much harsher velvet ropes and covers than the ones here. Lots of gray, austere furniture and original artwork on the walls give this place a modern, vaguely swank yet comfortable feel, and mirrors in the back help add at least the illusion of elbow-room. Just be careful as to how far you back that "thang" up.

The Four-Faced Liar

165 W. 4th St. (6th & 7th Aves.)
West Village 212.366.0608

The truth about the Four-Faced Liar is that it's a decent, no-frills pub that somehow manages to avoid the obnoxious hooligans who populate the neighboring bars in this little B&T nightmare of a neighborhood. It's easy to see how this place might maintain its privacy—the Four-Faced Liar doesn't offer anything spectacular: one TV, 10 beers on tap, and what they claim to be among the city's best Guinness pours. Neither posh nor dingy, with knick-knacks lining the walls and cluttering the front window, it's a good place to knock back a few pints sans distractions or entertainment. (A reading series is offered on Sundays, though.) Hungry for the standard pub grub that's commonly found in places like this? This spot's lack of a kitchen provides the Four-Faced Liar one surprise.

1492 Food

60 Clinton St. (Rivington & Stanton Sts.)
Lower East Side 646.654.1114

In 1400 and 92 Columbus sailed the ocean blue, and over 500 years later we have this warm, comfy Spanish restaurant to enjoy. With a beautiful garden patio out back, 1492 sets sail with delicious tapas that run from $6-$10 and appetizers like beef tenderloin with asparagus and empanadas with tuna that go from $8-$14. There's often a wait for dinner, so grab a mango margarita or strawberry caipiroska to savor at the bar. 1492's marvelous sangria is also worth getting punch-drunk for. Be sure to ask for a table out back, even if it means waiting a bit longer.

420 Bar & Lounge

420 Amsterdam Ave. (@ 80th St.)
Upper West Side 212.579.8450

This low-lit lounge lures mostly young, professional Upper West Siders into its embrace. Though early in the week 420 is a virtual ghost town, Wednesdays heat up with karaoke night, which seems to be a requirement for uptown bars. Fortunately, a DJ spins on Fridays and Saturdays. There are three bars to choose from, with plenty of dark corners for carousing and canoodling, but the retro/cheesy tiger-print barstools and curtains would've been cool about 10 years ago, and come to think of it, so would the majority of the patrons. It's hard to see what the draw is, but there's no accounting for taste—especially when your drinking buddies are accountants.

Frank's Cocktail Lounge

660 Fulton St. (@ S. Elliott St.)
Fort Greene 718.625.9339

Don't let the divey exterior fool you—there's nothing sketchy about this Christmas lights-trimmed neighborhood watering hole. With a long bar in front and booths and tables in back, Frank's has a diner-like feel and a social atmosphere filled with genuinely friendly regulars thrilled to be done with work for the day, night, or weekend. The few poseurs sprinkled in among the mostly legit crowd don't spoil the divey cheer. Not a place for persnickety drinkers or booze connoisseurs, as the bartenders aren't the most brilliant in the business, this is the perfect spot for an after-work drink before heading to the real nightlife bars. Though things pick up once the DJ starts spinning, it's better for a quick drink than a long-term commitment.

Frank's 410

410 W. 16th St. (9th & 10th Aves.)
Chelsea 212.243.1349

You've been looking forward to seeing Frank's 410. In fact, you even called ahead to make sure your reservation was intact. And now…it's closed? Located on an otherwise socially desolate block (read: loading docks, warehouses, and the like), the ultra-understated façade, consisting of a few overhead lights and a row of papered-over, glass-paneled front doors, practically invites newcomers to conclude that the place is no more. Au contraire. Recently relocated, the old-school steakhouse, originally established in 1912, is alive and kicking. With a walk-through butcher shop

Frank's 410

connecting the restaurant to the expansive Chelsea Market upstairs, Frank's does steaks to an alarmingly delicious effect. Check out their impressive wine list while you wait for your medium rare to be barely cooked to perfection.

Fraunces Tavern
54 Pearl St. (@ Broad St.)
Financial District 212.968.1776

This tavern looks like it's seen better days—in 1768, the very first New York Chamber of Commerce originally met here, as did the Sons of Liberty, who roused support for the coming revolution. George Washington was also a frequent visitor, and chose this spot to give his farewell speech after the Revolutionary War. Revolutionary artifacts and battle murals still grace the tavern's hallowed walls, but these days it's mostly Wall Streeters and financial types who come by for post-work brouhahas. The classic menu is hearty if a bit bland—there's a 16-oz. New York strip steak and chicken with a garlic glaze—but it's the boisterous 4pm-6pm happy hour with $3 drafts that makes after-work visitors' sobriety a part of history.

Freddy's Bar & Backroom
485 Dean St. (@ 6th Ave.)
Brooklyn 718.622.7035

Going by the decrepit blue shade hanging outside Freddy's, you might mistake this worn-in Brooklyn classic for an underachieving dump. Not that Freddy's isn't a delectable dive—the cheap beers, a "whatever" 'tude, and scruffy gaggle of all-hours regulars attest to that. A former speakeasy, bowling alley, and cop bar, Freddy's is best-known as a fringe art space. Its large backroom doubles as a gallery for local artists and the Rev 99 (a TV airing improv television), while the stage sports unknown bands belting out everything from bluegrass and folk to "Minimalist Brooklyn Chick Jazz"…woo-hoo! All the fun is cover-free, as is the clientele-published literary zine, "Lurch." Freddy's also has foosball, board games, random books, and monthly meetings with the Brooklyn Libertarian Party. How's that for an underachiever?

Frederick's
8 W. 58th St. (5th & 6th Aves.)
Midtown 212.752.6200

A SoHo house that's still cool, a Friars Club for the un-funny, a cocktail stop for the *Eyes Wide Shut*

crowd; there are a lot of ways of seeing this place, but seeing it is a must. One of the more elite lounges in town, this half-members, half-civilians hotspot is straight out of a movie. Anyone looking to enter this modern haunt of old-school exclusivity should dress up and be on their best behavior. If that seems like a hassle, apply for a $1,000 membership and enjoy the private member's room of this two-room haunt. (There is technically a third room with a few chairs, but they put you right under the nose of a stoic sushi chef.) Drinks are $12-$14 and they taste like a million bucks in these chi-chi confines.

Frederick's Madison
768 Madison Ave. (@ 66th St.)
Upper East Side 212.737.7300

When uptown restaurants try to appear "downtown," they often come across like obese Midwesterners who think that tight pants will make them look thin. Frederick's is an Upper East Side indulgence that knows who it is and what it's doing. A small upscale restaurant with bistro nuances and perfect service, this cozy place is picking up where neighbors like the now-defunct Le Cirque and certainly endangered Harry Cipriani left off. The servings here are labeled "Mediterranean," and with French and Italian influences, the menu spans its regional shores. Entrées in the $16-$42 neighborhood include a wonderful rack of lamb, but seafood figures most prominently. The crowd varies from elderly mon-eyed locals in Polo shirts to young nouveau Upper East Siders who dress to the nines before taking the complimentary in-house limo to Frederick's club space on 58th Street.

Freemans
8 Rivington St. (@ Freeman Alley)
Lower East Side 212.420.0012

Most alleys offer urinating drunks, homeless people looking for food, and Robert Downey, Jr. Thanks to a rightfully popular hipster restaurant, Freeman Alley is different. Tucked into a hard-to-find LES/SoHo netherworld, this fancied-up shack is packed wall-to-wall with taxidermy and good-

Freemans

looking people. Fittingly, American comfort food is what's for dinner and from sea to shining sea, and from wild boar to mashed potato, the wild frontier theme is complete. Maybe it's also part of their shtick, but Freemans doesn't take reservations, so only the strong, and patient, will endure the wait. The staff is rather friendly so long as you're not a Bush twin: It was reported last year that Texas's version of the Hilton sisters were told there'd be a four-year wait when they arrived here after their daddy's re-election.

French Roast
78 W. 11th St. (@ 6th Ave.)
Greenwich Village 212.533.2233

This French bistro is open around the clock and it seems to always be teeming with a bustling crowd. There's the morning crew doing the coffee and croissant thing, a lunch crew doing croquets, dinner dates sitting on the banquette with steak frites and glasses of wine, and late-nighters slurping one last beer. Sure, there's a bar, but French Roast isn't the place to go for anything but a coffee drink or maybe a glass of wine. And while French Roast has a romantic atmosphere, it's not going to score you any first-date points; it's more of a "been married for a while and got a sitter for the night" kind of place. Still, if you're sick of the Starbucks that are slowly taking over the Village, head to French Roast for a non-corporate caffeine fix.

The Front Bar (@ the Four Seasons Hotel)
99 E. 52nd St. (Park & Lexington Aves.)
Midtown 212.754.9494

If Gordon Gecko from the movie *Wall Street* was a real guy—and we're sure he's a dime a dozen—he'd be hanging out at the Front Bar, and your poverty-stricken ass wouldn't be allowed anywhere near the place. This oddly retro bar (tucked in a corner of the legendary Grill Room) feels ripped out of the "Greed is Good" '80s handbook, right down to the black leather and slightly scary sharp brass-needle sculpture hanging from the ceiling. The bar is full of heiresses, VIPs, and captains of industry trying to woo their next trophy wife over a plate of wild boar. Front Bar's staffed with attentive and talented bartenders, but they're only going to indulge you until the next mogul or robber baron takes a stool. And with $15 cocktails, this swank place screams BYOB (as in bankroll).

Fubar
305 E. 50th St. (1st & 2nd Aves.)
Midtown 212.872.1325

FUBAR may be army-speak for "f**ked up beyond all recognition," but this neighborhood dive bar is anything but. It's clearly identifiable as an oasis of cool amidst a sea of dull, identical pubs. Fubar feels like it should be on Bleecker Street, not in the heart of corporate New York. It's artfully grimy and dismal (without being gross), and has some of the cheapest beer deals in the neighborhood; during happy hour, all drinks are $1 off and Miller Lite draughts are only $3, and on Wednesdays, margarita pints are only $5. A pool table in the back feels as welcoming as the one you used to play in your friend's parents' basement; but here, you don't have to worry about his folks busting you for sneaking a beer.

Fuelray
68 W. 3rd St. (LaGuardia Pl. & Thompson St.)
Greenwich Village 212.995.1900

Pick up a drink, a spring roll, and a date at Fuelray. This intimate lounge has two bars, lounge areas, and a fauna-filled outdoor patio—and more than one couple has rounded second base in these seductive surroundings. If you're looking for

Fuelray

something to nibble on besides your date, there's a great selection of finger foods, like fondue and skewers. If Jäger on tap isn't up your alley, let the inhibition-loosening libations, 21 in all, do the trick—we like the Thai Me Up, but that's really more of a fetish thing, isn't it? Once the liquor kicks in, kick back on a banquette and raise a glass to Fuelray.

Fujiyama Mama
467 Columbus Ave. (81st & 82nd Sts.)
Upper West Side 212.769.1144

This uptown sushi restaurant didn't just hop on the sushi bandwagon—it's been around since the late 1980s. If you've got the 15 bucks required to get a table, start your night right by having the friendly staff bring you a seaweed salad or Tomiyama chan (spicy soup with shrimp and veggies). Then wrap your chopstick around fresh fixin's from the reasonably priced sushi bar, while the live DJ shuffles laidback house music. Or, put all your chump change towards a Japanese import at the bar. You can't go wrong with one of their cocktails, especially the Bonsai (sake and plum wine, $6).

The Full Shilling
160 Pearl St. (Wall & Pine Sts.)
Financial District 212.422.3855

The Full Shilling could be a poster child for the authentic Irish pub—not only do the bartenders and the Bushmills hark from the Emerald Isle but so do, in fact, the entire carved wooden bar and other furnishings, all of which were shipped over from Belfast. The draft selection will keep you busy throughout the night—Old Speckled Hen or Smithwick's Ale, anyone? The decent pub grub draws a sizeable lunchtime crowd. It'll cost ye more than a shilling, but the blackened catfish ($13.95), Portobello burger ($10.95), shepherd's pie, and bangers and mash (for the uninitiated, bangers go great with Guinness) will all stick to your ribs nicely. Now THIS is what we call a cool, real-deal Irish pub.

Funhouse
160 N. 4th St. (Bedford & Driggs Aves.)
Williamsburg 718.302.4300

Move over Galapagos—the Funhouse is where it's at. On weekends, this raw warehouse-sized space becomes a futuro-circus-esque party filled with Williamsburg's prime movers and shakers. Peel back the plastic drapes and find yourself in a coolly lit private room where white plastic bag-chic floors offset the long couches. Or pull up with a $3 Bud to the main "stage" where poets attempt to entertain the half-listening crowd of ultra-hip artists and people, who, you know, happen to have a couple of projects going on right now that might just happen to be funded by Mommy and Daddy. On Monday nights, the victor of the ping-pong tournament walks away with 20 free drink tickets. Welcome to the Funhouse—a haven for the weird and beautiful.

Fusion
818 10th Ave. (54th & 55th Sts.)
Hell's Kitchen 212.397.1133

Don't let the fancy name cause confusion—Fusion isn't some über-hip, velvet-roped club. Thank God. Instead, it's an upscale hangout blending after-work media types, Hell's Kitchen regulars, and new-to-the-'hood hipsters. The space is great to look at—a blend of modern fixtures and art up front and retro furniture and bright walls in the back. Keep going and you'll hit the garden where you can smoke or grab a table and order food that's imported from a nearby diner. Happy hour runs daily from 4pm-7pm, offering a buck or two off beer, wine, and fruity cocktails like Lola's Lazy Juice or the Mango Mojito. The best deal is the Fusion Rewards Card that earns you a $20 drink credit for every $100 spent.

Fuzion on A
211 Ave. A (@ 13th St.)
East Village 212.533.5188

This trendy-looking yet sparsely populated bar and restaurant is not the place to go to get wasted and dance on a table. But if you're looking to have an intimate conversation with a friend or lovahhh, the dark, candlelit décor and comfy, pillow-lined seats lend themselves to the task, as do the Pan-Asian hors d'oeuvres menu with treats like shrimp tempura and yam fries and the $8 menu of sake-infused martinis with names like Concubine, Iron Monkey, and Sweet Samurai. The indoor waterfalls and dragon head over the bar add to the atmosphere, although the service is a little slow even when not busy. Slightly upscale but without attitude, Fuzion on A adds a touch of swank to a neighborhood that mostly values stank.

G Lounge
225 W. 19th St. (7th & 8th Aves.)
Chelsea 212.929.1085

We all know that personality gets you only so far in life. In Chelsea, it ain't that far at all. And at this haughty nightspot, your friendliness, sense of humor, and intelligence don't amount to one of the bar's $8 cosmos unless you've got the looks to back it all up. G, you see, may as well stand for glamour. At first, this place seems rather clique-y. After a few minutes, it starts seeming really, real-

G Lounge

ly clique-y. So why do people come here if they're anything short of David Barton poster boy status? One look through the large arched window reveals eye candy that's simply worth the effort. If one walk around the circular bar doesn't net results, make the second one a strut and you just might get some G-male.

Gabriel's Wine Bar & Restaurant
11 W. 60th St. (Broadway & Columbus Ave.)
Upper West Side 212.956.4600

There's a constant sense of collision and competition at Gabriel's Wine Bar and Restaurant. Its fine reputation and close proximity to Lincoln Center guarantees a prudish pre-opera crowd, but its mutual proximity to Midtown adds a hearty dash of the trendy post-work, pre-dangerous liaison playground. Matrons, mavens, and hawks rub elbows along the bar and spacious dining area while the artwork competes for attention: cool, polished wall murals by owner Gabriel's wife, artist Christine Keefe, abutting a crazy spread of children's finger paintings—original artwork (signed and titled, of course) by Gabriel's son's preschool class. Even the plates are painted, and those works of art are best viewed after chowing through this restaurant's renowned Northern Italian cuisine. In the spirit of spirits, wine and cocktails are their specialty, and their bar olives are the best around.

The Gael Pub
1465 3rd Ave. (82nd & 83rd Sts.)
Upper East Side 212.517.4141

Toto, I don't think we're on the Upper East Side anymore. This gothic-looking bar is incredibly minimalist and gives off the impression that it's trying to be a non-UES high-class lounge, but when you spot the U2 posters, you wonder why the owners spent money on them when they could've hired a decorator. Gael has an impressive display of booze, but it's unclear whether they spent enough money on advertising, given its lack of anything resembling a crowd. One thing about Gael that trumps venues within a 30-block radius, though, are the beautifully designed restrooms, which look like they cost more than all three Brother Jimmy's locations combined.

The Gaf
401 W. 48th St. (@ 9th Ave.)
Hells Kitchen 212.307.7536

One small step into the Gaf is one giant leap for Midtowners looking to duck the 9-5 hydraulic press of drones desperate to get their fivers' worth at neighboring watering holes. Sure, the Gaf draws a crowd, but it's not the work-in-the-area defacto set. Barstool banter runs the gamut of so-how-small-is-your-apartment and where-are-you-from, but plenty of patrons steer clear, obsessing instead over a rack of videogame terminals. Women—more comfortable here than in many Ninth Avenue wood-paneled pens—often commandeer the machines, with pints of Guinness at their side. Drink hearty: You've found the Irish bar every wage slave in this ZIP code is hunting. And if you've found a seat, even better still. Now order a Gaf Brew Irish Amber, watch the overhead TVs, and discover why this Irish pub's name translates to "place to go."

Galapagos Art Space
70 N. 6th St. (Kent & Wythe Aves.)
Williamsburg 718.782.5188

Galapagos Art Space

The wall sconces at varying heights seem like they'd be a pain to light, but they lend a star-spangled quality to this cabaret institution. Snippy bar staff and a strict door policy are minor hindrances worth overlooking for the wide variety of entertainment; the large stage hosts everything from rock 'n' roll puppets to burlesque starlets. Ample tables and barstools allow patrons to take a load off at this one-time mayonnaise factory. The deep reflecting pool passed on the way in is smartly

lined with handrails to prevent embarrassment or worse. Specialty cocktails include the $8 Green Tea or the $9 Tortoise. Simpler tastes and smaller wallets can opt for "G": the $4 house beer on tap made just for the venue. Minimal covers often apply.

Galaxy Global Eatery
15 Irving Pl. (@ 15th St.)
Gramercy 212.777.3631

For a head trip out of this world, visit the Galaxy Global Eatery. The space-themed and spaced-out restaurant rocketed to stardom after being featured on the Food Network for its innovative lunar-hippy menu and has been packed ever since. The restaurant features dishes containing hempseed, which has numerous "nutritional" values—among other things. A great place to get and cure the munchies, Galaxy's jap chae is a favorite, as is the down-to-earth turkey meatloaf. No entrées are over $15 and the view is cool too; gaze up at the star-covered ceiling while relaxing in a far-out, oversized, black vinyl booth and sipping one of the restaurant's 15 creative cocktails. This kitchen is so strong that it sometimes makes nearby Irving Plaza smell like weed when bands like Fischer-Spooner play.

The Gallery (@ the SoHo Grand)
310 W. Broadway (@ Grand St.)
SoHo 212.965.3000

Still a great spot to see the ridiculous vanities of celebrities up close, the Gallery at the SoHo Grand gracefully looks past its $5,000 suites to cater to the rank and file. Occupying a minimal, tastefully decorated dining room, the Gallery is all understated charm. Drinks range from $8-$15, and the weekend brunch is open to the public. Regulars (is that Bobby Brown over there?) swear by the Bloody Marys, too. Check out the rotating photography exhibits on your way out to the back garden, which is as friendly as the yard you grew up in back in Long Island. You'd think this place would risk ridicule, being the late-night stomping ground of so many *Us Weekly* refugees, but the Gallery at the SoHo Grand maintains enough down-home humanity to retain a plainly comfortable everyman appeal.

Gallery Lounge (@ the Gershwin Hotel)
7 W. 27th St. (Madison & 5th Aves.)
Murray Hill 212.447.5700

Inside the trendy Gershwin Hotel is the Gallery Bar—a shrine to art, Austin Powers, and Prohibition. Walk past the long, wavy bar and be greeted by a huge room with high ceilings and plush, bright red- and orange-hued furniture under huge flowers that are painted onto the walls. Despite the hipness, most people here are friendly, and that covers the patrons, staff, and DJs who spin in the "secret" backroom, which looks like it was created solely for the purpose of storing bootlegged hooch. No need for moonshine here—just order a bottle of beer, bottle service, or a serviceable specialty drink, and enjoy the far-out scene, man. The artsy hotel above is pretty cheap, as it's clearly going for a modern and new-fangled Chelsea Hotel appeal.

The Garden of Ono
18 9th Ave. (Gansevoort & 13th Sts.)
Meatpacking District 212.660.6766

There are hotels, and then there are HOTELS. The Gansevoort just added another layer of activity to its general premises and it comes in the form of a big, lush, and hip outdoor space called the Garden of Ono. (Technically, the Garden of Ono isn't a part of the Gansevoort Hotel, but this seasonal outpost butts up against the Meatpacking District's sole hotel.) Hipness grows in these lush confines, which were a joint effort between BPC, who built Miami's Sky Bar, and Jeffrey Chodorow, whose Ono restaurant sits a tuna roll's throw from this new space. A velvet rope separates passerby from this reservations-recommended greenery where a light sushi menu is served to trend-obsessed scenesters who come here pre-clubbing when weather permits. There are four private cabanas for the moneyed set that likes to go out and be left

The Garden of Ono

alone, but plebeians can enjoy Asian-inspired cocktails at the tables, which abound.

Gardens Bar
493 Myrtle Ave. (Hall & Ryerson Sts.)
Fort Greene 718.783.9335

The collection of old-timers, oddballs, and pseudo-slick Pratt students watching sports while surrounded by faux-wood paneling and sparse furniture at this dive bar evokes the feel of hanging out in your neighbor's musty basement while life outside passes by unnoticed. It's not exactly a "garden" as billed, but the immense back deck is pretty much this 15-year-old neighborhood bar's greatest asset. This bar rates a zero on the hip scale, making it either totally unappealing or the best undiscovered place in the neighborhood, depending on how many beers you've had. Bottles of Bud are just $2.75; but then again, a tall one at the bodega will cost you just two dollars—so for 75 cents less, you can get pretty much the same experience drinking alone on your fire escape.

Garvey's
270 W. 45th St. (@ 8th Ave.)
Hell's Kitchen 212.997.6400

Garvey's is a surprisingly warm neighborhood bar (in Times Square of all places), the kind of joint where you can kick back with a beer and forget the tourist trap that surrounds you. Tucked beneath the Milford Plaza Hotel, the bar's only a few steps down but it's like a step into another world. Maybe it's the red walls, the vintage arcade games, or the bartender's winning smile, but Garvey's is not a place that's easy to leave—although, when 2 million tourists are shopping for knock-off handbags just outside, any place would be hard to leave. Regulars from the neighborhoods come in to cheer on their pals in the Tuesday night pool league while enjoying 18 beers on tap—ask them why, and they'll tell you: "Charm."

Gaslight Lounge
400 W. 14th St. (@ 9th Ave.)
Meatpacking District 212.807.8444

If you still find the Meatpacking District's posh and pretty condition a little intimidating, Gaslight may be the perfect place to get your feet wet—not to mention your beak. On a scenic corner separating the Hotel Gansevoort's cobblestone-lined road from Western Beef's sidewalk of stink, Gaslight is a crowded and jovial hangout for the young, pretty, and less well-connected. Welcoming and social, this place rocks on Thursdays when the crowds are minimal but lively. And don't be thrown by the velvet ropes outside—it's not a hate pit where evil doorman lurk, but rather a sectioned-off smokers' hangout with a little flair. This is one

Gaslight Lounge

of those places that's very party-friendly, so calling and planning a visit might net your group seating and a say in the music that's played.

The Gate
321 5th Ave. (3rd & 4th Sts.)
Park Slope 718.768.4329

The Gate

How better to spend a balmy summer evening than outside with beer in hand, dog by your side, surrounded by a bevy of Park Slope 20-something singles? In recent years the Gate has definitely felt a seismic shift from folksy local to modern hipster haunt, as has this neighborhood. The outdoor garden doubles the bar's capacity, and there's a portioned dart room, which cuts down on drunken impalements. As with many neighborhoody Brooklyn bars, the Gate is probably at its best on Saturday afternoons when it becomes more or less a day in the park, complete with roaming pooches.

Gatsby's Bar & Lounge
53 Spring St. (Lafayette & Mulberry Sts.)
NoLita 212.334.4430

F. Scott Fitzgerald would probably roll over in his grave if he chanced upon this less-than-great frat boy-infested pub named after his debonair hero Gatsby. Any association between the two is, well, nonexistent, though you can't fault them for trying: Gatsby's mint julep ($10)—bourbon whiskey, syrup, and sprigs of mint—is on offer, as are 22 kinds of Scotch, and the menu sports a quote about the Great Gatsby's legendary parties: "People were not invited…they went there." And

Gatsby's Bar & Lounge

that kind of free-for-all mayhem pretty much sums up this spot. If getting tanked in a dark, rambunctious, meat-market pub is your idea of a good time, then you'll probably love this place—as do the hordes willing to stand on line to get in on late-night Fridays and Saturdays. There's also decent pub grub to soak up the alcohol if you actually have to, like, work the next day.

Geisha
33 E. 61st St. (Madison & Park Aves.)
Upper East Side 212.813.1112

There's a plethora of strange little "members only" Japanese piano lounges in this area, and they're all hoping to capture the imagination of homesick Japanese businessmen hoping to live out a fantasy or two. Geisha seems to take that idea to a fun, practical, and slightly commercialized extreme. That, and they throw excellent modern Japanese cuisine into the mix. Pumpkin, curry—you name it and you'll smell it on Geisha's well-slathered fish entrées. (There's pork and chicken as well, but the seafood shines.) As you might image, the sake list is extensive and expensive, but specialty cocktails

like the green tea Zen cocktail ($12) are not to be ignored. The louder downstairs area is roomy and lively, but the smooth lounge upstairs is quite intimate.

General Store
29 Ave. B (2nd & 3rd Sts.)
East Village 212.254.0055

The old-timey wooden interior of glass cookie jars and stacks of coffee cans behind the bar, combined with the gourmet-yet-familiar breakfast skillets and out-of-this-world coffee, make General Store the perfect spot to dish with your pals while surfing the Sunday morning hangover wave. The easy vibe matches the comfort food and a fair list of wine and beer gets along well with mixed drinks like cider and mimosas. The daytime hours make for a folksy afternoon experience, but those looking through the oversized windows are more likely to see bed-headed hipsters and shopping cart-pushing crackheads than they are horses and buggies. Items like pecan pie are to be expected, but this General Store surprises with things like lobster pot pie.

The George Keeley
485 Amsterdam Ave. (83rd & 84th Sts.)
Upper West Side 212.873.0251

The George Keeley is a bit of a McPub—not veering in the slightest from the staid décor and expected amenities found in most of New York's Irish bars. (Dartboard, jukebox, etc.) For the unde-

The George Keeley

cided drinker, there is a beer sampler, consisting of four 5-oz. tasters for $7. Happy hour consists of $3 pints Monday through Friday from 4pm-8pm. If listening to live music is your cup o' Guinness, they offer it up on Wednesdays, and there's also an open mic night on Tuesdays. There are no alarms and no surprises here, which seems to be exactly what these locals want from their neighborhood pub.

Giggles
115 W. 40th St. (@ Broadway)
Midtown 212.840.1900

Keeping a shingle hanging in the New York restaurant business for 25 years is no laughing matter. Giggles has done it, though, and it's still boasting some of the heartiest, most committed regulars this side of the Soup Nazi. Giggles is the destination of choice for the Garment District after close-of-business. It stands two enormous floors tall, teeming with tables, walls covered with kitschy posters, and gads of antique touches throughout, though the big, friendly wooden bar downstairs is the centerpiece for it all. Burgers and steaks are popular, and everything's cheap ($7-$14 for entrées). Smart money says the fish bowl booze is what really keeps 'em coming back; stick a straw in one of those for a mere $14. Yep, you'll be giggling alright.

The Gin Mill
442 Amsterdam Ave. (81st & 82nd Sts.)
Upper West Side 212.580.9080

Like the Olsen twins, there isn't much of a noticeable difference between the Gin Mill and its twin Jake's Dilemma around the way (similar bar menu, cheap drink specials, and alternative rock juke jams). However, if it's sports that you want, Gin Mill is your bar. Sporting a more restaurantly than loungey set-up in back, the Gin Mill is perfect for joining local fans and frat-types in rooting for the home team. And with more boob tubes per capita than Jake's, it's the perfect spot for sports fans who usually miss most of the first inning after fighting with your friends about what sport (or team) you're gonna watch.

The Ginger Man

The Ginger Man
11 E. 36th St. (5th & Madison Aves.)
Murray Hill 212.532.3740

A mega-pub for mega-drinkers, the Ginger Man doesn't tread gingerly on the subject of beer. With 63 drafts and 120 bottled brews, this upscale tavern has been a jolly haunt for hops-lovers since it hit the "ale-ing" Murray Hill scene in 1997. For old boys who frequent the joint, there are 20 single-malt Scotches and fine imported cigars. The dark wood, amber-lit lounge comes complete with lots of leather sofas, wooden tables, and cozy corners for all, plus a huge mahogany bar where worker bees swarm for after-hours boss-bashing. Sandwiches, cheese plates, and bratwurst are served to soak up the suds, though the "Guinness Stew" will probably add to your beer buzz. Despite the upscale surrounds, the Ginger Man gets dive bar-style rowdy on weekends and after work.

Ginger's
363 5th Ave. (5th & 6th Sts.)
Park Slope 718.788.0924

Between the cheap drinks at happy hour, pleasant outdoor seating in the patio garden, and the Friday night DJ, Ginger's is the consummate party bar for the ladies who love ladies. Things can get a little rough-and-tumble in the back pool room, but from the looks of the "one person in the bathroom at a time" sign, it seems most patrons here like it that way. The jukebox kicks up the fun with the grrl-friendly rock of Melissa Etheridge, Tracy Chapman, and "Ginger's Mix," while the orange retro chairs and velvet couches house lots of girls who know what girls want: a no-frills, no-gimmicks, neigh-

Gaslight is open seven days a week and 365 days a year.

DJ spinning nightly

Never a cover/Never closes early

Great for private parties or corporate events (20-400 people)

"The Gaslight is an anomaly. The Gaslight is a refuge. Best of all, no one comes to impress; they come to enjoy."
—*THE NEW YORK TIMES*

"One of the world's best bars."
—*BESTBARS.COM*

"Truly one of the pioneers of the Meatpacking District movement, Gaslight has stayed strong and true to its original mission."
—*SHECKY'S 2005*

"It's so comfortable. It's like being in your living room but with a lot of extra perks!"
—*THE VILLAGER 2005*

400 W. 14th St. (@ 9th Ave.), Meatpacking District • Phone: 212.807.8444 • Fax: 212.807.8555

**Coming soon...
VIP private party room for 100!**

High ceilings and a handmade marble bar are the centerpieces of the MPD's newest addition.

Private banquettes, overstuffed handmade furniture & ornate tin ceilings envelop you as the DJ spins. Great for private parties (20-400 people).

"A new version of the Meatpacking District's hottest bar, Gaslight."
—*SHECKY'S 2005*

"'NYC's best place to throw a party and the Meatpacking District's most comfortable venue. The jewel of the Meatpacking District... a diamond in the rough."
—*SHOW BUSINESS WEEKLY*

"A perfect sequel to the original Gaslight!"
—*THE VILLAGER 2005*

Available for photo shoots, private parties & corporate meetings.

Open to the public Thursday, Friday & Saturday for weekend and holiday parties; call in advance— we've been sold out since opening day!

39 Ninth Ave. (@ 14th St.), Meatpacking District • Phone: 212.807.8444 • Fax: 212.807.8555

borhood lesbian bar with no surprises…like a penis. Everyone's invited to this party; gay, straight, bi, or just curious; so round up a pleasure-seeking posse and go down to Ginger's.

Giorgio's of Gramercy
27 E. 21st St. (Broadway & Park Ave. S.)
Flatiron 212.477.0007

Asking someone on a first date can be tough. Picking the right place can be tougher still. At Giorgio's velvet curtains and banquettes set the mood and the long, gleaming wooden bar and the open kitchen, visible behind glass blocks, show that you are a dater of impeccable taste. But with so many picky eaters out there, how are you to know what kind of cuisine your date digs? No fear here, because diversity is Giorgio's middle name—the $17-$28 entrées combine Italian, American, Greek, and French faves. And even if the date doesn't work out, these prices aren't astronomical, so you'll still have some spending money left over to try again tomorrow. While a lack of specificity stops this place from being an "All-City" star, the something-for-everyone approach makes it a local favorite.

The Girl from Ipanema
252 W. 14th St. (7th & 8th Aves.)
West Village 212.807.0150

This is the kind of place that your friends insist you visit because it will be funny—a real trip—but you just leave feeling depressed and dirty. Women should beware the geriatric Latin lovers who insist on dancing at the least inopportune times and the aggressive pool sharks dividing their time between brooding and ogling. And was that working girl skulking around the billiard room once the *boy* from Ipanema? Those are big hands for a chick. Still, one drink could be the impetus for a colorful evening, if not an intriguing sociological study. More than one drink here, however, could lead to an out-and-out disaster. This place has all the "charm" of a border-town bar, and while it's just outside of the Meatpacking District, it's still worlds away.

Girlsroom
210 Rivington St. (Pitt & Ridge Sts.)
Lower East Side 212.677.6149

Are lesbians as enjoyable to watch in real-life as they are on TV? The ladies who pack Girlsroom every Tuesday through Saturday seem to think so. DJs spin nightly, Saturdays offer $5 cosmos and apple martinis, naked karaoke is on Tuesday, and an energetic clientele defies the norm at this lesbian bar. Never mind that the furnishings are bare and crummy-looking, the beer selection dismal, and a humongous, horn-shaped piece of driftwood adorns the wall above the bar. The creative gyrations on the dance floor make up for the college dorm room look. One caveat—with its abundance of young cuties and XX chromosome combos (straight and gay), Girlsroom is not the right spot to meet a life partner, or ponder queer theory aloud—this place is hopping, and the dark corners aren't meant for talking.

Gladys' Comedy Room
145 W. 45th St. (6th & 7th Aves.)
Midtown 212.832.1762

If you've got one of those friends who's always laughing harder than anyone else at his own jokes, you might want to exact revenge by talking him into signing up for this laugh shelter's Talent Night (Wednesdays, 7:30pm-11pm). By the time you've ordered the requisite $6 table minimum (food or beverages, Gladys isn't picky), the audience will have thrown their beers and/or burgers at him and you will have proven once and for all that Michael Jackson jokes are so last year. On a funnier note, Gladys' offers a discount for any adult under five feet (with proof of height). Minors are allowed inside too, but the comedians here won't censor their acts. Dave Chappelle isn't likely to pop in here, but for $8 cover, Gladys' is worth a try.

Glass
287 10th Ave. (26th & 27th Sts.)
Chelsea 212.904.1580

What the pretty people waiting in line to get into Marquee don't know is that the giant translucent window they're primping themselves in is actually a bar, not a public mirror. And luckily for those people, Glass is a close swanky second to the A-list clubs they were unable to get into. Glass's glossy bar top and matching walls form a cooling sensation that sets the tone for a rather roomy outdoor back area which is perfect for drowning your "evil doorman" sorrows. Semi-translucent tables emit pastel colors, further adding to a sleekness that walks the line between over-the-top and unique. Even the cocktails spell breeze and ease—caiprinhas and flavored mojitos like the mojito rosa—proving that on many nights, "top club" rejections are a blessing in disguise.

Glo

431 W. 16th St. (9th & 10th Aves.)
Chelsea 212.229.9119

If you're going to "do" an all-access club kind of thing, you do it like Glo. You probably won't find Cain or Bungalow 8's A-list crowd here, but you also won't find doormen who make you feel like an A-hole for not being a model. Formerly Powder,

Glo is a well-designed space where everybody can see and be seen, whether they're on the main-floor dance space, the slightly elevated VIP area that wraps around it on three sides, or the second-floor terrace area on the fourth side. Big screens abound, flashing images of the cosmos, flowers, and all things trippy. DJs spin hip-hop and some pop, with Bon Jovi and AC/DC riffs begging for sing-alongs and encouraging the all-boroughs crowd to throw their hands and plastic cups in the air. Think 3/4 Avalon and 1/4 Marquee.

Gold Rush

493 10th Ave. (37th & 38th Sts.)
Hell's Kitchen 212.244.5165

Wanna hook up with an off-duty cop or firefighter? Go west, young man…or woman. Yes, housed within an utterly out-of-place '49er mill house on 10th Avenue is Gold Rush, Hell's Kitchen's salute to westward expansion. Inside, you'll find stuffed animal heads, Western paraphernalia and, of course, the aforementioned blue-collar fellas blowing off a bit of steam. With a jukebox featuring mostly loud American rock and midriff-baring bartenders who call you "honey," you may forget you're in Manhattan. The food prices—high for mediocre saloon fare—will bring you back to the

Glo

borough. Get your bargain brews during happy hour or on union nights ($2 beers and bring proof of membership!)—that's when the West (or at least this version of it) gets most wild.

Gonzalez y Gonzalez
625 Broadway (Bleecker & Houston Sts.)
NoHo 212.473.8787

The tacky yet captivating flashing sombrero outside of Gonzalez y Gonzalez is an accurate sampling of the festivities that one is about to encounter at this enthusiastic south-of-the-border celebration. Presenting a colorful array of red chili pepper lights, lanterns, piñatas, and a city block-long bar, Gonzalez y Gonzalez keeps its patrons drunk y drunk with $4 frozen lime margaritas and $3 draft beers during happy hour (Monday-Thursday 12pm-7pm; Friday-Sunday 12pm-4pm). For dinner, handsome groups of local and touristy 20- and 30-somethings feast on the standard Mexican dishes of chimichangas ($8.95), enchiladas ($7.95), fajitas ($8.95-$13.95), and burritos ($7.95-$8.95), but only after they've located the nearest bathroom. From Thursday through Saturday, late-night live salsa, meringue, bachata, reggaeton, and house tunes keep the Cervezas flowing and the local Latin music fanatics grooving.

Good Restaurant
89 Greenwich Ave. (Bank & 12th Sts.)
West Village 212.691.8080

If you've always wondered what it would be like to eat in an upscale farmhouse, you needn't look any further. This highly original downtown eatery boasts hanging farm tools and kitchen utensils, flower buckets adorn the tables, and countertop splays of grass complete the overall "Americana" effect. Good's cuisine is traditional Contemporary American, albeit with a twist—they've occasionally got corn dogs (but they're made with chicken), the mac 'n' cheese is prepared with green chili, and the donuts are made with orange sour cream. Wash down any of these creative dishes with a Sandia Limonada Martini, which is made with watermelon vodka. Basically, nothing here is what it seems, and that's a good thing.

Good World Bar & Grill
3 Orchard St. (Canal & Division Sts.)
Lower East Side 212.925.9975

Life can be Hell when trying to find Good World Bar & Grill. But once inside the cozy confines, it's easy to forget about time and responsibility. After work, tasty jazz spills out of the speakers and tasty beers (over 100 bottled types) like Carlsberg, Hoegaarden, and De Koninck (all $6 or $7 each) spill from the taps. The menu is Swedish, and it might take a while for the food to get to your table, but hot diggidy, these Swedes can cook. The Swedish meatballs and house burger are superlative, as are the potato pancakes and grilled *vasterbotten* sandwich. DJs have their fun on Friday and Saturday nights, and an occasional band might sing their ditties. The bar's open late every day of the year, because it truly is a good world.

Gotham Bar & Grill
12 E. 12th St. (University Pl. & 5th Ave.)
Greenwich Village 212.620.4020

Gotham Bar & Grill is one of those restaurants that you always hear about and always mean to go to. Having been around for over 20 years, Gotham is something of an institution. The food is consistently raved about; and how can people not talk, with their impressive selection that includes foie gras, miso-marinated black cod, warm upside-down banana rhubarb cake, and a daily assortment of pastas, desserts, and other seasonal menu items. The space is grandiose and elegant, with ceiling-high windows, flowers, and an overall warm, casual vibe. The restaurant is typically packed with couples making goo-goo eyes at each other, though, and the attractive bar holds the singles overflow. A great date spot for amazing food and atmosphere—especially if you don't want to dress up for it.

Gotham Comedy Club
34 W. 22nd St. (5th & 6th Aves.)
Flatiron 212.367.9000

People who endlessly quote *Seinfeld* episodes (we know where you live!) will love this place. Aspiring comedians attempting to glean the tricks from stand-up geniuses like Mr. Seinfeld, Ellen DeGeneres, and Dave Chappelle (all of whom have graced the stage here) might be better off taking one of Gotham's eight-week Stand-Up Comedy courses (or buying *The Complete Idiot's Guide to Stand-Up Comedy*). But people who would rather laugh than be laughed at will enjoy Gotham's nightly shows—the names of which are silly enough to put a smile on your face before the curtain goes up (Homocomicus, Chopshtick). Stars from HBO and Comedy Central come here to try out their acts at "NYC's most elegant, upscale comedy club." Now if hearing "upscale" and "comedy club" in the same sentence doesn't make you laugh, what will?

Gowanus Yacht Club & Beer Garden
323 Smith St. (@ President St.)
Carroll Gardens 718.246.1321

On a starry summer night, nothing seems better than hosting a BBQ with friends on your backyard patio. Unfortunately for most New Yorkers, though, being in actual possession of a backyard is about as likely as the subway fare staying the same price before the year ends. That's where Smith Street's Gowanus Yacht Club comes in; the all-outdoor patio space not only serves beer ($1 cans of PBR) and wine ($5 a glass) to the urban masses, but it also grills up hamburgers (just $4!) and hotdogs ($1.50 for the traditional kind, $3 for a vegan "Not Dog") for them, too. The result is an easy escape from another summer spent sweating in your studio apartment and a nautical-themed backyard porch to adopt as your own.

Gramercy Tavern
42 E. 20th St. (Park Ave. S. & Broadway)
Flatiron 212.477.0777

This perennially popular place attracts everybody from the wealthy to the very wealthy. Gramercy Tavern is a NYC standard for ladies who post-shopping lunch and businessmen who power-lunch. Dinner's a big deal in this warm and sparse space, and the tavern portion of the room doesn't take reservations so visitors actually stand a fighting chance of "popping-in." Jackets are suggested in the dining room, and we don't mean Members Only. The Creative American cuisine is rightfully world-renowned, as it's simple but flavorful with beef being the strong suit. Should the $95, eight-course tasting menu sound too daunting, come by after work for a glass of wine; their superb selection of over 300 bottles makes oenophiles squeal in delight.

Grand Bar and Lounge (@ the SoHo Grand)
310 W. Broadway (@ Grand St.)
SoHo 212.965.3000

Grand Bar and Lounge

Brassy in its overall look, if not its overall attitude, Grand Bar and Lounge at the SoHo Grand is a de rigeur New York experience. Blending in seamlessly with the rest of this opulent hotel, these guys charge a pretty hotel standard $12-$15 for cocktails, but there's plenty of complimentary eye candy. Marisa Tomei and Brooke Shields still saunter around for nightcaps, but they hardly stand out here. The SoHo Grand's sprawling lobby spaces remain one of New York's most consistently enjoyable closing-time refuges, and its modern, Euro-flavored bar is the crown jewel. During the summer months, the adjacent area, The Yard, becomes a very popular spot. But you're not THAT welcome: Unless you've won an Oscar, you may need a reservation toward the weekend. And notice we didn't say, "Unless you were nominated…"

Grand Central
659 Grand St. (Manhattan Ave. & Leonard St.)
Williamsburg 718.387.5515

Grand Central is a great live venue—if you want to see goateed dads in shorts rock their socks off with their Creed cover band. This place tries, it really does; the side room is decked out with retro sectional couches forming conversation pits and seemingly half-assed artwork on the walls, but it misses the hip mark. This is a dive, pure and simple. The drunkard glued to the bar will ask your name over and over after drinking from the puny grain alcohol selection and limited domestic beers on tap. Cheese curls are set out on the bar, but a quick glance around will make you think twice about swapping germs with this crowd. One bonus is the free grill-your-own BBQ.

Grand Press
284 Grand St. (Roebling & Havemeyer Sts.)
Williamsburg 718.218.6955

What it may lack in individual character, Grand Press makes up for in the fact that it's a bar. That serves alcohol. And sometimes, that's all you need. The vibe is somewhere between an Irish pub, a sports bar, and a Phish-y place, but the marquis feature is raised wooden booths conducive to big-group socializing and inviting in newly made friends. There are plenty of toys in back to keep you entertained: a pool table, foosball, and a jukebox, not to mention air hockey (when the DJ isn't using it as a turntable stand). Happy hour does you right with $2 domestics and $3 wells, imports, and draughts. Hungry? Bar policy is that you can order in from any one of the multitude of nearby restaurants—how grand.

Grand Saloon
158 E. 23rd St. (Lexington & 3rd Aves.)
Gramercy 212.477.6161

It was considered grand when it opened in 1880 but now the Grand Saloon is just plain old. And that's not necessarily bad, as its classic New York bar helps to attract a different crowd from the frat bars around the corner. Rather than be ensconced by 20-somethings getting trashed here, you'll get a mixed bag of neighborhood types ranging in ages from the just graduated to the just retired. Service is slow, but the pub grub is worth a short wait. You might try ordering online, as it'll take less time to get your burger to your apartment than to your table. It's friendly, neighborhoody, and cheap, and while the pressed-tin ceilings still provide a bit of charm, the TVs provide considerably more entertainment.

Grassroots Tavern
20 St. Marks Pl. (2nd & 3rd Aves.)
East Village 212.475.9443

Boing…boing…splash! Don't forget your orange life vest because the waters at this dive run pretty deep. The name says it all at Grassroots Tavern, a throwback watering hole. No nubile waitresses wander with trays of Jell-O shots, and if the jukebox is on the fritz, the bartender just might entertain you with stories of horseracing. Hospitality aside, one can't help but sense contempt toward the changes to the St. Marks scene undergone since the Ford administration, none of which have hit Grassroots: It smells stale and the floors are wobbly, but that's not why you're here. You want the $2-$3 happy hour drafts and a bag of popcorn for a buck. Grassroots is a dinosaur, maybe, but after 30 years in the biz, it's also the wise man with a rich secret.

Great Jones Café
54 Great Jones St. (Bowery & Lafayette St.)
NoHo 212.674.9304

Look for the Elvis head with Mardis Gras beads

Great Jones Café

and you've come to the right spot. This gutsy little Southern eatery is NoHo's answer to the Big Easy, with hearty, spicy creations sure to get you all shook up. Dig into the gumbo with shrimp and andouille sausage or jump into the jambalaya, and then sop it all up with a big 'ol hunk of jalapeno cornbread. Those Southerners know their cocktails—start off your weekend right with one of their superb Bloody Marys over brunch, chased down with some ice-cold Southern suds. The jukebox spews out alternately languid and toe-tapping country and hillbilly rock on old 45s, slow-cooking this joint into a comfortable simmer that'll make you want to hang out long after you've finished your Cajun eats.

Great Lakes
285 5th Ave. (1st St. & Garfield Pl.)
Park Slope 718.499.3710

Despite the dead fish mounted on the wall, the boat motor hanging above the bar's large mirror, Salvation Army-ish furniture, and the map of upper New York and Lakes Erie and Ontario above what used to be the live music space in the back, the aquatic theme of this no-pretense, comfortable neighborhood spot on burgeoning Fifth Avenue is commendably subtle and does nothing to distract one from higher purposes—namely, drinking, socializing, and listening to good music. Great Lakes' outstanding jukebox features everything from the Stones to the Clash and Massive Attack, all of whom do much to keep the spirit of this place rockin', especially on the weekends when it hops with young Brooklynites. The cheap drinks and good company are enough to keep you hooked.

Green Room
286 Spring St. (Varick & Hudson Sts.)
SoHo 212.929.8560

You won't find any anxious actors pacing back and forth in this green room, because, alas, the glory days of this upscale nightspot and its starry-eyed, starlet-filled days may have passed—and it's barely a year old! Once sizzling, the Green Room—with its "rider" bottle-service options—has suffered from the cruel fact that the crowd it wants would rather be within stumbling distance to Meatpacking District and West Chelsea clubs. As if you needed more proof, just listen closely while the DJ spins lost classics like "Mary Mary, why you buggin'?" before throwing a Michael Jackson remix on the turntables. The Olsen twin knock-off tending bar might not know how to make a margarita, either, but she says she'll work it out. So wait patiently and take a seat on the low banquette of smooth leather running around the square room and plan your escape to hotter clubs of NYC's here and now. Maybe the DJ will play Hilary Duff's song, "Anywhere But Here," on your way out.

Greenwich Brewing Company
418 6th Ave. (@ 9th St.)
Greenwich Village 212.477.8744

A perpetual hangout for locals and tourists alike, the Greenwich Brewing Company could be considered something of an institution. An institution in the study of beer, that is (that's "cerevisiological" research, for all of you bar-hopping trivia buffs). The boisterous chit-chat and periodic sound of clinking beer glasses proves this neighborhood bar is a mainstay of the Village. The food is standard pub grub and the music selection lacks edge, but you'll be overjoyed by the bar selection—eight home brews, 11 imported micro brews (we dare you to order the 12-ounce Dulle Teve "Mad Bitch"), 26 single-malt Scotches and cordials, and 12 types of wine. If you've got a bad case of cenosillicaphobia (fear of an empty glass), get to the Greenwich Brewing Co., stat.

Groove

Groove
125 MacDougal St. (@ 3rd St.)
Greenwich Village 212.254.9393

Like Kenny's Castaways and a slew of other cheesy, touristy, student hangouts, there's nothing about Groove that's very catchy or rhythmic. The food served here is no surprise, the noise level can be extreme, the dudes are forever out in force, and if you're a single female you'll get bombarded with lame come-ons all night. Every night features a long list of local funk and R&B bands you've never heard of. If you're really a glutton for punishment, come on Wednesdays for the open mic to see people who couldn't get gigs on a normal evening. While you're there, munch on the creatively named Grooveburger while deciding on which of the standard-issue drinks you'll have to meet the minimum drink requirement.

Groovedeck
530 W. 27th St., 6th Fl. (10th & 11th Aves.)
Chelsea 212.594.4109

Groovedeck is the closest an NYC club will ever get to Miami—vices and all. The building it houses feels like the South Street Seaport of West Chelsea, minus the cheesiness. Swank lounge BED is on the highest indoor floor and topping it all in more ways than one is this breathtaking rooftop lounge. Groovedeck's view doesn't rival that of its hotel-topping peers (Pen-Top, AVA), but its lack of high-rise neighbors is a huge plus and the crowd here is infinitely hipper than that of any Midtown bar under the stars. The well-handled bar serves drinks designed by the legendary Dale DeGroff. Big, weather-proofed beds line the perimeter, and

a canopied wooden deck runs down the middle, where a light mist sprays passersby.

Grotta Azzurra
177 Mulberry St. (@ Broome St.)
Little Italy 212.925.8775

"Dis neighborhood ain't what it use ta be and neither is dis restaurant." There's some good and some bad in hearing that. Grotta Azzurra was once Sinatra's favorite restaurant, and that was back before it renovated after years of boarded windows, this time bringing a little ring-a-ding-ding for its newly upscale neighborhood. (Now days, we call that "bling.") It seems only right that this landmark would stand watch over Little Italy's most definitive corner. The front of the room is bathed in gold and marble matched in subtlety only by the Vatican. There is a bar in back for old-timers, and while polished, it's a bit more sedate. Downstairs is a classy, table-stocked wine cellar that doubles as a lounge and private party room. Regardless of the aesthetic changes, Grotta Azzurra's pricey modern-classic menu is impressive and even. Wine is the beverage of choice here—go with it and don't argue.

Grotta Azzurra

Grotto
100 Forsyth St. (Broome & Grand Sts.)
Lower East Side 212.625.3444

Tucked underneath Monterone espresso bar on a quiet block in the outskirts of *Chinatown* is the surprisingly chic Grotto. Seating is plentiful in the rear garden, but expect to get up close and personal with the person next to you at the infinitely long table inside the tiny, dimly lit main room of this Italian eatery. Formerly known as Nautilus, Grotto offers light bistro fare along with classic cocktails such as the Martini Nero, a twist on the standard concoction that's served with roses. The crowd here seems to skew international and isn't as rowdy as at some other downtown hotspots. Grotto is the type of place that people like to keep to themselves…so choose who you bring along carefully.

Gstaad
43 W. 26th St. (Broadway & 6th Ave.)
Flatiron 212.683.1440

Let's get it gstaaded in here. Like the ridges cut into the crisp snow on a fabulous ski weekend in the Alps, so are the clean lines and geometrical shapes that abound in the Swiss lounge Gstaad. Slanted lines, cylinder lights, oval tables, and even square seats with circles cut into them emit the freshness of a bright winter day in Switzerland. The room is big, but conversation-friendly and intimate. A mirror runs the length of the wall so subtly scoping singles is doable. A large projection screen shows short films opposite the long bar that has backlit slats of wood along its base. Gstaad's high ceilings, new age music, and affordable drinks make it a good substitute for that Swiss ski vacation you missed this winter. Pull up a tree stump and enjoy a night among friends.

G2
39 9th Ave. (@ 14th St.)
Meatpacking District 212.807.8444

There's nothing like standing in front of a velvet

G2

rope to take you back to your childhood; the pain, the humiliation, the degrading sense of inadequacy. And people do this for fun? Thankfully, G2, Gaslight Lounge's upscale sister, is waiting patiently to collect our weary souls and scuffed high heels after being rejected by its trendier neighbors. Far friendlier and more welcoming than anything else in the 'hood, G2 is a solid option for those who prefer the mild stench of raw meat in these parts to the social bloodbath at nearby Lotus. Cozy, curtained booths with separate light controls, a DJ Tues-Sun, and a wood-heavy rustic décor give this hangout a warm, fun vibe for those nights when you'd rather chill out than be snubbed by a pock-marked, 400-lb. community college dropout.

Gypsy Tea
27 W. 24th St. (5th & 6th Aves.)
Flatiron 212.645.0003

When it started percolating in late 2004, Gypsy Tea became a gossip-column mainstay with a line down the block and two floors full of A-listers. Despite the name, there's no Stevie Nicks vibe here—just your basic hip-hop blasting and well-heeled crowds occupying private tables and enjoying bottle service. The two decidedly different floors each house their own DJs and downstairs is a fantastically elaborate fish tank that flanks the VIP area. Gypsy Tea definitely pulls out all the stops. Located on a block of similarly fashionable nightclubs, Gypsy Tea is a prime destination to look for celebrities, but on many nights, this, the VIP of the new 24th Street nightlife strip, somewhat lacks the cachet of the nightlife cluster a few blocks west.

Gyu-Kaku

34 Cooper Sq. (Bowery & 5th St.)
East Village 212.475.2989

If Benihana and Bennigan's merged, the result would be something like Gyu-Kaku. Don't get us wrong; the food at this charcoal Japanese BBQ lounge is fantastic (it is served "yakiniku"-style, which means there's a tiny grill in the center of each table for you to cook your own meat) and well-priced; it's just that the service is overly bright and chipper for the subdued ambiance the place strives for. Happy hour runs from 10pm to close and the beers and entrées are more affordable than most other spots in the 'hood. Adventurous diners will be delighted at the prospect of grilling up their own slab of beef tongue, while their more weary friends can numb their fears with one of Gyu-Kaku's hot or cold sakes and reward their bravery with savory S'mores.

Hacienda de Argentina

339 E. 75th St. (@ 1st Ave.)
Upper East Side 212.472.7577

Rivaling Dr. Frankenstein's lair, Hacienda de Argentina's décor is seeped in darkness that's offset by the abundance of flickering candles lining the bar and gothic candelabras topping tables. This Argentinean steakhouse attracts meat-lovers with its succulent carnivorous delights, like the Entrana ($16.50), a skirt steak grilled Argentinean-style and topped with chimichurri sauce. The dining room is mostly outfitted with large, bulky chairs and the occasional cowhide; the old-world feel is perfect for a romantic date or anniversary. Carnivore intoxication abounds here, though there are vegetarian-friendly items (gnocchi, $14.50) on the menu. Sit back, have a glass of Argentinean wine, and soak up the haunted mansion ambiance; just avoid eye contact with the eerie suit of armor standing guard near the kitchen.

The Hairy Monk

337 3rd Ave. (@ 25th St.)
Murray Hill 212.532.2929

Luckily there is no hirsute holy man theme at work here—it's just a name. Votive candles adorning an oak mantle and subtly dimmed Tiffany lamps aim to provide a touch of swank to the atmosphere, but underneath it all the Hairy Monk is just a good, solid Irish pub. Sixteen beers on tap and 17 more by the bottle offer a wide selection to those who appreciate a brew, and the bar top that lines the outside wall lends for a cozy place to socialize with this pretty down-to-earth clientele. The place gets pretty lively when either variety of football plays on the telly, but it's all in good fun.

The Half King Bar

505 W. 23rd St. (@ 10th Ave.)
Chelsea 212.462.4300

Don't let the romantically rustic pub façade fool you—this seemingly innocuous little working-man's drinkery nestled on the upper regions of Chelsea is actually a thriving hub of artistic activity. Named after a 12th-century Seneca American Indian chief, the Half King does indeed keep true to the cultural roots of its neighborhood, offering a regular Monday night reading series in cooperation with the likes of *Vanity Fair* and *Harper's* magazines, as well as ongoing six-week photojournalism exhibits in the dining room and live music every Sunday evening. Featuring a made-to-satisfy menu of traditional pub fare complemented by a few surprisingly eclectic offerings ($13 ostrich burger, anyone?) at prices even the lowliest peasant can afford, come on in and take a load off your crown at the Half King, where you'll be treated like true royalty. And yes, that is Sebastian Junger at the bar.

Half Wine Bar

626 Vanderbilt Ave. (@ Prospect Pl.)
Prospect Heights 718.783.4100

Inspired by the sleek sake bars they visited in Japan, intrepid vino lovers Max and Patty Jerome endeavored to steer Brooklyn's grape trail east of Park Slope by opening the pint-size Half Wine Bar two years ago. Mellow scenesters and wine aficionados alike will dig the reasonably priced glasses and half-bottles of choice wines from around the globe; there's also a shortlist of intriguing, wine-infused cocktails like the Prospect Park (sake, watermelon juice, and lime). A café by day, this narrow, brightly painted lounge attracts laptop-toting locals in need of a WiFi hotspot with their latte. At night, prepare to be pressed into the long bar or back patio for your panini and pinot; tiny Half can get as full-bodied as the fine wines they pour.

Hallo Berlin
626 10th Ave. (44th & 45th Sts.)
Hell's Kitchen 212.541.6248

Before Hallo Berlin, you may have thought that sausage came in only one flavor: "hot and sweet." But at this meat-laden German beer, wine, and food hall, you'll discover the best of the wurst, including wiener schnitzel, goulash, and bratwurst. Here, the beer comes in steins, humpers, and pitchers—and they have so many kinds (16 imported German draughts and bottled beers, seven 17-ounce special imports including Weissbeer, and three imported German wines), you'll want to try them all. Neither the *vieners* nor the *bier* will disappoint, but eat quick, because *herr* manager will inform you that you'll have to say "goodbye Berlin" when they stop the sausage party at 10pm. A biergarten it ain't, but Hallo Berlin is still a great spot for a "gute nacht."

The Hangar
115 Christopher St. (Bleecker & Hudson Sts.)
West Village 212.627.2044

Fashionistas, gym bunnies, and the cast of *Queer Eye*—the Hangar attracts none of them. Real men rather than reality TV stars pack this popular, friendly neighborhood bar. Though it's crowded on weekends after the bar begins its beer blasts at 2pm, it's worth stopping by any night—Wednesdays host the $100 pool tournament and on Sundays chiseled cuties compete in a go-go contest. And for the gay man who possesses the stamina to go all night long, the Hangar offers an extra-long happy hour on Thursdays from 3pm-10pm. But the fun doesn't end there: On Tuesdays the happy hour lasts all day long. Decorated with an aviation theme, the Hangar's cheap drinks and tight flight suit-worthy clientele are sure to raise your barometric pressure.

The Hanger
217 3rd St. (Aves. B & C)
East Village 212.228.1030

This very cute little bar provides everything you could ask for from a neighborhood bar: $2 cans of Old English, $3 Staten Island Iced Teas (vodka and tea mix), $12 cocktail pitchers, fun-sized chocolate bars, and vintage clothing that's for sale. Okay, so this combination clothing store/rock bar is on the unique side, but it all works very nicely. Formerly Plant Bar, The Hanger is one of those cute and not-so-accidentally-hip East Village haunts that people are just going to love once they realize there's life this far off the beaten path. (Most of the nicer clothing is put away when drinky time comes, but there are still cabinets and window displays to peruse.) The best part of this place is the charming staff, who could just as easily sell you a Budweiser or a string of pearls.

Hank's Saloon
46 3rd Ave. (@ Atlantic Ave.)
Boerum Hill 718.625.8003

Maybe it's the cinderblock façade or the old boozehounds falling asleep into their beers at 9am, but Hank's looks like it belongs somewhere off the New Jersey Turnpike rather than Boerum Hill. Not that this gritty Brooklyn dive should change anytime soon—Hank's is a haven for local tightwads, bringing scraggly old drunks and scraggly young hipsters together over dirt-cheap drinks and cover-free live music. Bartenders serve up $2 cans of PBR with a smile (even when neighborhood cheapskates skimp on tips) while a hit-and-miss lineup of jazz, metal, and country bluegrass bands jam in the back most every night of the week. On Sundays, BBQ grub grilled on the street corner is served for free. Don't forget to hit up an ATM before you hit Hank's—not that the cash-only joint will be hard on your wallet.

Hanratty's
1410 Madison Ave. (97th & 98th Sts.)
Upper East Side 212.369.3420

Hanratty's is a charming little restaurant stuck in an absolute no-man's land of commerce. The exposed brick walls give a quaint, almost Little Italy-type feel to the proceedings, though the menu is fairly standard bar fare, replete with burgers, steaks, and the like. Unfortunately, no one will ever know this—despite the seemingly swanky address, most of the chic Fifth Avenue denizens would rather be caught in a Kathy Ireland pantsuit than venture this far north. Which is a shame, because they'll miss out on a great happy hour that boasts $3.50 pints of Stella and $4 well drinks. Then again, when you can afford to use Ben Franklin as a toilet paper substitute, drink specials just don't hold the same luster.

Happy Ending
302 Broome St. (Eldridge & Forsyth Sts.)
Lower East Side 212.334.9676

Appropriately enough, Happy Ending occupies a former massage parlor. And all the glass and tile surfaces make it that much easier to clean up after the full-capacity crowds that sweep through. This popular yet semi-secret, bi-level late-night destination specializes in edgy dance music, and the clientele specializes in edgy haircuts. A range of fairly priced, frilly specialty drinks are available, like the Cowboy Special, a PBR with a well shot of your choice for $6. Celebrate all this socioeconomic inclusiveness on Tuesday nights, when the place is packed with eager dancers. Downstairs, the saunas have been turned into "party coves" and the street-level bar includes intimate red-velvet booths where you can give your special someone their own "Happy Ending." We mean an impromptu neck rub, of course.

Harbour Lights
89 South St., 3rd Fl. (@ Fulton St.)
Financial District 212.227.2800

Yet another South Street Seaport bar/restaurant boasting views of the river and all three lower Manhattan bridges? Not so much. The open-air deck sets this one apart; al fresco dining without the ground level hubbub. There's somewhat of an Irish theme reflected in the décor, if not the menu or the unobtrusive "adult contemporary" background music. The attentive staff is usually better-dressed than the patrons, who, true to the typical Seaport crowd, are mostly from out of town, which could account for their chattiness. It's certainly no place to get rip-roaring drunk and dance around with a lampshade on your head, but if you want to strip down and jump into the East River, no one's going to stop you. Of course, re-entry could be a problem.

Hard Rock Café
221 W. 57th St. (Broadway & 7th Ave.)
Midtown 212.489.6565

The Hard Rock Café hardly rocks at all, which everyone surely knows before coming here for the familiarity that Midwesterners oddly seem to seek when they travel. With fewer surprises than a Phil Collins CD, this theme joint delivers rock history paraphernalia, mediocre and pricey comfort food, and gimmicky drinks like Red Rocker, Hurricane, Sangrita, etc. Non-stop music videos careen wildly between awesome classics and mediocre crap-rock, à la VH1. The gift shop is probably this place's primary draw, allowing tourists to go home with wearable proof that they saw New York City…more or less. Those finding themselves forced to entertain three generations of family may find this place useful, but "Hard Rock"? Hardly.

The Harrison
355 Greenwich St. (@ Harrison St.)
TriBeCa 212.274.9310

Rather than going for TriBeCa cool and distinction,

The Harrison

this restaurant gives off a whiff of stodgy country club refinement. Much to its credit is the big outdoor corner where cool air often blows in from the Hudson, adding a little yacht club vibe to the al fresco seating. Inside it's all white linens and soft lighting. The male staff wears striped buttondowns, blue ties, and white aprons. The crowd generally consists of 20-somethings who live in the area or work in the nearby Financial District. At around $20-$25, the small but flawless menu, which includes a peeky toe crab appetizer and sautéed skate, veers toward the expensive side. The drinks are strong and the whiskey concoctions recommended. There isn't a lot of soul in the bar scene, but the dining is rather civilized.

Harrison's Tavern
358 Amsterdam Ave. (@ 77th St.)
Upper West Side 212.724.3600

Boston fans looking for a "Noo Yak baw" where they can cheer on the Sox without getting a Bronx-style beating just love good old Harrison's. Despite the chants of "Suck it, Jeter!" this no-nonsense sports bar is a routine pop fly. An older, primarily male crowd assembles at primetime to watch sports while drinking one of the seven beers on tap. Multiple TVs are tuned into different games while one larger projection screen displays the main event for fans sitting at the bar or at one of the checkered tablecloth-covered tables. Harrison's offers better-than-concession-stand appetizers in the ballpark of $7-$8, sandwiches and burgers for $9-$10, and entrées such as shrimp Cobb salad or steak tip dinners for $12-$13.

Harry Boland's Pub
297 9th St. (4th & 5th Aves.)
Park Slope 718.369.8269

This straightforward Irish pub feels gentlemanly, if a little uninspired, with an imposing mahogany bar and interior, multiple dartboards and electronic card games under a sign reading "players please," and patrons who are likely to be discussing politics or religion over three fingers of Johnny Walker Red. The low-hanging bar lights and beige décor seem best-suited for older folks who feel, well, low-hanging and beige. Still, Harry Boland's manages to ride the line between grown-up and boring without tipping too far into the snooze zone, and despite the pop-oriented jukebox, milder patrons may appreciate being able to hear themselves think. Stop in early for a Scotch and revel in your own maturity.

Hearth
403 E. 12th St. (@ 1st Ave.)
East Village 646.602.1300

If *The Restaurant* was the best example of how *not* to run a restaurant (or better yet, who not to hire), then this downtown eatery is the how-to guide for pan-roasted entrepreneurial success. Founded by two NYC restaurant talents (Marco Canora and Paul Grieco, both formerly of Gramercy Tavern), Hearth serves up a friendly, upscale dining experience. The restaurant's commitment to excellence and hospitality is evident in items from their seasonal menus (entrées include braised veal breast), the careful selections on the extensive wine list, and attentive service from a pleasant and professional wait staff (as opposed to those who provoked Rocco's temper tantrums). Most come to Hearth for dinner, but the bar serves specialty literature-inspired cocktails such as the Huckleberry Ginn (ginger beer, huckleberries, and Boodles Gin).

Heartland Brewery Radio City

1285 6th Ave. (@ 51st St.)
Midtown 212.582.8244

Heartland Brewery Radio City is one of the best places in New York to meet a group of salesmen from the Midwest. Try the free mini-mug samples in order to decide which classic or seasonal brew you want to nurse on, like the Red Rooster Ale, Farmer Jon's Oatmeal Stout, or Summer Apricot Ale. Heartland Brewery adheres to every standard a microbrewery should have—big copper vats, inoffensive pop rock, some obligatory Americana, and souvenir glasses and t-shirts. The smell, taste, and look of the pub grub—BBQ chicken quesadillas, mini-burgers—is almost too good to believe…until you see the Midtown prices. The Brewery is usually packed with an after-work crowd seeking good bar food, hops-packed brews, and the chance to roll up their sleeves and "crunch some numbers."

Heartland Brewery Union Square

35 Union Sq. W. (16th & 17th Sts.)
Flatiron 212.645.3400

The Heartland Brewery Union Square is one of those nondescript, perpetually busy restaurant/bars you see all over town—and at least four of those are also called Heartland Brewery. A WASPy, white-collared crowd, Pier 1-chic design, and generic pop music round out a risk-free formula. What somewhat distinguishes this place is its stellar beer collection. Heartland's microbrews are amazing, and they always carry at least eight different varieties. Another perk is the outdoor seating, which provides nice views of the park across the street. And even if you come during the after-work chaos, the two-floor design keeps crowding to a minimum. Plus, the food ain't half bad. If you must visit a vanilla pedestrian pub, walk on over to this one.

Heaven

579 6th Ave. (16th & 17th Sts.)
Chelsea 212.243.6100

Nonstop Madonna, Britney, Christina, Kylie. To some, that might seem like downright torture, but to those who pack this tri-level club for its Saturday night "Gay College Party," it's pure Heaven to their ears. Each Saturday, hordes of devilishly cute, young (age 18 and over) gays and lesbians work themselves into a frenzy while dancing to all their revered goddesses of pop. The gates of Heaven are also open throughout the rest of the week. Whereas Wednesdays and Fridays are lesbian nights, Thursdays lure Latin *papis*. Regardless of which night you come, be sure to pray that when you order a vodka tonic, you actually get to taste the vodka. The drinks in Heaven are often so weak that you'll wonder if you're actually in some perverse version of Hell.

Hedeh

57 Great Jones St. (Bowery & Lafayette St.)
NoHo 212.473.8458

Named for its chef, Hideyuki (Hedeh) Nakajima, NoHo's sushi newcomer is the hedeh the class. Owner Isami Nagai, who also owns the more casual Go on St. Marks Place, succeeds in creating a stylishly minimal raw fish experience with his restaurant/bar. An impressive collection of backlit Sapore bottles grace the entire back wall, all the more reason to order the tasty sake sangria. The bartender might even reveal that Jean-Michel Basquiat overdosed in the studio upstairs, which sort of makes Hedeh the Chelsea Hotel of the sushi world. After a round of very spirited "hellos" from the endearingly enthusiastic sushi chefs, it's dinnertime—but know that while the menu is minimal, the prices are not. Still, it's cheaper than actually going to Tokyo.

Helen's

169 8th Ave. (18th & 19th Sts.)
Chelsea 212.206.0609

In a part of town known for putting on airs, Helen's offers a much-needed escape from the exhausting travails of being a gay New Yorker. Overall, this year-old piano bar is extremely friendly and chill, so much so that even the hetero crowd feels at home. Humming along to the piano tunes, bartenders measure generous proportions of alcohol into the $8 mixed drinks, and the occasional lonely regular engages newcomers in a spirited debate over the greatest musicians of the past century. While the interior has a stagy dressing room look to it, the decorative bands of light along the ceiling are perhaps more evocative of Toys 'R Us. As for the bizarre display of floristry in the front window, it's probably best just to ignore it.

Henrietta Hudson
438 Hudson St. (@ Morton St.)
West Village 212.924.3347

Frisky is the best word to describe this lesbian lounge. Though the $5 cover can be a slight annoyance, the jovial pink and orange neon lights that bejewel the entranceway will lighten your mood, as will the hip-hop and '80s dance music spun by DJs (Wed-Sun). A go-go dancer gyrating on the bar top provides further entertainment, and the specialty cocktails with cutesy names such as "Naughty Girl" and "Tempted to Touch" come with glow-in-the-dark stirrers. Unless you have a saccharine-sweet tooth, however, stick with simpler libations from the vast wine and beer selection. If you're a girl looking to meet Ms. Right (or Ms. Right Away), hooking up at this Sapphic spot couldn't be any hotter.

Henry Street Ale House
62 Henry St. (Orange & Cranberry Sts.)
Brooklyn Heights 718.522.4801

After work, the blue-oxford-and-khakis set gathers at Henry Street Ale House, a bar that can't decide if it wants to be a modern lounge (the bathroom entrance is lit in red and blue sconces line the walls), an old-timey neighborhood hangout (a wrought-iron fan hangs from the ornate tin ceiling), or a diner (every last table carries a greasy ketchup bottle). Formerly the Park Slope Brewing Company, this neighborhood bar is heralded for its friendly service, delicious, non-pub grub-tasting pub grub, and a hefty list of beers on tap (over 15 to choose from), including Old Speckled Hen and Boddington's. This neighborhood staple is a safe haven to cool off with a cold one any day or night—especially if your home-brewing plans backfire and your bathroom's flooded with beer.

Hi Fi
169 Ave. A (10th & 11th Sts.)
East Village 212.420.8392

Formerly the super-cool music venue Brownie's, Hi Fi is a quintessential Avenue A hipster bar, which means it's probably losing popularity as you read this. The area by the bar is spacious enough for standing around and chatting, and the beers are reasonably priced, although the jagged island in the middle of the back area can make it tricky to get to the pool table or the three bathrooms, which, in classic Alphabet City form, are unisex, making the line an adventurous proposition. If your group manages to snag one of the coveted booths, you're golden. Hi Fi has a terrific MP-3 jukebox that plays thousands of songs and monitors show classic music videos. Should your ADD be in overdrive there are a couple of videogames and a pinball machine as well.

Highline
835 Washington St. (@ Little W. 12th St.)
Meatpacking District 212.243.3339

When you see gaggles of pointy-shoed girls and striped-shirted guys walking through the Meatpacking District, it's safe to say that this is one of the stops they're considering. Named for the old railroad line that once passed through this area, Highline is "New MPD." Three floors hold a waterfall that trickles into a downstairs fountain in a futuristic white room that can get a little messy when crowded. Upstairs there are beds which, appropriately enough, might be the most tired idea in nightlife since parachute pants. The Thai cuisine here is both tastier and less expensive than one might expect from this nightclub theme park of a neighborhood. There is no shortage of dizzying details here, and it results in a hyper-stimulating vibe that's fueled by clever $11 cocktails.

Hi-Life Bar and Grill
477 Amsterdam Ave. (@ 83rd St.)
Upper West Side 212.787.7199

This bar and restaurant's regulars love the Hi-Life, and thanks to its 1930s atmosphere accented with modern touches, you'll at the very least be impressed. It's hard to find a restaurant where you can order steak and gin martinis one night and sushi and saketinis the next without spending a night in the emergency room, but Hi-Life handles the fusion cuisine well, with entrées ranging from $8-$20, and drinks starting at $5. And with outdoor seating and popular half-price sushi nights on Mondays and Tuesdays, living the Hi-Life isn't as hard as one might think.

Hi-Life Restaurant & Lounge
1340 1st Ave. (@ 72nd St.)
Upper East Side 212.249.3600

The name could use a little more kick, but the tasty menu at this Upper East Side sushi bar/restaurant/lounge comes through loud and clear. However, the décor is a bit on the tacky side (pin-ups, neon signs, and retro lamps? Where are we, Colin Farell's apartment?). At Hi-Life, all sushi and sashimi is half-off on Mondays, cosmos cost $5 on Thursdays and Saturdays for ladies, and it's $5 off a bottle of wine on Wednesdays and Sundays. You can't find a better deal anywhere in this neighborhood unless you have a friend who works at Bloomingdale's who can give you her employee discount. So head to Hi-Life and skip Bloomie's; because after you load up on the hearty food (steaks, burgers, pasta), you probably won't fit into those designer jeans anyway.

Hiro Lounge (@ the Maritime Hotel)
371 W. 16th St. (@ 9th Ave.)
Chelsea 212.727.0212

Nur Khan, the club owner largely responsible for Wax and Sway, has become a nightlife hero with

Hiro

this subterranean scene. Low-arching ceilings, brown paper-like windows, colorful lanterns, and pricey themed cocktails like the Double Dragon set the tone in this faux-seedy hotel lounge that looks heavenly, but is delightfully sinful. Is that the Rolling Stones playing along with a little Public Enemy? Yes, it is. Is that Jay-Z and Sum 41? Get out! Seriously, get out before you're thrown out. Leather pants and rock tees are as common as $2,000 suits here, but lose the tie or visitors like Mick Jagger and Famke Janssen are going to think you're an idiot. The big, beautiful adjacent ballroom continues the Japanese theme; performers like Beck have done surprise shows on the ample stage.

The Hog Pit
22 9th Ave. (@ 13th St.)
Meatpacking District 212.604.0092

Proving that the Meatpacking District is big enough for two dive bars with "hog" in the name, the Hog Pit is a mellow alternative to being belittled by the door thugs at Lotus. This Southern-style eatery counts among its accomplishments the fact that it is a staple for New York barbecue connoisseurs, and with good reason. It serves up large, delectable portions of farmland friends, from juicy burgers or savory pulled pork to super-tasty ribs. Cheap beer can be had, pool and videogames can be played, and country music can be heard. You want fries with that?

Hogs and Heifers
859 Washington St. (@ 13th St.)
Meatpacking District 212.929.0655

Hogs and Heifers

This quintessential biker bar might seem like just the place to go if you want to get punched in the mouth, but the Hell's Angels and wannabes that frequent this classic dive are nice guys out to have a good time. Of course, a biker's idea of a good time is usually a rowdy night that includes people yelling "Wooooo!" at the top of their lungs. If you do get punched, it's more likely to be by one of the feisty female bartenders who have worn through the layers of the plywood bar by dancing on it in their cowboy boots (and they can drink you under the table). The dead shark on the wall is covered with hundreds of bras, presumably from "heifers" caught up in the spirit of place.

Holiday Cocktail Lounge
75 St. Marks Pl. (1st & 2nd Aves.)
East Village 212.777.9637

"Cocktail Lounge"? This dingy hole in the wall only sells beer by the bottle and there sure as hell aren't any blenders behind the bar. What that equates to is a clientele of hard-drinking outlaws who won't be putting their cell phones on the bar and talking a lot of shit. The spirit of Gram Parsons hangs over the unique horseshoe bar and lives in the superior jukebox, but it's the shadowy booths and tables in back that truly make Holiday a destination spot for dark and seedy adventurers. Men outnumber women, but it's not a pickup spot at all. That said, try your luck and see what happens.

(Either way, it won't be good.) Just don't get too rowdy—the ancient bartender gets cranky on weeknights and the place closes at 1am.

Holland Bar
532 9th Ave. (39th & 40th Sts.)
Hell's Kitchen 212.502.4609

Holland Bar

Do you remember that t-shirt that read, "Beer ain't just for breakfast anymore?" Well, just once, everyone should get hammered at 8am and find out what that means. Get off the A train during your morning commute, call in sick, and ante up at this Hell's Kitchen bar so you can get the first pint o' the day. This hole-in-the-wall is heaven for those who work all night and need happy hour when everyone else needs an IHOP. Located just yards away from the Lincoln Tunnel, the Holland Bar is a real dive—the beer is cheap, the jukebox works (usually), the walls are covered with old newspaper clippings, and the video poker machine will steal your money if the crackheads outside don't do it first. God bless America.

Home
532 W. 27th St. (10th & 11th Aves.)
Chelsea 212.273.3700

There are so many clubs on this block that they've now resorted to putting several into one building. At 530-532 W. 27th St., Spirit's on the bottom floor, BED and Groovedeck are on top, and the appropriately house music-spinning Home is in-between. In terms of over-the-top star power, this dark, crowded, and very lively spot is only literally in the neighborhood of Cain, Bungalow 8, and other high-rent residents. But thanks to its tucked-away, windowless, top-of-a-long-staircase confines, Home might be where our heart is as an after-hours or spillover club. Low-slung sofas and stools beg to be danced on and they're just as accommodating for bottle service. Shades of red abound in a setting that's more comfortable than it is revolutionary, but an unassuming sense of familiarity is what allows these Home-bodies to let loose.

The Hook & Ladder Pub
611 2nd Ave. (33rd & 34th Sts.)
Murray Hill 212.213.5034

This is the bar for firemen and the women who love them...or so you'd think. Firemen don't come here that often anymore, but most of NYU's medical school does for the Thursday night all-you-can-drink special or for the expansive outdoor space complete with covered pool table and TV. Prices are low, patrons are friendly, and they have a kick-ass jukebox with varied CDs, including a little bit of country and a lot of rock 'n' roll. If you're feeling competitive, play Golden Tee or darts. But if you're more of a lover than a fighter, the happy hour specials will help you do something about that fire in your pants.

Hookah Café
309 E. 60th St. (1st & 2nd Aves.)
Upper East Side 212.980.7998

Feeling nostalgic for your teenage days when you may (or may not) have enjoyed sucking on a bubbling water pipe? (We bet your substance of choice wasn't cantaloupe-flavored.) Here at the Hookah Café, overshadowed by the Queensboro Bridge and Scores (it's right next door), you can get comfy with friends on furniture that's not any

fancier than what you had in your dorm room. Choose from a flavored tobacco menu, fire up, and chill out. There's no alcohol served here (what, you want to smoke and drink?), but you can indulge in the munchies with inexpensive snacks like hummus and pita. If you're looking for a place to continue the party after the bars close, stop by for a smoke, as this small spot is open much later.

Hooligan's
1804 2nd Ave. (93rd & 94th Sts.)
Upper East Side 212.289.2273

Look up "Irish dive" in the dictionary and you'll find an entry for Hooligan's. Look up "lousy Irish dive" and you'll find a whole spread devoted to this Upper East Side hole. Not even the bowling game and Golden Tee can justify spending more than a second in this dump. The regulars look like they haven't moved from the barstools in about 300 years and if you're under 30, you'd better expect to be glared at by everyone in the place, especially the bartender. Should you even smell like soap, Irish Spring or not, you can expect to be labeled a yuppie. Hooligan's is the anti-fun; you'd be better off getting recreational chemo treatments than setting foot in here.

Hooters
211 W. 56th St. (Broadway & 7th Ave.)
Midtown 212.581.5656

You know you're in a classy joint when the sign above the men's-room door reads "Used Beer Dept." The food is generic and silly and the beer selection is ample, but hardly exotic: With 22 on tap and a dozen more from the bottle, selections barely stray from domestic and Irish. Covering the hot sauce stains on the walls are placards with witticisms like "Hooters waitresses are flattery operated." Ugh. Apparently this breast-themed joint is also operated by boobs. And if you're going to bring a date to this exemplar of refinement, impress that lucky someone with the Gourmet Chicken Wing Dinner: 20 wings and a bottle of Dom Perignon.

Hop Devil Grill
129 St. Marks Pl. (Ave. A & 1st Ave.)
East Village 212.533.4467

Hop Devil Grill

The devil went down to St. Marks, and it's clear he's a drinking man. With over 20 beers on tap and 100 in bottles ($5.50), Hop Devil should placate even the pickiest of beer connoisseurs, while a generous menu featuring fajitas, steaks, burgers, and BBQ will hide your beer gut under a layer of fat. An adjacent bar area dubbed the Belgium room serves (duh) Belgian food. Despite its beer list, however, Hop Devil is a restaurant first, which means there's relatively little space to hang out and enjoy your drink and plenty of tables to sit down and gorge on French fries. Either way, it's worth dropping by Hop Devil, if only to say, "I'll have a Smuttynose Old Brown Dog Ale, and a Dogfish 60 Minute IPA for my friend."

Horus Café
93 Ave. B (@ 6th St.)
East Village 212.777.9199

Despite an extensive menu of mixed drinks, booze is not the main attraction at this laidback but hopping bar with over 40 flavors of hookah tobaccos ranging from double apple to piña colada. Wise patrons will forgo anything in a spill-able glass and pull up to one of the huge wooden chairs or a pillow on the floor next to the fireplace and toke on exotic tobaccos while savoring the flavor of a wood-smoked burger or kebab from the café's cheap and tasty menu. A helpful staff stands by to assist the hookah-shy or inexperienced, and while you won't get high on what you're smoking, you will be on cloud nine from the awesome atmosphere and footage of belly dancers shakin' what their mamas gave them on the projection screen.

House of Brews
363 W. 46th St. (8th & 9th Aves.)
Hell's Kitchen 212.245.0551

House of Brews

This is the Disney World of bars…or maybe just the IHOP of beer. Promising to take you around the world with its selection of over 75 beers from 30 countries, the House of Brews carries such beauties as Rogue Chipotle Ale ($11), Delirium Tremens ($16), and Hitachino Red Rice ($9). The tourists that drift in from Times Square make the bar feel even more international as they mix in with after-work crowds to throw back Corsondonks (brown ale made by Belgium monks, $10) and watch a game on one of the five flat-screen televisions. And as the drunken guy at the bar next to you chugs Smuttynose Pale Ale from a 96-oz. beer bong while singing Elton John in German, you realize, right here on the cusp of Times Square, that it really is a small world after all…maybe even too small.

Houston's
378 Park Ave. S. (26th & 27th Sts.)
Murray Hill 212.689.1090

Despite the hugeness of the restaurant, the bar feels crowded at this dark, leathery after-work cavern for suits and their dates. The circular bar near the entrance lacks any sense of intimacy or leisure as the numbing chorus of business-types chortling at their own brilliance sabotages conversation; in fact, that's the number-one reason to avoid this giant yet empty-feeling establishment. The surf and turf food is fine but overpriced, a facsimile of the fare at every after-work schmoozefest for the neighborhood's office-choked maw. (The house spinach dip and chips is a really nice surprise.) There's nothing terrible about Houston's per se—it's just not the kind of place that anyone without a tie, an MBA, and a soul-sucking job would want to patronize. Think Denny's for yuppies.

Hudson Bar (@ the Hudson Hotel)
356 W. 58th St. (8th & 9th Aves.)
Hell's Kitchen 212.554.6343

There's a Starck difference between Hudson Bar and most hotel lounges. That "Starck difference" is designer Philippe Starck, who also did the Paramount and Royalton hotels. Looking somewhat like a pop art museum, Hudson Bar mixes antique furnishings with modern lighting and odd murals, combining class and character. The drink menu, which follows suit, is known for its cosmos, but the signature cocktails incorporate oddities like lemongrass and such. The chi-chi crowd is considerably more serious about the experience, as evidenced by their willingness to splurge for bottle service. Founded as an Ian Schrager property, Hudson Bar and its arguably over-the-top ode to the '80s décor can easily be interpreted as tacky and even a bit kitschy, but there's undeniably something cool about the place.

Hudson Bar & Books
636 Hudson St. (@ Horatio St.)
West Village 212.229.2642

Libraries have never been much fun to hang out in—too much shushing and dusty stacks—and Hudson Bar & Books does nothing to stop the Dewey Decimal System's downward spiral. The staff here is overdressed in costume formalwear, and while books line the shelves, you'll spend more time reading your bill: Cocktails available to appease the two-drink minimum on the weekend are all overpriced. You can smoke here, but if you don't buy the bar's tobacco, add a $2 surcharge to your already outrageous bill. Once you factor in tax and a service charge of 20% for any group of six or more, you'll be feeling like a kid who just got busted for reading the Cliff's Notes.

Hudson Place
538 3rd Ave. (35th & 36th Sts.)
Murray Hill 212.686.6660

If you live in Murray Hill, your parents are in town, and they didn't like the Third Avenue sports bar where the local hussy knew you by name, try Hudson Place. This mellow neighborhood hangout has a warm and airy feel that goes well with a pasta-heavy menu that creatively works lobster and red meat into the mix. There are a few TVs over the bar, so if the game is on, you can keep an eye on the score while Mom rambles on about relatives you don't really remember. There are a few tables outside where 25 wines are available by the glass and 30 by the bottle.

Hue
91 Charles St. (@ Bleecker St.)
West Village 212.691.4170

Hue may have long relinquished its standing as the hottest club in Manhattan, but they held onto the velvet rope—perhaps for sentimental reasons, because there's so little door man discretion that David Cross doesn't even need to tell a joke or show his SAG card to get in. Those craving the designer scene should ditch Hue and walk the few blocks to the Meatpacking District. But if it's sugary, sake-based cocktails, tasty French-Vietnamese fare, or simple clubbing sans Manolos you want, stay put. Hue makes it easy to linger, too. The wood walls, exposed stone, and leather banquettes lend a warm, sophisticated air to the upstairs lounge. Downstairs at La Cave, folks with fat wallets and bottle-service dreams relax on long couches covered in colorful pillows. This little club-turned-restaurant made the cross-over with its integrity intact.

Hunter's American Bar & Grill
1387 3rd Ave. (78th & 79th Sts.)
Upper East Side 212.734.6008

You probably wouldn't believe that there's a hip, groovy lounge hidden in the Upper East 70s, a place that's causing that grey-haired neighborhood to rock out just a little bit to the beat of a downtown drum. Well, you'd be right, because there's no such joint. Hunter's is just another standard pub, but this time, it's done up like a hunting lodge. Typically filled with retirees, publishing execs, and young yuppies living off of Daddy's dollars, Hunter's isn't all kitsch and killjoy—the food is quite good, and the redwood bar is exquisite—but come by for a visit and you'll find yourself trying to remember anything interesting about your experience the day after.

Hurley's Saloon
232 W. 48th St. (Broadway & 8th Ave.)
Midtown 212.765.8981

Even if the name brings up bad memories of unsuccessfully mixing hard liquor and beer, Hurley's is a must-see authentic Irish pub located in the heart of Times Square. Not only does it display fire department and naval hats atop tin ceilings and wood moldings, but the bartender greets his costumers in a soft Irish accent with a "how's your day," and hails from what he calls "the Noble Country." Although it changed locations five years ago, Hurley's has existed in this city since 1894. Having recently moved from Rockefeller Center, its new digs provide old-time charm without any old-time smells. Thanks to a somewhat standard pub grub menu, this old-new pub works well as an after-work or post-theater stop.

Hurricane Hopeful
139 N. 6th St. (Bedford Ave. & Berry St.)
Williamsburg 718.302.4441

They have great conch fritters and coconut drinks in the Florida Keys, but it's a pain getting all the way down there, the crowd is Spring Break '94, and it's Florida. Save the airfare and take the L train to this surf shack and your journey to a tropical paradise is complete; it's as if a hurricane plucked this place off a sandy beach and plopped it in downtown Williamsburg. All the accoutrements are accounted for: a surfboard ceiling, string lights, a sandy back deck, aloha shirts, beach boardwalk knick-knacks, and best of all, an extensive tiki drink menu with fog-cutters, rum-runners, and piña coladas. The formidable chowder menu and fried seafood baskets give this concept bar Caribbean cred.

i Restaurant & Lounge
277 Church St. (Franklin & White Sts.)
TriBeCa 212.625.0505

i Restaurant & Lounge

This small bricolage of a bar conveys the charm of original personality. Let's play "i spy": The entrance consists of black double doors that open out onto the street, the floor is cracked marble, and glowing red lamps hang from the ceiling. Placed about the bar are a baseball bat, small football helmets, a bronze statue of a Great Dane, a collection of comic books, funky artwork, and a fish tank. The beers on tap aren't the usual suspects, either—the wide selection of bottled microbrews includes Heavyweight Stickenjab. The bartenders here are usually DJing from a laptop, while patrons play backgammon at one of the booths. The kitchen serves comforting dishes like macaroni and cheese with bacon. We know there's no "i" in team, but the quirky eclecticism of this hangout feels more like "we."

I Tre Merli
463 W. Broadway (@ Houston St.)
SoHo 212.254.8699

Location, location, location. That's what keeps this bi-level Italian restaurant buzzing (it's certainly not the nondescript food). Set on one of SoHo's main drags, I Tre Merli packs in homesick Italian tourists and revelers who want to carb-load before an evening out on the town. Stick to the most basic menu options to avoid a disappointing brush with overcooked meat or undercooked pasta (the proscuitto sandwich on warm focaccia bread is a reliable choice). If necessary, drown your sorrow for a good recipe gone wrong with a few glasses of vino from the well-stocked wine list. Boring European lounge music fills the cavernous industrial-chic room; opt for sidewalk seating to avoid it, and to appreciate the restaurant's finest asset.

ICON (@ the W Hotel – The Court)
130 E. 39th St. (Lexington & Park Aves.)
Murray Hill 212.592.8888

ICON is an oasis amid the over-hyped bar scene that has become synonymous with the W Hotel enterprise. This swanky lounge on the ground floor of the W Court Hotel is a welcome refuge, marked by a tony boutique hotel décor sans snooty atti-

tude. Visitors are treated like customers and not annoyances as friendly wait staff and bartenders keep the martinis filled and satay skewers coming with a smile. A hearty appetizer menu of cross-cultural delights tempts post-work revelers with something a bit more substantial. Looking for something sweet? Try a sip of the S'moretini ($12)—the memories will take you back to summer camping days past, but with more booze and fewer bugs. The crowd here is hardly cutting-edge, but considering the direction hotel bars can take, they're chic enough.

ICU Bar
765 Washington St. (12th & Bethune Sts.)
West Village No Phone

When it's that bad, when nothing else can fix what ails you, convalesce at ICU Bar. This dive has what you need, including psychotherapy administered by zany regulars, who have all the answers—even if you don't pose the questions—with stories so insane that the imbalances in your life will suddenly level off. Expect one regular to bloviate about his castle in Jersey, conquests with Spanish kings, feuds with the Mexican Mafia and his friend, Lawrence of Ohio, who relocated to the New Ghetto. The orderlies will monitor your medication, by means of 10 bottled beers ($5) and a numbing stock of liquor. If this intensive care is too much, find serenity in the garden, hustle the frat boys at the pool table, or jam with the band downstairs.

Ideya
349 W. Broadway (Broome & Grand Sts.)
SoHo 212.625.1441

Stepping off the sidewalks of SoHo into Ideya, you'll feel like you've just entered the parlor room of a modest Havana villa. The subtle décor is an homage to simpler times—white brick textured walls, wooden floors weathered to a comfortable hominess, a patterned tile bench, and colorful sounds beating to the rhythms of the live salsa music. The staff at this Latin bistro is casual and friendly, the music always fits the vibe, and the menu items—empanadas, tomato and mango soup, ginger tuna, and *bebidas* like the mango mimosa—are fairly priced so you'll leave with a few pesos in your pocket. Pucker up and taste Ideya's signature mojito with fresh mint leaves that taste like they've just been picked off a home-grown bush out back.

Iggy's
1452 2nd Ave. (@ 77th St.)
Upper East Side 212.327.3043

Downtowners know Iggy's Keltic Lounge on Ludlow Street, but on an equally busy strip of the Upper East Side is his twin brother Iggy's, who's every bit as divey and unpolished. However, this uptown kid is the talented one in the family: With a 1pm-8pm happy hour and nightly karaoke from 10pm on, this place gets noisy if nothing else. St. Patrick's Day in this semi-fratty Irish pub is a nightmare for the ages or a dream come true depending on your tastes…not to mention your sense of smell. The crowd is decidedly like its neighborhood—suits during the day, shorts and athletic supporter tees by night, with the two coming together at happy hour for $3 domestic drafts and bottles. For better or worse, it is what it is.

Iggy's Keltic Lounge
132 Ludlow St. (Rivington & Stanton Sts.)
Lower East Side 212.529.2731

Since opening a few years back, Iggy's has plugged itself as the black sheep of Ludlow, and for a time the bar could bask justifiably in its reputation as a rough but friendly dive. While Iggy's may still be an anomaly among its haughtier neighbors, it has lost some of its defiant cachet. Less a hangout for LES rebels than a cesspool for LES rejects, weekends here are crawling with tourists, frat boys, and other enthusiasts of the Bud and PBR drink specials. It's on weekdays when Iggy's original flair shines through. The mock street lamps really are welcoming, the juke-box remains true to its gritty Irish roots, and the two unisex bathrooms just may be the dirtiest ones this side of Houston.

Iguana
240 W. 54th St. (Broadway & 8th Ave.)
Midtown 212.765.5454

Found: an unpretentious and satisfying Mexican saloon for tourists and locals alike in the Theater District. Follow the 30-foot iguana and enter the main bar and restaurant area that literally jumps to the baseline pumping from the dance floor below. The bustling upstairs area empties out a bit by 10pm, leaving behind a few lonely regulars looking to chat up slightly buzzed females. The food is appetizing and well-priced for the area (the pre-theater fixed menu is your best bet) but the drinks are pricey. Still, the nightly specials are always interesting (Cadillac margaritas?) and it's not hard to get a little extra punch in your drink by befriending the spirited wait staff. Opt for anything "on the rocks" to avoid the dreaded mix machine.

Il Buco
47 Bond St. (Bowery & Lafayette St.)
NoHo 212.533.1932

Be ready to spend big bucks for the small portions at NoHo's most charming and consistent Mediterranean hideaway. According to legend, this country-themed antique-store-turned-restaurant's 200-year-old candlelit wine cellar inspired Edgar Allan Poe to write *The Cask of Amontillado*. Il Buco's extensive, award-winning wine list offers vintages from some of the best international wineries, including a notable selection of Umbrian wines. With its rustic setting decorated with arti-sanal chandeliers and illuminated with kerosene lighting, this "oozing with romance" hotspot has the rare ability to be old-world and chic at the same time. Unless you're prepared to eat your garlicky baked fish and tapas at the bar, reservations are a must on the weekend.

Il Cortile
125 Mulberry St. (Canal & Hester Sts.)
Little Italy 212.226.6060

While not possessing much of a bar scene, Il Cortile is a fantastically ornate restaurant. Right in the center of Little Italy, the enormous interior is packed with plants, hanging and otherwise, and scores of potted trees. It sort of brings to mind the rainforest exhibit at the Museum of Natural History, but here it's OK to eat what you see. Most of the cavernous space is taken up by dining tables, and way in the back, past the fountain, the bar area is all but deserted. The music is unimaginatively tuned to an oldies station, but there's something to be said for the echoed hum of a dozen dinner conversations floating in the same air as Percy Sledge.

Il Posto Accanto
190 E. 2nd St. (Aves. A & B)
East Village 212.228.3562

This bar's name means "the place next door" in Italian, which is fitting as it's located right next door to its big sister restaurant, Il Bagatto. The perennially packed big sister loses people to this cozy wine bar when lines get long and patrons desire a more casual atmosphere. With its exposed brick, fire hydrant (clearly, it's dog-friendly), and scant tables, Il Post Accanto caters to small groups of people—mainly dates—who want to sample their 200+ bottles of wine (60 by the glass) and snack on the salty, bready treats on the countertop before ordering from a handful of authentic Italian dishes. Follow the grapevines intertwined along the ceiling overhead to the pricier Il Bagatto, or just pretend you're rich by association.

In Vino
215 E. 4th St. (Aves. A & B)
East Village 212.539.1011

You'll be drenched In Vino at this Italian wine bar. An offshoot of Max restaurant in Alphabet City, it's stocked with over 20 wines by the glass and 400+ by the bottle. This cavernous, rustically charming date spot has a tasty and inexpensive menu; the friendly, knowledgeable staff is inviting, and the young, local clientele experiences shorter waits than at any of the other neighborhood spots. All the wines served are Italian, and the food is too—

enjoy authentic homemade pastas or, if you want something to nibble on, order a cheese and meat platter to complement your vino. They don't serve beer or liquor here, so if you don't partake of the vine, you'll have a sober time...so do as they do in Rome and drink up.

Indochine
430 Lafayette St. (Astor Pl. & 4th St.)
NoHo 212.505.5111

Indochine

Upon entering Indochine, you'll feel that you've entered a VIP room in the jungle. The aromatic and beautifully arranged French and Vietnamese cuisine at this consistently popular NoHo favorite has been giving new meaning to "Good Morning, Vietnam!" for over 20 years. The moody décor consists of bamboo wainscoting, banana leaf wallpaper, and plantation shutters. People-watching doesn't get any better than this. From Warhol lookalikes to music and fashion industry execs to the comically uncomfortable first dates, Indochine hosts a truly mixed blend of downtown characters. Order one of the many signature cocktails at the bar including the very popular Indochine Martini (pineapple- and ginger-infused vodka, fresh lime juice, and triple sec) and look forward to another 20 years of excellence.

Ini Ani
105 Stanton St. (@ Ludlow St.)
Lower East Side 212.254.9066

Ini Ani is a tempest in a teacup, but it's a very well-decorated teacup. A fairly recent entry into the revved-up gentrification of the Lower East Side, this terminally cute wine/coffee bar occupies a former apartment. And the size of the space proves that out. No bigger than your living room, the space still manages to fit scads of small art-deco tables (and on weekends, a DJ station). Though coffee is served by day, at night the wine's the draw, and if the list seems short consider how much space there is to store it. A totally unpretentious local crowd gives way to far-flung (read: B&T, uptown) beautiful people on the weekend. Go for the evening happy hour after a tough day at work: $2 off most anything, for a couple hours starting around 5pm. $6-8 paninis and sandwiches round out the frilly friendliness of this polished little LES gem.

'ino
21 Bedford St. (6th Ave. & Downing St.)
West Village 212.989.5769

Itsy-bitsy 'ino is the perfect combination of fancy-shmancy wine bar and comfy-womfy neighborhood hangout. Funky alternative music sets the tone while you dilly-dally over the extensive wine list (over 125 to choose from). Don't worry, though; this is not your regular hoity-toity wine joint—the unpretentious wait staff makes navigating the list easy-peasy, even for novices (selections are available by the bottle, half-carafe, or glass.) The exposed brick interior is rustic and cozy without being fuddy-duddy; and while 'ino may be too small for large groups, this Italian café is super-duper for catching up with close friends. If you want to look like a hot-shot in front of your honey-bunny order her up a panini sandwich and an espresso before trying some hanky-panky in one of 'ino's candlelit nooks. Okey dokey?

'inoteca
98 Rivington St. (@ Ludlow St.)
Lower East Side 212.614.0473

You've seen this place before without realizing it. It's the romantic, airy wine bar on Rivington that, amidst grungy lounges and tenement houses, looks absolutely out of place. Yet with the culinary boom that's overtaking the LES, it's no wonder that this wee wine bar (which is more like a ridiculously well-stocked cellar of over 350 vinos) is part of an epicurean rejuvenation of the neighborhood. You know that poser oenophile you hang out with that just loves wine and claims to be more knowledgeable than the *Sideways* guy? Put his money where his grape-swilling mouth is and dare the windbag to navigate this wine list. Remember: in vino veritas. (Loosely translated, that means "There is truth in wine." In essence, intellectual beer goggles.)

Inside
9 Jones St. (4th & Bleecker Sts.)
West Village 212.229.9999

Inside's fresher-than-fresh seasonal menu puts a new spin on old favorites, and the subtle lighting, simple but elegant décor, and speakers that breathe a delightful selection of jazz standards complete the comfortable atmosphere. If you try the Newport steak, an unusual cut of lean sirloin served with black olive relish and white runner beans, you'll be in for a treat. The long hall of tables isn't cluttered, either, making Inside a great place to take a date; and if the wait is too long, the bar in the front is a friendly alternative to table service. Elegant without pretension and delicately exotic, this restaurant from Charleen Badman and partner Anne Rosenzweig is the place to go for classic New England cuisine, and you won't pay Newport prices.

International Bar
120 1/2 1st Ave. (7th & 8th Sts.)
East Village 212.777.9244

From the name you'd think this bar brings together a conglomeration of global festivities and patrons. So brace yourself. This dive, on first appearances alone, reminds passersby that they're a block away from gritty Alphabet City. Once you've passed the neon sign-filled front window and entered this dimly lit bar, head to the backroom and settle in for the 2-for-1 happy hour wih $3 well drinks. Take in the scenery (a Christmas tree hangs from the ceiling) and listen to tunes blasting from the functional jukebox, but if you're feeling overwhelmed by the gothic décor (a makeshift fireplace, dusty candelabra, and a deer head), take a cigarette break in the garden. Regulars here don't have the best foreign relations skills, but then, again, neither does the United States.

iO

119 Kent Ave. (@ N. 7th St.)
Williamsburg 718.388.3320

iO, a mini-complex of restaurant (Italian), bar (well-stocked, polished-looking), and club (Friday features live jazz and on Saturdays the DJ spins Latin salsa), is not your typical Williamsburg haunt. Food is available in the formal dining room located in the front section of iO, and with urban development taking over the waterfront, this might actually become a nice place to take in the East River rather than to try and rubberneck past abandoned lots and industrial buildings. The 100-year-old restaurant has survived a lot of change in the neighborhood, so when the wrecking balls come in to whitewash Willy B. with glistening condos, this classy establishment is likely to keep on marchin' on.

Iona

180 Grand St. (Bedford & Driggs Aves.)
Williamsburg 718.384.5008

Iona is one cool Irish-ish bar. Picture vacationing with friends at your grandmother's upstate house—all the older set has gone to sleep, leaving you guys to revel in ping-pong, Yahtzee, and the well-stocked liquor cabinet. Lit like a library, Iona definitely caters to a faux-hawked intellectual set that not only appreciates but sometimes even buys the art on the walls (it's all for sale!). In contrast to the majority of morose hipster scenes, Iona's jolly vibe doesn't cause visitors to feel self-conscious about whether or not their outfits are ironic enough. Cute little raised nooks sandwiching the entrance to the bar make for cozy drinking corners, and the window panes that separate them from the smokers in the garden make for a fun, people-watching dynamic.

Iridium

1650 Broadway (@ 52nd St.)
Midtown 212.582.2121

Ever since Iridium moved from the LES to Times Square with its conspicuous neon "Jazz" sign, it's left New Yorkers feeling like they've caught a glimpse of the Emperor's new clothes. Music to match the bland mushroom risotto panders to a receptive crowd of people who were likely alive when Les Paul (who plays here on Monday nights) first picked up an electric guitar. Apart from the requisite long-haired guitar enthusiast, most come not to pay tribute to the legend, but rather as a stop on their list of "must-see" attractions. Though Iridium's wine list hits a high note with 200 bottles, the high prices are way off-key, further adding to a fabricated Big Apple that hardly resembles the real New York—which is probably why the tourists love it.

Irish Pub

838 7th Ave. (53rd & 54th Sts.)
Midtown 212.664.9364

In some "Irish" pubs, the only hints of actual Irishness are a few decorative shamrocks on the walls or a picture of James Joyce tucked away in a corner. This place, however, despite the obvious name, is a charming and authentic pub. One gets the feeling Swift and Yeats might have come here for a pint if they somehow found themselves in the area, perhaps waiting for *Hairspray* to begin. Bartenders and a good number of customers even speak in actual Irish accents. The wood-paneled room, decorated with paintings and pictures of the Emerald Isle, has a slightly old-fashioned feel to it.

The atmosphere is relaxed, which makes it good for a leisurely, low-key afternoon or evening Irish coffee…or better still, a pint o' the ale.

The Irish Punt
40 Exchange Pl. (William & Broad Sts.)
Financial District 212.422.7868

The Irish eyes are smiling upon ye at this warm, casual pub that sits in a snarl of streets in the heart of Wall Street. Lunchtime draws lively crowds of financial types who come to gather and jaw over the fine pub fare, from juicy steaks to seafood, including the requisite fish and chips. Come nightfall, the same Wall Streeters return, this time to knock back a few pints, along with locals and the occasional stray tourist. Like all good Irish pubs, there's a worn bar where you can park yourself for the night, and friendly bartenders who'll listen to your woes while plying you with pints. One lick of the dense foam topping a monster glass of Guinness and you're cured. No surprises and no complaints here.

Irish Rogue
356 W. 44th St. (8th & 9th Aves.)
Hell's Kitchen 212.445.0131

Irish Rogue is the kind of place you either love or hate. Big greasy food is found, TVs abound, beer oozes from 22 taps, and U2 reigns supreme. Yes, this is Midtown/Hell's Kitchen at its most "after work." Dark wood and stone walls and pressed tin ceilings dress this spot up more than one might expect from such a place and on occasion the crowd dons something other than standard-issue khakis. There is a heavy sports bent at Irish Rogue, but when football season is in hibernation, Monday night is wing night, where three bird arms go for $1. Black-and-white author photos hang from the walls, completing a theme where these patrons like to celebrate, but don't necessarily read-Joyce. (Say it quickly.)

Irving Plaza
17 Irving Pl. (15th & 16th Sts.)
Gramercy 212.777.6817

Irving Plaza has earned its high rank among the city's most rockin' downtown music venues. It's also one of the only rock clubs left that still hosts all-ages shows, so on nights when bands like CKY play, the line usually wraps around the corner and far down the block. Big-name acts such as Coldplay, Old 97s, System of a Down, and Better Than Ezra have played here—and some nights the crowd is so into it that the balcony shakes. It's impossible not to hear the band no matter where you are in the venue—at one of the two full-service bars, lounging by coat-check on a torn-up velvet couch, or scoping out the people down on the main floor from the top-floor balcony.

i-Shebeen Madiba
195 Dekalb St. (Adelphi & Carlton Sts.)
Fort Greene 718.855.9190

You've heard about Cain—now meet the city's other, lesser-known South African bar and restaurant. Sidewalk tables replace celebrity-packed banquettes, and inside a treasure trove of art, crafts, knickknacks, and other African paraphernalia, including a giant Warhol-style portrait of Mandela, sets the tone. The gourmet-ized but otherwise very authentic South African cuisine is delicious, and the cocktails (not "Brooklyn cheap" at mostly $8) are made with fresh ingredients and go down nicely. No one said that travel was cheap, but sitting amongst these many tables of large and small groups talking, laughing, and meeting each other justifies the slightly inflated prices. Don't think you can cut back by skipping the tip—i-Shebeen only feels like another country.

Isis @ Union Bar
204 Park Ave. S. (17th & 18th Sts.)
Flatiron 212.674.2105

S'cuse me, hey, yo, barkeep! It's loud and crowded at Isis @ Union Bar after work, but when you finally get the bartender's attention and swig that first Woo Woo Martini ($11), you'll become part of the herd at this location's latest reincarnation. This

25-and-up professional contingent is only trying to blow off steam and the music helps, with a mix of throbbing soul and dance beats. Loosen that necktie because the Union Burger ($9) is a lot to swallow, or get sweet with grilled shrimp mango skewers ($11). After that, expect the typical bar fare until 11pm. Tense? Nine draughts and 10 bottles ($6) will loosen you up (and dropkick you under the table), as will the bevy of reds ($6/$39), whites ($7/$35), and single malts ($11).

IXTA
48 E. 29th St. (Park & Madison Aves.)
Murray Hill 212.683.4833

The hottest tamale in an otherwise flavorless strip of Murray Hill, it's no wonder this tiny and trendy hacienda was named after a Mexican volcano. Under the glow of candlelit wall sconces, IXTA erupts with fiery food, décor, and fiesta. Couples squeeze into green banquettes (and, in warmer weather, at outdoor tables) to taste inventive New Mexican dishes like squash blossom quesadillas, seafood ceviche, and tortilla-crusted tuna, while singles take to the stools along the elegant wood bar. Don't drink the water, because the cocktail list is more than a cut above Jose Cuervo, featuring 35 varieties of tequila and several inspired approaches to the margarita. Save some *dinero* during happy hour (Monday-Friday, 4pm-7pm) when drinks are 2-for-1, and homemade tortilla chips, fresh salsa, and tomatillo sauce are on the house.

Izakaya Izu
9 E. 13th St. (5th Ave. & University Pl.)
Greenwich Village 646.486.7313

Located beneath the already popular neighborhood sushi restaurant Izu, Izakaya Izu is a karaoke lounge with a quirky, cosmic décor that makes about as much sense as Jane Fonda in army fatigues. Unlike so many of the city's dingy karaoke dens, this venue suggests the inside of a luxury spaceship, from the neon lights of the bar area to the plasma-TV screens in the private karaoke rooms. While the bar ("Izakaya" means "bar" in Japanese) boasts over 25 premium

sakes, the most popular cocktail is the "UFO Chaser," a mix of Alizé, Wild Passion, Malibu Mango, and pineapple and cranberry juice; it's all you need to get up the nerve to belt out "What's So Funny About Peace, Love & Understanding?" for the crowd.

Jackie's Fifth Amendment
404 5th Ave. (7th & 8th Sts.)
Park Slope 718.788.9123

The lone outpost of genuine Brooklyn grit in a gentrified, trendified neighborhood, this dark little bar belongs to the diehard alcoholics. Stalwart bartenders will help you drown your sorrows with a standard selection of beers and cocktails, or, for a treat, your own personal bucket of tiny bottled beer. Whether it's the middle of the morning or the middle of the night, this place is somehow always open, a haven for the huddled masses to watch the game, punch some Billy Joel in the jukebox, or just cry into their beer. Newcomers are not terribly welcomed, and should be warned that this place refuses to be co-opted into an ironic gesture.

Jack's Restaurant and Bar
147 W. 40th St. (Broadway & 7th Ave.)
Midtown 212.869.8300

Jack Nicholson's character in *Chinatown* would have loved the classic noir-ish perfection of this Midtown bar and restaurant's interior—a long, white bar greets you on entry and sleek booths along the wall draw you into the dining room in back. Seductive ivory white lamps and light emanating from the front windows will make you feel like you've suddenly stepped into a black-and-white close-up all your own. And you won't need an alibi to leave—nor will you want one. Three generous portion-filled plates of tapas will cost you only $24 and the bartender serves up custom-made martinis. So make sure to wear your best vintage suit; Jack's will make you feel sexier than Orson Welles in *Touch of Evil.*

Jacques-imo's NYC

Jacques-imo's NYC

366 Columbus Ave. (@ 77th St.)
Upper West Side 212.799.0150

Nothing says Big Easy quite like a leg lampshade in fishnet stockings; and you'll find such an accessory resting on the bar at this Cajun/Creole joint. If that's not your first clue that this N'awlins joint just wants you to have fun, show up on Mondays for "Bingo for Booze." If you still aren't feeling the festive vibe, invoke the spirits with a hurricane ($8; $20 pitchers on Mondays) or the Purple Haze beer (it'll give you a heave-ho into the spirit of Mardis Gras, ensuring that you'll be cross-eyed and searching for beads before the night is through). At its heart, Jacques-Imo's is a family-friendly atmosphere where kids under eight eat for free, while the rest of this place is a one-way street to the glitz of Bourbon Street.

Jake's Dilemma

430 Amsterdam Ave. (80th & 81st Sts.)
Upper West Side 212.580.0556

The Living Room at Jake's Dilemma is to alcohol what *Friends'* Central Perk was to coffee: A comfy

spot with mucho seating and a mismatched décor, specially designed for cozying up to a date or chilling with your homies while cradling your favorite drink. The dilemma lies in the fact that the entire Upper West Side has that same thought in mind. If you can't snag a place to sit in the Living Room, try the private party-friendly space or the main bar area itself…beer pong anyone? You and the gang can exchange quips over a round chosen from the 48 bottles of beer on the wall, and on Thursdays, $10 pitchers of shots beat Must-See TV.

Jake's Saloon

875 10th Ave. (@ 57th St.)
Hell's Kitchen 212.333.3100

A place called Jake's Saloon sounds like it ought to rock all night long like a neighborhood bar filled with young people (wearing beer goggles) pounding (cheap) beers and singing along (badly) to (tacky) lost classics. Instead, this neighborhood bar is a tried-and-true (albeit subdued) establishment where everyone is more concerned with the impressive and appetizing beer selection than the bar's ambiance or hipness factor. The décor has a masculine feel and the pub grub is greasy (though it's a little on the pricey side); you'd think that because of its far, far, away location, Jake's Saloon would be more aptly named Jake's 7-11 or Jake's Parking Lot, if it weren't for the loyal (and thirsty) regulars.

Jameson's
975 2nd Ave. (51st & 52nd Sts.)
Midtown 212.980.4465

Old gents bump elbows with construction workers and salary men at this Midtown spot. And Jameson's scores big points for drawing customers from the homeland; unlike most of the cookie-cutter pubs in this part of town, you can actually hear Irish brogues at the bar, not just behind it. The staff is friendly and competent, the Guinness is a good pour, and the bangers and mash are as authentic as you can find outside of the Emerald Isle. Celtic cred aside, there's not much to set apart this dim and quiet spot; it's just an honest-to-goodness bar for folks looking to quietly get drunk. Here at Jameson's, it's polite to utter euphemisms like "May God not weaken your hand"—especially if your mate's clutching a freshly poured pint.

Jane
100 W. Houston St. (Thompson St. & LaGuardia Pl.)
Greenwich Village 212.254.7000

Fellas looking for a warm, clean-cut, cultured, sophisticated gal will find respite with Jane. Quite possibly the most tried-and-true low-key eatery the city has to offer, this little gem of a wine bar nestled on the western edge of Houston Street is virtually guaranteed to reduce your stress levels as soon as you cross the threshold. Furnished in cool, contemporary mod chic, which somehow, amazingly, exudes calm and comfort amongst a dizzying array of square shapes (from seats to lights and even the ceiling paneling), you'll immediately notice an abundance of pleasantly numbing beige tones—chestnut, taupe, cream, off-white—that gently whittle away the day's concerns as if by magic. Of course, the tasteful menu and 80-plus selections of old- and new-world vino don't hurt either.

Japas
11 St. Marks Pl. (2nd & 3rd Aves.)
East Village 212.473.4264

Smack-dab in the middle of the city's teeming breeding ground for teenage rebellion and over-priced lifestyle staples, Japas's understated outside is punctuated by the buzz-and-be-let-in policy that might make it easy to miss. Even to those who have seen the inside, this karaoke bar maintains its air of secrecy with low, sloping ceilings and brick walls, making it feel like a karaoke cave. The policies here are straightforward, though; leave your credit card at the bar and pay $1 a pop to wail away on Journey classics while you sip your mandated mixed drinks, sakes, or beers. Karaoke nerds may note that the music selection is limited, but the atmosphere is comfy for newbies, and the bartender might give you an A+ for your rendition of "Open Arms."

Jarrod's Lounge
198 Union St. (Broadway & Montrose Ave.)
Williamsburg 718.963.9300

Jarrod's Lounge is a little bit of smooth flava that happens to be located across the street from the 90th Precinct police station. A hip-hop bar for clientele who'll dress up to go out but don't want to haul to Manhattan just for a good time, Jarrod's kind of feels like you're in a Captain Morgan's ad; a good-looking urban crowd in tube tops and button-downs are shooting pool and taking it easy. Each light-blue pleather booth is furnished with its own flat-screen TV (just in case you missed the last episode of *Cops*, though you can catch the live version right outside), and since everybody's having a good time, the bartender's likely to do some ass-shaking to the music while she fixes you a drink.

The Jazz Gallery
290 Hudson St. (Dominick & Spring Sts.)
SoHo 212.242.1063

Though technically a museum, the Jazz Gallery features two sets of crazy jazz by hepcats each and every night. Jump on over to this "international jazz cultural center"; it's the perfect place to take parents who need evidence of your ever-heightening sophistication or that older special someone you've been seeing on the side. Music buffs will appreciate the quality music and legendary grand pianos. But unless you're Herbie Hancock, call ahead and make reservations because this bar/performance space fills up quick (though there's always the option of becoming a member). Tickets will set you back a cool $15, but with the cost of a movie quickly approaching that price tag, what's a few more rubes to experience some real culture? You don't want to be a "square" now, do you?

J.D.'s
206 E. 52nd St. (@ 3rd Ave.)
Midtown 212.751.7353

Like the Emerald Isle itself, this Irish pub is caught in a tug-of-war between two different masters. Only in this case, theme trumps politics and J.D.'s finds itself at the mercy of both "quaint Irish tradition" and "modern Southern dive," implying "J.D." might stand for Jethro Donnelly. Because for each Irish ying (shepherd's pie and the very tasty and quite affordable "famous wee burgers"), there's a Southern yang ("peel-and-eat shrimp") lurking somewhere in the background. But don't fret, because just when it seems that the bar has exhausted all possible U2 and neo-So-rock standards, it surprises with its own unique, muddled charm. And anyone can see why, after more than three decades, customers keep coming back for a wee bit of this bar's blarney brand of Southern comfort.

Jean-Luc
507 Columbus Ave. (84th & 85th Sts.)
Upper West Side 212.712.1700

Not an oyster is out of place at this impeccable, well-executed uptown venue for the 30-something after-work set. Candlelight and meticulously tarnished mirrors that just might be antiques create a spacious and tasteful provincial French atmosphere perfect for an after-work soiree or a night out with the girls. The ambiance and suave clientele are worth the jaunt uptown, though the uninspired wine and beer selection leaves a bit to be desired. The bar and restaurant are well-populated after work, but the scene is pretty relaxed compared to some neighboring bars. Whether you sally up to the bar for some pinot or relax at a table for crab cakes and caviar, be sure to take a jaunt downstairs along the luxurious, candlelit spiral staircase.

Jekyll & Hyde
91 7th Ave. S. (4th & Barrow Sts.)
West Village 212.989.7701

Don't let friends or out-of-town guests gaslight you into visiting this theme restaurant "for eccentric explorers and mad scientists." You'd have to be mad to want to endure a meal here. Old horror movies play on the TVs and spooky sound effects add to the "atmosphere." A tourist trap if ever there was one, the only mystery at Jekyll & Hyde is how they lure patrons into their lair. A staff of actors portrays kooky characters, interacting as you eat your meal and inducing indigestion with cringe-worthy puns. But don't be too hard on them; they're just trying to make a buck. Truly, the only monstrous thing here is the beer selection, which is impressive, but not a selling point. Sink your fangs into a real meal elsewhere.

Jeremy's Ale House
228 Front St. (Peck Slip & Beekman St.)
Financial District 212.964.3537

Happiness is a bottle of Miller Light and a shot of tequila that costs $4. For over 30 years, this crusty downtown tavern has been serving up suds, tequila, and seafood to a beer-guzzling crowd that's evolved over the decades from longtime fishermen and workers on break from the South Street Seaport fish market to 20- and 30-something Wall Streeters who like the uncomplicated vibe and the 32-oz. beer for about five bucks. That quart of beer dips to $1.75 during happy hour, weekdays from 8am-10am (yes, am, as in morning). Don't skip the seafood here; Jeremy's fried clams served with heaps of fries will get you refueled for the next 32-ouncer.

Jerry's

101 Prince St. (Mercer & Greene Sts.)
SoHo 212.966.9464

People who shudder at fluorescent lighting and grease will find Jerry's diner façade kitschy, fun, and refreshing. Those looking for anything resembling an actual diner should go to a diner. Most go to Jerry's for the cocktails like the key lime and watermelon martinis and the food, which is a far cry from diner both in taste and price. The "SoHo see and be seen" attitude compensates for the otherwise anti-climactic dining experience. By dinnertime the lights have been dimmed and the candles lit, which makes it suitable for some late-night gazing and grazing. Brunch is rumored to be one of the eatery's highlights and perhaps a better opportunity to enjoy Jerry's diner-chic décor.

Jezebel

630 9th Ave. (@ 45th St.)
Hell's Kitchen 212.582.1045

Like a coquettish Southern temptress, Jezebel lurks behind a nondescript corner of Ninth Ave., but peek behind the scarves that adorn the windows and you've found yourself a lady for the night. Inside is a magical mix of Southern, French, and African décor: swinging porch chairs, chandeliers, and intricate fabrics draped everywhere. More restaurant than bar, Jezebel serves pricey soul food to the pre-theater crowd and moneyed locals. On Fridays and Saturdays, the bar area turns festive with live piano music. The service can be a bit snooty and the drink prices are high, but who ever said a night out with Jezebel would be cheap? And c'mon. How many $12 WooWoos (peach schnapps, vodka, and cranberry juice) do you really need?

Jim Brady's

75 Maiden Lane (William & Gold Sts.)
Financial District 212.425.1300

A large, upscale Irish pub with red leather booths and lots of brass, Jim Brady's feels like a relic from an era past. Maybe it's the ornate bar, which was transplanted here intact after an earlier, more glamorous life at the legendary Stork Club, a place of guns, diamonds, and champagne. Now the excitement rarely extends beyond pints of beer and plates of buffalo wings. The vibe here is one of ease and that's reflected by easygoing bartenders who practice their skill with a smile. Nights at Brady's vary, but during lunch most days, it's full of masticating suits and other area workers. TVs play all of the big sporting events, but they're not the center of attention. Near the front lies a tribunal altar to 20 former customers who perished on 9-11.

Jimmy Walker's

245 E. 55th St. (2nd & 3rd Aves.)
Midtown 212.319.6650

Like Johnnie Walker's younger, surlier brother, this place enjoys its reputation as a local tough with just a hint of Irish humor i.e., novelty signs hanging behind the bar. (Who would ever believe that a place called Jimmy Walker's wouldn't be dyn-o-mite?) Though it's reminiscent of the grungy billiard halls mothers used to warn their children about, complete with a pool table and outdated videogames, Jimmy Walker's lacks both the excitement and cheap drinks one would expect from a place with its "charm." Comprised almost exclusively of no-nonsense regulars, this is a place where you don't want to cross the line—whether it be during a game of darts, or while chatting up one of the hard drinkers at the bar. Enjoy your apple mint martini.

Jimmy's Corner

140 W. 44th St. (6th Ave. & Broadway)
Midtown 212.221.9510

Perhaps the only establishment left to get that Times Square pre-Giuliani vibe, boxing-themed Jimmy's Corner is a dive bar institution. Offering a menu strictly of a liquid variety, patrons can choose from 15 different vodkas, among other spirits. Filled with loads of pictures and pugilism memorabilia, this museum-like place is tour-worthy. Established 33 years ago, this bar has surely seen it all. Shellacked photos on tabletops capture the many good times patrons have had at Jimmy's in the past. When slow, this is the kind of bar where you can strike up a conversation with a stranger at the tight bar and no doubt hear a great yarn. Go for the booze and stay for the characters. Just be careful you don't go down swinging.

Joe's Bar
520 E. 6th St. (Aves. A & B)
East Village 212.473.9093

Year-round Christmas lights, a classic country jukebox boasting Willie, Patsy, and patron saint Johnny Cash, and a selection of 60-cent chips above the bar complete the trifecta of dive bar greatness at Joe's. The friendly Midwestern feel keeps this 100-year-old establishment packed even on weeknights. Despite kitschy touches like the heads of Bambi's cousins mounted on the walls and the back-lit case of thrift-store trophies, Joe's is essentially a place to enjoy a cheap beer, play some pool, and get to know your urban neighbors. You won't find any event nights or specialty cocktails here, just sports on TV, and a barkeep who addresses the customers by name. Beer is your best bet, but the booze—like the design scheme—is cheap.

Joe's Pub
425 Lafayette St. (Astor Pl. & 4th St.)
NoHo 212.539.8770

To honor Shakespeare in Central Park founder Joseph Papp, Joe's Pub was added to the adjoining Public Theater in 1998, and culture vultures have been coming in for port wine/champagne cocktails dubbed Lady Macbeths while being entertained by an impressive mix of live music, dance, comedy, and poetry. Large-scale entertainers like Emmylou Harris, Joss Stone, David Byrne, and Alicia Keys have played this intimate setting, and late nights at Joe's Pub feature some of New York's hottest up-and-coming bands and DJs who spin a variety of R&B, hip-hop, electro, and global grooves. Grab a seat on a plush, comfy couch and you'll feel that you're enjoying all the downtown hipness in your very own living room.

Joey's
186 Ave. B (11th & 12th Sts.)
East Village 212.353.9090

Perfectly straddling that line between East Village dive and neighborhood haunt, Joey's is a cozy little joint for this area's locals, all of whom seem to get around the 9-to-5 in some way or another regardless of age or interests. Sufficiently jaded yet refreshingly unaffected, Joey's staff has a steadfast reputation for fast, friendly service and dishing out lip-smackin' comfort food. Televised sporting events play at the front bar, while the rear outside patio, which is decorated in the tried and true tradition of mismatched grandmotherly furnishings from yesteryear, makes a brilliant setting for Scrabble, backgammon, chess, or any one of a dozen parlor games. Ready and willing opponents are never further than a table away, so swing on by for a few rounds and indulge your inner sportsman.

John Street Bar & Grill
17 John St. (Broadway & Nassau Sts.)
Financial District 212.349.3278

You have to descend a steep set of stairs before you enter this scrappy, low-ceilinged cavern of amusements: lots of TV sets showing baseball and horse racing (there is an OTB right next door), dartboards, a pool table, speakers crackling with Black Sabbath and Beatles, and old men with moustaches, beards, and glasses manning the bar. No surprise that this deluxe adolescent basement is mostly male-populated. There's a large backroom for private parties, and the establishment gives you incentives to drink just about every day of the week: Thursday has $10 all-you-can-drink draft beer (17 choices) from 5pm-8pm; Fridays from 5pm–8pm offer $6 pitchers and $3 kamikaze shots.

Johnney's Fish Grill
250 Vesey St. (@ World Financial Ctr.)
TriBeCa 212.385.0333

Boasting some of the stiffest drinks and biggest dishes in Manhattan, Johnney's at first sounds like a pudgy slice of the Midwest. Seeing it in the context of a big suburban-looking mall drives the image home even further. Tucked in a corner of the expansive World Financial Center food court, Johnney's is a glassy constellation of booths set around a sleek, oval bar. The menu is all fish and game, bringing Texas to mind and attracting financial sector carnivores in droves. Prices are very fair: Half a roasted free-game chicken runs $12.95, and the hanger steak is just under $16. But if you're going to come, come for the fish. There are daily seafood specials, including exotic treats like paella and the always satisfying sea bass.

Joshua Tree
513 3rd Ave. (34th & 35th Sts.)
Murray Hill 212.689.0058

Joshua Tree is the pillar in a trifecta of nearly identical Murray Hill bars. But unlike its clones, Mercury Bar and Bar 515, Joshua Tree caters to a younger crowd who spent last year paying their roommates to write their thesis papers. Like its brothers (or "bros") Joshua Tree gets packed early, so don't be surprised if you can't find a seat and you wind up waiting for a beer. Famous for the friendly service and collegiate vibe, Joshua Tree has a ton of beers on tap; the food menu is extensive, the brunch is inexpensive, and the game is always playing on big-screen TVs. Joshua Tree also boasts a colorful desert nightscape for those art majors—not that you'll find art majors here.

Joshua Tree
366 W. 46th St. (8th & 9th Aves.)
Hells Kitchen 212.489.1920

Despite being better groomed, in a more prominent location, and even a little better-looking than his older brother, the Hell's Kitchen Joshua Tree seems less-known than its more-sporty Third Avenue sibling. Perhaps it's the mild sophistication of the pre-theater crowd that calms this sports lounge and restaurant down a bit? Huge TVs hang from otherwise bare brick walls behind the bar as

Times Square refugees inhale upscale burgers and bar food in two levels of seating. This spot opens for lunch and operates 'til the early morn. Like the hours it keeps and the food it serves is Joshua Tree's crowd, which is rather unassuming and middle of the road. In fact, if Rande Gerber tried to do an Irish pub/sports bar hybrid, it would look a little something like this.

Josie Wood's Pub
11 Waverly Pl. (Greene & Mercer Sts.)
Greenwich Village 212.228.9909

Josie Wood's Pub

This basement bar right off of Washington Square Park has the charm of a college bar in Anytown, USA. With a menu of tasty appetizers, burgers, and bar fare and a slew of happy hour specials ($3 beers from 4pm-9pm, $5 martinis from 4pm-7pm, and $11 draft pitchers all day), this pub is a great place to hang out no matter what your age. The chipper staff makes conversation while blending your special drinks, and beyond that there are pool tables, darts, and an Internet jukebox to keep you amused. The prices are all reasonable, and the drinks seem to get bigger as the night goes on, so you could easily stop in for a pint of the house ale and end up hanging out until the wee hours. Just be sure to change out of last night's clothes before heading to class.

Journey's Lounge (@ the Essex Hotel)
160 Central Park S. (6th & 7th Aves.)
Midtown 212.484.5119

After walking into the luxury Essex Hotel, ask the

staff to direct you to Journey's Lounge and they'll probably tell you to head straight and then turn left at the second glistening chandelier. Once inside, you'll find a mixed crowd made up primarily of hotel guests, including business and leisure travelers imbibing overpriced drinks (beers for $8; wine and cocktails for $10 or more). Depending on the hour, there's a selection of entrées and desserts that you would expect to find on a typical room-service menu. It's temporarily interesting to feel like you're in an upper-crust lounge from another era, but the novelty quickly wears off—unless, of course, you've brought your Hugh Hefner robe and you plan on enjoying a cognac by the fire with Miss May and Miss July.

Joya
215 Court St. (Wyckoff & Warren Sts.)
Cobble Hill 718.222.3484

Try to get a few inches of bar space on a weekend night at this Cobble Hill Thai joint and you'll likely find a mass of trendy locals eying you suspiciously as they clamor for tables. The restaurant serves delicious, moderately priced Thai food, but waiting at the bar isn't such a bad deal either. DJs spin unobtrusive electronica while the smell of curry and garlic floats in from the open-air kitchen. Pillows line the benches of the large garden space in the back, and oh-so-beautiful waiters and waitresses whisk in and out to take your order. If you can stand the wait, try their signature pad thai, or be more adventurous and get the banana rolls. Just make sure to hit the ATM before you go—Joya is cash-only.

JP Mustard
22 Fulton St. (@ Water St.)
Financial District 212.785.0612

When the sun is shining and the seaport is buzzing, JP Mustard's massive outdoor seating area makes it a choice spot for soaking in rays and wondering, aside from the Gap, where these tourists buy their clothes. Weekends are a carnival. On overcast weekdays, JP Mustard feels a little like a cafeteria with a tiny, almost irrelevant bar that's an afterthought to the sandwich and cafete-

ria shop. The crowd here ranges from old to young, but can skew slightly male when hubbies grab a seat while their wives hit the South Street Seaport's plethora of shops. The cobblestone streets, shady trees, and old buildings make for good scenery and the "ocean" air is relaxing, but in any other location, Mustard probably wouldn't cut it.

J.P. Warde's Saloon
12 Ave. A (Houston & 2nd Sts.)
East Village 212.477.9050

Never in a million years did we think we'd be saying it, but J.P. Warde's is an Irish bar that is actually a breath of fresh air. Completely out of place on hipster bar-saturated Avenue A, this non-hip, non-pretentious haunt is a welcome change from the horn-rimmed glasses and Converse-clad masses. The bar itself is fairly small, with a giant projection screen, the requisite pool table, and a huge American flag behind the bar as well as various tchotchkes bearing the bar's name. Every night from 4pm-8pm, J.P. Warde's has 2-for-1 drafts and mixed drinks, while Tuesdays offer half-price drinks for the ladies from 8pm 'til closing. Plus, there's nothing quite like banging down a Gray-Headed Slut shot ($5).

Julep
14 Ave. A (Houston & 2nd Sts.)
East Village 212.254.2442

Julep

Ladies, consider yourselves warned. The majority of Julep's clientele seems to be composed of single, drunken men of every age and description, few of whom qualify as Southern gentlemen. They no doubt come to chat up the friendly and down-home, pretty bartenders. Single ladies will certainly feel like the belle of the ball at Julep. Unfortunately, it's a monster's ball. Prices are appreciably modest, and that includes delicious barbecued meat that's best enjoyed on the patio out back. The Southern rockin' 2-for-1 happy hour might tempt you to cross the threshold, while the obnoxious patronage will more than likely drive you to drink…somewhere else. This is a good place to shoot a little pool, and ladies, having that big wooden stick in your hand will help in beating away the boys.

Jules Café
65 St. Marks Pl. (1st & 2nd Aves.)
East Village 212.477.5560

Hey, hepcats—tune into the laidback scene at Jules Café, where there's always fantastic live jazz, and never a cover. Throw in a killer wine list (80+ selections) and a heavily French-inspired, yet agreeably diverse, European lunch, brunch, and dinner menu—including everything from schnitzel to brochette to oysters on the half shell, as well as an amazing array of sinfully sumptuous desserts (check out the addictively delicious Le Fondant au Chocolat, $8.50)—and you're good to go, Daddy-o. Unobtrusively tucked into the often-obtrusive East Village, this jazzy haunt is one block off of the St. Marks madness so it's convenient to those who seek it out, but under the radar of the bar-hopping half-wits who ruin many of the places in this 'hood.

Julian's
802 9th Ave. (53rd & 54th Sts.)
Hell's Kitchen 212.262.4800

Though Julian's is primarily a restaurant offering assorted dishes (such as goat cheese ravioli, grilled lamb chops, and mahi-mahi), its wait staff of European beauties won't pressure you to dine. They realize you may be there for the three types of sangria (red, white, and rose with white zinfandel), the 10 seasonal cocktails (named after Mediterranean islands), or their solid list of wines.

The bar in the back, nestled amid a deep-red sea-faring décor, seats about six but it's a romantic place for an early-evening cocktail or post-theater nightcap wherein you can easily hear your date speak. In warm weather, Julian's outdoor seating doesn't hug the curb or clog the sidewalk and their side patio offers shaded outdoor seating.

Julius
159 W. 10th St. (@ Waverly Pl.)
West Village 212.929.9672

One of the city's oldest gay bars, Julius attracts a regular crowd of patrons that look as if they've been coming here since the bar first opened about 140 years ago. But that's OK, because naughty older gay men need love too. Julius is an average bar filled with average men—no fashionistas, Chelsea boys, or East Village twinks. Even so, everyone is welcome here; the guys are always eager for a good conversation to go with their beers. Named after a dog, this tiny bar is filled with small statues of dachshunds. While they don't bite, you'll definitely want to satiate your appetite by sinking your teeth into one of the bar's huge burgers (because biting the sexy customers isn't exactly polite—even if it appears they might like it).

Juniper Suite
44 W. 56th St. (5th & 6th Aves.)
Midtown 212.586.4737

In an area that's better known for tourist traps than chic hangouts, Juniper Suite is a welcome surprise. The botanical-themed, two-story restaurant and lounge starts with a downstairs bar that's packed with 30-something professionals during happy hour (5pm-7pm), and later. Diners can feast on a small plates-heavy menu ($6-$14) of green fries (asparagus), duck confit spring rolls, and chipotle-braised short rib either upstairs or downstairs, but the tastefully woodsy second floor offers a sprawling view of…Midtown. Entrées ($14-$29) like the almond-crusted chicken are delicious, but they can't compete with the lime-flavored Junipertivo cocktail ($12), just one of the many highlights on the impressive alcoholic and non-alcoholic cocktail list.

Junno's
64 Downing St. (Bedford & Varick Sts.)
West Village 212.627.7995

Global-thinking, community-active, and budget-friendly, Junno's is the answer to the "What ever happened to the student union crowd?" question. While they may have abandoned their food service aspirations, Junno's quenches its patrons' thirst for culture in the form of Junno's Tuesday Night reading series. Junno's also offers an array of drink specials that would have kept Charles Bukowski from throwing his typewriter out of a window ($4 well, wine, and beer selections until 8pm). And while the casual observer might get the wrong impression walking past the vaguely under-the-sea-themed interior, Junno's is a pseudo-cultural epicenter that's populated by an intelligent, arty crowd that clamors to check out their free film screenings. You'll find this crowd fighting for admirable causes—intoxicated literacy and personal space via the ample seating.

Justin's
31 W. 21st St. (5th & 6th Aves.)
Flatiron 212.352.0599

Unlike most celebrity culinary ventures, Justin's refuses to die—despite the fact that the black-clad, no-nonsense staff seems to dubiously await some imminent hipster party. Those with short attention spans can ignore their companions in lieu of giant flat-screen TVs that blast remixed music videos and sports events. The spacious bar, which spills out onto suede brown couches and chairs, provides a full view of the adjacent dining area, where salivating drinkers indulge in over-priced Southern and Caribbean comfort food. If your New York visit isn't complete without a pilgrimage to this P. Diddy shrine, at least visit Wednesdays or Thursdays for half-priced happy hour martinis. Otherwise, you'll pay $12 for Justin's Player's Punch, a seven-liquor shot drink that's disturbingly named after the Renaissance man's 11-year-old son.

K Lounge
30 W. 52nd St., 2nd Fl. (5th & 6th Aves.)
Midtown 212.265.6665

Burning incense, kitschy sculptures, Bollywood films playing in the background, tasty kebobs, samosa treats, and cocktails like the Passion-tini offer a delicious taste of little India in Midtown. Bring your date on a whirlwind trip to the sexy, Kama Sutra-inspired K Lounge. Plush couches in the pillow room are great for relaxing (and snuggling), and the lingering smell of curry coming from the Bombay Palace restaurant downstairs is almost enough to put you in a curry coma. But that's where the music (everything from hip-hop and reggae to '80s dance beats) comes in—to keep patrons awake and give them an excuse to lean in close to each other.

Kabin
92 2nd Ave. (5th & 6th Sts.)
East Village 212.254.0204

Remember when vacations went by in a blur of kayaking, hunting, and campfire songs? Kabin brings back all of those fond remembrances with wilderness kitsch lining the walls—a "Camp-run-a-muk" sign hangs over the bar, and a sled is affixed near the pool table, which is sectioned off by a log cabin wall. The third room continues the summer camp-meets-winter-hideaway scheme with a fireplace, large mirror, and a few chaises, catering to the more "mature" crowd. This back-woods revision will give you a little mini-vacation after work with their TVs, Belgian ales, 2-for-1 happy hour (5pm-8pm), Big Buck Hunter II game, DJs (Thu-Sat), and salsa music. It's the perfect escape; no bug repellant necessary.

Kaña
324 Spring St. (Washington & Greenwich Sts.)
SoHo 212.343.8080

Hoping for a romantic tête-à-tête? Kaña's dim lighting, rustic brick walls, and quiet locale on

SoHo's outskirts won't disappoint. At dinner, you'll see plenty of longing glances, handholding, and knee-nuzzling across the tiny tables, even if it's just due to a lack of space. Sample some tasty tapas ($5-$14) served by a friendly, relaxed staff that seems like it just awakened from an afternoon siesta. But things change around 11, and you'd best watch your back while tables are moved to transform Kaña from lover's lane to a Latin dance party (Thursday–Sunday) that packs the tiny space with a diverse, attractive, largely Spanish crew. Your mojito may lack moxie, but you won't care when you're shaking your tail feather. On Fridays & Saturdays there's sometimes a cover, but on Thursdays and Sundays you can salsa for zero *dinero*.

Kanvas
219 9th Ave. (23rd & 24th Sts.)
Chelsea 212.727.2616

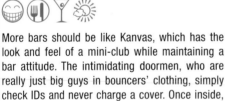
Kanvas

More bars should be like Kanvas, which has the look and feel of a mini-club while maintaining a bar attitude. The intimidating doormen, who are really just big guys in bouncers' clothing, simply check IDs and never charge a cover. Once inside, the young Chelsea crowd is loud, friendly, dancey, and ready for action. Sure, this place pales in comparison to the nearby West Chelsea super-clubs, but it's looking for a crowd that those clubs stay up too late to accommodate. A lot of afterworkers hit the upstairs lounge and clubby downstairs area, which are run by the same operator behind Hell's Kitchen bars Social and Latitude. Appetizers like big bowls of French fries and fried fishy snacks work nicely. The patio space ain't so bad either.

Karavas Tavern
162 W. 4th St. (6th Ave. & Cornelia St.)
West Village 212.243.8007

If you make the mistake of going to this pub before 3am, try to have a sense of humor about it. Karavas is crawling with (mostly lesbian) middle-aged women who wake up and go straight to this low-key bar for 15 or 20 "warm-up" drinks before they go on the prowl for fresh college meat. And that's just the wait staff. The half-hearted décor, featuring an excess of light-wood paneling (which we imagine was modeled after a little town called "Margaritaville") and the broken jukebox don't help much either. This place is good for getting in another beer and a greasy burger before you go home empty-handed. But who knows, maybe you could talk a respectable girl into coming here. Good luck!

Karma
51 1st Ave. (4th & 5th Sts.)
East Village 212.677.3160

Even before you enter, the reddish glow emanating from this sexy, no-attitude East Village rarity conveys its swanky disposition. A sundry crowd, ranging from a tattooed set to guys in khakis to anyone who just wants to freely mix their tobacco and alcohol habits in the age of the smoking ban perch on barstools to pretend this is an A-list lounge (and with the sumptuous décor, attentive bartenders, and cool music, it's easy to fool yourself). Twenty bucks will snatch two beers and a hookah; bring a date and snag one of the intimate red couches in the back and you might get even more. If a luscious cocktail is your kismet, you can't go wrong with the chocolate-covered strawberry martini; maybe then she'll be Nuts About You.

Kasadela
647 E. 11th St. (Aves. B & C)
East Village 212.777.1582

A rare find: A timelessly traditional, aesthetically pleasing, and reasonably priced authentic

Japanese kitchen and sake bar discreetly nestled in the heart of Alphabet City, Kasadela is a delectably delicate gem just waiting to be discovered and appreciated. The modest space and contemporary minimalist décor, accompanied by the incomparably hospitable and courteous demeanor of the staff, makes this an equally perfect locale for relaxed socializing, solitude, or romance. The menu features a generous selection of agreeable but not outstanding appetizer-esque fare and a few staple entrées, but feel free to forego the food. Sake is the undisputed house specialty, available in a dizzying array of draft-aged, filtered, fermented, and specially brewed varieties (try the grilled blowfish fin variation for a kick). If you haven't been here yet, go now!

Kate Kearney's Pub & Grill
251 E. 50th St. (2nd & 3rd Aves.)
Midtown 212.935.2045

Even though it's in Midtown, Kate Kearney's turns out a fun, laidback mix. The after-work crowd prefers the bar, where Dublin-born bartenders serve up eight beers from the tap. If you can't snag a barstool from one of the regulars, try your Irish luck at a table in the spacious backroom, and if you still have an appetite after listening to an endless playlist of Phish and O.A.R., order drinks and bar munchies from the prompt cocktail waitresses. Retired frat boys and grad-school yuppies dominate the rear backroom sports bar scene, complete with a pool table, dartboard, and eight televisions tuned to ESPN. Tuesdays and Saturdays turn especially Midwestern, when Beirut is played. For those who don't know, it's basically beer pong, but don't let any of these folks hear you saying that.

Katen Sushi Bar (@ the Marriott Marquis)
1535 Broadway, 8th Fl. (45th & 46th Sts.)
Midtown 212.398.1900

Described as a "traditional Japanese restaurant in a sleek and modern setting," Katen serves sushi and traditional American versions of Japanese food in a semi-tacky space (the floor pattern's dizzying wiggly lines clash with the boldly striped stools). With so many sushi places littering this town, Katen doesn't quite qualify as a cut above. However, if you're at the Marriott for any variety of reasons, it's not a bad place to fill up on raw tuna and sake. Though we can't believe many of the Midwestern families who frequent this Times Square standard hotel would dig kicking back a saketini or dining on raw fish eggs, the surprisingly delicious cocktails such as the Rising Sun and the Bonsai Blossom could make you forget what you just ate.

Katwalk
2 W. 35th St. (5th & 6th Aves.)
Midtown 212.594.9343

Katwalk

The "K" in Katwalk very well could stand for "klean," as that's the biggest of many renovations which have taken place in the litter box formerly known as Catwalk. (Mind you, that was with a "C.") In addition to having changed the spelling of their name, the new guys have also changed the entire staff, décor, etc. Though not purrrfect, Katwalk Bar and Lounge makes a noble attempt at reaching out to the male corporate crowd and the ladies who love them with '80s and pop-rock DJs, and big screens that show anything from sports broadcasts to fashion shows. To entice local kittens, Katwalk extends a ball of yarn in the form of drink specials.

Kavehaz
37 W. 26th St. (@ 6th Ave.)
Chelsea 212.322643.8632

The dramatic vault-like ceiling and luxurious display of handcrafted hardwood furniture are romantically fueled by an ever-present abundance of candlelight at this relocated jazz and wine bar. Relax, unwind, and sip a selection from the endless array of inviting beers, wines, cocktails, and blended caffeinated liqueur choices. Peruse the consistently rotating display of original artwork (by upcoming independent artists from around the world) adorning the walls or chow down on a few of Kavehaz's contemporary American dishes (including a separate menu exclusively dedicated to focaccia) and a tempting, tasteful array of entrées, salads, and desserts. And don't forget to enjoy the great live jazz bands playing seven days a week. Click your heels three times, say "Kavehaz" over and over, and you'll be transported to pure pleasure.

Kemia
630 9th Ave. (@ 44th St.)
Hell's Kitchen 212.582.3200

Kemia

Remember that episode of *Beverly Hills, 90210* when Brandon goes to the rave and has to exchange an egg for directions? Finding Kemia is

almost as annoying. First you'll discover that it shares the address of an office building/theater, then a sleepy security guard will direct you around the corner. Once inside, you'll find the same interior design of every other "swanky lounge" in NYC—dark, subterranean, high prices, experimental trendy food (here tapas), and uncomfortable seating. Tea candles and velvet are so 1999, but apparently the designer-clad bellini- and martini-guzzling patrons of Kemia didn't get the memo. It's too dark to see or be seen here, but if you like the Campbell Apartment and can't get in, stop by Kemia on your way back to New Jersey.

Kennedy's
327 W. 57th St. (8th & 9th Aves.)
Hell's Kitchen 212.759.4242

This Hell's Kitchen pub feels more like the average neighborhood bar with an Irish accent than a Dublin saloon. While many of the bar's regulars do share the bartenders' Gaelic twangs, the atmosphere—complete with ESPN-tuned TVs and celeb headshots—is suspiciously American with an Irish identity about the size of a leprechaun. Yes, the rosy-cheeked barkeeps can draw a shamrock in the head of a pint of Guinness and whip up a mean Nutty Irishman, but the lines of Carnegie-Hall-goers streaming in post-concert don't exactly scream "Erin go bragh." The charm of the bar lies in the jovial staff and the characters that frequent it, including a drunk Irishman permanently planted at the end of the bar muttering to himself and anyone who will listen while a presidential portrait of the bar's namesake stands watch.

Kenny's Castaways
157 Bleecker St. (Sullivan & Thompson Sts.)
Greenwich Village 212.979.9762

Marooned somewhere between Black Beard's dream bar and a hunting lodge, this bar/venue is a curiosity to be experienced. Complementing the assorted lanterns, swords, and chains hangs possibly the most impressive collection of Elvis memorabilia this side of the Mason-Dixon line. The soft, magenta window lights hint that a throng of strip-

Kenny's Castaways

pers might emerge, but that's when a band erupts from the back of the bar on a small stage, which can be seen from either the table seating downstairs or the small upstairs balcony area. A high, vaulted ceiling completes this interior decorator's nightmare. But after all, this is a beer drinker's bar, and with 14 beers on tap, Kenny's is a great place to bring a large group for a night of quirky novelties and hearty laughs.

Kettle of Fish
59 Christopher St. (@ 7th Ave. S.)
West Village 212.414.2278

The bookshelf at Kettle of Fish features a copy of *Baseball Prospectus*—the bible for statistics-loving baseball nerds; for reasons less known, the far corner is home to a taxidermist-stuffed dog, and the underlying "Wisconsin" theme—complete with Milwaukee Brewers games on the TV and Green Bay Packers paraphernalia on the walls—is not a beer-induced figment of your imagination; the owners hail from the Cheese State. Just after your first sip, though, it all blends together, and forms an atmosphere that can best be described as sports bar-eccentric. A backroom furthers the homey vibe set forth by the bartenders, with dartboards, an arcade machine, and board games. This is one of those landmark bars that's altered a bit from time to time, but it's always homey.

Kevin St. James
741 8th Ave. (46th & 47th Sts.)
Hell's Kitchen 212.977.5984

Somewhere between the super-divey hole-in-the-walls and the post-frat pubs that line Eighth Ave.

is Kevin St. James, which certainly has elements of each—too many TVs blaring sports, high-fiving white guys woo-hooing and doing shots, excessive amounts of beer posters and signage. But the incredibly accommodating staff, the better-than-it-needs-to-be food, and the swanky upstairs lounge area set Kevin St. James apart. Available for private parties, the second-floor lounge is cozy and warm and has a bar of its own. If you'd prefer rubbing elbows with the locals and tourists who flock here, stay down below. If you can, come for $5 happy hour beers, sit up front and watch the weird Times Square periphery as it crawls with Theater District escapees.

Keybar
432 E. 13th St. (Ave. A & 1st. Ave.)
East Village 212.478.3021

Keybar

At first glance, this Hungarian bar seems to be high on crowded and low on atmosphere, but further inspection reveals subtle sprinklings of charm. Take for example specialty drinks including the orgasmic $5 chocolate and vodka Rollo shots, which are made even better by the extra-long 2-for-1 happy hour. (6pm-10pm). A comfy lounge is tucked away in the back, but already short on space, the DJs and drink specials don't help Keybar's spatial matters much. Have a seat at the interesting lit bar that's color changes from time to time. Surprisingly, this love shack somehow finds space enough for a working fireplace. If Keybar were a better-kept secret, it would be your favorite bar in town. All things considered, it's still a good one.

KGB Bar

85 E. 4th St. (2nd & 3rd Aves.)
East Village 212.505.3360

KGB Bar has a long, illustrious history of patronizing under-aged drinking, gambling, and bootlegging. Now that's the kind of place we can grow attached to! Officially called Kraine Gallery Bar because you can't name a business KGB, CIA, or FBI in New York State, KGB is a former Ukrainian social club with a checkered past. This small, somewhat cramped, dark neighborhood bar gets packed on the weekends by those sober enough to stumble up the stairs to this hideout. You can still get cool local flavor here in the form of their Sunday and Monday night poetry and literary readings, or get educated by checking out the Marx-era photos and posters on the walls. There's a book about this legendary drinking spot, and there's no better place to read it than at KGB.

Kili

79 Hoyt St. (State St. & Atlantic Ave.)
Boerum Hill 718.855.5574

The *Divorzio all'italiana* poster on the wall is the beginning of Kili's cozy and smart aesthetic, and it's followed by candlelight, a fireplace, couches, and choice brew. In the early evenings the bar is quiet, save the doo-wop, jazz, and other dusty yet comforting music drifting from the speakers. Talk comfortably with that first date, who'll be impressed that you picked this place. Intimacy is this Boerum Hill hangout's selling point, but after 11pm on weekends, it can get rather collegiate. Superb for spring, Kili's doors open and hints of sunlight subtly brighten the cracks and corners. Have the wings with blue cheese dressing and a Stella Artois while wistfully staring at the Christmas lights, which add to the cabin-themed "Holidays with the Hipsters" vibe.

Killarney Rose

80 Beaver St. (Pearl St. & Hanover Sq.)
Financial District 212.422.1486

The Killarney Rose is reminiscent of an Irish pub in many respects: the witty, loquacious, Irish-born staff; Gaelic proverbs beautifully and meticulously painted onto the exposed wood beams; a Guinness clock hanging over the bar. But then there's the after-work crowd of brokers, traders, and other denizens of the financial underbelly, most of whom equate Ireland with puking up green beer on St. Patrick's Day. Come late-night, after the Goldman Sachs company cars turn into pumpkins and the financial set heads home, it quiets down, save for the occasional drunken girls in their early 20s dancing to *Thriller*-era Michael Jackson. Open since 1968, this enormous spot has ample seating on two floors, and the upstairs includes a mysterious lounge—mysterious only because the door is generally locked.

Kimono Lounge

62 Thomas St. (Church St. & W. Broadway)
TriBeCa 212.964.7777

If not for Megu, the über-upscale restaurant downstairs, a lot of people would ask if they could just order food at this bar. Ample mood lighting and cozy white leather booths complement Kimono Lounge's walls, which are lined with striking bolts of patterned silk. The drinks, like the décor, are sleek and expensive. While the "Blessing" is touted as Kimono's specialty, a more unique offering is the frosty pear/ginger concoction known as "Autumn Rain." The warm staff is happy to walk you through an extensive sake selection and the half-dozen or so signature cocktails. Things can be a little sleepy here on off nights, which isn't to say the room doesn't work for couples and small groups who are happy with the party they brought.

Kin Khao

171 Spring St. (W. Broadway & Thompson St.)
SoHo 212.966.3939

The name of this established Americanized Thai SoHo spot means "eat rice." But the place is all about "eat nice." It's not exotic; it tilts toward the conservative and refined. Kin Khao boasts a handsome design, soft lighting, and an open kitchen partially, and artfully, shielded by hanging floral-patterned mosaics made of pieces of colored plastic. However, David Byrne incongruously plays overhead, and the dinnertime crowd waiting for their tables at the small bar is an interesting and attractive mix of young professionals and foreign tourists. (Think several blond Swedes with martinis.) You can get some tropical flavor by sampling house drinks such as the $11 Pineapple Pat Pong, a vodka, rum, and juice pleaser. Kin Khao is part of the mini-empire that includes the two Kelley & Ping restaurants.

King Cole Bar
2 E. 55th St. (Madison & 5th Aves.)
Midtown 212.339.6721

If Mr. Peanut were a real person, this is where he would get drunk, along with the guy from Monopoly and Scrooge McDuck. Monocles and tuxedos are more likely to be seen than jeans and Jeter t-shirts, but the Bloody Mary was allegedly invented here (to this day still known as the "Red Snapper"). A huge mural depicting the "Old King Cole" nursery rhyme faces patrons, and the bartenders can't be beat. The room sets a mood that is hardly matched anywhere in Midtown, and—haughty crowd aside—if you dress nicely and use the word "charmed" a few times, you'll enjoy yourself. Bring a date, a suitcase full of Franklins to pay for the drinks, and study "Old King Cole," and there's no way you won't impress whomever you're with.

King Size
21 Essex St. (Hester & Canal Sts.)
Lower East Side 212.995.5464

This narrow silver space seems like something from a hipster-o-matic. Want "ironic" bar snacks? They've got Pepperidge Farm goldfish. Board games? You bet your colorful fake money they've got them. Techno-spinning DJ? You'll pass him en route to the plush couches in the rear. No one's going to say this place doesn't try. The bartender will even order your dinner from the beloved East Village trattoria Il Bagatto, whose owner is a partner. Despite the niceties, there are some raw

King Size

edges here. The front room has no-nonsense barstools, echoing the old-school LES, and the sofas seem designed for Ludlow/Rivington Street spillover. It's easy to be a part of the action, but tough to feel a sense of privacy at the smallish space that calls itself King Size. Happy hour runs from 5pm-8pm Tuesday through Friday.

King's Head Tavern
222 E. 14th St. (2nd & 3rd Aves.)
East Village 212.473.6590

The rock 'n' roll renaissance is alive and kicking at that noblest of noble "Union Squ-area" grog halls, the King's Head Tavern. Tired of swilling the same old suds? Never fear, m'lords and ladies—stop on by and change up your chugging routine with one of the daily shot-and-cocktail specials, check out

King's Head Tavern

the beer of the month, or have one of the irresistibly lovely serving-wenches fetch a $3 afternoon draft special from the well. Join the predominantly male, boisterously rowdy revelers as they quest for fair maidens, or take a seat at the seemingly endless bar while waiting for a knight in shining armor to appear while rocking out to one of the most hardcore jukeboxes in the entire kingdom.

Kingsland Tavern
244 Nassau Ave. (@ Kingsland Ave.)
Greenpoint 718.383.9883

If you make a habit of visiting Kingsland Tavern, you may discover a new bar every time you go. Some days, it's a place to have a quiet drink, while on others you can watch sports and enjoy complimentary treats like kielbasa and buffalo wings. You may also find an insane dance club some nights—complete with a disco ball that spins while a live band or the jukebox plays at full blast. The tavern itself is enormous and somewhat reminiscent of suburban bars, but it's retained its old-school charm via the high ceilings, pinball machine, jukebox, pool table, sports playing on the TV, and an enormous backroom for private parties. Don't come to savor an aged Scotch; this is a place to get tipsy and socialize.

Kinsale Tavern
1672 3rd Ave. (93rd & 94th Sts.)
Upper East Side 212.348.4370

An Irish pub on the Upper East Side sounds about as generic as bran flakes and a Coldplay album. But Kinsale doesn't suffer from the overabundance of similar establishments, as it's located just far away enough from the Second Avenue Shamrock Orgy. As far as the inside goes, it's everything you'd expect an Irish bar to be: rustic-looking and filled with plenty of TVs (11 plasma, two large) and old boozehounds who look like they exited the womb with a pint in hand. Regulars aside, Kinsale does a decent job of packing 'em in, as well they should be, because they sure as hell aren't getting any competition from neighboring Coogan's Parrot Bay.

Kitchen & Cocktails
199 Orchard St. (Houston & Stanton Sts.)
Lower East Side 212.420.1112

Kitchen & Cocktails

The name pretty much sums it up. They've got a kitchen. They've got cocktails. What this cool little place also has is a very red façade that opens onto Orchard Street forming a walk-up bar and semi al fresco tables. As you may have noticed, every aspect of this place is pretty upfront. Even the kitchen, where "American bistro" fare is cooked up, is open for public viewing. There's really no secret to the fact that good looks are a prerequisite for aspiring servers and bartenders, who certainly bring their own brand of hipness to these minimalist and stylish confines. Kitchen and Cocktails is an offshoot of San Francisco's popular Luna Park, where similar comfort food is served. Try the Dr Pepper cocktail.

Kitchen 82
461 Columbus Ave. (@ 82nd St.)
Upper West Side 212.875.1619

Kitchen 82 is the quintessential Upper West Side experience. A trendy metropolitan couple cuddles and smooches between sips of champagne while, one table over, youngish, well-to-do parents discuss international vacation plans with their seven-year-old daughter. The wait staff is quick to greet but slow to serve at Charlie "Metrazur, Aureole, CP Steak" Palmer's latest uptown venture; reservations aren't accepted, so line up behind the locals and get ready to wait. Your patience will be rewarded with a $25 prix fixe and à la carte menus, complete with recommendations from a tasteful, modest wine list of $25-$35 bottles. The folksy music and friendly banter will lull you into complacency as you lose yourself in eavesdropping, champagne kisses, or if you prefer, the flat-screen TV hanging over the bar.

Knickerbocker Bar and Grill
33 University Pl. (@ 9th St.)
Greenwich Village 212.228.8490

From the looks of it, the owners of Knickerbocker Bar and Grill seem to have purchased this restaurant from a Pizzeria Uno franchise that went out of business years ago. You know the look—brass railings, glass dividers, a worn-out wooden bar, and a few white cloth-covered tables strewn about. Really, Knickerbocker is more restaurant than pub; the food is decent and they offer a hefty bistro menu (try the Black Angus Meatloaf if you're feeling decadent, hungry, and have no plans to work out the next day). The crowd is older but by no means stuffy and the jazz music is conservative but by no means boring. That said, by no means should anyone under 40 want to find themselves drinking at Knickerbocker on a Saturday night.

The Knitting Factory
74 Leonard St. (Broadway & Church St.)
TriBeCa 212.219.3132

An incubator for fringey music since its early '90s inception, the Knitting Factory has become a more inclusive venue over the years—and one of the city's best. Three floors showcase local and national touring acts nightly, and "the fringe" still makes regular appearances. Everything from free jazz to salsa share calendar space with straight-ahead rock and more downbeat acoustic acts. The snooty staff can be off-putting on bad nights, and no room ever seems properly ventilated, but the barroom in front is big and inviting with high ceilings and long bay windows overlooking the smokers outside. Somewhere between being a CBGB's for grownups and the Bowery Ballroom for musicology snobs, this NYC standard is a must for live-show junkies.

Koi
40 W. 40th St. (6th & 7th Aves.)
Midtown 212.921.3330

Beautiful servers. Modern Japanese. And a space inside an upscale NYC hotel. Yes, it's cliché, but despite being open for just a short time, the trendy residents of Manhattan are already able to see past all of that. As the East Coast outpost of the Los Angeles celebrity hangout—its VIP number was one of those hacked from Paris Hilton's Sidekick—this restaurant is sure to attract its own flock of "Page Six" regulars, thanks to its location inside the Bryant Park Hotel, just steps from the center of the Fashion Week universe. Inside, the multilevel space allows diners to survey the room while indulging on top-notch sushi, salad, and cold dishes, all the while keeping an eye out for a star seated nearby. Or at least a Hilton sister or two.

Kori
253 Church St. (Franklin & Leonard Sts.)
TriBeCa 212.334.4598

Try to find a better, or even another spot to get soused on Korean brews. A love letter to all things from the land with Seoul, this small dining room of muted wood tones is bustling with connoisseurs of Asian cuisine and, yes, Asian booze. Try the $8 ginger kamikaze made with ginseng, giving Red Bull some competition. The dira is a cosmopolitan made with soju, a Korean vodka. And OB and Hit beers are in supply. On the menu are a range of lunch specials ($9 lunch boxes featuring fish, chicken, and vegetarian fare) as well as a sprawling selection of soups, dumplings, fish, and noodle dishes. Kori is named for its owner, who clearly had a vision for his restaurant. In a fickle neighborhood, Kori has found a lot of love.

Korova Milk Bar
200 Ave. A (12th & 13th Sts.)
East Village 212.254.8838

Let's face it—you've always been different. You were an outcast in high school, and all the cool

kids made fun of you. But not to worry; there's an eccentric bar in Alphabet City made just for you. Korova Milk Bar pays homage to the cult classic *A Clockwork Orange* in every way, going so far as to feature milk on its menu. But if you're lactose intolerant, check out the rest of the drink menu, with over 10 different types of frozen drinks, and an excellent happy hour special Monday-Thursday featuring $3 domestic pints. But chug too many of these relatively inexpensive drinks, and you might start to believe that the army of naked man-nequins embedded in the wall are pointing invit-ingly to the host of TVs showing horror movies.

Kos

264 Bowery (Prince & Houston Sts.)
Lower East Side 212.343.9722

When Lenny Kravitz, his cousin Kevin Conner, and Denzel Washington opened this unmarked, retro-ish LES lounge in 2004, they were about the only ones who could get in. Now that they've put a neon sign in the window and loosened the velvet ropes a bit, less-famous people are welcomed, and this intimate lounge screams "open for busi-ness!" A small green and black lounge leads to the VIP "Kitty Room" in back, which is covered top-to-bottom in brown shag carpeting. DJs play rock and soul tunes at the perfect decibel level, so you can still hear the pretty people at your table. Drinks hover around the $15 range, ensuring that

the club retains its A-list clientele; for some, though, it's a small price to pay to drink alongside celebrities.

Kush

191 Chrystie St. (@ Stanton St.)
Lower East Side 212.677.7328

These days, the knock-off Middle Eastern aesthet-ic reigns, be it trendy belly dancing classes or Chinatown vendors hawking cheapo bangle bracelets. Amidst all the faux, Kush is a breath of fresh air. Step off of battered old Chrystie Street

and into a calm Moroccan mansion where, provided expense is not an issue, one can puff flavored smoke from a hookah and sip a cool chai martini by calm candlelight. Decorated with hanging lanterns and strategically placed sculptures, Kush is a true sensory experience, with its winding hallways and plethora of shadowy alcoves perfect for either whispering sweet nothings or making a little less conversation, as the King might've suggested.

Kyma
300 W. 46th St. (@ 8th Ave.)
Hell's Kitchen 212.957.8830

If your parents who are visiting from Indiana made you see *The Lion King* a third time, quench their thirst for "adventurous" food with Kyma (it means "wave"). This Greek restaurant has just enough swank to impress the folks without breaking the bank (theirs, of course; when the 'rents come to town we know who is paying!). But don't be fooled by the massive brass chandelier and excessive use of linen here; this clean, well-lit tourist trap is strictly family. Ply Mom and Dad with Kyma's tasty spinach pie, fava beans, or grilled octopus while tinny Greek music plays overhead. Luckily for you, it's so noisy here it's difficult to have a conversation; order some Greek mountain tea before you finally tell them you're dropping out to become a Rockette.

La Bottega (@ the Maritime Hotel)
363 W. 16th St. (@ 9th Ave.)
Chelsea 212.242.4300

As if the Maritime Hotel hasn't brought enough seafaring nightlife to NYC, with its funky porthole windows and yacht-like rooftop bars, now there's the ultra-hip outdoor La Bottega. A trattoria by day, La Bottega turns into a swanky bar with a gorgeous crowd by night, when it seems like it hopped right over the Atlantic and landed in Chelsea. Italian posters spot the white tiled walls and blue-and-white-striped umbrellas dot the impressive outdoor terrace. Hundreds of wine bottles lining the huge bar may inspire you to start inhaling bread to help soften the blow you'll be doing to your liver. Flaky pizzas browned in the wood hearth oven and the Chicken Under a Brick are crowd favorites; but collegiate diners beware—you might get swashbuckled by the prices (desserts start around $8 and a martini will cost you $12).

La Cave
91 Charles St. (@ Bleecker St.)
West Village 212.691.4170

Below the snazzy French-Vietnamese restaurant Hue lies the newly sectioned-off La Cave. Whereas you used to be able to saunter downstairs after your chic meal, now you must get in line to sip with the well-heeled VIPs. Since its siphoning, La Cave has become a private party destination for big-bucks business types and the ladies who love the corporate bling. Dance on a leather banquette or sink into black and tan suede couches in one of the two basement rooms. This cavernous space feels like a high-end rec room, where turquoise-outfitted cocktail waitresses stand out from the sleek, all-black-adorned crowd, and pay special attention to bottle-serviced tables. The doormen are on hand to make sure the crowd is "mixed" (meaning, it doesn't become a sausage party).

La Caverna
122-124 Rivington St. (Essex & Norfolk Sts.)
Lower East Side 212.475.2126

Descending this place's staircase is akin to falling through a rabbit hole and into the proverbial belly of the LES. The bar, which offers liquor, beer, and a few specialty drinks, draws a hard-to-label variety of patrons, most presumably there to view the unique interior design. Faux stalactites jut out of the ceiling above the large, island-like bar that serves as center stage. The musty air and plaster adds to the, ahem, cave theme, while patrons rock out to house and '80s DJ tunes. There's plenty of seating and the menu's standard Italian offerings effectively complement well-picked bottles of wine that start around $25. Had the Flintstones been Italian, they would've hung out in a place like La Caverna.

La Churrascaria Plataforma Tribeca
221 W. Broadway (Franklin & White Sts.)
TriBeCa 212.925.6969

You're going to want to save up before you come to this Brazilian steakhouse, but you'll be glad you did. The $50 prix-fixe menu includes a first course—a banquet-style buffet offering casseroles and vegetables—and for the main course, waiters offer your table select cuts of beef, pork, lamb, or chicken sliced right from the skewer. For dessert (provided you have room), there's a tough-to-choose selection of Brazilian pastries, pies, and cakes. The décor is just as opulent—marble fixtures resembling something from a Frank Gehry building, overflowing plants, high ceilings, and tuxedoed gents stroking a nearby piano. Stick around long enough and you'll enjoy free appetizers; now try to say "obrigado" with your mouth full.

La Linea
15 1st Ave. (1st & 2nd Sts.)
East Village 212.777.1571

When a bar's only dress code states that "neat appearance is required," you could probably walk in wearing the clothes you rolled out of bed with—as long as you remember to brush your teeth and put on some deodorant. But La Linea's patrons, who sit neatly perched along the monstrous windows facing First Avenue, have obviously taken great pains to do more than that. After all, with a happy hour from 3pm-9pm, it's no wonder everyone is smiling and laughing while the city rushes by them on the other side of the picture window-ish glass. The mini-sized bar is lit by small, cone-shaped blue and yellow lamps and the walls look like whoever started the paintjob never finished when they discovered the nearby kegs. But, hey, no one's perfect (even though they seem to be).

La Prima Donna
163 W. 47th St. (6th & 7th Aves.)
Midtown 212.398.3400

There are two reasons for dining and drinking in Times Square: The food is phenomenal, or you're from out of town, have tickets to the theater, and don't know any better. La Prima Donna is...well, good for a pre-*Hairspray* meal. Sandwiched between the Pig N Whistle pub and a deli, this Italian restaurant's front bar area exudes a strong European flavor, thanks to its international, 30-ish crowd, the '80s-era glamour girl artwork, and the piped-in Julio Iglesias. Fried mushrooms ($7.95), pollo boscaiola ($15.95), and sautéed filet of halibut ($19.95) can be enjoyed in the elevated dining room, where the walls are adorned with Venetian paintings. La Prima Donna's far away from Venice—geographically and culinarily speaking—but for this neighborhood, it's a decent option.

La Streghe
331 W. Broadway (@ Grand St.)
SoHo 212.343.2080

Perched on the corner of Grand and W. Broadway, La Streghe occupies prime people-watching real estate. To aid its patrons in this pursuit, large mirrors have been mounted behind the bar, reflecting the motley crew of tourists, bureaucrats, and brokers passing by the large outside window. This, along with the bar itself (a strikingly modern structure of studded metal intriguingly at odds with the rustic continental décor), provides an intriguing reason to peer in. But while the scene outside may be lively, inside it's a different story; this Italian bistro's small space and high prices make the formation of a boisterous clientele difficult. Even the affable European bartenders and the movie-inspired bar name don't help to liven things up.

La Tour
1319 3rd Ave. (75th & 76th Sts.)
Upper East Side 212.472.7578

Classic and camp converge at La Tour. Kitschy relics like a Statue of Liberty lamp and disco balls belie any pretension within this French bistro's warm rouge ambiance. Not surprisingly, wine is the predominate drink, and it's served by helpful, chatty bartenders who also know how to shake a mean cocktail. Arrive between 5pm and 7pm for 2-for-1 bar specials; also note free champagne lures female patrons during Monday's Ladies' Night. But you'd miss out if you didn't grab that drink and mosey back to the intimate, comfortable dining area, where for $18 you can divulge in unlimited gargantuan bowls of mussels with three different sauces, fries, and sticky French bread. Don't feel embarrassed about ordering thirds; just be careful to splash the sauce on the bread and not your date.

Laila Lounge
113 N. 7th St. (Berry St. & Wythe Ave.)
Williamsburg 718.486.6791

A couple of years ago, when Williamsburg first became the "it" 'hood of the moment, Laila was a happening hotspot for the post-Planet Thai crowd, with live music and an animated cast of hipsters. Now that the neighborhood has fully blossomed into a gimmicky, post-modern paradise, this loft-style bar's subdued digs have become more of a sanctuary for the 30-something set of laidback artists and professionals. With a comfy backyard, free WiFi access, Sunday BBQs, and an active musical stage (OK, so the stage only looks big enough for a two-person act or a midget rock band), Laila will retain its staying power as a neighborhood hangout that keeps the purists satiated—you know, the people who lived in Williamsburg before it was cool (or so they say).

Lakeside Lounge
162 Ave. B (10th & 11th Sts.)
East Village 212.529.8463

So engrained into the hipster conscious that it's raised itself from the "dive bar" status it so deafeningly screams, Lakeside Lounge has become more of a neighborhood bar, but for a dive-mentality neighborhood. Never mind the faded, chipped cement walls and floors, and huge steel pipes that seem to hold up the ceiling. You'd be hard-pressed to find anyone here without a big grin plastered—and we do mean plastered—across their face,

including the token canine that turns a deaf ear to the bands that manage to play in a very cramped corner. Grab a friend or two and take a seat in the infamous photo booth, close the curtains, and document an evening you might not otherwise remember. In case you're wondering, there's no "lake" in the area.

Landmarc
179 W. Broadway (Leonard & Worth Sts.)
TriBeCa 212.343.3883

Since opening over a year ago, this neighborhood addition has been gaining praise from the crowds, and the critics, for its contemporary approach to French food. Part brasserie, part bistro, this bi-level space packs them in nightly and it's sometimes three-deep at the bar, where you'll have to wait it out for a table. Known for its innovative and reasonable half-bottle wine list, Landmarc is proving that sometimes a half is better than a whole. As for food, you'll want to eat it all. Try one of Chef Marc Murphy's special entrées, such as boudin noir or crispy sweetbreads, or keep it simple with a roast chicken or moules frites. Satisfy the red meat lover inside by choosing your cut of meat (hanger, strip, or rib eye), a sauce (including peppercorn, chimichurri, or béarnaise), and a side. Get the fries, but save room for dessert. $15 will buy you a dessert plate to die for.

L'Angolo Café
108 W. Houston St. (@ Thompson St.)
Greenwich Village 212.260.8899

Perhaps it's the jumble of dusty vintage velvet sofas. Maybe it's the long list of coffee drinks and the abundance of focaccia on the menu. Could it be the out-of-place reggae music? Whatever it is, there's something about the L'Angolo Café that screams "1992" (and we don't mean that in a feel-good nostalgic way). Sure, the whole "funky, dingy Euro living room" vibe used to be all the rage, but at L'Angolo's it just seems played out, not a throwback to the "good ol' days." They do stock plenty of wines by the glass, and offer a primo selection of ports, snackable petite wine and cheese plates, and even some obscure Italian sodas, but it's just not enough to overcome the antique atmosphere and the "been there, done that" vibe.

Larry Lawrence
295 Grand St. (Roebling & Havemeyer Sts.)
Williamsburg 718.218.7866

So, which is it? Larry or Lawrence? Named after the owner's friend whose self-dictated persona makeover served for many a joke, Larry Lawrence is one of Williamsburg's neighborhood bars that caters to a regular crowd by providing a comfortable, cigarette-friendly hangout in a discreet and out-of-the-way setting. And by out-of-the-way, we mean a little weird—it's at the end of a hall in a seemingly residential complex with no appropriate signage indicating anything at all. With specialty cocktails like the coconut margarita, Larry Lawrence is a big comfortable joint sure to be a hit with the locals even if it never catches on to a crowd outside of this building, let alone Grand Street. Music ranges from Hank Williams to indie lite, but despite their best efforts, the crowd is more Wilco than Johnny Cash.

Latitude

Last Exit
136 Atlantic Ave. (Henry & Clinton Sts.)
Cobble Hill 718.222.9198

For seven years now, Last Exit has brought life and vitality to this part of Atlantic Avenue. The friendly (and attractive) bar staff mixes stiff drinks at this neighborhood anchor; the Bloody Mary is almost always delicious, but the Bloody Maria (made with tequila) is even better. And what Brooklyn bar would be complete without a Pabst Blue Ribbon special? Last Exit offers six cans of PBR for a mere 10 dollars. Check out the garden in the back, a romantic respite from the city where ropes of paper lanterns dangle over a small, tree-lined courtyard. On the first and third Monday of each month Last Exit offers a pub quiz and Karaoke Tornado, hosted by Texas Rob. Heavy drinking is encouraged, if not mandatory.

Latitude
783 8th Ave. (47th & 48th Sts.)
Hell's Kitchen 212.245.3034

Hell's Kitchen's latest hangout is called Latitude, but they could have called it Longitude because with four levels, you're going to be climbing a LOT of stairs. Start your journey on the first floor, where a 47-foot-long bar, booths, TVs, and a fireplace welcome an after-work crowd munching on pastas, sandwiches, and salads. A red pool table awaits players in the second-floor billiards room, next to a table-filled room overlooking Eighth Avenue. On the third floor, a small, loungier nook faces a spacious rooftop bar, and if your legs are still working, pass yet another lounge and go up one more flight to a second outdoor bar, where you can cool off with a margarita and wipe the sweat off your brow. You may need Magellan's powers of navigation when exploring this maze-like bar/lounge, but with five full-service bars, who's complaining?

Laugh Lounge NYC

Laugh Lounge NYC
151 Essex St. (Stanton & Rivington Sts.)
Lower East Side 212.614.2500

The problem with Midtown comedy clubs is that they often lack that raw and inviting vibe that's necessary for off-the-cuff humor. After all, can you really share common ground with a crowd comprised of Midwesterners, suburban Long Islanders, and vacationing Germans? Laugh Lounge, located on a decidedly less-touristy stretch of the LES, allows local comedians like Todd Berry to take such liberties. Besides, you're only paying a $10-$15 cover so the joke's on you if you're expecting family-friendly Gallagher stuff. Upstairs is a comfortable lounge with comedy albums on the wall and a staff that clearly cares about the craft, even though they can't see the shows from up here. Downstairs, temporary-seeming chairs and tables face a small, no-frills stage where the ha-has happen.

Lava Gina
116 Ave. C (7th & 8th Sts.)
East Village 212.477.9319

Let the two words in the name get cozy, give it a French twist, think like Austin Powers, and you might get the theme the owners of this East Village tapas bar were aiming for. Scintillating advertising aside, Lava Gina is worth visiting for its sexy, intimate lounge décor and specialty drinks. And people at this self-proclaimed "world music lounge" really know how to get down. Each night there's a different theme, like Latin Tuesdays and Arabian Thursdays. Patrons hoof it from all five boroughs to shake their derrieres to authentic, energetic global music; others come to scope out the exceedingly good-looking crowd. The few tapas options they have (food is only served Monday-Thursday) are a nice touch, but this candlelit lounge gets patrons hungry for something else.

Lava Gina

Le Refuge
166 E. 82nd St. (3rd & Lexington Aves.)
Upper East Side 212.861.4505

Anyone without an AARP card and a Civil War pension should consider skipping this old-fashioned snooze-fest of a faux-posh French bistro. Catering to the Upper East Side's diehard old-money seniors, this utterly cheesy pre-theater establishment feels more like an elegant crypt than a place to eat, much less drink. The barely-there bar was seemingly installed so the owners would have somewhere to linger and hit on chicks, but it hasn't drawn much of a following as most of the clientele is in bed "clapping" their lights out by 9pm. The modern country-leaning French cuisine is certainly serviceable and the desserts are quite tasty, but save for the dozen or so outdoor tables, there isn't much here that justifies the high prices.

Le Souk
47 Ave. B (3rd & 4th Sts.)
East Village 212.777.5454

Hookahs, dancers, hummus, and clubbing? This Middle East meets East Village fantasyland serves up something for everyone. If you're not familiar with the menu of Northern African cuisine split into mezze, plat principal, brick oven, and African specialties, the helpful wait staff will navigate you to grilled fish or jumbo rack of lamb. Those feeling more moody than foodie gravitate to plush couchettes, tiled tables, colorful hanging lanterns, specialty cocktails, and nightly (8pm-9pm) belly dancers in this bizarre bazaar. Bring friends and pass the dutchie with Alice in Wonderland-type hookahs. Romantics may want to take advantage of Tuesday's belly dancing lessons and surprise the hell out of their dates later on. And those thugs harassing passersby on the sidewalk aren't going to mug you—they're the surly bouncers.

Lea
230 Park Ave. (45th & 46th Sts.)
Midtown 212.922.1546

Because it's almost hidden in the heart of Manhattan, the only thing harder than finding Lea is locating an empty table within the place itself. Tucked away in East Helmsley Walkway (next to Grand Central), Lea's in-the-know, high-rolling regulars mix it up with the common commuters who just happened to stumble upon the low-key lounge. Eating sushi and sipping Tokyotinis at these little coffee tables can be a challenge, but one worth pursuing. Larger groups that make arrangements are better accommodated, whether they are gathered at the bar or intimately dining in high booths in back. The gorgeous staff is as diverse as the menu, which features both small and sharable portions of sushi and tapas.

Leisure Time Bowl
Port Authority, 625 8th Ave., 2nd Fl. (40th & 41st Sts.)
Hell's Kitchen 212.268.6909

No one goes to the Port Authority's bowling alley to meet the man/woman/sugar daddy of their dreams. Not surprisingly, they don't come to the over-lit, sporty bar for the bistro menu, either. The main attraction at this bar/bowling alley is its location; here, lonely hearts wait for their busses to Jersey by knocking down pins. Leisure Time is there to keep the pitchers coming during their all-you-can-drink/all-you-can-roll "disco bowling." And on weekends, there's a young crowd bumping their cares away to appropriately blaring and atrocious music. The special is a steal, though, at $17 for one hour ($27 for two) Sundays through Wednesdays. Candlepin, anyone?

Lemon
230 Park Ave. S. (@ 18th St.)
Flatiron 212.614.1200

Never sour, Lemon serves moderate-to-expensive American cuisine with a heavy dose of Asian influence. The ground floor consists of a self-consciously swank dining room and bar, and the upstairs has a more casual café feel to it (sink into slick blue U-shaped booths or cushy red couches).

Most of the customers here appear to be groups celebrating birthdays, which helps to amplify the jovial air, as do the $5 apple martinis during happy hour. The crowd—like the neighborhood at-large—is affable, attractive, and smug. The staff is pleasant, if a bit haughty, as if working here is somehow a reward in itself. Lemon is great for dates or downtown debs wanting to celebrate their birthdays with 30 of their closest friends.

Les Halles
411 Park Ave. S. (28th & 29th Sts.)
Murray Hill 212.679.4111

Among the many French brasseries that populate the city, Les Halles has a certain "je ne sais quoi." (That's a good thing.) The long wine list reads like a French novel, and the swanky wood-trimmed interior and classic steak frites menu makes this perpetually crowded (and understaffed) bar/restaurant a near-perfect watering hole for the local MBA set. It's not cheap, but judging from the crowd, Les Halles is geared toward "les rich" who are willing to stand around the limited-seating bar tipsy on "le vin." But be warned—if you're not a briefcase-toting keyboard jockey, you might feel out of place among the almost entirely professional clientele. Don't worry about kitchen cleanliness—this is the home base of Chef-at-Large Anthony Bourdain, who penned *Kitchen Confidential*.

Les Halles Downtown
15 John St. (Broadway & Nassau St.)
Financial District 212.285.8585

This dimly lit French brasserie draws suits and local residents for after-work drinks and solid meals that justify this popular place's lack of elbowroom. The entire place is decked out in dark wood and the ceilings are high. Behind the long, wide bar, upon which rest medieval-looking candelabras, are impressive wine racks; Les Halles' list includes more than 60 different bottles. The 25 single-malt Scotches complete a healthy listing of drink choices. And with all this, Les Halles offers more sensual appeal and atmosphere than many of the other establishments down here near Wall Street, where options are many, but variety is limited.

Levee
212 Berry St. (@ N. 3rd St.)
Williamsburg 718.218.8787

So, you drove your Chevy to the levee and it was dry? It must not have been this Levee, where the beer pours like wine and the wine pours like—well, cheap wine by the glass. Quiet literary types saddle up beside the jukebox, play pinball and pool, and speak in hushed conversations. They're nibbling vegetarian bar food and doing $4 Evan Williams shots with PBR chasers in between debates over whether Jonathan Safran Foer has any talent. This isolated Williamsburg haunt, which used to be known as the Antique Lounge, has to be sought out, but once you find it, it'll become either your favorite quiet drinking hole in the 'hood or you'll just be bored and never go back.

Level V
675 Hudson St. (@ 14th St.)
Meatpacking District 212.699.2410

The sole nightclub in the BR Guest restaurant family is everything one might expect from the juggernaut that brought, among other things, Ruby Foo's, Blue Water Grill, and Vento (which sits atop this subterranean hotspot). It's not hard to believe that this cavernous club of stone walls and iron bars was a sex club in its previous incarnation (not that single people are going home alone now). Level V (it's a V, not a 5) is run with flawless proficiency, meaning the suit-clad door staff can't be coaxed, and no reservations means a slim chance of getting in. The main space is always crowded with trendsters; those wanting privacy can reserve one of the small private party rooms, which are wired so you can play the Marvin Gaye collection on your iPod.

Lexington Bar & Books
1020 Lexington Ave. (@ 73rd St.)
Upper East Side 212.717.3902

This classy cigar bar is the kind of place where you might bump into the guy who tormented you in prep school or the girl that you had your eye on at that fundraiser. If it's the guy, take him past the

Level V

classics lining the bookshelves into the backroom and clear the air over a cigar and Remy Martin. If it's the girl, sit her down at a cozy, dimly lit banquette and keep the champagne cocktails (four varieties) coming. The greeter at the door will inspect your footwear (no sneakers) and the waitresses, dressed in red cocktail dresses and single-strand pearls, will measure your manners. Order a Pimms Cup or a Dark & Stormy before asking your company, "Weren't you a Kappa at Duke with my sister Muffin?"

Libation

137 Ludlow St. (Stanton & Rivington Sts.)
Lower East Side 212.529.2153

Amidst tiny creperies and sketchy tattoo parlors sits Libation, a three-story affair that sometimes becomes a halfway point between the Lower East Side and New Jersey. Semi-clogged with a fun-loving weekend crowd and condo owners of the new LES, this place itself is a genuinely nice and unique place without being a misfit. The ground floor is crowded with groups of people who park themselves in the middle of the bar, often getting underfoot. The second floor is calmer, housing a smaller bar and bank of tables where patrons can look down on the heads below. The penthouse dance floor is as straightforward as $11 specialty cocktails like Tangerine Crush. Through it all, the staff is both prompt and courteous.

The Library

7 Ave. A (Houston & 2nd Sts.)
East Village 212.375.1352

At this Library, you don't have to whisper. As a matter of fact, you'll probably have to shout to be heard over the happy noise of ongoing drunken revelry at this casually hip, beautifully boisterous East Village den of iniquity. Peopled by the young and unpretentious crowd who are just too cool to worry about having fun and always do, this is a prime destination in everyman's quest to let their hair down, forget about the past-due rent, the final notice from the electric company, and that idiot that just broke up with them. Who needs a psychiatrist to work out their woes when you have sassy tough girl and cool dude bartenders like these?

Library Bar (@ the Hudson Hotel)

356 W. 58th St. (8th & 9th Aves.)
Hell's Kitchen 212.554.6000

This swanky bar, located in an incredibly trendy hotel that houses a total of four bars, is worth the trip if you're willing to shell out. Whoever designed this place had winter in mind—the huge tan leather furniture, cherry-wood paneling, purple-felt pool table, and the perpetually roaring fireplace all whisper warmth and comfort in the darkest months. About two-thirds of the way up the walls of the high-ceilinged room, the "library" begins—a movie set's worth of fake books on shelves that cover the walls and reach to the ceiling. Below the books, the walls are dominated by giant photos of costumed cows (actually, apparently it's the same cow over and over). It's worth rubbing shoulders with turtleneck sweater-wearing Euro snots and jaded American businessmen just to drink in the middle of such surreal surroundings. That is, if you've got $15 to blow on a delicious, fresh fruit-laden cocktail.

Library (@ the Paramount Hotel)
235 W. 46th St. (7th & 8th Aves.)
Midtown 212.764.5500 Ext. 2598

Past the Phillippe Starck lobby and up a candle-lined set of stairs lies the Library at the Paramount Hotel. If you haven't been here, you're overdue. With its mahogany paneling, dim lighting, and heavy use of lounge-standard orchids, this is a calculated departure from the fanny-packs and naked cowboys of nearby Times Square. On a weekday happy hour the backroom is full of professionals reclining in leather furniture and trying to pretend their second home isn't a cubicle. Neighborhood standard $12-$14 cocktails are fair enough, but overall, the bar's sophistication feels a bit like Madonna's British accent—undeniably forced, but still enjoyable every so often. Cheapskates beware: Bartenders will automatically reach for the top-shelf if you can't swallow your pride and ask for the Popov.

The Library (@ the Regency)
540 Park Ave. (@ 61st St.)
Upper East Side 212.759.4100

Some bespectacled, buttoned-up, bun-wearing librarians are not what they seem—and neither is this upscale uptown lounge. It's not stuffy or pretentious, despite the plentiful antiques worthy of custody battles between Christie's and Sotheby's and floral arrangements that'll make you wonder if they were leftovers from Trump's wedding. The Library is surprisingly comfortable and relaxed for its Park Avenue address. Books, newspapers from

around the world, dark wood bookshelves, and a seating area decked out in a color scheme of burgundy, hunter green, and gold give the room a homey rather than stuffy feel. Munch on complimentary M&Ms while you plan your next chess or backgammon move, then order a late-night study snack (food is served until 1am)—decadent options include shrimp and crabmeat cocktails, thin-crust pizza, and coconut crème brulee.

Life Café
343 E. 10th St. (@ Ave. B)
East Village 212.477.8791

Life Café valiantly attempts to exude the fashionably understated, cosmopolitan image of contemporary urban hipness its name implies, but falls drastically short of the mark. The brightly colored, hand-chalked wall menus, spacious al fresco dining area, and agreeably trendy, reasonably priced comfort food menu (ranging from $3 yam potato fries to "mega burritos" for $7.95) fails to compensate for the needlessly pretentious attitude and outrageously lackadaisical service provided by the wait staff, who attend to their duties with such insincerity and relaxed indifference that patrons are often left to feel that they're doing all of the work. The food ain't bad, but the staff needs to get a life.

Light
107 Ave. A (6th & 7th Sts.)
East Village 212.253.4934

Light represents a new breed of East Village restaurants and bars—homey, reasonably priced, and especially appealing to the yuppies-in-training now renting in the neighborhood. With a rustic-chic décor featuring rust-colored banquettes and exposed brick, Light features rotating artwork and an extensive wine list of over 70 bottles. If you believe that liquor is quicker, you can try one of a few specialty drinks that include fruit-flavored martinis in watermelon and lychee. The menu features American staples with a creative French twist, and while there's no garden, you can enjoy your salmon al fresco if you sit up front where the enormous windows open onto Avenue A. If you're sick of the dark, dank dives scattered all around Alphabet City, let this be the Light at the end of your tunnel.

Light
125 E. 54th St. (Park & Madison Aves.)
Midtown 212.583.1333

At the end of the metaphoric Midtown tunnel of awful bars, there is, at last, a Light. A swanky lounge that rocks hip and underground dance music, this place all but promises a long line and big bouncers. If you want to see the Light without forking over a $15 cover, stop in on Thursday nights, when the after-work hours are extended until way past bedtime, and entrance is totally gratis. In true club style, table status here requires a bottle purchase, and there is otherwise little room to dance. Being tucked into the heart of Midtown, Light attracts an all-borough crowd, but so long as you're not dressed like a gym rat, the velvet noose shouldn't be a problem. Live DJs rock the house and the occasional celeb does a drop-by.

Lilly Coogan's
102 1st Ave. (6th & 7th Sts.)
East Village 212.420.9668

Assuming that Lilly Coogan is anything like her bar, she must be a relaxed local chick who likes beer. You won't find any pretension, B&T, or attitude at Lilly Coogan's, which is a rare thing for modern-day East Village bars. (After all, this place shares a wall with an enormous McDonald's.) You will find a fantastic jukebox with "new classic rock," including Porno for Pyros. The backyard looks like an abandoned garage sale with chairs, old grills, and even a stray mirror hung up. Inside and out, these grounds are dark so come here with a new date or simply to hide from the one that went awry. If you used to come here when it was the crappy Old Homestead, let us be the first to welcome you back from prison.

Lincoln Park Bar & Grill
867A 9th Ave. (56th & 57th Sts.)
Hell's Kitchen 212.974.1803

Sunken a few steps below ground level and sporting a dark interior with antique Guinness signs hanging on smudgy red walls, Lincoln Park is remotely reminiscent of a cozy British pub. But that aside, Guv'ner, this indie and classic rock jukebox is decidedly American, and the "football" they celebrate here is the kind where players had better use their hands and the big games are played on Monday night. The universally appealing happy hour is on weekdays from 5pm-7pm, with drink specials like $3 wells and glasses of wine. There are no surprises with these laidback bartenders and post-work young professionals, but getting to know them will require some yelling as this is a tough place to exchange sweet nothings, something best not done with this mainstream, predominantly male, neighborhood set.

Link
120 E. 15th St. (@ Irving Pl.)
Gramercy 212.995.1010

This place is for squares—literally. There are squares on the walls, square seats, square light fixtures, a square-shaped bar, and even the adjacent bakery is called 3 Square. There's something of an obsession going on here, and it doesn't stop at the décor. They're equally compulsive about their food, to the benefit of all who eat here. Everything is marvelous, although it does help to have some familiarity with fancy-sounding menu items. For example, what the hell is a spatchcock? No matter, you really can't go wrong with anything. And if you're only in the mood to sample, they offer their "amuse" menu in the lounge, which consists of several tasty and cheap appetizers. Square or not, you're in good hands here.

Lion's Den
214 Sullivan St. (Bleecker & 3rd Sts.)
Greenwich Village 212.477.2782

Don't confuse this live music spot with the cooler, less-pretentious Red Lion a few blocks away. If the gaggle of college kids out front holding their skateboards, kicking a hackey sack, and bemoaning the general suckiness of this season of *Punk'd* won't turn you off, perhaps the $8 cover charge on a Wednesday night will (it's $10 on weekends). Devil's advocates will argue that you might see an up-and-coming band before they make it big, but feel free to point out that you may just as easily see a bunch of no-talent hacks trying to be the next Phish, and your eight dollars would be better spent on a pitcher of beer down the street.

Lips
2 Bank St. (Greenwich Ave. & Waverly Pl.)
West Village 212.675.7710

Lips

Dining is a real drag at this place—and that's what makes it fun. After all, it's been way too long since you and Cher last had lunch together, but luckily, you girls can catch up on Thursdays at Lips, where various drag queens glam themselves up as celebs to create "The Ultimate in Drag Dining." Or drop by on Wednesdays for Bitchy Bingo to compete for cash prizes. The entertainment is a treat, but the food's quite a show as well. Each dish is named after a famed drag queen, so go ahead and bite into RuPaul (grilled chicken breast, $14.95) or snack on Cashetta (lobster ravioli, $17.50). Either way, the glamazons serving you will make sure you get good Lips service.

Lit Lounge
93 2nd Ave. (5th & 6th Sts.)
East Village 212.777.7987

Don't wash your hair, grow a little stubble, show off your tats, and brush up on your history of indie rock before venturing to this East Village staple, which is poised to become the next CBGB's, if only by default. The dimly lit, grungy upstairs room of this bi-level rock 'n' roll bar overshadows the Fuse Art Gallery in the rear. Upstairs, DJ Jason Consoli spins hard rock classics Thursday nights; head downstairs for celeb DJs who play tunes to complement the not-yet-retro '80s décor or live bands channeling a rock/punk vibe, including the always exuberant Fiona Sand. With the Lower East Side's recent return to a post-mod sensibility, complete with tatted rocker chicks, overdrawn eyeliner, and pseudo-intellectual art-speak, this borderline dive bar is a haven for the nouveau rocker (and rocker hangers-on) set.

Little Branch
20-22 7th Ave. S. (@ Leroy St.)
West Village 212.929.4360

Little Branch

Impress a date with your style, taste, and super-secret know-how by bringing them to this hidden speakeasy brought to you by the owners of the elusive Milk & Honey and East Side Company Bar. A nondescript brown door with a tiny sign leads down a dark staircase to a small basement room with charmingly unrefined low ceilings, Venetian-plastered walls, candlelight, and small tables that give the illusion of being haphazardly thrown together. Classic jazz and bowtied barkeeps bring it back to the 1930s, and unique cocktails (there are over 300 to choose from) like the Ward 8 and the Hemingway Daiquiri come to your private table on a silver platter. House rules help weed out hooligans and keep the joint classy: No fighting, play fighting, or talking about fighting; no name-dropping or star f***ing; and don't bring anyone here that you wouldn't leave alone in your own home.

Live Bait

Live Bait

14 E. 23rd St. (Broadway & Madison Ave.)
Flatiron 212.353.2400

Manhattan is a long way away from the wetlands, and at Live Bait, that feeling really hits down-home. This too-contrived dive is not so much about the bayou as it is about boozing—Live Bait has long been reeling in ex-frat types with its jumbo frozen drinks, oyster shooters, and corn-fed cocktails like Lynchberg Lemonade (Jack, sour, grenadine, and soda) and the Redneck Martini (vodka and jalapeño sauce). Fake alligators, rusty Coke signs, Mardi Gras beads, and other backwater kitsch are just a backdrop for the bright, chalk-drawn drink menu above the bar. Southern grub like pulled pork and fried chicken ($13.95) is finger-lickin' good, if overpriced; hillbillies with a hankerin' can grab a booth in the diner at the back, or stagger into the wooden oyster shack on their way out the door.

The Living Room

154 Ludlow St. (Stanton & Rivington Sts.)
Lower East Side 212.533.7235

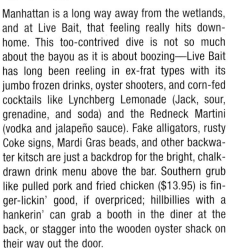
The LIving Room

Torn between the comfort of *su casa* and the thought of a cold one in the company of complete strangers? From its backroom stage to the main bar and the private lounge upstairs, the Living Room is all about homey comfort, which isn't to say it isn't ambitious. Known as a laidback playground for low-key performers like Norah Jones and Jill Sobule, the Living Room broadcasts its own online radio station and even fetches sandwiches for their hungry masses from nearby Grilled Cheese restaurant. Happy hour here runs from 2pm-7pm Friday-Sunday, at which time pints and mixed drinks are $3. Even when there are performances, there's no cover. This is almost as cheap as staying in for the night, but it's a lot more fun.

The Living Room (@ W Hotel – Times Square)

1567 Broadway (@ 47th St.)
Midtown 212.930.7447

Loosen your tie, unbutton your collar, and sink into the white pleather ambiance of the Times Square W Hotel's seventh-floor lobby bar, the Living Room. With a design theme that wants to be both modern and welcoming, the Living Room is neither kick-back comfy nor the exclusive and swanky lounge one could expect from the people who keep bringing us "Whiskey" bars. Instead, this bar becomes a sometimes uncomfortable mix of business meetings and public groping. With low-slung seats, semi-private booths along the wall, very, very low lighting, and a crowd who generally doesn't hail from here, but wouldn't mind meeting a few locals, the Living Room can look as much like an awkward swingers party as an upscale concept lounge. There are nights where it works, but come here with a plan B.

Lobo
218 Court St. (Warren & Baltic Sts.)
Cobble Hill 718.858.7739

188 5th Ave. (@ 2nd St.)
Park Slope 718.636.8886

Ignore the kitsch of Lobo's overly Western décor (we're talking horns, saddles, sombreros—the works) and order yourself a giant margarita ($14 for 4 oz.)—guaranteed to be among the best you've ever had. Lobo has two floors of wooden roadhouse, um…charm, and a menu full of hearty Tex-Mex favorites fit for a sheriff…maybe even a sheriff named…Lobo. The main attraction is a menu of over 60 hangover-inducing tequilas, from the mainstays to the hot, hot, hot jalapeno variety. What could possibly go wrong? If you happen to get thrown out, take you and your worm to the other location.

Local Café East
1004 2nd Ave. (@ 53rd St.)
Midtown 212.755.7020

Always packed to the max, this bar's outdoor seating and prime Second Avenue location make it a much-welcomed pit stop for those in need of an after-work blowout. Grab a patio table as early as you can, and hang on to it all night; it's practically guaranteed that someone will try and pick you up, even if it's just for your seating status. With an after-work rush that doesn't end until after 10pm and a menu of pretty standard bar food, Local is a Midtown staple that does what it needs to do and little else—just like its clientele. There's something to be said for reliability and Local Café East says a mouthful.

Local 138
138 Ludlow St. (Stanton & Rivington Sts.)
Lower East Side 212.477.0280

The mullet of the Lower East Side, Local 138 is total frat boy up front and indie out back. There are two big private booths in the front while the back-room is more of a hipster lounge. The décor in the back is very '80s *Miami Vice*, compete with a small side rail for drinks with mirrors hanging overtop. Should you and some of your drinking buddies' tastes in mates be about as similar as tequila and red wine, then mix it up at Local 138. The happy hour is from 4pm-9pm, which amounts to a whole lot of happiness. Weekends here can get suburban, but weekdays, as the name says, are pretty "local."

Local West
1 Penn Plaza (@ 33rd St.)
Midtown 212.629.7070

Boasting a rooftop deck and patio across from Madison Square Garden, this newbie is where high-rollers will be trying to salvage their evenings with a few cocktails after witnessing a near-nightly pummeling of the Knicks. The local team may want to come here for inspiration as the menu fills some tall orders. Local West's nachos have definitely got game and being jalapeno-studded gives them "mad hops." The painstakingly arranged potato chips on the counter come off a little fussy, but in this part of town, upscale spots looking to stand above the local franchises have to stretch things a bit. After all, where else can you stand in a vestibule gawking at Tyson and Gisele while hearing the Penn Station announcer declare that you just missed your train? Don't believe us? Read the "Page Six" clippings that plaster these walls.

Lodge
318 Grand St. (@ Havemeyer St.)
Williamsburg 718.486.9400

In Williamsburg, where trucker hats and flannels are ironic, this rustic joint brings an authentic New

Libation Bar, Restaurant, and Lounge is a three-level , 6,000-sq.-ft. venue of exquisite décor and sophistication, offering endless possibilities for a unique event experience. We specialize in all events, such as corporate outings, cocktail receptions, movie premieres, magazine launches, birthday parties, bachelorette parties...the list goes on!

Whether it's a gathering of 20 or 600 people, this three-floor, three-bar establishment can cater to any of your party needs. Boasting a mouthwatering American tapas menu, as well as amazing passed hors d'oeuvres and buffet-style packages created to perfection by chef John Donnelly. Mixed with an addictive specialty cocktail list, the Manhattan dining experience suddenly got a lot less ordinary.

LIBATION

137 Ludlow St. (Rivington & Stanton Sts.), Lower East Side
For more information, call 212.529.2153
or e-mail PartyPlanner@Libationnyc.com or visit www.Libationnyc.com

Hampshire log cabin feel in a neighborhood of kitsch. The wood-paneled walls, hanging ferns, and low-priced food remind us of Denny's, but don't expect rubbery Moons Over My-Hammy: They use only high-quality fresh ingredients, prepared simply. The turkey meatloaf sandwich, grilled whole brook trout, and skirt steak with cumin and coriander bordelaise, served with farmer's market sides and home-baked bread, are all under $13. The bar area features porcelain deer antler chandeliers created by artist Jason Miller, big brass beer taps, a shag rug, and cross-section log coffee tables with padded stump stools, made from wood from the owner's land upstate. The wines are classy, but the beers are canned (PBR for $2).

Loki Lounge
304 5th Ave. (2nd & 3rd Sts.)
Park Slope 718.965.9600

This cavernous, couch-filled bar encompasses a sizable space containing a pool table and dartboard (free to play, but only three mismatched darts are available) and a high-ceilinged oasis in the back, dimly lit and filled with your grandma's rejected furniture on which meatheads pursue girls with too much makeup and painted-on jeans. The mixed drinks are strong and not so mixed—add that to the décor and clientele, and but for the cathedral-like feeling of the architecture, you'd think you were at a bad college party, except everyone looks about 10 years too old and there aren't any drugs. A jukebox loaded with oldies favorites and takeout menus from local restaurants can't redeem this place from being what it is—a pick-up bar where you're not likely to see anyone you want to pick up.

Lolita
266 Broome St. (@ Allen St.)
Lower East Side 212.966.7223

Thank heaven for little girls, and thank heaven for charming and eclectic bars like this one. Trendy without trying, Lolita exudes a quiet coolness as it sits alone on its dark corner just east of Little Italy. Choosing a seat from the array of vintage chairs that are scattered about merits more considera-

tion than ordering a drink as the selection is rather modest. Beers are $5 ($3 during happy hour) and specialty drinks ring in at $8, and they're both served up by fast and friendly bartenders. The back area is ideal for either discussing Nabokov and the allure of youth, or simply licking your big lollipop while tossing come-hither stares to the mature wise men at the bar.

Long Tan
196 5th Ave. (Berkley & Union Sts.)
Park Slope 718.622.8444

This Asian fusion bar/resto is so Park Slope it's painful. Well, it's not actually that painful. In fact, it's actually quite pleasant if you can get beyond the crunchy-yuppie crowd. A simple design and country soundtrack help to stave off pretension, and the basic, yummy Asian classics (pad thai, spring rolls, etc.) are affordable and filling. Although there are tables many choose to eat at the bar, creating an air of social congeniality, though most people come in couples or groups and stick together rather than chat with strangers. Their two happy hours (after-work and late-night) are generous, and daily cocktail specials like a ginger kamikaze are affordable and delicious. Laidback and unpretentious, it's a great place to bring your date—especially if he/she's in the co-op.

L'Orange Bleue
430 Broome St. (@ Crosby St.)
SoHo 212.226.4999

This colorful SoHo Moroccan restaurant updates the sophistication of Humphrey Bogart's Casablancan watering hole with a glossy veneer. Instead of freedom fighters and spies, you get chatty African tourists, guidebook-toting Midwesterners, and a smattering of urbane *bon vivants* who seem to know everyone in the room. Expect to see people guzzling large mugs of dark coffee in between glasses of wine, but that doesn't stop the conversation from flowing or dampen the exuberant familial atmosphere. Throw in the occasional belly dancer (performances happen on Mondays, Fridays, and Saturdays) and some killer couscous, and you've got the beginning of a beautiful friendship.

Loreley

7 Rivington St. (Bowery & Chrystie St.)
Lower East Side 212.253.7077

Loreley

While you won't see any St. Pauli girls swinging from Loreley's wrought-iron chandelier, this German pub exudes European civility and cheer. With a dutiful, accented wait staff offering 12 German brews on tap, and a Jäger machine gleaming from behind the bar, your friends will be reminiscing over their college semesters abroad before you can say, "Spaten, please!" As for décor, Loreley's furnishings best fit the low-budget/bistro category. In the boisterous adjoining beer garden, patrons—mostly stylish brainiacs—squeeze onto pine benches that smell of sawmill, while the odd middle-aged male duo labors over plates of schnitzel.

Los Dos Molinos

119 E. 18th St. (Park Ave. S. & Irving Pl.)
Gramercy 212.505.1574

With hanging cacti, license plates, and other fiesta-inspired tchotchkes, this Gramercy bar and restaurant looks like the State of New Mexico post-Los Alamos implosion. Since "Molinos" means "chili grinder," it's no surprise that all food here is hot; the menu states that they don't do

mild, so don't ask. That means sissy-tongued gringos will just have to douse the flames from their relleño dinner with one of 10 fruit-flavored margaritas, including the typical prickly pear and not-so-typical tamarind. Or there's always the option of numbing your tongue first with one (or all) of 20 tequilas. How many fingers are we holding up? Dos? Tres? Ouch-o! This place is closed on Sunday and Monday, so catch a siesta and try another day, si?

Lotus

409 W. 14th St. (9th & 10th Aves.)
Meatpacking District 212.243.4420

The club that launched the modern era of arrogant bouncer behavior and velvet rope drama may never die, but it certainly has become much less relevant in the wake of super-clubs like Cain and Marquee, where the doorman may not let you in, but at least he won't send you home crying. Thursday night's "Rewind" party is a retro good time for the well-connected models who manage to eek past the line; less than haute monde "Fashion Week" coordinators still throw big parties here from time to time, but the club's current crowd grooving to DJs are visitors of the hotel-package variety, not the international jetsetters that once swept through to enjoy table service featuring $275 bottles of Absolut Vodka. These same owners have recently opened nearby Double Seven, but if you can't get into Lotus, you can't get into that, either.

Lotus Lounge

35 Clinton St. (@ Stanton St.)
Lower East Side 212.253.1144

Through the cracks of the LES's concrete hipness grows Lotus Lounge, where it's still possible to overhear conversations about Irish poetry and community gardens, as opposed to chatter about where so-and-so got her new pair of designer jeans and timeshares in the Hamptons. By day, coffee and sandwiches are served to a largely neighborhood-based crowd poring over newspapers or pecking away on laptops. At night, things pick up as a rotating lineup of DJs work the tables from behind the bar which they share with a friendly staff. Lotus Lounge's busy but non-over-crowded scene means the wait for the bathrooms downstairs is mercifully brief. Here's to hoping the Jimmy Choo-wearing hordes don't descend.

Louis 649
649 E. 9th St. (Aves. B & C)
East Village 212.673.1190

"Beyond the Invisible, Beyond the Silence." No, we're not talking about *Batman Begins*. We're referring to the motto of Louis 649. This noteworthy new kid on the block is well on its way to earning icon status as a unique enclave for the artistically inclined, aesthetically inspired, young and beautiful. Named after Louis Armstrong, the jazz at this gem is so cool, it's red-hot seven days a week (without a cover). Feed your head on the way-cool tunes, give your taste buds a treat, or purge your cocktailing urge with drinks from the extensive, exotic menu of chilled vodka selections. The service is so attentive and sincerely personal, you'll want to take the staff home with you. What are you waiting for?

Low Bar
81 Washington St. (York & Front Sts.)
DUMBO 718.222.9880

Low Bar almost seems like an afterthought—it's as if the paternal owners of the restaurant Rice decided to let their art-student child have a place of his own in the basement. Low is only open on Fridays and Saturdays, but this is one of the very few places left in DUMBO where you can get a stiff drink, sample an inventive menu (skewers!), and listen to occasional live jazz, or attend a reading series in an unpretentious space that has a *Dead Poet's Society* feel (but without the sentimental dialogue). If you're one of the billy-goat gruffs living under the bridge, you're likely to make this raw space (exposed brick, unfinished bar, sparse lighting, and bench-style seating) your home away from home. Swing Low and channel your inner Chuck Palahniuk.

LQ
511 Lexington Ave. (47th & 48th Sts.)
Midtown 212.593.7575

Think of this tropically decorated, elegant club as an underground Latin city. LQ, short for Latin Quarter, is two levels of almost constant Latin-themed nightlife. Come by on Wednesdays for the after-work salsa party and return on Friday to try out your moves to the beat of Latin music. LQ's lower level features a sprawling dance floor with a VIP area and four full bars, packed to the gills with fans and other Midtown curiosity-seekers most every weekend. A full tapas menu comes highly recommended by the attentive staff as well. You can even book your next corporate event here. But if your inner Casanova still isn't aroused, at least get in on the happy hour ($2-off drinks every day before 8pm).

Luca Lounge
220 Ave. B (13th & 14th Sts.)
East Village 212.674.9400

Do you like bars, but aren't so big on hopping? Rest your legs and hit the Luca Lounge, which is like four different über-cool destinations conveniently rolled into one. The main bar is pure Wall Street suave, ensconced in dark wood and accompanied by an impressively debonair bartender for the serious cocktail crowd. Just beyond, walk into the enclosed veranda complete with mismatched couches, Pac-Man, and a well-worn foosball table, and fall into your typical East Village lounge. Journey into the dining garden and enjoy an Italian dining experience under the stars. Or, venture across the way into the party room, where you can collapse in a drunken stupor with 80 of your closest friends on furniture so decrepit and threadbare that even your half-senile grandmother would banish it from her sitting room.

Lucien
14 1st Ave. (1st & 2nd Sts.)
East Village 212.260.6481

Sure there are several bistros in the East Village where you can find mustard-colored walls featuring faded Lillet and "laughing cow" ads, a tin ceiling, tile floors, rickety chairs, and romantic amber lighting. But Lucien is a classic—the Balthazar of the East Village. Maybe it's the photos of Michael Stipe and Keith Richards blessing the casually hip crowd, or the people-watching from the large front windows, or rustic entrées such as duck with candied turnips and figs ($22), and roasted squab with wild mushroom risotto and foie gras jus ($28). Although it goes on and off the menu, regulars know to order the juicy, exquisitely peppered burger on a baguette to sop up a night of drinking in the East Village or Lower East Side.

The Lucky Cat
245 Grand St. (Driggs Ave. & Roebling St.)
Williamsburg 718.782.0437

Being open from the morning (9am) 'til, well, the morning (4am) leaves plenty of time for variety. Lucky Cat's front room feels like the perfect coffee shop, an anti-Starbucks with mosaic-tiled tables, puffy vintage couches, board games and books on loan, and a ramshackle bakery case with homemade sweets, while the red sultry backroom showcases gothy paintings and hosts an array of events. Weekly "Piano Parlor" and "Keyboard Karaoke" is the cat's meow, but is played on an old upright—not a baby grand—so nix those fantasies of lounging atop it while crooning "A Kiss is Just a Kiss." If you prefer to leave the live music to the professionals, the Cat hosts bands and solo acts frequently, with everything from acoustic folk to psychobilly, which isn't that bad after a spicy green bean martini.

Lucky Cheng's
24 1st Ave. (1st & 2nd Sts.)
East Village 212.473.0516

Forget the fortune cookie—just keep your eyes sharp around the "ladies" of Lucky Cheng's, or a guest appearance on the *Maury Show* could be in your future. Peddling Pan-Asian food, cleverly named cocktails (Tobell's Ebony and Ivortini, $9), karaoke, and some fierce queens, Lucky Cheng's

has been entertaining locals and tourists alike for over a decade. The restaurant, outfitted in full Asian regalia (paper lanterns and gold stenciling), resembles a backwards (in more ways than one) geisha house. This mainstay ups the ante on Fridays and Saturdays with The Savage Men: Male Model Revue. Bachelorettes not satisfied with just a lap dance can take some of the action home…in the shape of an erotic cake ($75; order three days in advance). And for those wanting to relieve tension, make a dash for karaoke and Bingo on "Blingo Bingo" Mondays. "Dude Looks Like a Lady," anyone?

Lucky Jack's
129 Orchard St. (Rivington & Delancey Sts.)
Lower East Side 212.477.6555

Even the Lower East Side needs a sports bar and this one is suited for even the coolest of indie rockers. Lucky Jack's is a big, juicy venue with a bar that spans a city block. (Actually, it's as long as the distance between the pitcher's mound and home plate.) Connecting Orchard and Allen Streets, this long and narrow room offers a roomy billiard area complete with a well-maintained red pool table. Spillover from the nearby Bowery Ballroom tunes into Jack's TVs to catch local scores and they do so while Nirvana and the Smiths play overhead. Despite the occasional sea of Yankees caps, Lucky Jack's attracts a lot of creative types, which shows that not all art-school dropouts are allergic to the sun and sneakers.

Lucky Strike
59 Grand St. (W. Broadway & Wooster St.)
SoHo 212.941.0772

Keith McNally (of Pastis, Pravda, Balthazar, Schiller's Liquor Bar fame) may be the best non-French Frenchman since Oscar Wilde. Along with Odeon founder Edward Youkilis, McNally opened Lucky Strike in 1989 and its SoHo bistro vibe, complete with the copper-topped bar and Coppertone-tanned crowd, is as popular now as it was then. Franco/American cuisine keeps downtown hipsters in their seats until late-night DJs bring them to their feet with pop, dance, and old jazz tunes. Lunchtime starts at noon daily and that's a good time to be here, particularly for those who work on Wall Street or shop on Broadway. The French Martini is right on time no matter when you drink it.

Lucky 13 Saloon
273 13th St. (5th & 6th Aves.)
Park Slope 718.499.7553

Thursday may be Ladies' Night here, but girls looking for a bargain should be warned—it may not be worth descending into this post-adolescent nostalgic sausage-fest. With the grunge rock posters on the ceiling, gremlin and goblin figurines, darts, Japanese monster or horror movies playing on the TV, $2 PBRs, and the "white trash special" (Rheingold or PBR with a shot of Wild Turkey), Lucky 13 is like the basement of every lame guy you dated in the '90s. And chances are, they're here, talking about how rock died the day Kurt Cobain killed himself. Supposedly business picks up at midnight, but don't count on it. So unless you just shaved off your rat-tail to keep up with the trends, you'll want to avoid this dive.

Lucy Latin Kitchen
35 E. 18th St. (Broadway & Park Ave. S.)
Flatiron 212.475.5829

Take a break from shopping for overpriced furniture in this super-stylish, Latin oasis headquartered next to ABC Carpet & Home. You won't find any traditional tacos or burritos here; instead, you can choose from such scrumptious (and pricey) delicacies including $32 lobster paella, $24 Cuban pork, and $23 Peruvian stew. The watermelon and mango mojitos are creative and the sangria is supposedly "legendary." Just make sure you've got a lot of time to kill. Service is impossibly slow, and waiters range from aloof to rude. If only management knew the benefits of administering the occasional hot tamale suppository, they'd have a much better place on their hands. Come for the style and food, stay because the servers give you little other choice.

Ludo
42 E. 1st St. (1st & 2nd Aves.)
East Village 212.777.5617

Chez Es Saada used to be one of the most romantic restaurant/lounge combos in all of downtown, despite its unsteady kitchen. Eventually, the beautiful bi-level space behind unmarked brick walls lost its way. Now it's back on track and marked with its new name Ludo painted discretely at the entrance. Though romantic, the sometimes sleepy upstairs bar area plays second fiddle to a beautifully appointed lower-level lounge and restaurant. The subterranean semi-Moroccan lower level has its own bar, and behind exposed brick walls with candle insets, an ash-colored room and a sultry red-furnished one share a cement floor. In the Meatpacking District, there would be a month-long wait to sample Chef Einat Admony's (Odea, Patria, Danube) Mediterranean-influenced fare in a setting this chic. Here, last-minute planners have a fighting chance. At $20+ for entrées, Ludo will test just how gentrified the area really has become. At $22, this is no cheap polenta-crusted skate, but it is good.

Luke & Leroy
21 7th Ave. S. (@ Leroy St.)
West Village 212.645.0004

Wicked loud, even when there's nobody there, Luke & Leroy offers an after-work/all-night transitional location with a bi-level space for flirting and boozing. The crowd is young, good-looking, fired up, and scheming for a little action on most nights. This shabby-chic scene is an organic relief from that of super-high-priced A-list clubs, and the occasional second-tier celeb does roll through, generally for Saturday night's über-popular MIsShapes hipster extravaganza. (See Chloe Sevigny and Salma Hayek, to name a couple.) The upstairs dance floor is a bit old-school and kitschy, and that does make for an environment that's conducive to acting like a fool. The vibe here is the right kind of low-budget; DJs from major rock bands play, but such events generally aren't advertised.

LuLu Lounge
134 N. 6th St. (Bedford Ave. & Berry St.)
Williamsburg 718.218.7889

Thought Williamsburg was too hip for karaoke? Not at this underground lounge, where 20-somethings decked in logo t-shirts and Vans let their inner William Hung shine through. Thursday through Saturday, the über-chic bar allows fans of the low-brow pastime to maintain their hip New Yorker status. Thursday nights here are known for the regulars, so come early and avoid the scramble for one of those plush seats. No cover charge, $4 beers, and great appetizers make it a great date spot. Assuming you don't mind letting your date hear your chalkboard-scratching rendition of "I'm Every Woman."

Luna Park
Union Sq. Park (16th & 17th Sts.)
Flatiron 212.475.8464

With a Caribbean feel, Mediterranean food, and New York City prices and attitude, Luna Park is quite the international mix, nestled right in the heart of Union Square. Festooned with a floral décor, the inviting seasonal bar and restaurant is the type of place you'd want to go to forget your worries. Once you're seated and have been served (neither of which is a small feat), sit back and relax with Luna Park's bustling happy hour scene. It's always packed with everyone from the beautiful people to laptop junkies enjoying wireless Internet on the steps. Plus, you'll be able to enjoy a cocktail and the lovely Union Square scenery at the same time—without being pestered by protesters and petition-wielders.

Lunasa
126 1st Ave. (7th & 8th Sts.)
East Village 212.228.8580

If there's a soccer match on (European football to all you newbie imports), make sure you pack your earplugs and get ready to meet your next 15 best friends over an endless succession of priced-to-please pints ($5-$6) at Lunasa, where the revelry is rowdy, free, and fierce, no matter who wins the big game. If you don't dig sports, or have an overstated appreciation of bright lights and designer suits, stay home. This is the undisputed East Village Mecca for the unapologetically unglamorous 20- to 30-something, "jeans and jersey" ilk of international games fans. If it's a televised team competition involving some kind of ball, you'll find it blaring on the tube here—so bring your "A" game and grab a stool.

Lupa
170 Thompson St. (Houston & Bleecker Sts.)
Greenwich Village 212.982.5089

Do you speak Italian? Fluently? If the answer is no, you'll sure wish you did at Lupa. This fabulous Greenwich Village eatery features a menu so ethnically correct that you may require a translator—or a patient waiter. But don't despair—Mark Ladner and Mario Batali's Roman osteria speaks the international language of "yum." Work up an appetite perusing the 350 varieties of aged grapes, then tackle some authentically old-world culinary delights like lamb sausage or whole roasted fish. The mid-priced menu is divided into courses, so just in case verdura, carne, insalate, pesce, prima, secundi, and Piatto Del Giorni are Greek to you, remember that the cheaper things at the top of the menu are essentially appetizers, and if you order one of each, you'll need a stomach pump when the entrée arrives.

Lure Fish Bar
142 Mercer St. (Prince & Houston Sts.)
SoHo 212.431.7676

If you think P. Diddy has been having all the fun, reel in a date to this downtown seafaring bar and restaurant for a little yacht-owning, private island-ownership fantasy action. Start by ordering a strawberry-basil martini for her and a sake martini with fresh cucumber juice for yourself while you discuss the advantages of docking in Manhattan. Complete the fairytale by telling her how "your designer" decorated the mainliner room with nau-

Lure Fish Bar

tical-themed furniture and real porthole windows. If she stays long enough to hear the end of your fish tale, order up the fresh potato chips served at the bar before dining on some of the freshest catch in town (oysters, sea bass, and tuna). Lure's impeccable service and stylish menu guarantees you'll be smooth sailing from here on out.

Lyric Lounge

278 Nassau Ave. (Morgan Ave. & Hausman St.)
Greenpoint 718.349.7017

After fleeing the bodega down the block, Monica the cat has been given permanent residence status in the Lyric Lounge, where she'll keep you company in this sparsely populated and dark establishment. If you scratch her behind her ear she might lead you to a pool table in the backroom. An ample beer supply includes seven different taps, one of which is for Guinness. Mixed drinks ($4 for well) and pints ($2) keep the wallet happy, and occasional live music, a decent jukebox, and a couple of old videogames serve as entertainment. A backyard hosts smokers and private parties.

M Bar

349 Broome St. (Bowery & Elizabeth St.)
Little Italy 212.274.0667

Tucked away in the no-man's land where Little Italy meets Chinatown, this urban lounge swells on the weekends with a party crowd. Swanky it's not—the cut-rate furnishings have seen better days, the bathrooms are dingy, and sports blares from the overhead TV—but there's a certain kitsch appeal to the "glamorous" 1920s nightlife murals on the walls, fusion cocktails, and retro beers like Pabst Blue Ribbon. By Manhattan standards, you can get liquored up for relatively cheap, with $7 cocktails and $4 drafts on most nights from 9pm to midnight. Rotating DJs play techno and deep house on "subkulture" Thursdays and '80s pop, hip-hop, reggae, and funk on Fridays. The dim

M Bar

downstairs lounge, with its mirrors, hanging beads, and shades of brown, could have been ripped right out of a low-budget '70s porn film.

M Shanghai Bistro & Den
129 Havemeyer St. (Grand & S. 1st Sts.)
Williamsburg 718.384.9300

Upstairs at the restaurant portion of Williamsburg's M Shanghai Bistro & Den, owner and hostess May Liu buzzes around to each table, welcoming her patrons. There are long wooden banquet tables where you can taste the eclectic Chinese fare, and a busy L-shaped bar for those looking for something liquid or light. Downstairs, at the eponymous den, post-dinner-goers settle down lounge-style while slinky overhead red bulbs and candlelit tables cast a sultry glow. The wooden, pillow-backed benches and romantic nooks are perfect for nights out either in a group or in a pair, although the den does get cozy on the weekends. If you don't want a Shanghai Surprise, check the calendar before you go—the den is often host to a variety of DJ parties and live local music.

MacDougal Street Ale House
122 MacDougal St. (Bleecker & 3rd Sts.)
Greenwich Village 212.254.8569

Don't watch where you're going and you'll walk right past this Greenwich Village hole in the wall. Take a walk down the stairs and you'll find $2.50 PBRs, Buds, and Bud Lights. That's likely to draw in a college crowd, but anyone else who happens to enter this pub may just find that there's a reason smoking should be reinstated in the NYC bar scene. A pool table, darts, Ms. Pac-Man, and a jukebox add to the dive bar ambiance. So grab your baseball cap and baggy frat khakis and pull up a stool—a few pints of one of the 10 beers on tap is a surefire way to a good time.

Macelleria
48 Gansevoort St. (Greenwich &
Washington Sts.)
Meatpacking District 212.741.2555

The long, marble bar stretched along this Italian steakhouse's main wall is a prime spot to drink a glass of pinot grigio while watching guests seated at the rustic wooden tables. The venue is known for its wine (boasting 100 bottles on the menu and even more downstairs in its wine cellar) and fresh meats, pasta, and cheese selections (the chef chooses them daily). Exposed brick, high ceilings, and dim lighting give Macelleria an intimate feel, yet the long tables can easily seat bigger parties, making it the perfect spot for any Italian family reunion. Saddle up at an outdoor table, enjoy the view of the cobblestone streets, order another glass of vino, and practice saying "Capiche?" in your best Italian accent.

MacMenamin's Irish Pub
89 South St., 3rd Fl. (@ Pier 17)
Financial District 212.732.0007

Let's get this out of the way: South Street Seaport is a tourist trap, and the only good reasons to be down here are being a tourist, escorting tourists, or buying some tees at Abercrombie. Still, MacMenamin's does help soften the blow. Located on the third floor of the Pier 17 mall in a space normally reserved for Sunglass Huts or an Orange Julius, this pub dishes out $5 pints and tasty, reasonably priced burgers. If you have flashbacks to that Bennigan's from college, just step outside to the terrace and fugheddaboudit with the view of downtown Brooklyn across the river—then have another pint and remember that you were once a tourist too.

Mad River Bar & Grille
1442 3rd Ave. (81st & 82nd Sts.)
Upper East Side 212.988.1832

Be sure to study up on your Boston College trivia before heading into this Golden Eagles-heavy bar. It's a good bet that you'll always find a group of girls on the dance floor, as drinks flow freely, with relatively fast bartending service considering the crowding around the bar. Arrive at 11, throw down eight or nine vodka tonics, and plan your next move. Girls here travel to the bathroom in packs and assertive men looking to hook up travel in numbers as well. Drink prices are decent, but this is the kind of place where SoCo and lime shots are a rite of passage, and the $60 you took out from the ATM probably won't last you past midnight.

Madame X
94 W. Houston St. (LaGuardia Pl. & Thompson St.)
Greenwich Village 212.539.0808

Madame X

With the exception of Neverland Ranch, sex and kitsch generally don't go together. At Madame X, where velvet furnishings and sexy cocktails crack the whip, it's easy to feel comfortable (and a little naughty). The pick-up scene is in full-effect as locals, NYU students, and out-of-towners gather for music that's not very loungey: a little U2, a bit of Beyoncé. There's a doorman and he's looking for…who knows what? Odds are pretty good that everybody is getting in, but Madame X occasionally hosts private parties that you might not be invited to. The bar up front is wild enough, but the backroom lounge is for the already hooked-up. And for those who smoke after Pussy Galore, it flows freely. Oh, behave—it's a cocktail!

Made
330 W. 38th St. (8th & 9th Aves.)
Hell's Kitchen 212.465.2200

When Made (then called Lobby) first opened it drew models and celebs out of the woodwork despite its deceptively labeled Fashion District

locale. Now things are starting to make a little more sense. The occasional A-list party still happens here from time to time, but on many weekends, this spot's proximity to Queens and Jersey becomes more pronounced. The girls are still pretty and the guys still have credit cards, but the Hilton sisters are less likely to come than the Ramada Inn twins and the black Amex cards are a deeper shade of pale. Subtly bathed in beige with plants all around, the bi-level room looks great—especially from the VIP lounge upstairs. Made isn't recommended for a one-night-only-in-the-city experience, but it merits an occasional look.

Maggie's Place
21 E. 47th St. (5th & Madison Aves.)
Midtown 212.753.5757

Maggie's Place is like an aging model that needs to retire, but no one has the heart to tell her to hang up her stilettos. Still, Maggie's has been hanging on for over 30 years, providing her guests with comfort food pub grub and a great selection of 20 draft beers, another 30 in the bottle, and an expansive variety of whiskeys. The friendly staff is usually accommodating and Maggie's munchie menu offers standards such as jalapeño poppers and chicken fingers. The upstairs section, with its open balcony, emits a romantic vibe—and it's unlikely you'll be disturbed. Maggie's is now closed on weekends in the summer, though; so you'll have to get the hair of the dog somewhere else.

The Magician
118 Rivington St. (Essex & Norfolk Sts.)
Lower East Side 212.673.7881

"And for our next trick, we'll make snottiness disappear and cut your discomfort in half!" The Magician's coffee shop ambiance is provided by rustic-looking chairs, Formica tables, a tiled floor, and a quaint display of mini-blinds. The only tricks you'll find in this warm, sedate, dimly lit bar are the conspicuous clocks and the sound of Patsy Cline crooning in the background. Bookish couples come here for peaceful, low-key dates, but the oftentimes academic conversations can puncture the silence you crave. When they start in on

13

35 east 13th street
@ university place
union square nyc 10003

212.979.6677 www.bar13.com

MON: Poetry. Sponsored by Team Union Square.
Open Mic. Slams. Guest Artists.

TUES: Live Acoustic Music

WED: Karaoke with Live DJ

THURS: love+evol rock-n-roll dance party

FRI/SAT: Dance Central. Hip-hop, funk,
soul, R&B, disco.

SUN: "world famous" 8 years running-
Shout! Party (www.shoutnyc.org) with
the Notorious Shout! DJ's Steve & Pedro

Open 7 days a week

Established 1996

mAnnAhAttA
restaurant ★ lounge

11am - 4am 7 days a week
2 for 1 HAPPY HOUR 5pm-8pm

Full Tapas Menu
Private Parties + Live DJs

www.mannahatta.us
212.253.8644

316 Bowery @ Bleecker St. NYC 10012

Russian verb conjugation, you may find yourself looking for a trap door…or a saw.

Magnetic Field

97 Atlantic Ave. (Henry & Hicks Sts.)
Brooklyn Heights 718.834.0069

Only in a bar straddling three Brooklyn neighborhoods can a retro/Western/'50s/sci-fi décor work. And never has a bad case of schizophrenia paid off so well: This self-proscribed "rock and roll cocktail lounge" hosts local bands and touring acts on its ample stage every weekend, throws parties with guest DJs, has an excellent MP3 jukebox, and holds literary readings and short movies, too—not to mention the twice-monthly live band karaoke where you can channel your inner rock star. Magnetic Field pulls off being the most versatile neighborhood bar with as much style and flair as its red-felt pool table. And judging by the band of loyal local followers coming in every weekend, this is one neighborhood favorite that's here to stay.

Maker's

405 3rd Ave. (28th & 29th Sts.)
Murray Hill 212.779.0306

Based on name alone, you might think that Maker's was a whiskey bar. You'd be way off the mark. Still, drinkers don't go home empty-livered: This Murray Hill hangout carries a full bar with over 10 bottled beers, four drafts, four wines by the glass, and well, call, and top-shelf liquor, all at reasonable prices. Like a Vegas casino, you can scarcely tell what time of day it is in here due to the dim lighting and the sole window at the front of the bar being covered in paint. But we suppose there are worse ways to lose track of time than by drinking yourself silly, challenging the genial patrons to a game of pool or Golden Tee, and keeping the jukebox busy.

Makor

35 W. 67th St. (Central Park W. &
Columbus Ave.)
Upper West Side 212.601.1000

On the whole, Makor is about as kosher as bars get in Manhattan—the patrons are excruciatingly courteous, the hard liquor is nonexistent, and Shabbat is observed on Friday night. Kosher can border on the annoying, however, when the crotchety security guard you must pass by (Makor is located on the bottom floor of the Steinhard Building) requests to eyeball your stuff, all the while cracking jokes about WMD. Inside, Makor is pleasant enough, but candlelight does not altogether offset the college cafeteria atmosphere, or the attitude emanating from behind the bar. Frequent live music draws a surprisingly diverse crowd, and despite the $10-$25 cover charge, the $5 beer tastes pretty good. But once the music stops, Makor transforms into a massive J-Date.

Malachy's

103 W. 72nd St. (@ Columbus Ave.)
Upper West Side 212.874.4268

Malachy's is the type of bar where you'd expect to find a lot of blue-collar guys having an after-work drink, but this is the UWS, where few construction workers or masons reside. Except for being surprisingly bright inside, there are no surprises here: just older men hanging out with one another while watching one of the four TVs overhead. Because of its long bar and many tables Malachy's is the kind of place where groups can move in and take over, much to the pleasure of the bartenders who probably don't mind the occasional change of pace. Try Wednesday and Thursday nights from 10pm to close, when pints of Newcastle are only $3.

Mama's Bar

200 E. 3rd St. (Aves. A & B)
East Village 212.777.5729

Mama owns three restaurants, so it's no surprise that she needs a drink. Last year, she opened Mama's Bar around the corner from her popular food shop. The interior looks like someone was going to peel the paint and re-do the place, but forgot in the midst of the project…and that's part of its charm. Unlike other local bars, Mama's manages to attract mostly locals despite the throngs of suburban weekenders who just discovered this area. How? "We don't serve mojitos," says a friendly bartender. Instead, they offer six infused vodkas ($5-$8), including ginger and vanilla coffee. Mama's features DJs on Tuesday through Saturday and a great juke when no one's spinning. Plus, you can order off of Mama's fantastic comfort food menu, making this one of the tastiest spots in town.

Manchester Pub
920 2nd Ave. (48th & 49th Sts.)
Midtown 212.935.1791

Unlike the American version of the hit British TV show, *The Office*, this Yankee version of a British staple is a good thing. Plus, the female bartenders at this authentic British pub become instantly hotter once you realize that they're actually British and not just some surly out-of-work actresses. The only element that seems out of place is the "touch-screen" jukebox. In a bar selling itself on old-world British pub-style charm, being able to download 50 Cent's "Candy Shop" just seems downright wrong. Be sure to order from the tasty menu offering Irish Nachos Chips—a basket of English chips served with imported malt vinegar—wings, or Grandma Sticks (handmade mozzarella sticks) and catch a variety of sports playing on the "telly" while tossing back a few pints.

Mancora
99 1st Ave. (@ 6th St.)
East Village 212.253.1011

For the ultimate in unmistakably addictive south-of-the-border cuisine, check out Mancora, the new kid on the hipster block that is busily making a name for itself in circles that recognize and appreciate truly kick-butt Peruvian chow. This mouthwatering destination shares the name of a small coastal village in northern Peru, where the world's most perfect and even surfing waves break. And even though the staff seems to have such a laidback customer service attitude that it suggests they'd rather be at the beach, the spicy

menu delights—ceviche, Pulpo al Olivo—and fruity cocktails (like the Bahama Mama) will calm your nerves and numb your mind to the concerns of place and time, like the sound of crashing waves (or visions of South America's topless beaches).

Manhattan Grille
1161 1st Ave. (63rd & 64th Sts.)
Upper East Side 212.888.6556

A Manhattan aberration, this enormous steakhouse (five dining rooms seating 275 people) that stretches along First Avenue yearns to be upscale. And by outsider standards, it would probably be the fanciest restaurant in town; but in New York City, it seems faded and outdated. Manhattan Grille's small, classic (as in the dearly departed Astor Hotel that your grandparents talk about) mahogany and oak bar hosts 10 stools lined neatly under a pressed-tin ceiling, among Persian rugs, heavy velvet curtains, and floral arrangements throughout. The décor may go with its too-classic offerings (melon, Caesar salad, chicken parmagiana, cheesecake, and a coffee prix-fixe dinner for $25, for instance), but the VIP Card (which gets you a 15% discount on dinner Sunday-Tuesday) is so 1980s.

Manhattan Lounge
1720 2nd Ave. (89th & 90th Sts.)
Upper East Side 212.9875555

Welcome to another installment of "Completely Out-of-Place Drinking Establishments." This week's entry is the upscale Manhattan Lounge, located in the heart of Irish pub/frat bar territory. The drinks are standard fare, although given that you're hanging out in a place that's masquerading as a trendy lounge, be prepared to pay trendy lounge prices. But you can't fault them for trying to break the UES mold, right? Unfortunately, most flip-flop-clad frat dudes in this area are likely looking for a place to crush beer cans on their foreheads, not balance a well-made martini. Fairly inconsistent hours don't help establish any sort of regularity here, either, although that won't stop the staff of neighboring Pat O'Brien's from shutting their own bar down early and dropping by Manhattan to knock a few back.

Manitoba's
99 Ave. B (6th & 7th Sts.)
East Village 212.982.2511

Raise your Bic lighter high in the air, puke all over the Converses of the guy next to you, and swill your fill of cheap suds like it's 1973 at this no-nonsense rock bar. Owned and run by "Handsome" Dick Manitoba of punk rock band The Dictators fame, you'll feel the vibe of rock-god glory days gone by. Reminisce about the heyday of garage bands at the photo gallery wall, which depicts images of musicians so streetwise cool that half of them died of suspiciously unnatural causes. Grab a game of pool in the basement while you wait for the next band, but be fore-warned—the ever-present musty stench in the bar's nether regions is best stomached by those already under the table.

Mannahatta
316 Bowery (@ Bleecker St.)
NoHo 212.253.8644

Mannahatta

One of many upscale nightspots on the once-seedy Bowery, Mannahatta is well-planned, large, and luxurious, yet intimate. And though some local residents might take exception to this place, they're either doing so from their brand-new luxury condos or the cardboard box they've occupied for 20+ years. Mannahatta's comfy couches ease after-workers into a happy hour which features $3 beers, $6 cosmos, and Mediterranean/Asian/American tapas ($5-$11). Monday is movie night, Tuesdays feature karaoke, and weekends are positively bumping with preppy transplants enjoying the swanky upstairs vibe and grooving in the downstairs lounge. Though $12-$16 would pay for a cover charge, beer, and potentially a lap-dance from a tattooed reveler at CBGB's across the street, it'll only get you a cocktail here—but this crowd can afford it.

Maracas
317 E. 53rd St. (1st & 2nd Aves.)
Midtown 212.593.6600

Situated on a block of upscale nightspots catering to locals, Maracas does little to buck convention. Its clientele consists of neighborhood professionals in search of fun (but nothing too crazy) and the décor only suggests exoticism, with tiny skeletons and alluring string lights adorning the brightly colored room. You can bank on some good drink specials, though—every Monday, all super-strong margaritas (mango, prickly pear) are $1, as is sangria on Sundays. Live flamenco guitar is another offering every Thursday and Saturday at 8pm. The food runs the Mexican gamut (quesadillas, taquitos), but it'll cost you a heap of pesos. Still, for $1 margaritas we can do the Mexican Hat Dance all the way to Midtown.

Marie's Crisis
59 Grove St. (@ 7th Ave.)
West Village 212.243.9323

Can't pay the rent? Can't find your bottle of hairspray? Feel like there's a phantom haunting your room? If your crisis involves a show tune, then come to sing about it at Marie's Crisis, where you'll find *les miserables* just like yourself who enjoy belting out their favorite Broadway songs. And since we all know that we kinda sorta (but not really) sound better after a few drinks, a one-drink minimum charge at this West Village piano bar ensures that alcohol lubricates everyone's throats. Fridays and Saturdays attract a mostly straight crowd, but the rest of the week features gays and lesbians channeling Norma Desmond. Regardless of the night, there's never any shortage of drunken divas singing about their crises.

Marion's Continental
354 Bowery (4th & Great Jones Sts.)
NoHo 212.475.7621

So many bars strive for that perfect retro feel, something Marion's Continental insouciantly pulls off (they've been here, after all, for 55 years) with panache. Orange walls and plastic cup-style lighting supply character sans the desultory clutter. A few dozen martinis provide ample drinking options, and the more mischievous can ask for an "XXX-Rated" drink list, which is discreetly wrapped in brown paper carrying the appropriate warning. Combine a Brassy Blond with Marion's eclectic fare at the front bar; if "Fondue Sunday" (chocolate or cheese, pick your pleasure) doesn't sound filling or fulfilling to you, come by for Monday night "Date Night," when you and your squeeze eat for the price of one.

The Mark Bar
1025 Manhattan Ave. (Freeman & Green Sts.)
Greenpoint 718.349.2340

Any establishment that has a bidet is worth a visit (hence the Mark Bar patrons' proud boast, "the cleanest derrieres this side of the river"). Other than the reward of a squeaky-clean tush, there are many reasons to visit this cozy little pub—a kick-ass jukebox, pool table, a plethora of beers, and cocktails like the ginger martini. The staff is friendly, and the Mark Bar is proud of its eccentric

regulars, yet welcoming to newcomers. The décor is sophisticated with an arty twist, courtesy of the rotating gallery featuring local artists. A new garden adds to its allure, so plant your derriere here before it becomes overrun with party-crashing dirty bums.

Mark's Bar (@ the Mark Hotel)
25 Madison Ave. (@ 77th St.)
Upper East Side 212.606.4544

The dress code at Mark's Bar says it all: "smart casual." Filled with velvety green armchairs and seats upholstered with rose-printed fabric, a floral rug, and a gold-rimmed mirror, this hotel bar's décor is as "clubby" as your dorky dad's basement-turned-cocktail-bar where he wants to "like, hang" with you and your friends. Plop onto an overstuffed chair and pick something off the cocktail menu or kick back and peruse the wine list for a few hours (there are 378 bottles to choose from). One doesn't stumble into this bar; either you're a guest of this nondescript gem of a hotel, you live within a five-block radius, or you sell European designer clothes from a Madison Avenue boutique. Snacks include hors d'oeuvres like jumbo shrimp, spring rolls, and crème brulee.

Markt
401 W. 14th St. (@ 9th Ave.)
Meatpacking District 212.727.3314

Don't sweat it if you can't speak French or Dutch—this popular Belgian bistro is stuffed with a trendy neighborhood crowd who wouldn't understand you anyway. Watch your head under the low-hung pub lighting, lose yourself in a Belgian beer, and rub elbows with a steady crowd of fashion slaves shifting in their heels at this crowded bar. Despite its über-trendy surroundings, Markt has an inviting aura bolstered by bartenders from the Northeast who don't mind at all if you butcher the pronunciation of everything on the menu. Outdoor seating is the icing on the cake (or waffles, as the case may be) at this unpretentious, but still sceney Meatpacking District locale.

Marlow and Sons
81 Broadway (Wythe Ave. & Berry St.)
Williamsburg 718.384.1441

By day it's a quirky gourmet café/market, serving mostly organic tastes and treats (like Jacques Torres chocolate). By night, the few (and the lucky) Williamsburgers who are in-the-know spend cozy, intimate evenings at the bodega-like back raw bar/restaurant/cocktail bar, where foodie savants serve an array of well-priced plates ranging from deliciously briny West Coast oysters and artisanal cheeses to a dish of succulent olives; both are perfect with a pomegranate martini or a half quartino of wine. Marlow and Sons' owners are also responsible for Diner, the ever-popular Williamsburg establishment right next door. Grab a table before the rest of the 'Burg scopes it out. With a place as perfectly date-worthy as Marlow and Sons, it shouldn't take long.

Maroon's
244 W. 16th St. (7th & 8th Aves.)
Chelsea 212.206.8640

There's a lot of spunk at this Southern/Jamaican hybrid. Chill at Maroon's with a Maroon's Madness ($10) or let the live jazz help digest your brunch on Sundays. Either way, they aim to be comfortable here. Reservations are helpful at this eat-first, drink-later joint, but the bar crowd is loyal, drawn to cocktails that range between $10 and $15. The menu pulls from the South and Caribbean, with two-ounce fried crab cakes to start, a spring herb salad with champagne vinaigrette, and Cujo's Jerk Chicken with macaroni and cheese and collard greens for a solid, belly-filling finish. But the Montego Bay Broiled Filet Red Snapper with garlic spinach and fried grits ($24) is the kitchen's bounty. Maroon's reminds us that Manhattan's an island, too, mon.

Marquee
289 10th Ave. (26th & 27th Sts.)
Chelsea 646.491.0202

Marquee

Nearly two years after opening its doors, Marquee has finally found the one thing it can't do, which is remain brand-new. Opening to unparalleled fanfare, Marquee was once the 700+-person venue that 6,000 people per night wanted to enter. Now, the velvet rope rejections have been reduced to 2,000 a night or so, but this is still a home base for A-listers, B-listers, and the occasional striped-shirted weekender as well. A big main room splits the space with two smaller lounges, all of which share a wishbone staircase. A $20 cover applies to those not on the list but odds are good that a bottle purchase will be required to make the cut on most nights. Because of its size Marquee is a popular event space, but more often than not, "private party" means open to some, but "not to you."

Mars Bar
25 E. 1st St. (@ 2nd Ave.)
East Village No Phone

Prices may have gone up to $3.50 for a Bud and $4.25 for a mixed drink, but this throwback to the old East Village is still a headfirst dive into a pool of safety pins, brass knuckles, and false teeth. Show up wearing Polo and you'll be laughed out of the place—if you're lucky. Every square inch of this hole in the wall is covered in graffiti—especially the bathrooms, which can be smelled from the front door. Since there aren't any tables (just a long, carved-up bar protecting an abuse sponge of a bartender), the eccentric punks, Bowery boys, and slummers who call Mars a second home (and sometimes a first one) can usually be found screaming into the pay phones, blasting the Stooges on the jukebox, playing video poker, or cursing the smoking ban.

Mars 2112

1633 Broadway (@ 51st St.)
Midtown 212.582.2112

Deep below the surface of bustling Times Square lies a world of glowing craters and intergalactic travelers. Mars 2112 is truly out of this world—especially if your world is one of good taste. Filled to the brim with tourists, prepubescent birthday parties, and the occasional corny corporate event, it's improbable that there's intelligent life on Mars. For those less interested in running between a plate of Nebula Chili Nachos and the crater video arcade, there's a separate Mars Bar. If you must, hang out for the generous $2 beer-and-wine happy hour (plus a mozzarella stick and buffalo wing buffet), or try a couple cosmic Marstinis (the $9 Meteor Shower is suspiciously similar to an apple martini) and a celestial shot special like the Astral Projection.

Marseille

630 9th Ave. (@ 44th St.)
Hell's Kitchen 212.333.3410

Situated on one of the better blocks in one of NYC's seedier nabes, this swanky restaurant/lounge boasts more than 150 wines, smooth jazz, and romantic lighting that will transport you out of Hell's Kitchen without using your third and final wish. Backed by a Moroccan-themed décor (tiled floor, a mirrored column in the center of the room) Marseille touts Chef Andy D'Amico's Southern French Mediterranean menu of assorted mezzes, crispy *gourjons* of fluke, jumbo lump crabmeat pasta, and alluring desserts. Although the sleek, metal-rimmed bar at

Marseille stays open late, you can also enjoy a liquid meal in Marseille's candlelit, cave-like lounge, Kemia.

Martell's

1469 E. 83rd St. (@ 3rd Ave.)
Upper East Side 212.879.1717

This friendly neighborhood bar and restaurant is an after-work hangout for locals who want a short drunken walk when they're ready to stumble home. Though one in a chain of three, this locale feels unique, with its attentive bartenders, friendly wait staff, and crowd of happy regulars. The plentiful outdoor seating on both sides of the restaurant is appealing in the summertime, when people are willing to wait for a seat to chow down. The bar itself is often crowded, and seats may be hard to come by, but you can always amuse yourself with the digital jukebox while you wait. But if you're looking for a place with more sass and personality than a Dilbert cartoon, avoid the train ride to this 75-year-old haunt.

Martignetti Liquors

159 E. Houston St. (Eldridge & Allen Sts.)
Lower East Side 212.995.0330

There's no cover at all in this shabby-chic LES rock club, which occupies the former Carnaval space, but there could be. Located halfway between Eldridge Street's hip-hop corridor and Ludlow Street's hipster row, Martignetti Liquors is literally and figuratively somewhere between funky and rockin'. Upstairs, a subtle safari motif of bamboo and palm tree-patterned walls enjoys rock and reggae in the early part of the evening, then partakes in hip-hop and harder rock as the night grows later. Downstairs, it's models, bottles, and bad behavior in an environment that's consciously seedy. By comparison, bottles here are cheap (all under $200) and there's even "White Trash Bottle Service," which amounts to a $120 case of cold beer. Two parts small club and two parts dive bar, Martignetti Liquors is all right, albeit an oddball in this 'hood. (Think Suite 16 meets Max Fish.)

Marty O'Brien's
1696 2nd Ave. (87th & 88th Sts.)
Upper East Side 212.722.3889

No relation to Pat O'Brien's across the street, Marty's is yet another in a long line of Upper East Side bars with Irish monikers whose existence owes a lot to an undiscerning local crowd. The local fratties must all be playing Beirut at Pat's, because you'd be lucky to find more than three people at any given time in Marty's, and the likelihood of any of those patrons possessing so much as a GED is the only thing in here that's slim. If you inexplicably find yourself here, you can at least take comfort in live music on Thursday through Saturday, and rightfully cheap booze, which is incredibly necessary to surviving this experience.

Matchless
557 Manhattan Ave. (@ Driggs Ave.)
Greenpoint 718.383.5333

Just across the street from the ever-popular Enid's, Matchless has done well in carving out a name for itself other than, well, "that bar across from Enid's." It's not hard to see why, either, with generous happy hour ('til 8pm) specials—$4 margarita pints, $2 well drinks, and $2 PBRs—served in a dark, big, sexy space with local artwork hung on the brick walls; several "nights" like trivia, open mic, and motorcycle (not to mention the regular drinking and drawing contest); and a great selection of 16 beers on tap, from Blue Point Toasted Lager ($4) to Rogue Dead Guy Ale ($5). For those who never quite left the rec room '70s behind, Matchless has a dartboard and pool table as well as one of the few foosball tables in the city. The crowd's fun, too—a little more cool Williamsburg to Enid's occasionally Park Slopey vibe.

Matt's Grill
932 8th Ave. (55th & 56th Sts.)
Hell's Kitchen 212.307.5109

People who work within a few blocks away and are too lazy to go somewhere better seem to be the primary clientele for this standard-issue, dull bar and restaurant. From the non-descript, dark-wood interior to the sports on TV and the collection of pre-sundown drunks and lonely dudes who lack savvy friends to steer them towards a cooler after-work spot, Matt's Grill screams generic. The food—overpriced typical American fare—is OK, and the beer selection is fine, but who wouldn't prefer to use their imagination a little and spend their time somewhere that's not the upscale NYC equivalent of Bennigan's or TGI Friday's?

Max Fish
178 Ludlow St. (Houston & Stanton Sts.)
Lower East Side 212.529.3959

A perennial hipster favorite, this place has been around so long that the bar's O.H.s (Original Hipsters) are now well into their forties. A cigarette still hangs over the door, reminding us of the days before smoking became passé. Waifish Max Fish pool sharks—who look as though they haven't been outdoors since MTV debuted—hang out in the back of the room, occasionally moving the billiard table for events, including an annual rock guitar contest. Students and part-time philosophers chill along the sidelines, playing videogames, swilling bottled beer, and selecting songs from the legendary indie-and-more jukebox. On weekends the place can become a B&T tourist trap, but on the "city days" (Sunday-Wednesday) it's pretty great. This is easily one of America's best dive bars.

Maya Lounge
14 E. 33rd St. (Madison & 5th Aves.)
Murray Hill 212.685.6275

A new entry to Murray Hill nightlife, Maya Lounge was designed with an attention to detail normally reserved for sculptures. Each piece of furniture, from the glass bar, to the bed-style couches lining the walls, to the bead-and-cloth curtains surrounding them, to the floor lighting blinking up throughout the main room, was custom-made. Further craftsmanship appears in house specialty drinks like the $11 house-recipe Mayatini. Indian

Maya Lounge

food is in the offerings, and dishes like samosa and tikka are guaranteed to please the gods. The doors are always open, but promoters rule the day; note the snazzy DJ booth. And if all this should fail to entice you, feast your eyes on the hypnotic Bollywood/Hollywood flicks running on the corner projector screen.

McAnns Irish Pub
14 E. 58th St. (5th & Madison Aves.)
Midtown 212.688.2710

"Ninety-nine bottles of beer on the wall…" OK, maybe McAnns is only serving up 28, but this old-school Irish pub (founded in 1945) still has enough ale to give you double-vision. After work, the sophisticated (but still fun) Midtown crowd jams into the back dining room for mozzarella sticks and chicken wings, while the ladies kick off their heels and mingle around the high-tops. The budget-minded can chow down on the free popcorn for dinner and still have enough cash to buy their buddies a couple of rounds. McAnns may be entering her golden ages (the pub turns 60 this year), but she's kept in stride with the times; the menu features a Starburst drink and Atkin's Diet options.

McCormack's
365 3rd Ave. (26th & 27th Sts.)
Murray Hill 212.683.0911

While McCormack's is one of a handful of Irish pubs in this section of Murray Hill, their staunch regulars might stop drinking if it were ever to close down. This 11-year-old bar and restaurant serves Irish staples like Guinness and shepherd's pie to loyal locals of all ages, and they also offer a large menu of generic pub grub and complimentary wings during happy hour. You read that right— "complimentary," as in free! The exposed brick walls, wood paneling, and Tiffany lamps are old-school and, unless there's a football or rugby match on one of McCormack's TVs, the down-home vibe is downright civil. On game day, all bets are off.

McCoy's
768 9th Ave. (51st & 52nd Sts.)
Hell's Kitchen 212.957.8055

It's tough to avoid jokes about "the real McCoy" at this establishment because it offers little variation from the millions of other Irish pubs in NYC. The one defining characteristic, though, is the multitude of signs that hang among the traditional pub trappings—darts, slogans on the wall asking you not to "cuss, brawl, or throw chairs," and "My Goodness, My Guinness" posters. Well, at least there's something to read while you're waiting for your pal to arrive. And if you're too lubed on Guinness to know which pub you're at, stay calm, watch sports on one of the 10 TVs, and soak up the alcohol in your stomach with some pub grub. Happy hour is all day until 7pm, serving $3 domestic beers and well drinks.

McFadden's Saloon
800 2nd Ave. (@ 42nd St.)
Midtown 212.986.1515

Just another Midtown pub? Perhaps. But apparently, this McFadden guy isn't without his charm. Something seems to be working for this slightly polished joint, which draws the usual suspects of beer-guzzling ex-jocks and the girls who love, or at least settle for, them. There is a nightlife scene here and it seems to work for the pedestrian crowd that doesn't need a whole lot. Surely, that crowd remains forever vexed by the boneless chicken wings. Like its clientele this joint compensates for its lack of imagination with good attendance—they're open 11am-4am daily. Also matching its customers tit for tat, McFadden's dress code is "casual, but neat." There are daily food and drink specials, but Thirsty Thursday's $10 top-shelf open bar lasts all the way from 6pm-7pm.

McGee's
240 W. 55th St. (Broadway & 8th Ave.)
Midtown 212.957.3536

Freedom's just another word for nothing left but to booze at McGee's—a cheery Irish-ish pub that's amazingly neighborhoody for a bar on the outskirts of Times Square. A friendly crowd gathers early to eat standard American fare that seemingly comes with French fries no matter what it might be. Diner-style booths fill the front of the room and large wooden tables pack the back, evoking a slightly more unique version of your typical Applebee's/Bennigan's/Friday's. Later, the bar takes a turn for the drunk, as the "beer bongs" are

filled (six beers in one giant canister for as low as $15), drained, and filled again. Offering a plethora of options on tap and a surprisingly large selection of frozen girly drinks, these surroundings provide a fine place to watch the game.

McHale's
750 8th Ave. (@ 46th St.)
Hell's Kitchen 212.997.8885

Welcome to another standard American sports bar scene: baseball and hockey snapshots on the walls, a game on the TV, and a bunch of guys glued to it. Upon entering you'll find booths of boys with pitchers of beer and, further back, a dining room that resembles a barbecue joint, complete with burgers aplenty. The clientele is about as diverse as the beer list—there are only four beers on tap from which these armchair quarterbacks can fill their pitchers. But hey, no one's complaining: This is definitely a spot for "escaping the girlfriend." The bar itself doesn't much care for drama either—cash only.

McKenna's Pub
245 W. 14th St. (7th & 8th Aves.)
West Village 212.620.8124

This grubby, no-frills bar is the perfect place to kick back, relax, and skip the drama of the neighboring Meatpacking District. A 2-for-1 happy hour that extends from noon-9pm daily ensures you can stretch your hard-earned dollars a long way. A jukebox selection ranging from ABBA to AC/DC and a bartender who'll call you "hon" makes McKenna's appealing to an eclectic crowd of locals, lesbians, and slumming hipsters, as does the decent beer selection. The large outdoor patio accommodates smokers, $5 burgers accommodate carnivores, and $2 cans of Pabst Blue Ribbon accommodate anyone wearing a trucker hat. If you choose to stumble over to McKenna's for a pint, you'll lose a few hours of your life, but not your life's savings.

McKeown's

1303 3rd Ave. (74th & 75th Sts.)
Upper East Side 212.452.2011

The brightness of the red paint of this Irish pub's façade gives away McKeown's young age. Formerly known as Pioneer, this spot aims to please—12 beers on tap; half-priced beer during happy hour from 4pm-7pm Monday-Friday; wine and well drinks; a jukebox; and a full, inexpensive menu that includes burgers, bangers and mash, Irish stew, and shepherd's pie. What you might not expect are the white tablecloths, stone wall, grilled tuna steak with herbed caper butter sauce, and a kid's menu. Rest assured you can rough it at the bar without the white tablecloths with a tall, cool pint. Things are mixed here; for example, roasted chicken comes wrapped in Irish bacon and a mushroom whisky sauce. Sure, you could have it plain, but that would take away the fun.

McSorley's Old Ale House

15 E. 7th St. (2nd & 3rd Aves.)
East Village 212.473.9148

McSorley's

Who's your grandaddy? This 150-year-old bar is filled with guys old enough to have seen Hailey's Comet more than once, but if you don't mind a few wrinkles and gray hairs, you'll actually enjoy this old relic. A drink menu that consists of two beer choices—McSorley's Light and McSorley's Dark—makes it easy for Gramps to remember what he ordered. McSorley's floor sports a carpet of sawdust and the kitchen whips up boiled ham, burgers, and French fries all day long. On the weekend nights the line to get in can stretch down the block, so hit this time warp while it's still daylight. Who cares if you're buzzed by sundown? Two beers for $4 equates to meeting the locals. The "back in my day" stories are on the house.

McSwiggan's

393 2nd Ave. (22nd & 23rd Sts.)
Gramercy 212.725.8740

Does anyone still live in Ireland? It seems as though everyone from the Emerald Island has come to Manhattan to open a bar and none of them made it west of Third Avenue. We're not saying that's a bad thing. Spanning 9pm-midnight, McSwiggan's $10 all-you-can-drink Wednesdays are a waitident aksing to happen…or we mean, an accident waiting to happen, officer. (Yes, they make Thursdays difficult!) There's a jukebox, pool table, dartboard, frat boys, TVs, and supermodels…except for the supermodels. It is what it is at McSwiggan's, and by that we mean beer, beer, beer, and another beer. Hey, with 16 on tap, that still leaves you 12 more beers.

MeBar (@ the La Quinta Inn)

17 W. 32nd St. (5th & 6th Aves.)
Midtown 212.290.2460

For egotists who think this is a spot just for them, be aware that MeBar, pronounced "May Bar," is actually just paying homage to its location by using the Korean word for "mountain" to describe its rooftop space. Found on the 14th floor of the La Quinta Inn in Koreatown, MeBar is a small indoor/outdoor bar perfect for an air-conditioned after-work drink, or somewhere to listen to a DJ on Thursday nights while enjoying a smoke on the patio. While it's a hotel bar, and does afford a killer view of the Empire State Building, most of the clientele is 20- to 40-somethings catching a quick drink on the way to Penn Station. Call ahead before heading over, as they're often booked for private parties, and there aren't many similar bars in the area otherwise…unless you're looking for a karaoke bar, and then you're in luck.

Meet
71-73 Gansevoort St. (Greenwich & Washington Sts.)
Meatpacking District 212.242.0990

The problem with hotspots is that they don't stay hot forever. More lukewarm than sizzling, Meet seems to have cooled off since its opening in 2002. Now that the crowd of svelte "it" girls and boys in designer duds has migrated elsewhere, what remains is a pretty restaurant with somewhat pricey food. Feng Shui experts seem to have used neutral tones and natural materials to give Meet a warm, minimalist glow. And the food is similar—favorites like roasted halibut ($27) and grilled salmon ($23) have just enough flair to justify the prices. Stop by on a Sunday night to sample small plates from their "Sunset Menu." And even when waif-like models aren't sauntering down Meet's illuminated catwalk, it's quite a sight. Besides, in their absence, there'll be far more eating going on.

Mehanata
416 Broadway (@ Canal St.)
TriBeCa 212.625.0981

You are lucky to be reading this because unless you a) work at Mehanata; b) are Bulgarian; or c) have a thing for thick accents, you might never find this bar. And that's a shame. Although there's not much going on here—besides a $5 cover on weekends after 10—this shamelessly kitschy space is somehow endearing, just like that foreign exchange student in high school who liked to wear suspenders. Why is the bar decorated tiki-style? Who knows—we couldn't even tell you where Bulgaria was on a map if you spotted us Latvia and Turkey. For stories your pals will never

believe, seek this place out. Look for the open door and head up two flights. When you see the flag, you've arrived.

Mekong
44 Prince St. (Mott & Mulberry Sts.)
NoLita 212.343.8169

Long beaded curtains separate the kitchen from the dining area in this mid-sized Vietnamese bar/restaurant, providing somewhat of a mystique until you peer through the chunky wooden beads and see, well, a very ordinary kitchen. The décor is rounded out by whitewashed brick walls, black-and-white photos presumably taken in Vietnam, and a corner that hosts a devotional shrine. However, the steaming bowls and dishes emerging from behind the curtain are fresh and inviting, tasty drinks like orange-basil mojitos and raspberry margaritas hit the spot, and the staff is friendly without being cloying. The crowd is neighborhood-based, or at least appears to be, self-consciously sporting all the latest fashions and occasionally dancing to the somewhat-eclectic musical selection, which ranges from the Sugar Hill Gang to Tom Jones.

Merc Bar
151 Mercer St. (Houston & Prince Sts.)
SoHo 212.966.2727

Taxidermied deer heads? A wall of antlers? Giant paintings of dogs? The miracle here is that the urban ski chalet décor inside Merc Bar almost works. The locale (a stone's throw from gorgeous eateries Mercer Kitchen and Lure) screams upscale, but this SoHo institution is down-to-earth, with a relaxed atmosphere to boot (wood walls, dim, golden lighting, and cozy tables). And if you're lookin' for love, you may get picked up, but you might not want to seal the deal because Merc Bar's days of models and A-listers are a thing of the past. So knock back a couple of liquid "Loves" (Sauza, Cointreau, OJ, lime juice, and Chambord, $12) instead and you won't feel so self-conscious about flirting with the co-workers that you came here with.

Mercadito
179 Ave. B (11th & 12th Sts.)
East Village 212.529.3566

As a young boy, present-day restaurateur and culinary king Patricio Sandoval spent innumerable hours shopping with his mother in the small-town produce markets of his native Mexican. These habitual sojourns quickly made an indelible impression on the adolescent Sandoval, inspiring a lifelong interest in and dedication to the preparation and presentation of a diverse spectrum of Mexican cuisines, and culminating in the development and creation of Mercadito (Spanish for "little market"). Owner-run and operated (Sandoval is also the master chef), this irresistibly appealing East Village restaurant and tequila bar delivers both simplistically straightforward, widely recognized "staple" dishes and complex, little-heard-of delicacies. Make a run for the border, and don't forget to down some tequila on the way.

Mercantile Grill
126 Pearl St. (Wall St. & Hanover Sq.)
Financial District 212.482.1221

Wall Street is crawling with pubs, but the long-time, Irish-owned Mercantile Grill is easily a notch above the others and has the historic heft to prove it. A tavern has occupied this address since Prohibition, and the original brick walls, detailed tin ceiling, and 45-foot bar remain. A friendly bar staff that's always glad to top off a pint glass sees a huge lunch crowd of Wall Streeters, techies, and the usual suspects. Come nightfall, it's the same crowd, only happier and more inebriated. Don't leave without tucking into the tasty pub eats; from a Cajun chicken quesadilla topped with a creamy mound of guacamole to a grilled calamari salad tossed in a sherry vinaigrette, and juicy burgers, Mercantile Grill isn't just about drinking—but that's a big part of it.

Mercer Kitchen
99 Prince St. (@ Mercer St.)
SoHo 212.966.5454

Much like the incarnation of Williamsburg's Sea in the film *Garden State*, the impeccably decorated, upscale Mercer Kitchen is more like a parody of a restaurant than the real thing. The eclectic, vault-like downstairs dining room features lots of dark corners (good for dates), a few communal tables (could be good for getting dates), and an open kitchen so patrons can ogle chefs as they prepare American Provencal cuisine with sophisticated prices (something you'd come to expect from a Jean-Georges haunt). It's not exorbitant by New York standards, but certainly too pricey for a place that might keep you waiting 45 minutes past your reservation. Hit the Mercer Kitchen for a quick drink and stay long enough to take in the atmosphere and gawk at the visually appealing clientele. Then head somewhere else.

Merchants
112 7th Ave. (17th & 18th Sts.)
Chelsea 212.366.7267

Merchants is not the kind of place where anybody "bellies up" to the bar. Here, you approach the elegant bow-shaped, marble-topped counter, and squeeze in between the beautiful people. Or sit down to order a couple Snickertinis (think of the candy bar), or pair one of 30 wines with a plate of tuna carpaccio. Finding a table outside or on the mezzanine makes for a more tranquil experience than shuffling around the narrow bar area, since Merchants does a brisk business even in the early evening. The bartender CD-DJs just what you'd expect: house music and some chilled-out downbeat mixes. This is Chelsea, after all, and the opulently fashionable vibe is belied only by a big TV, which hangs precariously over the bar like it's about to fall off its bracket.

Merchants NY
1125 1st Ave. (@ 62nd St.)
Upper East Side 212.832.1551

Get your stogies out! One of the few cigar bars in the city, this Merchants (there's also one in

Chelsea) has a downstairs space of nooks and crannies with premium cigars and liquors on display and for purchase. Two fireplaces warm the two levels, including the upstairs smoke-free lounge. The pretty staircase sets the stage for a geometrically patterned floor, clubby seating areas, and couches, all in muted shades of brown, gold, and red. Have a beer from the rotating selection that might include Lindeman's Framboise or Ithaca Nut Brown to accompany your yellowfin tuna club sandwich or firecracker spring rolls with sweet Thai chili sauce. There's live jazz every day except Monday—stick that in your pipe and smoke it.

Mercury Bar
493 3rd Ave. (33rd & 34th Sts.)
Murray Hill 212.683.2645

Mercury Bar is where most post-grads go when they get lost after trying to go to neighboring Joshua Tree or Bar 515. Since the three bars all seem to be cloned from the same genetic material of some state college bar in New Jersey, most Murray Hillers can't be blamed for not knowing which bar they're actually in. However, most lost souls end up sticking around, since Mercury Bar is the scene for those still craving deafeningly loud music and some decent drink specials. The food here is also a step up from the "free wings, $1 hamburgers" you may have grown accustomed to. On Friday and Saturday nights, Mercury Bar airs college football on 11 satellite TVs so you won't ever feel homesick again.

Mercury Bar & Grill
659 9th Ave. (45th & 46th Sts.)
Hell's Kitchen 212.262.7755

This solid, dependable neighborhood bar covers all the bases without spreading itself too thin. Weekdays beckon youngish after-work Midtowners to a 4pm-7pm happy hour. On weekends, young and slightly older customers alike make use of Mercury's outdoor seating and brunch menu (standard American fare at standard prices). But if sports are what you're after, Mercury serves again, with seven TV screens above the bar counter. Red velvet and leather semi-circle booths can accommodate a ladies' night on the town or smaller dinner tables can work for dates, but know that the later it gets, the younger, louder, and more single the crowd.

The Mercury Lounge
217 E. Houston St. (Ludlow & Essex Sts.)
Lower East Side 212.260.4700

Since the demise of Brownie's (and now the possibly soon-to-be-defunct CBGB's), Mercury Lounge has reigned as the favorite child of the downtown NYC music scene. This 250-capacity, two-room music venue/bar has hosted countless indie rock legends and cutting-edge acts such as Lou Reed and Ryan Adams; it also harbors an interesting history, since the space used to be a tombstone store and quarters for servants who worked at the Astor Mansion. Now, rock 'n' rollers feel like they're one step closer to rock royalty once they've played this Lower East Side standard. Just be weary of the door lady; she's as tough as they come and she won't fall for any cockamamie explanation as to why you should be let in even though your name's not on the guest list.

The Mermaid Inn
96 2nd Ave. (5th & 6th Sts.)
East Village 212.674.5870

Can't escape to the Cape this summer? If you can live without the beach part, Mermaid Inn is a close second. You might need a reservation if you hope to score some lobster at this East Village eatery. Great seafood and a well-edited wine list make empty tables scarce at this perennially packed, upscale fish shack. Amidst the rough-hewn ceiling beams, polished tables, and antique nautical maps, diners have their choice of fresh seafood staples and a mouthwatering array of oysters, clams, and shrimp. Get the raw bar sampler and request a patio table to invoke the true spirit of seaside summer dining—without the sea-sickening boat ride or smell of dead fish.

Merrion Square
1840 2nd Ave. (@ 95th St.)
Upper East Side 212.831.7696

The interior of this bar/restaurant has a beautiful wooden finish, and the beer selection is to die for, with 16 beers on tap and 20 by the bottle. This is a really nice bar in a neighborhood that's not very fun at all. The traditional bar food isn't half-bad either and it's served by a staff that would probably hang out in a bar just like this one on their days off. Cheese fries, spring rolls, and bruschetta? Not too shabby. Merrion Square is also a great place for watching the game, and it even seems refined—classy if you will. We shouldn't recommend coming here from Brooklyn, but those who live up here needn't leave the 'hood to drink among people who dress like grown-ups.

Mesa Grill
102 5th Ave. (15th & 16th Sts.)
Flatiron 212.807.7400

Thanks to the popularity and driving force of celeb chef and owner, Bobby Flay, Mesa Grill thrives today as it did when it opened 15 years ago. The difference is that it's now more popular with tourists and Food Network viewers than locals. This colorful space has high ceilings and colorful columns depicting a wide-open Southwestern theme, which is reinforced by matching cuisine and 28 tequilas. The yellow corn-crusted chile relleno ($20) has been on the menu for years, and is still prepared expertly, with a tender pepper in a crunchy shell and warm, melted cheese inside. Mesa serves the original prickly pear cactus margarita ($12), and has a few other specialty margaritas, including a tasty white peach version ($12). The excellent kitchen more than offsets the mediocre crowd.

Metrazur
Grand Central Terminal, East Balcony (@ 42nd St.)
Midtown 212.687.4600

Check out that view (or just glance at the celestial ceiling) here and you'll understand how Metrazur can justify their $10.25 martinis in over 13 varieties. Located in Grand Central Station's East Balcony, this bar exudes an expansive, open feel that nicely contrasts with the stuffy, cramped cubicle where you've likely been stuck for the past eight hours. You'd be wrong to dismiss it as a tourist spot, when more likely urbane after-work 30-somethings munching on appetizers and sipping Swedish Tiramisus congregate around the two full bars. Tuesday is Ladies Night, though both genders receive reduced-priced cocktails before 6pm any night (and at those prices, you'd better arrive early.) The balcony allows patrons refuge from the massive crowd scurrying below while simultaneously basking in some of Manhattan's most beautiful architecture.

Metro Café & Wine Bar
32 E. 21st St. (Park Ave. S. & Broadway)
Flatiron 212.353.0200

You might think you've stepped into an AA member's version of the *Twilight Zone* or simply discovered a wine aficionado's wet dream. Metro Café & Wine Bar offers 100 wines by the glass and 120 by the bottle (yes, we counted correctly) from Italy, France, South America, Australia, Germany, California, and Oregon. The large, airy space is romantic enough for a first date, impressive enough to bring business associates, and casual enough for a leisurely dinner with friends. The eclectic menu (burgers, pizza, meatloaf, and a dim sum bar menu) is sure to satisfy a broad range of palates. The menu items are priced a bit high ($8.50 guacamole and chips?), but if you get all tingly when you hear words like "fermentation," come on in.

Metro 53
307 E. 53rd St. (1st & 2nd Aves.)
Midtown 212.838.0007

Though it may seem like your average Midtown bar scene—corporate, martini-drinking 30-somethings all totally hammered at 7pm—Metro 53 actually has potential to be a really fun bar. This bar's high point is the half-off happy hour. So, while you might need double the alcohol just to stand the mediocre crowd, Metro 53 has one big advantage over its neighboring joints and "big" is that advantage. The key is to bring all of your own friends—and your own fun. Bar tables are plentiful and the music is hip enough, even if the people dancing to it aren't. Did we mention the happy hour? Quieter times can be had in the upstairs lounge, the Upper Deck.

Metropol
234 W. 4th St. (@ 10th St.)
West Village 212.206.8393

Metropol

Finally starting to realize that pounding back shots of Jägermeister at your local frat bar isn't that cool when it's been a good decade since you've cracked open a textbook? It's time to get acquainted with Metropol, a new West Village hangout for grown-ups. Perched on the prime corner of W. Fourth Street and W. 10th Street (yes, apparently that is possible), this smallish, seductive French bistro woos couples with an artsy black-and-white décor, dim lighting, romantic nooks, and piped-in, Euro-flavored music. (A DJ spins Thursday-Saturday, including weekend brunch). Wine is the poison of choice, and there's a healthy list with which to complement your filet

mignon or sea scallops. While Metropol may be a slam-dunk third-date dinner spot, its late hours—4am nightly—give singles the chance to ask, "Voulez vous couchez avec moi?"

Metropolitan
559 Lorimer St. (Metropolitan Ave. & Devoe St.)
Williamsburg 718.599.4444

Williamsburg is a little gay everywhere you go, but the highest concentration of "the new SoHo"'s hip gay population congregates at Metropolitan. It's not too queeny, and the clientele has been out of the closet long enough to be comfortable with it; in other words, talk of sample sales and sparkly half-shirts aren't common here. It seems, though, that everyone here has slept with one another already (or they're working overtime to get it on later that night). Party girls and boys come for the fab music (Saturday night's "GAG" dance party is a hit), cheap drinks, huge backyard, or to giggle at passersby primping themselves in the mirror at the front of the bar that ostensibly faces the street.

Metropolitan Café
959 1st Ave. (52nd & 53rd Sts.)
Midtown 212.759.5600

Surprisingly, this family-friendly restaurant draws a decent bar crowd, even on weekends. Chalk it up to the charming bartenders or a wine list as long as the wait for a table, but the dinner crowd here only leaves a few spots open at the bar. The tables are usually filled with stodgy Midtown types, but the scene is a refreshing, more sophisticated break from the frat house reunion going on down the street. The live jazz/fusion music on Tuesday nights and the garden in back help to erase your memory of the bar's 9-5-centric locale. If you're feeling flirty, try your moves on a lawyer-type perched at the bar. Or just hit on the bartender—he may just pour that second glass of chardonnay on the house.

Mexican Radio
19 Cleveland Pl. (Kenmare & Spring Sts.)
NoLita 212.343.0140

California transplants can finally stop their whining thanks to Mexican Radio. With salsa so fresh and salty that you may be tasting it weeks later, this NoLita bar/restaurant is a mainstay for those who take their Mexican to heart…burn. Order up a raspberry/black cherry margarita ($9) or a few glasses of the bartender's special rum punch ($9), and you'll soon be tuning into different frequencies of incoherence. With its random assortment of Mexican kitsch (think fake flower collages and stencil art), Mexican Radio provides the obligatory fiesta, while the pleasantly blunt wait staff seems to take a genuine interest in the patrons, who range from talkative after-work and trendy student types to sauced diehards grinning mischievously from barstools.

Mica 51
252 E. 51st St. (2nd & 3rd Aves.)
Midtown 212.888.2453

As another sultry, candlelit martini lounge trying its Western hand at fusion, Mica 51turns out to be an Asian culture clash. Gold embroidered pillows and an Indian décor accompany a menu of sushi and tapas, and while it's no surprise that dumplings plus mojitos do not equal Asia de Cuba, even that equation was so 2004. The low-lit bar and lounge does manage to attract a chill, swanky crowd on Thursday nights when a DJ spins on the first floor. Lounging around leather booths, the FIT students sipping guava cosmos and red wine are easily the hippest option on this venue's ambitious if not slightly confused menu. If only everything were as easy as peanut butter and chocolate. These guys have a second location in Murray Hill.

Mica 587
587 3rd Ave. (38th & 39th Sts.)
Murray Hill 212.661.3181

At press time, this Mica sister bar was getting prepped for a little reconstructive surgery. Here's the "before": The lower level of this bi-level, multi-room bar/restaurant gives off the feel of a more traditional, high-end bar and performance space (there's live entertainment twice a week), while the top half is more of a loungey eating area. Mica regulars are probably crossing their fingers that the retractable roof above the downstairs area will remain intact after its extreme makeover. But with enough rooms to suit an array of personalities, copious specialty martinis, and well-favored food and wine menus, this bar will continue to please. Mica 587 is a refreshing departure from the standard fare of loud, flavor-of-the-week sports bars that seem to be the bedrock of the Murray Hill bar scene.

Mickey Mantle's
42 Central Park S. (5th & 6th Aves.)
Midtown 212.688.7777

Mickey Mantle's is to sports as the Red Sox's 2004 World Series victory is to inexplicable miracles. Mantle's sports a variety of impressive sports memorabilia, and the proprietors have thought of everything—the waiters are decked out in Yankees No. 7 jerseys, huge games from bygone eras play on big-screen TVs, and the washroom attendants offer anabolic steroids (just kidding, Giambi fans!). Like all good themed restaurants, Mantle's offers a wide selection of souvenirs (some of which are actually genuine artifacts) so patrons can walk away with a little bit of Yankees magic. Still, Mantle's should stock up while they can, because after last year's post-season, that magic might be a little harder to come by.

Micky's Blue Room
171 Ave. C (10th & 11th Sts.)
East Village 212.375.0723

This Alphabet City favorite knows how to keep its customers happy (and coming back). Besides the 5pm-9pm/1am-4am happy hour featuring $3 beers (in the bottle or on draught) and well drinks (and $1 off everything else), Micky's hosts a quality jukebox and a pool table that only costs $1 per game. Two live acoustic performances on Tuesdays and Wednesdays showcase New York's up-and-coming talent. And if you're looking for some laughs, stop in on Thursday nights between 8pm-10pm when the comedy hour is in full effect. If you have the strength to hang, Micky's generously shows appreciation to its loyal locals by offering Late Night Happiness Sunday through Thursday with free pool from 1am 'til 4am. Oh, Micky…you're so fine, you're so fine you blow our mind!

Milady's Bar & Restaurant
160 Prince St. (@ Thompson St.)
SoHo 212.226.9340

Whether or not they still live around here, the displaced SoHo ex-patriots and rent-control survivors will always regard Milady's as their neighborhood bar. A pool table in the back stands watch over a classic rock and funk jukebox, both of which get plenty of use from local legends and off-duty bartenders. The darkened bar feels like something out of a woodsy lodge, where guys in fishing caps watch Yankees games on the overhead TV, and the bartender seemingly knows everyone inside. Small, standard kitchenette tables are spread about the joint—that's where groups order standard pub grub before starting in with the heavy drinking. The occasional celebrity will pop in, but if they do, it's because they want to be left alone; and this down-to-earth crowd will happily oblige.

Milano's
51 E. Houston St. (Mulberry & Mott Sts.)
NoLita 212.226.8844

Don't let the fancy name fool you—Milano's is about as Italian as a pint of Guinness. Plastered with photos of regulars and good times past, the walls of this Irish saloon display memorabilia like NYC subway signage, an homage to both JFK and horseracing, and a road marker pointing towards County Kerry. Those tired of breathing the air of NoLita pretension will like this little getaway. Happy hour (Mon-Fri, 4pm-7pm) offers $1 off their already dirt-cheap drinks, including $3 Pabst and Bud and $5 mixed. Squeeze past the narrow bar, plop yourself down on a stool, and maybe you'll find your face up on the wall some day.

Milk & Honey
134 Eldridge St. (@ Delancey St.)
Lower East Side Unlisted

The first rule of Milk & Honey is don't talk about Milk & Honey. Or is that *Fight Club*? Don't mistake the two—there are lots of strange rules to this semi-private non-VIP lounge and one of them prohibits talk of fighting. Another rule forbids the wearing of hats and there's yet another that requires that men who wish to meet ladies must first go through the bartender. Oh, play along—it's fun. Behind the soundproofed façade of an unmarked dry cleaner lies this railroad layout, which offers a single long row of booths under pressed-tin ceilings. Owner Sasha Petraske, who's designed cocktail menus for lounges including the Church Lounge, Double Seven, Little Branch, and East Side Company to name a few, places a serious emphasis on well-crafted cocktails and their presentation in this modern-day speakeasy.

Mini-Bar in the District (@ the Muse Hotel)
130 W. 46th St. (6th & 7th Aves.)
Midtown 212.485.2999

Finding this upscale drinkery is like playing with a set of those Russian matroishka nesting dolls or getting to the center of a Tootsie Roll Pop. Tucked away in the back of District restaurant inside the Muse Hotel, this cozy little joint appeases foodies and barflies looking for a little sustenance before curtain time. Mini-Bar has no beers on tap and only a few in the bottle, but brews are often not what guests here crave; they come for the large selection of wines and cocktails like the potent martinis. Theater-goers have the option of snacking on Mini-Bar's free sacks (gummy worms and other candies), which they can sneak into the Broadway play of their choice.

Miracle Bar & Grill
415 Bleecker St. (Bank & 11th Sts.)
West Village 212.924.1900

On any given night at Miracle Bar & Grill, you'll see groups of young women sharing plates of fried calamari and fish tacos (let's keep it clean, you sick-o!). This place is a goldmine for single men as it's a starting point for trendettes destined for a night out in the West Village. As sure as Long Island dudes wear striped button-ups, $9-ish mojitos and sangria are favorites here. The flavorful Tex-Mex cuisine favors fruity salsas, and most things are share-friendly. Miracle Bar & Grill can occasionally over-flavor, but because its efforts are bold, we'll cut it some slack. So long as you avoid the back door and its unfortunate proximity to the sometimes smelly alley, Miracle Bar & Grill provides a worthwhile olfactory experience that's as pleasing to the senses as the pretty crowd and tasty culinary servings.

Miracle Grill
112 1st Ave. (6th & 7th Sts.)
East Village 212.254.2353

Unless it's pouring, don't even *think* about eating inside this hip downtown restaurant, because all of the action happens in the stunning (and mammoth) backyard dining area, where you can eat and chat (and smoke!) al fresco amidst sparkling white lights, sloping trees, and quaint green patio tables. Naysayers may harp about Miracle Grill's "chi-chi" attitude, but you're better off seeing for yourself because you'll find that Miracle Grill lives up to its name. The drinks are yummy and the Southwestern fare menu is diverse and delectable enough to satisfy even the pickiest of palates. You might overhear a heated conversation about Prada sample sales, but it's a small price to pay for heaven.

Miss Williamsburg Porta Via
228 E. 10th St. (1st & 2nd Aves.)
East Village 212.228.5355

Manhattanites who do "miss Williamsburg" will enjoy this Brooklyn transplant, which has a bigger sister across the river. And like everything that makes the leap into the city, Miss Williamsburg Porta Via has had to make some sacrifices; the roomy indoor space and 200-capacity garden they

have over the bridge translates to a simple basement dining area here. The more traditional Italian menu offered east of the river has also been scaled down, but the "Ultimate Lasagna" is all one really needs. For $14.75, cheese fondue lasagna is covered in pesto sauce, resulting in a big, sloppy culinary gem. (For $100, these guys will ship the Emiglia Romagna Lasagna almost anywhere in the US.) A wine list of 30+ options ranges from $22-$110 and each vino works for toasting this place's arrival.

Mission
217 Bowery (Prince & Rivington Sts.)
Lower East Side 212.473.3113

Mission

There are places that you go to and really dig, but deep down, you also know such a place's time will pass. At Mission, time has kind of stood still, which makes this well-planned, mostly hip-hop lounge/club a welcomed oasis among the rapidly changing Bowery and its rags-to-riches identity crisis. The main room is dark and it sits in the shadow of a tall DJ booth, which doubles as a small VIP area. There's a lower level here and when it isn't serving as a private party space, it works out as a less-busy alternative to the energetic top floor. Celebrities and socialites don't darken this doorway as they once did, which means more lingering space for a mostly downtown and other-borough crowd. Covers, parties, and music vary each night.

Mixx Lounge
84 7th Ave. S. (Bleecker & Grove Sts.)
West Village 212.243.7888

The velvet ropes hint at exclusivity, but once inside the familial bar staff makes it known that all are welcome in this West Village hangout. Mixx hosts an eclectic patronage, some of whom can be witnessed getting body-painted, and others who are just here for the 2-for-1 happy hour drinks (Tuesday-Friday, 5pm-8pm) and free buffet on Thursdays and Fridays. Hip-hop and Top 40 play overhead, although no room for dancing invites the next best thing—head bobbing—from deeply reclined regulars. More of a house party than a hotspot, this is a great place for resting your Manolos after navigating cobblestones all night. Grab a Mixx Martini and take a break from the bustling neighborhood without paying a cover or getting snubbed by the doorman.

MJ Armstrong's
329 1st Ave. (@ 19th St.)
Gramercy 212.358.9946

MJ Armstong's

If "square inches of video screen" were gold, MJ Armstrong's would be the Sultan of Brunei. Such television real estate makes MJ's a haven for the sports-inclined, who come in droves during football season to enjoy 50-cent wings and assorted drink specials during weekend games. Anchoring a growing bar district across from Stuyvesant Town, MJ's employs two floors with two bars to provide live music, while the inviting front façade of large windows and cozy interior attract all ages and genders. Families and females are frequent,

but let's not kid ourselves; with $2 beers during "Pub Night" and Fridays complementing an arcade's worth of parlor games and sprawling acreage of football games, the fellas are likely coming here to avoid their women, not meet new ones.

MOBar (@ Mandarin Oriental Hotel)
80 Columbus Cir., 35th Fl. (59th & 60th Sts.)
Upper West Side 212.805.8826

The ambiance at this 35th-floor, Asian-themed hotel bar is elegant, refined, blah, blah, blah. At the leather-padded bar, posh, moneyed singles order really dirty $17 martinis, and in the padded-leather recliners beyond, gray-templed suits kick back aristocratically before chowing down on some MObites, MOBar's imaginatively named snacks. Of course, the real question is, who doesn't like feeling that the genteel young bartenders, who stand dutifully at attention, exist solely to fulfill your every immediate need? And with a bird's-eye view of Midtown Manhattan stretching before you, you may also begin to wonder why you don't come to MOBar mo' often. The answers to these questions will be revealed once your bill arrives on a silver platter. There is often a long wait for tables and they're dealt with on a first come, first served basis.

Moda
135 W. 52nd St. (6th & 7th Aves.)
Midtown 212.887.9880

Entering Moda is a bit like walking into a hotel lobby where the desk clerks are so inattentive you start thinking how badly you need a drink—and then suddenly, you spy a bar in the corner. This dark, quiet indoor bar is impeccably designed, with sleek black chairs, leather benches, and an art-deco-ish wall of glass windows that breaks the room in two. The bar menu consists of overpriced, high-end Southern Italian appetizers, a substantial amount of vegetarian options, and $8-$12 cocktails served in funky glasses. The outdoor area in a spacious causeway is the place to hang, though—especially on weekend nights when Moda shows free movies and hands out complimentary wasabi peas. It's perfect for that evening when you want to show off that new pair of designer chinos.

The Modern
9 W. 53rd St. (5th & 6th Aves.)
Midtown 212.333.1220

Danny Meyer finally lets uptowners skip the 6 train. Now, they can flag a cab over to his new restaurant at the re-opened MOMA, where Chef Gabriel Kreuther is breathing life into the otherwise drab world of museum dining and drinking. Up front in the Bar Room, reasonably priced plates are divided into ones, twos, and threes, presumably telling you how many people they will feed; order a bottle of wine no matter how many people are in your group. Flusher clientele prefer to sit in the back to enjoy the three-course prix fixe for $74 as they overlook the Abby Aldrich Rockefeller sculpture garden. The food is as fine as the art next door, with Kreuther creating French-influenced masterpieces nightly. Try it all: the front room, the backroom, the food, the wine, and the desserts. Unlike the museum, the only line you'll be waiting on belongs to the phone, because reservations are a must. Fortunately, however, this is one list you won't have to shell out too much cash to be on.

Moe's
80 Lafayette Ave. (@ Portland St.)
Fort Greene 718.797.9536

Moe's rates highly among Fort Greene's sincerely cool bars with its moody lighting, deceptively large space with tons of tables and chairs for small or larger groups, and a DJ whose spinning chops reconcile a great soundtrack with easy conversation. The mixed crowd is all-inclusive and remarkably hipster-free, with young locals, slightly older after-work types, groups of friends, and a handful of attractive singles on a subtle prowl. Best of all, happy hour boasts 2-for-1 beers—a bargain that makes the bar's one drawback (tiny bathrooms) well worth it. Moe's is the kind of place where people from all boroughs and walks of life can feel at home (and you will when you sit on the garage sale-like furniture). You'll come back for "moe."

The Molly Wee Pub
402 8th Ave. (@ 30th St.)
Chelsea 212.967.2627

It's Sunday at the Molly Wee and scarcely a bar seat is to be found at this single-room Chelsea restaurant/pub. A regular stopover for Knicks fans pre- and post-game, Molly Wee's service is quick and friendly and Guinness is the pint of choice. This place definitely has character. Molly Wee is Irish for "yellow hill"; the bartender is Irish, as are most of the regulars, and a proud Irish flag flies behind the bar. U2 plays on a retrofit digital jukebox, and the head waitress is named Sinead. Sitting at the bar, expect to hear a couple Irish accents, as well as a few outrageous drunk stories. Overall, this is a good place to come and enjoy a pint and a snack before letting the Knicks ruin your night.

Mona's
224 Ave. B (13th & 14th Sts.)
East Village 212.353.3780

If you've had a crappy day and are feeing inclined to find somewhere dark, dank, and depressing to watch the day turn into night, wallow in your depression surrounded by like-minded individuals, and swill drinks priced to deliver you into a more mellow, painless place. C'mon in, you miserable wreck, you. A string of tired, older regulars is always in attendance, and for the cost of a pint they'll be more than happy to listen attentively to whatever woes you have. Grab a few of your equally sad sack pals and take a game of pool, or just get blitzed on $3 beers from the tap. (Guinness pints are $3 all day on Thursdays.) Tomorrow is another day, and if things don't get better, Mona's is open seven days, 3pm-4am.

M1-5
52 Walker St. (Church St. & Broadway)
TriBeCa 212.965.1701

This bar's name refers to the city's local zoning policy, but if it brings to mind WWII bombers...you've got the right idea. Ambitiously approaching the size of an airplane hangar and coated in dark red paint, M1-5 combines the low-lit sexiness of TriBeCa nightlife with the egotism of New York City at-large. Don't expect attitude at the door, though; there's no dress code, and drinks are priced for the proletariat (wells and beers go for $4-$5, exotic fruity concoctions run $8-10, and there's $1 off drinks during happy hour from 4pm-7pm and until 9pm on Fridays). Management isn't opposed to bringing out the projector TV for a big game on the weekends, either. Wooden booths lining the dimly lit main space are perfect for cooing into someone's ear; just set your libido on autopilot.

Monkey Bar
60 E. 54th St. (Park & Madison Aves.)
Midtown 212.838.2600

As the name suggests, there's lots of monkeying around going on at this 89-year-old institution. Well, on the walls anyway. In fact, the restaurant at the Monkey Bar offers a history of the 46 monkeys painted on the walls of the bar, who are doing everything from juggling to getting liquored up. And there's plenty to get drunk on—the Monkey Bar features a specialty cocktail list with over 10 drinks, including the signature cocktail, the Banana Hi-Ball. If you're hungry for more than a banana or a liquid dinner, though, you can enjoy a bar menu all day. But keep the Tums handy—Monkey Bar's steak-heavy menu has gi-normous sides like black truffle creamed spinach. Nightly you can swing over to the piano bar to sing a song and toast the wonders of evolution.

Monkey Temple
558 Broome St. (6th Ave. & Varick St.)
SoHo 646.613.1620

We're not sure what it is about this understated lounge that draws swells of women, but the Monkey Temple is full of subtle charms like that. The small room is full of recline-friendly furniture and lit by a fire hazard row of votive candles lining one wall (the effect is worth the calamity). The menu is mostly cheeses and salads (toasted brie, pear salad). Management is friendly to celebrants:

The room can be rented for free; have your birthday there, and they'll throw in a bottle of champagne and a cake. Regular poetry readings and art shows are frequent too. Enjoy the many charms of the Monkey Temple, but beware running into your ex in its tight confines...she may try to maneuver your gelled hair over to those candles.

The Monster
80 Grove St. (4th St. & Waverly Pl.)
West Village 212.924.3558

A blend of K-Mart décor and Mexican restaurant festivities makes the Monster a beast of bad taste. Despite its vivid colors, unpretentious ambiance, and fiercely loyal patrons, this aesthetically void gay bar exudes a more funereal than fun vibe. Those who must visit (and far more creative spots permeate the area) can mingle on the downstairs dance floor or grab a comfortable booth by the large windows that provide a panoramic view of Christopher Park and W. Fourth Street, a visually pleasing contrast to the Midwest-looking middle-aged crowd inside wearing clip-on cell phones and highwater jeans while sipping equally unoriginal frozen margaritas. This Monster really does bite.

Montero's Bar & Grill
73 Atlantic Ave. (@ Hicks St.)
Brooklyn Heights 718.624.9799

Back when it opened in 1947, Montero's Bar & Grill was a neighborhood hangout for merchant marines. While the décor hasn't changed much—think model ships, fishnets, and a sign that proclaims "company and fish stink after three days"—the clientele has...a little. Some of the more grizzly types seem like they've been around since the East River was a major port of call, but look past the stack of Bud cans and you might just see a curious hipster-type hoping to sneak in a pool game with the local sharks. So if you want to see a true old-school dive, strap on your life preserver and head towards the BQE. But don't expect any frills—there are no beers on tap, and the barmaid won't take any lip.

Mooney's Pub
353 Flatbush Ave. (Sterling St. & Park Slope Ave.)
Park Slope 718.783.9085

You may have graduated from college just to get away from this type of bar, but Mooney's is probably your first stop for a homecoming. A typical ole Irish pub complete with posters of Ireland, dartboard, and rowdy locals, Mooney's is a stomping ground for older Brooklynites looking to watch the game with a cheap cold one. The bartenders are super-friendly and happy to give you the most up-to-date stats on every sport (except water polo). Mooney's is a home away from home for the local pub-goers at this dingy bar, except for women—you'd have to be a leprechaun to fit into the ladies' room.

Moonshine
317 Columbia St. (Woodhull St. & Hamilton Ave.)
Red Hook 718.422.0563

Only in the outer-reaches of the Red Hook/Carroll Gardens border would you find a bar like Moonshine (or at least north of the Mason-Dixon line). This bar's well-stocked with cheap beer (as in PBR, not Brooklyn Lager, for all you wandering yuppies) and shot specials, and the jukebox plays honky-tonk blues. There's an upright piano that's up for public use, and in a *coup de grâce* move that you only wish more neighborhood dives would imitate, a big backyard with a BYOM (as in "bring your own meat") grilling policy. Moonshine's location ensures an always interesting mix of older locals and young 'uns, but you won't find a more welcoming place in all of Brooklyn. Grab your burger patties and get friendly with the F line.

Morgan's Bar (@ the Morgan Hotel)
237 Madison Ave. (36th & 37th Sts.)
Murray Hill 212.726.7600

How pretty can one bar be? At this intimate lounge, blue flowers glow across the bar, candlelight plays off the lush décor, and DJ-spun music hums through the room. This place is wonderful, from the super-friendly staff to the frilly menu (champagne is practically a staple). The menu includes updated favorites like blood-orange margaritas and raspberry mojitos, as well as a selection of scrumptious tapas. There is a $20 minimum per person, but everything here is so sweet and lovely that you'll fork it over without a blink. And after a few sips of your Morgan's Martini (vanilla vodka, strawberries, and coconut), you'll have to forcibly restrain yourself from making out with whoever's beside you on the low-slung sofa.

Morrell Wine Bar & Café
1 Rockefeller Plaza (@ 49th St.)
Midtown 212.262.7700

Morrell is across the street from Rockefeller Center—but wait, you hip New York compatriots, don't shriek and run back downtown yet. Morrell is a wine lover's paradise, with 150 wines available by the glass, a daily rotating list, and several thousand bottles. Their obscenely enormous wine list includes short paragraphs about each wine, so that connoisseurs can sniff about the poetry and novices can know what the heck to order. Jazzy music, French posters, and a curvy, modern metallic décor complete the romantic, sophisticated, but unpretentious vibe. So hold your breath and push past the Midwesterners in fanny-packs to get there, and maybe even admit that the front outdoor seating overlooking Rockefeller Center is lovely.

Morrisey Park
121 St. Marks Pl. (Ave. A & 1st Ave.)
East Village 212.979.1459

Yes, folks, the clouds have rolled in on the former Openair and the winds of change have taken hold. This is one of those places that seem to change names and identities every year or so and now, Morrisey Park is hoping to settle this spot down and make an honest lounge of it yet. St. Marks locals drift in here during the week, and the weekends are shoulder-to-shoulder with trucker-hat honeys, dry-clean-only yuppies, and Adidas hipsters hanging by the bar and chilling on leather lounge furniture. The bar packs few surprises—$6 draughts, $5 bottles, and a small wine list. DJs spin every night and there's no cover, unless it's a hot name. This place isn't reinventing the wheel, but it gets to where it's going.

Mo's Caribbean Bar & Mexican Grille
1454 2nd Ave. (@ 76th St.)
Upper East Side 212.650.0561

Mo's is the ideal spot for those who spent Spring Break cleaning their parents' gutters or working to pay off their college loans. You'll find no-holds-barred comfort in the beer pitchers and buckets of bottles, tequila shots, 50 kinds of margaritas, scorpion bowls, and specials galore—like Krazy Karaoke Tuesdays featuring $2 light beers and $1 draughts, cheap margaritas for ladies on Wednesdays, all-you-can-eat Thursdays, and a $9.95 fresh lobster special and $5 mussels on Mondays. And the night wouldn't be complete without trying this festive Caribbean-themed bar/restaurant's Killer Kool-Aid during happy hour. Kick back with a bowl of Mo's Three Alarm Chili or their Honey Cannibis Lager, find someone to hook up with later, and thank Mo's for kickin' it island-style.

Mosto Osteria
87 2nd Ave. (@ 5th St.)
East Village 212.228.9912

Mosto serves up what most recovering South Beach dieters crave—hearty, carbo-loaded staples like gnocchi, lasagna, and spaghetti, a big basket of bread, and some olive oil. Crowd-pleasing favorites like Penne all'Arrabbiata and the ricotta ravioli are offered along with an array of specialty martinis and a robust selection of over 20 red wines and 10 whites. Be sure to stop by during warm weather, though, when the windows are thrown open and you can sip a margarita or mojito and observe the onslaught of bar-hopping undergrads bustling along Second Avenue. Reliable, if uninspired, Mosto is a dependable

choice in the proliferation of East Village Italian joints; it's just chic enough to fit in, but not enough to outshine its more seasoned neighbors.

Moto
394 Broadway (Hooper & Division Sts.)
Williamsburg 718.599.6895

Located in the middle of a Nowheresville part of Williamsburg in a flatiron-shaped building—the entrance to which is marked only by a hanging bicycle—resides Moto. Moto is a work of art in itself, really—beautifully crumbling walls, weathered wood, and endless intriguing curiosities make just setting foot in this place an experience (it's as though the owners captured the essence of a silent black-and-white film). The slate-topped bar mimicking the V-shape of the building serves up a tasty selection of beer and wine, including the scrumptious Corsendonk Belgian brown ale. Musical acts equally bizarre and awesome as the bar perform every evening here, and the kitchen's influences stretch from the Middle East all the way to the Bayou.

Motor City
127 Ludlow St. (Delancey & Rivington Sts.)
Lower East Side 212.358.1595

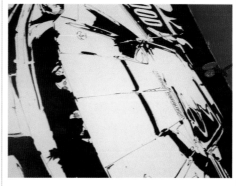

Naysayers who claim that the LES has lost its edge need to check out Motor City. This dive bar is a shout-out to Detroit with its road signs and license plates from the city that gave us Eminem. They don't serve 40s here, so you can't tip one in the memory of your missing bros, but you can give props to your pals on the "Leave a friend a drink" board instead. If you're just passing by, take a pit stop at Motor City along your highway to hell. It's pretty hard not to stop inside this rockin' hub of heathenism—especially once you get a look at the bucket seats, chrome car memorabilia, or the curvy, gold bikini-clad go-go dancer gyrating to rock tunes in the window.

Movida

28 7th Ave. S. (Bedford & Leroy Sts.)
West Village 212.206.9600

Pack some Dramamine when you come aboard this new "luxury vessel," because Movida—finally open after about a year in the works—is rocking the boat. This swanky, quasi-nautical-themed West Village restaurant and lounge offers three futuristic levels for enjoying international dishes and cocktails. Like the Titanic, the top level's primarily VIP, but the hip "main deck" and subterranean, blue and green "aqua room" will keep the little people happy. Your cruise directors on this rock glam voyage include Jason Swamy (DJ for Le Souk, Table 50, and Crobar), nightlife fixture Johnny T, celebrity photographer Dah Len, and Chef Sam De Marco. A rotation of nightly parties and DJs—and musical styles—is offered, but sorry, Charo won't be stopping by this love boat.

Mr. Biggs

586 10th Ave. (@ 43rd St.)
Hell's Kitchen 212.246.2030

Mr. Biggs is the perfect spot to go to if you're with people you don't want to talk to. Why worry about holding a conversation when you can stare at sports all night? With enough TVs covering the walls of the bar (AND the bathroom) to make your eyes cross, Mr. Biggs is the quintessential sports bar in Manhattan. You won't have to clean up after downing about 50 wings (they're 25 cents apiece on Monday nights) and there are plenty of people to talk stats with. Stuff your face with half-priced appetizers and drinks during one of the bar's two nightly happy hours happening seven days a week, big guy.

Mr. Dennehy's

63 Carmine St. (7th Ave. S. & Bedford St.)
West Village 212.414.1223

Maybe it's the crane-shaped taps, the live music vibe, or the flickering candles across the room, but Mr. Dennehy's is a date bar waiting to happen. An open beer garden in the summer, off-Village locale, and friendly staff with ample mixing skills

Movida

all give Mr. Dennehy's a certain charm that doesn't seem force-fed or overdone, even on nights when NYU kids are playing "grown-up." Even the Michelob promotional girls quietly hand you a free "Ultra" just for sitting there, not even demanding your e-mail address or making you guess how many calories are in a bottle. Subtlety is the name of the game here, and with understated prices to match, it's a great spot to begin your night in the Village.

Mugs Ale House
125 Bedford Ave. (N. 10th & N. 11th Sts.)
Williamsburg 718.384.8494

Mugs Ale House

As Williamsburg continues to expand, no place seems safe from becoming a sleek dining spot or kitschy boutique. Mugs, however, is a stronghold of the neighborhood vibe that's rapidly waning. Attracting a varied crowd with over 30 beers on tap and an impressive menu, the bar stays low-key as high-rises and legwarmers continue to plague the area. A quick wait staff is pleasant to regulars watching a game on TV as well as the younger set playing songs on the jukebox. With not much in the way of décor, cheap drinks and the popular 20-oz. mug of beer for only $4 are reason enough to stick around. Spacious and full of tables, Mugs is a fun place to spend time on the Bedford Avenue of old.

Mulberry Street Bar
176 1/2 Mulberry St. (Broome & Grand Sts.)
Little Italy 212.226.9345

The next time someone annoyingly bemoans the gentrification of New York City, bring them here. This old-school joint has been around for almost a century and looks it. From the straight-talking name to the bare-bones décor—a worn bar, a couple of tables, and little else—this good-natured dive is Little Italy's quintessential cheap liquor shack. Through the decades, wiseguys, locals, and cops have warmed the barstools and longtime regulars still come by for a cold one, but these days the bar also draws hipper downtown types who like to think they're slumming it for the night. Lots of them commit karaoke crimes on the weekend until somebody has the sense to put Frank on the jukebox.

Muldoon's
692 3rd Ave. (43rd & 44th Sts.)
Midtown 212.599.2750

If you've been to any Irish pub anywhere, you've been to Muldoon's. And, as you may have surmised from drinking binges past, that isn't necessarily a bad thing. There are no surprises in the décor: Tiffany lamps, a few TVs, bright lighting, and Irish paraphernalia reminiscent of a TGI Friday's, with Monty Python-esque fingers distinguishing the ladies' room from the gents'. A few things that set it apart include $3 domestic drafts daily, a nice patio out back with a handful of tables, and a staff that's as friendly as the day is long. If you're not a member of the mile-high club and would like to be, try your luck with the flight attendants who drink here when they stay at the hotel across the street.

Mulligan's Pub
267 Madison Ave. (39th & 40th Sts.)
Murray Hill 212.286.0207

Like a pair of old sweatpants, this Midtown pub is scruffy, but convenient; it's the ideal destination for those who don't know better or don't care to search beyond a typical local Irish pub. Dim lighting emanating from small wall lanterns keeps a gratefully low glow over the mauve walls, wood paneling, TVs, and aging Ireland-themed, dorm room-style posters. In the after-work weekday hours, Mulligan's holds court to tables of 30- and

40-something diners chowing down familiar pub and diner-style food. The long wooden bar is usually crowded with local office drones donning Irish smiles and bloodshot eyes. Mulligan's décor and ambiance is nothing fancier than what you have at home (if it is, please find a girlfriend stat), but with its unpretentious vibe, it may be just as comfortable and inviting.

Mundial
505 E. 12th St. (Aves. A & B)
East Village 212.982.1282

There are certain bars that serve a very specific purpose—to provide their patrons with the four basic food groups: baseball, basketball, football, and soccer. Mundial takes this philosophy a step further, focusing intently upon the latter, as in the game known as "football" everywhere else in the world and "soccer" here in the States. Two huge flat-screen TVs hover behind the bar, the lounge has TV tables, and a large projection-screen television shines up front. Mundial is huge and has lots of room for smokers out back; and if there are no soccer games on, the bartender will gladly turn the channel to a lesser sport. The clientele tends to be European males or worldly, sporty locals. No food, live music, or dancing, though; this place is strictly for competition-thirsty voyeurs.

Murphy's Bar & Grill
977 2nd Ave. (51st & 52nd Sts.)
Midtown 212.751.5400

If you ask a bartender how long Murphy's has been around, he'll respond, in a thick Irish drawl, "forever." A true neighborhood pub, Murphy's continues to draw the old-school, local crowd left unimpressed by the surrounding played-out lounges. Offering little else to do but eat, drink, and chat, this isn't your best bet for a Saturday night, but for those in the mid-50s (age or street name) this joint works during the week. Late-night menus are available at the bar, and solid lunch and dinner crowds gather around tables in the adjacent back dining room. Rude managers, dark lighting, and backless wooden barstools would have Murphy's bordering on a dive; just substitute

pool-playing hipsters for corn beef sandwiches and bartenders who check IDs…twice.

Murphy's Law Bar & Restaurant
417 E. 70th St. (1st & York Aves.)
Upper East Side 212.628.3724

If the old adage that is Murphy's Law holds true (you know the saying; this isn't remedial Philosophy), it may just be the luck o' the Irish that a bar by the same name is situated across the street from a hospital emergency room. In fact, (single gals, take note), it's a favorite hangout for drained docs to sip away post-surgery stress after a grueling shift. Guinness on tap is the chaser of choice, of course, and the pool tables add comforting touches to this perfectly respectful—if a bit predictable—pub. You won't need your stomach pumped after eating the pub food either, but you might want to feign discomfort to get the attractive, scrubs-wearing physician sitting next you at the bar to "play doctor."

Mustang Grill
1633 2nd Ave. (@ 85th St.)
Upper East Side 212.744.9194

Itching for a taste of Mexico, but can't schedule a Spring Break now that you're old enough to legally drink? Have no fear, Mustang Grill is here. *Muy grande* margaritas are priced at $6.75-$12.50, but you're on your own for bad weed and cheap leather goods. Mustang Grill's menu is rife with affordable Mexican fare, from fajitas ($11.95-$15.95) to burritos ($11.95-$13.50) to mesquite-grilled chicken ($13.95) and yellow fin tuna ($16.75). The one downside to this tasty menu is the layout—it's easy to feel cramped, though the space problem is somewhat alleviated as the mercury rises, enabling patrons to take advantage of an outdoor seating area in the front as well as in the rear. The American dollar still goes pretty far up here in faux Mexico.

Mustang Harry's
352 7th Ave. (29th & 30th Sts.)
Chelsea 212.268.0719

"Ride Harry, ride" just doesn't sound quite right, and fittingly, neither does a $13.95 fish and chip platter in a place with franchisey, "anywhere" atmosphere. However, for a spot that survives largely on pre- and post-game visitors from nearby Madison Square Garden, this place is, if nothing else, reliable and universally agreeable. Got family coming to visit? Here's your spot. With 11 beers on tap, you can't go terribly wrong. There are no surprises here except for an extremely strange and private table at the end of the bar. Not for claustrophobics, this oddity is walled in on all sides by art-deco glass panels like an old-timey phone booth. Should you be working out a shady deal, you may want to come calling.

Mustang Sally's
324 7th Ave. (28th & 29th Sts.)
Chelsea 212.695.3806

Imagine a sports bar so elegant, fellas could almost take a date there and still get laid. Between all the etched glass and varnished wood, walking into Mustang Sally's feels like stepping inside a giant grandfather clock, only one that keeps the score and not the time. Be careful about letting your attention wander over to either of the two Jumbotron projection screens or any of the 13 flat-screen TVs covering every imaginable sport. Mustang Sally's has 11 brews on tap and no wine, and while that's largely what puts the "almost" in our taking-a-date-here scenario, it's not always a deal-breaker. However, answering "I love you," with "Oh—did you see that tackle?" is never a good idea.

ñ
33 Crosby St. (Broome & Grand Sts.)
NoLita 212.219.8856

Where have SoHo's hipsters gone? To ñ, that's where. At this unassuming tapas bar, the elusive breed perches on high stools and calmly sips from a selection of sangria, wines, and cocktails such as mojitos, caiprinhas, and pisco sours. On Friday and Saturday nights the low-lit room fills to capacity with arty types and those who wish they were, while an assortment of upbeat, self-consciously un-Top 40 tunes provide a festive soundtrack. Days are mellow—weary fashionistas, Eurotrash tourists, and SoHo locals nibble on better-than-average tapas like Manchego cheese, toasted almonds, and garlicky shrimp (you won't be overwhelmed by the quality, but with prices starting at a low, low $2.75 for a plate of olives, your wallet won't be either). Interlopers, approach with caution or the cool flock will scatter.

NA
246 W. 14th St. (7th & 8th Aves.)
West Village 212.675.1567

Gone is NA's hotspot reign of a year ago when it appeared in "Page Six" almost daily. However, Nell's existed in this very space for nearly two decades—so there might be something more to this bi-level club than flash-in-the-pan pizzazz. Like its predecessor, NA sells membership key chains, there's still a small stage upstairs, and the downstairs is the darkened dance space it's always been. But there are some little things that make NA very much its own thing. Cover girl Petra Nemcova and actor Chris Noth still own shares, famed designer Tara Subkoff designed the main level, and celebrity photographer Patrick McMullen keeps an office upstairs, so models, moguls, and media players still make the rounds. Plebeians should expect to pay a sliding cover.

Naima
513 W. 27th St. (10th & 11th Aves.)
Chelsea 212.967.4392

Sure this brand-new Italian wine bar and restaurant is popular and stylish, but where's the arrogance that comes with success in this neighborhood? West 27th Street is the hottest nightlife stretch on earth and this former garage, which starts with a cozy modern bar and more lofty rear dining area, is worthy of sharing a wall with Bungalow 8. Resting in upright wine racks, wall-mounted shelves, and anywhere they'll fit, wine bottles are everywhere. The menu, a mid-priced sampling of Capri cuisine, is heavy on dried pastas and seafood. An exceptionally friendly staff takes care of the vino pairings.

Naked Lunch

17 Thompson St. (@ Grand St.)
SoHo 212.343.0828

It's never a good sign when more than one girl in a bar is wearing a tiara. If you love the sensation of being on a packed subway car full of drunken junior yuppies, this is surely your spot. Unfortunately, the well-thought décor—walls covered in tobacco leaves, hand-painted Moroccan design adorning the wooden floor, and antique radios—isn't enough to save this bar from patrons who wouldn't know the source of the bar's name if they were hit on the head by the book itself. The mirror above the bar reflects the blissfully ignorant crowd that's dancing sloppily to the DJ's crowd-pleasing, mainstream tracks by artists such as Britney, Whitney, and, horrifyingly, Bon Jovi.

Nam

110 Reade St. (Church St. & Broadway)
TriBeCa 212.267.1777

Save those frequent flyer miles because all you'll need to feel like you've been transported to Southeast Asia is a trip to this handsome Vietnamese restaurant. The dim lighting and dark wood and bamboo décor make this exotic eatery date-friendly. And if your knowledge of Asia doesn't extend past that Leonardo DiCaprio film, strike up a conversation about the pendulum-like lights hanging on the walls that feature family portrait-like photographs of Vietnamese families while you wait for a table. On a good night, the wait is lengthy, so sip on a lychee martini before sampling Vietnamese staples such as jasmine rice, sautéed shrimp and beef, and noodle dishes (entrées cost between $12 and $20). Instead of cute belly-baring waitresses, though, you may get an Asian metrosexual.

Nancy Whiskey Pub

1 Lispenard St. (@ W. Broadway)
TriBeCa 212.226.9943

Nancy Whiskey Pub

This old-school pub is named after an Irish ballad about a man's undying love for…whiskey. Enough said. They also have one of the few bank shuffleboards in Manhattan, above which hangs a sign that reads "Fuck Communism." In contrast, Nancy Whiskey serves working-man's pitchers of Bud and Bud Light for $7. Power to the people, comrades. Nancy Whiskey's been around since 1967, and looks like it too, with a scarred wooden bar, an old-style cash register that slides open with a nostalgic "ka-ching," vinyl barstools with bits of stuffing popping out, and a working payphone in the corner. Sure, everyone on Earth now has a cell phone, but back in the day, this was a hangout for telephone repair guys from the nearby AT&T building during the TriBeCa renaissance. These days, there are still plenty of old-timers along with a smattering of corduroy-wearing hipsters and slumming Wall Streeters, all pulling together to drink beers, make a little noise, and fuck communism.

Nassau Bar

118 Nassau St. (Beekman & Ann Sts.)
Financial District 212.962.0011

The main draw of this dive bar seems to be the scantily clad barmaids and its roadhouse atmosphere. Unfortunately, the combination of near-naked women and alcohol invariably results in the exchange of verbal threats between patrons. Female customers who come to this low-scale watering hole should abide by the unwritten "enter at your own risk" rule, as the place is usually littered with grope-happy men looking for cheap thrills via the moderately priced beverages and copious amount of exposed flesh. So unless you're looking to enjoy the irony of the closest thing to a "titty bar" in the Financial District, head north to the original purveyors of suds 'n' sin, Hogs & Heifers.

Nathan Hale's
6 Murray St. (Church St. & Broadway)
TriBeCa 212.571.0776

With the gritty charm of one of Her Majesty's trash collectors, Nathan Hale's serves all the roles of a proper London local to a T. Trimmed in unpretentious wood tones and affixed with a smattering of British sports pennants, the aesthetic combines recreational *élan* with a stiff upper lip. It's perfect for a foggy afternoon, or else go for the English football televised live; a schedule of upcoming matches is available by phone. Don't come on Sundays, though, because the house is closed. Imbibe six daily drink specials in the smallish barroom, or tuck into the Monday-Wednesday three-course prix-fixe meal at a table in the back. (A good deal at $19.) The menu is self-described as typical British pub fare: as humble, direct, and no-nonsense as anything about this tough yet lovable downtown spot.

Nation Restaurant & Bar
12. W. 45th St. (5th & 6th Aves.)
Midtown 212.391.8053

Nation Restaurant & Bar is an all-American place that might get you thinking, "Hey, America is a damn fine country," over a cool brew, even if the large portrait of the Native American chief brings to mind one of our country's less finer moments. Steps set against the red brick walls lead to two upper levels. You'll be proud to be an American here once you discover "Martini Mondays" ($5 well martinis, 5pm-9pm), Saturday's "Groove Nation" night ($5 for a beer and a burger), "GirlNation Saturdays," and a weekday happy hour from 4pm-6pm that offers $3 Buds and margaritas. If you want to spend a lot of time at this patriotic Midtown bar, consider joining the VIP club, which lets you drink and eat your way to a trip to Vegas, among other prizes.

Neary's
358 E. 57th St. (1st & 2nd Aves.)
Midtown 212.751.1434

Neary's is an anachronism in modern-day New York. From the carpeted floors to the Tiffany lamps to the presidential pictures to the chandeliers, this place screams "grandparents." Neary's opened in this three-floor brownstone in 1967 and it hasn't changed a lick since. Fax? Nope, they don't have one. E-mail or website? They couldn't even tell you what those are. That said, if you're dining with anyone from the pre-Boomer generation, bring 'em in for a square meal of meat 'n' potatoes (and a veggie). In fact, there's even a dress code here, which means no shorts or t-shirts (it is a "conservative" restaurant, according to the owner). The septuagenarian behind the bar warns that this place is crawling with senior citizens, so unless you're a card-carrying AARP member, move on.

Negril
362 W. 23rd St. (8th & 9th Aves.)
Chelsea 212.807.6411

Craving Jamaican food? No problem. Feast on jerk chicken and other Caribbean delights at Negril; after dinner, move over to the bar and "Stir it Up" with the Island Punch, which will make you feel more blitzed than Jimmy Cliff with a .38. Sure, it's no Montego Bay, but if you're craving savory "home-style" Jamaican cuisine (Bahamian Mussels, the Jerk Sampler), heart-thumping reggae music, and exotic drinks and rums from over 40 islandy origins that will leave you singing "Songs of Freedom," you will most definitely enjoy Negril. Now do you get it, mon?

Negril Village
70 W. 3rd St. (Thompson St. & LaGuardia Pl.)
Greenwich Village 212.477.2804

This is the kind of place you accidentally walk into once, and then continue walking into on purpose, generally with a date. Perhaps you've been waiting to ask that certain someone out and you want to show your in-the-know yet outside-of-the-box side. Suggest this cozy spot in the Village, with authentic Jamaican décor, food, and service. The bartenders not only adeptly mix the cocktails, but also coolly explain how obscure ingredients like "ginger beer" give it the extra kick. Head downstairs to the Rhum Lounge for a genuine Caribbean vibe, or remain up top and enjoy the laid-back atmosphere created by unassuming three-piece bands, agreeable food, and accommodating staffers. The crowd can be anywhere from hoochie to Gucci, and unfortunately there are few "Ya mon, I totally love reggae" Connecticut types.

to 20-somethings who are old enough to remember OJ's white Ford Bronco (a replica of which is parked inside and used as VIP seating) but young enough to forget that it's not a terribly funny gimmick, Nerveana lays it on thick with murals of a *Basic Instinct* Sharon Stone and the Spice Girls, a Snoop Dogg hip-hop lounge serving 40s, a life-size cutout of the *90210* cast, and glass-enclosed Monica Lewinsky and MC Hammer costumes. Cocktails like the John Wayne Bobbitt, the Heidi Fleiss, and the Pearl Jam add to the theme, as does a random mix of tunes from the Gin Blossoms, Mariah Carey, Counting Crows, and Sir Mix-a-Lot. With a $20+ cover most nights (the club is open only Thurs-Sun), Nerveana seems to be setting itself up for a crowd that values kitsch over taste and money.

Neogaea
4 E. 28th St. (5th & Madison Aves.)
Flatiron 212.889.4840

All those hundred-dollar bills weighing you down? Neogaea is more than happy to help you unload them. This high-rollers lounge picks up where some of its operators left off at Pangaea. That means you'll be spotting celebs while handing over big bucks for the privilege of sitting in one of numerous neutral-toned bottle-service banquettes in the exposed-brick main room, which sits under a domed rendering of an ancient map. A long, pink-hued resin bar in the back serves up $15 cocktails like the Fresh Rome Apple Martini, while a velvet roped-off staircase in the middle of the room leads up to a small balcony where two or three people can look down on the scenesters bobbing their heads to thump-thump music. A second VIP room in back offers A-listers refuge, but with these prices, just about everyone's A-list.

Nerveana
179 Varick St., 2nd Fl. (King & Charlton Sts.)
SoHo 212.243.1999

Come as you are—or were—to Nerveana, the new 1990s-themed club that would have Kurt Cobain rolling over in his grave. Certain to appeal

Nevada Smiths
74 3rd Ave. (11th & 12th Sts.)
East Village 212.982.2591

Nevada Smiths is an Irishman's idea of the ultimate sports bar, lest the bar's slogan, "Where football is religion" should leave you confused. The barrage of flat-screen TVs won't let you forget that the Red Sox are up in the 9th—and neither will the enraged fans guzzling cheap draughts. The carefully scheduled soccer games shown during the course of the day are wisely advertised outside. If your team loses, head downstairs to Chrissy Mac's to ingest one of the many signature cocktails to lift your sprits. With a congregation that's always happy to talk stats and a pulpit full of TVs, this "church" is perfect for faithful sports fans.

New York Comedy Club
241 E. 24th St. (2nd & 3rd Aves.)
Gramercy 212.696.5233

Comedy clubs are a funny thing. At least that's the idea. New York Comedy Club has neither the history nor pedigree of many of its contemporaries, and perhaps that's why it keeps covers, drinks, and food prices below standard comedy club rates. Tickets here range from $10-$12 and though less-recognized, the talent is noteworthy. There are lots of theme nights, including Monday and Thursday open mics, Saturday's Latino Laughter, and that sort of grassroots thing; there are also classes and workshops on premises. There are two spaces here and they both provide fantastic sightlines. The main room, which seats 175, is where you'll see bigger acts, though the @24 lounge area also has well-known names. Comic Strip Live this isn't, but for casual comedy fans, it's just fine.

Newgate Bar & Grill
535 LaGuardia Pl. (Bleecker & 3rd Sts.)
Greenwich Village 212.358.7995

This year-old pub took its name from an old prison, and it's a well-planned break from all of the nearby tourist traps. Those looking to do time inside NYU's walls, and hoping to avoid angry staffers and kids who can't control their liquor, could do worse than a perp walk down Newgate's bar, which follows a straight line to wide-screen video golf. This place isn't reinventing the wheel, but it knows the drill: Outside patio tables sit chest-high, the nachos supreme ($11) delivers generous hacks of grilled chicken, the 14 beers on tap come in grippable glasses, and the plasma-screen TV is as easy to watch as it is to ignore. Trivia nights and flavorful cocktails like the Chocolate Cake are almost as good as a pardon from the governor.

Niagara/Lei Bar
112 Ave. A (@ 7th St.)
East Village 212.420.9517

Niagara's one cool customer. How can we tell this? Well, the light-blue bulbs that soak the room might be a dead giveaway. There's a DJ here, but no one cares where else he's played before. That pretension-free spirit is reflected by a battered Monopoly pinball machine and an old-school photo booth that forever preserves drunken moments. (Yeah, we love those too!) Past the bar there's a generous amount of seating, making Niagara an ideal spot for you and your entourage to set up shop. If you're really feeling adventurous, take a peek downstairs to the Lei Bar, tricked out in tiki décor and featuring even more amateurish live music

than nearby Sidewalk Café. The hipster alert is on Code Red here, but the weekends get a bit fratty at the bar.

Nice Guy Eddie's
5 Ave. A (@ Houston St.)
East Village 212.253.1666

Nice Guy Eddie's

Ah, Nice Guy Eddie's. While it's very refreshing to find a place so utterly indifferent to keeping up appearances this close to Houston Street, we're not entirely sure what to make of this everything-but-the-kitchen-sink bar. Red-and-white-checkered tablecloths and greasy bar food reek of TGI Friday's, while a pool table and televised sports suggest a sports bar that Alphabet City so desperately needs but doesn't want. Eddie's older crowd makes no bones about dancing poorly to Joan Jett and a cadre of '80s rock, while frat boys pop in for drink specials. But despite plenty of room and a prime location, there aren't enough patrons to fill the space, which isn't such a bad thing.

Nightingale Lounge
213 2nd Ave. (@ 13th St.)
East Village 212.473.9398

This celebrated dive bar (which used to hold court as one of the edgiest music venues in town) has had a case of *Extreme Makeover* blues—and now this remade bird ain't singing quite as cheerfully. Second Avenue's rents have sky-rocketed since Nightingale Lounge opened over a decade ago, so we'll cut them some slack for filling the events roster with an open mic and occasional reggae DJ nights—but a velvet rope and a cocktail list that's pasted with stickers taped over the old prices? At least there's a pool table. The not-so-new-and-improved dive-turned-lounge is losing fans…didn't they see what the addition of Cousin Oliver did to the *Brady Bunch*?

Ninth Avenue Saloon
656 9th Ave. (45th & 46th Sts.)
Hell's Kitchen 212.307.1503

Who said all the action is on Eighth Avenue? Go west, gay men—one avenue over, where you'll find even more fun at this Hell's Kitchen drinkery. In case the rainbow flags here don't clue you in, then Village People songs blaring from the jukebox should make it clear that, "Young men, there's a place you can go," because the Ninth Avenue Saloon offers a gay old time. With dirt-cheap drink specials, your limited savings account can write checks your liver has to cash. The gay male clientele is of the burlier, macho persuasion, but that doesn't mean you won't hear a lot of conversations that start with, "Top or bottom?"

Nisos
176 8th Ave. (@ 19th St.)
Chelsea 646.336.8121

Nisos brings some favorites from the Greek Isles to the heart of Chelsea, an unlikely place for quality Mediterranean food. The energy and the atmosphere are very inviting, and the regulars are friendly and festive. Nisos' menu is on the steep side—pricier than other stops on the same stretch—but there's an extensive list of Greek appetizers and entrées, heavy on the shellfish. (Don't miss a generous helping of the grilled calamari.) French doors give way to a comfortable spillover into the street, weather permitting. The lobster tank makes for pretty lively décor, as do the upscale gay and straight couples who take advantage of having a little slice of Pelion on the block.

No Idea
30 E. 20th St. (Park Ave. S. & Broadway)
Flatiron 212.777.0100

If you work in the Flatiron District, chances are you've been to this bar. No Idea exerts a strong-yet-unexplainable gravitational pull on all the 9-5ers within a five-to-10-block radius. No Idea is designed for fun, boasting multiple rooms, low prices (their "everyday" special is a $5 cocktail), and a festive air. However, don't expect anything too fancy; this no-frills dive bar is all about the basics. You won't hear anyone discussing existentialism or world politics here either, but after working eight hours, who wants to talk about that anyway? If you happen to arrive when your moniker is chosen as the "name of the day," you get to drink for free. That alone should be reason enough to come back, Rufus.

No Malice Palace
197 E. 3rd St. (Aves. A & B)
East Village 212.254.9184

More like a sexy dungeon than a palace, this narrow, candlelit bar is constantly buzzing with good-looking 20-somethings who know a good time when they see it. A bar, lounge, and outdoor drink spot rolled into one, No Malice offers prime seating in the garden (get there early), with a comfy couch holding court near the faux fireplace inside. Mondays bring live music; friendly bartenders and reasonable drink prices bring patrons one step closer to cirrhosis. No malice, sure, but show up around midnight on a weekend and you'll find yourself at the end of a long line out front. Note: No Malice has no sign, but you can find it by the dark awning where the name of the former occupant, Delia's, can still be seen under a coat of paint.

Nolita House
47 E. Houston St., Mezz. (Mulberry & Mott Sts.)
NoLita 212.625.1712

The retro allure of a big old plate of mac and

cheese is hard to resist. Here at Nolita House, it's a gooey mess of four cheeses topped with a crisp layer of breadcrumbs, which you can wash down with a Red Tail Pale Ale at the homey bar. The one-room-schoolhouse aesthetic—hardwood floors, pegs where you can hang your coat, a school map of the United States, and chalk scribbles on the walls—makes the Americana comfort food and brews taste that much better. Or, indulge in a plethora of fine cheeses, including Spanish goat's milk cheese and a pungent Portuguese, best paired with one of their excellent wines or tart sangria. Treat yourself to cookies and brownies for dessert before heading out to get your buzz at one of the area's livelier bars.

Nooch
143 8th Ave. (@ 17th St.)
Chelsea 212.691.8600

OK, Nooch probably means something in some other language, but we don't care. What we do like is that it's a hip enough place in a hip enough neighborhood and the noodles have been well-received from here to Singapore and back again. (Nooch is a multi-national chain.) Lunchtime in these colorful and geometrically dizzying confines is laidback, but on weekend nights, DJs spin techno to a pre-clubbing crowd of graphic designers, animators, and other not-so-corporate types. Further discouraging the expense account crowd, Nooch doesn't accept credit cards. $9-ish Japanese/American dishes like eel-based chili

beef ramen blend nicely with similarly priced Thai items like sweet roasted duck with poached lychee. A $7 "Bangkok Martini" menu further prepares this crowd for a night on the town.

North West Restaurant & Lounge
392 Columbus Ave. (78th & 79th Sts.)
Upper West Side 212.799.4530

For an UWS establishment that serves over 70 different kinds of wine, you might expect something of a disaster scene. But the coast is clear: Those timid highbrows, stuck drinking champagne in their penthouses, can emerge. With its mini-blinds, track lighting, and giant potted plant, this Tuscan-style bar/restaurant aims for the sophistication of a Union Square Café and achieves the Pottery Barn showroom effect, even more so when you consider that practically all the decorative black-and-white photographs, which range in subject from Italian-American actors to Venetian canals, are for sale. Regardless, the patrons don't seem to mind gazing at Joe Pesci over a glass of pinot noir, and even the staff appears quite content swapping their life stories at the tiny front bar area.

Northsix
66 N. 6th St. (Wythe & Kent Aves.)
Williamsburg 718.599.5103

Northsix

Down by the docks, on what has become the hippest street in Williamsburg, the Northsix venue hosts the most rockin' acts this side of the East River. This spacious concert hall accommodates the young rock-craving crowd with bleacher-style seating, plenty of standing room, and multiple bathrooms. The front room is a lounge and bar area, complete with a pool table and couches for those who want to chat, grab a brew without a crowd, or escape a blaring band. Since Northsix opened its door three years ago, the roster has been solid, with acts as varied as Sonic Youth, Lydia Lunch, members of MC5, and the Roger Sisters. As of late, this industrial space has opened its near-claustrophobic downstairs area to bands, usually of the punkier and raunchier variety.

Nowhere Bar
322 E. 14th St. (1st & 2nd Aves.)
East Village 212.477.4744

Nowhere Bar describes itself almost too well. A neighborly drink-and-let-drink attitude and the usual bar trappings draw a primarily gay crowd that's amiably cruisey but not creepy. Frayed, musty couches and peeling wallpaper provide an ersatz thrift-store insouciance that, depending on your taste, charms or repels. Those uninterested in pinball or Galaxian can hold a fireside conversation thanks to a jukebox that doesn't drown the entire bar. Friendly bartenders, a karaoke machine, and cheap drinks made cheaper by a daily 3pm-9pm happy hour contribute to a this-bar-could-be-anywhere feeling. NYU students congregate in corners, 20-something lesbians seize the pool table, middle-aged men sip Bud Light at the bar, and a leashed, panting Corgi near the Ms. Pac-Man machine is loved by all.

Nuyorican Poets Café
236 E. 3rd St. (Aves. B & C)
East Village 212.505.8183

With its high ceiling, intimate tables, and brick walls clad in colorful paintings, the Nuyorican embodies the coolness that many clubs in the city strive for, even after more than 20 years in the biz.

This cultural legend has remained a stronghold against the gentrified trendiness occupying much of Alphabet City. Like all small venues, the Nuyorican suffers its fair share of dreadful performances, and on livelier evenings you may find yourself pressed against someone's armpit, especially during the famed Friday night poetry slams. The fun, artsy vibe and largely urban crowd are always welcoming, so bring your rhymes and they won't laugh you off the stage. And with just $10, you can get in the door for some Latin-spiked jazz and still buy yourself a beer.

The Oak Room (@ the Algonquin Hotel)
59 W. 44th St. (5th & 6th Aves.)
Midtown 212.840.6800

The spirit of New York-style cabaret is still alive and swingin' at this legendary Midtown haunt. The performers holding sway here include a veritable who's who of popular singers, and the old-fashioned lyrics and arrangements you'll hear will take you back 80 years. Though more hip-replacement than hip, and not likely to host any Brad and Angelina make-out sessions anytime soon, the Oak Room is a refreshing blast from the past that reminds us all that New York City was cool well before PM and Marquee came along. You won't have to shell out for bottle service, but you will have to fork over $55-$60 for cover, plus food and drink minimums. A sugar daddy will come in handy.

Oasis Bar (@ W New York)
541 Lexington Ave. (49th & 50th Sts.)
Midtown 212.486.1590

New York now has a handful of W hotels, and to fulfill each one's manifest destiny, David Rockwell has filled each of them with stunning bars. Unlike other hotel chains that work hard to seem like an oasis of sameness among the many changes of the road, the lobby bar Oasis works hard to look and feel different from other bars, while being in essence, the same. At this Lexington Avenue

Celebrity Hot Spot In Style Magazine

"This is lounge dining defined" Black Book

"ONE returns laid-back lounge dining to the culinary scene" Gotham

"A good place to get together with a group to start a night out" Town & Country

Nominated as one of the hottest new restaurants and lounges Time Out New York

Best Group Dining and Best Bar Scene Citysearch

Located in the heart of the Meatpacking District - Manhattan's most explosive entertainment area. One has the best of both worlds in the restaurant and nightlife scenes.

LITTLE WEST 12

1 Little West 12th Street (@ 9th Ave.), New York, NY 10014
T: 212.255.9717 E: info@ONELW12.com www.ONELW12.com

Available for Private Functions and Special Events

ONE AND ONE

"....ONE AND ONE IS THE NEXUS OF THE UNIVERSE"

Located on the corner of 1st Street and 1st Avenue, this modern-day Irish bar has it all! Come to sip a beer and watch an afternoon game, enjoy the outdoor seating, or indulge yourself with appetizers, entrées, and salads. We feature such famous dishes as One and One's 'Fish & Chips,' beer-battered the Dublin way.

The newly opened traditional fish & chip shop has an exciting new menu that offers take-out and delivery! Call 212.254.FISH.

The new lounge has created a sophisticated and sexy atmosphere with the hottest cocktails and DJs spinning the night away, attracting a cool and hip crowd.

76 E. 1st St. (@ 1st Ave.)
East Village, NYC
212.598.9126

incarnation, the white-covered furniture gives the feeling of a Crate & Barrel showroom, with an array of tall lamps and perfectly arranged plush pillows and plants. Guests can celeb-spot and gaze down upon the rest of the crowd from the balcony while sipping cocktails like the lavender margarita. While not perfect, the Oasis does offer a slice of paradise.

O'Connor's

39 5th Ave. (Bergen & Dean Sts.)
Park Slope 718.783.9721

There's no mistaking or missing this Brooklyn legacy. It's a squat (but tidy) brick bunker just off Flatbush Avenue that's been friendly to drinkers since Prohibition. And by friendly, we mean $3 shots of Jameson (all the time, no less), and $2.50 well drinks (all the time). As you can see, it's always happy hour here, as the bartender, an original Brooklynite, will explain. This attracts old-timers and true sots, but younger ones come in, too, including the kids who've just moved into the neighborhood. O'Connor's is weathered and worn, and it still has a fine and good Irish spirit.

Odea

389 Broome St. (Baxter & Mulberry Sts.)
Little Italy 212.941.9222

With its dim gas lamps and faux marble busts, Odea's décor is a loungey alternative for a neighborhood that usually counts red-checkered tablecloths and baskets of garlic bread as decoration. And then there's the wait staff, shimmying and skulking behind the orangey onyx-lit bar, bringing you stiff drinks like the black raspberry mint martini and small plates like avocado pâté and empanadas. Enjoy them at the small tables or barstools up front, or gather your group and head into one of the private curtained-off areas. At its core, Odea is undoubtedly a serious pick-up joint, the kind where beautiful, cash-laden ladies and gents exchange furtive glances, numbers, and sometimes more—all to the beat of a clubby soundtrack.

Odessa

119 Ave. A (7th & 8th Sts.)
East Village 212.253.1470

We're not entirely sure if it's fair to classify Odessa as a bar, but given the fact that they serve alcohol, we're willing to give it a shot. Still, no one's hitting up Odessa for a night on the town, but it's an outstanding place to go to afterwards. What alcoholic worth their weight in Cuervo shots doesn't love finishing a drunken bender with greasy diner food and perhaps another beer? Odessa's got all the food you can stuff down your gullet for moderately cheap prices and will stay open super-late to ensure that you will wake up regretting the fact that you ate a bunch of crap right before bed and

Odea

now have to drag your lazy ass to the gym. As far as appearances, take everything you know about a diner. Then don't change one iota of that mental picture. That should give you a pretty good idea of what Odessa's all about.

Off the Wagon
109 MacDougal St. (3rd & Bleecker Sts.)
Greenwich Village 212.533.4695

Off the Wagon

Walk into Off the Wagon with 20 bucks and an open mind, and you just might leave with a belly full of beer and wings and the phone numbers of two girls you never intend to call (one of whom you made out with in the back corner). A good time is had at nearly any hour at this NYU alum-heavy bar, offering a dizzying array of drink specials too numerous to remember and a pitcher-and-hot-wings special that's such a steal you'll want to keep it to yourself. Fix your eyes on the glowing neon sign to this neighborhood dive, and head for the light. Down enough brands of the 14 beers on tap, though, and you're liable to see the sun come up.

O'Flaherty's Ale House
334 W. 46th St. (8th & 9th Aves.)
Hell's Kitchen 212.581.9366

The walls at this Irish-American pub are lined with books, the bar is worn and inviting, and you can just imagine Dylan Thomas or W.H. Auden cozying up to the bar with a Guinness and a good read. But if they did that, they would've missed out on the daily pub-tastic live music performed nightly in the backroom. Everyone gets drawn in, and by the second or third song of the set, the entire bar seems to be singing along, belting out the words

to songs they've known forever. As James Joyce might have said, "Never underestimate the curative powers of a good tune, a laugh with a friend, and a glass of beer." It's all right here. And who are we to argue with Joyce?

O'Flanagan's
1215 1st Ave. (65th & 66th Sts.)
Upper East Side 212.439.0660

At first glance, O'Flanagan's could be considered a sports bar (they've got four 50" flat-screen televisions airing sports around the clock). But if your idea of being a team player involves the good ol' Irish pastime of "Pass the Guinness," then you've hit gold. O'Flanagan's has procured one of those newfangled jukeboxes that plays MP3s instead of CDs, but at around 11pm the jukebox is unplugged and the band starts playing. Now you've got a choice—watch TV or the band (you'll want to watch the band, of course). O'Flanagan's cocktails are not very large, but their prices make up for that. Because even if you have to keep going back for refills (a good excuse to chat up a cute biddy at the bar), you won't spend your whole paycheck.

O'Hanlon's
349 E. 14th St. (1st & 2nd Aves.)
East Village 212.473.5542

O'Hanlon's

You know you're in good company when one of the world's top dart players is pouring your drinks. Greener dart tossers might want to stay at the bar on Mondays and Tuesdays while the big boys compete in league action; Sundays have a pool league. Seven TVs will certainly keep your attention as the 12 draughts (between $3 and $5) intend to medicate your ADD inclinations. The atmosphere is friendly, but it's not that they like you or they're happy to see you. It's just that, well, they're drunk. And then the softball team walks in. They've been drinking since the first inning, and they intend to keep the rally going. Just watch out for flying darts when you make your way through the rowdy crowd to the bathroom.

O'Hara's
120 Cedar St. (Trinity Pl. & Greenwich St.)
Financial District 212.267.3032

In Donegal a hangover is "something occupying a head that wasn't used the night before." At O'Hara's you'll find the three Irish commandments—cold ale, good humor, and satisfying pub food—reminding you that Irish folks are basically just a bunch of glad guys and gals in search of a good time. The bar, a huge, wooden behemoth in the front room, is surrounded by plenty of extra space for impromptu conversation among strangers (which you can expect). During the afternoon, it's as well-lit as a greenhouse and unavoidably cheerful. Much of the traffic is tourist run-off from Ground Zero, but O'Hara's bread and butter is the Financial District. The menu is a bit pricey, with burgers starting at $9.95, but O'Hara's is one of downtown's more upscale Irish watering holes.

Old Town Bar & Restaurant
45 E. 18th St. (Park Ave. S. & Broadway)
Flatiron 212.529.6732

It's never a good sign when upon entering a bar your companion mutters, "The lighting in here looks like it's already last call." And it's 11pm. True, Old Town Bar could put their dimmers to better use, but how much hipness can you really expect from a bar that's been around for 113 years? A great space for after-work drinks or blind-date cocktails, this classic bar provides a friendly, easygoing atmosphere with stiff drinks and bar space a-plenty. In short, it comes highly recommended for when the Saturday morning hangover lasts until Saturday night, when your flannel-wearing big brother comes to visit, or better yet, when you need a stiff drink to put things in a better light.

Oldcastle Pub & Restaurant
160 W. 54th St. (6th & 7th Aves.)
Midtown 212.471.4860

What Oldcastle Pub & Restaurant lacks in overt excitement, it makes up for in authenticity. The majority of the wait staff is the real Irish deal—expect brogues, pithy drinking aphorisms, and Guinness that looks and tastes almost like the stuff across the pond. Oldcastle's clientele is older and less touristy than in most spots so close to Times Square. The pub's other draw is the multiple TVs, which lure sports fans throughout the week. And on big game nights the crowd can become a rancorous mob. The pick-up scene is non-existent; however, if your one true love is football and you're looking for a place to load up on grease and carbohydrates before continuing your wanton drinking binge, this pub comes highly recommended.

Oliva
161 E. Houston St. (@ Allen St.)
Lower East Side 212.228.4143

"We serve the best mojito in Manhattan," claims the bartender, and they are indeed damn good. This Basque-inspired bar/restaurant is a bit different from most of the spots in the neighborhood, in that it's neither jammed full of hipsters nor budding investment bankers. Four pitchers of sangria stand at the ready on the bar, while frenzied dancers work it between the tables in this tiny, candlelit spot. Jazz, Cuban, and salsa bands somehow squeeze into one corner four nights a week, much to the delight of the aforementioned dancers. Outside, yellow cabs career down the street and frat boys stumble loudly past, but inside Oliva, it's possible to pretend you're in Basque country, especially with all the Spanish being spoken. Just don't turn around and look out the window.

Olives (@ W Hotel – Union Sq.)
201 Park Ave. S. (@ 17th St.)
Gramercy 212.353.8345

Just trying to get inside Olives can be intimidating; you need to wait until the hotel doormen open the door for you. Not that they'd deny you entry, but they'll give you a quick once-over, seemingly making sure you're hip, pretty, or rich enough to enter. And you'd better be—this light and airy-feeling restaurant/lounge is not for the down-and-out. Prices are exorbitant and the crowd is super-stylish. If you think you've got what it takes, however, you're in for a treat—long, low couches, Oriental rugs, and an open fireplace invite you to stay a while. Be careful not to dribble Chef Todd English's signature tart filled with olives, goat cheese, and caramelized onions on yourself, because Union Square passersby are gawking at you through the enormous windows.

One
1 Little W. 12th St. (@ 9th Ave.)
Meatpacking District 212.255.9717

One

In a neighborhood full of competing meat markets—Aer, Lotus, Plunge, Ono, Cielo, etc.—One holds its own. Though it may not be the coolest kid on the block, this massive three-roomed hotspot of glittering candles and brown suede furniture has plenty of room to hold the aspiring models and metrosexuals who stop by as an alternative to the vicious Lotus scene. One's enormity also makes it a popular party spot, so expect to hear several choruses of "Happy Birthday" before the night is over. Though One has a discerning door policy, it's fairly easygoing; if you can't get past this velvet rope, cut your losses and hop on over to the Hog Pit, because you won't have better luck in this too-cool-for-school area.

One and One
76 E. 1st St. (@ 1st Ave.)
East Village 212.598.9126

One and one isn't just named for its location on First Street and First Avenue; it's also the Dublin saying for fish 'n' chips. With a relaxed, low-key, non-sporty sports bar atmosphere, candlelit tables that assist in unwinding the tensions of the workweek, and a bar that features strategically placed plasma TVs that guarantee you a perfect position for the game (usually European "football" matches) whether you're outside or in, One and One scores a 10 on the hang-out-ability scale. One and One serves food until 11:30pm on weekdays and 2am from Thursday to Saturday. The limited outdoor seating is a coveted prize for people-watching and the weekend picks up the pace when DJs spin an eclectic mix of rock, reggae, R&B, hip-hop, and '80s tunes. A traditional fish 'n' chips shop is next door.

One 91
191 Orchard St. (Houston & Stanton Sts.)
Lower East Side 212.982.4770

Dressed from front to back in more leather than Whitesnake and Rick James combined, One 91 oozes suave sensuality. Leather-tassle lights and stapled leather walls might muster a picture of tackiness, but here, the hide-a-rama polishes the Euro-chic vibe with circa-1950s black-and-white floors and artwork, as well as a cherry-wood bar picked straight from the UK. Rest in the dining room for Mediterranean cuisine or just dive

One 91

straight past to couches waiting to swallow languid bodies out back. Don't sleep through New York's best-kept patio garden, which is the only part of One 91 where your friends from PETA might actually stop whining for a few minutes.

O'Neals'
49 W. 64th St. (Central Park W. & Broadway)
Upper West Side 212.787.4663

The Upper West Side's 40-year-old dining establishment has the flavor of a classic New York Irish pub with a dash of "fancy restaurant" thrown in for good measure. The bartenders could just as easily be fronting the Pogues as tending bar (if only they were actually Irish). Patrons dine on above-par, fish-oriented fare while celebrity look-alikes dressed in disco-era clothes glare down at them from the massive mural adorning the back wall. The people in the painting may resemble Al Pacino or John Travolta, but these bar-hoppers aren't Hollywood's leading men. They're ballet dancers posing alongside original O'Neals family members in the famous portrait called "Dancers at the Bar." This fair-priced pub is a great place to enjoy a pre-Lincoln Center meal and soak up a little Manhattan history.

O'Neill's
729 3rd Ave. (45th & 46th Sts.)
Midtown 212.661.3530

If your idea of a good time is getting drunk among the suits with whom you're paid to spend the workday with, O'Neill's happy hour has your name all over it. Throw down some potato skins and jalapeno poppers along with $3 pints and you'll soon be a little closer to the cardiac arrest you're probably hoping for at this point. Though the office boys might not appreciate it, you'd be flummoxed to find a nicer staff in Midtown, and you've got to give it up to the lads and lassies that can work this crowd with a smile. There's nothing wrong with this run-of-the-mill pub, but there's nothing right about the unfortunate crowd.

119 Bar
119 E. 15th St. (Park Ave. S. & Irving Pl.)
Gramercy 212.777.6158

A hole in the wall? Yes, but a great hole in the wall nonetheless. People coming from Irving Plaza love this place, as it's cheap, mellow, and unpretentious. But this dark, seedy bar has been here for a while and isn't going anywhere soon, not as long as there are concert-goers looking to get their hearing back over some suds. The patrons playing pool enjoy it as the stale smell of smoke still hovers above their heads. If you're beat from a day at the design studio, take a load off on one of the shabby (but not chic) sofas, or just hang at the wood-paneled bar by yourself, as this is a place where you can definitely come to drink alone.

169 Bar
169 E. Broadway (@ Rutgers St.)
Lower East Side 212.473.8866

This dive bar is so close to Chinatown, you can smell the fish—and it's not coming from the fish tank inside. The locals will tell you that the bartenders know exactly how to make your favorite drink—and they're right. The first Sunday of every month gives new meaning to J-E-L-L-O; with GLOW, the Gorgeous Lushes Of Wrestling. Come in at 6pm and get ready to rumble, or if you just like to watch, put on a rain slicker, because nothing says "messy" like flying gelatin. This bar is happy to ignite the fire inside you by serving up plenty of beer, which is exactly what you'll need to make it through a long night of wrestling.

Onieal's Grand Street
174 Grand St. (Lafayette & Mulberry Sts.)
Little Italy 212.941.9119

Walking through Little Italy on an empty stomach, you get an idea of how celebrities must feel when the paparazzi strike—waiters shouting menu specials, trying to win your business and the contents of your wallet. But if all that bustling European flair is more than you can handle, then Onieal's Grand

Street will instantly remind you that you are still in the greatest city in the world. Onieal's is quite possibly one of the best-looking bars in the city (massive windows, a hand-carved mahogany ceiling), and it has a rich history—during Prohibition it was a speakeasy, complete with a secret tunnel that currently serves as a wine cellar. It was also the bar that hunky furniture designer, Aidan, owned in that "sexy" HBO show we're not going to mention by name.

Ono

18 9th Ave. (@ 13th St.)
Meatpacking District 212.660.6766

Just when you thought the Meatpacking District couldn't get any hotter, Jeffrey Chodorow lights the grills at his new restaurant "concept." Billed as a multilevel restaurant/lounge/sushi bar/robata grill, this addition to the Hotel Gansevoort is the biggest neighborhood import since Spice Market. Cocktails will set you back $14, but that's nothing compared to the sushi rolls that range from $12 for the screaming "O" to $16 for a spicy crab. The older crowd doesn't seem to mind the pricey tabs and large groups are fighting for reservations. For a quieter experience, reserve a table upstairs where you can peer down on the Garden, which overflows with Blushing Geishas (the signature cocktail) by springtime.

Onyx

168 Sullivan St. (@ W. Houston St.)
Greenwich Village 212.533.9595

A long list of delicious cocktails go for just $6 during happy hour here, which, lucky for parched after-workers, goes strong until 7pm all week long (and all night long on Wednesdays). Try the Drunken Monkey—the mixture of 99 Bananas, Malibu rum, and pineapple juice is sure to take you to paradise no matter what the weather is like outside. Get your dance on with the Friday-Saturday DJ while you slug back 20 different varieties of brew. The vibe of this lounge is laidback and because of its proximity to NYU, Onyx is a hit with students wanting to be seen at anything but the usual undergrad dive. There are drink specials

every night and if you're in the mood for some nosh, there's a full bar menu.

Opal Bar

251 E. 52nd St. (@ 2nd Ave.)
Midtown 212.593.4321

Opal screams "sports bar" through enormous flat-screen TVs, though the deafening jukebox makes everything else inaudible. And why does this neighborhood-friendly bar need a bouncer? Go ahead and ask him—he's rarely busy. But don't totally dismiss Opal Bar—a spacious, open atmosphere where chatty bartenders provide a comfortable after-work or first-date meeting spot—particularly if you have no interest in actually hearing your companion. A varied beer selection of 10 on tap, exotic martinis, and surprisingly popular Bellinis (champagne with fresh peach or mango puree) make Opal more varied drink-wise than the average Midtown bar. Much like the Palm-Pilot-and-pleated-khakis crowd that comes here, Opal's mini-hamburgers, pizzas, and quesadillas look better after a few drinks.

Opia

130 E. 57th St. (Park & Lexington Aves.)
Midtown 212.688.3939

You're a tourist who doesn't want to leave the hotel for fear of being mugged. Or perhaps you want to impress a less-than-discerning date with an elegant dinner? Maybe inflated prices and pretension are your cup of tea? Wow, do we have a place for you! Opia's French-inclined breakfast and brunch plates lure in a foodie-lite crowd, and the after-work cocktail time draws what one might expect from the neighborhood, but evenings see more Eurotrash and WASPs than a David Hasselhoff concert. This spot was co-owned by Frederick Lesort, who's nearby, semi-exclusive Frederick's, does this same vibe, but they do it much better. Opia's main draws are the 400-bottle-strong wine list and second-floor balcony, where folks smoke their Silk Cuts and for a few minutes are right in feeling above everyone else.

Opus 22
559 W. 22nd St. (@ 11th Ave.)
Chelsea 212.929.7515

Opus 22 aims to be the CBGB's of turntabling, but rather than junkies in dirty jeans, they draw a crowd that tries on everything in the closet, plucks their eyebrows, then comes out to dance. The atmosphere here is friendly, thanks largely to the hands-on proprietors. Sunday through Tuesday from 5pm-10pm is open mic night, but we're not talkin' 'bout tourists doing show tunes—this open mic is for DJs. Professional mix masters spin everything from trance to house and it's almost always cover-free. Though the shows generally start at 10pm, Opus 22 opens its doors at 5pm and the after-work crowd is welcome to come by for cheese, fruit, and seafood appetizers. It's not a stretch to think that local club owners will be using this place as a recruiting ground for new talent.

Ora
39 E. 19th St. (Park Ave. S. & Broadway)
Flatiron 212.777.2201

Ora is everything one could ask from a chic, contemporary restaurant and lounge. Sophisticated Mediterranean fare and fruity martinis accent a tastefully minimalist aesthetic, that just screams, or more so calmly says, modern Manhattan. The diverse dishes all have their own special twist; the roasted butternut squash soup is poured over amaretti, sage, and green apple, and thinly sliced French baguettes. Sumptuous meals are washed down with specialty cocktails like the Nightcap or ginger margarita, which are just a sampling of an extensive cocktail list. Digest it all under soft lighting and subtle floral prints. This is New York dining at its most chic.

Orange Valve
355 Bowery (3rd & 4th Sts.)
East Village 212.979.1818

Orange Valve appears to be the missing link between the cardboard boxes that bums on the Bowery call home and the ridiculous Bridge and

Tunnel clubs that have been sprouting up along the strip. Classier than swigging a 40 outside of BLVD, but without the class system-invoking velvet rope, Orange Valve stays popular with the kids by offering 25-cent appetizers, finger foods, and cheap, exotic drinks during happy hour. There's an ambitious menu, chatty bartenders, a huge TV for karaoke in the basement, and special events such as Bingo on Tuesdays to keep you entertained. But don't be fooled by the brightness of the orange-colored walls inside; if you think you see daylight, it's probably just because you've been having hours and hours of Tang-alicious fun here.

Orchard Bar
200 Orchard St. (Houston & Stanton Sts.)
Lower East Side 212.673.5350

Orchard Bar is the embodiment of the LES haunts that are battling places that coddle gentrification and urban renewal (like Crash Mansion). A haven for grungy bands and cheap beer, Orchard Bar has a stronghold on the super-skinny-rockers-with-tattooed-vamp-groupies demographic. For those who wanna rock all night long, this LES bar is more of a museum exhibit showcasing this neighborhood's seedy past, as evidenced by the creepy knickknacks adorning the walls and shelf above the bar—skulls, bamboo, and odd sculptures. There are no tapas, the person making your drink is a bartender, not a mixologist, and not all of the patrons bathe—so what?

Orchid
765 6th Ave. (25th & 26th Sts.)
Chelsea 212.206.9928

Facing the sidewalk with 10 glass-paneled frames, this greenhouse exterior houses a bizarre concoction of decorating styles, though there's no mistaking that you're in the Flower District. Palm trees form a line down the center of this spacious, lofty bar, with scattered, minimalist cube seats, booths, and the odd leather couch keeping a mix of hip 20-somethings, yuppies, and the middle-aged firmly planted on their keisters in this open space. Oddly shaped cut-outs in the wall give the impression that the attempted new twist on exposed brickwork was not quite a success, and live jazz music on weekend afternoons isn't going to do much for the nightlife scene. While the staff is friendly, the variety of drinks impressive, and the menu of pasta and burgers tasty, Orchid still has some growing to do.

Orchid Lounge
500 E. 11th St. (Aves. A & B)
East Village 212.254.4090

Get here now before this Asian fusion lounge gets too crowded. Seriously, drop what you're doing immediately and head to Orchid Lounge, where specialty cocktails like the $8 China White Lily is made from house-infused coconut vodka, Bailey's, and fresh cinnamon. The music is loungey and hip, but thanks to a gong behind the bar, the ring of percussion means free ginger-infused vodka and fresh lemon shots. Paper lamps line Orchid's tables, birdcages hang from the ceilings, and modest hipsters try to decide between keeping time with the friendly staff and securing a cozy sofa. A lite, all-Asian menu makes this a good place for groups to meet early in the evening, but Orchid Lounge serves best as an intimate late-night date spot.

O'Reilly's Pub & Restaurant
54 W. 31st St. (6th Ave. & Broadway)
Midtown 212.684.4244

Take away the rather elaborate frozen drink menu and O'Reilly's is almost indistinguishable from any other Irish pub in the city. But please don't take those yummy concoctions away. Due to its proximity to Penn Station, you get exactly what you'd expect at O'Reilly's: a steady crowd of suits from 4pm-7pm tying one on, then stumbling out to catch a train along the LIRR. Weekends here buzz with tourists and a blue-collar crowd, all popping in to grab a bite before plotting their next move. God bless 'em, because O'Reilly's is all about convenience if nothing else—they open at 11am on weekdays and Saturdays, and noon on Sundays. This place marks a great escape from the Knicks fans that start pouring out of Madison Square Garden at the end of the third quarter.

O'Reilly's Townhouse Tavern
21 W. 35th St. (5th & 6th Aves.)
Midtown 212.502.5246

This is not the type of place that gets written up for sweeping architectural style, decadent ambiance, impeccable service, or a super-hip menu. In fact, you probably won't get lucky at O'Reilly's either, unless you count buybacks, or the ability to pass time here comfortably before a game or concert at Madison Square Garden. O'Reilly's follows the standard pub mentality of good food, good drink, good prices, and good people. It's the kind of place where you can knock back a few pints during happy hour and be treated like a regular in an irregular world, an unfortunately dying trend that O'Reilly's has kept alive since it opened in 1975. It's not just Irish eyes that smile in O'Reilly's (at least not after a few pints).

The Otheroom
143 Perry St. (Greenwich & Washington Sts.)
West Village 212.645.9758

East meets West at this sedate downtown hideaway; East and West Village, that is. The minimalist décor, hip soundtrack, and perfectly tousled bartenders give this West Side gem a decidedly East Side vibe. Well-dressed 30- and 40-something couples recline on velvet chairs to reminisce about their misspent youths. An oenophile's dream, the Otheroom boasts a vast wine list (20 by the bottle, 20 by the glass), and almost as many draft and bottled beers. So comfortable it's like lounging at home, the Otheroom is a top-notch wine bar that personifies class via its impressive drink selection and "tomorrow may never come" European vibe. Plan accordingly—think of plenty of sweet nothings to whisper in your date's ear as you top off a bottle of wine (or two) together.

Otto Enoteca Pizzeria
1 5th Ave. (@ 8th St.)
Greenwich Village 212.995.9559

Otto Enoteca Pizzeria

When the gaggle of hostesses informs you of the inevitable 15-minute wait at Otto, you receive a "train ticket" to a particular Italian destination. The old-style train display board (which flips to your town when your table is ready) verges on theme park, and the iPod-fueled sound system blasting "Appetite for Destruction" is a little confusing, but the ambiance overcomes these obstacles to settle into a noisy, bustling bistro. The real attraction at Otto is the 700-bottle wine list and encyclopedic bartending staff, though their knowledge often goes unappreciated. Still, the pizza, antipasti, and gelato on the menu, coupled with their wine classes and tastings, pack 'em in every time to this peculiar pizzeria.

Otto's Shrunken Head
538 E. 14th St. (Aves. A & B)
East Village 212.228.2240

While you're sipping Pang's Punch at this hip bar you'll start to wonder what the semi-tropical décor has to do with the very rock 'n' roll biker vibe— assuming the large, burly fellas loitering outside didn't deter you from coming inside in the first place. Though wet-your-pants-intimidating at first, Otto's tough-guy customers are harmless, and like you, they just want to enjoy the rockabilly-heavy jukebox and the vintage photo booth. DJs and rock bands keep the backroom busy with throbbing beats. Otto's sports a twisted bamboo ambience and yummy rum-based drinks, which won't shrink your head but may not improve your IQ. If you're looking for real adventure, Saturday nights at 2:30am Otto's serves the semi-secret "Slice of Heaven" (deep-fried bacon and a shot of your choice). Elvis would have approved.

O2 (@ the Time Hotel)
224 W. 49th St. (8th Ave. & Broadway)
Midtown 212.246.5252

Trashing your hotel room is so passé. Instead, take the glass elevator to the second floor of the Time Hotel to O2 (formerly known as La Gazelle). The burnt-orange color scheme, backlit wood paneling, faux-leather chairs, and globe-shaped water fountains reveal this Midtown lounge's Holiday Inn-like attempts to pass itself off as a swanky W or Paramount Hotel lounge. But don't fret; the friendly bartenders and yummy cocktails over-

Otto's Shrunken Head

come the obvious culture strain. O2 is an intimate lounge that comes to life late on Friday nights, when tipsy patrons dance to the DJ's set. O2's backroom (The Crystal Room) can be rented out for semi-private parties, but it never seems to get too crowded. A little O2 is a breath of fresh air in the midst of tourist hell.

Ouest

2315 Broadway (83rd & 84th Sts.)
Upper West Side 212.580.8700

The clientele of this Upper West Side outfit is definitively swank–it looks like most of them happily traded in their Birkenstocks and cargo shorts for white collars and ties. The food is "meat and potatoes" American, the wine selection is overwhelming, and the beer selection is mostly Belgian. The space is deceptive, though; upon arrival, an entryway bar is crammed with baseball fans eating barside. Beyond, Ouest opens up to intimate booths lining a wood-and-platinum expanse–the luscious chic one might expect of entrepreneur Tom Valenti. The bar staff, though often engaged in gossip-mongering or romantic interludes, will gladly mix up the sought-after Ouest Martini upon request. As for another signature drink, the Hipster–well, that should probably be left to the LES.

Outpost Lounge

1014 Fulton St. (Grand & Classon Aves.)
Clinton Hill 212.636.1260

This hot new spot off of the Clinton-Washington stop on the C train isn't just a great place to go for coffee. From their finger sandwiches at high tea, to the selection of wine and beer, to the friendly baristas, everything at Outpost is done with a subtle eye to beauty and perfection. Art from local artists hangs in the gallery space; for their official opening, filmmaker Gus van Sant's watercolors and celebrity photographer Greg Gorman's photos graced these exposed-brick walls. On sunny days, take your drink outside and enjoy the secluded back garden. Outpost is a great place to get your buzz in this up-and-coming area—whether it's from the coffee or the beer.

Ouzerie @ En Plo

103 W. 77th St. (@ Columbus Ave.)
Upper West Side 212.579.7777

En Plo shouts Greek love top to bottom, with a good-looking seafood restaurant upstairs and a swank lounge nestled in the dark, decadent basement. En Plo means "set sail," and in the subterranean lounge Ouzerie you'll navigate your way through the dudes or drop anchor on one of the fancy love seats under a sea of stars shimmering down from the ceiling. The lounge is open from Thursday to Sunday, but things don't get going until very late. Upstairs, the menu boasts a wild selection of "provincial Greek savories" and a selection of charcoal-grilled fresh fish that's priced by the pound ($17.50 to $24). At Ouzerie, veritably sail away to the Mediterranean by watching the belly dancer keep rhythm to Greek music while you down an Ouzupolitan and snack on mezzes, dreaming of John Stamos.

O.W.

221 E. 58th St. (2nd & 3rd Aves.)
Midtown 212.355.3395

"The only way to get rid of a temptation is to yield to it," proclaimed 19th-century writer Oscar Wilde, after whom this bar was originally named. And there are plenty of temptations at this Midtown drinkery: a daily happy hour from 4pm-8pm, a smoke-friendly outdoor patio, and plush, black leather couches to slouch and/or make out on. But the best attraction to O.W. is what the bar claims to be the city's only digital jukebox. With more than 140,000 songs on board, you're bound to stumble across one to dirty dance to while imbibing one of O.W.'s $7 martinis. Nightly shows (including a drag competition called "Drag Wars" and the hilarious game, "Bingorama") ensure that there's never a dull moment at O.W. The dandyish Wilde would have fit right in.

PLAN B
BAR • LOUNGE • GALLERY

2 PRIVATE ROOMS

Perfect for Special Events o
Birthdays

Be the Organizer and drink
on us all night

Reservations are recommended
for weekends

339 EAST 10TH ST.
(CORNER OF AVE B)

TEL: 212-353-2303

WWW.PLANBNY.COM

ALWAYS HAVE A PLAN

P & G Café
279 Amsterdam Ave. (73rd & 74th Sts.)
Upper West Side 212.874.8568

This hard-living dark wood box has been ridden hard and left out wet since she opened her doors in 1942. Part dive, part neighborhood watering hole, P & G draws grizzled old timers, middle-aged patrons, and younger customers all at once. The old-timers have a monopoly on the section of the bar closest to the door. There are stories to be told at this bar, with a favorite being of Mariah Carey having come in one night wearing shades, getting drunk, and flirting with the locals. Most nights here are nowhere near being that exciting. P & G's location is a plus—being close to the action of the Beacon Theatre and where Amsterdam and Broadway split, varied and sundry drop-bys provide a little variety.

Pacific Grill
89 South St. (@ Fulton St.)
Financial District 212.964.0707

Pacific Grill is big on the sea theme—from the oversized seahorses and crabs hanging on the walls, to the verdigris "scaled" posts behind the bar, to the lobsters displayed in tanks, innocent of their fate. Too bad the theme isn't extended to the soothing sounds of the ocean. Disconcerting, beat-heavy dance music makes for a frenzied dining experience, as twin fabric and wooden sail-like sculptures sway lazily overhead. Plenty of outdoor seating gives the worst of both worlds: There's not enough of an escape from the circa-'96 clubland techno, and you're also within earshot of the "bands" on the boardwalk at the same time. This spot would be perfect for a date, if you don't care to hear anything each other say, and you're both nostalgic for the Tunnel.

Paddy Reilly's
519 2nd Ave. (28th & 29th Sts.)
Murray Hill 212.686.1210

THE Irish bar to be at on Manhattan's east side,

Paddy Reilly's provides Irish goodness in a way that your ancestors who bestowed your 8% bloodline intended. The "first and only all-draft Guinness bar in the world," there isn't a single draft beer save for waterfalls of that dark brown goodness at Paddy's and seven days a week you can do the jig to live Irish tunes. The blood-red walls at Paddy's are marked with wise Irish proverbs and there's a large room for you and your friends in back, but smart money says you'll be meeting plenty of new faces before the night is over. Double your pleasure at happy hour, Monday-Friday from opening to 7pm; Guinness is $4, well drinks are $4, and bottled beer is $3.

Palace Cafe Inc. (aka Goodman's)
206 Nassau Ave. (@ Russell St.)
Greenpoint 718.383.9848

You can feel the soul of working-class Brooklyn in this place, which just may be the last vestige of Irish Greenpoint. Better known in the 'hood as Goodman's, this family-run hangout boasts a mahogany, horseshoe-shaped bar and a tough Brooklyn barkeep, who serves up $4 Bud, Coors, and Killian's drafts and bottles and $4.50 mixed drinks. A diverse crowd enjoys reasonably priced home-cooked meat and potato fare, with a rocking jukebox kicking in later in the evening. You'll probably see more than one wrinkled fella drinking up his Social Security check in between lamenting the loss of the Brooklyn Dodgers and his old neighborhood. Palace Café has wake party specials. Top that, Bungalow 8.

Paladar
161 Ludlow St. (Stanton & Houston Sts.)
Lower East Side 212.473.3535

The name of this Pan-Latino restaurant is the Cuban word for small restaurants that are run out of people's homes. And though the vibe is more '80s Miami than modern hip, Chef Aaron Sanchez has designed a tempting cocktail menu and an array of colorful, authentic dishes such as chilled melon soup with crab salsa and the pan-roasted market fish served with coconut clam rice. On weekends, Paladar offers exceptional brunch menu items such as mango cheese empanadas. Wash it down with a Michelaada or a pint of Dos Equis Lager with a salt rim and lime juice for $5. If beer isn't your thing, sip on an El Vampiro, a margarita prepared with hibiscus flower juice, cayenne pepper, and a salt rim…then dare someone to kiss you.

Palais Royale
173 Mott St. (Broome & Grand Sts.)
Little Italy 212.941.6112

What do they call a bar in France? A Palais Royale. Not really, we just felt like throwing in a *Pulp Fiction* reference. The recently opened Palais Royale is literally a hole in the wall; you could walk right past it and fall into the hole in the ground that leads to the same-owned Double Happiness. But why prove yourself to the doorman at Double Happiness just to squeeze in elbow-to-asshole with girls from New Jersey bopping to tech-step when you can get a Styrofoam cup of beer for $6, listen to punk rock, and play pool at Palais Royale? Offering an impressive bourbon selection, Palais features velvet seats, a fish tank, and a jukebox. The movie-buff bartenders have been known to bring in DVDs to play on the big-screen; tap your inner Faye Dunaway, order up a bourbon, and make a request for the Mickey Rourke classic, *Barfly*.

Palmiras
41 Clark St. (@ Hicks St.)
Brooklyn Heights 718.237.4100

Great for families and large, cheesy birthday parties, this huge, airy restaurant serves up standard Italian-American food (steak, specialty pizzas, and a wide wine selection) in a prime location in central Brooklyn Heights. With a long marble-topped bar and three spacious rooms, Palmiras can accommodate several parties simultaneously, and the wait staff doesn't disappoint in the friendliness and cheesiness department. They seem like the type that would jump at the chance to sing "Happy Birthday" to you and your quirky relatives. A pool table awaits in a room dubbed "The Library." Still,

Palmiras is more upscale prom-and-wedding-reception-hall than rustic ristorante; so if you're seeking any level of coolness, hipness, or anything of the kind, this cheerfully stereotypical restaurant may not be the place for you and your slick self. Otherwise, take your "ironic" 30th birthday party to Chuck E. Cheese.

Pangea
178 2nd Ave. (11th & 12th Sts.)
East Village 212.995.0900

Few East Village venues can claim they've been around since the '80s, but this sexy restaurant/café has; and to use a familiar phrase from its early days, it's "totally awesome." While Pangea's focus is mainly on the food (a variety of Mediterranean fusion fare), the large wooden wraparound bar situated in the restaurant's center is a hangout that draws mainly neighborhood types and regulars. The long, lovely wine list is nicely supplemented with a selection of seasonal drinks—fruity refreshments in the summertime and more cuddly cocktails in winter. The bar's signature specialty, the Pangea, is an intoxicating blend of pomegranate juice, tequila, triple sec, and lemon; go in and ask for it by name, and you'll feel like a regular.

Panorama Café
1640 2nd Ave. (@ 85th St.)
Upper East Side 212.288.6868

This bi-level Italian eatery is aptly named, affording patrons a sweeping view of the hustle and bustle about its busy intersection. Panorama Café, with its friendly staff and atmosphere, is a great place to have an authentic Italian meal at prices that won't leave you without lira. There's also an outdoor dining area for those sultry summer nights. The bar is serviceable, though the selection isn't terribly extensive. At $7 per glass, the sangria simultaneously provides a booze buzz and a sugar high. Stop by Panorama for a meal, order the chicken parm ($12) and the lobster ravioli ($15), and then cap your dining experience off with a couple of drinks at the bar before heading out for your evening.

Paradou
8 Little W. 12th St. (9th Ave. & Washington St.)
Meatpacking District 212.463.8345

Now that smoking is as illegal as dancing (thank you, Bloomberg) in NYC restaurants, those with outdoor seating seem to be getting away with murder. OK, make that mediocrity. Such is the case with Paradou, a tiny French bistro with a backyard that's pretty, but not pretty enough to make up for the overpriced menu and small portions it offers. However, the (mostly blonde) clientele is too busy trading sample sale information with their old sorority sisters to notice. Thankfully, the sound system playing soothing Parisian tunes helps to drown out the banter, as does the liquor menu (offering 30 wines by the glass, eight champagne cocktails). The only thing worth pairing either of these saving graces with is the freedom of a cigarette with your meal.

Paris Commune
99 Bank St. (@ Greenwich St.)
West Village 212.929.0509

Now you know where rich old people go to get sloshed in the West Village. Formerly Nadine's Bank Street Bar & Grill, the Paris Commune is an upscale restaurant that caters to older folks in the neighborhood with a full menu of Frenched-up fare. Unfortunately, Paris Commune continues to prove the theory that service has depressingly declined in New York City and unapologetically so—maybe they're still working out the kinks. Still, if you have lots of time on your hands and you want to take your parents somewhere nice and reasonable, hit the Commune—especially for brunch. Just don't go there looking for a bar in which to get ripped up. This won't cut it—unless you really, really like wine, of which there is an abundance.

The Park
118 10th Ave. (17th & 18th Sts.)
Chelsea 212.352.3313

Coming from the folks who brought us B-Bar and the Maritime Hotel, it's no surprise that the Park is a popular trendy bar for all seasons. An outdoor space with heat lamps and soft lighting draws dinner and cocktail crowds in for cool summer nights. In the winter, fashionistas and B&Ts head indoors, where three big fireplaces illuminate bearskin

The Park

rugs, creating literal and figurative warmth. We're not sure whether this spot was named for the park it's created as an outdoor space or the former parking garage that once inhabited the giant lot, but this is an ideal place to idle if you can get a seat and afford the high-end cocktails. Pricey Mediterranean-influenced eats are also an option, but this spot's more about the scene than it is cuisine.

Park Avalon
225 Park Ave. S. (18th & 19th Sts.)
Gramercy 212.533.2500

One of the many trendy hotspots lighting up Park Avenue South, Park Avalon's only real distinction is that it manages to come across as even more stylish and sophisticated than its competitors. Too intimidating for most tourists and average Joes, Park Avalon is the perfect playground for the well-heeled and well-to-do. The dining room is over-the-top elegant, with cathedral ceilings and candles galore; and the bar, with its neat rows of illuminated liquor bottles, looks like it could be on the cover of a design magazine. The food is pretty standard hoity-toity fare ($24 Chilean sea bass, $26 filet mignon), but the prices aren't priced for the Nan Kempner set. The extensive wine list, not to mention some interesting cocktails (we recommend the Velvet Margarita), make this posh lounge a drinker's delight.

Park Avenue Country Club
381 Park Ave. S. (@ 27th St.)
Murray Hill 212.685.3636

This country club's for frat boys who want to watch multiple games on multiple screens and stuff themselves with beer and wings. The only polo to be found here is the logo on 90% of this crowd's shirts. Not that there's anything wrong with that. And if you're interested in checking out the NBA playoffs or, God forbid, the Superbowl, make a reservation ahead of time because big games are big business here. That said, a huge menu, a solid beer selection, and a pick-up scene right out of the pages of the Alpha Beta playbook are bonuses. Plus, if the World Series is on but you want to watch the World's Strongest Man compe-

tition instead, chances are they'll turn the channel on one of their 50 TVs just for you, sporto.

Park Bar
15 E. 15th St. (Union Sq. W. & 5th Ave.)
Flatiron 212.367.9085

Park Bar

Park your pals at Park Bar, but hope that they don't mind sitting on each others' laps, because this itsy-bitsy bar is practically wallet-sized. Thankfully there are no Napoleon complexes here; a dark interior, friendly staff, and tasty drinks like the French martini make this easygoing watering hole worth squeezing into, even if it means going on a diet first. West of Union Square, Park Bar offers a respite from the hordes of NYU students, hipsters, and protesters just outside, providing the feel of a neighborhood haunt minus the drunk at the jukebox. Dark wood walls and a matching U-shaped bar further add to the "intimacy," but when the big bay windows swing open, this little place suddenly becomes huge…for a phone booth anyway.

Park Blue
158 W. 58th St. (6th & 7th Aves.)
Midtown 212.247.2727

Upscale sophisticates lounge here to the jazzy sounds of Frank, Louis, and Ella, but on occasion, the room buzzes with A-list visitors, which have included Oasis' Gallagher brothers, among others. But executive chef Eric Simeon, former sous chef at Aquavit and Piccholine, is the real wonder wall here. This perfect park-side locale makes for as good a business lunch as it does for a romantic dinner. Cushioned pinstripe "stools" can be hogged by fat cats looking to stretch their legs or for couples who don't mind getting a little close. There are no desserts, but the chocolate martini with specialty Debauve and Gallais chocolate will suffice.

Park Slope Ale House
356 6th Ave. (@ 5th St.)
Park Slope 718.788.1750

A longtime local favorite, the Park Slope Ale House is a no-thrills pub best suited for the Homer Simpsons of the world. Dark, paneled floors, brick-faced walls, and high-backed booths may scream ordinary, but the down-home service makes up for any lackluster décor. In fact, you can probably get kicked out for saying fancy words like décor, fusion food, or valet. Standard pub fare like burgers and French onion soup are served daily, but on Tuesdays, 30-cent wings score a home run with sports fans and Sunday brunch-goers can grab huevos rancheros or the $9.95 prix fixe, which includes a cocktail. Though the neighborhood is chock-full of pubs, beer connoisseurs won't snub the Ale House's 20 drafts of tasty microbrews. And at $5 a pint, who would?

Parkside Lounge
317 E. Houston St. (Aves. B & C)
Lower East Side 212.673.6270

The Lower East Side has become so trendy that even the dive bars are crowded with over-styled hipsters in premium denim. Sometimes it's a relief to buy a brew in a dive where the hats aren't ironic and the t-shirts aren't designer. Parkside Lounge is one such place. In business for half a century, this laidback dive hasn't changed too much in its lifetime, except now the indie bands that play here have electric guitars. Stop by before 8pm and sample $3 domestics from their array of 12 drafts; stop by anytime and enjoy a fun mix of entertainment, from comedy to live music to salsa lessons. A foosball table, jukebox, videogames, and $3 pints of Pabst also give you a reason to park it here.

Parlay
206 Ave. A (12th & 13th Sts.)
East Village 212.228.6231

Beware the wax and wane of the crowd at this wannabe lounge. Good nights are dictated by good promoters, and other nights will leave you pounding your head into the padded vinyl walls, wondering whoever got the idea that the East Village ever needed lounges. Ergonomic stools line the glass bar and futuristic-looking booths surround the dance floor, all of which is coated in ultra-violet light (did you know if you write your name in detergent you can read it in the dark? But you didn't get that idea from us). Specialty drinks are reasonable at $4 to $10 a pop, but that may not be worth the risk of walking into a dark, empty room on the wrong night. Aim for the weekends, when the odd celebrity DJ floats by.

The Parlour
250 W. 86th St. (@ Broadway)
Upper West Side 212.580.8923

Rather than the homey feeling you'd expect from an Irish bar called the Parlour, this 86th Street institution is enormous and bare and overflowing with the vibe of a suburban sports bar. Stocked with your average selection of beers, the Parlour is a friendly enough place to have a drink and watch the Arsenal game (they show Premiership football), which probably more honestly reflects the Irish ex-pat community, most of whom are here, after all, to get corporate jobs, not to open up quaint pubs with tin-roofed ceilings. The dinner menu is a bit pricey (the $20 prix-fixe "early bird" special is only cheap for the neighborhood), but the beer specials aren't—on Tuesdays, pints of Pilsner are just $6 (starting at 9pm) and refills cost just $4

Parnell's Pub
350 E. 53rd St. (1st & 2nd Aves.)
Midtown 212.753.1761

Parnell's suffers from badlocationitis. Located in a veritable no-man's land, Parnell's attracts an older (think great-grandparents) and younger (think babysitters and sittees) crowd, but hardly anyone in the middle. Parnell's seems to be fine with that, though; it's a low-key place with great outdoor seating, a typical American bar food menu, and a dining room for those who want to pretend to eat out formally (in a bar). Despite the "antique" décor—tin ceilings, exposed-brick walls, and hunting pictures, there's a good deal of drinking going on, and the beer steins hanging from the ceiling are indicative of that. If you're in the 'hood, there's no reason not to stop by. And if you're not in the 'hood, there's no good reason to go out of your way.

Pasha

70 W. 71st St. (Columbus Ave. & Central Park W.)
Upper West Side 212.579.8751

Decorated like something from the *Arabian Nights*, Pasha is a moderately priced Turkish restaurant catering to a combination of locals, tourists, and the Lincoln Center crowd. Appetizers run from $4.50 to $6.50, and dinner runs from $12.95 to $23.95—which is a bargain for this level of service and quality. Be warned, though, that things can get quite busy, and when they do, they charge a $20-per-person minimum during peak hours. Of course, some of Pasha's regulars think it's worth 20 bucks just to hang around in the warm ambiance with a glass of wine. If you're looking for the perfect first-date restaurant or an evening out with good friends, Pasha makes for a nice alternative to the overplayed lounge scene.

Passerby

436 W. 15th St. (9th & 10th Aves.)
Chelsea 212.206.7321

The multicolored lit floor at Gavin Brown's vibrant lounge may make you expect to see Jamiroquai moon-walking, but you're probably more likely to see Napoleon Dynamite busting some "sweet moves" here instead. In this wee funhouse of a bar, frenetic techno ricochets off of the mirrored walls and funky, beautiful artists spill over to mingle with a crowd more on par with the East Village.

Still, it works (in spite of the pricey drinks no less), somehow because Passerby is worth a drop-in when you're in the mood to feel like you're in-the-know (hence the bar's sign-less entrance). Don't pass this by.

Pastis

9 9th Ave. (@ Little W. 12th St.)
Meatpacking District 212.929.4844

This French bistro (a creation of Keith McNally of Balthazar and Schiller's fame) is a scrumptious little slice of Paris set on the cobblestone streets of the Meatpacking District. And, if you're willing to pay the price ($3.25 for a cup of coffee, $10 for a Bloody Mary during brunch, and $14 for eggs benedict), it doesn't disappoint. Antique mirrors and artistically arranged rows of glass bottles line the walls, and well-heeled patrons create a constant din. There's always a crowd here. And if there's a line at the door, you won't get a table without ordering food. So unless you're willing to empty your wallet in order to dine with NYC's glitterati, don't even walk through the old-world-style wood and glass doors.

Pat O'Brien's

1701 2nd Ave. (@ 88th St.)
Upper East Side 212.410.2013

Hey baby. You want to get drunk and go crazy? No, we're not talking about that Pat O'Brien, the booty-calling entertainment reporter—although drunk-dialing is practically guaranteed thanks to 25-cent 16-oz. beers on Fridays from 6:30pm-7:30pm. With hours that are more sporadic than your child support payments, Pat's isn't much for punctuality. And if you're a night owl, don't even think about boozing here late night, as the staff routinely closes well before 4am. When POB's actually is open, it can be one of the more enjoyable joints on the UES, as they do have an entire back room devoted to Beirut, and those aforementioned cheap brews. Leave the phone at home, you horny bastard.

The Patio
Dag Hammarskjold Park (47th St. @ 1st Ave.)
Midtown 212.980.9476

Like those lovely, form-fitting spaghetti-strap tank tops, the Patio only comes out when it's warm enough. This completely al fresco Midtown bar, located across from the U.N. Plaza, offers the after-work crowd a haven to enjoy tropical (yet pricey) summer cocktails in a glorious, low-key setting. The nearby ornamental fountains of Dag Hammarskjold Park and the dangling blue Christmas lights don't quite camouflage the towering buildings of the U.N. (or the bustling traffic), but the Patio is relaxed enough to bring your dog, yet polished enough for its Gucci-wearing patrons. On Fridays, the Patio's clientele groove to live Brazilian jazz guitar. The Patio is small and doesn't serve food, but it's a worthy after-work place for the powerbrokers of international politics (or at least their interns) to kick up their heels and talk about something besides oil-for-food.

Patrick Conway's Pub
40 E. 43rd St. (Vanderbilt & Madison Aves.)
Midtown 212.286.1873

"Build it and they will come." And indeed they do, largely thanks to a locale that's both a strength and a weakness. Sitting the slightest of derailments away from Grand Central Station, Patrick Conway's Pub is a fine Irish bloke who gets a little dressed up regardless of the occasion. White linen covers the tables and the mahogany bar is as solid and reliable as the Worcestershire sauce-doused Black Jack burger. As one might expect, the after-work hours are rather busy here, and because of this joint's two-parts classic knickerbocker style and two-parts accessible pub ambiance, the crowd is often a disjointed, incongruent mix with no commonality outside of working in Midtown. Old pictures of Grand Central hang from the walls, along with photos of Ireland which are lit by Tiffany lamps. There's talk of renovation so keep your eyes open and hard helmet on the ready.

Patrick Kavanagh's
497 3rd Ave. (33rd & 34th Sts.)
Murray Hill 212.889.4304

Could an Irish pub be more generic? From the "My Goodness My Guinness" framed posters to the three televisions which broadcast British football matches to the after-work crowd that lingers long after happy hour is over, Patrick Kavanagh's is exactly what you would expect from an American version of the Irish classic. It's nothing special, but if all you want is a pint of Guinness and a little Erin Isle nostalgia, this is the perfect place, and the friendly bartenders would probably be more than happy to join you in a rousing late-night chorus of "Danny Boy." Yes, the pints, the pints are calling.

The Patriot Saloon
110 Chambers St. (Church & Hudson Sts.)
TriBeCa 212.748.1162

The Village Idiot is gone, but its mongrel-chic sister lives on in this after-work spot near City Hall. Scantily clad female bartenders greet you with almost-convincing enthusiasm and sell beers starting at $2. (Pitchers begin at a mere $5.) The menu's cheap, too, with nothing costing more than $1.50. Yes, you read that right—$1.50. It's just the basics: burgers, fries, rings, etc. There are bars on both floors and a pool table upstairs, but don't expect shelter from the screaming jukebox by the door. The large frat boy clientele must've politicked for some CCR...the rest is pure, throwback country, catering to the older drunks tearing into their beers in the corners. Come to think of it, maybe THAT'S what frat boys look like when they grow up.

P.D. O'Hurley's
174 W. 72nd St. (Amsterdam & Columbus Aves.)
Upper West Side 212.873.1900

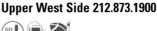

P.D. O'Hurley's is definitely a "guy's place," with its mahogany taproom, wide selection of single-malts, working gas-burning lights, and commitment to showing NFL games on satellite TVs. Not priced for a student budget, but not overpriced either (expect $14 pasta dishes and a $20 steak), O'Hurley's offers 17 beers, pints of Guinness Extra Cold, and some decent finger food. All in all, P.D.'s is a jolly good pub; after all, it's owned by a real Irishman, and it's located close enough to Lincoln Center so you can catch the last half of the Jets game after seeing that opera the wife dragged you to. (Just be forewarned—she might insist on a trip to Bed, Bath & Beyond as retribution.) P.D.'s also offers a special pre-theater dinner menu, though we doubt many of these patrons subscribe to *Playbill*.

Pearl Oyster Bar
18 Cornelia St. (4th & Bleecker Sts.)
West Village 212.691.8211

If you're lusting for a lobster roll but can't make it up to the Cape, Pearl Oyster Bar is a treasure well worth diving downtown for. The airy ambiance is pure seafood shanty chic; think Red Lobster meets Martha Stewart. The settings at the long marble bar come complete with a tiny packet of oyster crackers to get diners in the mood for succulent, slippery seafood menu items, from small plates of chilled oysters and shrimp to New England clam chowder, Prince Edward Island mussels, or a hearty bouillabaisse. Pearl Oyster Bar tends to pack 'em in like sardines, though; so get here early, drop anchor at the bar, and have a laugh at the landlubbers waiting for seats.

Peasant
194 Elizabeth St. (Prince & Spring Sts.)
NoLita 212.965.9511

The Italian fare may have been born from humble roots, but the prices are geared towards the lords and ladies at this chic restaurant. Nonetheless, this rustic spot is well worth the splurge; their selection of age-old Italian delights with a twist, such as gnocchi topped with wild mushrooms, prosciutto with fruit, and "asparagi e uovo" (crisp asparagus and grapes), is reminiscent of supping in a well-appointed country manor. Communal dining unfolds at long, family-style tables, and

Peasant

bright copper pots hang in an open kitchen fronted by brick arches. If you're here to get drunk on wine (highly recommended), park yourself at the bar or, better yet, head downstairs to the wine lounge, with low ceilings, low chairs, low lighting, and, refreshingly, low prices (starting at $6) for selected wines.

Peculier Pub
145 Bleecker St. (Thompson St. &
LaGuardia Pl.)
Greenwich Village 212.353.1327

Peculier with an "e"? How...unusual. Such is the world of NYU students and Greenwich Village barflies, both of whom take advantage of the 600 bottled beers and 24 drafts at this dive bar (the brews' ethnic origins are as diverse as the nearby university's student body). Mixed drinks start at $5 and many beers cost much less, making this a tough study hall for anyone majoring in topics outside of Alcoholism 101. The hardwood bar top and booths are lit primarily by neon bar lights, and if the Bleecker Street crowd isn't already lit on the way in, they're sure to have a glow on the way out. Peculier Pub just might sport the most impressive (and only) beer bottle-cap mosaic.

Peep
177 Prince St. (Thompson & Sullivan Sts.)
SoHo 212.254.7337

Funky lighting abounds as you step into yet another trendy downtown Thai spot. Settle in at the long front bar for a cocktail or two and notice how

Peep

much better your date looks bathed in a neon pink glow. Hungry? The Thai fusion menu has quite a few delectable entrées like macadamia nut-crusted salmon and deconstructed hung lea blackened strip steak, but no worries, if you're not into going too exotic, the pad thai is a solid choice. Don't worry about those windows in the bathroom—the folks out there can't see in. Are reasonable prices and a fun décor enough to set Peep apart from the rest? Maybe not, but it's worth checking out just in case. The B&T alarm rings loudly on weekends, but such is the price of fame.

Pegasus
119 E. 60th St. (Park & Lexington Aves.)
Upper East Side 212.308.6729

Dismiss any pre-conceptions about this lounge. Despite its name, Pegasus is more mild-mannered than mystical, attracting a conservative navy-blazer-and-pleated-khaki crowd. Just about everything about this lounge brings to mind that *Sesame Street* song, "Which one of these things is not like the other?," from the décor—Ralph Lauren-ish framed horse prints, a beautiful wooden bar, round, café-like tables, and a giant disco ball—to the bar's mismatched gay events (Strip Karaoke Challenge on Saturdays, "a dark, rugged cruisy men's night where muscle bears, daddies, and frat boys meet!!" on Wednesdays, and "Professional Thursdays"). The friendly bartenders don't make up for the paltry alcohol selection at this gay-friendly, karaoke-obsessed bar featuring "fetish visuals" and "live erotic shows." Pegasus is as baffling as any winged horse would be wandering around NYC.

Penang
109 Spring St. (Greene & Mercer Sts.)
SoHo 212.274.8883

One might expect Penang to have a stronger grasp on feng shui than this place demonstrates. Large alien tubing runs ominously down the length of the dark ceiling, and the semi-open kitchen is close enough to the bar that its heat can be felt. Clunky, built-in tropical gazebos make up the dining area and they block any sense of flow through the front half of the space. The faux-sheet-metal bar is not appealing, and the shovel handles that serve as seat backs at the bar feel like…well, like having shovels in your back. Penang's popular lychee martinis ease pain and dinner parties at the large wooden tables give the room some energy. The Malaysian food isn't without value, and at lunch time, it comes on the cheap.

The Pencil Factory
142 Franklin St. (@ Greenpoint Ave.)
Greenpoint 718.609.5858

Formerly the Miltonian Social Club, the Pencil Factory draws back to the days when Greenpoint was the pencil-making capital of the country and its neighborhood pubs poured pints for local dock workers. (The now-defunct pencil plant, which closed over a century ago, is across the street.) Sporting original wood-plank floors, rich mahogany décor, and sidewalk seating, this place is sharp. The Pencil Factory's selection of single-malt Scotches, plus 15 draught beers at $4-$5 a pint, satisfy laidback Brooklynites looking to tipple somewhere other than a Polish social club. For now, the Pencil Factory is as wholly unpretentious as its roots, but we can't promise that the masses won't eventually erase that situation.

The Pen-Top Bar & Terrace (@ the Peninsula Hotel)
700 5th Ave. (@ 55th St.)
Midtown 212.956.2888

There are few hotels anywhere whose rooftop bars and cocktail prices match those of the Peninsula Hotel and its Pen-Top Bar. Due to the older monied crowd that stays in places of this price range, the air up here is one of slight pretension, but it's not stifling. In the early evening, the blue blood gets an infusion of red from the sprinkling of after-work 30-something "youngsters" who out-earn all those poor grunts who are stuck sucking suds at the plethora of bars 23 floors below. There are a few TVs in Pen-Top's enclosed parts and they're usually tuned to sports, so on occasion, for one glorious moment, the state-school kids get to gloat over their Ivy League drinking companions as Kansas State puts a beating on Stanford. Alas, tomorrow's another day…and the bill is yet to come.

People Lounge
163 Allen St. (Rivington & Stanton Sts.)
Lower East Side 212.254.2668

Are you a People person? If you live in New York, that answer depends on how crowded the subway gets during your morning commute. One of the first LES upscale ventures, People's young, diverse singles scene is far from hip, but fun nonetheless. Happy hour offers half-priced drinks like the People-tini and People-jito. Pop on those beer goggles and cruise downstairs to find a partner, then seal the deal upstairs where there's a warmer, more seductive vibe (if you can push your way to a velvet loveseat). Striking out? Refuel with the basics (burgers, spring rolls, and satay, all around $5) and get your flirt on (there are plenty of drunk dancing girls and dudes to choose from). People gets bonus points for being a stylish, sophisticated spot that's attitude-free.

Pequeña
86 S. Portland St. (@ Lafayette St.)
Fort Greene 718.643.0000

They weren't kidding when they named this Mexican cucina; even on a Manhattan scale, Pequeña is small. But the vividly painted façade of this delightful little café promises a colorful experience—and Pequeña delivers. With its folk art-covered walls and brightly enameled furnishings, this eatery boasts a festive, yet cozy atmosphere. And though the service is unpredictable, the tasty and judiciously spiced dishes are made with crisp, fresh ingredients (they even use fresh squeezed lime juice for their margaritas). And it's a good thing you can order the entrées (ranging around $8-$16) and traditional Mexican fare (tostadas, tacos, and quesadillas) in either dinner or appetizer portions; because most likely, you'll fill up on good conversation, and the homemade chips and pico de galla served before your meal.

Perdition
692 10th Ave. (48th & 49th Sts.)
Hell's Kitchen 212.582.5660

Just when you thought this area didn't need any more bars, Perdition is a welcome addition to the area (and to the island's plethora of Irish pubs). The venue, owned by two Irishmen and two New Yorkers, is the perfect mix of accommodating pub (replete with 16 draft and 16 bottle beers) and modern New York establishment, granting patrons both a long black bar and a cozy backroom with plush seating. The bartenders, their accents authentic, are beyond friendly and happily offer myriad draft, shot, and cocktail specials for the unpretentious after-work and evening crowds. Perdition has also thrown in a few flat-screen TVs for major sports games, a weekly DJ, and a Sunday jazz band. Appropriately, Perdition is located in Hell.

Peter Dillon's
130 E. 40th (@ Lexington Ave.)
Midtown 212.213.3998

Outside some suits are making a business deal; inside the rest of the suits are talking fantasy baseball. Try to find a girl in that sentence. Peter Dillon's stands as yet another entry in the crowded field of Midtown Irish pubs. Its following is loyal, though, and enthusiasts at the bar swear the place is packed with young cuties after work later in the week. Apparently there've been confirmed sightings. What's the drawing card? World Cup qualifying rounds are televised in-house, and then there's a pool table. OK, try the happy hour: $3 Stellas, Monday through Friday from 6pm-8pm. This is no Bavaria haus, but that doesn't mean they don't host many a beer-soaked sausage party. Remember the early '90s? This jukebox can't seem to forget them.

Peter McManus
152 7th Ave. (@ 19th St.)
Chelsea 212.929.9691

Peter McManus

These folks claim to have the oldest family-owned bar and restaurant in Manhattan. The place is so unaffected and unassuming that we'd believe pretty much anything they tell us. Bartenders pull pints of McManus Ale from behind the long oak bar. While neighborhood celebrities have been spied at the drinking end of the counter, these proprietors either don't know or don't care who they are. TVs play the local sports, regular folks discuss regular barroom topics, and a jukebox plays an inoffensive if unexciting mix of pub tunes: U2, Coldplay, etc. Sandwiched between the Meatpacking District and the West Chelsea club scene, this old Irishman keeps doing its thing and that's why locals love it. Peter McManus' isn't groundbreaking, but there's something to be said for simply being grounded.

Peter's Bar & Restaurant
182 Columbus Ave. (68th & 69th Sts.)
Upper West Side 212.877.4747

How do delicate-looking statues of naked women and enormous fake flower arrangements wind up in the same bar as a Golden Tee videogame and an enormous projector television? Welcome to Peter's, where Italian ambiance (translation: empty wine bottles and funny-looking murals) meets the rabid, 30-plus singles set of the Upper West Side. Along the sprawling bar, women in sweater sets chat nervously, and a funky mix of gents, from suits to flannel-clad frats, take in sporting events and/or eye lustily at the bottoms of passing members of the opposite sex. Meanwhile, the efficient wait staff serves up plates of jalapeño poppers and crocks of chili (yes, crocks), and overhead, Phil Collins issues a heart-felt lament.

Pete's Candy Store
709 Lorimer St. (Frost & Richardson Sts.)
Williamsburg 718.302.3770

Pete's has that intimate, dark, and romantic feel (soft lighting, antique wood paneling, mellow music) that is so conducive to meaningful thoughts and deep conversation. Just don't expect any of that before 10 on weeknights as the place is crawling with playas, and we're not talking about badass goumbas—we're talking Scrabble, Bingo, trivia, and spelling bee participants. Free live music and book readings go on seven nights a week in the skinny railroad car-esque backroom, while love connections are made in the back patio under the gorgeous glow of Christmas lights. The panini and cocktail menus change with the seasons, so in summer, expect citrusy refreshers, and in winter, warming spicy drinks like Dark & Stormies or ginger sours (both $7).

Pete's Tavern
129 E. 18th St. (@ Irving Pl.)
Gramercy 212.473.7676

It's no surprise that Pete's Tavern has been serving patrons for nearly 150 years—especially if the atmosphere was as warm and low-key at the turn of the century as it is now. The peculiar "forgotten '80s" soundtrack doesn't exactly catalyze a dance party, but it does provide a calm backdrop to enjoy a pint or one of Pete's various Monday-Wednesday night dinner specials. Romantics looking to slink away from the narrow front bar can find peaceful seating in the red-lit Skylight Banquet Room or at one of the outdoor tables peppering the sidewalk. With cheap drinks and a strong regular following, Pete's Tavern epitomizes your prototypical neighborhood bar. The historical landmark where O. Henry double-fisted with a pint and a pen is still going strong.

Petrosino
190 Norfolk St. (@ Houston St.)
Lower East Side 212.673.3773

Petrosino is pleasing to both the eye and the palette. The ever-so-dim romantic lighting, paired with a reasonable bottle of red procured from the extensive Southern Italian wine list, promises a good date or at least a good setting for one. Keep in mind, though, that Petrosino will not be held responsible for awkward conversation and highly deceptive Internet profiles. More of an eatery than a nightspot, the true brilliance of this Southern Italian gem is their food, which includes a healthy devotion to seafood. Sure, we can complain about the long-gone days of Lower East Side scum (well, almost long-gone), but thanks to places like this we'll keep quiet.

Phebe's Tavern & Grill
359 Bowery (@ 4th St.)
East Village 212.358.1902

Drifting off at work again? Imagining a simpler time and place where you could blow off your term paper and throw back a few pints with your friends instead? Don't despair! Salvation is much closer than you think! Phebe's has all the down-home comfort of your favorite upstate college bar without the hassles of tuition, townies, and tons of TVs. A jukebox provides the loud (and sometimes questionable) background music, and a friendly staff provides the ample food and drink. The large selection of beer is matched only by the large selection of seating options, which include two dining areas as well as bar seating. If this place looks familiar, it's because it used to be Fuel @ Phebes. Being decidedly more spit-shined that Hooters and that kind of thing, NYU students are more likely to be on dates than on the prowl here.

Philip Marie
569 Hudson St. (@ 11th St.)
West Village 212.242.6200

Best known for its private "tasting room," an 18th-century farmhouse kitchen that became a speakeasy in the Prohibition '20s, this folksy bistro also offers a cramped but cozy bar area where affable, buttoned-down bartenders create 18 signature martinis like "The Grey Lady" (hot apple pie martini, $10) to please a diverse crowd that mingles in the mahogany confines. A homey décor and friendly ambiance make Philip Marie an appropriate spot to impress parents or out-of-towners and a welcome relief from the area bars' trendiness. Bar patrons tend to be waiting for a table, where hungry boozers can munch on critically lauded dishes like chicken pot pie. Best deal: Saturday's $15.95 unlimited mimosa brunch, a welcome excuse for late-morning alcohol consumption that packs a nice buzz for afternoon shopping on nearby Bleecker Street.

Phoenix
447 E. 13th St. (Ave. A & 1st Ave.)
East Village 212.477.9979

With all the hip gay venues dotting the East Village, it's nice to know you can rise above it all at Phoenix—the bar that time seems to have left behind. Though only six years old, this place looks like it's pushing 60. But that's OK, because cheap drinks (like $1 beers on Wednesdays) and cute, laidback men make up for any lack of décor. But fellas, beware: Not only will you have to compete with each other for attention, you'll also have to compete with a woman—Ms. Pac-Man. The bar's videogame always seems to draw the attention of guys looking to keep time with her more so than each other, which brings up an interesting question: Is that a roll of quarters in your pocket or are you just happy to be here?

Phoenix

Pianos

Piola

Phoenix Park
206 E. 67th St. (2nd & 3rd Aves.)
Upper East Side 212.717.8181

On first impression, this neighborhood bar looks like any other Irish pub. But after spending some time here, you'll start to notice the growing number of die-hard Mets and Jets fans—and despite the Greek alum crowd, you'll want to stay a while. Phoenix Park is a sports bar with the requisite jukebox playing classic rock and on a typical Saturday night, the barstools are filled, but it's not like a subway car during rush hour—you can still walk around without having to fight for your own personal space. At Phoenix Park the pub food is sublime and the drinks are made to perfection. After all, as the bartender's t-shirt reads, Phoenix Park has employed the finest "Drinking Consultants Since 1998." The t-shirt does not lie.

Pianos
158 Ludlow St. (@ Stanton St.)
Lower East Side 212.505.3733

Despite the occasional party-pooper "no dancing" Gestapo-like employees working at this downtown music club/bar/restaurant, Piano's has held court as one of NYC's most-treasured hotspots. A venerable launching pad for "it" bands (and a magnet for "it" fans—David Byrne of Talking Heads fame has been spotted here), Pianos has hosted some of indie rock's hottest music acts. The comedy and "Stitch 'n Bitch" knitting nights are also a hit. And the clientele isn't the only thing that's sure to make your mouth water—the delectable menu offers pastas, seafood, burgers, desserts, and mango-, ginger-, or apple-cinnamon-infused vodkas. With three floors that include two stages (the main space and an upstairs space for acoustic performances), and a recording studio, Pianos gets music lovers wet by hitting all the right keys.

Pieces
8 Christopher St. (@ Greenwich Ave.)
West Village 212.929.9291

When you see the kaleidoscope of bright rainbow lights adorning this bar's window, you should think only one thing: You're here, you're queer, you might as well have a beer! Luckily, happy hour stretches from 2pm to 8pm on weekdays at this small bar that's big on friendly waiters and patrons—they actually smile back at you here. Or maybe they're just smiling nervously wondering if you realize that you're butchering your favorite Cher song on Tuesday's karaoke night, hosted by drag diva Blanche. So if you missed the *American Idol* tryouts, go ahead and take Pieces' stage. After all, who's a harsher critic? Simon Cowell has nothing on the catty West Village crowd.

Pig N Whistle
165 W. 47th St. (6th Ave. & Broadway)
Midtown 212.302.0112

The Pig N Whistle stakes claim that it is "the best Irish pub in New York City," but mostly this Midtown barroom is just fool's gold made of exposed brick and polished wood, requisite Paddy O'McShanahan and "Old Country" praises, and a skillfully placed red phone box. Located in close proximity to the TKTS Booth in Times Square, the Pig N Whistle attracts tourists and hand-slapping frat boys. The food is better than the overpriced chains in the area, but if you can't think of a better bar, whet your whistle here for just a few bucks (16 bottled beers and 12 on draught) and in between bites of the standard pub fare, talk with your friends about which train you need to take to get downtown.

Pigalle
790 8th Ave. (@ 48th St.)
Hell's Kitchen 212.489.2233

Move Pigalle 30 blocks north or south and it'd be a hip place to hang out. Instead, this Hell's Kitchen brasserie is a cute spot that would benefit greatly if amputated from the conjoined Day's Inn. But if you don't face the windows, you'll be charmed by this sepia-toned bar that's great for pre-theater noshing and upscale after-work drinks. The French fare is pretty standard, but the drinks are noteworthy. The wine list boasts more than 80 bottles, and beers—both bottle and draft—are mostly French and Belgian. The most interesting libations are the $7.95 champagne cocktails and $6.50 versinthe (absinthe) drinks. Pigalle is open 24 hours a day, although the neighborhood tends to be a little creepy around 4am. But like so many things French, at Pigalle, you take the good with the bad.

The Pinch Bar & Grill
237 Sullivan St. (3rd & Bleecker Sts.) Greenwich Village 212.982.5222

They're not exactly reinventing the wheel at Pinch. In fact, this is simply another spoke in NYU-Ville's tire-d old one-speed cycle of all-things-obvious. One plasma-screen TV hangs behind the bar while another plays behind a stage in the back of the room where singer/songwriters croon over sports fans' cries of "Down in front." The place bills itself as "Irish," which apparently translates to "Long hours, $6 pints, and greasy food." The kindly staff dons uniform shirts that add a corporate vibe to a place already lacking in imagination. (Red Bull and vodka as a "specialty" cocktail? Come on!) The strange thing about this area's bars is that their patrons often appear too old to be undergrads and too simple to be master's candidates, yet they want to hang out with school kids. Pinch us if we're wrong.

PineTree Lodge
326 E. 35th St. (1st & 2nd Aves.) Murray Hill 212.481.5490

With a vibe as creepy as a David Lynch movie set, it doesn't help that the PineTree Lodge is also a geographic outlier. Located mere footfalls from the FDR, but enjoying close proximity to NYU Medical School dorms, this oddity of a bar has the look of a deserted garage. Potted plants and bric-a-brac fill the room, and a tiny room with sofas and shelves sits in back. Kibbutz back there with friends or take a seat at the giant wood-slab bar in front and try your luck with a self-selected motley crew of regulars. Weekday happy hour runs 5pm-10pm (drafts and well drinks are 2-for-1). Curiosity-seekers and anyone wondering about

med school nightlife may be eager to try the ol' PineTree. The rest of you are advised to watch *ER* reruns.

Pink Pony Café
176 Ludlow St. (Houston & Stanton Sts.) Lower East Side 212.253.1922

Delicious French and comfort food is served at this boho eatery that feels like a literati's loft space. There's not a speck of pink or pony in this place—except for the ceiling-high barn-like doors leading to the backroom. What there is a speck of, and there's actually more of a splatter, is scenesters. A longtime favorite of locals and first-time LES'ers, the Pony offers a delectable (and moderately priced) brunch, hot chocolate made with real chocolate, and a friendly staff that is happy to give you an oral history of the place (but they're likely unable to explain the surrealistic literary scribbles on the walls). Come on, ride the Pony—and on your way out, let yourself be mesmerized by the illusionist mirror in the bathroom.

Piola
48 E. 12th St. (@ Broadway) Greenwich Village 212.777.7781

The word "piola" in Venice means a wine bar on the canals where people go after work to eat and get sloshed. In New York, Piola is an upscale pizza bar with unique, international pizzas and booze—draw your own conclusions. The menu of "world pizzas" feature ingredients that sound odd together, but taste great: the Eastern European pizza with fontina cheese, roast beef, mozzarella, and chili peppers; and the South American pizza with fresh mozzarella, sliced avocado, hearts of palm, baby corn, and tomatoes. You can also get primo pasta and of course wine while you dine. Piola's already a hit in Miami, Argentina, and Italy...Ay! Wadda yous waiting for?

Pioneer Bar & Restaurant
218 Bowery (Rivington & Prince Sts.)
Lower East Side 212.334.0484

This LES watering hole's ubiquitous elbowroom makes it a fave for social gatherings. Empty tables and spare stools are always at the ready, and a big-screen TV above the bar broadcasts soccer matches. Less sedentary patrons can shoot pool, or, given the magnitude of the bar's front room, play their own soccer match. Ironically, the seeds of Pioneer's success are grafted to its shortcoming. In spite of its hip Celtic vibe, genial bartenders, and relaxed local clientele, Pioneer often feels empty and drafty. All fine if you're looking for a final resting place, less so if it's fun you seek. To escape the mausoleum effect, consider crashing a birthday party in the much cozier backroom. These same guys own the Meatpacking District's Brass Monkey.

Pipa
38 E. 19th St. (Broadway & Park Ave. S.)
Flatiron 212.677.2233

Clearly feeling the pressure of matching the ABC Carpet & Home store to which it's attached, Pipa goes all out with a tastefully planned Cuban gypsy décor of antique chandeliers, gauze tapestries, and shells and candles, all of which fill the cozy space between sandblasted wood walls. Where do you go from there? How about Douglas Rodriguez's stellar kitchen, which churns out funky "Pan-Latin" cuisine that, unlike most places which make the claim, can rightfully claim the "tapas" label. Mucho sangria is a given. Drink enough and you'll forget that you just blew $2,000 on a rug next door.

P.J. Clarke's
915 W. 3rd Ave. (@ 55th St.)
Midtown 212.317.1616

Sick of bars that aspire for a we've-been-here-since-forever atmosphere? Stop reading. A buttoned-down Midtown institution with quirky old-school relics, it's possible your great-great-grandfather downed a few at P.J. Clarke's. This bustling, noisy drinkery reeks of fresh oysters and old money—or at least as old as its conservative and primarily Caucasian Brooks Brothers-clad clientele, which doesn't seem to mind shelling out for 18-year-old Macallan and 12-year-old Glenlivet. Friendly, no-nonsense bartenders serve up 30 types of bottled wines (only a dozen by the glass) and a fairly diverse beer selection. P.J.'s adjacent raw bar provides familiar munchies, and hungrier patrons can venture back to the Sidecar for standards like chicken pot pie and fish 'n' chips.

P.J. Kelly's
90 Fulton St. (William & Gold Sts.)
Financial District 212.406.1380

This Irish pub's most charming attribute, advertised on a board in front on the sidewalk, is the daily special: burger deluxe and French fries with draft beer, soda, or juice for $10. The burger is substantial, and as the co-owner/barkeep will tell you, the solid 20-oz. Imperial Pint is far superior to the skimpy so-called pints some places serve these days. The Guinness temperature is almost perfect, and $5 apple martinis can be had all day on Mondays. The place is still hopping between the lunchtime business crowds and late-evening workers, thanks to a following of neighborhood residents who camp under these six televisions, which show golf and soccer. This isn't a bad place to make a small Wall Street deal or plan an escape by sea.

The Place
310 W. 4th St. (Bank & 12th Sts.)
West Village 212.924.2711

Resembling something between a bar, a restaurant, and a closet, the Place's ambiguous atmosphere gives it a certain forbidden charm. The food portions seem to correspond to this eatery's size, and the term intimacy takes on new meaning here. This hideout is a great place to take your mistress (or your college roommate's girl, depending on your year of graduation), because it's dark, and after your illicit date sits down, there's little

The Place

room for anyone else. Even the outdoor seating area makes you nearly invisible from the street, with its shady canopy. The Place has an interesting wine selection, and the friendly staff is quick to make a recommendation. Having an affair? You don't even need to make up a code name, just meet at "the place."

Plan B

339 E. 10th St. (Aves. A & B)
East Village 212.353.2303

Plan A for the evening? Plan B. The crowd is young, and the atmosphere at this East Village locale feels like foreplay. Red neon lights offset ample seating and zebra-skin upholstery, and new and old-school hip-hop sets the beat. Drink prices are on the steep side—two drinks plus tip runs about $20. A comfortable vinyl lounge provides relative calm if dancing isn't your bag, though the bar itself rocks a vertical pole, much to the men's delight. Women dance on the bar as though they're being paid for it, which may or may not be the case. Stiff drinks and a strong potential to hook up make the former Drinkland a good place to shake what your momma gave you in the East Village.

Planet Hollywood

1540 Broadway (@ 45th St.)
Midtown 212.840.8326

Like the real thing, Planet Hollywood is a place of contradictions: friendly, funny staff; atmosphere that reeks of a brightly colored nursing home; music stuck in 1992. John Steed's hat and umbrella from *The Avengers* is next to a utility belt from *Spy Hard*. Hand-dipped milkshakes are surprisingly delicious and the predictable menu of greasy American food will give you a heart attack, albeit probably later than sooner. Maybe it's the sickly sweet Indecent Proposal and Interview with a Vampire cocktails talking—or the hot staff—but like an over-the-top B-film, there's something endearing about this tourist-heavy, notoriously cheesy bar and restaurant. Planet Hollywood, you had us at…five cocktails.

Planet Rose

219 Ave. A (13th & 14th Sts.)
East Village 212.353.9500

As faceless as a phone booth but for the oversized rosebud in the window, Planet Rose somehow soldiers on as yet another karaoke joint. The pinkish lighting's as tacky as a neon sign and seeing the leopard and zebra-skin upholstery in the lounge may inspire you to knock a few light bulbs out. Pacifists in this little corner of nowhere can take comfort in their $6-$12 well drinks, and maybe try challenging the bartender to a round of '80s vocalizing; apparently, the entire staff has to "audition" on the system before getting hired. Otherwise, just mingle with the madding crowd that keeps showing to bellow like a banshee in their own private room.

Planet Thailand

133 N. 7th St. (Berry St. & Bedford Ave.)
Williamsburg 718.599.5758

While a ton of other Williamsburg joints might be suffering from a cooler-than-thou pretension, Planet Thailand has the reputation to back it up.

Seven years and running, Planet Thailand is still the best deal in town, with a sleek atmosphere and delicious Thai/Japanese cuisine belying the low price range (vegetable pad thai = $6.95). This expansive former factory has an art installation of a leaking rowboat hanging from the ceiling, which gives you something to look at as you sip on drinks and wait for an ever-elusive table. The bar itself is a work of art; multicolored beer bottles grouted into the lit bar create a Lite-Brite effect. A DJ spins on the weekends.

Plantain

20 W. 38th St. (5th & 6th Aves.)
Midtown 212.869.8601

Without a doubt, Plantain is the top banana—if you want a memorable dining experience in Midtown, that is. This brightly lit establishment gives off an airy, tropical feel with a number of refreshing cocktails available such as the Plantain Punch, mojitos, caipirinhas, and an ample supply of sangria. Mondays night is Salsa Night and glasses of sangria are $2 at the bar, making this is an ideal place to shake your rump early in the week. The tiny lounge upstairs offers a quieter setting. The high quality of Plantain's Caribbean and Cuban dishes and two reasonably priced, scrumptious tasting menus more than make up for this tapas bar/restaurant/lounge's sub-par location.

Playwright Tavern

202 W. 49th St. (Broadway & 7th Ave.)
Midtown 212.262.9263

Many things set the Playwright apart from the typical schlock of the touristy nightspots that infest the Theater District, not the least of which is its abundance of charm. You can tell the management is Irish by the exclusively Celtic cast of playwrights that adorn the menu. Entering into the downstairs bar can seem off-putting (it's usually full of boisterous frat guys and other punters), so stroll up the stairs for a more embracing experience in either the restaurant or upstairs bar. Priced on par with the neighborhood, the menu offers everything from chicken fingers to rack of lamb. And the well-stocked bar features a dozen beers on tap and a selection of frozen specialty drinks—enough to keep the likes of famous literary drunks like Joyce and Yeats satiated.

Plunge (@ Hotel Gansevoort)

18 9th Ave. (13th & Gansevoort Sts.)
Meatpacking District 212.206.6700

Now that stilettos are as synonymous with the Meatpacking District as pig entrails, a bar on the penthouse rooftop of a billion-dollar hotel doesn't seem so out of place. If you're more interested in the scenery than the scene, get there before sunset while the suits' expense accounts are still lying dormant in a cubicle fifty blocks uptown, and breathe in the 360-degree view, which is what that $15 martini you're about to order is really paying for anyway. On weekend nights the music thumps until 3am, and while the heated pool boasts underwater tunes, unless you're a hotel guest it may as well be a song played on the tiniest violin you will never hear.

PM

50 Gansevoort St. (Greenwich & Washington Sts.)
Meatpacking District 212.255.6676

Choosy doormen guard the ropes at this exquisite nightclub where table service generally bears a two-bottle minimum (read: 500 dollars). If you can stand the wait or can talk your way in, you'll be surrounded by an intense Haitian décor and a true party theme, complete with balloons and palm trees. Mind the tabletop performers and dance yourself sick to an actual mix of old-school, new-school, and rock classics. Open a tab if you dare or just splurge on a pretty $7 bottle of Norwegian water, insisting it's for health and not financial reasons. PM hosts the "it" and "almost-it" crowds until the wee hours, and while it's not the madhouse it was when it opened a couple of years ago, that's not really a bad thing.

Pop
127 4th Ave. (12th & 13th Sts.)
East Village 212.767.1999

Inundated with long-haired, eyebrow-waxing, fake-tanned, wannabe Abercrombie model-types (and the women, we assume, who love them), Pop's only purpose seems to be to serve as shelter in case a hurricane or tornado suddenly swept through Union Square, and every other place was flooded or locked. The drinks at this rainbow-colored lounge (the color scheme would make Dorothy feel like she's tripping out—fire engine-red benches, blue pillows, pop art) are overpriced, the layout feels cluttered, and to say the service is slow would be giving the staff false hope. The only redeeming factor at this beehive of narcissism is the friendly, knowledgeable bar staff, who mercifully pour liberally. But it would take about 15 drinks to cause you to eventually black out, and save you from such brightly hued mediocrity.

Pop Burger Lounge
58-60 9th Ave. (14th & 15th Sts.)
Meatpacking District 212.414.8686

Do you know Roy Liebenthal, the restaurateur who brought us Café Tabac, Pop, and the Lemon? What about Roy Lichtenstein, the '80s pop artist? This fast-food hipster lounge could've been designed by either one, but it belongs to the former. The front area of this hyper-futuristic diner looks like something out of the *Jetsons*. The back lounge is more of the same, but with a sexier and darker vibe more befitting the Meatpacking District. Oddly, the security staff is generally friendly and the wait staff is generally dismissive. The wonderfully thick burgers and fries are to die for, and the kitchen stays open until 4am during the week and 5am on weekends. That said, the huge video screens and inviting pool table in back make getting to sleep no easy feat.

The Porch Bar
115 Ave. C (7th & 8th Sts.)
East Village 212.982.4034

Just imagine...lazing about in a rocker, mosquitoes shut out by the screen, and friendly neighbors walking by waving, because of course, you know everyone in the neighborhood. But wait—the porch (in back) at the Porch Bar is nothing like they have in the South. With candlelight filling the space, this place is more lounge than neighborhood bar. During the blistering summer days, the swing in the garden, the Porch Hard Lemonade ($6-$8), and the tropical wall painting will transport you out of this concrete jungle. Though the summer heat is excruciating, chilly winters seem to go by slower, so the Porch Bar has filled the garden with heat lamps to entice year-round activity. Bring a parka and a warming drink.

Porcupine
20 Prince St. (Elizabeth & Mott Sts.)
NoLita 212.966.8886

And you thought you'd never drink a Porcupine. Well, sidle up to the polished, carved bar, ask for Porcupine's signature cocktail (dark rum, ginger syrup, fresh lemon juice, and soda water), and think again. Despite its thorny name, Porcupine is as friendly as an upscale NoLita bistro gets. The intelligent staff patiently explains seasonal cocktails ($8-$11) and their 42 wines while you drool over the creative New American menu ($16-$25 dinner, $8-$16 lunch, $12 prix-fixe brunch). Lonely singles beware: The walls glow golden as the night progresses, and this place is so damn romantic you'll either attack one of the cute bartenders or make out with the mirror in the candlelit bathroom.

Port 41
355 W. 41st St. (8th & 9th Aves.)
Hell's Kitchen 212.947.1188

Sharks, begin circling. This new, dim tavern in the side of Port Authority offers four pool tables in a spacious backroom. Beyond the felt-top fest, the bar seems pretty bare-bones. You can get cashews from a coin machine and shelled peanuts from a mammoth Tupperware someone seems to have forgotten across from the wooden bar. The two-room space feels like an unused stage set; so far, pool opponents are harder to find than open barstools. But that's bound to change. Commuters with aggression to expel or tourists with time to kill are sure to find this port, and already the sleek TVs behind the bar give the passersby a reason to take shelter. Rack 'em up!

Porters

216 7th Ave. (22nd & 23rd Sts.)
Chelsea 212.229.2878

Porters

If the phrase "modern throw-back" wasn't an oxymoron, it would describe Porters to a T. This dark wood and marbleized bar is mod and classic, swanky and subtle, and, well, expensive. This hobnobbing Mecca for the up-and-coming CPA and Wall Street set might have come off as cool and retro à la *The Great Gatsby*, but the hint of pretension that comes with so many of Manhattan's chardonnay-sipping nouveau riche is enough to send most casual diners and drinkers elsewhere. The sidewalk and garden cafés, though, offer brief respite from the backless barstools and dim mood lighting. There's no doubt that the service and presentation is impeccable (right down to the tightly knotted bow ties), but the rigidity of the atmosphere is sure to hurt even the most dedicated swinger's game.

Posh

405 W. 51st St. (9th & 10th Aves.)
Hell's Kitchen 212.957.2222

If you were a Spice Girl, which one would you be? OK, so maybe you're just too, well, posh to care since that was sooo nine years ago. But this swanky lounge isn't just for the Victoria Beckhams of the world; it's also for the sporty and scary. Theater queens, Chelsea boys, and everyone in between mingle at this Hell's Kitchen drinkery. What was once a neighborhood bar has of late lured a diverse group of gays from all over the city. Posh's metallic bar, hip red lighting, and comfy backroom couches create a chill, yet "see and be seen" atmosphere for drinking and cruising. Plus, the outdoor area is perfect for relaxing with a cosmo while you ponder your future as the fifth Spice Girl.

The Pourhouse

790 Metropolitan Ave. (@ Humboldt St.)
Williamsburg 718.599.0697

Location, location, location. The Pourhouse doesn't worry about this real estate maxim; it's located on the margins of Williamsburg on an otherwise bar-free block, allowing it to single-handedly serve as a social hub for the surrounding community. The bar consists of two rooms; the first looks like your run-of-the-mill tavern—bar, barstools, pool table, and jukebox. The backroom is a performance space replete with murals and a ring of couches. Saturday and Thursday are Ladies' Nights, with 2-for-1 drink specials. Monday is Boys' Night, when the Pourhouse offers free hot dogs with the purchase of a beer. No need to make dinner reservations. Bring your date here and if she doesn't throw her beer in your face after you hand her the ketchup to top off her meal, she's a keeper.

Pravda

281 Lafayette St. (Prince & Houston Sts.)
NoLita 212.226.4944

It's easy to miss this underground caviar bar—but only because it's tucked discreetly under Lafayette Street. But once you're inside, you'll find out that this Russian hideaway is super-chic and full of trendy people wearing shoes that cost more than most people's paychecks. Lovers of the fermented potato will be elated to find an extensive list of over 80 flavored and imported vodkas. The décor is intended to be Russian and the vaulted ceilings give it the feel of a hush-hush speakeasy. Pravda's friendly bartenders (clad in white dentist coats) serve up a plethora of specialty cocktails that are just tasty enough to merit their $11 price tags; many of them are concocted from such luxurious liquors as coconut vodka and apricot rum. Raise a glass to the end of the Cold War.

Press 195
195 5th Ave. (Union & Sackett Sts.)
Park Slope 718.857.1950

This establishment is a good little sandwich joint with a drinking problem. The bright yellow walls, blue ceiling, and small tables give the place an innocent appeal, somewhat reminiscent of a kids' classroom—and indeed, mothers and their children stop by during daytime hours. There are more than 30 kinds of tasty pressed sandwiches on the menu, going for up to $9 a pop. (They offer delivery and catering services as well.) However, along with this sunny, sweet sandwich side, Press 195 sports a no-joke list of more than a dozen wines and a dozen beers. Under the umbrellas in the back garden is a good place to enjoy them. Just behave yourself—there are families here.

Pressure
110 University Pl. (13th & 14th Sts.)
Greenwich Village 212.255.8188

Though it garners its name from the pressurized bubble that houses it, Bowlmor Lanes' lounge space, Pressure, nevertheless vexes singles who can't decide which nubile coed to target. But stay away from the pool tables because, at $26 per hour, they'll put a strain on your wallet. This sprawling 16,000-square-foot room presents itself well with subtle lighting and a serviceable

menu including nachos and very affordable $7 spring rolls. The space is very willing to be co-opted for big corporate events, but if you just want to hold down your own little corner of this game-world-theme-park-meets-nightclub, spend a couple hundred bucks on a bottle and a table will soon be yours.

Prey
4 W. 22nd St. (@ 5th Ave.)
Flatiron 646.230.1444

Prey

Prey is a rare confluence—it's a nightclub that's health-conscious. Management openly declares the target demographic to be 20- and 30-something professionals with style, aka "the beautiful people." So decide for yourself if the menu flatters you. Low-carb versions of your favorite frozen drinks stand out, and while there's a kitchen, you'll find no bar food thereabouts—it's all light tapas. All of this may have you thinking that maybe there's a roomful of treadmills somewhere. Prey has all the New York lounge basics too—sleek, black, glassy surfaces bathed in ultra-violet lighting, and a lot of hot bartenders stationed at the two bars. Check out happy hour from 5pm-8pm; you might be inspired to splurge with a few rounds, but then you'll want to do some sit-ups in the bathroom.

Prime 54 Lounge (@ Hotel Rihga)
151 W. 54th St. (6th & 7th Aves.)
Midtown 212.468.8888

In the Hotel Rihga, Halcyon has traded its name and menu to become Prime 54, an Italian steakhouse. The food is rich, and if you want some, you should be, too: The oversized drinks carry inflated prices to match. This is a great date spot—dark and quiet, casually elegant with comfortable table seating—provided you don't run into Uncle Bob, who may not notice this easy-listening music is better suited to a dentist's office. On that subject, the overly serene vibe smacks of Novocain. After work, sink into a single-malt Scotch, unwind with one of nearly a hundred wines, or even grab a grappa. For fruitier patrons, the bar offers flavored martinis and sangria, a summer special.

Private Park (@ the Hudson Hotel)
356 W. 58th St. (Broadway & Columbus Ave.)
Hell's Kitchen 212.554.6343

This lush oasis located in the courtyard of the über-trendy Hudson Hotel is open to the sky and surrounded on all sides by the walls of the hotel's reportedly tiny rooms. Stepping through the dark, futuristic lobby and into the surreal daylight of Private Park feels a bit like a trip to Wonderland, complete with giant furniture—watering cans overflowing with begonias and flower pots taller than the bar's patrons—and carpets of 40-foot-high ivy climbing every vertical surface. The brick patio is covered with exotic bohemian-chic benches, chairs, and couches on which unwinding businessmen, wealthy Europeans, and too-slick-for-

Times-Square tourists recline luxuriously. The gorgeous cocktails are made with fresh fruit and go down like silk, but the prices ($14-$18) may be out of any sane New Yorker's price range.

Prohibition
503 Columbus Ave. (84th & 85th Sts.)
Upper West Side 212.579.3100

With its velvet curtains and wine-bottle lighting, this popular speakeasy has the feel of a '20s-style jazz club, minus the flappers and bootleg liquor. Instead, yuppies strike animated poses over plates of roasted meat and pricey cocktails that contain more sugar than booze. Patrons are advised to call ahead for the acts here, as the music can range from grunge rock to exuberant cabaret. If you can elbow your way to the bar, the service is quite efficient and friendly, but those who get seated in the dining area will have to endure the harried wait staff stumbling amidst the densely packed tables, advising customers to please get their personal items out of the way. Doing something legal (i.e., drinking yourself into a stupor) never felt so good.

Proof
239 3rd Ave. (19th & 20th Sts.)
Gramercy 212.228.4200

Tee off at Proof, the archetypal sports bar in Gramercy. This sleek, tri-level bar features TVs for your sports events-viewing pleasure, a small menu of specialty cocktails, and bar food so you can dine while you whine like most of the fresh-out-of-college clientele who have recently discovered that Daddy's credit cards have been cut off. You won't find Bud Light posters or sawdust on the floor here, though. What you will find is a couple of comfy lounge areas and nightly drink specials that include daily 2-for-1 Absolut drinks from 5pm-9pm (except on Tuesdays, which offer an open bar from 5pm-8pm). Despite the plush surroundings, ultimately this place serves as proof that you can take the kid out of college, but you can't take college out of the kid.

DINE UPSTAIRS

PROVIDENCE
NEW · YORK · CITY

PROVIDENCENYC.COM

"(EXECUTIVE CHEF) MARGHERITA
ALOI'S MEDITERRANEAN CUISINE
IS EFFORTLESSLY GOOD"
—THE NY SUN

311 WEST 57TH STREET / BTW 8/9 AVE NYC / 212.307.006

DANCE DOWNSTAIRS

"FOR THOSE TIRED OF THE
VELVET ROPE GAME AT SUCH
ÜBER-CLUBS AS MARQUEE AND
CROBAR BUT STILL IN THE
MOOD TO DANCE" —SHECKY'S

TRIUPH
ROOM

TRIUMPHROOM.COM

Proseccheria
447 3rd Ave. (@ 31st St.)
Murray Hill 212.679.2551

Tucked in the back corner of Pasticcio, an "artisan" Italian restaurant, this wine bar tries—but fails—to have its own shelf-life independent of the whole. You can't enter the bar without walking through the restaurant, and the scarcity of seats isn't enough to make it feel like an actual bar. Proseccheria's pleasant-but-drab atmosphere may be irrelevant to real (or wannabe) wine connoisseurs, who can choose from a multitude of vino options, and the soft lighting is semi-romantic, but since this wine bar doesn't really function separately from the restaurant, it has a perpetually unfinished feeling that prevents total relaxation and silly drunken behavior. Besides, it's tough to pronounce oenology correctly when you've slung back a few too many merlots.

PS 450
450 Park Ave. S. (30th & 31st Sts.)
Murray Hill 212.532.7474

Class is in session at PS 450, but the lusty red and dark wood décor is more along the lines of "Hot for Teacher." This "cafeteria" opens at 11:30am and serves from an American fusion menu until 3am (the bar serves until 4am), but public school never plated asparagus and beef negimaki skewers ($10) or wood-grilled hanger steak over chorizo hash topped with lobster butter ($20). The music makes it a great after-work and late-night spot, and the staff is devilishly charming—like that flirty cheerleader who never did give up her digits. Take notes from the TV at the front bar, blend in at the middle lounge, or hang with the troublemakers in the back. With four beers by the bottle, five by draft ($6 each), and endless mojitos, detention is the objective.

Public
210 Elizabeth St. (Prince & Spring Sts.)
NoLita 212.343.7011

In a city where space is at a premium, Public is an industrial-chic anomaly. Lofty ceilings preside over spacious dining rooms of whitewashed brick walls and exposed concrete floors, all of which is nicely counterbalanced by a mini "library," complete with quaint card catalogues, just as you might find in a public library—and hence the name. Global fusion cuisine reigns in this wide-open space: Tender grilled kangaroo tops a coriander falafel ($13), and snail and oxtail ravioli comes with pickled shiitake mushrooms ($12). Fusion food calls for fusion cocktails, something to which Manhattan is no stranger. Here, the exotic pairings actually taste good. Try a vanilla and mango mojito ($11), and settle in at the burnished bar or the appropriately dim rear lounge, all soft leather and warm orange hues.

Puck Fair
298 Lafayette St. (Houston & Prince Sts.)
SoHo 212.431.1200

It looks Irish and smells Irish and yes, they know how to pour a proper pint of Guinness, but there's occasionally a whiff of too-slick marketing going on at Puck Fair. Still, an infectious spirit pervades, especially when the roaring, post-work crowd starts loosening their ties after a day on the trading floor. Their beer-fueled mating rituals are on boisterous display, living up to the legend of the testosterone-driven, mythical "Puck," for whom the too-big-to-be-a-pub-too-blasé-to-be-a-club thing is named. Comfy corners abound amid the gleaming wood, brick walls, and skylights. Couples and co-workers populate the corner retreats that are reminiscent of "snugs," separate rooms that were once the only place in a pub that ladies could frequent. Like every Irishman, Puck Fair has sisters: Swift and Ulysses.

Punch
913 Broadway (20th & 21st Sts.)
Flatiron 212.673.6333

A taste of the tropics on an otherwise sleepy strip of Broadway, this spot is islands elegant; it's decked out with wicker chairs, dim lights, and hanging tapestries. The bar occupies the front of the space and with its own menu of small plates (summer risotto with green tea-flavored bamboo rice, the cold cucumber sandwich, and crispy duck confit) and a variety of specialty drinks including fruit-infused vodkas, Punch attracts a crowd of low-key locals. A full menu is also available at the tables in the back of the restaurant, where groups can dine under the soaring ceiling. Definitely a great spot to grab a cocktail or quick bite before a big night out, but not quite exciting enough to become a destination, Punch lacks just that.

Punch and Judy's
26 Clinton St. (Houston & Stanton Sts.)
Lower East Side 212.982.1116

Dark and sensual as a cabernet sauvignon, Punch and Judy's is a pioneer among the recent crop of sophisticated hotspots springing up in this once desolate area. If the ambiance doesn't immediately tip you off that this is a wine bar, the full-bodied stems waiting expectantly at each place setting probably will. Whether you're an i-banker or a social worker, you'll be able to afford to drink here since wine is served by consumption: choose between a 4-oz. taste, 8-oz. large glass, or 16-oz. mini-carafe. Should the vibe feel too stuffy for you, just look at the bar's rubbery Homies figurines who are busy keepin' it real.

Puppets Jazz Bar
294 5th Ave. (1st & 2nd Sts.)
Park Slope 718.499.2627

This Park Slope jazz hangout opened in mid-2005, but it's already generating local buzz for its talented performers and classic feel. From blocks away, eloquent jazz leads you by the ear to this tiny venue with its simple unfinished wood interior, collection of little tables, and a bar that's little more than a glorified table. A $5 cover and two-drink minimum may seem steep to non-jazz aficionados, who will find conversation difficult during the two nightly sets (three on Fri and Sat nights). But there are no other strings attached at Puppets, which is geared toward those who love to sit attentively and listen to high-quality live jazz at a hot new dish in Park Slope's Fifth Avenue nightlife smorgasbord.

Pyramid
101 Ave. A (6th & 7th Sts.)
East Village 212.228.4888

Whether you dream of being a goddess on a mountaintop or you're just hungry like the wolf, Pyramid's 1984 party on Friday nights will have you believing that heaven really is a place on earth. The drinks may be weak at this dive, but you'll still have fun singing and dancing like a fool to Belinda, Madonna, Duran Duran, and other one-hit wonders and legends from two decades ago. And if you get tired of dancing in the dark upstairs, head downstairs, where you never know whether you'll catch an episode of *Dynasty* or *Jem*. While Fridays are truly outrageous, the club's other nights, including hip-hop on Tuesdays and new wave on Thursdays, don't draw nearly as huge a crowd. Best to skip them.

Q Lounge & Billiards
220 W. 19th St. (7th & 8th Aves.)
Chelsea 212.206.7665

How this corny pool hall/sports bar/hetero meat market manages to make it in hip, happening Chelsea is a mystery. Generic-looking 20- and 30-something happy hour-types try to pick each other up while the 20 giant TV screens, 16 wine-colored pool tables, and DJs assault the senses and the playful menu items (White Castle burgers, pigs 'n' blankets, nachos) miss the ironic bull's-eye; it's like being trapped at a Chuck E. Cheese for grown-ups. The hottie waitress in the lounge's low-budget TV ad teases, "We won't stop 'til you say 'Thank Q'!" Please, for the love of respectable Chelsea nightlife, somebody just say "Thank Q!" and maybe, just maybe, they'll stop already.

Q56 Restaurant & Cocktails
65 E. 56th St. (Park & Madison Aves.)
Midtown 212.756.3925

If you're drinking in Midtown and the Yankees game isn't playing overhead, you're in a hotel lobby. Tourists staying at the Swissôtel get the sanitized New York City they came to see via $13 "Sex and the City" martinis at Q56. The bar attracts a solid cocktail hour and dinner crowd, and while prices are geared toward expense account-ers who sign without looking, the bartender isn't cheap; be nice and your Q-tini or Cosmo might get "topped off" with the leftover liquor. Candlelit tables and comfortable lounge seats make for an intimate setting, which could explain the groups of 40-something men crammed into the limited bar tables. A suit and tie aren't required, but after 7pm, a Midwestern accent seems to be.

Quench
282 Smith St. (@ Sackett St.)
Carroll Gardens 718.875.1500

Quench wants very badly to be THE Smith Street swanky lounge. And it has all the requisite accoutrements—the sexy one-word name, the kitschy bright-colored wall lined with curvy, asymmetrical couches, and two large round mirrors perfectly positioned behind the bar for working on that perfect pout or fixing errant hair. The bartenders are wearing the official tank top and tight jean uniform, too, and most of the patrons look as though they're on the prowl (while trying to look aloof). Why is the vibe, well, a bit off here? Sometimes there's a little thing called trying too hard, and for a bar as self-conscious as Quench, that pretty much comes standard, too. Break in your brand-new $200 jeans by heading here for a glass of their stellar hot chocolate, but don't expect to be blown away.

Quhnia
45 E. 1st St. (1st & 2nd Aves.)
East Village 212.529.3066

Quhnia's great food and homemade vodkas create a potent pleasure mix for any day or night of the week. Offering a collage of Eastern European specialties, this intimate East Village nook is ideal for dates. The restaurant (Quhnia is the Polish word for "kitchen"), with its highly attentive wait staff, makes you feel like you're attending an intimate dinner party with friends. From the black truffle

garlic hanger steak, to simpler dishes such as the goat cheese panini with Moroccan olives and sun-dried tomatoes, or a bowl of the white borscht, the kitchen here will appease anyone's palette. The bar features an impressive French wine selection along with specialty cocktails such as the Perfect Love Martini, which would make even Aphrodite blush.

Quigley's
313 1st Ave. (@ 18th St.)
Gramercy 212.253.9440

It's no surprise that Quigley's attracts an older crowd—the proximity to Stuyvesant Town makes that inevitable. Still, the bar's friendliness and cheap drinks also draw the whippersnappers from nearby SVA who are more likely to carry a fake ID than a fraudulent Medicare card. With seven TVs—three of which are 42" plasma screens—Quigley's also entices sports fans who want to chug $3 happy hour beer while complaining that the Yankees aren't leading by more than five runs. A quiet garden makes this neighborhood hangout a nice addition to this sleepy strip of First Avenue, where usually the most exciting thing to happen is a cardiac arrest at nearby Beth Israel.

Quo
511 W. 28th St. (10th & 11th Aves.)
Chelsea 212.268.5105

Already a hit on the Chelsea club scene, Quo is bound to impress first-timers as well. You'll have to get a little glamorous to get past the ropes, but once you do, you'll dread that "Last Dance." You won't forget the "Jetsons go to Miami" feel of this neon wonderland that spins spaciously into three rooms revolving around the stone and wood main bar. Plenty of tables and banquettes make space for dining or champagne consumption (Quo has 12 bottles to choose from). Or, cut loose and order the Grey Goose, which comes in a hand-carved ice tube. And if you manage to leave with your credit card still intact, keep an eye out for the return of the infamous "Loungewhore Sessions" Sundays.

Quo

R Bar
451 Meeker Ave. (@ Graham Ave.)
Williamsburg 718.486.6116

Real locals wielding true Brooklyn accents, $2 Rolling Rocks, Ladies' Night Wednesdays, pool, darts, and a bowling video game give this Williamsburg bar a casual, neighborhoody feel, which is something that can't be said for most of the establishments in the area. Hipsters, fashion plates, and wannabe rock stars be warned—this is not your scene. However, if you're willing to leave your ego (and trucker hat) at the door, you're more than welcome to enjoy the daily 5pm-9pm happy hour and kick-ass jukebox. Not surprisingly, it's not uncommon to see regulars playing long games of Scrabble, Twister, and Jenga here. The R Bar (or "our" bar as the owners like to call it) is truly a little slice of normalcy in a sea of pretension.

Raccoon Lodge
59 Warren St. (@ W. Broadway)
TriBeCa 212.766.9656

A jukebox filled with generic tunes seems to be just the thing for the 30- and 40-something crowd filling this no-frills bar. Expect a monolith of after-work suits and the co-workers they're still trying to pick up now that the day's meetings are over. The interior design isn't too starched, though, even if it is utterly ordinary (think the bar version of Chili's "wacky" décor). Prices are run-of-the-mill, too, with domestic beers at $4, imports at $5, and PBR at a low $2. Jaw with the bartender about his girl problems or watch sports on the corner TV, lest you wind up like one of the mute hippies staring into space. A pool table in back rounds out what has to be one of New York's most thoroughly undistinguishable neighborhood holes.

Radio Perfecto
190 Ave. B (11th & 12th Sts.)
East Village 212.477.3366

The downtown branch of this hip Mexican café is a necessary pit stop along Avenue Bistro. Seemingly less crowded with the weekend-warrior types who gather in Alphabet City, Radio Perfecto manages to be both a great place to eat and a cool place to hang out. The drinks are fun and imaginative (try the Hendrick's Martini with rose petals and cucumber-infused gin) and the back garden is a spacious, festive place to enjoy them. The menu is notable for the roast chicken that comes in a different sauce every day of the week; it also includes plenty of appetizers to share, and incredible desserts like cinnamon gelato.

Raga
433 E. 6th St. (Ave. A & 1st Ave.)
East Village 212.388.0957

If you avoid walking down E. Sixth Street because of the army of "free glass of wine"-touting waiters/salesmen attempting to lure you into their restaurant, fear no more. Just put in your iPod earphones and quickly duck into Raga. This treasured restaurant's inventive Indian-French fusion menu, including the bestselling wild boar and "famosa samosas," in addition to their huge martini menu, make this hotspot worthwhile. Chic yet casual, Raga hosts a 2-for-1 happy hour every night until

8pm in the summer; during the open mic night on the first Friday of each month, local poets, singers, and comedians can come in and perform. Grab one of the big booths in back and enjoy the comfortable setting and crafty dishes that make this more than your typical curry house.

Rain
1059 3rd Ave. (62nd & 63rd Sts.)
Upper East Side 212.223.3669

The menu at this large space is safely Pan-Asian (read: Thai, Malaysian, Cambodian, and Vietnamese) and like the food, the service is just on the high side of average, keeping complaints (and maybe repeat customers) low. There are six Asian beers to choose from and the cocktail concoctions are tasty (pomegranate and champagne, various martinis made with fruit from Southeast Asia). Still, although Rain's music selection could use revamping, the prices are fair, the food is reliably mediocre, and the décor isn't too hard on the eyes—wood-slat ceiling, wooden booths, and brightly lit lanterns hanging above. Let one of their specialty cocktails like the Rain Sangria (white wine, peach schnapps, OJ, blue curacao, and brandy; $8.50) relax you like soothing, pre-programmed rain sounds from your alarm clock.

Rain Lounge
216 Bedford Ave. (@ N. 5th St.)
Williamsburg 718.384.0100

Who would have the thought that on modern-day Bedford and N. Fifth the native Latino population of Williamsburg would still have a place to groove? Standing out among the hipster bars in the area is Rain, a hip-hop lounge/dance spot where "jiggy wid' it" is gotten. When that door opens, the tops get tighter, the pants get baggier, the women get surlier, and the men are just lookin' to get some action. Don't panic—you're still in Williamsburg. A, um, lovely velvet painting of a nude lady sets the tone for the front room, but people are too busy dancing to notice her. Out back is a patio, and karaoke is offered on Tuesday nights. Overall, the place has a house party feel and Mom won't be home until late.

Rancho Café
570 Amsterdam Ave. (87th & 88th Sts.)
Upper West Side 212.362.1514

Not so much a bar as it is a somewhat pricey attempt at a Mexican cantina, the Rancho Café attempts to appeal to the young and hip, with decidedly mixed results. The food isn't spectacular—better and more authentic Mexican food can be found in the many taquerias in the neighborhood—but the open-air seating is a nice setting for enjoying one of their legendary frozen margaritas on a hot summer night. These icy delights come in a slew of flavors, and they're priced right at two for $7 during happy hour, Monday-Thursday, 4pm-7pm. And if you're hungry, the alambres (skewers of seasoned roasted meat and veggies) come highly recommended. Unfortunately, the occasionally sub-par service and long wait for a table can slow your salsa down to a waltz.

Rare
416 W. 14th St. (9th Ave. & Washington St.)
Meatpacking District 212.675.2220

Rare

A discreet entryway keeps this live music spot slightly hidden from the trendsters—how rare. Here, a wide range of shows by underground artists (no one you've heard of) play while a youngish crowd of regulars and new-to-the-neighborhood folks dance awkwardly in the red-and-black-colored cavernous space that offers little in the way of atmosphere (save for the occasional zebra pattern). The adjoining barroom is only slightly better lit, but it's certainly more conducive to enjoying conversation as you sip slickly named drinks like The Cooler and watch the crowd filtering in and out from all sides. Expect to pay an $8 cover on weekends for something a little different than the multiplying swanky lounges popping up like Gremlins all over these cobblestone streets.

Rare View (@ the Shelbourne Murray Hill Hotel)
303 Lexington Ave. (@ 38th St.)
Murray Hill 212.481.8439

It's rare to hang out on a rooftop bar and actually have room to move around. But on this swank rooftop, you can stretch out on plush banquettes or lounge by the bar, where you can score complimentary wasabi peas or gourmet snack mix. Savor the free grub, though, as drinks don't come cheap. $9 for a Bud on tap?! Don't ask how much the specialty drinks (like the kiwi mojito) are. It's typical for seasonal bars to make up for the little time they're open by charging more, but Rare View tacks on an extra $4-$5 than you'd pay elsewhere just for the pleasure of drinking there. However, it does offer fantastic fauna and views of the Empire State and Chrysler Buildings. So bring a client, your expense account, and enjoy the rare view.

Rathbone's
1702 2nd Ave. (88th & 89th Sts.)
Upper East Side 212.369.7361

On first inspection, Rathbone's looks like every other bar you've been to. On the second, you start to feel like Bill Murray in *Groundhog Day,* but there's something endearing about it. Maybe it's the old-school, devil-may-care attitude this joint oozes, or the fact that it's a bar on the Upper East Side that people actually seem to like going to. Navigating the place can be tricky, as the narrow space between the bar and seating area makes relieving yourself difficult; but if you make it to the back you'll be rewarded not only with bathrooms but videogames as well. The food is decent, especially their hamburgers, but easily the greatest aspect is the sidewalk seating, where you can sit and drink a 'Rona on a lazy summer afternoon.

The Raven
194 Ave. A (@ 12th St.)
East Village 212.529.4712

Edgar Allan Poe might've been a bit creeped out by this haunted-house-meets-goth rock bar. After a walk around this neighborhood's weekend warrior joints, he would've probably come back to this aged haunt for a drink. Old, but not as old as most of the standbys of Alphabet City, this dark little dive packs pinball and pool into its faux-morbid space, with the odd frill. Mojitos, for one, are served on Mondays, and there's most always a DJ in the corner. The Raven and its crowd long for the East Village of yore, grogging to Johnny Thunders and the Ramones on the house PA, and sticking close to that era of dress as well. Whenever you're in the mood for some dyed spikes and a $4-$8 beer, the Raven's your bird.

Rawhide
212 8th Ave. (@ 21st St.)
Chelsea 212.242.9332

Are you still looking for your daddy? Does he have a moustache, wear jeans and a t-shirt, and drink lots of beer? Well, good news! We've found him. He's here at Rawhide, along with plenty of other daddies eager to reward you with a spanking. But don't worry. Though the bar's blacked-out window gives an ominous appearance, the scene inside is anything but. Sure, there's a motorcycle hanging over the pool table. Sure, a lot of these dudes are clad in tough-looking leather and spikes, but on average, they're quite friendly. As the song goes, "Don't try to understand 'em, just rope, and throw, and grab 'em…Rawhide!"

Reade Street Pub and Kitchen

135 Reade St. (Greenwich St. & W. Broadway)
TriBeCa 212.227.2295

You can always tell a good pub by how many regulars fill the room at any given time, and Reade Street's loyals get there as early as 10am some days. This 100-plus-year-old haunt is the kind of neighborhood bar that you'd find all over the outer-boroughs, but rarely in Manhattan; and it's better during happy hour than on weekends. The prices aren't criminal (pitchers for less than $10!) and the wait staff is genial—it's as though they're willing to work for tips rather than expecting them. But epicureans beware—the menu isn't fusion or "neo" anything; it's tailored more for those who spend their weekends watching ballgames instead of going to the opera.

Red and Black

135 N. 5th St. (Bedford Ave. & Berry St.)
Williamsburg 718.302.4530

One of the more eclectic locales this side of the Williamsburg Bridge, Red and Black is one part hip-hop, one part disco, one part Texan, and six parts rockin' bar. Various DJs spin a combination of dance-inspiring music nightly (sometimes it's accompanied by live conga drumming). Lounge-friendly booths in back show signs of what could be a not-so-lonely evening, but you might be more tempted to smoke out in the patio or hang out by the fully functional fireplace that separates the pool table from the rest of the bar. Order up the nightly drink special and witness the occasional unabashedly awful dancer. If you're clever enough, you'll figure out how to eavesdrop by sitting in one of the booths located in a corner under the vaulted ceiling.

Red Bench

107 Sullivan St. (Prince & Spring Sts.)
SoHo 212.274.9120

There's a red-light special on Sullivan Street. Red Bench may be young (it's only been around for a year and a half), but like the NYU grads pervading the area, this youthful bar is more experienced than its age lets on. The candlelit room is extremely dark and cozy, and sexy bartenders pour your drink fast and strong to ensure that you'll stay a while. Red Bench is filled with plenty of inviting, romantic nooks that are suitable for getting up close and personal. Be careful, though; everyone appears to look good in the dim red lighting–so if you didn't come in with a date, you'll probably leave with one, though we can't vouch for the actual attractiveness of your special someone in broad daylight. Red Bench is soon to become a staple night spot; the 3-for-2 happy hour is thrice the fun.

The Red Cat

227 10th Ave. (23rd & 24th Sts.)
Chelsea 212.242.1122

Don't pussyfoot around. For the cat's meow in the dreamily discreet area west of Eighth Avenue, make a date with your best-loved soul mate (or your favorite forbidden crush) and slink on over to one of the city's best destinations for a picture book-perfect romantic rendezvous, the Red Cat. Flatter your special someone with an array of sumptuous selections from their temptingly chic, Contemporary American steak and seafood menu, or just gaze longingly into each other's eyes as you wile away the evening below antique lanterns over sangria. Or you could spend the night sampling selections from their expansive (100-plus) wine list, and fall in love all over again. Lonely hearts and sports fans—don't bother darkening this door.

Red Lion

151 Bleecker St. (@ Thompson St.)
Greenwich Village 212.260.2959

If you enjoy cover bands and the people who love them, you'd be hard-pressed to have a horrible time at the Red Lion. For 25 years the Lion has provided fast service and all the music patrons can handle; original acts also play. Still, the place has earned a bad rap for featuring second-rate cover bands and playing host to drunken NYU coeds. Naysayers can drown their pretentiousness in a couple of bottles of Bud Light and ask one of the many singles to dance to "Living on a Prayer." It's a far cry from a lounge, and you may never hear any of the bands featured on MTV, but for a fun night of butchered versions of your favorite tunes (think *American Idol*), you could do worse than this Village mainstay.

Red Rock West Saloon
457 W 17th St. (9th & 10th Aves.)
Chelsea 212.366.5359

When your friends from home roll into town and they're begging to go to Coyote Ugly to see girls dance on bars because they liked the movie, flex your "I'm a New Yorker now" muscles, clue them in about the leather-clad bartenders over at Hogs & Heifers, and then throw a curveball and suggest the grittier, less touristy Red Rock West Saloon instead. They'll ooh, aah, and ogle at the bar occasionally being set ablaze by the sassy female bartenders and the wannabe models in the crowd covertly sipping mixed drinks. The girls behind, under, and on top of the bar are not only fire-breathing and sexy, they have legitimate drink-mixing abilities; so order up, steal a glance at their curves, and enjoy a drink made with surprising aplomb.

Red Sky
47 E. 29th St. (Park & Madison Aves.)
Murray Hill 212.447.1820

Laidback locals like to drop anchor here, but thanks to the addition of a rooftop deck, warm weather sees even more young preppy types setting their sails for Red Sky, a bar/lounge off the coast of Park Avenue. Come quittin' time, a youngish after-work crowd descends on the downstairs bar to cheerfully booze on $4 appletinis and cosmos and $3 domestic drafts during happy hour (Mon-Fri, 4pm-8pm). By nightfall,

Red Sky

sailors in search of a "first mate" cruise up to the second floor, not so much to hear the DJ's typical rock/pop mix, but to canoodle with other on-the-prowl singles among the fluorescent fish tanks. On the third floor, the mingling masses can take a breather on the new, tiki bar-esque roof deck, where fresh air and fresh drinks help keep the party going long into the night.

Redd's Tavern
511 Grand St. (Union Ave. & Lorimer St.)
Williamsburg 718.218.9429

Established in 2002, Redd's is the type of bar that can quickly become a second home. There are huge, comfortable couches sprawled out in the front of the room, where the smell of popcorn lingers in the air. The crowd is just as cozy, like the neighborhood dudes who gather to toss darts and drink beer or the girls who sit on the patio smoking cigarettes like they're in their own backyard. No matter what it is, Redd's is a great place to hang out and kill time. With happy hour running from 4pm-7pm and in-the-know patrons streaming in all night long, this true-blue neighborhood institution makes it easy to feel like you've found a barstool to call your own.

Redemption
1003 2nd Ave. (@ 53rd St.)
Midtown 212.319.4545

It might be somewhat telling of a neighborhood when the owners optimistically name their social spot Redemption. This newbie is stuck in the armpit of Midtown, but that hasn't prevented a cavalry of pretty boys on a hair-gel overdose, poor little rich girls, and token fuzzy dudes with tired, red eyes from stopping by for a night out. Aiming for an upscale martini crowd, Redemption is what you might expect to find in a European airport, with colored neon lights angled against a white ceiling, $9 cocktails—heavy on the ice—and $10 hamburgers. The DJ plays music to jiggle to, but no cabaret license means no white-man's-over-bite, for better or worse. On the bright side, there's a strong showing of debutantes, and they're hot, if that's any, sigh, redemption.

Reif's Tavern
302 E. 92nd St. (1st & 2nd Aves.)
Upper East Side 212.426.0519

You know how people say that Central Park is "New York's backyard," but they never really spend much time there? Make up for it at Reif's Tavern, by checking out a game, having a drink, or grilling your own food on the patio. Yep. Grilling. Yes, you read correctly—they give New Yorkers fire and pointy utensils! Reif's also has pool tables and darts, which really makes the place feel like a local bar in the boroughs rather than on the bourgeois UES. Prove your dedication to Reif's by drinking there often enough to join the softball or darts teams (because a tattoo that says, "I heart Reif's" is just too much).

Relish
225 Wythe Ave. (N. 3rd St. & Metropolitan Ave.)
Williamsburg 718.963.4546

Don't be fooled by the cute diner shtick. Relish delivers some of the best food and atmosphere in the neighborhood, hands down. Dressed-up classics such as the $9 sirloin burger are delicious, complementing the noteworthy cocktails. The surprisingly swanky joint is always hopping, whether inside or in the back garden, as the decidedly young and foxy clientele drink the night away or nurse their hangovers at the popular weekend brunch. Despite being the cool kid on a block of less appealing choices, Relish lacks an attitude and seems to manage both the locals and the occasional adventurous Upper East Sider with no

problem. The costs are a bit beyond those of a traditional diner, but in this part of town, irony is priceless.

Remedy Bar & Grill
974 2nd Ave. (51st & 52nd Sts.)
Midtown 212.754.0277

Claiming to be "the cure for your mid-week blues," Remedy delivers with just the right combination of sleekness and comfort. Locals come for the best happy hour in the neighborhood (starting at 5pm, drafts and margaritas are $4), exceptional bar food (especially the sirloin burger), specials like Wednesday night's $5 martinis and $6 burgers, a decent jukebox, and sports on TV. Thursday is Ladies' Night; from 5pm-9pm ladies pay only $4 for cosmos, draughts, Bud and Bud Light bottles, or a glass of wine. Guess that makes up for pantyhose and PMS. Remedy is great if you're sick of the hum-drum of Midtown.

Remote Lounge
327 Bowery (@ Great Jones St.)
East Village 212.228.0228

This voyeur's dream is probably what people in the 1960s figured 2005 would look like. Now, it's more kitschy than anything, but still worth a look. Desktop machines resembling 1970s IBM prototypes can be found all over both floors of this spacious bar. You should be warned that while you're looking into your monitor, someone's looking back at you...so get that finger out of your nose pronto. Not even Rick Solomon has this many cameras in one place, but the technology here pales in comparison to modern web cams and such. However, the addition of inexpensive drinks takes visitors back to the future and the bartenders are very open to requests. DJs are frequently on hand so while the see-and-be-seen bit is fun, this place would still work just fine if there were simply *Golden Girls* reruns on those screens.

Remy Lounge
104 Greenwich St. (Rector & Carlyle Sts.)
Financial District 212.267.4646

Bring your singles (as in George Washingtons and your unattached friends) and guzzle as many $1 drinks as you can before midnight at this Financial District lounge. Once you've secured a buzz, you'll notice the throbbing music. Then you see the girls. But it's only a flash, because your pupils have to adjust to the blinding darkness that sets the mood inside this play space. Feel your way to the bar, open a tab, and everything will come into focus. Dress for success, though, because it's too loud inside to work your game. The wine selection is unimpressive, so most people come here to drink from the well, dine on upscale bar food (shrimp fajitas, Cuban sandwiches), and dance it off to Top 40, Latin, and hip-hop music.

Republic
37 Union Sq. W. (16th & 17th Sts.)
Flatiron 212.627.7172

One of the few remaining affordable restaurants in Union Square, this bustling noodle house teems with life. Its huge interior is filled with large wooden, picnic table-style tables that are perfect for groups but impractical for an intimate night out. There's often a wait for a sidewalk table, but it's worth it to score one of the best people-watching spots in the city; watch out for the circulating panhandlers, skaters, protestors, or religious fanatics, though. Inside, the bustling hubbub can make conversation difficult, but there's something exciting and very New York about the medley of sights, sounds, and smells. Save your super-private chats for another night and enjoy a refreshing mango martini and a bowl of glass noodles.

Reservoir
70 University Pl. (10th & 11th Sts.)
Greenwich Village 212.475.0770

Don't be fooled by this NYU staple's seedy exterior. It has all the ingredients of a frat bar, but it

Reservior

comes out of the oven resembling a sports bar, more Jets-fan-since-1968 than *Girls Gone Wild*. The jukebox has some range, but sometimes gets stuck in the mid-'90s. Blind Melon plays while the pool table entertains locals who choose from 16 beers on tap. Grab some wings or burgers to go along with your brew and settle in at the long, comfortable bar for some good conversation with a friend or friendly strangers. Where these blue-collar old-timers now live is a good question. The kids in the purple sweatshirts are less of a mystery.

Resto Leon
351 E. 12th St. (1st & 2nd Aves.)
East Village 212.375.8483

If you're dreaming of an afternoon at a quaint Parisian café, but there isn't a chance in hell that you'll be getting any vacation time soon, this French bistro is for you. Out front, genuine Europeans (bred specifically to leisurely smoke and drink coffee, not the substandard American versions that thrive in these parts) nibble on French Provencal cuisine and smoke, smoke, smoke. Inside, the vibe is just as charming with a kitschy, cluttered space, friendly staff, and relaxed atmosphere. Bon vivants of all nationalities lounge at the bar or small tables and enjoy the typical steak and seafood bistro fare or the weekend brunch (both are well-priced for the already-cheap American dollar). So grab an exchange student and some Gauloises and get ready for an afternoon of ex-patriotism.

Revival
129 E. 15th St. (Irving Pl. & 3rd Ave.)
Gramercy 212.253.8061

A good Union Square area bar is neither too cutting-edge nor overly "khaki-fied." Revival unquestionably fits that bill. After-work hours welcome a business-casual set with $3-$4 happy hour pints (4pm-7pm daily) while late nights see a local crowd that includes a few NYU students and sprinklings of Irving Plaza concert-goers (a late-night happy hour runs Sun-Thurs, 11pm-1am). An upstairs lounge/faux-study and backyard garden add to what is essentially a pretty normal neighborhood bar, but one that has the intangibles going its way. There are TVs over the bar, but they're not centerpieces. Thursday's "iPod battles" allow locals to put their stamp on the place by taking turns playing their playlists, and as the event suggests, the 20-something-to-crusty-barfly ratio favors the whippersnappers. Darkened nooks and crannies provide privacy while the main bar is quite lively and generally friendly.

Rhône
63 Gansevoort St. (Greenwich &
Washington Sts.)
Meatpacking District 212.367.8440

Rhône has maintained its status as one of the top spaces in this hyper-hip district. The blue pod-like chairs add a touch of chic to the minimalist décor, and so do the well-groomed patrons. The sophisticated crowd here loves a scene, and the outdoor tables remain the perfect spot to sit back and sip a lychee martini while you dangle your Prada mule from your well-manicured toe. Rhône's interior betrays its warehouse past, with high ceilings and concrete walls, and the DJs warm the atmosphere by spinning hip-hop and house music. As its name alludes, the venue pays as much attention to libations made from grapes as to those shaken, not stirred (the wine list features more than 150 bottles).

Rialto
265 Elizabeth St. (Houston & Prince Sts.)
NoLita 212.334.7900

If Daniel or Bouley are way beyond your paltry paycheck, come to this romantic French-Italian-American bistro. From the dark brown curtains at the entrance and the aged mirror behind the bar to the orange lamps that cast a warm glow onto the cozy tables, Rialto exudes a sultry Parisian ambiance that'll turn any first date into an all-nighter. Cozy up in one of the red booths and seal the deal with a fine vintage of hearty French red or a pitcher of fruity sangria. Feeding each other steamed mussels also helps. If you're in the mood for the hard stuff, try one of their potent coconut or apple martinis, or the Rialto mojito, with fresh mint, lemon Bacardi, and lime juice.

Ribot
780 3rd Ave. (@ 48th St.)
Midtown 212.355.3700

And they're off! Actually, they're quite "on" at this upscale Mediterranean restaurant, which was named after Italy's most storied racing horse. Italian influences run through Ribot's thoroughbred menu, where $16 rock shrimp ravioli pasta sets the pace for $24 roasted lamb chops or $22 glazed baby poussin. Chef Patrick Woodside's desserts are a steal at $8—he was the pastry chef

Ribot

at Windows on the World. With only 50 indoor seats, Ribot calls out to the power-lunch crowd looking to impress clients with a showing of exclusivity. Business turns to pleasure in the form of a comparably sized outdoor terrace where sunset dinners are popular. (There's also a tastefully small bar and lounge for those in-between times.) Boasting more than 500 bottles, Ribot's wine list is anything but limited in size.

Rice Republic
134 N. 6th St. (Bedford Ave. & Berry St.)
Williamsburg 718.218.7889

Sharing a space with Peruvian restaurant Tacu Tacu, these two eateries have one of the loveliest spaces around, with an indoor waterfall and a balcony wrapping around the dining room. The Southeast Asian fare takes few risks (Thai duck salad, flaming snapper), but it's affordable and tasty, making Rice Republic a hit with the struggling artists permeating the area. The menu (including the one for Tacu Tacu), along with a full bar, is available until midnight, and Rice Republic is the perfect pit-stop before a night of indie music at one of the nearby clubs. But if you're looking for some real nourishment, head to nearby Sea or Planet Thailand.

Rise (@ the Ritz-Carlton)
2 West St. (Battery Pl. & West End Ave.)
Financial District 212.344.0800

If you can't afford a room at the Ritz, you can pretend you're staying there by parking your imitation Jimmy Choo-wearing self at the bar on top of this chi-chi hotel. Once you've arrived, you won't be taking in the view of Lady Liberty; you'll likely be more interested in the polished clientele—and some PDA between the financial sector refugees and their leggy secretaries. The atmosphere is sleek, with opaque tones and tons of mirrors, and the prices are pretty steep—spring rolls at $14 and mini-burgers at $25. If you want to impress your arm candy, you can order the $45 lobster or the Hawaiian rib eye-steak, which is sure to thin out your wallet. It's $70.

Riviera Café & Sports Bar
225 W. 4th St. (@ 7th Ave. S.)
West Village 212.929.3250

Riviera Café

Like viewing *Star Wars* on a Sony Watchman, drinking at Riviera has the right attributes, but the setup is less than spectacular. Too few stools and strange placement of the actual bars make grabbing a table pretty necessary in this sports bar, which is one of the only places in town where Red Sox fans can cheer for their team out loud. Plenty of Mets fans can also be found sitting at the bar, where their plate of fries and half-eaten burgers present a bit of an obstacle course to those reaching for their freshly poured pints. There are lots of all-boys bars in the West Village, but here, the patrons aren't on dates, which isn't to say there isn't a fratty, ass-slapping, homoerotic vibe in the air. Outdoor tables make for great summertime people-watching.

Robert Emmett's
694 8th Ave. (@ 44th St.)
Hell's Kitchen 212.302.9999

There are good ol', down-home, scuffed-marks-on-the-bar pubs, and then there are overpriced yet cheap-feeling versions where the music's all wrong, the clientele is too drunk or too dowdy, and, well, it just doesn't feel right. Exhibit A: Robert Emmett's. If you live in the area and are having an affair, this is a good place to meet (and possibly do more at one of the cubicle-like booths) before looking for that last hotel on the square that rents by the hour. Never fear, you won't run into anyone you know here. Somehow the masses haven't fallen for a menu of bar food (plus "international" cuisine) and specialty cocktails like the Sex in the City. There's also a pre-theater kids' menu. How's that for sexy?

Robin des Bois (aka Sherwood Café)

195 Smith St. (Baltic & Warren Sts.)
Carroll Gardens 718.596.1609

Where else can you dine on an open-faced croquet monsieur in "Sherwood Forest" and listen to the Misfits? This relaxed neighborhood spot attracts hipsters and young parents alike with its kitschy, "more is more" approach to decorating. Countless light fixtures (including one made of antlers) dangle from the red-painted tin ceiling, European ad posters cover the walls, and a *Playboy*-themed pinball machine stands next to a worn, chipped Virgin Mary statue. The effect is somehow cozy, which complements the menu of French comfort food (think skirt steak au poivre with potato au gratin) and cocktails like the Lilletini (Absolut Mandarin and Lillet). In the eccentric back garden, groups of friends gather around patio sets and share the Sherwood Special, a rustic cheese and meat plate topped with figs and nuts.

Rock Candy

35 E. 21st St. (Broadway & Park Ave. S.)
Flatiron 212.254.5709

Unwrap Rock Candy, Flatiron's new site for "Page Six" photo ops, and you'll find celebs grooving alongside mortals who haven't been told they're not famous yet. It's one big music video set here, which is perfect for those that practice their moves in a full-length mirror at home, but a nightmare for those that are already "so over" the next hot thing. The club holds two bars staffed with the prototypes for "Bartender Barbie" and "Bartender Ken" and stocked with ingredients to make some of the best—and priciest—specialty cocktails around. Try the Honey Pot with honey vodka, Citronge, and a flaming orange zest ($15), or the Idle Class with Patron Silver, Chambord, peach brandy, and lime juice ($17). On your way out,

grab a piece of candy from the candy bar to eliminate alcohol breath before you try to get Bijou Phillips' digits.

Rock Star Bar

351 Kent Ave. (@ S. 5th St.)
Williamsburg 718.599.1936

At first glance you'll wonder if Rock Star is a dive or a faux-dive. Well, the verdict is in and this true-blue dive bar beneath the Williamsburg Bridge has an oddly country roadhouse feel—more Johnny Cash than Mick Jagger. Boasting a lively pool table, musical acts, and some of New York's most enlightening graffiti in the horror movie-esque ladies' bathroom, Rock Star provides a real venue for folks who are out to get drunk and surly. Even the hipsters seem a little scared of this place—but who's complaining? In the midst of Thai restaurants and luxury apartment buildings in Williamsburg, Rock Star Bar is keeping it real.

Rockwood Music Hall

196 Allen St. (Houston & Stanton Sts.)
Lower East Side 212.477.4155

It's kind of funny that they call this place Rockwood Music Hall, when in fact it's about the size of a closet. What it's not small on is charm. A tiny stage holding a beautiful antique piano sits in the corner of this wood-enshrouded room where wine-bar sensibilities and a folk-rock heart draw local music aficionados for live performances that are reminiscent of the old Living Room scene. And what could be better than live music seven nights a week? How about live music in the afternoon? That's right. On this rapidly developing strip where the East Village meets the Lower East Side, this little joint is doing a bit of a café thing, but with liquor. There isn't a bad seat in the house at Rockwood Music Hall, but on that note, there aren't many seats at all. Arrive early and expect a one-drink minimum.

Rock Candy

Rouge

Rockwood Music Hall

Rocky Sullivan's
129 Lexington Ave. (28th & 29th Sts.)
Murray Hill 212.725.3871

There are so many Irish pubs in this city, some of them just get lost in the shuffle. Luckily, the proprietors of this establishment have figured out clever ways to make this pub stand out by capitalizing on Irish lore and kitsch. Apart from offering enough Guinness too nourish a small village, Rocky's hosts the political humor series "Satire for Sanity" on Tuesdays. On Wednesdays there are literary readings (Frank McCourt and Roddy Doyle have read here) and they offer Irish language classes in their backroom every Tuesday and Wednesday night—and by Irish language we mean Gaelic, not the "git the feck off me back!" stuff you may be used to hearing. But what really has Rocky's patrons doing the jig is their famous (it's NYC's longest-running) Thursday night "Pop Quiz." The live music is nothing to squawk at, either. Rocky's is a drunk (but cultured) Irishman's dream.

Rodeo Bar
375 3rd Ave. (@ 27th St.)
Murray Hill 212.683.6500

Giddy up! This might not be Dubya's idea of a cowboy hangout, but then again, Dubya isn't most New Yorkers' idea of a real cowboy. As the peanut shells covering the floor suggest, Rodeo Bar is the type of place to kick up yer spurs and let it all hang out. The kitschy interior resembles something akin to Dolly Parton's basement—a huge, hairy buffalo hangs over the bar, antique beer signs and a grain silo adorn the walls, a chandelier made of deer antlers lights the front room, and a sticker-covered trailer sits idle opposite the bar. Croon along with the daily live country music offerings and lasso a dish from the standard BBQ/Tex-Mex fare (Texas beef and bean chili, Cowboy Kisses, and desserts like the Fat Elvis).

Rogue
757 6th Ave. (25th & 26th Sts.)
Chelsea 212.242.6434

If the words "after-work bar" conjure the sound of bad music, the feel of sticky vinyl booths on your work clothes, the torture of office banter, or the chance that you might run into your micromanaging boss, try this swanky lounge. Here you can meet up with colleagues in a big, modern space and listen to decent lounge music without feeling like you need to go home and change out of your suit and tie. The wine list is what you might expect from a stuffier establishment, the broad selection of beers will satisfy beer snobs who crave Smithwick's or Blue Moon, and recessed flat TVs appease sports fans. Three suspended metal beams hang in the windows, advertising Rogue as a bar, lounge, and restaurant. Rest assured Rogue measures up.

Rolf's
281 3rd Ave. (@ 22nd St.)
Gramercy 212.477.4750

Though officially a German restaurant, everyone knows Rolf's as a great place to get drunk, especially around Christmas time when drunken patrons sing dirty renditions of holiday carols. ("Rudolph with your 'what' so bright?") From the land that brought us Santa Claus, this elaborately decorated institution always reflects a season: spring/summer brings lush leaves on very real-looking trees, from October to Thanksgiving the décor is Oktoberfest, and from Thanksgiving to the end of January evergreen garlands, wreaths, a mini-town display, and a creepy collection of kewpie dolls beckons a few wise men and maybe even a virgin. When not turning Jesus' birthday into a potty mouth convention, Rolf's features a large menu of German beer and food, including potato pancakes and a whole lot of 'wursts.

Romi Restaurant & Lounge
19 Rector St. (@ Washington St.)
Financial District 212.809.1500

Romi is a bi-level playground for the Wall Street set, where financiers evidently go to unwind after work by drinking and talking about, well, work. Two large, antique mirrors hang over the crowded L-shaped bar, and dozens of cocktail napkins litter the floor suggesting that the brokers warming the barstools might have engaged in a mock ticker-tape parade. Amuse yourself by observing how many people accidentally drag around the cocktail napkins stuck to their shoes as they amble drunk-enly around, past the red booths and brown leather ottomans—but that's where the fun ends. Start a tab at Romi's if you're rich, square, and don't feel comfortable having a drink without hearing the phrase "business trip" from at least three people in a one-foot radius.

Rooftop Bar (@ Hotel Metro)
45 W. 35th St. (5th & 6th Aves.)
Midtown 212.279.3535

You don't have to be a big name to access this no-name rooftop terrace, offering urban views and stripped-down booze in the shadow of the Empire State Building. The concrete vistas from this well-tread wooden deck send out-of-towners into a tizzy, oooing and ahhhing, and pointing frantically at LaGuardia-bound airliners that fly by the famous skyscraper looming just overhead. Tourists share their Kodak moments with Midtown desk jockeys who clamber up for after-work imbibing May through September. Despite appearances, the tiny white bar on-deck is well-stocked for basic drinks, and the hospitable bartenders pack a lot of vertigo-inducing punch into the plastic cups. Grab a coveted table or bench to soak up early evening rays while you sip, and as the sun sets, prepare to stand in a long line for one slow elevator back down.

The Room
144 Sullivan St. (Prince & Houston Sts.)
SoHo 212.518.8769

Hey, lovebirds...get a room! The Room is a cozy, candlelit little nook with over 30 wines by the bottle, 10 by the glass, and over a dozen types of beer. Because of its size, the Room is perfect for small group gatherings and even more appropriate for an intimate date. The darkness and wine that flows plentifully are sure to make a date go in the right direction. There's not much room to dance, though, so you'll have to carve out a niche in order to rock what you got to the beat of the bartender/DJ's tunes.

Room 18
18 Spring St. (Elizabeth & Mott Sts.)
NoLita 212.219.2592

At Room 18 you can repose on low couches and sip pricey concoctions like white chocolate martinis served with a kiss—a chocolate one, that is. Like so many of New York's buildings, Room 18 has had a host of former lives. Once an apartment, it's now decked out like a hip friend's stylish pad. The savvy owners managed to conserve its turn-of-the-century roots, including tin ceilings and elegant French windows. For nibbles, try out the eclectic menu of Latin food with a Japanese flair, from duck tortilla heaped with avocado and salsa to spicy crabmeat rolls.

Rope
415 Myrtle Ave. (Clinton & Vanderbilt Sts.)
Clinton Hill 718.522.2899

This naturally hip neighborhood bar has figured out the recipe for attracting a perfectly balanced crowd. Busy but not packed, friendly but not pushy, and cool but not trendy, these elements combine to create an evenly mixed scene of neighborhood regulars, after-work colleagues, friends, and chill bar-hoppers, all of whom fit perfectly in this spare yet cozy space. With a bartender who actually cares how your drink tastes and plush seating, Rope has many assets—and let's not forget the jukebox, which manages to please all with its indie rock, nostalgic pop, and hip-hop selection. Whether you stop by for one of the Sunday night movies or any other night, you'll be happy to tie one on at Rope; provided you're able to spot the signless door adorned only with a sailor's knot.

Rosa Mexicano

1063 1st Ave. (@ 58th St.)
Midtown 212.753.7407

61 Columbus Ave. (61st & 62nd Sts.)
Upper West Side 212.977.7700

Getting into one of these *muy loco* upscale Mexican joints is tougher than crossing the US/Tijuana checkpoint with a Spanish accent, fake passport, and piñata full of weed. Yes, these are popular thresholds with the uptown crowd. Inside Rosa Mexicano's relatively unremarkable bar areas, ravenous diners-in-waiting kill time and brain cells by filling up on pomegranate margaritas ($10) before FINALLY sitting down and shoveling down an avocado orchard's worth of fantastic guacamole, which is made at the table with cilantro, onion, tomatoes, and jalapenos. (As one might imagine, the Columbus Avenue locale draws a stately Lincoln Center crowd while 58th Street sees Midtown office folk.) The swanky but festive décor tells you that this is a ritzy run for the border, and despite what you've heard, your American currency doesn't go very far here.

Rosemary's Greenpoint Tavern

188 Bedford Ave. (N. 7th & N. 6th Sts.)
Williamsburg 718.384.9539

This tavern's working-class clientele bonds with hipster transplants over 32-ounce Styrofoam-cupped "Big Buds" at a meager $3.50. The plain setting is livened with the help of owner Rosemary's private collection of rotating seasonal decorations (and her snowy-white beehive hairdo). See a local laborer swigging beer beside a cuddly teddy bear in a Santa hat at Christmas, or a construction worker hollering at the TV next to a papier-mâché turkey at Thanksgiving. The light-up eagle and 9-11-inspired art hanging from the ceiling and bar provide the non-ironic touches that patrons love. Rosemary won't tolerate any rowdy customers, either. This place has been here long before the hipsters invaded (it's been open for 50 years), and it ain't goin' nowhere.

Rose's Turn

55 Grove St. (Bleecker St. & 7th Ave. S.)
West Village 212.366.5438

And what a turn it is. This cozy West Village piano bar has been entertaining New Yorkers since 1990 and the cabaret space upstairs has been around for almost 50 years. A winning happy hour and nightly live music ensure that every night here is always different. There are cabaret performances on the weekends and if you don't mind the cover plus the two-drink minimum, get ready for a show that will open your eyes and ears to glorious culture "day and night, night and day." Rose's Turn is great if you're looking for an alternative to the usual bar crawl. And yes, you can have your turn too—bring out your inner Judy Garland and Ella Fitzgerald during the week and take the stage at Rose's Turn's open mic.

Rothko

116 Suffolk St. (@ Rivington St.)
Lower East Side 212.475.7088

Mondays are one of the few nights that don't include a cover at this club; could it be because it's hip-hop karaoke night? You tell us. Trying its damnedest to give Pianos a run for its money, Rothko features *SPIN* magazine-worthy acts like the Donnas, Ambulance Ltd., and the Dandy Warhols. Located on a dead-end street, bands and music snobs hang outside to discuss the new Interpol record and examine everyone's outfits. It's the place to see and be seen; just make sure your Converse sneakers are appropriately worn in, and your vintage AC/DC shirt has holes in it—otherwise, you'll look like a poseur. We'll bet you a Rapture CD you can't figure out how to work the sink outside the bathroom.

Round Bar (@ Royalton Hotel)

44 W. 44th St. (5th & 6th Aves.)
Midtown 212.944.8844

With a wine selection fit for the high-class, the

Round Bar at the Royalton Hotel spins you right round, right round with its cozy, intimate vibe. And once you discover the posh prices, you'll soon realize that you're paying dearly for the atmosphere. Tiny round tables and square leather chairs are ensconced by ceiling-high, curved, leather walls atop M.C. Escher-like checkerboard floors. The service is slow considering the lack of customers and the bartenders have been known to be stingy on the pour, but at these prices, you'll be sucking the ice cubes in your empty glass just to buy some time.

Route 85a
85 Ave. A (5th & 6th Sts.)
East Village 212.673.1775

Navigate a flight of stairs and you'll find yourself in Route 85a's subterranean confines. Favoring what works over the road less traveled, Route 85a falls into the pseudo-lounge genre, which means it has red lighting, comfy banquettes, and charges $5 for a Bud Light, though a TV and a license plate-heavy décor scream "neighborhood bar." DJs play everything on the map and drinks put regulars on the road to no good. If tourists give you road rage, avoid Sunday-Wednesday's State Night, where 4-for-2 drink specials await those with a valid ID from a designated state. If you've ever wondered how it must've felt to have been Albert Einstein, swing by on Alabama Night.

Roxy
515 W. 18th St. (10th & 11th Aves.)
Chelsea 212.645.5157

When it comes to gay institutions, Roxy ranks right up there with Liza and Cher. Every Saturday night, the main dance floor morphs into a sea of skin as shirtless Chelsea boys bump and grind to hard techno/house sounds. Meanwhile, those who keep their wife-beaters on can also be found grooving to pop music upstairs, where—ready for this?—they play TONS of Madonna. If this doesn't entice you, then perhaps $1 drinks from 11pm to 12pm will. "But I'm not gay," you say to yourself. Don't worry—Roxy has a night for straight people, too, although nothing's gayer than roller skating to disco on Wednesday nights. And nothing's more fun than "accidentally" crashing into someone you like in a roller rink.

Royal Oak
594 Union Ave. (@ Richardson St.)
Williamsburg 718.388.3884

Royal Oak

An oasis in the middle of an industrial desert, Royal Oak is a step back in time. Its interior is reminiscent of an early speakeasy, with plush, mahogany leather booths, velvet wallpaper, a secretive backroom, and dark wood accents. The lengthy tiled bar holds an impressive array of liquors, reflected in the full-length mirror that gives the room added dimension. Draft beers are crowned with ceramic characters: a unicorn, a soldier, and a vampiress to name a few. The only thing that keeps Royal Oak visitors rooted in the modern age is a fine rotation of cool indie tunes, an über-hipster crowd, and of course, beer specials—don't miss the lil' $5 Miller High Life Pony and shot specials. Giddy-up!

Ruby Falls
609 W. 29th St. (11th & 12th Aves.)
Chelsea 212.643.6464

Ruby Falls

Once an overdone club trying to squeeze in all of the latest nightlife gimmicks, Ruby Falls has mellowed into a cool spot to play at on a Saturday night. The music is upbeat and the quirky disco lights manage to provide a funky atmosphere without the laser lightshow headache. The expansive skylight and occasional art exhibits add a nod to class. The crowd and staff have less 'tude and more clothing than most competing clubs of the same size. However, ladies beware—it's still a sausage fest, so the crowd will likely include a few button-up shirts consuming Long Island Iced Teas. The best perk is that the scantily clad professional dancers have taken a backseat so amateur club-goers can shake their assets on the various platforms.

Ruby Foo's Times Square
1626 Broadway (@ 49th St.)
Midtown 212.489.5600

Perhaps the best known of Steve Hanson's themed mega-restaurants, this dining standard combines sushi and dim sum under one "palace." Complete with a red Asiatic gate, giant fat-bellied character, lacquer details, and generic brushwork décor, Ruby Foo's is an understated Disneyification of the Orient (besides Japanese and Chinese, some Thai standards make an appearance). On the upside, the bar is comfortably discreet and offers fused (if not confused) cocktails like the Ginger Mojito, Sake Blossom, and Opium Martini (from $9 to $12). The service is super-friendly and a refreshingly pleasant surprise for a Times Square attraction. With décor and drinks being on opposite ends of the spectrum, and the tie-breaker coming down to cuisine, Ruby Foo's wins big. This isn't Mr. Chow, but it's not as far from it as the waiting line of tourists might imply.

Ruby Lounge
186 E. 2nd St. (Aves. A & B)
East Village 212.387.9400

OK, so the owners could have come up with a more imaginative name to describe this cozy tapas lounge. Still, it's better to have a lame name than a lame bar. Ruby Lounge, as the name suggests, has red couches and chairs in loungey configurations, and the requisite specialty drink menu includes over 20 cocktails such as Ruby's Caipirinha and the Ruby Haze. The Mediterranean tapas menu features faves like dates stuffed with almonds. And if all that sipping and munching doesn't get you in the mood, perhaps sucking on a long, slim appendage will. Ruby Lounge has a hookah on each table with a tube through which you can suck on over 10 kinds of tobaccos; be prepared to send smoke signals out to some single patrons.

Rubyfruit Bar & Grill
531 Hudson St. (Charles & 10th Sts.)
West Village 212.929.3343

Ask any gray-haired butch which way to Mecca, and chances are she'll point you in the direction of Rubyfruit. This infamous hangout has been around the block AND through the Lincoln Tunnel, and so have its grisly but high-spirited regulars, typically out professionals. Inside Rubyfruit, Applebee's for lesbians goes Art Nouveau, and old-school Madonna plays almost continuously. While the beer selection is nothing to write Ellen about, and martinis will set you back 11 buckaroos, the standard pub grub (compliments of the candlelit restaurant downstairs) generally hovers above par. Favorites include Sappho's Salad ($7) and Debbie's Sizzling Strip ($20), supplying patrons with some much-needed sustenance before slumming at nearby Henrietta's for baby dykes.

Ruby's Tap House
1754 2nd Ave. (91st & 92nd Sts.)
Upper East Side 917.684.6756

Ruby's may be the last great bar on the Upper East Side. Built on the brilliant idea that you can never have enough beer, Ruby's boasts over 25 beers on tap, which basically blows all of the neighboring bars out of the water. And Ruby's has a partnership with Atomic Wings, enabling a most holy matrimony of beer and chicken. The locals are fiercely loyal to this place, but unfortunately it too suffers from Upper East Side-itis, that most unfortunate of maladies that has crippled this neighborhood. It's truly a shame, as there's no more engaging an owner in the neighborhood than Stan, whose gift of gab makes you feel immediately at home.

Rudy's Bar & Grill
627 9th Ave. (44th & 45th Sts.)
Hell's Kitchen 212.974.9169

Rudy's Bar & Grill is the kind of place you walk into, but eventually get carried out of. You might have heard that Rudy's isn't what it used to be (the famous free hot dogs and popcorn aren't always available, since the clientele has expanded from the bikers, teamsters, and shifty-eyed gangsters of yore to include hipsters, grad students, and yes, finance types), but the fact of the matter is, Rudy's is still one of the greatest watering holes in Hell's Kitchen—and that's quite a feat. Marked by a giant waving pig wearing little more than a red sweater and a mischievous grin, Rudy's has a no-frills courtyard and enough cheap beer (just $3 for their house ale, Rudy's Red) and booze to make you as happy as a pig that just escaped the Jimmy Dean factory.

Rue B
188 Ave. B (11th & 12th Sts.)
East Village 212.358.1700

If you're looking for a place to savor amazing food, drinks, and live music, do yourself a favor and head to Avenue B, where you'll find a narrow, sofa-lined space with a New-York-meets-Paris bistro. The bar was opened by Peter DuPre, an actor/bartender who was the advisor to Tom Cruise in the movie *Cocktail*, and the libation menu reflects this adventurous owner's tastes. If jazz is not your thing then come early to grab a delicious panini and a pint. Otherwise, be prepared to soak up some great music, munchies, and a lot of well-mixed booze. Happy hour is every day from 4pm-8pm with every drink at half-price.

Rufus
640 10th Ave. (45th & 46th Sts.)
Hell's Kitchen 212.333.2227

Rufus is the kind of bar you'd expect to find in Brooklyn—it lacks attitude, has a neighborhood feel, and features a killer jukebox and friendly service. Which is why it's nice that you can enjoy this right in Hell's Kitchen. The space is tricked-out in comfy rec room furniture and they serve up a mean key lime martini. Snag a table up front if you can; otherwise, grab a stool and chat with locals or the bar staff. And while there's a TV for Yankees game viewing, this understated yet memorable bar feels blessedly little like a sports bar. Drinks are reasonably priced, especially if you hit happy hour ($2 pints and $3 well drinks). Located on the most up-and-coming avenue in Hell's Kitchen, Rufus is one of those places you'll want to discover and then tell no one about, for fear you'll jinx it. Good thing we can keep a secret…oh, whoops.

The Rum House (@ the Edison Hotel)
228 W. 47th St. (Broadway & 8th Ave.)
Midtown 212.869.3005

"Yo, ho, ho, and a bottle of. . ." Well, you know. A whole bottle of rum is exactly what you'll need to enjoy this nautical-themed piano bar off the lobby of the Edison Hotel. The Rum House was surely one of those glamorous, smoke-filled Broadway haunts back in its heyday. But these days, with the smoking ban and the insistence of tourists on wearing sweats to the theater, the bar seems to have lost its charm. Cabaret chanteuse Karen Brown adds a desperately needed touch of class, though, by crooning Sinatra covers and show tunes into the wee hours, while a touristy crowd gathers to listen and gawk at the yellowing array of actor headshots on the wall. Elaine's, it ain't, but there are worse hotel bars in which to sing the blues.

Russian Samovar
256 W. 52nd St. (Broadway & 8th Ave.)
Midtown 212.757.0168

Nicole Kidman, a rabbit, and a lamb walk into a bar…If there's one thing about Russian Samovar, it's that the menu and the restaurant's celebrity guests are no joke. Braised rabbit, marinated leg of lamb, traditional cold borscht, and Norwegian salmon are just some of the impeccable dishes offered at this upscale Mikhail Baryshnikov-owned establishment. Inside the dark, cavernous dining room, patrons listen to the resident pianists while sampling the exotic, buzz-inducing, home-made vodkas (try the horseradish or apple flavors). You always knew the Ruskies did vodka, but who knew they did it this well? Russian Samovar offers a $28 pre-theater dinner and at less than $20 per carafe of vodka, you can challenge your friends to your own space race, and wind up with a tab that won't have you seeing red.

The Russian Vodka Room
265 W. 52nd St. (Broadway & 8th Ave.)
Midtown 212.307.5835

This Midtown anchor has a happy hour that will make you "strong like bear." From 4pm to 7pm, patrons can order any of the Russian Vodka Room's homemade vodkas for a meager three dollars. And these are not ordinary well brands or any paltry drink-it-in-the-bathroom-at-the-prom vodkas. They're strong enough to have kept Lenin embalmed. From horseradish to apple to pomegranate, the Russian Vodka Room has a vodka for every taste. But if you're not looking for a liquid lunch, you can enjoy Russian classic dishes while the pianist in the corner plays a little music for you to relax (and digest) to. The Russian Vodka Room's intimate, windowless interior might lead some to think they're sitting in a Cold War interrogation room, but others will long for the Motherland.

Ryan Maguire's Ale House
28 Cliff St. (Fulton & John Sts.)
Financial District 212.566.6906

The confusing part about this neighborhood pub is that there are two bars named Ryan within a couple of blocks of each other. But this Ryan is closer to the water and located smack-dab in the middle of the circus-like atmosphere of the Seaport. It's an unassuming spot that's bustling during the day with a business lunch crowd. Ryan is also decidedly Irish, right down to the friendly, jocular bartender. The backroom features plenty of seating, drawings of scenes from Olde New York, and porcelain Irish knickknacks protected from greasy fingers by a plate of glass. The jukebox features a generous representation of Irish bands—the Corrs, U2, and the Pogues; but Ryan is a true Irish treat, so it's hard to hold their odd music tastes against them.

Ryan's Daughter
350 E. 85th St. (1st & 2nd Aves.)
Upper East Side 212.628.2613

Congratulations Ryan, it's a bouncing baby bar. It's hard to put your finger on what exactly separates this joint from all the clones in the neighborhood—perhaps it's the placement, positioning itself somewhat off the beaten path on 85th Street, the inexpensive drinks, or the gregariousness of the staff, but one thing's for certain—the mere presence of a second level immediately distinguishes this one from the pack. The bar is generously sized and has a large area in the back where drunkards can hang out and shoot pool. Ryan's is also a favorite of the bar-crawl set and since this is the Upper East Side, these packs even have t-shirts printed up. Then again, if they're that fanatical and they like it here, this place is doing something right.

Ryan's Irish Pub
151 2nd Ave. (9th & 10th Sts.)
East Village 212.979.9511

For good bar food and beer, Ryan's Irish Pub is as good as any place of its kind. While the staff can be curt during busier hours, the burgers are always good and the pints are poured with love. That said, there isn't much that makes Ryan's or its crowd stand out. The place is very dark, and while they do have some outdoor seating, space is limited and the servers can forget it's there. It's a good place to go if you want an uncomplicated night out with friends, and despite the al fresco option, Ryan's is at its best in the winter when locals and NYU students snuggle into booths for a hot toddy or a blood-warming Guinness.

Ryan's Sports Bar & Grill
46 Gold St. (Fulton & John Sts.)
Financial District 212.385.6044

Trends? We don't need no stinkin' trends. Welcome to Ryan's Sports Bar & Grill, where they've turned their backs to the fads. Sometimes all you want is a bar with taps and bottles. They've got that here, and a kitchen to boot. It's quiet and comfortable after work, where you'll see administrative assistants giggling over a pitcher ($9 domestic, $13 imported) and mozzarella sticks ($4.50), as well as the token older guy in the corner with bags under his eyes and a glass of white at his fingers ($3.50). Five TVs hover around the bar, all tuned to the sporting world. The college crowd comes in when the sun goes down and the atmosphere becomes young and frisky. If only your social life could be as simple as Ryan's.

Saga
329 Lexington Ave. (@ 39th St.)
Murray Hill 212.682.8288

Neither bar, restaurant, nor lounge, but a little of all three, Saga combines a huge range of drink specials with a lengthy menu for a genuine nightlife event. Peopled mostly with 30- to 40-somethings, presumably from this higher-rent neighborhood, the barroom and dining room exhibit a design marrying shadows with dark earth tones. Dirt-cheap prix-fixe meals beckon those who might think they're in over their heads: $13 and you're set. Higher-end seafood and steak dishes ($15-$25) round out the entrées, with a range of finger foods on the shorter bar menu. The house's Sagatinis—very fruity martinis—are

popular. Twenty-somethings on the prowl for a sugar daddy are going to strike gold at Saga.

Sake Bar Satsko
202 E. 7th St. (Aves. B & C)
East Village 212.614.0933

Sake Bar Satsko

The ancient art of sake-making is honored in this petite (blink and you'll miss it) East Village bar. With over 40 sakes for the sampling, including the house special, "made from the pure waters of the Sierra Nevada," Shochikubai, this can be a learning experience, albeit one you're unlikely to remember if you do it right. Other drink choices are a little limited; a handful of bottled beers accompany a menu of Pan-Asian fusion dishes. Space is at a minimum in this kitschy '60s-esque den and you might end up knowing more about your neighbors than you'd intended. Luckily, the crowd tends to be friendly and somewhat interesting in this far-flung corner of the city.

Sake Hana
265 E. 78th St. (2nd & 3rd Aves.)
Upper East Side 212.327.0582

Somewhere between Sushi Samba and that half-priced sushi place on Avenue A rests the perfect sushi bar—Sake Hana, who, along with its sober twin Sushi Hana, will soon dominate the Upper East Side with its romantic décor and specialty rolls like the Dragon. Despite the surrounding competition, this bar lures in the local crowd with its lychee blossom martinis and sake sours. Even if sake isn't your thing, there's no excuse for passing up this honey of a *hana*. Add a 12-ounce Sapporo to your sushi roll or not-so-shrimpy shumai, and you'll see why Sake Hana is the next big thing. Just don't show up dressed like Gwen Stefani's crew of Harajuku girls—this is still the Upper East Side, you know.

Sala
344 Bowery (@ Great Jones St.)
NoHo 212.979.6606

Named for the Spanish word for "living room," this sexy downtown tapas bar and restaurant looks quiet on the outside, but inside the fiesta always seems like it's been going strong all night long. Sala is sure to turn you on to the European style of enjoying nightlife—that is, arriving late and staying late, and eating, drinking, and dancing until you collapse. The rustic décor (a brick archway, tiled ceiling, and antique-looking lanterns) gives Sala its sexy vibe and the food—seafood paella, fried goat cheese—is delectable enough to put you in the mood. Patrons who book the private party room downstairs are likely to stay there almost until the sun comes up. After a few too many glasses of sangria, you'll want to too.

Salon
505 West St. (@ Jane St.)
West Village 212.929.4303

Oh, how we long for the good old days. Pairing a stylish 1920s décor with modern sensibilities, this two-story newbie starts with a dining room swathed in warm orange tones, velvety wrap-around banquettes, and paintings depicting Weimar Germany. Flavorful dishes can be enjoyed in these swanky confines or at the outdoor tables. Cocktails like the Salon Kitty (Grey Goose, fresh raspberries, and ginger beer) are best sipped at the bar. Upstairs, a large room decked out in black-and-white tile opens for private parties and late-night lounging. Salon is going for the exclusive thing, and being this far west and unheralded, they just might get more of that than they want.

Saloon
1584 York Ave. (83rd & 84th Sts.)
Upper East Side 212.570.5454

Saloon bills itself as "the best of both worlds," due to its split club/pub personality. Well, they're half right. While it certainly delivers on the "both worlds" claim with separate bar and club spaces, they're slacking a bit in the "best" department. Really, what you get is more of a watered-down version of each. At the same time there's plenty of beer, booze, and youngsters to party with in the pub or on the seriously large (and often rocking) dance floor that's usually filled to the gills. Decent for happy hour and beyond, though, Saloon solves the dilemma of the friend who hates clubs and the friend who hates bars; park one in each room and you can dance if you want to, without leaving your friends behind.

Salt Bar
29 Clinton St. (Houston & Stanton Sts.)
Lower East Side 212.979.8471

When did the base price of an entrée at an LES joint start around $17.50? Luckily, Salt Bar is more about drinks than food; because what you're really paying for is the clean-lined, sophisticated ambiance (dark-stained communal tables are off-set by lemon yellow walls and candlelight) that's apparently become the neighborhood standard. A mid-sized space offering a tiny bit of everything (a romantic table-for-two section, a tiny window-seat lounging area, and even an itty-bitty, easily overlooked open-air kitchen that abuts the bar), Salt Bar fits a broad range of evening agendas. There's even a long, German beer garden-style table for those looking to make friends with the sassy and chic patrons next to them. A stylish staff makes drinking here a pleasure, and a sweet wine list leads to delectable possibilities.

Sambuca
20 W. 72nd St. (Central Park W. &
Columbus Ave.)
Upper West Side 212.787.5656

A popular destination for large groups and families, this Southern Italian eatery is reminiscent of that one restaurant in your average small town that all the locals go to celebrate proms, graduations, birthdays, and everything in between. Everyone comes a bit dressed up to enjoy Sambuca's dinner entrées (priced in the $20-$25 range) in the spacious front dining area with its large circular tables. There's a soft ambiance at Sambuca that could also be appropriate for a date, though. In the back, a smaller room (with atrium seating) offers additional flexibility for larger parties and outdoor dining. There's a bar too, if you'd like to order some licorice-flavored liqueur; but this Sambuca is less chug-from-the-bottle-in-your-dorm-room and more long-black-skirt-and-pressed-white-blouse-family-reunion.

San Marcos
12 St. Marks Pl. (2nd & 3rd Aves.)
East Village 212.995.8400

The slap-dash, Tex-Mex décor that lines the walls of this restaurant would do just as well were it left in the cookie-cutter Southwestern design book it was ordered from. Aside from the uninspired tidbits—desert animal skulls and faux cacti—the room's bring-your-own-party vibe is welcoming, and the staff is perennially chipper. Even better news for NYU students and Village regulars: The prices are well within reason. You're sure to get sloshed on cheap pints of any of the 16 tap beers or fruity frozen margaritas, which are perfect for washing down the nearly foot-long burritos or pile of Nachos San Marcos. Patrons gather out in the smoker-friendly sidewalk café to chat and snicker at passersby who are sadly sans margarita. (Get 2-for-1 drinks during the daily happy hour, 3pm-7pm.)

Sandia
111 W. 17th St. (6th & 7th Aves.)
Chelsea 212.627.3700

Spanish for watermelon, this restaurant/lounge

Sandia

combo fuses Latin and Asian cuisine. As you step down into Sandia, you'll walk into a world of color—fuchsia walls line the narrow restaurant while the lounge in the front is cradled by windows that open onto the street. Start off with a watermelon martini—their signature drink—then move on to their unique cuisine. Each dish merges Latin and Asian ingredients, creating a spicy tuna roll in a crispy plantain ($11) and grilled churrasco over green rice in a tangy peanut sauce ($22). Every Wednesday night there is a live Latin jazz band (no cover) and every night the bar and lounge stays open late, serving off their tapas menu for a late-night treat. So cha-cha over and check out Sandia.

Santa Fe
73 W. 71st St. (Columbus Ave. & Central Park W.)
Upper West Side 212.724.0822

Formerly located on 69th Street, this neighborhood staple has been going strong in its new location. More of a restaurant than a bar, Santa Fe features a fairly exhaustive menu that goes beyond mere Mexican, with a number of seafood entrées and a few special creations like the black bean and sweet potato burrito or the nacho pizza. Lunch can be had for eight bucks and under, but dinner gets pricier, with entrées ranging up to around $20. The welcoming dining room, while sparsely

Sapa

furnished, is decorated in warm Southwestern colors, and the prominently featured bar is well-stocked. And while the food has the kick to beat out most poseur Mexican restaurants in the city, Santa Fe doesn't have half the personality of that Chihuahua from those Taco Bell commercials.

Sapa
43 W. 24th St. (Broadway & 6th Ave.)
Flatiron 212.929.1800

Despite being sandwiched between two nightclubs (Select and Gypsy Tea), this modern bistro/brasserie/dojo might be the nicest-looking place on the block. In the vein of scenester eateries like One, Sapa is a very fashionable way to start the evening, and with its diffused interior of soft white tones, tall plants, and decorative pools surrounded by stones, this space could almost double as a day spa. Sapa's front half is split between a formal dining room, a roll bar, and a long cocktail bar from which visitors can spy into the immaculate kitchen. Behind a subtle divider is a hipper dining space, which is where the pre-club set prefers to hold court. Equaling the impressive aesthetic is a French/Vietnamese menu where cultures are merged in the form of moderately priced appetizers and entrées. On Sundays and

Mondays, bottles of wine are half-off. Put on your beret, take off your shoes, and let these folks *aimer vous* long time.

Sapphire Lounge
249 Eldridge St. (Houston & Stanton Sts.)
Lower East Side 212.777.5153

Finding a space to dance in this city without fielding a painful $30 cover charge or angry Cabaret Law Police is becoming a perennial problem in this city. Luckily, this itty-bitty (though thankfully well-ventilated) club comes to the rescue with a mere $5 cover (after 10:30pm), a surprisingly diverse crowd, and an overwhelming excitement for dancing amongst its patrons, whether they're good at it (the majority) or not (a cheerful and lovable minority). The house/hip-hop music mix gives Sapphire Lounge a more notable bootylicious repetition than most other joints, too. Sneak off to the (nearly) secret room to rest, gossip, or get some. During Sapphire's new Girl Meets Boy party, ladies drink free all night long with a cover.

Sasha's
255 W. 55th St. (Broadway & 8th Ave.)
Midtown 212.265.5555

Fellow comrades, if what you crave is a great Russian nightlife experience, then head to where all the other Ruskies go—Brooklyn. Sure, the staff at this Midtown bar is Russian, but you get the feeling that the only patrons from the Motherland are Russian Manhattanites too lazy or snobby to emigrate from the island for a night. "Dress Sexy, Be Sexy," instructs a promotion for Sasha's Sunday night party. But for whom? Strangely enough, the women so greatly outnumber the men here that you'd think you walked into a lipstick lesbian bar. In the end, it seems the most Russian thing you can do here is order a vodka shot. This is definitely one Russian joint you should be rushin' out of.

Satalla
37 W. 26th St. (Broadway & 6th Ave.)
Flatiron 212.576.1155

As kind to its patrons as it is to the huge range of musicians who cross its stage, Satalla is a monument to inclusiveness. The house specialty is world music—all the genres excluded from most rock venues. That goes for everything from bluegrass to Latin hip-hop to Irish music and straight-up American blues. Settled into a large orange room, Satalla's stage dominates one wall with tables spanning outward on two levels. Come for the tunes, but stay for some food; the menu goes in a few different directions, but sticks mostly to American dishes. The one-drink minimum charge can go towards one of the house specialty drinks, all of them enticing fruity concoctions. Think of Satalla as post-collegiate diversity training, with better booze and a very savvy music booker.

Satelite
505 E. 6th St. (Aves. A & B)
East Village 917.941.7023

Why do they spell Satelite with only one "l"? Because the owner thought it looked funny with two. That's the way this quirky little spot operates. A small stage offers small bands an opportunity to try new stuff on open mic Tuesdays and Wednesdays. There are only four beers on tap here, but at $3-$5 a pint, it's tough to be picky. A subtle celestial décor hints of a theme, but despite the few colorful planets painted onto the walls, this is a neighborly, down-to-earth, no-frills bar where locals get together, play pool, and sometimes become regulars.

Savalas
285 Bedford Ave. (Grand & S. 1st Sts.)
Williamsburg 718.599.5565

Savalas

A sleek lounge among South Williamsburg's dives, Savalas is asking sophisticated locals "Who loves ya, baby?" Cross-sectioned logs make up one wooden wall, exposed brick another, and a groovy geometrical diamond-print trademark is ubiquitously emblazoned throughout the wallpaper, cutout hanging lanterns, mod wall sconces, coasters, and even on event flyers. The flattering red lighting and discreet dance floor in the back melt away inhibitions at this DJ-driven bar. Let Chaka Khan tell you something good on disco night and come back for hard rock 24 hours later. Held every other Thursday, Rio Deal goes way south of the border with '70s soul, samba, and Brazilian funk. Best of all, there's no cover charge, which leaves extra cash for the already reasonably priced cocktails and beer.

Savoy
70 Prince St. (@ Crosby St.)
SoHo 212.219.8570

Straighten your collar and wipe your nose, junior—Savoy is a place of refinement. The fresh flowers and exquisite décor immediately declare that this bar is for those who are looking to savor their drinks. In its tiny nook on the corner of Crosby Street, Savoy is primarily thought of as a restaurant, but the small slate bar offers a perfect place to perch, if you're planning on behaving yourself. Green olives and taro chips are complimentary with your cocktail of choice, and though the hostess might sneer, the polished bartenders warm up to even the dreggiest of folks as they describe in detail the tannins and faint undertones of the wines you're sampling.

Scenic
25 Ave. B (2nd & 3rd Sts.)
East Village 212.253.2595

Is it odd that a club called "Scenic" would be a revolutionary sonic venue? Perhaps, but any way you look at it, this is a spot to behold. Formerly the infamous Save the Robots, then Guernica, this bi-level venue has it all. Still upset about Brownie's closing? Cry no more. Downstairs, a stage and a DJ booth pump rock-oriented tunes through a raging sound system. Upstairs, the bar area is a little more geared towards just hanging out, but there is comfort and continuity throughout. Scenic's kitchen doubles as an outpost for the East Village's The Burger Joint, where the priciest item on the menu is a $2.50 double cheeseburger. Cover downstairs goes from $5-$20, beer ranges from $3-$6, and we suggest the Colt 45 32-ouncer. (Billy Dee Williams seconds that notion.)

Schiller's Liquor Bar
131 Rivington St. (@ Norfolk St.)
Lower East Side 212.260.4555

This place is so hoppin', you'd think drinking just

Schiller's Liquor Bar

became legal and it was the only place open for miles. That's exactly the effect owner Keith McNally (Balthazar and Pastis) was aiming for when he opened this post-Prohibition-style bar and restaurant. The yellow-hued back lighting, set against black-and-white tiles, antiqued mirrors, and stainless-steel accents make you feel like you've stepped into a glamorous era of days gone by. Getting to the bar is no easy feat, mind you; you'll have to push your way past the stylish diners and wait staff, and then find an open crevice of this perpetually packed bar to stand in—but the clever lighting design will make you feel hot and sexy once you get there.

Scopa
79 Madison Ave. (28th & 29th Sts.)
Murray Hill 212.686.8787

This swanky lounge will sweep you away with its beautiful 140-foot bar, delicious food, and delectable drinks. The seafood-focused menu has reasonably priced Northern Italian food, including grilled pizzas, crispy calamari, and lobster ceviche. Tables situated by tall windows overlooking Madison Avenue allow for plenty of the timeless NYC pastime of people-watching while you drink and dine. Happy hour is daily (from 5pm-7pm), and so is the live music. Impress your date with the expensive-looking, artfully presented, yet reasonably priced food. Thursdays bring a DJ and crowds, so get there early to claim your spot at the bar. You can also have a swanky soiree in this intimate setting of gaudy Italian art and embellishments (gold fixtures, anyone?).

The Scratcher
209 E. 5th St. (2nd Ave. & Bowery)
East Village 212.477.0030

This cozy subterranean hangout is decorated with minimalist strands of lights and wooden tables with benches to facilitate a communal drinking experience...and possibly a hookup. Locals flock here on weekdays for inexpensive drinks in the company of fellow East Villagers. Weekends bring throngs of uptowners seeking refuge from the velvet-roped lounges on the Bowery who get down on it with '80s tunes. While there's no food served at night, on weekends you can enjoy the coveted hearty, traditional Irish fried breakfast (known in the homeland as "Fry"—eggs, beans, Irish bacon, toast, and pudding) with fellow Irishmen and anyone else who enjoys a Guinness in the morning. And who doesn't? Few would dare contend the wisdom of the aging "Guinness is Good for You" sign hanging inside the bar.

Scruffy Duffy's
743 8th Ave. (46th & 47th Sts.)
Hell's Kitchen 212.245.9126

Scruffy Duffy's

This Hell's Kitchen spot is sort of like the love child of a sports bar and an Irish pub. The décor consists of several large-screen TVs broadcasting ESPN, nostalgic photographs, street signs, and an oddly placed moose head jutting from the wall. The clientele is largely male, and not surprisingly, a bit scruffy. In fact, the décor suggests that the owners (it's a family business) probably look back on the old, less-sanitized version of Times Square with some fondness. However, the scruffiness doesn't descend into sketchiness here and everyone is relaxed, friendly, and ready to play a game of pool or darts. During "Matsui Madness," Scruffy's promises to buy everyone in the bar a drink if Hideki or Kazuo Matsui hits a homer; now how's that for bringing rival fans together?

Sea Thai Bistro
114 N. 6th St. (@ Berry St.)
Williamsburg 718.384.8850

Sea's ultra-modern interior was featured in one of the opening scenes in cult flick *Garden State*. It was supposed to be set in LA, which makes sense because Sea is the clubbiest destination in Williamsburg—without being a club. The drink menu offers some interesting choices (mint tequila gimlet, passion fruit saketini, pomegranate mojito), but it would be a sin not to chow down on the cheap but yummy Thai food (Drunk Man's Noodles, for one). Try to grab a wooden art-deco table for two beside the trademark reflecting pool for maximum Zen effect. Sea offers many distractions while you wait for a table (and you will wait)—you can hang in the glass egg-shaped chair or sit on the white pea pod-like seats surrounding the DJ booth.

Seaport Café
89 South St. (@ Pier 17)
Financial District 212.964.1120

This outdoor eatery is the kind of place where tourists flock, convinced they're getting a big, thick slab of genuine New York. It's also the type of place where fanny-packers are sure to whip out a video camera in order to document the experience of eating burgers with their friends. Situated right on Pier 17, the Seaport Café could be a decent place to wile away a summer afternoon in the sun (live music is occasionally featured nearby), if it weren't for the grating sounds of parents yelling at their kids to stand up straight while they wind their disposable cameras. Breezes coming off the East River and surprisingly affordable ($5) drinks are pluses, though, and the view of ships against the Financial District backdrop is surreally picturesque.

Second Nature
221 2nd Ave. (13th & 14th Sts.)
East Village 212.254.2222

Second Nature might seem like just another late-night beehive of primped singles set up on the street to annoy partiers on their way to grimier, more down-to-earth East Village haunts. But there's a good reason why they're waiting to party in this loungey bar: There's plenty of space, with private rooms available for reservations, an area in the back for billiards, and a lengthy bar in the front room. Come by and enjoy $8 specialty cocktails or bottle service, and soak up the tunes and the Warhol-ish paintings on the walls. And guys, get your wallets ready—there's a $10 cover for males. Just the way nature intended.

Second on Second
27 2nd Ave. (1st & 2nd Sts.)
East Village 212.473.2922

With the influx of karaoke joints taking over the city, you'd think one of them would catch a case of *American Idol*-itis and host a karaoke contest. Luckily for competitive Kelly Clarkson wannabes, this bar/karaoke lounge offers just that. Catering to a crowd of trendy 20-somethings, Second on Second specializes in the art of wielding a microphone while drunkenly trying to read lyrics, with a large TV screen commanding more attention than the diva-like singers and an enormous selection of over 30,000 songs from Depeche Mode to Bollywood ballads. Cheap beer soothes throats stretched by attempting Whitney Houston's high notes, while the food is a Thai version of pub fare, with greasy pot stickers and spring rolls. Don't arrive too early, though; the troubadours can be a pretty hapless lot before everyone's had enough to drink.

Select
49 W. 24th St. (5th & 6th Aves.)
Flatiron 212.255.9200

On a block full of instant hotspot nightclubs, Select holds its own. Decorated with large stained-glass

Select

windows, arched ceilings, and red everything, this Steve Lewis-designed Vatican-meets-strip-club room "selects" a rowdy weekend crowd that dances the night away. The DJ sits in a booth above the crowd spinning dance tracks while the beautiful people lounge in luxe booths enjoying bottle service. Regular folks should double-fist it at the bar, as the wait for a drink can be a bit long. Lacking the pretension of other area clubs, Select is the place to choose if you're hungry for a taste of the high life. Those with some cash to spend might want to request seating in the elevated VIP area, as it offers a godly cathedral altar appeal. A dress code is in effect here.

Señor Swanky's
513 Columbus Ave. (84th & 85th Sts.)
Upper West Side 212.579.2900

Perhaps you witnessed the collars-and-khakis crowd doing the Macarena up Columbus when this abysmal Mexican-themed lounge relocated 11

blocks north. Its other unfortunate following is the collection of celebrity photographs onto which the smiling Señor himself has been superimposed, a narcissistic touch that surprisingly hasn't yet been tacked to the dartboard in the corner. By far the most inspiring feature of this so-called speakeasy is the assemblage of fake chili peppers over the bar. Luckily, Swanky's chipper wait staff, daily happy hour specials (4pm-7pm, 10pm-close), and endless supply of tortilla chips (beware the salsa) may reconcile some cranky patrons to their less than *bueno* surroundings. And with 26 tequilas on offer and an astonishingly decent wine list, even the most embittered drinkers may find themselves shouting, "Ole!"

Serafina

393 Lafayette St. (@ 4th St.)
NoHo 212.995.8442

If there were such a thing as a chain lounge, the stale Serafina would be it. Mired in a manufactured vibe that attracts, not surprisingly, loud crowds of tourists, this deceptively named lounge is the anomaly to the arty, sophisticated vibe of its locale. As the night marches on, the B&T brigade gets increasingly lubricated and even more annoying, letting out giddy hoots to deafening house and '80s tunes, giving the tourists something to tell the folks back home about ("Another crazy night in the Big Apple!"). Serafina is palatable if you arrive early enough to enjoy the simple, hearty, and relatively inexpensive Italian fare before the masses descend. Savor your meal and then escape to a bona-fide lounge, which is anywhere but here.

Serena

222 W. 23rd St. (7th & 8th Aves.)
Chelsea 212.255.4646

Whether you're a fan of the Sex Pistols or Leonard Cohen, Arthur Miller, or Arthur C. Clarke, chances are you've already made the pilgrimage to the Chelsea Hotel. But you might have missed the discreet sign for Serena on the iron steps that lead down under the hotel. Make a point of going back and descending, and you won't regret it. You'll discover a crypt-like series of rooms connecting a candlelit bar to quiet pillowed nooks—and the most attractive staff in the city. Of course, that might just be the lychee martinis talking, or an optical illusion caused by Serena's sultry semi-darkness: This lounge smolders with seductiveness, thanks to a red glow of Moroccan lanterns and maroonish walls. In fact, it might be said there's never been a room in this building so bathed in crimson since Nancy Spungen checked out upstairs.

Session 73

1359 1st Ave. (@ 73rd St.)
Upper East Side 212.517.4445

If you thought all UES bars were filled with chest-baring, shot-guzzling Tara Reid-types (though she has been spotted here), you'll be pleasantly surprised by the fun, down-to-earth crowd and impeccable bar service at Session 73. There's usually a band playing the main bar area, and surprisingly enough, there is no cover charge. Nuzzle up to the bartender while seated atop one of countless stools in the polished-looking front room. Sunday night is Tango Night, so the beautiful parquet floor fills quickly. But if you don't like your toes getting stepped on, sink into one of the comfy couches and watch the action from afar, while you sip a chardonnay and dine on tapas or Asian or Nuevo Latin dishes. Session 73 is a hip, uptown bar with an easy-going, downtown feel. Finally!

7B

108 Ave. B (@ 7th St.)
East Village 212.473.8840

You know that old man on the corner who seems disoriented and damaged, but when forced into a conversation, is actually lucid and charming? He follows the Yankees, sees what's "hip," and knows everybody. Welcome to 7B, the East Village's grandfather, who, at 21 years old, has wild tales it'll never share. Also known as Horseshoe Bar, 7B's u-shaped bar offers Natty Light in a can ($4) and 26 drafts in a glass ($3.25-$6). As for the crowd, there's a group in the corner who probably inspired an episode of *The Sopranos*, while a pair

17

of punks canoodle at the bar as the Polo-clad loner waits for his friends. An old jukebox plays Guided by Voices and other smart rock and the bartenders have beef jerky and chips at their fingertips.

17
37 W. 17th St. (5th & 6th Aves.)
Flatiron 212.924.8676

One of the first clubs to spice up the Flatiron District, which has turned into a mini Meatpacking District over the last year or so, 17 is a party palace for those who can sneak past the velvet rope. The space begins with a narrow entrance-way leading to a crowded bar, with two levels of banquettes further back. DJs spin for these party-minded, designer jean-wearing pretty people, who aren't opposed to shaking a little booty now and then. Though the area's influx of nightclubs has dampened 17's hip factor, specialty parties like Sultry Thursdays still draw a crowd. Whether they stay here or move on to Gypsy Tea, Select, Prey, Duvet, etc., is another matter.

17 Home
17 Stanton St. (Bowery & Chrystie St.)
Lower East Side 212.598.2145

The entrance to 17 Home offers possibilities, but the backroom feels sterile with its mono-white interior and tall, padded, box-like booths warmed by yellow candlelight. It's dark downstairs and broken up into separate rooms that provide ample nooks and crannies for various "activities" of a private nature. A standard assortment of cocktails (including the sour raspberry martini), beer, and wine is delivered by a friendly wait staff for around $7 a pop. The clientele mimic the bar in that they are both nicely accessorized, but not terribly note-worthy. Neither terribly warm nor pretentious, 17 Home is a safe bet when attempting to please new acquaintances or a group with varying tastes.

17 Murray
17 Murray St. (Church St. & Broadway)
TriBeCa 212.608.3900

Before its current tenure, 17 Murray was former New York Met Ron Darling's vanity project, Legends. Now it's just a whitewashed dining room with a bar. Distinctive as a Holiday Inn lobby and about as well-decorated, it's no surprise owner-ship couldn't think of a name for this faceless pocket of downtown. A conservatively dressed wait staff serves from a menu of burgers, hero sandwiches, and a few shrimp dishes on the glitzi-er end. Food runs about $8-$16 and drinks go for $5-$7. The crowd is older, and as buttoned-down as anything about the place; you won't meet the love of your life, but you may run into your accountant. What does make sense about 17 Murray is that it closes on weekends, wrapping up by 11pm with plenty of time for the Westchester commute.

Shades of Green
125 E. 15th St. (Irving Pl. & 3rd Ave.)
Gramercy 212.674.1394

You'll be green with envy if you don't stop by this friendly neighborhood bar. A casual pub for Irish ex-pats, Irving Plaza-goers, and locals, Shades of Green has been serving up Guinness and fish and chips for over 15 years. Décor is a veritable Irish wallpaper, with posters of the Emerald Isle on the walls and pictures of famous Irish folk that look upon the bar, plus the dining room's plush leather booths. Despite tourists who are in the 'hood to see a show, there is a staunch group of regulars who are surprisingly welcoming, and will tell you stories about when seedy tramps inhabited this space. If you drink too much you'll be okay: There's a guest house upstairs.

Shadow
229 W. 28th St. (7th & 8th Aves.)
Chelsea 212.629.3331

Unlike some more pretentious dance venues, Shadow is a dark, sweaty, straight-up club where grown men and women can get their grooves on. The door policy is strictly "No Scrubs"; guests must be at least 23, and no blue jeans, sneakers, or other offending clothing items are allowed (so leave your Flava Flav clock necklace at home). The large dance floor is always packed with patrons enjoying old- and new-school hip-hop and R&B jams, and it can get hot and heavy in the smaller reggae room, where beats drive serious bump-and-grind action. Strictly for weekend warriors (and wannabes), Shadow is open Thursday-Saturday nights only; singles nights and special nights featuring special guest stars like Salt 'n' Pepa's diva of a DJ, Spinderella, are not to be missed.

Shag
11 Abingdon Sq. (Bleecker & 12th Sts.)
West Village 212.242.0220

Are you horny, baby? Fancy a Shag? Nestled somewhere between the ubiquitous van-lining carpet that lines the walls here and Jon Bon Jovi's haircut, this Shag also happens to fall somewhere between a dive and a lounge. A mostly 20-something crowd indulges in tasty drinks (try the lime daiquiri) and campy food selections (munch on the "Almost Corner Bistro Mini Burgers") at this kitschy West Village joint. The bright ultra-white décor and orange S-shaped chairs exude '60s chic; however, it contrasts heavily with the Top 40 tunes being pumped over the speakers, sometimes giving the space an awkwardness comparable to a 1990 Camaro blasting Mendelssohn's "Piano Concerto No. 1" at a red light. And, like a Camaro, leg room inside Shag is limited, so call ahead if you plan on bringing a crowd.

Shalel Lounge
65 1/2 W. 70th St. (Central Park W. &
Columbus Ave.)
Upper West Side 212.873.2300

Easy to miss if you're not looking for it, this subterranean lounge is something like an exotic oasis among the UWS's painfully ordinary neighborhood watering holes. Shalel's stone and brick interior appears as though it was carved out of the earth and when combined with the dim, candlelit room and nook-and-cranny floor layout, the bar feels like a small old-world catacomb. Of course, it's the kind of old-world catacomb where drinks and appetizers are served while a Middle Eastern techno soundtrack plays in the background. This alcove is sufficiently isolated as is, but those needing extra, extra privacy can move into one of the semi-private rooms, including a "honeymoon suite" which features a trickling waterfall.

The Shark Bar Restaurant
307 Amsterdam Ave. (74th & 75th Sts.)
Upper West Side 212.874.8500

Officially called the Shark Bar Restaurant (not to be confused with the Spring Street Lounge, which is often called the "Shark Bar" due to the large, stuffed toothy one hanging on its wall), this Southern-style bar/restaurant hasn't got much bite. The interior looks oddly neglected and half-finished—empty shelves line the walls and there's plenty of space where no imagination has been applied. There are no beers on tap, either, but the soul, Southern, Creole, and Cajun-style dishes coming from the kitchen lure in people hungry for Georgia Bank catfish strips, seafood okra gumbo, or sweet potato pie. But if you're hungry for soul food that comes with authentic Southern hospitality, swim further upstream to the legendary Amy Ruth's and skip this cold fish of a restaurant.

Shebeen
202 Mott St. (Spring & Kenmare Sts.)
NoLita 212.625.1105

Proof that fusion is still a buzz word in NoLita, Shebeen's owners are South African (the bar's name is South African slang), the music's eclectic (DJs spin tunes from hip-hop to down-tempo), and the cocktails are a zany mix. Fall brings pumpkin martinis, summer yields watermelon concoctions, and Red Bull addicts can get that same buzz from an espresso martini, with a potent shot of espresso, vanilla vodka, and Kahlua. All the requisite trendy lounge accessories are present: exposed-brick walls, flickering candles, low white sofas, and lots of deep nooks, like the windowless, bunker-like back lounge—formerly the kitchen, that's now sealed off with a heavy door. The hospitable bar staff might even let you into the "secret" room in back. Just ask politely.

Ship of Fools
1590 2nd Ave. (82nd & 83rd Sts.)
Upper East Side 212.570.2651

Ship of Fools

This mega-sports bar with numerous large screens, Golden Tee, and pool is a home away from home for die-hard sports fans. Whether they're watching Jeter take a swing or Tiger getting a birdie, this crowd is all about the sports, except during commercials, when it's all about scarfing down wings and chicken fingers, and making more room for beer via active urinals. If you think Joe Torre is a character on *The Sopranos* walk the plank and get your nightlife kicks elsewhere, sissy. Otherwise, put on a jersey, pull up a chair, and root your way to the final buzzer. Ship of Fools also has one of the city's friendliest staffs.

Shore
41 Murray St. (Church St. & W. Broadway)
TriBeCa 212.962.3750

Shore is as comfy and low-key as an ol' clam shack where you can shuck shells, eat shrimp, and drink "beeaz" all summer by the "sho'" while watching the Red Sox. At this NYC Shore, though, seafood and beer go together like baseball and pinstripes. Shore speeds up a few knots with a menu of fresh catches and plenty of brews to choose from (served in bottles, pints, and mugs). Don't worry about the red tide either; "We always get clams from somewheres," a chef jokingly told an inquisitive customer. Grab a bucket and get your gastronomic patriotism (and a good buzz) on at Shore. Those in-the-know say the wine list is better than expected; but if beer and seafood aren't on your GPS screen, you're fishing at the wrong hole.

Show
135 W. 41st St. (6th Ave. & Broadway)
Midtown 212.278.0988

This swanky, flamboyant nightclub, located smack-dab in the middle of Times Square, is, despite its Disney-fied location, a decent place to go for a wild night out if you're too stubborn to go downtown. The impressive red design, which utilizes sweeping, elegant drapes and shiny satin furniture, is lit by soft, glittering lamps. There are a number of hang-out areas to choose from, ranging from the packed dance floor to the Crow's

Nest, mezzanines, and the elite upstairs VIP lounge. Show's "Victorian-style" stage is regularly used for all sorts of theatrical events, from musical performances and album release parties to private receptions and displays of exotic dancing— you'll be treated to an eyeful of burlesque performers. Show is particularly well-known for their bachelor parties, which feature the Times Square Hunks, who are accurately called "the best built men in the business."

Siberia

356 W. 40th St. (8th & 9th Aves.)
Hell's Kitchen 212.333.4141

The perfect dive bar requires a few key elements: cheap drinks, crappy décor, seedy clientele, and loud music. How does Siberia stack up? Check, check, check, and check please. If you venture inside the bar, marked by a red light and sometimes a sketchy-looking bouncer, the drinks will run you around $5. Luckily, they're poured pretty stiff. And that's just the kind of fortification you'll need here—especially if you want to say, visit the bathroom, a Petri dish of yuck. Live bands play upstairs or down and vary in quality but never in volume (loud). Also consistent is the variety in Siberia's crowd. Salty neighborhood types mingle with journalists, regulars, and the occasional slumming celebrity to create one of the oddest, dirtiest, and most interesting bars in New York.

Sidecar

205 E. 55th St. (2nd & 3rd Aves.)
Midtown 212.317.2044

Hello, Schweetheart...lookin' for a Prohibition-era-type bar where only the coolest cats and kittens in town can get in? Try Sidecar, the bar on the side of P.J. Clarke's. Despite its young age, this place looks as old as its 120-year-old sibling bar with its back-lit brown banquettes and of course, Sinatra playing in the background. Sidecar is more upscale than P.J.'s, with a power lunch menu featuring steaks, a raw bar, and a wine list of over 50 bottles. Sidecar is often booked for private parties, so the after work-crowd varies by night. Only the crème de la crème get in, though, so make a reservation or get a Sidecar card to check out this swingin' scene.

Sidewalk Café

94 Ave. A (@ 6th St.)
East Village 212.253.8080

With the demise of the amateur-embracing The Spiral and Coney Island High, Sidewalk Café has become one of the most popular launching grounds for relatively new and inexperienced musical acts. It's not entirely clear why, as a wall obstructs 25% of the performance space depending on the angle. A lot of the credit goes to Monday night's "The Anti-Folk Hootenanny," a brilliantly twisted weekly open mic night which features musicians of all kinds, from undiscovered greats to misguided souls who wouldn't sound out of place in a rousing symphony of 10,000 nails on a chalkboard. The staff tends to enforce a two-drink minimum during open mics, but Sidewalk's reasonable prices and occasional ear-bleeding vocalists will make you glad you shelled out for those two Amstels. In the restaurant portion, every night seems to be amateur night for cooks and waiters.

Sin Sin

85 2nd Ave. (@ 5th St.)
East Village 212.253.2222

Check your conscience at the coat check before entering Sin Sin. (We know, Sin Sin's a Gaelic term, but we're doing the double-entendre thing.) The temptation in this East Village establishment, from its patrons to its happy hour, is sweltering. With a "buy one, get one" lasting from 1pm 'til 8pm seven days a week it's easy to see why no one is wearing halos. Its sultry atmosphere— composed of lush black curtains, red lighting, a mini-disco ball, and mirrors—presents the perfect setting for seduction. An added bonus to this sinfully delicious den is the Leopard Lounge, conveniently located upstairs, spinning music nightly. Sin Sin provides a double dose of dancing and debauchery. The faint of heart should stay away.

Sin-e
150 Attorney St. (@ Houston St.)
Lower East Side 212.388.0077

It may not be the Sin-e you know and love, but the new locale still serves its rock pretty hard. Now an official Lower East Side resident, this Sin-e has seen the likes of the Yeah Yeah Yeahs and the Walkmen and plays host to lots of lesser-known bands. The main rock room comes equipped with amps and groupies while the smaller bar around the corner is a great place to have a beer while listening to aspiring musicians wield some bitchin' cover tunes. And since it's on the outskirts of the Lower East Side's super-trendy epicenter, grungy audiophiles need not worry that Jeff Buckley and the like are spinning in their graves.

Single Room Occupancy
360 53rd St. (8th & 9th Aves.)
Hell's Kitchen 212.765.6299

Once upon a time in the seedy New York of the '70s and '80s, tourists were afraid of the subway and Times Square was known for smut. You won't find the missing filth at Single Room Occupancy, but urban legend has it that a blue light similar to the one outside this basement bar once signaled an underground house of ill repute. You can't buy sex so easily these days, but take comfort in the fact that places like SRO leave behind the snobbery of secret, underground scenes and instead opt for thoughtful décor and beverages. With a

heavily local beer and wine list (no liquor here) and an intimate feel, SRO doesn't replace smut houses of yore, but it does give you someplace cool to impress your friends with.

6s and 8s
205 Chrystie St. (@ Stanton St.)
Lower East Side 212.477.6688

It's quite a coincidence that 6s and 8s got its name from the game of craps because all bets are off when it comes to the service here. Patrons might want to yell "Hit me" before the bartenders will deal out drinks like the Sin City Cosmo. However, the atmosphere wins the jackpot. Downstairs hosts a blackjack table and slot machines line the walls at this '70s-inspired lounge. Velvet black posters of old-school rockers and giant playing cards set the scene for an evening of rocking and high-rolling. So head on over to 6s and 8s if you're a gambling man, because when it comes to getting a drink it's a crap shoot—but the ambiance is a sure bet.

The SkinNY
174 Orchard St. (Houston & Stanton Sts.)
Lower East Side 212.228.3668

Happy hour on a Saturday? We're there. Though the SkinNY sounds like either a strip club or a Mary-Kate Olsen fan club, sweet drink specials and an even sweeter jukebox make this LES addi-

The SkinNY

tion a welcome one. Here's the skinny: The draft choices are lean—zilch, in fact—but all that extra space behind the bar leaves room for liquor on tap. Take a chilled Jägermeister shot ($4) from the tap machine before heading to the upstairs lounge area, fully stocked with lots of pillows and turntables to help you burn off some calories with a dance session. This place's unpolished odds and ends are very LES: Rent is so high that they have no money left for furniture and similar niceties.

Slainte
304 Bowery (Bleecker & Houston Sts.)
NoHo 212.253.7030

If you shun traditional Irish watering holes because most of them are more accurately collegiate Greek, then this pub's for you. Yes, there's the requisite sports on the telly and Guinness on tap, but overall this spacious spot with brick walls draws a more refined crowd who appreciate fresh, messy sandwiches and an Irish breakfast as good as any fried up back in Dublin. A chatty bar staff facilitates a happy hour of 2-for-1 drafts (5pm-8pm). Plus, these guys have both McSorley's and Smithwick's on tap. Slainte is still a young pub but the three Irish lads who own it (along with Dempsey's and the Baggot Inn) have a good thing going on. Here's an amusing little drinking game: If you can say Slainte (pronounced "salon-chay") three times fast, it's time for another beer.

Slane
102 MacDougal St. (Bleecker & 4th Sts.)
West Village 212.505.0079

Slane is a young bar in a hurry to grow up. The low, Latin arches of this Irish bar and restaurant have been repainted to suggest the interior of a castle, or an impeccably kept wine cellar. The exposed brick and candles give the room a warm, European feel (and you thought all Irish bars looked lived-in and smelled of spilled beer and Bailey's), and the furniture throughout resembles items straight out a Crate & Barrel catalog. However, the chill vibe gets trampled as quickly as anything that stands between an Irishman and his beer, thanks to overpriced drinks and the loud

satellite radio music. Slane needs to lower the volume and remember that it's not the size that matters; it's what you do with what you've got. Ah, youth, so naïve.

Slate Plus
54 W. 21st St. (5th & 6th Aves.)
Flatiron 212.989.0096

The inverse solution to a sports bar day care center for boyfriends who are forced to go shopping with their shoe-obsessed girlfriends, Slate Plus is an upscale hideaway for girls whose beaus have 8-balls on the brain. Formerly known solely as Slate, Plus now occupies the top floor of this bilevel, warehouse-sized Chelsea pool hall. Pool tables were lifted out, replaced with cushy sofas, and *voila!*, Slate Plus was born. Happy hour is from 4pm-7pm Monday-Friday, so grab your girl a stiff pink drink, and get your game on before she claims you love sports more than her. Slate and its baby sister Plus are enjoyable enough to melt the heart of the most-committed dive bar enthusiast, while pushing the boundaries of nightlife design. Who says opposites don't attract?

The Slaughtered Lamb
182 W. 4th St. (6th & 7th Aves.)
West Village 212.727.3350

Inspired by the horror flick *An American Werewolf in London*, this pub is more schlock than shock. The bar features three roaring fireplaces and ye olde Ms. Pac-Man table, and the kitschy downstairs dungeon is adorned in manacles, iron bars, and a few well-placed skeletons. Truly, the only thing supernatural about this place is the extensive selection of imported beers, microbrews, and potent cocktails like the $8 Bloodbath. There are no werewolves in sight, and the only silver bullet on premises is Coors Light. If there's a full moon and you need to let off some steam, this is the place. The downside may be the curse of a hangover, one that only a little hair of the werewolf that bit you can cure.

The Slide
356 Bowery (4th & Great Jones Sts.)
NoHo 212.420.8885

Be prepared to descend into a sanctum of seediness at this East Village underground dive. The wood paneling and dimly lit interior looks as though it has remained unchanged since the 1880s, when this place was home to the city's first openly gay bar. While discreet gentlemen likely came here more than a century ago, today the men who flock to the Slide are anything but gentle and the go-go boys who gyrate nightly don't seem to know the meaning of discreet. A trashy 20- and 30-something crowd packs this place—especially on Saturdays for the Slide's "High Life/Low Life" party, hosted by drag queen Sweetie. A daily happy hour from 5pm-9pm ensures that your slide into sleaze is all the more stimulating.

The Slipper Room
167 Orchard St. (@ Stanton St.)
Lower East Side 212.253.7246

It's amazing how what goes around really does come around (like people in Williamsburg who are wearing acid-washed jeans again!). But one of the more confusing recurring trends is burlesque—the practice of the old-fashioned striptease. It's as if we've moved backwards to a time when pasties and cellulite were sexy. Chubby girls with bona-fide boom-boom routines stomp around the stage at this cocktail lounge, kicking up their heels in a full-on scissor move. But the question is, are people digging it because it's sexy? Or because it's weird? (Or perhaps because it's funny?) Maybe it's all of the above. Either way, the Slipper Room is worth visiting at least once for the feel of bygone sleaze. The Slipper Room also features live music, sketch comedy, and vaudeville performances.

Sly
310 Spring St. (Greenwich & Hudson Sts.)
SoHo 646.546.5860

Recess is over. And so is Noca. So was this neighborhood until recently. Now Sly, which used the aforementioned names in previous lives, this room is still smaller, darker, louder, and way more likeable than Martin Lawrence. An agreeable space, this is nightlife for those burned out on West Chelsea clubs where they're turned away for being unfamous, unconnected, underdressed, or whatever the big clubs' doormen might be thinking. A non-stop mix of '80s-'00s party music plays

Sly

to a racially, economically, and geographically diverse crowd that orders corny-named $8-$12 cocktails, all using the word "Sly" in their titles. There are a few tables in the back of this room, but they fill up in a hurry. The tiny, shabby-chic backyard has a nice Miami feel to it, as does the understated and relatively attractive crowd.

Small's
183 W. 10th St. (@ 7th Ave.)
West Village 212.675.7369

Big news for Small's fans: Downtown's best jazz venue is now "new and improved." New, meaning recently reopened, and improved, meaning "liquor license." Acts range from Latin-influenced quartets to traditional trios, all booked by the owner (who doubled as an electrician during renovation). Small's feels like a labor of love, though, not just another local watering hole. So if you're sick of trendy, plastic-looking bars, and you can't stand the music in a student/tourist pub, escape to this dim basement and the dulcet tones of a saxophone. There's no food menu, but the bartender will provide a cup of fresh-popped popcorn on request. Expect a $20 cover—10 bucks goes toward two $5 poker chips, redeemable at the bar. Small's is big on good old-fashioned whoopee.

Smith & Wollensky
797 3rd Ave. (@ 49th St.)
Midtown 212.753.1530

Despite being a chain founded by the TGI Friday's gang, Smith & Wollensky's earned a reputation for serving some of the primest rib this side of Adam. A signature green and white façade fronts a brown leather and wood dining room. Old pictures line the walls, surrounding carnivores who scarf down power lunches of Fred Flintstone-sized steaks and enormous supplemental sides of onion rings and creamed spinach. Dinner is big business, with businessmen and their clients bringing an old boys' club feeling to the joint. After work you can scarcely reach the bar as patrons wait (and wait and wait) for their tables. There is a pick-up scene here, but it's of the last chance, third marriage variety. The martinis are stiff, as are the dudes who order them.

Smiths
708 8th Ave. (@ 44th St.)
Hell's Kitchen 212.246.3268

Smiths is like good ol' grandpa—it's old, it's clean and tidy, the seasoned barkeeps wear crisp white shirts and ties, they wake up early, and they handle a lot of booze. Open daily from 6am to 4am, Smiths is both a bar and restaurant serving traditional New York bar food for breakfast, lunch, and dinner in an old-fashioned corner of Times Square. The patrons are mostly salty but friendly regulars who call the bartenders and each other by name.

Beer is the beverage of choice and never runs you more than $5 a pint. Live music plays Monday–Friday, but don't worry, it doesn't class the place up too much. After 50+ years in Times Square, there's little danger of that.

Smithwicks
191 Smith St. (Warren & Baltic Sts.)
Cobble Hill 347.643.9911

Smithwicks is a Smith Street rarity: an authentic Irish pub that cares more about its meat and mash than its score on the neighborhood trend chart. The result is a cozy, unadorned space with bar, tables, and an outdoor garden—a simple equation that always works. Maybe the well-poured Irish drafts have Smithwicks' proprietors a little tipsy, but it's hard to ignore their boasts of having the "best burger in Brooklyn." The friendly crowd and oh-so-tasty fish and chips more than hold their own against the meat patties, plus there's live Irish music every Thursday during the summer. A traditional place like this on such an über-popular street seems like a simple and unremarkable plan that ranks up there with putting dictionary listings in alphabetical order.

Smoked
103 2nd Ave. (@ 6th St.)
East Village 212.388.0388

Bringing new style to an old idea, this East Village restaurant is the hottest thing that's happened to

Smoked

barbecue since charcoal. It's a small place, but giant windows and French doors belie its size. The crowd is as diverse as the neighborhood, and even the salads come off the grill. From the executive chef at Ida Mae, these eats are definitely worth digging into: Wings, ribs, and shrimp are all great, but don't leave without trying the sweet potato ravioli. Sit down for a nice dinner, and stick around after-hours because when the lights go down, the candles come out, and Smoked turns into a…barbecue lounge? Trust us, it works.

Snacky
187 Grand St. (Driggs & Bedford Aves.)
Williamsburg 718.486.4848

Tucked away on a tree-lined street a few blocks from the bustle of Bedford Avenue, this affordable Asian treat lives up to its name. The menu is a catalog of tiny snacks with mysterious, whimsical names, like "popsies" (delicious mini-burgers) and "Tiny Juicy Buns." Apart from its tastiness and novelty, the menu's best feature is the prices—no item is over $10, which also holds true for the myriad drinks. Snacky offers a variety of creative cocktails for $5, almost all made with sake or soju in various fruity, but not-too-sweet concoctions. Everyone seems remarkably happy here, especially for Williamsburg; they're hunched at little tables removing bright yellow chopsticks from cheerful dispensers, chatting with the Japanese school girl-chic waitress, and smiling amid the campy Pan-Asian décor, enjoying their snackies and drinkies.

Snapper Creek
1589 1st Ave. (82nd & 83rd Sts.)
Upper East Side 212.327.1319

There are some unspoken rules followed by Upper East Side natives, and one of them involves avoiding First Avenue like the plague. Part of the reason could be attributed to the awfulness of Snapper Creek. Bad music and an older crowd condemn this neighborhood bar to a life of mediocrity. Snapper Creek has six beers on tap, 10 bottles, and a wine selection that could be counted on two hands; there's no food but patrons are allowed to

order in. What they can't order in is a little excitement, which is what this boring bar desperately needs. We would say that Snapper Creek gives new meaning to the word dull, but that would be too inventive for these guys.

Snitch
59 W. 21st St. (5th & 6th Aves.)
Flatiron 212.727.7775

With owners like rock stars Scott Weiland, Duff McKagan, and Brett Scallions, this less than "Plush," minimalist space won't have to worry about becoming a "Big Empty" anytime soon. Past the doorman, a stairway to heaven leads underdressed in-the-know types to the second-floor lounge where TVs show muted fashion, music, and sports programming. Tables along the walls of the lofty space facilitate the bottle-service crowd, but Snitch doesn't seem like "that kind of place." A small stage near the center of the room hosts live shows that occasionally attract an "unplugged" big shot. Initially, Snitch comes off a bit under-produced and no-frills, but its musical and aesthetic complexities eventually shine through, making for a good time. How grungy.

S.O.B.'s
204 Varick St. (@ Houston St.)
SoHo 212.243.4940

It's not what you think—this S.O.B. stands for "Sounds of Brazil." If you're looking for the samba sound of the land of Carnivale and Cachaça, then S.O.B.'s is a must. Neither fans of funk nor Fela Kuti followers should miss the monthly Afro-beat party, Jump N' Funk. Typically the music is provided by DJs, but S.O.B.'s also books a range of hot acts, sometimes offering free salsa lessons for the early crowd. The only temptation here that's greater than the urge to get up and dance is the temptation of delicacies like the lobster empanadas. Some might find the jungle room décor tacky, but the fake palm tree doesn't block your view of the stage and if it inspires the cool clientele to get all hot and sweaty, who cares?

Social Bar & Lounge/ Fusion at Social

795 8th Ave. (48th & 49th Sts.)
Hell's Kitchen 212.459.0643

Social seeks to be all things to all drinkers. Each of its three floors has its own unique décor, bar, and music, allowing folks to bar-hop without leaving the building. The ground floor harbors a long bar counter down one side and tables and chairs on the other. A few flat-screen TVs show sports, but the after-work 20s-40s crowd isn't watching. You can satisfy any food craving including bar basics like wings, fries, and burritos. Sometimes the upper floors are closed on weeknights, but if not, Social climbers can venture upstairs to the cozier and less sporty second level for a quaint Irish pub of dark-wood paneling. The top floor, Fusion at Social, is a swankier lounge with couches and a DJ that extends to an outdoor deck, which is often reserved for private parties.

Soda Bar

629 Vanderbilt Ave. (Prospect Pl. & St. Marks Pl.)
Prospect Heights 718.230.8393

Soda Bar made the switch from root beer to real beer many years ago, but its old-school charm hasn't gone flat. The former soda fountain, nestled in the heart of Prospect Heights, caters to local devotees who would sooner die than see their favorite juke joint succumb to the likes of the Seventh Avenue sect. The vibe is still mellow—a laidback mix of young hipsters and yuppie-lite parents with stroller-bound kiddies in tow fill the worn barstools and backroom couches to chat over indie rock tunes and swig a stout or micro-brew for a mere $3 during happy hour (daily from 2pm-8pm). The pub grub, highlighted by shoestring fries, is not to be missed, though some would pass on the DJs that take to the outdoor garden on weekend nights.

SoFo

550 Court St. (9th & Garnet Sts.)
Carroll Gardens 718.222.3535

SoFo aims for comfort, and this neighborhood bar has all the luxuries of an unpretentious living room—free chips for TV watchers, a jukebox full of straight-up rock 'n' roll to play during a game of pool, a patio out back to bring your freshly grilled bar burger to, and a super-long weekday happy hour that lasts until 9pm. It doesn't get much better than that. A homey-feeling bar that straddles two neighborhoods—Red Hook and Carroll Gardens—this is one that you'll keep coming back to. SoFo's pep is matched by its boldly painted walls (orange) and ceiling (blue).

SoGo NY

337B W. Broadway (@ Grand St.)
SoHo 212.966.2113

Why wok when you can roll? Situated on prime SoHo real estate, Sogo NY adds inventive Mexican and Malaysian ingredients to its lengthy list of sushi rolls. Hate fish but inexplicably love sushi? The honey nuts roll comes with roasted honey nuts, avocado, and cucumber, and not the teeniest bit of raw fish. The alligator roll counts shrimp tempura, eel, and tobiko as ingredients, and every bite is worth savoring. While you're trying to get the hang of your chopsticks, take a moment to soak in the Zen-like setting, made modern by a front bar and colored lights. Of course, nothing goes better with sushi than sake, and there's plenty of it. Sogo's Sak-e-to-ya! Sake Hour (Mon-Fri, 5pm-8pm) serves up healthy doses of strawberry shortcake-, lemon-, and pear-infused sakes. Sounds good? So go already.

SoHo:323

323 W. Broadway (Canal & Grand Sts.)
SoHo 212.334.2232

Palm fronds sway, scantily clad damsels swivel their hips, and permanently tanned playboys look on lustily...but you're not in the Bahamas, silly; you're at SoHo:323, downtown's version of the tropics. This two-level space combines landmark-protected architecture with cushy banquette seating along its exposed-brick walls, rattan ottomans, and gauzy fabrics to create a little chic island flava. Mainstream hip-hop, pop, and R&B are a hit with the flashy clientele; stop by on weekdays for a hipper, more glamorous cohort (and less hubbub among everyone trying to get in). The bouncers look a little intimidating, but really they're just big, black-clad teddy bears. Just don't forget to pack your wallet; there's a $20 cover and the fancy cocktails aren't cheap.

Solas

232 E. 9th St. (2nd & 3rd Aves.)
East Village 212.375.0297

Solas is like the bar version of the girl next door. The main floor is laidback and pub-style friendly, and the upstairs hosts a sexier, more intimate, red-walled lounge. That said, this East Village stronghold is more than meets the eye. An additional side room accommodates DJs and dancing in ultraviolet dark and the back of the second floor has tables so you can gather with friends and let your dancing feet rest over good conversation and half-priced happy hour drinks (from 5pm-8pm). In fact, just about every corner of this nightclub has its own bar and distinctive vibe. Solas suits, no matter what mood you're in. Sunday through Thursday nights you can enjoy $6 cosmos, margaritas, mojitos, and the rotating specialty drink.

Sophie's Bar

507 E. 5th St. (Aves. A & B)
East Village 212.228.5680

It's ironic that Sophie was one of the most popular girls' names of last year, because the last thing you'll see in Sophie's is a family outing. This dive is dark, has no sign, and borders on seedy. Which is exactly why it's great: no frou frou drinks, no banquettes, and no credit cards accepted. Locals in their 20s and 30s inhabit the small bar on weekdays, but the B&Ts invade on the weekend. Sophie's has a few tables, a small bar, and a pool table, so it's a good place to come with a friend or two, as it can't accommodate many more people than that. Bring a buck to play the kick-ass juke with icons ranging from Miles Davis to the Stones

Sophie's Bar

to Johnny Cash to Elvis. If you're sick of "the scene," head to Sophie's 'cause you won't find any 'tude here.

Sortie

329 W. 51st St. (8th & 9th Aves.)
Hell's Kitchen 212.265.0650

Red walls, red velvet cushions, and a sea of candles make this cozy oasis an exit (consult your high-school French books) from the busy restaurant row-like area outside. An extensive beer list ($7-$11) is presented with an array of creative drink offerings, like the ginger-infused champagne cocktail ($12), the green tea martini ($11), and the namesake indulgence, The Sortie, with hibiscus-infused vodka ($10). The eclectic food menu has something for all patrons, like mussels Provencale ($9), steak frites ($19.50), the Black Angus burger ($13.50), and the cheese plate ($7). Attentive service, DJ-spun tunes Thursday through Saturday, and a certain "je ne c'est quoi" are starting to attract revelers, both for the long-haul and late night, but not to worry: There's plenty of seating, liquor, and amour for everyone.

Southpaw

125 5th Ave. (Sterling Pl. & St. Johns Pl.)
Park Slope 718.230.0236

Even staunch Manhattanites will take the F train out of the city to go to this unbelievably cool music club. Not only does Southpaw have a history (this space once housed a 99-cent store), it's also one of the coolest in NYC—from the plethora of acts who grace the stage (Ted Leo, TV on the Radio,

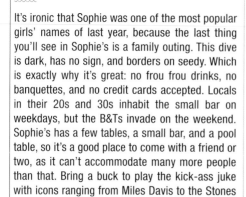

Clinic), right down to the jukebox, which features mix tape-like CDs made by the bar staff, local celebs, and bands who have played here. The set-up is a bit odd, though; the seating area faces perpendicular to the stage, but patrons are happy to crane their necks or stand up front to catch the near-perfect acoustics. On slower nights, the videogames, poker, pool, table tennis, and cool bartenders take center stage.

South's
273 Church St. (Franklin & White Sts.)
TriBeCa 212.219.0640

South's

Unlike most other TriBeCa hangouts, South's does-n't pretend to do its patrons a favor by serving them; it's a neighborhood bar and happy to be one, dammit! Here, you'll feel welcomed and you'll eat and drink better than almost anywhere else in the neighborhood. Granted, you won't find super-models or socialites swaying to classic soul at the long, wooden bar or among the tables at the back of the room, but that's a good sign—neither group is known for good sense, anyway, right? Um, yeah. Look for old-fashioned comfort food—the $9 Sunday brunch with its lumberjack-sized options plus coffee and juice can't be beat. If you're more interested in the sauce than sausages, mingle with the cool crowd that lives and works in the area during laidback weekday happy hours.

Southside Lounge
41 Broadway (Wythe & Kent Aves.)
Williamsburg 718.387.3182

You just started to get a decent buzz at Diner and they're closing up shop. A few doors down on Broadway you'll find Southside Lounge, a dimly lit, somewhat dingy haven of bare-bones late-night imbibing. The cave-like, red paper lantern-lined room is vaguely reminiscent of Mario Bros. fire levels after a few $3 happy hour Bloody Marys. Constantly spotted about town are flyers touting the venue's various DJ nights (the Red Light Party's nasty funk and classic hip-hop, Psychedelic Perversions, Club Weird Coldwave, postpunk, and goth, and so on and so forth), but neither the vibe nor the crowd changes regardless of the themed nights.

SouthWest NY
2 World Financial Ctr. (Liberty & Vesey Sts.)
Financial District 212.945.0528

It's easy to dismiss this as a cheesy corporate look at Mexico, but in the Mexican cities where this very same Wall Street set hangs out, places look just like this. Maybe that makes it authentic after all? The roomy waterfront deck is where after-workers feast on cheesy quesadillas, tasty lobster clubs, barbecued pulled pork sandwiches, and hefty burgers in between rounds of margaritas, Coronas, and shots of tequila. Downtown clears out on the weekends, but SouthWest NY doesn't—when the sun's out, a lively crowd of locals and financial guys pulling a long weekend at work come here to kick back and soak in the rays. After a few margaritas or one of the beer bucket specials, even the polluted Hudson starts looking like Cabo San Lucas.

Spaghetti Western
59 Reade St. (Broadway & Church St.)
TriBeCa 212.513.1333

Except for the Italian movie posters decorating the walls, there's nothing too spaghetti or western about this TriBeCa eatery. There's pasta on the menu, but the real focus is on the meat dishes, which are simply prepared and well-spiced, and priced under $15. The bar is small and standard, offering a few specialty cocktails (like the lurid Electric Lemonade), but beer buyers beware; even though it's listed with the other brews, the ginger beer contains no alcohol. It is, however, sweet and delicious. The young professionals drinking here like to get sloshed before 9pm, and their celebration can take over the entire place. The dining room might be unassuming, but the quality of the food indicates that Spaghetti Western is really a neighborhood restaurant disguised as a happening bar.

Spanky's BBQ
127 W. 43rd St. (Broadway & 6th Ave.)
Midtown 212.575.5848

Walking into this homey bar/restaurant, visitors are spanked with the rich, mouthwatering smell of sweet BBQ sauce. If that's not enough of an invitation to splurge on comfort foods like fried pickles and pulled pork sandwiches, the huge pig murals are welcoming. This two-story spot successfully authenticates the laidback Southwestern vibe with its open and airy feel, and its explosion of down-home kitsch doesn't hurt. A mix of tourists and Lincoln Tunnel-bound professionals fill out the bars on both levels. Whether dining or just drinking, do take advantage of the free beer sampling courtesy of the affiliated Heartland Brewery, because pale ale always works well with Southern spices and fried batter. And with non-Times Square prices, you'll be in hog heaven.

Spice
60 University Pl. (10th & 11th Sts.)
Greenwich Village 212.982.3758

199 8th Ave. (19th & 20th Sts.)
Chelsea 212.647.9218

1411 2nd Ave. (73rd & 74th Sts.)
Upper East Side 212.988.5348

It's a mod, mod world in this claustrophobic eatery, decked out with space-age lighting fixtures and sleek furniture. The noisy nook might try your patience as the bar area is small and usually cramped with patrons waiting for a table. When seated, don't expect intimacy, as diners are shoehorned in so close one whiff tells you that your neighbor had the curry special. Specialty drinks,

which are served "on the rocks," include a lychee mimosa and sake mojito kamikaze, and like the food, they're very affordable ($5-$6). Indulge in one too many sakes and you may mistake the pod-like bathroom for an escape hatch. Though the effect can be disconcerting, speedy service and bargain prices are the spice of life. This is sort of the Indian Sushi Samba.

Spice Market
403 W. 13th St. (@ 9th Ave.)
Meatpacking District 212.675.2322

Is it the food or the scene that makes this Jean-Georges Vongerichten/Stanley Wong venture a success? It's a little of both. While foodies often regard the tapas-esque "Southeast Asian street food" as a comparatively modest achievement for the man who brought us Jean-Georges, the pre-clubbing, pointy-shoed girls and spikey-haired dudes who cram into the upstairs restaurant's wooden tables just can't get enough. The downstairs portion of this huge, wood-heavy, Asian-Indian space is where loungers recline in style, but only if they have reservations. Spice Market looks like one of those exotic sets from *Indiana Jones* where Harrison Ford might go to meet the evil archaeologist who's stolen something sacred. And though possibly evil, this moneyed crowd isn't too adventurous.

Spike Hill Bar & Grill
184 Bedford Ave. (@ N. 7th St.)
Williamsburg 718.218.9737

The proximity to the Bedford Ave. L stop and the riff-raff that attracts may put you off from visiting this pub-style restaurant, but upon closer inspection, Spike's ain't half bad. It's attractive in a masculine way, with dark wood and vintage beer ad mirrors. The clientele is rather manly as well—they come in pairs on man-dates to drink from the extensive Scotch menu, pick from over 60 types of beers, eat cheap but above-average pub grub, and chat about life like they were in a Dublin watering hole. It may be a boys' club, but Spike Hill serves as a formidable date spot, with semi-enclosed private booths and a whiskey tasting menu featuring "flights" (tastings of four top-shelf whiskies). Between the booths and the booze, making out is bound to ensue.

Spirit
530 W. 27th St. (10th & 11th Aves.)
Chelsea 212.268.9477

This chameleon of a club (formerly Twilo) is regularly updating and improving its multi-room interior. The atmosphere reeks of a mini Crobar, complete with loud techno music, patches of fog, and a killer cover charge. While the door guys are friendly, you have to work hard to score a break on the $25 average entry fee (try calling ahead for the guest list). The calm crowd and dim lighting create a comfortable spot to let loose and dance your cares away, while the side seating allows a haven for everyone else to choose who they'll try and take home. The best part about Spirit are the hours—open until the wee hours of the morning, you can easily lose track of time (for once) in this bustling city.

Splash
50 W. 17th St. (5th & 6th Aves.)
Flatiron 212.691.0073

Ever wonder what REALLY goes on in a bathroom stall at a popular gay nightspot? OK, so maybe you don't have to "wonder," you perv. But that doesn't mean you can't also watch others "be there" and "do that" through the new, semi-translucent wall that lines Splash's bathroom. The fact that peeping Toms can only see Dick and Harry's silhouettes is probably what keeps this sex show improv legal. And if shadows aren't enough for you, head upstairs to watch go-go dancers being hosed down onstage. Popular with tourists, Splash is perhaps the only reliable gay venue regardless of the night (though Wednesday nights do boast $3 Long Island Iced Teas in 10-oz. jars). Just prepare to pay a cover that can vary depending on how attractive you are.

The Spotted Pig
314 W. 11th St. (@ Greenwich St.)
West Village 212.620.0393

You'll spot plenty of pigs at this boisterous, British-inspired pub that offers more character than space. The overstuffed animal-themed vibe (look for the lamb dissection chart) spills into a packed older crowd that politely shifts to allow waiters table access. Green-themed fabric stools promise a more comfortable drinking experience, though good luck finding an empty one. A limited beer selection nonetheless proves varied (including Anchor Steam, Sappora, and raspberry-flavored Lambic), but wine's clearly the focus with over 100 bottled reds and whites, though only seven each by glass. Most beers and wines hover around $9; food options include $13 chilled asparagus soup and $24 skirt steak. This is a "gastro pub," so those expecting a McSorley's West outpost will be sadly disappointed. Imagine Mario Batali, who consulted here, taking over Pete's Tavern.

Spring Lounge
48 Spring St. (@ Mulberry St.)
NoLita 212.965.1774

Spring Lounge serves its purpose. A trimmed-down watering hole that's a "lounge" in the same way a beer is a "cocktail," at least this spot offers a hint of variety in an overly swank-ified neighborhood. The all-wood interior and manly-man furnishings, such as oak barrels that act as tables and shark paraphernalia looming overhead, keep Spring Lounge properly under-swanked. The only mystery remaining is: How does a modest NoLita joint manage to attract so many frat boys? Come 5:01, button-down shirts descend on the place like vultures. Where were they amongst the svelte, Chihuahua-toting fashionistas during the daytime hours? Isn't Wall Street a mile away? Well, if you're a jocky, beefy dude lost in a sea of downtown trendiness, you've found your refuge.

Spuyten Duyvil

**395 Metropolitan Ave. (Roebling &
Havemeyer Sts.)**
Williamsburg 718.963.4140

Spuyten Duyvil is serious about beer. With over 100 different types of bottled suds and their very own beer engine, this bar means business. Attracting brew aficionados takes more than just selection, though, and this bar delivers with an eclectic, charming atmosphere featuring vintage subway signs and ashtrays (and the bathroom walls have been made into chalkboards). Spuyten Duyvil can feel a bit more Carroll Gardens than Williamsburg, however, as 30-somethings (occasionally with offspring in tow) lounge around the big table in back or outside in the sizeable garden. Mellow music and a good-natured, knowledgeable staff are the icing on the cake for this clean, comfortable space. This bar, named for the NYC folktale, is the spot where beer connoisseurs can have a duyvil of a time.

St. Dymphna's

118 St. Marks Pl. (Ave. A & 1st Ave.)
East Village 212.254.6636

There are restaurants and bars that make a great point of proclaiming how Irish they are by covering the walls with Guinness ads and overdoing St. Patrick's Day as if Hallmark had invented it. St. Dymphna's on the other hand actually has an Irish clientele, real Irish food, and an atmosphere that doesn't come off as at all contrived or themey. With a bright, spacious interior and a garden in the back, this pub is welcoming in all seasons. If you bring in your iPod, the friendly bartender will often be happy to hook it up to the stereo system and play your mixes. If you come at 4pm you can take advantage of both brunch, which is served until 5, and happy hour, which ends at 7.

St. Maggie's Café

120 Wall St. (Front & South Sts.)
Financial District 212.943.9050

Abuzz with stockbrokers, St. Maggie's Café has taken in Wall Street's worker bees for over 20 years now. And it's easy to find…just keep walking until you hit the river. Tucked away on far-east Wall Street, Maggie's heavy doors open onto a multilevel bastion of dining rooms, befitting the mid-day bustle of their busy lunchtimes. On the other hand, you're just a phone call away from scheduling a full room for your next dinner engagement (steak dishes come highly recommended). The bar is long, and as quiet as the financial sector after dark…try a martini the next time you need some peace, quiet, and booze. And don't forget the kindly help all around you: A number of them have been there over a decade, always a good sign.

St. Marks Ale House

2 St. Marks Pl. (2nd & 3rd Aves.)
East Village 212.260.9762

Got a hankering for greasy nachos? Aching to chug 24 draught beers? Missing the good old days of self-induced whiplash from watching games on 11 different TVs? St. Marks Ale House wants your business. The woody neighborhood bar has been serving up no-nonsense drinks since 1995, promising a safe haven for erstwhile frat boys who have lost their way on the infamously punky row. Here they can fuel up on brew and a surprisingly good jukebox, mustering the power to stumble back to the house in time to be hazed. Although now that there's a Chipotle across the street, maybe those frat boys aren't so out of place after all. God help us. What's next, a Whole Foods on the Lower East Side? Oh…right.

St. Marks 88

157 2nd Ave. (9th & 10th Sts.)
East Village 212.614.0138

For many, the idea of eating sushi at a place that also serves Chinese is scary as hell, but St. Marks 88 is one of those rare places that actually manages to bring Japan and China together peacefully. They have an excellent sushi bar, but since some like it hot, this lucky number does it all. But don't shy away if you aren't in the mood for a feast—they also have a fully stocked bar with loads of sake. For teetotalers there is a plethora of crazy drinks: frothy teas, green teas, black teas, smoothies, tropical juices, agars (a gelatin-infused drink), and milkshakes. The prices are very reasonable, making this place perfect for a weekday dinner or the first stop on a weekend night.

Stain

766 Grand St. (Humboldt & Graham Aves.) Williamsburg 718.387.7840

Stain

This area may not yet have little boutiques selling artsy clothes for 10 times the suggested retail price like nearby Bedford, but it does have its vestiges of artistic life popping up here and there. One is Stain: a spacious (after all, rent here is still relatively cheap) hodgepodge of velvety couches and antique coffee tables picked up curbside, and local artwork for sale. Stain keeps acts local by only serving beer, wine, and even soda made within the confines of New York State. Monday night is Craft Night, so bring some colored noodles and pompoms and start gluing. Get deep with a low-lit poetry reading on the small stage in the back, and duck out for a smoke on the patio if things get too heavy.

Stand-Up NY

236 W. 78th St. (@ Broadway) Upper West Side 212.595.0850

Stand-Up NY might be the only spot in NYC where a Mexican guy can riff on race relations without inviting a few fists to introduce themselves to his face. Anything goes at this Upper West Side laugh emporium where up-and-coming comedians (many of whom have appeared on Comedy Central) try to out-funny each other in front of a decent-sized crowd. Big names like Dave Chappelle and Jerry Seinfeld have been known to drop in too. On Saturday nights you can see three comics for the price of one. And at $16 a show and a two-drink minimum, you'll want to get your laugh's worth; otherwise, buy a wig and some costume jewelry and try to get in for free. Just tell the guy at the door, "I'm Rick James, bitch!"

Standings

43 E. 7th St. (2nd & 3rd Aves.) East Village 212.420.0671

Formerly Brewsky's, Standings is a baseball fan's dream come true. With about two-dozen seats all within a bat swing of one another, this small room is lit primarily by four big-screen TVs upon which it isn't uncommon to see Yankees and Red Sox games being watched with equal fervor. What could possibly go wrong when one of the $6-$7 imports on tap are thrown into the mix? On one wall, a series of chalkboards chart the "standings" of every team in major league baseball. (We're not sure if the name comes from this or the limited seating.) The opposite wall is covered in vintage pennants and rows of aged beer cans. Like major-league baseball itself, this spot is full of men in baseball caps. These guys have built it, but will "they" come?

The Stanton Social

99 Stanton St. (Ludlow & Orchard Sts.) Lower East Side 212.995.0099

A less rock 'n' roll little alternative to nearby Pianos, the Stanton Social is a sign of what's to come on the Lower East Side. It's very, very pretty. Decked out in leather, chrome, and china pattern-covered walls, the ambiance will smack you in the face faster than you can say "Le Cirque." Mercifully, the food (if not the wine) is a real bargain. Ceviche, always a welcome addition to a night out, is $12, and entrées range from $5 burgers to $17 for the hanger steak. The staff, dressed in 1940s uniforms that include Mary Jane shoes and seamed stockings, is courteous to no end. Maybe the Lower East Side has cleaned up its act; give Stanton Social a try, and see for yourself.

Starfoods
64 E. 1st St. (1st & 2nd Aves.)
East Village 212.260.3116

Anything from Chucks and jeans to stilettos and skirts will do in this East Village standard, which offers tasty Mediterranean fare for grown-ups along with playful Atari-paneled floors and a Galaga videogame for kids at heart. Venture past the packed bar into the backroom where DJs spin on the weekends; sexy singles, couples, artists, and actors looking to escape the workweek grind occupy the booths. The staff is beyond attentive and friendly and they're always ready to make menu recommendations, or serve you a can of Tecate with a salt rim and a slice of lime. Bottles start at $25, but the chance to shoot down alien spaceships is only a couple of quarters.

Starlight Bar & Lounge
167 Ave. A (10th & 11th Sts.)
East Village 212.475.2172

Starlight shines brightly in the East Village, drawing a hip, laidback mix of men in their 20s and 30s from all over the city. Perhaps the Chelsea boys, East Village punks, and UES preps converge at Starlight to down this drinkery's relatively inexpensive drinks (shots are priced nicely too). Or maybe they enjoy getting "this close" to each other underneath the entangled spaghetti-like chandelier along the super-narrow walkway that passes the bar. But if the front area gets too cruisy for you, head to the candlelit section of comfy couches in the back, where a stage hosts live music performances on Mondays. Though popular at any time, Starlight is "last chance" cruise central at the end of a night out, including Sunday night's "Starlette" party, when the ladies take over.

Stay
244 E. Houston St. (Aves. A & B)
East Village 212.982.3532

The East Village is never going to be mistaken for West Chelsea, and that's why places like Tribe, Plan B, Niagara, and Abaya, which successfully occupied this space for a while, tend to go over well in these parts. The multicultural crowd that doesn't do ropes or cover charges will be splitting their time between the aforementioned spots and Stay. A long wall of padded banquettes stretches from front bar to back bar in this rather long space, where house and hip-hop say "dance," but the vibe and (the city's archaic cabaret laws) fittingly say "sit…stay…good lounger." Thanks to funky, geometrically clever furniture and linear minimalism, there's a bit of a 2001 vibe to this simultaneously futuristic and retro spot—and we mean the movie and the year.

Steak Frites
9 E. 16th St. (Union Sq. W. & 5th Ave.)
Flatiron 212.463.7101

For a noisy dinner in cramped quarters, swing by Steak Frites around 8pm. For a quiet nightcap, come back at ten and take a seat at the long, dark wooden bar. Friendly bartenders pour glasses of wine or pop open one of the 110 that come by the bottle. Not wild about wine? The French brasserie's specialty drinks are surprising—how does an espresso martini or a peach vanilla mojito sound? Surrounded by original Parisian-inspired artwork and mirrors at every turn, this place is a bit labored, but it's highly forgivable. Plush leather booths line the walls and white tablecloth-clad tables take up the rest of the floor. Try to grab an outside table when the weather gets nice and say ooh la la to all of the passersby.

Still
192 3rd Ave. (17th & 18th Sts.)
Gramercy 212.471.9807

The sports bar/pick-up scene that was once

Stir

Tavaru is Still filled with flirty 20- to 30-year-olds, is Still crowded after work due to great happy hour specials, and is Still basically a neighborhood bar with a faux-classy twist. They did a great job of refurbishing: The blue tavern-like space now has red walls with framed pictures, dim lighting, and leather-lined barstools. And rather than a bottle-service lounge in the back, Still has a second bar for those who want to escape the TVs up front. There is a full menu of salads, pastas, and bar food, and an all-you-can-drink brunch on Sundays. The white-bread crowd has probably never been to Freaknick, but there are no objections when the DJ plays a little Jay-Z…or Will Smith.

Stir
1363 1st Ave. (73rd & 74th Sts.)
Upper East Side 212.744.7190

Frank Sinatra and the rest of the Rat Pack would have loved this place—that is, if they'd been of the female set. At this laidback lounge, martinis are topped with pixie dust, Pop Rocks, and Sweet Tarts to accompany the fruity concoctions being served up. Young professionals relax on comfy banquettes, enjoying tapas like the chicken kebabs and buffalo wontons. Happy hour (Monday-Friday, 5pm-8pm, and Saturdays) is the coveted time to unwind after work. Closer to the

weekend things start to liven up with "All Ladies Night All Night" on Thursdays ($5 cosmos) and DJs spinning from Thursday-Saturday starting at 10pm. On Sundays, the lounge reverts to its laid-back and chill temperament, with live jazz and acoustic performances so you can de-stress before the Monday grind.

Stitch
247 37th St. (7th & 8th Aves.)
Midtown 212.852.4826

"Midtown sucks!" you cry with an empty mug. But fret no more, because Stitch is here to sew the Garment District's tear. With eight choices on tap, 14 different bottles, four reds and whites each, and a fashionable happy hour, this place is dressed for business-casual success. One large screen floats above the bar and two plasmas are scattered, creating a comfortable after-work spot or pre-game stop for nearby Garden events. If the hustle and bustle of the mostly white-bread, dry-clean-only crowd bar is too much after your haute monde day on the runway, go upstairs and take a load off in the bar and lounge area. Munch from an American menu and sip on specialty drinks named after fashion items, which suit the locals. Allergy warning: fresh flowers abound.

Stone Creek
140 E. 27th St. (3rd & Lexington Aves.)
Murray Hill 212.532.1037

Stone Creek

What do you call a mature lounge in Murray Hill with patrons who don't wear baseball hats? A figment of your imagination? Stone Creek is the exception that might prove your sanity yet. Set on a quiet block off of the Third Avenue strip, Stone Creek could easily be the bar inside of Pottery Barn, if it had a bar. All the furniture is cool, comfy, and clean; think "farmhouse chic." This is a great date place to share lobster mac-n-cheese, and it's somewhere to unwind after work with a Belgian beer. Flat-screen TVs sometimes show rad surfing videos, dude, and other times they feature mood-enhancing visuals. If that gets you in the mood, grab your date by the hand, head to a banquette in the backroom, and let the drinks work their magic.

The Stone Rose
10 Columbus Cir. (@ 8th Ave.)
Upper West Side 212.823.9769

In the mezzanine of the ritzy Time Warner Center on Columbus Circle lurks nightlife entrepreneur Rande Gerber's baby, the Stone Rose. This fancy and spacious lounge boasts Trump-worthy views of Central Park and the Columbus Circle statue. The Stone Rose also offers the best vantage point to witness Time Warner executives getting sloshed after a hard day of toeing the corporate line. Waitresses provide fodder for customers' fantasies as they prance around in short, dominatrix-style black dresses and high black boots. Red walls, slender columns, brown leather seats, and marble floors set a posh scene for the mostly

after-work crowd and the occasional fashion show after-party elite to sip on martinis and indulge in the bar's more celebrated drink, Woodford Reserve bourbon fused with Grand Marnier, white-cranberry juice, sour mix, and simple syrup. DJs spin Wed-Sat.

The Stoned Crow
85 Washington Pl. (6th Ave. & Washington Sq. W.)
Greenwich Village 212.677.4022

The Stoned Crow prides itself on being perfect for a loud, brash bunch, whether they're current NYU students or former frat rats. The vaulted ceiling in the backroom makes Crow's billiards room an unusually spacious place to hang; there's plenty of room for large groups to spread out. Add some old movie stills and posters and you've got yourself one of NYC's most relaxed, fun-loving haunts. With beer priced way lower than textbooks or, at some bodegas, even a can of Red Bull (drinks are $5 and under), it's no wonder stressed collegiates gather here to blow off a little pre-finals steam. The famed owner, Betty, has made sure to keep the prices down and the rock up. Let's get hammered and beat up some "NEEERRRRRRRRRD-DDDDDSSSS!"

Stonehome Wine Bar
87 Lafayette St. (@ S. Portland St.)
Fort Greene 718.624.9443

Stonehome fits perfectly into its newly hip, yet longtime friendly, Fort Greene locale. Gracefully fusing a cozy charm with the streamlined sleekness you'd expect from a wine bar, the space is great for relaxing in the midst of unassuming sophistication. Not only is Stonehome a fantastic date destination, but it's also an ideal meeting spot for friends who want to dish about their boyfriends' "bedroom issues" without interruption. Pair some light fare like charcuterie or cheese plates ($8+), or maybe salads and pressed sandwiches ($8+), with an artisan beer ($5+) or one of the 32 wines available by the glass ($6+). There are also options aplenty for bottle-buyers: Stonehome's list goes roughly 140 wines deep

($20-$100). Should you struggle to find a good match for your red velvet cake, the bartender will gladly make a suggestion and he'll do so without an ounce of condescension.

Stonewall
53 Christopher St. (6th & 7th Aves.)
West Village 212.463.0950

The Stonewall is where it all began. Ever since the 1969 NYC rebellion that launched the gay civil-rights movement, Stonewall's reputation as a historic bar continues to lure older generations of gays and lesbians. But Thursday night's "Detention" pop music dance party ensures that this place caters to the new generation too. Most nights, however, attract mainly locals and tourists who come for happy hour and to cruise back in time. Indeed, the bar looks as if it hasn't changed much over the last three decades. But then again, neither have its patrons. Most continue to come here to pick up one of two things: a drink or a man. Anyone who considers him or herself a true New Yorker should warm a stool at the Stonewall; stop by and toast gay rights.

Stout NYC
133 W. 33rd St. (6th & 7th Aves.)
Midtown 212.629.6191

You'd swear you were in a London alleyway and not in Midtown at Stout, the new beer emporium just down the street from MSG. The stone walls and floors give this casual pub a cozy outdoor feel, even though the space is large enough for a lofted second floor which affords great views of the hub-bub below and a chance to perfect your spitting accuracy. With over 20 beers on tap and 125 in bottles, Stout refers to both the wide drink selection and the wide belly that typically comes with it. (Highlights include O'Haras Celtic and Rogue Shakespeare.) Stout also has a large food menu, but with all this beer, who cares? There are also flat-screen TVs so you can watch the game, because nothing goes better with a stout than a little groin-pulling.

Strata
915 Broadway (@ 21st St.)
Flatiron 212.505.2192

If you enjoy comfort food like mac 'n' cheese and chili, but are tired of high-end eateries charging exorbitantly for Mom's cooking, or you're a Prince fan and want to pretend you're at Paisley Park, surrounded by purple and blue, and you like cheesy hip-hop and house music and don't mind obnoxious servers, then Strata fits the bill. The recommended cocktails here are inspired,

Stout NYC

though—Stoli with pomegranate juice, the lychee margarita—as are the live music events that this Flatiron lounge/club has hosted—Elvis Costello, Moby, and Wyclef Jean. Strata boasts high-profile events such as celebrity book signings, movie and TV premieres, and the occasional bar/bat mitzvah. The plus-sized dance floor suits your private party needs, too; just be prepared to ask Mommy and Daddy to foot the bill.

Strip House

13 E. 12th St. (University Pl. & 5th Ave.)
Greenwich Village 212.328.0000

Situated among the scuzzy takeout joints on NYU's restaurant row, Strip House is a surprisingly luxe spot—even for parent's weekend. Draped in red leather, lit with red lights, and decorated with black-and-white photos, the charm of a classic steakhouse is supercharged at Strip House. This attention to detail is surprising, since the restaurant is part of a chain. The crowd tends to be chock-full of younger after-work professionals taking advantage of the prix-fixe meal before 6pm, and their slightly older counterparts enjoying some of the 600-plus bottles of wine that are available. With a celebrity following and super-sexy interior, Strip House is an asset to the college kids surrounding it—it's a course in contemporary classics.

Suba

109 Ludlow St. (Rivington & Delancey Sts.)
Lower East Side 212.982.5714

It's no secret that the service in restaurants is going way downhill. It's true of almost every less-than-four-star restaurant and it's true of Suba—a dining complex where décor is the main draw. A moat (as in a medieval castle) surrounds the dining area where high-end, Spanish-infused cuisine is served. Downstairs, a lounge serves potent and pricey cocktails—and after a few specialty martinis, no one seems to care that they had to wait two hours upstairs for paella. After all, haven't we all come to expect it these days? What you won't want to miss, though, is the dinner-and-a-movie series, which features a new film every week.

Subway Bar

527 Metropolitan Ave. (@ Union Ave.)
Williamsburg 718.218.7956

If taking the L train drives you to drink, head over to the Subway Bar for round two. The public transportation theme décor (subway signs, anyone?) won't blow your mind, and most likely, neither will most aspects of this bar. Don't get us wrong, the Subway Bar isn't a terrible place; but what sort of masochist wants to sit around reminiscing about riding the subway? The music is enjoyable if predictable, the staff is amicable, and the regulars are boring hangers-on and townies. B.Y.O.F. (bring your own friends) because you don't want to get stuck talking to the clientele. Don't get taken for a ride at the pool table; but if you do, you can just step outside to the subway entrance and head back to the city with a Bud tucked discreetly in a paper bag.

Subway Inn

143 E. 60th St. (3rd & Lexington Aves.)
Upper East Side 212.223.8929

The Subway Inn isn't about to replace Siberia Bar as NYC's best-loved dive bar, but the grungy décor and 70-odd-year history ranks it a close second. The sticky, red vinyl-checkered floors, ripped stools, dust-covered, garage sale throwbacks, and the ashtray-scented air provide a "home sweet home"-like atmosphere for bar-hoppers who would rather spend their last $4 on a shot than two overpriced subway rides. True to dive bar form, the Subway Inn only sells beer by the bottle, which may be a good thing, because we would be hard-pressed to know how often they've actually cleaned the taps (if at all) since opening somewhere around the 1930s.

Suede

161 W. 23rd St. (6th & 7th Aves.)
Chelsea 212.633.6113

When Suede opened a few years back, it was "the" club—a prototype of a mod, sleek, minimal-

Suede

ist lounge where divas danced, trust-funders trysted, and celebs made the scene. Things have cooled off since then, but the long and narrow, white-hued room is still your best bet if you're hosting out-of-towners who insist on doing the whole "club" thing. Suede's not a nightmare to get into and it's definitely still dressed well enough to impress. And while newer clubs have encroached a bit on Suede's "hip" turf, like a Botoxed actress making a killer comeback, the Chelsea lounge still has perfectly pretty, primped people and movie stars (Jake Gyllenhaal has been spotted here) coming to twist and shout.

Sugar Bar
254 W. 72nd St. (Broadway & West End Ave.)
Upper West Side 212.579.0222

Sugar Bar is a haven for UWS fans of classic R&B music. Owned by the songwriting and performing duo, Ashford & Simpson, the restaurant revives the fading tradition of the conventional lounge/nightclub with solid-like-a-rock live music acts every Thursday through Saturday night. An Afro-Caribbean theme pervades throughout, from the traditional African art and artifacts displayed on the walls to the menu (entrées average $20-$25). There's a $10-$15 cover and you'll need to order food if you want to sit at a table, but it's well worth it if you're looking for some sweet soul music. And if your rendition of D'Angelo's "Brown Sugar" during Thursday's popular open mic night is good, the crowd won't care that you don't have his washboard build.

Sugar Bar & Lounge
311 Church St. (@ Lispenard St.)
TriBeCa 212.431.8642

You might hear this from a range of spots around town, but Sugar claims to be the originator of the white cosmo. However, this TriBeCa lounge distinguishes itself well enough in other ways to make that claim believable. The overall look—African masks adorning the walls, white tables, and orange couches—is unique to lower Manhattan...let's call it "homey chic." And the sleek bar (with an even sleeker bartender) reminds you just what part of town you're carousing in. But then when you spy the limestone finish on the walls, you might feel like you're in the room where your parents kept the ping-pong table. Stick around for when the beautiful people show; but by then you'll be wondering if your brand-name jeans have already become outdated.

SugarCane
243 Park Ave. S. (19th & 20th Sts.)
Gramercy 212.475.9377

Think Sushi Samba. Now dim the lights, cut the room in half, and add a swanky bar crowded with sexy patrons looking to throw back a few $10 cocktails. Ladies and gentlemen, we have SugarCane, the newest creation from the owners of the well-known Japanese/Peruvian/Brazilian fusion restaurant next door. In fact, the two places are connected, making the narrow space feel like a mere extension of Sushi Samba. The dinner menu is a pared-down version of its neighbor's, divided into categories like Raw, Greens, and Crisps (fried food). Reservations are not accepted, so one of its cozy tables—or any space for that matter—comes at a premium. Large groups of partiers can commandeer the backroom; otherwise, it's up to you to fight the beautiful people for space, and their elbows are sharp.

Sui

54 Spring St. (Lafayette & Mulberry Sts.)
NoLita 212.965.9838

Where better than in an underwater-themed spot for suckling raw fish and sipping a Malibu rum, blue Curacao, and pineapple juice called Blue Buddha? Sui's décor leans towards kitschy—moving lights play against a blue wall to simulate the ocean depths—but becomes decidedly more authentic in the ample dining room, where large aquariums are embedded in the walls, and you can chomp on your raw fish with live ones looking on in terror. (For the record, the big bug-eyed orange creatures are puffer fish. Enjoy!) Sui is going through growing pains as it tries to become a swank sushi/Japanese fusion restaurant and not just another bar on Spring Street. Most nights of the week, you can sit at the quiet bar and talk with friends at normal decibel levels, and you'll have the newbie bartender all to yourselves.

The Sullivan Room

218 Sullivan St. (3rd & Bleecker Sts.)
Greenwich Village 212.252.2151

Techno beats turn this inconspicuous basement located in the heart of the Village's tourist district into a rocking party bar most evenings. If you have a quiet early nightcap in mind, the painted blue demons on the walls may well be your only company because the hip-at-heart don't show off their dancing skills until the late-night hours when the beats are hitting hard and loud and the dance floor is packed with more bumping and grinding bodies than that S&M club scene in *The Matrix Reloaded*. Decorated with ornate lighting, Persian rugs, and velvet couches, the Sullivan Room offers a subterranean refuge for those who love to break a sweat on the dance floor but don't want to spend an hour trying to talk their way past a snooty bouncer.

The Sunburnt Cow

137 Ave. C (8th & 9th Sts.)
East Village 212.529.0005

You might not spot Russell Crowe at this Aussie bar (he's probably still trying to make that one phone call—only this time it might be from behind bars), but you will be greeted at the door by a friendly bouncer, tiki torches, and a burnt-red cow. Inside, the down-under vibe heats up thanks to the house, soul, funk, and pop music that rips through the airwaves. Any night caters to your craving, from the $15 brunch on weekends with an endless supply of Moomosas or pints of Fosters to the Fiesta Cubana on Thursdays, offering a dinner special and free salsa instructions. With an upbeat crowd, friendly staff, and the specialty Moo Juice cocktail, this bar takes you to the Outback without having to leave New York.

Supercore

305 Bedford Ave. (@ S. 1st St.)
Williamsburg 718.302.1629

If Supercore were a superhero, one of his powers would be the ability to destroy wallets in a single visit—not that this Japanese sake shack is particularly pricey, but because every item on the menu is so inviting. Have you ever had sake-simmered carrot, lotus, and konnyaku? How about mackerel with ginger, white radish, and scallion? Imagine trying these unique foods under paper lanterns, behind wooden blinds, or in a powerful bar designed to bring Tokyo and America closer together than a mere mortal ever could. If that's not your thing there's a courtyard for nature lovers and regular ol' lovers to get away from the busy, decidedly hip crowd inside. Not just another faux divey Williamsburg joint, Supercore is the center of feng chic.

Supreme Trading

213 N. 8th St. (Driggs Ave. & Roebling St.)
Williamsburg 718.599.4224

OK, so you've heard that Williamsburg is the "next big thing" and you want to see what all the rage is about (but just for the record, people have been saying that about Williamsburg for the past 10 years). After a short ride on the L, amble over to Supreme Trading—a multiplex of dancing, drinking, and pool-sharking. This neighborhood bar is well-known for its art gallery and its Friday night "Crashin' In" party, which is usually packed with B-list celebs like Smashing Pumpkins' alum James Iha and the Yeah Yeah Yeahs' Nick Zimmer. Take a breather on the bleacher-like seats in the smoker's lounge or amble outside to the back courtyard, where you can giggle because now you know what all those Manhattanites are missing.

Sushi Generation
1571 2nd Ave. (81st & 82nd Sts.)
Upper East Side 212.249.2222

Contrary to popular belief, not all sushi is priced for the budgets of people living in this restaurant's neighborhood. And other than saving Upper East Siders a trip downtown to get their hands on some sticky rice, Sushi Generation offers little variation on quality or selection, save some creative menu options like the Hari-Kare Flambé for two and the Tiger's Eye roll. The sidewalk area invites locals who aren't shy about bringing their dogs along and a generous happy hour offers half-priced beers from 3pm-7pm, but this good deal goes undiscovered as on weeknights the place aches for customers to fill the bountiful seating area. Sushi Generation has little appeal as a bar, but it's a perfectly acceptable restaurant option for those unaware of the tastier raw fish options below 14th Street.

Sushi Samba Park
245 Park Ave. S. (19th & 20th Sts.)
Gramercy 212.475.9377

Sushi can be a frightening endeavor for skittish "meat-and-potatoes" eaters. But adventurous palettes rejoice; at Sushi Samba Park, you'll encounter a ton of fresh, creative ways to filet raw fish—like the Green Envy roll, made with wasabi pea crust, tuna, salmon, asparagus, and aji Amarillo key lime mayo. This upscale Gramercy restaurant/bar has cornered the market on hip ambience too—the glass wall facing the street is an art-deco arrangement of red, yellow, and green sections and upside-down white mushroom-caps pad the ceiling above the sleek sushi bar. Sushi Samba's antichuchos (shish-kabobs) and churras-

co (grilled steak and pork with beans and rice) are unbelievable. And sake-lovers have over 30 varieties to choose from. Über-trendy people seated nearby are gleefully tolerated in order to experience this swank, inventive establishment.

Sushi Samba 7
87 7th Ave. S. (@ Barrow St.)
West Village 212.691.7885

The second New York incarnation of the beloved Japanese/Brazilian/Peruvian-infused restaurant, this location offers rooftop lounging underneath a breath-taking atrium-like ceiling that's covered with criss-crossing ivy and fogged glass. Everything is exciting about this chic West Village hub—except for the predominantly Bridge and Tunnel patronage. Sushi Samba 7 tastefully blends exotic flavors (menu items include seviche, edamame, tuna tartare, churrascos, and vegetarian udon), and boasts an impressive cocktail menu punctuated by an intense saketini. A raspberry mojito will take the edge off of the fluorescent décor. Make your way to the unisex restrooms (read: equal-opportunity wait time), where communal washing occurs over wooden barrels surrounded by thick bamboo stalks. The expert bar staff is only slightly less friendly than the gruff bouncer, so dress nice and come bearing tips.

Suspenders
111 Broadway (@ Wall St.)
Financial District 212.732.5005

Owned and operated by former NYC firefighters, this jovial watering hole is a Dalmation and a pole short of being a station house. Until recently, the bar staff even gamely wore suspenders until it was deemed "too '80s." Make your way down the trash-strewn flight of stairs and your perseverance is rewarded with a tall cold one served up by a chatty female bartender at the 90-foot mahogany bar. Owner and former fire lieutenant Bill Ahearn heartily greets the crowd most nights of the week and as he puts it, "We're open when the market's open," which is to say, not on the weekends.

Sutra
16 1st Ave. (1st & 2nd Sts.)
East Village 212.677.9477

With two levels of mirrored hallways, banquettes just waiting to be danced upon, and bottle-service, Sutra—formerly the Flat—is ready to cater to a party girl's dreams in a tranny girl neighborhood. With a rotating schedule of theme nights including "Funk Monday," "Reggae Tuesdays," and the always-packed (and cover charge-free) weekends, this sexy lounge is a bit more glamorous than your average First Avenue nightclub. The bartenders and bouncers are relaxed and friendly, keeping in mind that in order to make it in this neighborhood, you actually need more than just a pretty face. Exotic fixtures and a red pool table in the backroom give Sutra a fun taste of bordello chic. Kama on in.

Sutton Place
1015 2nd Ave. (53rd & 54th Sts.)
Midtown 212.207.3777

Think a rooftop bar on a warm summer evening sounds like a great idea? Well, so do the other 600 people who try to cram onto Sutton Place's roof every night. The huge, table-filled, and overcrowded outdoor space tops off the two floors below it, each of which features a bar and dance floor. The bar's staff is surprisingly quick, and grabbing a drink is easier and less-expensive than you'd expect. Bar food is also served, but these girls would seemingly rather go home with a guy who wears Drakkar Noir than eat a greasy fry. (They're both bad for you, but fries don't borrow money.) Sutton Place could be considered a pick-up spot...if you're a guy; the girl-to-guy ratio reads like an episode of *The Bachelor*.

Sway
305 Spring St. (Greenwich & Hudson Sts.)
SoHo 212.620.5220

If you need a place to feel popular or show off your latest fashion buy, Sway is for you. Decked out in Moroccan style (colorful tiles, tall archways, red lanterns), Sway houses booths that are usually tagged with "Reserved" signs. But don't fret; snag one anyway and see how long your fabulousness will let you get away with it. Enjoying their reputation of being pretentious, the style-policing doormen and bartenders do their part to toe the trendy line. A DJ spins techno/hip-hop remixes that keep the young and oh-so-slim crowd (that's schooled on the art of emulating the young, rich, and famous) dancing until past 2am. Hey, if you can't hang out with Paris Hilton, why not hang out with 50 people who look exactly like her?

Sweet and Vicious
5 Spring St. (Bowery & Elizabeth St.)
NoLita 212.334.7915

Like a lot of other bars, Sweet and Vicious faces a tough Catch-22: To develop a reputation as a hotspot, you must attract people to the bar. However, as soon as it's achieved popularity, overcrowding becomes a liability, newer bars are born, etc. This cool bar itself has not changed—low-lying wooden benches still line a spacious room with exposed brick that's intimately lit with candle-stocked Gothic chandeliers. Sadly, Sweet and Vicious also features debris strewn on the floor as a weekend B&T crowd tosses back drinks and engages in vigorous make-out sessions near the bathroom. The after-work scene is more laidback and when it's open, the back patio's still pretty sweet.

Sweet Ups
277 Graham Ave. (Powers & Grand Sts.)
Williamsburg 718.384.3886

Like Royal Oak's parlor motif, but hate dancing to Interpol with a bunch of sweaty art-school students? Enter Sweet Ups, the Oak's mellower, blossoming sister. Located on the East Williamsburg/Bushwick cusp, Sweet Ups' clientele is mostly made up of neighborhood folk. Think coupled-off, late 20-something folks who want to chat and have a cheap yet classy cocktail (like the $6 gin bramble) in an antique setting (red-velvet wallpaper, dark-leather banquettes) while rocking to an indie soundtrack. And the ladies' bathroom is what all thrift-shopping girls wish their home loo was like—a vintage sanctuary with a marble table and ornate-looking glass, and that cheap strawberry candle smell. If your dream girl is Bettie Page, get a gander at the wooden pinup girls that serve as the beer tap tops.

Swift Hibernian Lounge
34 E. 4th St. (Bowery & Lafayette St.)
NoHo 212.227.9438

"May you live all the days of your life," said the great satirist Jonathan Swift, whose ironic gaze stares down from his enormous visage painted onto this bar's wall. Living a few of those days here isn't a bad idea. A long wooden church pew from Ireland is bolted to the wall behind the bar and it holds all the liquor. In the dim backroom, a DJ spins pop music atop a pulpit. The bar staff is friendly and the patrons, a collection of B-Bar refugees and locals, are cordial enough even when the standing area gets beyond crowded. Oh, and if you're thinking of leaving without finishing off your beer, Swift would remind you, "Better belly burst than good liquor be lost."

Swing 46
349 W. 46th St. (8th & 9th Aves.)
Hell's Kitchen 212.262.9554

Remember back in the '90s when swing dancing was all the rage? Y'all were jumpin', jivin', and wailin'—but hey, there are only so many times you can sweat it up to the Glenn Miller Orchestra, right? Not for the grand-daddy-o's and hep cats hitting the floor during busy nights at Swing 46. Nightly live jazz music will have you pushing the chairs out of the way the instant you walk into this happenin' joint. It'll cost you on weekend nights, though ($10 if you have dinner or $12 to just drink and cut a rug)—but dig it; when's the last time you hit a supper club and then did the Lindy hop until you needed a shower? Get out there and party like it's 1939.

TA Cocina Express
714 9th Ave. (48th & 49th Sts.)
Hell's Kitchen 212.586.0821

It's difficult to pass by this taqueria without being lured inside by the spellbinding sweet scent of Mexican food. And with a 2-for-1 margarita special Sunday through Thursday, you're likely to stay awhile if you do. Just about everything is designed to keep "gringos" happy and glued to their seats. The light Brazilian jazz playing in the background, paired with dim lighting, makes this a *bueño* place to impress a date. If you run out of things to say to

Swift Hibernian Lounge

each other, you can always check out the walls adorned with Frida Kahlo and Diego Garcia prints, hanging plants, and Aztec masks—or count the spices tucked beneath the glass on the tables. Food service is strictly takeout here, though; so order the Mexican-style pork chops and *vamos!*

Table 50
643 Broadway (@ Bleecker St.)
NoHo 212.253.2560

It's not that Table 50 is too pretentious to have a sign or any outdoor markings. It's just that this DJ lounge harks back to the Prohibition era, when it was a speakeasy, and only word of mouth could lead you here. Black, cast-iron stairs descend into this underground, brick-walled space that still exudes an illicit, yesteryear vibe; though when you get the cocktail bill, you'll be snapped back to the present-day soon enough. You won't find any bootleg moonshine here, but there's plenty of Grey Goose and potent fruity drinks like the Blackberry 50 (vodka and crushed berries). You can thank Table 50's cabaret license and big-name DJs like Grandmaster Flash for getting the crowd (like P. Diddy and Prince) to cut some sexy moves on the dance floor.

Table XII (aka Etoile)
109 E. 56th St. (Park & Lexington Aves.)
Midtown 212.750.5656

Though Etoile is still in action on Friday and Saturday nights, this space has been largely transformed into one of Manhattan's most stunning and exciting new restaurants. Created by restaurateur John Scotto, this new space is crowned with gilded accents, soft tones, and candlelight. A more casual and cozy front bar feels like a bistro, but the back bar in the main dining room features ceilings and original moldings built for William Randolph Hearst's castle, San Simeon. Geometric works of art hung on the walls make you feel like you've stumbled into one of Napoleon's castles that was eventually inherited by a rogue mathematician. Table XII is elegant without being stodgy, and the Italian cuisine (homemade pastas, veal paillard) is so good it lives up to the legend-inspiring gallant décor (and prices). Come on the weekend if you feel like dancing.

Taboon
773 10th Ave. (@ 52nd St.)
Hell's Kitchen 212.713.0721

When a restaurant located so far from civilization doesn't take credit cards, you'll have to scour the area for an ATM. But this posh Middle Eastern/Mediterranean restaurant will make you forget all about that (and those pesky ATM fees) when you sit down at one of the tables and you're

Table XII

greeted by warm, puffy bread and olive oil. The décor is romantic and the menu stretches far beyond your average hummus and kebab fare (we dare you to try the squab). Taboon becomes "the fire in Hell's Kitchen" with live Spanish guitar playing on Monday nights ("Flamenco Chill"). Sample the weekday happy hour (half-priced drinks from 5pm-7pm), but before you traipse over from Port Authority with a bankroll after dark, try their brunch and see how "Middleterraneans" treat a hangover.

Tai
223 Mulberry St. (Spring & Prince Sts.)
NoLita 212.965.0439

When lounge-hopping in NoLita gets old—and believe us, it does—try Tai, a sultry Thai joint with bamboo walls, velvet curtains, and arty black-and-white photos. Start your evening at the semi-swanky bar with a Lolita—cherry vodka, maraschino, and lemon juice—or choose from the fine selection of wines, and then move on to the candlelit tables for some superb Thai eats, from Ho Mok Pla (salmon filet wrapped in banana leaf) to Neua Yang (grilled sirloin steak with lemongrass sauce and green papaya salad). Once satiated, kick it upstairs at the soothing Velvet Lounge (generally only open for special events and sometimes on weekends) and test out your new Thai pick-up line, helpfully printed on the menu: "Tan arhan yen kab pom mai?" You know what we're talking about, hot stuff.

Tainted Lady Lounge
318 Grand St. (@ Havemeyer St.)
Williamsburg 718.302.5514

Deb Parker (of Beauty Bar and the since-closed Barmacy) tells the story of the "art" on display at her most recent venture: apparently a trucker's widow uncovered dozens of busty nudes on velvet canvases that her hubby had been painting from magazines for decades prior to his demise. Shocked by her husband's tasteless talent, the widow was more than happy to fork his "masterpieces" over to Deb, who has always harnessed the energy of tacky memorabilia in the best possible way. Campy soft porn emanates from the TVs,

but amicable bar-goers are too busy making new friends to notice. Fancy beers like Chimay, Duvel, and Framboise Lambic are options, as are cans of Miller and PBR. Try a signature cocktail named after a famous tainted lady: Lizzie Borden Extreme Bloody Mary or a Mae West's Red Kiss.

Taj
48 W. 21st St. (5th & 6th Aves.)
Flatiron 212.620.3033

PBR? What's that? Frown on downscale drinkeries? Are you the decidedly discriminating type who would never consider darkening the doorway of a sports bar? Here's guessing you lo-o-o-ve Taj. The well-heeled crowd is welcomed here with open arms and top-shelf service. Get a funky tribal groove on in their exotic-themed environ as you chill to a mix of DJ-spun tunes underneath Far East-inspired trumpet-like lamps. If you're flying solo, settle in with some French-American/Indian-influenced munchies or invite the whole harem down for some outrageously delicious cocktails. Weekdays, weekends, after work, or after dark—anytime is the perfect time to receive the royal treatment at Taj.

Tamari
201 5th Ave. (Union St. & Berkeley Pl.)
Park Slope 718.230.5636

This gentle, candlelit Japanese addition—not the only one by any means—to the impressive Fifth Avenue strip of bars and restaurants bills itself as a "sake and Japanese tapas bar." Sunday to Thursday from 6pm-8pm is "Happy Sake Hour" (which refers to alcohol and not to some prurient service advertised in the back of the *Village Voice*), during which if you buy one small sake ($5.50), you get one house sake free. Sashimi and various noodle dishes dominate the menu, but Korean kimchi and BBQ are also offered. Most entrées range from $7.50-$15. You won't hear any babies crying at this Japanese tapas lounge; the only infraction found here might be a discussion between two friends about the correct pronunciation of the fermented rice beverage they've had too much of.

Tamarind

41-43 E. 22nd St. (Park Ave. S. & Broadway)
Flatiron 212.674.7400

It's Friday night. You're a 40-year-old male. You've worked hard. You come to Tamarind's bar to let loose…and you see about seven more of you. Situated in the chicly soothing environment of one of the best Indian restaurants this side of Bombay, the bar plays second sitar to the amazing food in the restaurant and the eponymous tea house next door. But what the bar lacks in a social scene it makes up for in décor, music, and drinks like the Indian Kiss ($10) or tamarind margaritas ($9). If you're a 40-year-old woman looking to be treated like a Brahman, come on by. Otherwise, Tamarind is a restaurant best enjoyed by groups, with the bar being an afterthought.

Tao

42 E. 58th St. (Madison & Park Aves.)
Midtown 212.888.2288

The gossip columns and A-listers long ago said "ciao" to Tao, but this former hotspot still provides enough Manhattan chic for the *Sex and the City* fans and former pro athletes found in the cramped downstairs bar. Oh sure, some patrons might feel a little silly ignoring the terrific selection of Asian beers on the menu when they order that pricey saketini, but don't let the koi pond and giant Buddha fool you— despite Tao's reputation as "the largest and most popular Asian restaurant in New York City," it's largely a theme joint for people who really believe that starlets and rock stars frequent Planet Hollywood.

The Tapas Lounge

1078 1st Ave. (@ 59th St.)
Midtown 212.421.8282

Several plates of tapas, a lemonada, and a pitcher of sangria later, you may find yourself referring to your busboy as "mi amor" before you realize that you're at a velvety, candlelit lounge in Midtown. A swanky spot that draws a mostly international crowd, the Tapas Lounge is likely to bring you back to your college days when you studied abroad in Madrid, with a menu that could put a café in Plaza Mayor to shame. A bottle off of the impressive list of authentic Spanish wines (50 by the bottle) will leave you two *hojas* to the wind, but at very New York prices, stick to one glass and you'll only be half off your leather chair.

Tapeo 29

29 Clinton St. (@ Stanton St.)
Lower East Side 212.979.0002

Tapeo 29

Deep in the Lower East Side, Tapeo 29 has not only created the term "tapas bar-hopping," but they've also made their dark and intimate space a necessary stop on such bourgeois-bohemian excursions. With wooden shutters on the windows and just a small sign painted on a wood door, Tapeo is an inviting offer. The wine list has some range and glasses go for roughly $7 a pour while bottles top out at $65. Authentic "queso de Espana" and smoked meat dishes are recommended and the wait staff is good about helping with mixes and matches. Forget about tapping a keg and chill out at Tapeo 29 instead.

Taste
1411 3rd Ave. (80th & 81st Sts.)
Upper East Side 212.717.9798

Self-service café by day, sophisticated candlelit restaurant and wine bar by night, Taste errs on the fancy side. But after all, this is the Upper East Side, and its olive drab walls and dark marble bar do make it a bit murky. The wine list is expansive not only in offerings but also in the regions it spans. Taste's menu is impressive and changes slightly from day to day; on offer are the likes of Taku River King salmon, sardines with tabbouleh, and salad with endive and pecorino croutons. Dig the tasty complimentary olives on the bar, but otherwise be prepared to spend. Consider boning up on your wine vocabulary before bringing a date.

The Tasting Room
72 E. 1st St. (1st & 2nd Aves.)
East Village 212.358.7831

With just 11 tables and 25 seats, there's certainly a communal feel at work here. Despite a lack of space, the Tasting Room carries 300 wines by the bottle, and over 10 by the glass. There's no need for a bar here as neither liquor nor beer is offered—the drink menu reads like the props list from the movie *Sideways*. All of the New American dishes are made with local organic ingredients, and the items change daily. Tasting Room is a great place for a date or an intimate group, as they don't accept reservations for more than five people unless that group wishes to rent out the place, which basically means inviting another couple or two. There's no room for arguing that this dark little wooden room has an incomparable charm…literally.

Tavern on Dean
755 Dean St. (@ Underhill Ave.)
Prospect Heights 718.638.3326

Tavern on Dean is about as old-school as it gets in up-and-coming Prospect Heights. Born at the dawn of the hipster invasion, this cozy, three-room bar and grill is favored by Brooklynites yearning for their borough's days of yore, as well as neighborhood newbies willing to venture a few blocks off Vanderbilt Avenue for a bite and a beer. Because of this dual affiliation, Tavern on Dean tries to straddle the line between unpretentious and upscale—the laidback vibe at the long, mahogany bar is London pub-ish, while the prices seem better-suited for a typical Manhattan watering hole. Still, a solid menu and friendly staff have let locals take root. In back, an enclosed garden (open year-round) hosts an amalgamation of patrons, proving the bar's everyman appeal.

Tavern on First
1678 1st Ave. (87th & 88th Sts.)
Upper East Side 212.828.7820

We have to give Tavern on First some credit—despite looking, smelling, and sounding like a standard Irish pub, it manages to set itself from the pack. The beer selection is more than respectable and the bar's layout is spacious. Extra points are awarded for employing competent older bartenders rather than comely young lasses who flirt, giggle, and mix lousy drinks. This may not sit well with the khaki crowd, but Tavern on First's hardened drinkers know that an average girl and five beers trumps a pretty girl and no beer. (What that means for ladies is good odds and odd goods.) The outdoor seating area is another huge plus, as sun and suds go together like cigarettes and…more suds.

Tavern on Jane
31 8th Ave. (@ Jane St.)
West Village 212.675.2526

This unpretentious pub has a ye olde tavern-ish feel—exposed bricks, tin ceilings, and a location on an old, crooked street—but without the ye olde tavern-like gaiety. Where's the merriment? The singing? The hot, drunk Irish chicks and beefy bartenders spinning tales with mirth and high spirits? You won't find any of that here, that's for sure. Still, the hearty pub food is tasty, the single-malt Scotches are divine, and the joint is kid-friendly. Hear that? We said "kid-friendly." If that doesn't stop you from coming here, nothing will. But if you do have some little ones, steer the stroller over here for that once-a-month out-with-the-kids dinner.

Tavern on the Green
Central Park W. (@ 67th St.)
Upper West Side 212.873.3200

There's a lot of hype surrounding Tavern on the Green, most of which is true: It's overpriced. It's smarmy. It's crowded with theater celebs (if you're lucky) or out-of-towners (if you're not). Well, get over it. The Tavern is a New York institution that—overrated food aside—delivers an unbeatably swanky experience. Bypass the dining room and sit in the intimate upstairs alcove for a clandestine champagne rendezvous, or head to the garden from June to September. Sip sweet cocktails or sample an à la carte menu beneath Japanese lanterns and the occasional celestial (and maybe celebrity) body. Mixed drinks are 2-for-1 during happy hour; dancing, DJs, and live music are offered nightly to a diverse crowd. (Weather- and event-permitting; call ahead.) The bar stays open all day; "official" closing time is 10:30, but the real time varies—the staff always stays as long as the crowd.

Tea Lounge
837 Union St. (6th & 7th Aves.)
Park Slope 718.789.2762

The Union Street sibling of Park Slope's premier teahouse proves you can never get too much of a good thing. Only blocks away from its older sister, Tea Lounge draws a crowd of caffeine addicts and those who like their drinks "Irish." Enticed by the extra seating and expanded menu, everyone from Park Slope granola types to the yuppie stroller set frequents this neighborhood watering hole. Free wireless Internet and plenty of caffeine fuel the scores of writers and students that converge on the couches with a cup of chai to tap out the next breakthrough novel. During happy hour (daily 5pm-7pm), trade your English Breakfast in for a Moroccan mojito, a beer, or an $8.50 Greentini of vodka, green tea, lime, and grenadine.

Teddy's Bar & Grill
96 Berry St. (@ N. 8th St.)
Williamsburg 718.384.9787

Where do you go on a fourth date if you're 39? Teddy's beautiful old-school structure (stained-glass windows, wood molding, punched-tin ceilings) seems to be attracting an older set these days. But on occasion, one might see the odd hipster alone, crying into his beer at the end of the bar, complaining about gentrification. Even if you don't fit one of these profiles, Teddy's atmosphere is relaxed enough for all types to bring their friends or their emotional baggage for an easy drink in a scene-free spot. Though Teddy's does serve wings and burgers throughout the night, this joint is oddly classy.

The Telephone Bar and Grill
149 2nd Ave. (9th & 10th Sts.)
East Village 212.529.5000

Unlike other night spots, the gimmicks here are kept to a minimum, keeping the younger crowds at bay further downtown. The theme is an Anglophile's paradise, but native patriots will simply find a solid hangout. Food choices are ample, ranging from greasy appetizers to English specialties for curious risk-takers (English stilton cheese fritters, anyone?). Likewise, beer connoisseurs will find a rare selection of imported hops. For those looking to sit back and be entertained, there's poetry, comedy, and music, and movies are shown on an LCD screen in the rear lounge. Brits yearning for life across the pond can try dialing home in the antique-style red phone booths lining the front wall of this English-style pub; but they're bloody out of commission, so try one of the English beers on draught instead.

Temple Bar
332 Lafayette St. (Bleecker & Houston Sts.)
NoHo 212.925.4242

Serving as a discreet house of worship for the business-chic, as well as being a nice first date

fabulous fusion dinner menu
transforms into lounge with dj
exotic cocktails
private events
corporate parties
private vip room available

taj

48 West 21st St. NYC
212 620 3033 www.tajlounge.com

Temple Bar

spot, Temple Bar is a clandestine place for seedy dealing of every kind. The long, stained, cherry-oak bar, inviting cocktail lounge, dimmed backlighting, and velvet drapes set a romantic stage at this lover's den. Jazz favorites croon in the background, an extensive list of alarmingly strong specialty beverages further set "the mood," and with 70 types of vodka, this 17-year-old NoHo hideaway is a closer's best friend. Those wishing to do more than nibble on their date's neck or kiss their boss's arse can try the tasty salt-and-pepper calamari. If the high-end cocktails have already tapped out your wallet, dive into some complimentary popcorn.

Temple New York
240 W. 52nd St. (Broadway & 8th Ave.)
Midtown 212.489.7656

Looking to bring the club-goers and lounge-dwellers to Midtown is no easy feat and Temple has their work cut out for them. Despite the considerable dance floor, state-of-the-art sound system, and Moroccan vibe, another challenge may be getting people to forget this tri-level venue used to be Float. Still, the chic banquettes, hidden nooks, VIP areas, and muted lighting encourage excess, so indulge by overspending on bottle service and other acts of gluttony. In fact, Temple

seems to support such behavior—especially the bottle service. Not looking to drop a week's salary on premium vodka? Not to worry—there's a bar on each floor, along with a balcony overlooking the dance floor, so you can keep grooving to the sounds provided by the impressive roster of DJs.

Tenement
157 Ludlow St. (Stanton & Rivington Sts.)
Lower East Side 212.766.9028

This isn't the rundown dive you would expect from a place named Tenement, though it actually used to be one. Tenement's upscale décor and mixed-bag menu, which includes panini ($8-$11), po' boys ($8-$11), lamb ($18), and salmon ($16), make for a successful combination, despite a slight lack of focus. Housing 16 wines by the bottle, roughly half that many by the glass, a bit of bubbly, and a dessert wine list, Tenement's real treats are the mango margaritas ($11) and saketinis (a lavender-infused sake; $10). Take your drink upstairs and check out the lounge area. If you think it's intimate now, you should have seen it when it housed 10 families. Congrats to this place for fusing a touch of the old with a bit of the new in a neighborhood on the verge of an identity crisis.

Tennessee Mountain
143 Spring St. (@ Wooster St.)
SoHo 212.431.3993

If not for this themey, suburban-feeling place's having been here for 23 years, it would be easy to write it off as another gimmick that lacks Spring Street cred. A 4pm-7pm weekday happy hour of half-priced drinks including $1.50 Buds can attract some local action, but the North Carolina barbecue ribs and Texas pulled pork aren't here to impress Moby and the liberal intelligentsia. So here's the crux: Why open a touristy place that gives visitors what they come here to get away from? Ask Applebee's—it seems to work. The $9 house specialty, Tennessee Moonshine, doesn't answer any questions, but a few of them just might make the answers less important. Maybe a Red State infusion like this will help us city slickers figure out what everybody else is thinking.

Terra Blues
149 Bleecker St. (Thompson St. & LaGuardia Pl.)
Greenwich Village 212.777.7776

Big cities can be breeding grounds for the blues, but the music at this venue/bar is more of the my-baby-left-me than that-frat-boy-throwing-up-on-himself-will-someday-be-president variety. Candles flicker in the dark, second-story room where some sit at the bar, others grab a table, and a few even dance in front of the locals-friendly stage. Acoustic acts and one-man bands take the stage at 7pm every night, and later on, things start to get a little livelier when legendary bluesmen (like Little Milton, Edgar Winter, and Robert Lockwood, Jr.) plug in the heavy artillery. Thursday nights tend to draw the more impressive acts, but this place puts a little soul into a pretty evil stretch of bars. That said, NYU will surely be petitioning to buy this place or shut it down soon.

T.G. Whitney's
244 E. 53rd St. (2nd & 3rd Aves.)
Midtown 212.888.5772

One look at this bar's online dating-like photo album and you'll get the feeling that T.G.'s will do anything to attract young, clean-looking singles. So if you're more Nerve.com or Onion.com than Clubyuppie.com, T.G. Whitney's might not be the correct match for you. Offering staple bar food (greasy hamburgers, cheese fries), an after-work crowd, outdoor seating, and, like every other bar these days, karaoke, T.G.'s is the kind of bar that keeps the Midtown wheels well-greased. Still, as the pictures indicate, T.G.'s patrons seem to be having a grand old time. Head to T.G.'s if you're hanging with your by-the-books cubicle mates or looking to catch up with your old sorority and fraternity buddies. Otherwise, tell T.G. you'll take a rain check.

Thady Con's
915 2nd Ave. (48th & 49th Sts.)
Midtown 212.688.9700

It's been suggested that Thady Con's is a fake Irish bar, but not too many people complain about Pam Anderson's "fake" boobs, so what's the big deal? This isn't like the Olive Garden claiming to be Italian, or even Donovan McNabb trying to say he's from Dublin. The owners are off-the-boat Irish, and the bartenders speak with a brogue. The live music schedule features Irish surnames like "Deegan" and "Murphy," and the atmosphere is surprisingly cozy and inviting, whether you're looking to raise a Smithwick's and sing along with some Irish drinking song you've never heard before, or to impress a date with a cool pub in Midtown that has character to spare. Self-consciously themey, Thady Con's is as Irish as freckles, potatoes, and U2.

Therapy
348 W. 52nd St. (8th & 9th Aves.)
Hell's Kitchen 212.397.1700

Even in New York a whorehouse-turned-Zen-gay-bar raises eyebrows. This Hell's Kitchen drinkery's rock pond, wood walls, and stone floors is a little

Therapy

Pier 1ish, but the pseudo-tranquility somehow transports to the mature, mostly male crowd that exudes less attitude than Chelsea and more class than the Lower East Side. The 18 suggestive ("Oral Fixation," "Coitus Interruptus") and psychologically laden ("Freudian Sip," "Pavlov's Dog") signature drinks ($10) require little imagination and a well-padded wallet. More reserved drinkers might opt for six tap beers like Bass and Blue Moon or a glass of Pinot Grigio and grab a candlelit table downstairs. Go-go dancers on Thursdays encourage a friskier, more sociable crowd upstairs, but don't worry—bars grace both floors.

Third and Long
523 3rd Ave. (@ 35th St.)
Murray Hill 212.447.5711

Your hands might stick to the bar top here, but you'll be glad you visited the crown jewel of cheap-o Murray Hill nightlife. Pleasantly unadorned and armed with an ardently committed local fan base, Third and Long features drink specials, drink specials, and more drink specials.

Saturday nights it's "Kill the Keg" ($3 pints until, yes, the keg's empty). On Mondays and Tuesdays, $1 will get you a pint of Bud or Bud Light. Still, the bartenders claim the main draw here is that this is where "locals come to meet each other" (who says New Yorkers are cold?). For a fine community feel without a drop of pretension, Third and Long goes the distance.

Thirsty Scholar
155 2nd Ave. (9th & 10th Sts.)
East Village 212.777.6514

As you walk up to this unassuming Second Avenue watering hole, you might have the same thought as most: frat-urated. But don't be too quick to judge. The Thirsty Scholar betters all those baseball cap joints in the east teens. Yes, it's very NYU, but pay close attention to the bartender when he says they don't have nearly enough guys to go with all the girls. Plus, the Thirsty Scholar's interior is a cut above, with a suit of armor perched above the carefully lit bar, high ceilings, and rustic, exposed brick. Throw some darts with your $5 pint, and enjoy your improved chances with the ladies. Management is actually considering doing a Fellas Night. Beat them to the punch and show up with some buddies of your own.

13
35 E. 13th St. (@ University Pl.)
Greenwich Village 212.979.6677

A rooftop deck, chill crowd, and a 2-for-1 weekday happy hour make 13 a happening spot for any after-work get-together. The roof deck is smoker-friendly and the two spacious lounges downstairs pump danceable tunes so you can shake your booty with abandon. Cute bartenders make strong drinks, so if you arrive at 4pm for happy hour, you'll be sloshed by 8. 13 offers a relaxed, fun setting to meet someone for drinks for the first time; it's crowded enough that there's ambient noise, but you won't have to fight your way through the crowd for a good table or shout to your date. Come for karaoke on Wednesday nights if you want to channel your inner Donna Summer.

13 Little Devils

120 Orchard St. (Rivington & Delancey Sts.)
Lower East Side 212.420.1355

An all-boroughs crowd lives in sin at 13 Little Devils, where a projector screen on the back wall treats their devilish eyes to crazy film clips. Commit to the seven sins-themed cocktails or get gluttonous with the $5-$6 beers, relax slothfully on the cozy banquettes, lust after the hottie at the end of the bar, envy the person getting past the velvet ropes before you, show off on the dance floor, and get pissed at the peeping Tom downstairs looking up your skirt from the glass slats on the main level. And remember to take care of your servers—there's a special place in Hell for bad tippers.

Thomas Beisl

25 Lafayette Ave. (Ashland Pl. & St. Felix St.)
Fort Greene 718.222.5800

The food's the thing at Thomas Beisl, which serves eclectic and surprisingly affordable Austrian/French bistro fare in its warm, wooden dining space. Star chef/owner Thomas Ferlesch moved south to Brooklyn's Fort Greene after a long stint serving it up for the Upper West Side set, and the local scene—plus the nightly BAM-goers—has been saying "danke schon" ever since. Many of the patrons sitting at the busy bar appear to be regulars, and the after-work scene is especially lively. And after a few pints of the best Austrian beer, you won't be able to resist that sweet smell of goulash any longer. If you like buns and you can not lie give these mega-burgers a try.

Thom Bar (@ 60 Thompson)

60 Thompson St. (Broome & Spring Sts.)
SoHo 212.219.2000

There are no surprises about this charming boutique-like hotel lounge that's filled with well-heeled SoHo-lites, local celebrities, and fit wait-

Thom Bar

resses wearing tiny skirts. Everything runs with mechanical efficiency—right down to the leather club chairs and roomy benches that perfectly match the muted earth tones and plants. The corner seats are most conducive to people-watching. As found in neighboring hotel lounges, including the SoHo and TriBeCa Grands, it's hard to distinguish locals from hotel guests as they're the same cosmopolitan flavor. Ambient house tunes play in the background (DJs spin Thursday-Saturday) and they're loud enough to prevent the people next to you from eavesdropping. Thom Bar is a swanky place for a pricey pre-dinner cocktail—the wonderful Kittichai is right down the hall.

Three of Cups

83 1st Ave. (@ 5th St.)
East Village 212.388.0059

If a science fiction-reading, rock music fan living in his parents' basement were to open a bar, it might not be too different from Three of Cups. The smallish downstairs bar is decorated with rock music posters, stickers, photographs, and Christmas lights, as well as starry wallpaper and a "Fallout Shelter" sign. No-nonsense bartenders serve drinks that average $5 (or $3 during the daily 6pm-10pm happy hour) to a 30ish crowd that's civil, but not looking to meet their neighbors. Rock DJs spin five nights a week with Sundays reserved for live acoustic music; Mondays are when comedy acts do their thing. For a change of pace, move upstairs to the more refined dining room bar and tables for Italian food, including pizza from a wood-burning oven. (Entrées run $9-$18.)

Timboo's
477 5th Ave. (@ 11th St.)
Park Slope 718.788.9782

This cheap and unassuming dive takes you back to a time before bistros and Pilates studios populated the Slope. More trashy than trendy, no-frills drinking is the main aim of this Fifth Avenue bar. Neighborly bartenders, bargain domestic beer ($3-$3.50), a classic jukebox, and old-timers drinking whiskey all add to Timboo's shopworn charm. For a low-key evening (or morning) pull up a vinyl stool to Timboo's friendly bar, order a cheap draft ($2.50-$4), and shoot some pool. Who knows who you might run into—with buckets of Bud and wine by the box, anyone can have a good time.

Time Out
349 Amsterdam Ave. (76th & 77th Sts.)
Upper West Side 212.362.5400

This isn't your father's suburban sports bar, populated by local plumbers and shop owners perched on tiny stools and nursing Coors Light. No, Time Out is much more—from weekly karaoke sessions and beer pong tournaments to darts and billiards, this Upper West Side mainstay has something for everyone. Starting with the evening broadcast of SportsCenter, the bar's 25 TVs tune to any variety of sports that exists in the lower 48—and even some that don't. Although the room is dark and loud, it's rather civilized despite the glow of big screens and sport enthusiasts' cheers. Between innings, order anything from PBR to a local microbrew or any of the tasty bar bites. Appetizers are half-price during happy hour.

Tin Lizzie's
1647 2nd Ave. (85th & 86th Sts.)
Upper East Side 212.288.7983

We're not entirely sure why the stretch of 84th through 86th Streets on Second Avenue requires approximately 8,000 bars, but then again we're rarely sober enough to contemplate this conundrum for longer than the 10 seconds it takes to chug a can of Natty Light. Regardless, Tin Lizzie's fills the um, the uh…well it fills the void of not having to walk more than seven feet to stumble to the next bar. It's a fairly average-sized place—bar up front, larger dining/dancing room in the rear. Stop by during the day and you'll see middle-aged blue-collar men's men pounding brews; stop by at night and find recent college grads who haven't quite figured out that all the cool bars aren't nearby. Come in, have a brewsky, then continue on your way. Nothing to see here folks, nothing to see.

Tir Na Nog
5 Penn Plaza (8th Ave. @ 34th St.)
Midtown 212.630.0249

Sultry and dark, just like, sadly, so many other Irish joints, Tir Na Nog catches MSG run-off like an Irish setter going after dead ducks. Carved wood and exposed brick lend a mysterious Masonic craftsmanship to the place. But don't let it cloud your mind: You can find this elsewhere, with a much cooler crowd. There are regulars, though, and they can't all be overheated Knicks fans. If you've got some time to kill, why not grab a bite: Shepherd's pie is $14-$16, and the Irish smoked salmon is another recommendation at $10.95. (Not a bad deal.) Or stake your luck to the Irish bands playing Fridays and Saturdays. There's little gaiety in this Gaelic spot, but it does what it sets out to do.

Toad Hall
57 Grand St. (W. Broadway & Wooster St.)
SoHo 212.431.8145

Maybe it was a princess's kiss that made this SoHo stalwart just a bit too polished for dive status, but Toad Hall is a neighborhood stronghold whose posh neighborhood continues to become tougher on town hall-type drinking establishments like this one. The loyal locals who line the wooden bar seem to understand that change, which is probably why they smile and tolerate the yuppies that push their way to the pool table in the back. The jukebox tunes are a familiar mix of classic rock, blues, old country, and the occasional old-school crooner. The bartenders are always friendly and the beer is poured to perfection, which is why this pub has managed to remain down-to-earth despite the increasing peer pressure to conform to the neighborhood's inflating pomp and pretense.

Tommy's Tavern
1041 Manhattan Ave. (@ Freeman St.)
Greenpoint 718.343.9699

Tommy's Tavern is not the place to bring a date, unless you favor rough company. This bar doesn't pretend to be anything it isn't—they serve up $4 beers, lots of whiskey, "stiff" well drinks, and ear-splitting live music. It's not unusual to see a fight forming outside, but the place still maintains the feel of a safe neighborhood haven, albeit a very loud one. If you're in the mood for a no-frills night out with rafter-shaking music, Tommy's is the place for you. There's no sign outside, so just follow the scent of spilled beer and the sound of smashing barstools (we're kidding!). As of late, Tommy's has attracted a dance-crazy crowd that fills the place to the brim; so arrive early to mark your territory at the bar…and keep your eyes to yourself.

Tonic
107 Norfolk St. (Delancey & Rivington Sts.)
Lower East Side 212.358.1237

When the voice inside you cries out, "Feed me with experimental jazz! Bathe me in the tones of intellectual rock!" you can find the antidote at Tonic…and a shrink in the Yellow Pages. Not to be confused with the Midtown bar/restaurant of the

same name, this "avant-garde, creative, experimental" music venue is for those who take their tunes seriously (and don't mind silly band names like Video Hippos). The raw atmosphere features the sole adornment of red Christmas lights, an altar-like stage set up front, and your standard-issue bar in back. Don't try to push your way to the front unless you're willing to face the snarl of a crowd that has come to savor their music without interruption. Music nerds unite; Tonic is a breeding ground for the next generation of Rivers Cuomos.

Tonic and the Met Lounge
727 7th Ave. (48th & 49th Sts.)
Midtown 212.382.1059

Not sure if huge-screen TVs with a nonstop parade of pro sports is a good thing or bad? Meet Tonic. In what could either be considered an anti-social distraction from good-looking 20-somethings, or a cathartic break from the Midtown crowd, this place is abuzz with electromagnetic images. Tonic is a tale of two bars. With three similar levels of fun from which to choose, it serves its role as a Times Square attraction with gusto, as each level's busy color scheme is epilepsy-inducing. There is an after-work singles scene, but guys looking for guaranteed action can head to Lace, which is the strip club next door. Ladies are invited next door too, but if all the horny losers leave, they're better off staying right here.

Tool Box
1742 2nd Ave. (90th & 91st Sts.)
Upper East Side 212.348.1288

The best place for Upper East Side gays to meet is definitely nowhere near the Upper East Side. But if you're too lazy to commute to Chelsea, then Tool Box should suffice. Still, considering its small size and location, it's hard to justify paying a $3 cover on Tuesdays simply to look at go-go dancers. And another note to the thrifty: If you want to descend into the dark downstairs area, where women are not allowed (take a guess why), you'll be forced to buy a drink. Regardless, you get the impression that most of the guys here can't wait to leave—but only with someone else.

Tortilla Flats
767 Washington St. (@ 12th St.)
West Village 212.243.1053

Bar-hoppers looking to relive the good old days of the sleepovers when you stayed up all night playing games should haul their merriment-loving selves over to this fun-tastic bar, where there's something silly going on every night of the week: Monday and Tuesday nights it's Bingo, Wednesday is Hula Night, and anything goes on Sundays (when brave pajama-wearers get VIP treatment) with trivia, goofiness, and prizes. With outdoor seating in the summer, this Washington Street gem turns into a little slice of Tijuana. Offering a *caliente* menu of Tex-Mex dishes, Tortilla Flats deserves an extra two points for its back wall, which is entirely devoted to the illustrious career of beloved actor Ernest Borgnine. Bingo!

Total Wine Bar
74 5th Ave. (St. Marks Pl. & Warren St.)
Park Slope 718.783.5166

"Little. Wooden. Different." That's how Park Slope's Total Wine Bar describes itself, and after just minutes in this cozy space you'll totally agree. The bar houses a mere 16 patrons at a time, but what they lack in space is more than made up for in selection. With 36 wines by the glass ($4-$8), an array of bottled beer, and a tasty selection of small plates, Total Wine Bar would be a yuppie couple's dream haven, if it wasn't so, well…different. You won't find a hint of pretension here, and the staff, with its staggering knowledge of wines, will lead you through the menu with such good-natured ease that in the end even your date will forget that you couldn't tell a Merlot from a Shiraz if your life depended on it.

Town Crier
303 E. 53rd St. (1st & 2nd Aves.)
Midtown 212.223.3157

When the Yankees play the Red Sox, and you happen to be wearing a hat or shirt of the team presently in the lead, all of your drinks at Town Crier are half-price until they start to lose. This jumping on the bandwagon may be frowned on by sports purists, but it is greeted with fanfare by…well, drinking purists. The bartenders go out of their way to please—such as obtaining diet iced tea from a bodega to whip up an obscure drink order. Plus, there are beer pong tournaments on Mondays. Push the khaki pants-wearing stiff with his JP Morgan bag out of your way, order a Bud, and let the good times roll. But bring both a Yankees and Red Sox hat with you—just in case.

Town Tavern
134 W. 3rd St. (@ 6th Ave.)
Greenwich Village 212.253.6955

Pop quiz: Where can you party in the Greenwich Village without being surrounded by purple t-shirt-wearing, baby-faced NYU students whose hearts leap with joy when they get to hand over their IDs to prove that, as of last week, they're of drinking age? Town Tavern, where being 21 isn't good enough to get in—on the weekends, this neighborhood bar requires its crowd to be 23 and older. What that leaves is a gathering of grad students, locals, and a few seventh-year freshmen to chow down on burgers, bob their heads to a loud stream of music, and get friendly in the unisex bathroom. Sorry, kid—come back in two years…or during the week, when the age-limit isn't in effect.

The Townhouse
236 E. 58th St. (2nd & 3rd Aves.)
Midtown 212.754.4649

Before heading to the Townhouse, you'll need to decide if you're a have or a have-not. Of course, it all depends on how you see things. Perhaps you have money, but lack youth. Or maybe you're young, but kind of broke. Luckily, both groups can find each other at this gentlemen's bar and restaurant. The Townhouse's warm lights and sleek décor surround older men in suits sipping martinis ($8-$12) and Scotches ($6-$12) while younger gay men all but ask the question, "Is that a wad of cash in your pocket or are you just happy to see me?" The answer is both, it turns out; and that's the beauty of this refined and upscale bi-level bar that doesn't dare serve beer from the draft or allow in gents wearing hats or sleeveless shirts.

Tracy J's Watering Hole
106 E. 19th St. (Park Ave. S. & Irving Pl.)
Gramercy 212.674.5783

With happy hour daily from 3pm-7pm (Fridays from 12pm-7pm), karaoke Thursday-Saturday, a free buffet from 5:30pm-6:30pm Monday-Friday, seven TV screens, and a loud, festive crowd, Tracy J's has all the ingredients for after-work debauchery. The atmosphere is fun and irreverent, and typically packed with young, preppy professionals boisterously reliving their college days. Between dancing and drinking, this crowd tries not to bump into the brick walls and samples the moderately priced food, which includes everything from buffalo wings to burgers to Cajun meatloaf, served up by a happy-go-lucky staff. If you long for the days when the only important things were hooking up and getting drunk, this is your bar.

Trailer Park Lounge
271 W. 23rd St. (7th & 8th Aves.)
Chelsea 212.463.8000

Well, kiss my grits! This kitschy lounge proves to be more restaurant than bar, with scrumptious grilled fat dogs, decent sloppy Joes, and moon pies that you simply can't resist. Inside, chicks and dudes sip on specialty drinks such as the Paradise Hawaiian, Lover's Concerto frozen margarita, and Jim Bob's IQ while seated amongst the life-sized blue-and-white trailer, pink flamingos, and fake palm trees. The regular showing of old movies, mostly from the '50s and '60s, makes this spot the perfect destination for a first date...with your cousin. *Hee Haw* jokes and cans of PBR are protocol, but the beers are hardly trailer park-friendly at $4 a pop. Happy hour is daily from 4pm-7pm and the weekend creeps up early in this neck of the woods, with Wednesday's crowd giving Saturday's a run for its money.

Trash
256 Grand St. (Driggs Ave. & Roebling St.)
Williamsburg 718.599.1000

We see Julian, we see Sara, and we see Max ...Trash is *Romper Room* for Williamsburgers. There wasn't a single bar prop left out of this place: a pool table, a Ms. Pac-Man machine, pistachio, peeanut, and cashew nut dispensers, a jukebox, video trivia, karaoke, and an ATM in case you run out of cash for all this nonsense. The chairs are former car seats from the back of a Dodge Caravan or something of that ilk, and license

Trailer Park Lounge

Trash

plates from all sorts of vehicles adorn the walls. The clientele is punk-ish... or at least that's what the scribbling on the bathroom walls would have you believe. Take advantage of the free tater tots and hot dogs that retail for $2.

Trattoria Dopo Teatro
125 W. 44th St. (6th Ave. & Broadway)
Midtown 212.869.2849

Don't be fooled by this "after-theater" trattoria's intimate dining room. This lavish Italian restaurant harbors more than just homemade pastas. Hidden beneath the dining room are sequestered party rooms—the Theater room, the American room, the Grappa library, a wine cellar, and the Secret Garden complete with an eternal spring and stone waterfall. But if you're not looking to host noni's 100th or a rehearsal dinner for your little sister Tina, the 24-foot antique oak bar is the perfect place to discuss the extras on *The Sopranos* DVDs. And if you're into the emphatic gesturing of the old country or seeing some local stars of the stage, Trattoria Dopo Teatro can be a show unto itself.

Tre Dici
128 W. 26th St. (6th & 7th Aves.)
Chelsea 212.243.8183

Want to eat like a mogul but don't have the platinum credit card to do so? Tre Dici has got your back. This chic new Italian restaurant presents a creative, delicious menu of brick-oven pizzas, pastas, and seafood- and meat-oriented entrées, and nothing tops $26. Settle into a gray banquette (the candlelit dining area seats about 30) and feast on seared sea scallops, hanger steak accented with gorgonzola and mushrooms, and the mouthwatering 20-layer crepe cake. In addition to being a romantic date spot, Tre Dici should also appeal to an after-work crowd with its front bar area, complete with cocktail tables and a wall-length front window that faces the street, making for great people-watching.

The Triad
158 W. 72nd St. (Broadway & Columbus Ave.)
Upper West Side 212.362.2590

The Triad is an off-Broadway outpost that serves as a performance space for theater, live music, comedy, spoken word, and cabaret. A smallish venue, the Triad attracts a more local community of friends—although it has enough "cred" for the occasional celebrity to pop in now and then. Believe it or not, Slash of Guns 'N Roses fame has performed at the Triad. But so has Susan Lucci; so be forewarned—the Triad is a mixed bag of events and clientele. It's a crap shoot and you never know what you're going to get, so you might want to call ahead before you hoof it uptown to this joint. Cover charges range from $10-$20 and drink minimums (beer and cocktails are $7-$12) vary; light snacks are also served.

Tribe
132 1st Ave. (@ St. Marks Pl.)
East Village 212.979.8965

Toss your tattered Ramones t-shirt in the laundry and button up, because it's time you joined a more refined—but still frisky—hut of natives. Part of the adventure of the East Village is the dive bar scene, which is why Tribe is a stylish change. The DJ spins varied tunes (from Jay-Z to Sinatra to Al Green to salsa) for an equally eclectic crowd, and even the lit wall behind the bar changes colors like a mood ring. Choose from five draughts and five bottles ($5-$6), but the Tribe Lemonade ($10) ain't what Granny had in mind and the Mexican Mudslide ($10) has enough punch to bring Montezuma to his knees. During happy hour (5pm-9pm daily), drafts are $3 and apple martinis and cosmos just $5. Break from the dives, and groove with the tribe.

Trinity Public House
229 E. 84th St. (2nd & 3rd Aves.)
Upper East Side 212.327.4450

Ah, the blessed trinity—beer, jukeboxes, and...skiing? This relatively polished bar is just far enough off of Second and Third Avenues' stretches of stench to discourage fat ex-frats from wandering in on a late-night crawl, which keeps it relatively safe for local yuppies—aka, the UES's "other" white meat. During the winter Trinity's upwardly mobile crowd quite literally goes downhill. This bar is well-known for its group ski trips, which make it a bit of a resort in its own right. The brick-lined interior of this wee place exudes a ski lodge sense of community as well; young and old locals come to escape the area's alternatives, which seem to be more beer- and belch-oriented. Single women can enjoy British Isle beer at Trinity without being hassled.

Trio
167 E. 33rd St. (Lexington & 3rd Aves.)
Murray Hill 212.685.1001

Croatian-owned Trio marries a huge range of wines with the carefully selected Dalmatian ingredients that make the menu special. The classic bar inside is simple marble, with gilded surfaces lending a friendly touch. Summers bring prix-fixe meals to the menu (dinner runs $35 per person,

everything included). Entrées include pastas, meat dishes, and plenty of fish. Look for other flourishes on the menu in specialized Balkan treats from a culture often not given due respect for their cooking. Live piano rounds out the mix every Tuesday through Friday. Here's guessing the trio referred to is fine cuisine, great atmosphere, and the style of a little cultural legerdemain.

Triple Crown Restaurant & Ale House
330 7th Ave. (28th & 29th Sts.)
Chelsea 212.736.1575

Irish-owned and operated, Triple Crown has been a staple to the Chelsea sports bar scene for the past 10 years. This large venue manages to contain a warm and cheery atmosphere, from the friendly bartenders chatting behind the long wooden bar to the capable waiters serving the large booths and dining tables in the rear. You can't beat the combination of great food, expansive draft beer selection, and plethora of TVs complete with DIRECTV. The crowd varies from night-to-night—it's a genuine melting pot of business professionals, theater groups, tourists, and FIT students. While the TVs draw the boys, the bartenders would happily hedge their bets that few frat guys call this bar their second home. We'll raise a glass to that.

Triumph Room
311 W. 57th St. (8th & 9th Aves.)
Hell's Kitchen 212.307.0062

For those tired of the velvet rope game at überclubs like Crobar but still driven to dance, the discreetly located Triumph Room is here to win hearts. Located below the dramatically decorated Providence Restaurant, Triumph Room offers a large dance floor surrounded by cozy alcoves where colored lights splash the large but unremarkable crowd as a DJ spins tunes (which differ depending on the night). Triumph's bartenders can mix a mean drink, and they're actually friendly—apparently they didn't get the memo. This new space—formerly Le Bar Bat—has potential, but being halfway between Newark and Queens isn't going to help.

Trousdale
226 W. 50th St. (Broadway & 8th Ave.)
Midtown 212.262.4070

We know this much is Trou: The atmosphere at Trousdale is proudly posh; the décor is chic in an eclectic, immaculate kind of way, draped in swank checkerboard and striped blues, browns, and whites. However, this small, elegant (and well-hidden—it's located in the lobby of the Amsterdam Court Hotel) spot is actually quite inviting, even to those of us who aren't quite as posh as the geometric furniture. Friendly bartenders and a quiet atmosphere make Trousdale an attractive lounge for people looking for a spot to chat (or swap tips on furniture swatches). The drinks are tasty too; there's a long list of specialty cocktails and everything is reasonably priced: Well drinks are $6 during happy hour and one of the many martini options will cost you between $8 and $10.

Tupelo Grill
1 Penn Plaza (33rd St. bet. 7th & 8th Aves.)
Midtown 212.760.2700

If you're picking up your grandmother or old college roommate at Penn Station, and they're craving protein after a long train ride, Tupelo Grill offers a selection of top-quality steaks and plenty of booze to brace you for the pleasures of Granny's incontinence problem. Vegetarians beware, though; this celebrated restaurant caters to carnivores—the specialties include fish, lamb, and steak, including something called "Steak Elvis," which alone will get you thrown out of PETA. None of this will come cheap, however; the most inexpensive entrée will cost you $19. Located across the street from Madison Square Garden, Tupelo has several rooms to choose from—the main dining room, tap room, bar, a patio, and café in the park. And should "Steak Elvis" cause Granny to keel over in the toilet, the NYU hospital is a few blocks away.

Turkey's Nest
94 Bedford Ave. (@ N. 12th St.)
Williamsburg 718.384.9774

On any given night (or afternoon, really) you'll find at the Turkey's Nest a veritable cross-section of modern Brooklyn: Hasidic Jews huddled drinking 32-oz., $3.50 Budweisers at one corner of the roughed-up bar, skinny jeans-clad hipsters knocking back $2.75 Rheingold bottles at one of the many tables, and old-school Italian guys making a ruckus while downing $2.50 pints of "Turkey Beer," a gamey sort of microbrew that's usually on special—and all, of course, watching the game on one of many TVs arrayed around the friendly, happily drunk place. If watching sports isn't your thing, there's pool for 50 cents a game, Big Buck Hunter and Silver Strike Bowling video games, and a good jukebox that mostly stays jumping. All in all, the Turkey's a great joint for those who don't give a damn about being part of a scene.

Turks & Frogs
323 W. 11th St. (Greenwich & Washington Sts.)
West Village 212.691.8875

While Turks & Frogs bills itself as an "antique shop with a wine bar," patrons will likely choose vintage merlot over a Turkish vase. Other than five bottled beers and some herbal teas, this elegant, yet non-stuffy lounge offers over 30 white and 30 red wines, but no liquor. Wine amateurs needn't worry—a helpful staff and convivial ambiance dispel any *Sideways* pretension. A small bar is situated in the candlelit front, but far better ambiance prevails in the cinnamon-walled backroom (arrive early to snag a couch). Inside, the intimate vibe and innocuous yuppie techno buzzing in the background make this spot perfect first-date material. Not surprisingly, the crowd tends to be older, smarter, and better behaved than the frat boy and pseudo-model types that plague many nearby bars. And remember: You break, you buy.

Turquoise Seafood Restaurant

Turquoise Seafood Restaurant
240 E. 81st St. (2nd & 3rd Aves.)
Upper East Side 212.988.8222

Impress your date with this new hidden gem of a seafood restaurant, tucked away on a tree-lined street in an area where culinary improvement is always welcome. The menu boasts that "fish fresher than ours are still at sea," and from the list of offerings, no sea creature is safe. Chilean sea bass ($25), bronzini (whole fish, $29), and stuffed tilapia fillet ($29) are some of the highlights, complemented by starters like baked clams, grilled shrimp, tahini, and charcoal grilled babaganoush ($6-$11). A cozy bar offers an impressive Israeli wine list, while attentive service and a candlelit setting help you with the romance part of your date. And if the relationship doesn't pan out, call ahead for your next first-impression session: The crowds are starting to find out about this one, so reservations are recommended.

Turtle Bay Grill & Lounge
987 2nd Ave. (52nd & 53rd Sts.)
Midtown 212.233.4224

Although exceeding the expectations of those eyeing this spot as a total yuppie breeding ground,

this multilevel Midtown bar/grill/lounge is no more than a hotbed for an after-work crowd that hasn't discovered nightlife below 34th Street (psst! Those subways go up and down). The red fixtures, leather banquettes, exposed brick, and dim lighting suggest that this could be a location for a lascivious late-night activity, but despite the working fireplace, a sleek wooden bar, and an attractive staff, you'll be disappointed if you're looking for bawdy encounters. The drink specials and standard pub fare are priced fairly enough for the hard-working suits occupying the lower rungs of the corporate ladder, and the service is amicable and relatively fast, but like its locale, this pub struggles for an identity outside the 9-5 spectrum.

12"
179 Essex St. (Houston & Stanton Sts.)
Lower East Side 212.505.6027

12"

Twelve inches? Where do we sign up? This bar's name could easily lend itself to several celebrated jokes involving porn stars, but it was really chosen in praise of vinyl. And 12" always spins the jams. Framed record sleeves line the walls, and old lunch boxes and '80s and early '90s toys border the shelves. A Mad Dog cocktail menu and a $4 PBR or Rheingold with a Mad Dog shot special will take you back to those high school days when you were tapping for alcohol in the parking lot of a convenience store. 12" also boasts random pizza parties, champagne cocktails, sake, and soju cocktails—which promise no hangover—and its own 12" beer. This may be the best foot-long since Subway.

12:31 (@ the Hotel Chandler)
12 E. 31st St. (5th & Madison Aves.)
Murray Hill 646.218.4422

This 40-seat bar and lounge located inside of the Hotel Chandler doesn't have room for large groups, but it is a great place for an intimate moment. 12:31, named for its address, is a bit slicker than your typical hotel bar, with comfy ban-quettes where you can relax with friends or better yet, someone you want to get to know better. They have 10 signature specialty drinks, including the Yellow Polka Dot Bikini Martini with Bacardi Raspberry. On Fridays and Saturdays, belly up to the bar while a belly dancer swivels her hips; then try to make conversation with one of the many hotel guests filling the room. Who know? Maybe room service is in your future after all.

24-7 Bar & Lounge
247 Eldridge St. (Houston & Stanton Sts.)
Lower East Side 212.505.7600

If you want 24/7 convenience, hit the new 7-11. If you want 24/7 nightlife, you'll have to cool your heels until 9pm, make it past the velvet ropes, and keep a close watch out for the friends you're meeting, because they won't see you through this bar's black curtain and blacked-out windows. Though you might hear crickets chirping upon first arriving at this empty space, stick around and you'll eventually be joined by revelers who come

in to hear the DJ-spun hip-hop, reggae, and R&B tunes. Not nearly as lively as places like bOb, 24-7 does provide an alternative for those looking to escape the LES indie rock scene.

Twins Pub
421 9th Ave. (33rd & 34th Sts.)
Chelsea 212.564.7288

This neighborhood pub may just be the "Goofus and Gallant"—or Mary-Kate and Ashley—of the bar world. The upstairs bar is the kind of clean-cut place you'd take your mom for lunch, while the more straight-shooting barroom downstairs is exactly the place to get away from her. At Twins, duality is key—neighborhood folks rub elbows with the post-show run-off from nearby Hammerstein Ballroom and Madison Square Garden, and you have the choice of enjoying a civil meal or hoisting a few with some ornery Knicks fans after a loss. The buffalo shrimp come highly recommended, and the hungry crowd is big for a reason—the kitchen at this full-service nightspot has its act together. Burgers and sandwiches cost about $7-$9, so it's a good deal to boot.

Twist Lounge (@ the Ameritania Hotel)
230 W. 54th St. (Broadway & 8th Ave.)
Midtown 212.247.5000

Occupying a glorified corner of the Ameritania Hotel, the Twist Lounge has all the right moves, but none of the right attributes. To be fair, Twist offers an interesting menu of martinis and drinks, but so does the Chili's in your hometown mall. And despite Twist's best efforts, it seems like the owners followed the step-by-step instructions printed in some bar instruction manual: 1. Buy some nightclub rope; 2. Put it in a corner of your hotel; 3. Throw in some couches, stools, a bar, and wall decorations; 4. Wait until five to open on Saturdays, so you can fully alienate the Midtown tourist/theater crowd, but still manage to become a perceived hotspot for the after-work yuppies who think they're getting into Marquee later on; 5. Shake well. For a bar named Twist, we'd appreci-ate a surprise ending here and there.

2A

25 Ave. A (@ 2nd St.)
East Village 212.505.2466

This Alphabet City staple spells a good time for all, especially when you take the 2-for-1 happy hour special (4pm-8pm) into account. For East Villagers needing a stiff drink, 2A has a downstairs bar with a mini-lounge in the back where one can enjoy a mix of rock and punk music that reflects its patrons. Upstairs is a shabby-chic haven for post-grads who dig '80s music and chi-chi drinks. Prices are very reasonable, service is slow, and it's not the friendliest place in the world, as both the patrons and staff downstairs will give you 'tude. Your best bet is to stop by with a group of friends, commandeer the back lounge, and ignore the scowls you get by throwing back cheap drinks.

2 by 4

68 2nd Ave. (3rd & 4th Sts.)
East Village 212.254.5766

The sign out front says it all: "Free shots for ladies in nighties." 2 by 4 may be somewhat of a new-comer to the 'hood, but it carries on some long-standing traditions of sketchy East Village dives—namely, loud music, a pool table, cheap beer, and the occasional whiff of BO. But what really makes 2 by 4 special is its knack for bringing people together. On a typical night, you'll find white dudes with dreads playing Ms. Pac-Man, Harley guys guzzling $2 cans of PBR, and lesbians wielding cue sticks. Now if all this doesn't inspire you to hop on the bar and pole dance in your Victoria's Secret slip, then the bartenders will likely do it for you.

200 Fifth

200 5th Ave. (Union St. & Berkeley Pl.)
Park Slope 718.638.2925

Park Slope's sports bar 200 Fifth wants to cover all of its bases. This venue is one-part raging sports

bar with over 40 beers on tap and better-than-your-average-pub food, one-part family-friendly restaurant with butcher paper and crayons at every table, and one-part live music/DJ lounge that packs them in on weekend nights for a little post-game dancing. With such a diverse space, be prepared for a wide mix of locals. On big-game days, the median age of patrons can range anywhere from 21 to 41. But the gray-hair count drops considerably in the lounge on Saturdays, when you can witness competition of a different sort as Park Slope singles try to hit a few home runs of their own.

2i's
248 W. 14th St. (7th & 8th Aves.)
West Village 212.807.1775

You might feel a little apprehensive arriving at this two-level nightclub, especially after the pat-down from the brawny bouncer. But upon entering this haven for hip-hop heads, your fears should subside. The peeps are here to dance, and the club is drama-free. The DJs know how to get the crowd moving with a mix of hip-hop, R&B, and rap; Sunday nights cater to reggae lovers. The interior ain't pretty—in fact it's downright dingy—but the super-nice staff and gargantuan grooves keep everyone happy. The club also hosts two specialty evenings, Hunkmania male revue, and the startlingly different G Spot, the lesbian party—check the schedule carefully, ladies. Drinks don't come cheap and the cover charge varies, but there's a little something for everyone.

203 Spring
203 Spring St. (@ Sullivan St.)
SoHo 212.334.3855

It seems the more things change, the more they stay the same at 203 Spring, an erstwhile restaurant, lounge, bar, and—not that SoHo needs another one—a lounge again. The surprisingly spacious backroom has the requisite low couches, brick walls hung with Jackson Pollock-like art, and a discreet DJ booth in the corner that gathers dust during the week, but spews the latest tunes on the weekends. Bar food in the way of pizza and

fried calamari keeps the natives full. A long bar dominates the front room and faces an equally long mirror, the better to flirt with on jam-packed Friday and Saturday nights, when the heavy velvet curtains guarding the entrance are joined by heavy bouncers, though it's more for show because everyone gets in.

212
133 E. 65th St. (Park & Lexington Aves.)
Upper East Side 212.249.6565

You can't help but feel stylish at this scenester restaurant, which is about as cool as the Upper East Side gets. Amongst the European playboys and gaggles of local young women in their party dresses, a sprinkling of older patrons find the corporate refinement safe enough to risk the semi-high-energy scene. 212's bar menu takes five times as long to get through as the food menu. There's a drink for two served in a pineapple and even the mixers have some kick; there are 120 vodkas, including kosher and bison grass…whatever that is. Celebrities and sports stars have also been sighted here. The food is heavy on appetizers and salads, and it suits 212's slim patrons, fine as they're mostly interested in flirting with each other and the wait staff.

Ty's
114 Christopher St. (Bedford & Bleecker Sts.)
West Village 212.741.9641

When they're not putting out fires, the city's gay firefighters are starting them in the hearts of their admirers at this West Village bar. While you can probably find firemen turning up the heat any night of the week, the second Tuesday of the month is when they flock to this Western-style bar. Of course, if a fireman's overalls don't make your temperature rise, then cool off with a Cape Cod and flirt with the guys in jeans and leather. Yet regardless of what patrons wear, they're all fairly laidback men in their 30s and 40s who enjoy a good beer and good conversation (regulars are known for chatting up patrons). One visit and you'll want to make Ty's your neighborhood bar—no matter which borough you live in.

UK New York
22 Warren St. (Church St. & Broadway)
TriBeCa 212.513.0111

UK New York

This newbie is a cozy and inviting English/American establishment that's more laid-back lounge and restaurant than typical pub. While the narrow entrance is easy to miss (look for the London Underground sign), the long bar inside rewards your effort with a quality happy hour of $4 drafts (Boddington's and John Courage, among others) and $5 martinis, cosmos, and margaritas from 5pm-7pm Monday thru Friday. Further back, a lounge of comfy leather seats opens up to a small section of dinner tables with room for about 50. Less than a year old, the owners are still working to perfect their formula, with a downstairs lounge in the works and a new menu underway. For now, New Yorkers would do well to experience some of this British charm, just as it is.

Ulrika's
115 E. 60th St. (Lexington & Park Aves.)
Upper East Side 212.355.7069

Waterloo! It's all about the ABBA, people. From the Swedish pop group's classic tunes playing on the sound system to the IKEA-showroom décor, Ulrika's screams "Swedish!" so loud, you'd expect them to offer a plate of complimentary Swedish meatballs with every drink. As a restaurant, Ulrika's is cozy, offering a full Swedish tasting menu and giving off a cottage-like feel, thanks to

the rustic furniture designed by the Swedish furniture company's Svenssons Mobler. But as a bar, Ulrika's is about as boring as a foreign-exchange student who speaks perfect English and wears a chastity belt (you won't find the Swedish volleyball team here). Named for the establishment's chef, Ulrika's offers $11 raspberry martinis and the walls are covered with art by Swedish artists. Bring Mom and Dad here sometime.

Ulysses
58 Stone St. (@ Hanover Sq.)
Financial District 212.482.0400

Lit by candles and sexy, low-hanging light bulbs, and made darker by its sultry colors and distressed surfaces, Ulysses is a fitting match with the mysterious twisting streets New York's earliest forefathers designed for this part of town. It's not hard to tell ownership loves James Joyce; his picture is everywhere, and well, did we mention the place is called Ulysses? The menu abounds with Eurobrew, and then gets creative: Try a platter of shots or, better, a Ulysses Grand Platter ($98), the house's multi-tiered raw bar smorgasbord of oysters, clams, and other sea fare. A $15 lobster is served on Mondays but, unfortunately, the prices on the whole are very high. Joyce himself almost starved in his 20s…imagine the spite $10 nachos and $12 calamari would have inspired in him.

Uncle Ming's
225 Ave. B, 2nd Fl. (13th & 14th Sts.)
East Village 212.979.8506

The slightly hedonistic aura that Uncle Ming's exudes begins with an unmarked entrance; walk up the dimly lit flight of stairs to this second-floor bar and you get the feeling you're about to crash a wild private party. Inside, there's a hint of bordello in the predominantly red lighting, Victorian couches lining the walls or tucked into corners, and stripper poles embedded in the bar. (Yes, this was once a late-night den of ill-repute). Fortunately, the drooling men have been replaced with a good mix of laidback, unpretentious revelers who save their singles for tipping the bartenders. The décor, DJ- or bartender-selected

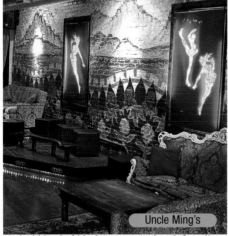

Located underneath the W Hotel Union Square, Underbar is certainly sexy, with its velvety booths, fuzzy pillows, dark red curtains, and a sloping, candlelit staircase. There's a somewhat seedy, lascivious feel to the place, but the sexiness (like the employees) is really just for show. The staff is seemingly made up of models and actors, and the crowd is dressed to the nines, in the New York uniform of all-black (hell, even the urinals are black). You can wait all night for some debauchery to occur, or you can make it happen yourself by closing the heavy curtains to your private banquette and getting to know your new friend a little better. But be forewarned—people outside can see your silhouettes.

Uncle Ming's

musical blend of hip-hop, pop, and rock favorites, and the drinks create a fun scene that's somewhat pick-up oriented, but not overly so—unless you want it to be.

Under the Volcano
12 E. 36th St. (5th & Madison Aves.)
Murray Hill 212.213.0093

It might not be as explosive as some of its neighbors (the Ginger Man is right across the street), but Under the Volcano is far from dormant. Come quittin' time, this cozy Murray Hill bar erupts with the din of after-work revelers, anxious to loosen their ties and down south-of-the-border specialties. The skulls-and-skeletons décor is very Dia de los Muertos, but the crowd is not nearly so morbid—youngish professionals cozy up on leather booths and über-friendly bartenders slip extra shots into the Volcano Margaritas ($9). For those who yearn for the worm, there are 15 different tequilas on hand, but beware: This bar gets loud when the crowd gets shot-happy. Thankfully, Under the Volcano cools off around dinnertime early in the week, so you can nosh on their fabulous empanadas ($6) in relative peace.

Underbar (@ W Hotel – Union Sq.)
201 Park Ave. S. (@ 17th St.)
Gramercy 212.358.1560

Underground
613 2nd Ave. (33rd & 34th Sts.)
Murray Hill 212.683.3000

Get down underground at this subterranean sports bar/local pub/comfy lounge. Underground has so many personalities, you could call it schizophrenic; but this kind of insanity is OK by us. If you're looking for a cheap drink in an atmosphere that's not so cheap-looking, pull up a barstool at the front sports bar (which boasts flat-screen TVs) and enjoy a cold beer as you take in the exposed brick and wooden beams of the classic-looking pub room. If you're on a date (and wanting to mate), hit the plush couches and tables à deux in the lounge and order alcoholic concoctions served by the friendly wait staff. If the weather's good, head outdoors to the back patio for a cold one on a hot day and you can take in any game on the TV.

Union Pool
484 Union Ave. (@ Meeker Ave.)
Williamsburg 718.609.0484

Williamsburg's hipster population would be wiped out instantly if Union Pool ever caught fire. Music changes nightly with rotating DJs playing vinyl ranging from '50s bluegrass to '70s funk in the main space where tattooed types and Johnny

Cash look-alikes congregate along the curved bar. Spontaneous dancing occurs religiously in the backroom, where local musicians take to the tiny stage. The doormen get serious about IDs, though, even if you clearly have gray hairs in your pompadour. The massive outdoor patio underneath the BQE is where regulars smoke, exchange iPod downloads, and grill hot dogs over the fire pit, which turns into a fountain in the summer. Inside, the antique photo booth that takes whitewashed pictures provides a cozy place to steal a kiss—but watch out for lip rings.

Union Square Coffee Shop
29 E. 16th St. (@ Union Sq. W.)
Flatiron 212.243.7969

We would like to take a moment to applaud the wait staff at Union Square Coffee Shop. They can understand the slurred words of drunken customers at 2am ordering their late-night fix. They can keep the place open 23 hours so that those of us who don't order their late-night fixes until 4am can do so. While they're not the fastest-moving people in the restaurant biz, these great-looking servers deliver delicious dishes that are a sophisticated spin-off of diner classics, with drinks to match. While the crowd can sometimes be nauseatingly hip, it's usually not overwhelming. So when you're jonesing for a late-night grilled cheese, stumble into the Coffee Shop. Coffee Shop also opens a nice outdoor area for those who come in really, really late…as in 10am.

The Upper Deck
305 E. 53rd St. (1st & 2nd Aves.)
Midtown 212.838.0007

Recently renamed the Upper Deck, the former Metro Loft extends itself as a small, intimate lounge resting above the rowdy Metro 53 Café. The Deck boasts two bars, a pool table, couch seating, and a deck-ish-type area overlooking Midtown construction. Hey, you can still pick up a cute pool player by tricking them into checking out "the view" with you. Come to the two-in-one bar for the half-price happy hour, but avoid the tired after-work crowd by moving upstairs for an almost

private room before 9pm. If you came to Metro 53 to revel in one night with a former frat boy, then you won't have to wait too long to (ahem) get him upstairs.

Upright Citizens Brigade
307 W. 26th St. (@ 8th Ave.)
Chelsea 212.366.9176

Not only are they owners, they're also performers. The four comedians who founded Upright Citizens Brigade, a sketch comedy group that offers cheap shows and improv classes to the masses, have resumes so impressive you'll wonder how it is you've gotten the chance to watch them for the price of a beer—which is also sold at the shows. Sketch and improv shows at the UCB Theater are done nightly and often feature performers you've seen on TV: Amy Poehler (one of the co-owners) is a regular on *SNL*. Tickets for these shows (costing you anywhere from nothing to $8) are cheap—especially in comparison to those other comedy clubs around the city. To top it off, there's no drink minimum, so put those twenties back in your wallet where they belong. Sketchy? No. Good sketch comedy? Most definitely.

Uptown Restaurant & Lounge
1576 3rd Ave. (88th & 89th Sts.)
Upper East Side 212.828.1388

In an attempt to inject some downtown appeal into the Upper East Side, Uptown Lounge is quite a departure from its Third Avenue neighbors. (And we mean "downtown" from here…as in Midtown.) This plasma screen-lined bar and pop DJ combo

Uptown Restaurant & Lounge

wouldn't work in SoHo, but it's more than trendy enough for this area. Uptown Lounge has one of the lengthier bar menus around, which is why happy hour easily bleeds into dinner time. It's a bit more hit or miss during late nights, but the crowd is more about quality than quantity. The actual bar area is rather deep, and the dining space is also fairly roomy. There's a second bar in the back which can be rented out for private parties, and it's in this skylighted area that Uptown shines.

Urge Lounge
33 2nd Ave. (1st & 2nd Sts.)
East Village 212.533.5757

When you have the urge for hot go-go guys and 2-for-1 happy hour drinks, hit Urge Lounge. This East Village gay bar is housed in a former funeral home, and flirty patrons are hoping to get "six feet under" with one another after a few $8 mango martinis and free appetizers (7pm-10pm) at the cash-only bar or back lounge area. Gay men usually aren't interested in fish, but the dual-level bar features a few fish tanks, as well as a round mini-tank suspended from the ceiling. There are flat-screen TVs, but sports are on about as frequently as an adults-only sleepover at the Neverland Ranch. And when you get hungry, there's nothing like some nuts in your mouth to hit the spot...the bar has two nuts machines.

Uva
1486 2nd Ave. (77th & 78th Sts.)
Upper East Side 212.472.4552

Upper Eastsiders, rejoice. In a neighborhood where Mo's Caribbean is a culinary standout, a wine bar with great pours and excellent Italian fare has finally arrived, thanks to the owners of UES establishments Lusardi's, Luke's, and Willie's. The inviting bar up front blends into the rustic candlelit atmosphere of the brick-lined dining room, where attentive servers are ready to answer questions about the extensive wine list (glasses start at $7.50; bottles at $22) or the menu of hearty Italian dishes (like the fantastically rich gnocchi in a black truffle sauce, $15). A backyard patio promises romantic dinners and leisurely chats over

espresso when the weather is right. For now, we'll take the cozy warmth of the bustling main room inside. And another glass of vino, please.

V Bar & Café
225 Sullivan St. (Bleecker & 3rd Sts.)
Greenwich Village 212.253.5740

This little delight is the best-kept secret in the West Village. The wine and beer selection is outstanding, boasting a number of tasty Belgian brews, and the laidback, neighborhood atmosphere of this place is so comfortable you'll wish it were your living room. The bar staff is friendly and quick to offer helpful suggestions about one of the many delicious beverages, and the high tables and stools are great for playing games, reading the paper, or taking in the calm of the bar's quiet location. The bookshelves, covered in flowers, books, and bottles, round out the quaint décor of this delightful bar. It's perfect for a first date or a chat with an old friend. Just try not to ruin it for everyone, will ya?

Vapor
143 Madison Ave. (31st & 32nd Sts.)
Murray Hill 212.686.6999

Now there's no need to go all the way downtown for a cool vibe and great drinks. This lounge from a co-conspirator of Duvet has three areas for reveling: an elongated front room with smoke (or vapor if you will) snaking from behind the main bar and misting from the bottle-service tables; a Diddy-like white room for VIPs featuring a light sequence that will either enhance everyone's looks or make your head spin; and downstairs, a second bar with different music in a cozy, candlelit space just screaming for nookie. The signature drinks concocted by bar master Kristopher Carr, like the Amazon Mist, Persian Cosmopolitan, and Toasted Almond Bellini, run $9-$10, and the crowd is very, very thirsty.

Varjak
923 8th Ave. (54th & 55th Sts.)
Hell's Kitchen 212.245.3212

If jazz is your game then Varjak's the name. Sure, it's a little bit out of the way for most people, but the soothing tunes and nightly live performances merit the trip to Hell's Kitchen. Or, if that's not enough to draw you back after work, come straight here when they open at 4pm and stay until 4am. See vocalists like DeeAnne Gorman while picking at the free finger food buffet from 5pm-9pm every day. The crowd here is mixed in every way imaginable, but all have the same goal in mind: listening to good music and relaxing. Play some video arcade classics and drink until the jazz starts working for you. The bartenders are friendly and quick to pour a well-made drink.

Vasmay Lounge
269 E. Houston St. (@ Suffolk St.)
Lower East Side 212.554.0688

There's nothing more boring than complaints about the "gentrification" of the LES, and when Meow Mix closed, the cattiness began. After painting "We'll-never-leave" slogans on the abandoned bar's exterior, the largely lesbian locals left, and a more hetero crowd moved into the thoughtfully divey Vasmay Lounge. Thankfully, a very attractive staff still provides plenty of eye candy for boys and girls alike, regardless of their "preferences." Vasmay's exterior is a strange shade of red that probably hasn't yet been named, and inside, a dark room with a new pool table and punk-rock jukebox hosts an old and young mix of LES barflies who won't go near Ludlow Street. The live music area downstairs is being remodeled, but the bands will be back soon and there will be no cover. Welcome to the neighborhood, Vasmay Lounge.

Vegas
135 Smith St. (Bergen & Dean Sts.)
Carroll Gardens 718.875.8308

With a name like Vegas one might expect this to

be an ode to the desert Disneyland of gambling and gluttony: ringing slot machines, overly glitzy attempts at glamour, neon, and Celine Dion. But this roomy bar foregoes the cringe-worthy aspects of its namesake and offers up something subtle, relaxed, and far, far classier. There's more than ample room around the pool table so amateurs needn't worry about sinking the cue ball in a neighbor's pocket. And both the bar's jukebox and bartenders have garnered something of a Carroll Gardens cult following. If you can make it before the happy hour ends at 7, you'll be rewarded with 2-for-1 drafts. But leave your poker chips at the door: The only high-stakes game here is the Scrabble board they keep behind the bar.

Vera
88 2nd Ave. (4th & 5th Sts.)
East Village 212.420.0202

Can we be Frank? And we don't mean "honest," we mean "Can we be very popular with scenesters, families, and couples the way that this East Village Italian restaurant is?" This always crowded eatery is locally famous for its Italian fare, and Vera, its neighboring bar, isn't so bad either. Never have hipsters and socialites coexisted so peacefully. This wee bar often overflows with diners who drown their impatience in wine while waiting for a table to become available next door, so despite the hipper-than-thou impression you may first experience, you won't be required to name three Bravery tunes for service. For a hipper scene still, not to mention formidable oven-baked pizza, try Frank and Vera's brother, Little Frankie's and its cool Big Cheech bar.

Vera Cruz
195 Bedford Ave. (N. 6th & N. 7th Sts.)
Williamsburg 718.599.7914

Vera Cruz has been witnessing Williamsburg's growth spurts like an awkward teenager for the past 10 years. Maybe it's the artsy Mexicano interior, the beautiful backyard garden, or the killer margaritas that keep this place afloat. Mosaic tile accents and a breezy, chaotic interior make the place so inviting, you won't notice any traces of

Williamsburg dinginess here. A great open-air front window where drinkers can see and be seen has you longing to come inside and join the fiesta. Fresh and tangy drinks more than make up for the semi-authentic food (although you'll want to order more than one *Elote a la Mexicana*, grilled corn on the cob topped with mayonnaise and mixed chili powder), and when you get to suck them down in the jungle-like garden, who's going to complain?

Verlaine

110 Rivington St. (Ludlow & Essex Sts.)
Lower East Side 212.614.2494

The Asian-Latin fusion trend may have spread itself all around town, but it's a rare and special thing when you see its influence in an entire cocktail menu. From the Chupacabra to the Saigon Bellini and the Suko Sangria, Verlaine has a sweet list of cocktails to match its tasty and trendy décor. Avoid the temptation to climb up the mystery ladder near the entranceway—unless of course you're looking to hang out with the DJ in his loft-like nook. High ceilings, comfy lounging couches, and local art on the walls keep the atmosphere intimate and stylish, yet relaxed. The errant French poet this bar was named for would certainly enjoy the decadent drink menu at Verlaine, which features enough intoxicating libations to hit all of your pleasure points.

Vertigo Bar & Restaurant

354 3rd Ave. (@ 26th St.)
Murray Hill 212.696.1011

There's nothing dizzying about Vertigo Bar & Restaurant, except for how fast it went from a dime-a-dozen local Irish pub to a comfortable, semi-swanky lounge. There are no traces left of the Abbey Tavern, and it's just as well, as Murray Hill could use a place like this. With flat-screen TVs, plush bar chairs, large tables, and an extensive menu (including "big salads"—thanks Seinfeld!), this is somewhere you can take a date, join your parents for brunch, or meet up with a group of friends. They have an impressive beer selection, with 18 drafts and 13 bottles, including the usual suspects like Amstel and Heineken and

the more obscure Widmer Hefeweizen. Happy hour from 4pm-7pm daily brings patrons to drunken heights with specials like $4 domestic beers and $5 imports, as well as $5 mixed drinks. If this is what Vertigo feels like, bring it on.

The Viceroy

160 8th Ave. (@ 18th St.)
Chelsea 212.633.8484

A tried-and-true Chelsea locale, the Viceroy flaunts floor-to-ceiling windows that create a bright, open space perfect for entertaining friends and a darker backroom that provides a spot for canoodling with your mate. The décor is casual, with a hint of Italian elegance and an expansive cocktail list that hosts everything from coconut mojitos to a "Chocolate Lick." Daily happy hours, weekend brunch, late-night food, and the Saturday night dinner show make this spot a one-stop shop for urban kings (or queens). With a friendly and catering staff to boot, this spot is more "nice" than "vice."

ViceVersa

325 W. 51st St. (8th & 9th Aves.)
Hell's Kitchen 212.399.9291

For you Italophiles out there, ViceVersa (pronounced in the proper Italian—although somewhat annoying—"Veech-eh-Verza") is your cup of cappuccino. More restaurant than bar, it really shines in the summer, when the outdoor veranda is opened up and patrons can enjoy the nice weather and romantic atmosphere. Steel bar tops and fancy floors can only take you so far, and with all the other options in the area, ViceVersa serves an excellent role as "restaurant," but the bar's usefulness extends mainly to those waiting to sit down. Not a real pick-up scene because most people are here on dates, the only real justification for coming would be to sit in the corner by yourself with a bottle of wine and a nice suit on, pretending you're "made."

The Viceroy

Viet-Café
345 Greenwich St. (Harrison & Jay Sts.)
TriBeCa 212.431.5888

For a menu with Far East flair, be sure to stop by the Viet-Café for their exclusive list of exotic cocktails and authentic cuisine. Linger at the bar with a delicious pomegranate margarita or a plum granita cascading over a mountain of ice. Their own Kaffir-lime lemonade is the secret behind their signature Viet-Cafe martini, along with splashes of ice-cold vodka and amaretto. Oh wait—you wanted to eat? Highlights from Chef Lan Tran Cao's menu include green papaya and beef salad, Vietnamese steak frites, and braised short ribs. If you want to replicate one of the dishes at home, sign up for a monthly themed cooking class. For after-dinner entertainment, browse through the exotic art housed in the neighboring Gallery Viet Nam.

The View (@ the Marriott Marquis)
1535 Broadway, 47th Fl. (45th & 46th Sts.)
Midtown 212.704.8900

Where better to see Times Square and the stampeding crowd shuffling along Broadway, making googly eyes at the flashy neon pantheon to our modern age, than up, up, and away on the 47th floor of the Marriott Marquis? At this aptly named rotating bar and restaurant, you can peer out the window for a 360-degree view of America's monument to its own capitalistic impulses, sup on overpriced "continental" buffet food, and sip "international" cocktails like the View Fizz and the Algonquin as the city that never sleeps sweeps around and around. The prices meet the tourist-trap requirement, with a $59.95 prix-fixe menu; but it might be what your out-of-town friends are craving. Keep watch over your cocktail intake, lest hundreds of unsuspecting tourists down below should get a motion sickness-induced vomit shower.

View Bar
232 8th Ave. (21st & 22nd Sts.)
Chelsea 212.929.2243

Ever walk inside a bar only to leave after realizing how empty it is? Conveniently, View Bar's oversized windows allow you to see how vacant this bar usually is without ever stepping foot in inside. Though the bar intends for its patrons to "see and be seen," not even drag queen puppet bingo, drink specials, and a *Desperate Housewives* viewing party can make patrons appear. It seems many either prefer Barracuda's drag shows around the corner or would rather sip lattes at the ever-popular Big Cup next door. In fact, you get the impression that the only people who come to View Bar are those who can't find seats at Big Cup. For those who just want a place where they can sit and have a drink, this is it.

Vig Bar
12 Spring St. (@ Elizabeth St.)
NoLita 212.625.0011

Vig is an old-school gambling term, but what's in a name? This NoLita lounge is more new-school, with an ultra-clean interior design that's accented by colorful booths, tea lights, and velvet curtains. Vig is your standard after-work, trendster bar where the more mature crowd stops in for libations that are a far cry from the $2 pint. The DJ is the highlight of the Vig experience, providing a cool retro soundtrack for couples that are one or two martinis away from dry-humping over in the corner. Either way, the crowd is a few cards shy of a full deck of balls-out fun; whether you choose to hit it up or pass all together is your call.

Village Speakeasy Pub
247 Smith St. (Douglass & Degraw Sts.)
Carroll Gardens 718.855.2848

Just how much do you love beer? So much that you would shell out $50 for membership in Village Speakeasy Pub's "Mug Club," which provides a personalized mug and frequent brewsky specials? Non-members needn't feel the sting of shame—the low-key, friendly wait staff is happy to point out the bar's myriad other amenities, including a Friday night comedy show, televised sporting events, beer game night, BBQ parties, live music, and standard American fare, which can be enjoyed in the family-friendly, first-floor restaurant, Village 247. Decorated in old-timey kitsch, this basement bar is a neighborhood favorite with a heavy contingency of paunchy, middle-aged dudes, but thanks to beer pong—which trails a naked sorority girl and a keg of Bud in the list of ultimate frat boy fantasies—there's a Greek element as well.

Village Tavern
46 Bedford St. (@ 7th Ave. S.)
West Village 212.741.1935

Come playoffs time, Red Sox fans usually take over this neighborhood favorite. Not that Yankees fans aren't wanted, but last time we checked, Red Sox and Yankees fans co-mingling usually ends in knuckle sandwiches and trips to the emergency room. Equally competitive are the Big Buck II and Golden Tee videogames which separate the rednecks from the country club-types. This West Village bar has a sophisticated list of Scotches and bourbons to complement the many beers on tap. Don't confuse the Village Tavern with a boring sports bar, though; the clientele is a delightfully mixed bag, and everyone's ready to have a grand old time…just as long as the Sox are winning.

The Village Underground
130 W. 3rd St. (MacDougal St. & 6th Ave.)
Greenwich Village 212.777.7745

Located in the basement of what was once the legendary club, Gerdes' Folk City (the Greenwich Village spot that sparked the folk-rock movement), and run by famed booker Steve Wietzman, the Village Underground has hosted performances by Bob Dylan, Evan Dando, Elvis Costello, and Patti Smith—so show some respect when you're outside on your knees, puking up another night at Down the Hatch. On Sunday nights, the Underground is packed to the gills with those vying for the attention of a Sony Records A&R rep during the open mic (stars like Mariah Carey and Stevie Wonder have been known to stop by for it). Slide into one of the booths in this historic music club and get schooled by the masters. Hey, it takes a village.

Village Vanguard
178 7th Ave. S. (Waverly Pl. & 11th St.)
West Village 212.255.4037

The Village Vanguard is a treasured New York City landmark chock-full of history and first-rate jazz. Repeat this to yourself when you're handing over a $20 cover and a $10 drink minimum. All of the greats have played or recorded at this "jazz center of the universe"—from Sonny Rollins to John Coltrane to Thelonious Monk—making it an absolute must-hit destination on any out-of-towner's "to do" list. But the Vanguard is well-loved by locals as well; they've been coming here to see the best sing the blues or jam and wail with the best of 'em since the Vanguard opened 70 years ago. And yes, some of the patrons are that old.

Villard Bar & Lounge (@ the New York Palace Hotel)
24 E. 51st St. (Madison & Park Aves.)
Midtown 212.303.7757

One of Villard's unique drink specialties, the Zeer martini, takes its name from the sumptuous Russian phrase "Zyrkalo Mira," which humbly translates into "reflection of the world." Indeed, you could not pick a more luxuriant spot in all of New York City to so idyllically upon gaze your surroundings. Whether you're with that special someone or a small group, the embracing and sultry ambiance makes this spot feel like a decadent home away from home. The menu offers an astounding array of wines, liqueurs, and specialty drinks like the lounge's namesake and the Salty D.O.G., as well as a variety of tempting espresso-related concoctions. Among the light fare served in the lounge are the citrus-crusted beef pinchos, rice flour crispy calamari, and the enticing Mediterranean dips. Just try not to spill any on yourself, hotshot.

Vince & Eddie's
70 W. 68th St. (Central Park W. & Columbus Ave.)
Upper West Side 212.721.0068

Popular with patrons of the arts—read: nobody you know—due to its proximity to Lincoln Center, Vince & Eddie's offers a menu of classic continental American fare (the average entrée costs $19) in a charming, semi-formal dining room setting. Guests are received in the front room, which features one of three cozy fireplaces. Drinks may be ordered here at the bar, which is separated from the dining area, or guests can proceed to hang their coats in the closet and walk through a short hallway to the larger dining room. At first glance, Vince & Eddie's décor might suggest a stodgy atmosphere, but the friendly wait staff quickly makes you feel at home—although now would be a good time to stop picking your nose with your fork.

Vintage
753 9th Ave. (@ 51st St.)
Hell's Kitchen 212.581.4655

Vintage is not for the indecisive. With over 70 types of beer and 200 kinds of martinis (the drink menu, like a bartender's bible, is broken down into sections according to liquor), you can spend a lifetime gaping at the menu before making a decision. But not to worry; Vintage is decked out with comfy couches on which to ponder your choices, and the super-friendly staff won't rush you. Young professionals who come to this laidback, "mature" restaurant dine on typical American fare—burgers, steaks, nachos, wings, and seafood—out on the outdoor patio. On Sundays and Mondays, things pick up thanks to live jazz. With any luck, you (and your intoxication preferences) will get wiser with age.

Virage
188 2nd Ave. (7th & 8th Sts.)
East Village 212.253.0425

Somewhere between a bistro and an all-night diner, you'll find Virage. Open 24 hours and busy through most of them, this cute corner spot is a perfect first date for the unadventurous. The room is inoffensive, if uninteresting, and Virage's able kitchen does as well with burgers and fries as it does with steaks and haricots vert. The drink list is pretty standard, with beer and wine being the most fitting libations. Not as loud as many places on this bustling strip of the Second Avenue corridor, Virage is a dependable standby, but not a destination. One thing's for sure—shrimp and crab burgers with shoestring potatoes are a great alternative to the usual 4am slice of pizza.

Virgil's Real Barbecue
152 W. 44th St. (Broadway & 6th Ave.)
Midtown 212.921.9494

Looking for some Memphis pork ribs and beer in Midtown? For a finger-lickin' good time in Times Square, look no further than Virgil's Real Barbecue. From their smoked Maryland ham to the sliced Texas beef brisket to their signature pulled Carolina pork, Virgil's brings the best of the South up north. Topping off the indulgent fare is an extensive beer list (or opt for a Cajun Swamp Water), a must to complement the flavors and bite of the stuffed jalapenos and beer-battered onion you can't refuse. Often crowded with out-of-towners, office folk, and displaced Southerners—as well as the occasional VIP getting their fix—the bi-level eatery with a roadhouse vibe is roomy enough to accommodate most BBQ fanatics and those just craving some hushpuppies and baked beans and a cold one.

VON
3 Bleecker St. (Bowery & Elizabeth St.)
NoHo 212.473.3039

The decade-old VON has amusedly witnessed NoHo's transformation. Long before the boutiques and upscale eateries set up shop, homeless people used to "do their thing" between the parked cars. Ah, those were the days. Happily, though, VON has managed to keep up with the times without losing its rakish charm. A pitbull named Happy bounds around the bar, occasionally slobbering on the regulars; black-and-white photos of the turn-of-the-century Bowery hang on the yellow and white walls; and the amiable bar staff cheerfully serves up pints and offers suggestions on the tasty selection of wines, including a Chilean merlot and an Australian shiraz. Suddenly gentrification doesn't seem like such a bad thing after all.

Voyage
117 Perry St. (@ Greenwich St.)
West Village 212.255.9191

Located in the heart of the only section of Manhattan where New Yorkers lose their way, it's well worth the time to seek out this hidden gem at the end of Perry Street. Voyage embodies New York chic but not the attitude. Once inside this swank bar and restaurant, let the "eclectic down-home global" menu take you away as you sit in the dining room enjoying a cocktail or two (or three). If you're out to impress a date, the moderately priced menu will let you do that in style. With entrées and appetizers ranging from $7 to $32, you won't be breaking the bank, and you can show off your globe-trotting tastes with menu items that are inspired by destinations such as the Caribbean, the American South, India, and France. All aboard!

Vudu Lounge
1487 1st Ave. (77th & 78th Sts.)
Upper East Side 212.249.9540

Vudu Lounge

This Upper East Side dance club provides a *Mad Hot Ballroom* experience for young jetsetters on the weekends. On Thursdays and Fridays, Vudu's DJs spin salsa and merengue, so everyone can show off the fancy footwork they learned on *Dancing with the Stars*. Later in the evenings, hip-hop and reggae are played, giving the club a tribal theme reflected in the décor. Sun mirrors hang over red leather banquettes with swirling backs, while a throne-like chair (lined with maroon velvet) sits before a mantelpiece between the dance floor and the bar, flanked by two small palm trees. A large mirror placed adjacent to the dance floor lets revelers watch their own moves during Thursday's happy hour, aka the "Latin After-work Party"—2-for-1 drinks, a buffet, and the only time admission is free. Sounds like it's time to put those moves to the test.

Vynl

824 9th Ave. (@ 54th St.)
Hell's Kitchen 212.974.2003

Vintage music-inspired figurines, including the Fab Four, stand above Vynl's soda-fountain bar, contributing to a colorful place that visitors will regard as either obnoxiously cutesy or a kitschy alternative to standard diners. The hipster-on-Prozac theme continues with bold tabletops, funky lighting created with 45s, and a chatty, hardworking staff that serves a young, kid-friendly clientele. Grab a black vinyl booth to enjoy a martini or specialty drink like Purple Rain ($7) to complement the eclectic sandwich-and-Thai fare. (Burgers and pad thai?) Unsurprisingly, the menus are buried within old record covers. It's all a little "Johnny Rockets," but still, there's something about the Dolly Parton doll that wins us over…

Waikiki Wally's

101 E. 2nd St. (Ave. A & 1st Ave.)
East Village 212.673.1689

This kitschy tiki palace (featuring a working waterfall and tropical murals) conveniently attached to drag queen mainstay and Chinese restaurant Lucky Cheng's is downtown's best tropical getaway. With the requisite fruity drinks coming in three sizes—mug, volcano, or scorpion bowl—bemused locals and adventurous tourists alike gather here to lose their inhibitions and eventually wipe out. If the packed bar isn't your scene, grab a table in one of the cave-like rooms and enjoy some Polynesian fare under the watchful eye of a tiki mask; the prix-fixe menus are served family-style and meant for sharing. Waikiki Wally's may be a bit too gimmicky to be your regular drinking hole, but it definitely makes a great vacation spot. Wally's also hosts pig roasts for your private luau.

Walker's

16 N. Moore St. (@ Varick St.)
TriBeCa 212.925.0796

It's not surprising to hear that the space that Walker's has occupied for 18 years has (since 1892) featured some manner of drinking establishment. Even on your first visit, it's hard to imagine anything here that's less than authentic. Wooden floors and just-so decorations make up the homey front room, with its smattering of tables and a long, comfortable bar leading off into dining rooms filled with smiling couples watched closely by the friendly staff. The prices are a pleasant surprise as well ($5 beers, $7 wines) and the menu is mostly American fare (delicious roasted organic

Waikiki Wally's

chicken, $13.25). Gaping windows showcase this pleasant little corner, providing passersby with a view inside of what could be a museum exhibit called, "Taking Care of the Locals."

Wallse
344 W. 11th St. (@ Washington St.)
West Village 212.352.2300

Austrian food gets a much-needed makeover under the direction of über-chef Kurt Gutenbrunner at Wallse. Spatzle is a star when paired with braised rabbit and wild mushrooms, while the wiener schnitzel with lingonberries is a must-have. Less classic dishes are equally as exciting, with standouts like foie gras terrine and cod strudel. It's all about the food, but let us not forget the wine. An extensive selection of Austrian wines with names like Guwerztraminer and Grüner Veltliner will be rolling off your tongue by the time you reach dessert. Viennese-inspired sweet things put the final touch on what might be one of the most interesting meals you'll have. West Village residents and downtown celebs seem to agree, and you can be sure to spot at least someone worthwhile during your visit.

The Warsaw
261 Driggs Ave. (@ Eckford St.)
Greenpoint 718.387.0505

Everyone should see their first rock show in a venue like this. Greenpoint's Warsaw (aka the Polish National Home) looks like an old gymnasium or a turn-of-the-century theater that has been converted into a concert venue. The space is enormous, the bands are top-notch (Frank Black, the Decemberists, the New Pornographers), and the crowds are genuinely excited to be here, further personifying its youthful, nostalgic vibe. Warsaw's main space is connected to a smaller one which houses a bar and a restaurant, where old Polish women serve up cheap beers in plastic cups and hot pierogies. There's even a balcony in the back of the concert space where you can sneak off to escape the crowds. Poles haven't been this much fun since strip clubs.

Waterfront Ale House
540 2nd Ave. (@ 30th St.)
Murray Hill 212.696.4104

Who knew ale could be so stale? Set far off the riverside in a tired corner of Murray Hill, the Waterfront Ale House is about as blah as it gets. Don't be fooled by the name—waterfront views don't abide here, unless you count the plate-glass windows facing a Kips Bay shopping plaza. And the misnomers don't stop there; sadly, this sleepy bar shares none of the charm of its sister institution in Brooklyn. No live jazz. No snazzy BBQ. No young Brooklynites. Just an ESPN-centric TV, some bland pub grub, and an ever-present crew of old booze hounds staring blankly into their pints. Yeah, there's a lot of ale, and it's reasonably priced during happy hour (Mon-Fri, 4pm-7pm). At least the bar kept up that part of the bargain, because on all other counts, it's a deal-breaker.

Waterloo Tavern
629 2nd Ave. (84th & 85th Sts.)
Upper East Side 212.535.4472

It's not entirely clear why Waterloo exists. Despite its generous size, which includes a large dancing area in the rear, there is literally nothing in this bar to set it apart from its boring brethren. A few cursory television sets aside, there's nary a pool table, darts, nor Golden Tee to pass the time. So why come here to meet your Waterloo? For whatever reason, it draws a good crowd that's not hard to look at either. However, upon entering, you'd better embrace your inner undergrad as the khaki-clad, baseball-wearing meatheads will try and grind on every girl in sight. Waterloo is best enjoyed during a warm Saturday afternoon when outdoor seating allows singles to watch yuppies as they push their strollers up and down the avenue while glaring back, bitterly remembering the lives they once had. On second thought, a look around this place tells you that they're probably better off.

WCOU Radio (aka Tile Bar)
115 1st Ave. (@ 7th St.)
East Village 212.254.4317

This bar is officially known as "WCOU Radio" but is most often referred to as the Tile Bar because…well, because the bar has tiles on the floor. Located on a relatively quiet corner in the East Village, WCOU is a simple, friendly place to have a drink or two with a few pals. Groups of three to five crowd around small tables to enjoy each other's company and listen to the eclectic music coming from a large, retro jukebox at the back of the bar. The most attractive reason to visit, though, are stiff drinks that cost just $5 each and don't require intense jostling for position and vision-blurring efforts to make eye contact with the barkeep. WCOU, Tile…call it whatever the hell you want, but do call.

wd-50
50 Clinton St. (Rivington & Stanton Sts.)
Lower East Side 212.477.2900

wd-50 may very well be responsible for the Lower East Side's metamorphosis from seedy nabe to the faux-hawked it-spot you know and secretly love. Named after owner/chef Wylie Dufresne (formerly of neighbor 71 Clinton Fresh Food), wd-50 serves up modest plates of New American fare for the foodie set. The seven-seater bar is perfectly nice, but not necessarily the kind of place where you pop in for a drink. Better to save your pennies and indulge in the whole shebang—dinner and one (or five) of wd-50's signature or seasonal cocktails, like the Royal Blush (vodka, lime juice, cherry puree, and champagne) or beet sangria (brandy, red wine, triple sec, beet juice, and orange salt). Don't get too drunk, though, or you won't notice the restaurant's cool but sparse design. Even the bathroom is meticulously designed, but the stalls are hard to work, even when you're sober.

The Web
40 E. 58th St. (Madison & Park Aves.)
Midtown 212.308.1546

Gaysians and their varied admirers enjoy getting caught up in a web of decadence at the city's only gay Asian dance club. Confucius say: For most fun on Mondays, check pants at door for "Boxers & Briefs" night. Of course, since it's not easy being easy while cavorting around in only your skivvies, the Web rewards anyone who does so with a happy hour-priced drink. Want more flesh? Drop by on the first Saturday of every month to ogle at the boys competing in a strip contest. And if you're looking to take the Orient Express to Bedroomville, come in to hear groovy music during topless night on Thursdays. Regardless of the night, what happens at the Web (especially during its wild Friday and Saturday dance parties), stays at the Web.

Webster Hall
125 E. 11th St. (@ 4th Ave.)
East Village 212.353.1600

This multilevel venue can seem a lot like a teenager who is going through a metal, indie rock, pop, and rebellious phase—all at the same time. Webster Hall searches for its true identity every night by offering live music (polar opposites like the Bravery, Avril Lavigne, Tegan & Sara), an amateur strip contest, Playgirl's Night Out, and Saturday night's Sexy Singles Auction. This mishmash of events can be downright disturbing; inside, the marble stairs, intricate carvings, and low lighting are reminiscent of a haunted mansion. Lines form around the block for the all-ages punk shows, making the plastic wristband a coveted accessory. All of this dichotomy might make you dizzy; so down their *Apprentice* "You're Hired" Ice Shot, kiss your 19-year-old date goodnight, and call it a night.

Welcome to the Johnsons
123 Rivington St. (Norfolk & Essex Sts.)
Lower East Side 212.477.5005

Drinking at Welcome to the Johnsons takes you back to raging in your friend's rec room when their parents were out of town, except now everyone is

Welcome to the Johnsons

of age. The beers are cheap (Pabst is $2) and come out of a full-size fridge, the walls are covered in family pictures and old trophies, and the plastic-covered furniture looks like it was on the losing end of a monster truck rally. The rec room look is complete with a pool table, Ms. Pac-Man, and an old TV with bad reception that was playing a documentary on animal mating on one recent visit. Ah, just like home—without the emotional baggage and guilt trips.

Westside Brewing Co.
340 Amsterdam Ave. (@ 76th St.)
Upper West Side 212.721.2161

The vibe of this pub has about as much appeal for local Manhattanites as your average suburban Elk's Lodge. Plus, the typical American fare— burgers and buffalo wings—is nothing to write home about, and the service is as lackluster as the interior. But a new generation of beer snobs will be sated with the selection of over 40 varieties, including local brews from Brooklyn and Chelsea breweries. Imports from as far as Japan and Germany offer patrons ales and lagers that are as tongue-twisting as they are tongue-tingling; try ordering a third or fourth round of the 16-ounce Aecht Schlenkerla Rauchbier and you'll have a newfound respect for the flustered waitresses who somehow seem to keep so many brands straight despite the omnipresent beer goggles and word-slurring.

Westside Tavern
360 W. 23rd St. (8th & 9th Aves.)
Chelsea 212.366.3738

Westside Tavern boasts exactly what the name suggests—a quintessential tavern on the West Side. What it isn't is your typical Irish pub with bartenders spilling genuine brogues. Though nestled in the heart of Chelsea, the venue proves to be a low-maintenance pick-up spot for any gender preference, a chill place to hang with friends, or a one-stop shop for a quick beer after work. The Tavern is equipped with all first-date essentials: draft beer and Jäger bombs, a pool table, an interactive jukebox, and a quieter atmosphere earlier in the week. While they don't serve food, you can bring in your own any night you want. Be sure to inquire about the Tavern's soccer team if you're looking to score.

The Wheeltapper Pub (@ Fitzpatrick Hotel)
141 E. 44th St. (Lexington & 3rd Aves.)
Midtown 212.351.6800

Take a ride on the Irish Amtrak, or at least feel like you're a kid visiting a train museum with your parents—except this time, while drinking. Wheeltapper's décor is more polished than your generic Irish pub, but bizarrely specific. Antique-looking architecture and dark wood creates quaint nooks for semi-private dining and drinking, and along with real artifacts like drivers' seats and mileposts, gives the impression that you're at a turn-of-the-century Irish railroad station. Especially popular for lunch among local workers and commuters, as well as visitors at the attached Fitzpatrick Hotel, the grub is upscale comfort food, with $16 cheeseburgers and $10 fancy cocktails. But for you Irish pub purists, a regular claims "the Guinness just tastes better here."

The Whiskey (@ W-Times Square)
1567 Broadway (46th & 47th Sts.)
Midtown 212.930.7444

The Whiskey sits underneath the W Hotel Times Square and like its brethren, strives to create the aura of exclusivity and swank. This incarnation is a disco/mod nightclub (colored circles light up the entrance's floor) where beautiful people go to burst their eardrums listening to seriously LOUD Top 40. Cocktails and martinis are mixed to perfection, even if the service is a little slow. (We wouldn't want the beautiful staff to break a sweat.) And though the crowd isn't always tourists, the "locals" aren't exactly Manhattanites, and a $20 cover on Friday and Saturday does little to change that. But if you're in the mood for adventure, the Whiskey's mission to create a space that blends "a chic and sexy nightspot with a soothing mix of intimacy and action" leaves plenty of dark corners to be explored.

Whiskey Blue

541 Lexington Ave. (49th & 50th Sts.)
Midtown 212.407.2947

Another Gerber baby, Whiskey Blue is an after-work haunt for the Midtown middle management-and-up crowd that generally foregoes bars full of TVs for $12 cosmos and opposite gender scenery once the clock strikes 5:01pm. On most nights the scene dies for a little while as the after-workers head home and the W Hotel guests dine elsewhere before coming back for a nightcap. Like with Starbucks, the W bars' strengths and weaknesses revolve around predictability. You know how to dress business-casual, you know to "write it off" to the company, and you know the music will be '80s and '90s pop-heavy. There's always a bit of a pick-up scene of sorts going on, but beware Bob from Accounting who's sitting at the bar and dying to tell somebody about his day at the office.

Whiskey Park

100 Central Park S. (@ 6th Ave.)
Upper West Side 212.307.9222

If the stench emanating from the horse-drawn carriages in Central Park doesn't impede your imbibing experience here, the cost of the drinks might. With steep prices (specialty drinks start at $12), and a liquor list long enough to make you feel drunk after reading it, this swank saloon attracts mostly young adults in linen pantsuits and golf shirts. Nonetheless, the big apple mojito is tasty enough to tempt even the thriftiest patron. The leather couches are inviting, but "Reserved" signs make the encounter a tad foreboding. The pool table seems oddly out of place, and the music is a bit loud for this spot. Whiskey Park is a sure bet for ladies searching for fetching fellows in a higher income bracket. Just watch out for the olfactory offender lurking outside!

Whiskey Blue

Whiskey River

575 2nd Ave. (31st & 32nd Sts.)
Murray Hill 212.679.6799

It's no surprise that whiskey flows at the aptly named neighborhood spot across from the Loews movie theater. Pre- and post-movie-goers aren't the only ones swimming in the extensive beer and whiskey list. Fratty types crowd the all-American Internet jukebox, where $1 will buy you the right to skip your competitors' songs. Drinking without a paddle? Just grab a pair of snowshoes, or any of the other outdoor gear that adorns the walls and get in the game. Though the stuffed bear is eyeing you to be good, the cigarette hanging from his mouth is telling you to be bad. Take it out back to the garden, where you won't be the only one trying to drown your sins.

Whiskey Ward

121 Essex St. (Rivington & Delancey Sts.)
Lower East Side 212.477.2998

Woo-hoo! A happy hour for people who don't have to work at 9am. Hit Whiskey Ward on a Monday or Tuesday night between midnight and 3am, and you'll be rewarded with rock-bottom late-night happy hour specials served by fantastic bartenders. Check out the Knock Out Drop ($6), a shot of tequila and whiskey that has late-morning snooze button written all over it. If you aren't feeling that bold, stick with The Parker—for $6 comes a Pabst and a shot of Wild Turkey or Jack. Feel like swirling a good Scotch or sipping a fine whiskey? They have you covered with an extensive selection of the browns. Hot spiced cider does well in the winter, and sangria ($15-$25) is served year-round.

White Horse Tavern

25 Bridge St. (Broad & Whitehall Sts.)
Financial District 212.668.9046

This isn't the White Horse of legend where Dylan Thomas drank himself to death. This one's for the financial sector that's more likely to be killed with boredom. The long wooden bar is packed with broker types who are out in spades at lunchtime and after work. Sure, you can drink here, but this is no one-trick pony. Burgers and other bar foods fill the menu, along with daily specials along the lines of steak, chicken dishes, and even Hungarian goulash. The place probably works best in the summertime—a long list of frozen drinks is available and it's unlikely that great poets come for melon balls and margaritas. Tourists and traders are a different story.

White Horse Tavern

567 Hudson St. (@ 11th St.)
West Village 212.243.9260

Once upon a time, Dylan Thomas may have drunk himself to death at the White Horse Tavern. So as long as you steer clear of drinking consecutive shots of whiskey, you should have quite a time at this piece of New York history (they've been going strong since 1881!). The White Horse has a wide selection of beers, featuring seven on tap and 13 bottled brews, guaranteeing that you'll find something to satisfy your palate (and the pub grub is superb). Whether you stop in after work or after midnight, with a group or with a date, the White Horse is always packed with New Yorkers out to have a good time. The assortment gathered here ranges from locals to students to tourists, so you're sure to meet someone interesting…like a dead poet.

The White Rabbit

145 E. Houston St. (Forsyth & Eldridge Sts.)
Lower East Side 212.477.5005

Follow the White Rabbit and you'll experience one hell of a rabbit hole. With double doors in the front that open up to the street and a projection screen in the back, there's plenty to watch. After 6pm the kitchen opens and serves a tasty menu of appetizers (empanadas, summer rolls), all ranging from $6-$7. The cocktail list boasts more tempting potions than you can shake your tail at, including $9-$10 chocolate hazelnut martinis, lychee apple martinis, and even a peach Manhattan. Live music (of the Latin variety) and DJs add to this rabbit's bag of tricks.

Wild Spirits
1843 1st Ave. (95th & 96th Sts.)
Upper East Side 212.427.7127

As if the Upper East Side needed another trashy dive with the word "Spirits" in its moniker, get ready to shrug indifferently at the latest addition to the area: Wild Spirits. Fresh off the spectacular failure that was the uptown version of Hogs & Heifers, Wild Spirits aims to pick up where that bar left off by being as loud, obnoxious, and predictable as possible. We do have to give the place props for hosting live music seven nights a week, even if the bands are worse than an unholy alliance of Creed, Lifehouse, and Nickelback combined. So if you're a fledgling band in search of a gig or on the UES looking for some amateur rock, you know you've come to the right place.

Willy's Bar & Grill
1538 2nd Ave. (80th & 81st Sts.)
Upper East Side 212.734.1888

One of the more striking things about this cozy, upscale, stylishly decorated (dark wood, white linen lining the tables) pub is how diverse the staff is—there's the friendly American bartender, Latin hostess, and Slavic and Asian waiters and waitresses. But while Willy's gets a blue ribbon in the foreign relations department, it also scores high points in the brunch and sidewalk dining categories. Willy's menu is big, with everything from burgers ($6.75) to rib-eye steak (just under $20), to salad nicoise, and a half-dozen pasta dishes. If you're looking to fill your stomach with carbohydrates before going out on a bender or if you're just in need of a quick drink, head to this uptown staple. No one ever seems to have anything bad to say about Willy.

Windfall Lounge & Grill
23 W. 39th St. (5th & 6th Aves.)
Midtown 212.869.4606

Where do frat boys go when they grow up? Trick question—they don't. But you'll find plenty of them in their older forms at Windfall Lounge & Grill. Think of this as a state college bar that graduated, got a job in the city, and wakes up every morning, looks at its hairline in the mirror, and wonders if it's receding. Like a tiny piece of cheese in the center of the rat race maze, Windfall's spacious setting attracts a genial clientele that is looking to unwind after a long day of playing computer solitaire—er, crunching numbers. Over two dozen different types of beer and a nearly 50-foot-long bar attract drinking men, while a New American menu with such fare as a Santa Fe Black Bean Crab Cake offers a nice alternative to standard bar food.

Winebar
65 2nd Ave. (3rd & 4th Sts.)
East Village 212.777.1608

Winebar

On this strange little strip of Second Avenue, not far from where Mars Bar's customers regard methadone as a fancy cocktail, wine is most often sipped from a paper bag. However, in this teeny oenophile's dream room, vino bottles literally line the dimly lit walls. Exposed brick abounds in Winebar's minimalist space where there are a dozen tables inside and a few more on the sidewalk. There's a lot to pick from—40 wines by the glass. Where they hide the kitchen in this tiny spot is a mystery, but light dishes with a Mediterranean influence are certainly coming from somewhere. This is a big-time date spot.

Winnie's
104 Bayard St. (Baxter & Mulberry Sts.)
Chinatown 212.732.2384

How did a Chinatown dive with mediocre drinks and a two-drink minimum become one of the hippest places in New York? That's easy—a little pact with the devil called pay-for-play karaoke. For a buck you can embarrass yourself by singing a song from Winnie's impressive song catalog while corny, low-budget Asian music videos play on the big screen behind you on stage. The combination of karaoke and cheap drinks brings together a wide assortment of patrons, from hipsters and Wall Streeters to employees from the nearby municipal court. Winnie's is a social melting pot where the great equalizer is who can belt out Sinatra or Chinese pop tunes like a pro. Think of William Hung, and you'll know what Winnie's is about.

Wogie's
39 Greenwich St. (@ Charles St.)
West Village 212.229.2171

Intended to be a little slice of Philadelphia in the Big Apple, Wogie's serves up delicious cheese steak sandwiches and wings, which you and a few friends can wash down with a cheap bucket of Rheingold for only $15. Some outdoor seating is available, but when the game's on, everyone will be piled in, waiting with bated breath for the final buzzer. It's no sports bar, though, and despite the frat boy name, the chill atmosphere is surprisingly lady-friendly. Wogie's houses a pretty tame, after-work crowd—even the edgiest kids in this joint look like recovering preppies. The high-backed booths provide a little privacy, but not too private—when those buckets start stacking up, you'll have gotten to know everybody in this friendly corner bar.

Wolfgang's Steakhouse
4 Park Ave. (@ 33rd St.)
Murray Hill 212.889.3369

Can't wait two months for a reservation at Williamsburg's Peter Luger's? Wolfgang's is heavily influenced by Brooklyn's king of steak...maybe because its namesake was the headwaiter at Luger's for over four decades. Wolfgang's follows Luger's lead with dry-aged porterhouse, fried German potatoes, and the widely craved creamed spinach. So what sets these two great steakhouses apart? Well, Wolfgang's replaces the simple wooden tables and old-world, down-home charm of Luger's with vaulted, tiled ceilings, an impressive wine and Scotch list, and upscale diners. Plus, their menu features more seafood options and Brooklyn-shy Manhattanites won't have to cross the Williamsburg Bridge. Grab a beer and raise a toast. Raising your cholesterol has never tasted or looked so good.

Wonderland
14 E. 27th St. (5th & 6th Aves.)
Flatiron 212.686.1400

Send in the Marines, because Wonderland appears to have more private nooks than an Al-Qaeda cave. Pairing a North Pole-like icy-blue color scheme with Miami-inspired palm trees, Wonderland isn't a place you'll find on any map. The new Flatiron lounge is outfitted with curtained-off private berths provided for the bottle-service crowd, while the more sociable and stingy among us can find a place around the glowing, 50-foot-long horseshoe bar while enjoying "bargain" $12 cocktails. A DJ in the center of the room spins a dance mix from an aqua-lit booth, and the upstairs level is designated for—what else—private events. In its infancy, Wonderland is still looking for the VIPs it needs, so stop in now before this party paradise starts playing the velvet rope game.

World Bar
845 UN Plaza (48th & 49th Sts.)
Midtown 212.935.9361

Upscale and overpriced, World Bar is where those who rule the world take a timeout. UN employees mingle over martinis while top lawyer-types hit on girls you know you've seen somewhere (*The Apprentice*, perhaps?). Fittingly, the bar is on the first floor of Trump's World Tower, furnished with swanky, tan, wraparound lounge seats and a very low-lit and sultry bar. Live Brazilian jazz is offered on Thursday and Saturday. Any lounge that offers a $50 "World Cocktail" requires a certain attitude and attire, so even if you stick with $7 glasses of economic punch, don't forget that you're in Trump's house. Still, for those who are so over over-impressing, there is always the low-key outdoor space, the Patio, right around the corner.

WXOU Radio Bar
558 Houston St. (11th & Perry Sts.)
West Village 212.206.0381

If you're not paying attention, you'll walk right past this inconspicuous little dive bar on Hudson Street. Unpretentious and straightforward, everyone needs to tune to WXOU. Beers and mixed drinks cost around five dollars, the jukebox pleases more often than not, and the generally laidback vibe gives this little space a lot of character. The bartenders are friendly and the mix of locals and students make for good company. WXOU is a great place to start off your night in the West Village. But watch out—the cheap prices and good tunes might ensure that you stay here 'til the wee hours; then you'll wonder how WXOU "Shook [You] All Night Long" (and you'd better have a good excuse to give your boss as to why you're still wearing yesterday's clothes).

XES Lounge
157 W. 24th St. (@ 7th Ave.)
Chelsea 212.604.0212

Pronounced "excess," this is your daddy's Chelsea. And we mean "daddy." Amateur go-go boy contests attract well-shaven night owls, and early birds dig the weekday 2-for-1 happy hour, which ends at 9pm. Friday's hip-hop beats bring a few gay-ngstas into the mix, but it's more dress-up than shoot-out. And what's the vibe? We said, WHAT'S THE VIBE? It's loud. Very loud. XES-sive, one might argue. There's little 'tude with these fun-loving dudes and despite guest DJs and cheap drinks, there's never a cover here. On occasion, XES has hosted parties for Log Cabin Republicans

as well. Come meet an Alex Keaton for Wednesday night's "Booty Dance" party, buy him some $1 shots, and let him explain how Dick and Bush understand gay issues.

Xicala
151B Elizabeth St. (Broome & Kenmare Sts.)
Little Italy 212.219.0599

Xicala

Bigger is better? Not always. This Tom Cruise-sized bar offers a unique house blend of strawberry and peach sangrias, "pequeño" tapas (omelets, pastries, you name it—if it's tiny and tasty, Xicala has it), moderately priced Spanish wines by the glass, and a weekday happy hour. This intimate wine and tapas bar is frequently packed with a hip, young, neighborhood crowd; and by "packed" we mean there are about 45 people inside—when we said Tom Cruise-small, we weren't exaggerating. Still, Xicala is oozing forth with palatable dishes and warm, friendly service, proving, yet again, that it's the little things that matter.

Xing
785 9th Ave. (52nd & 53rd Sts.)
Hell's Kitchen 646.289.3010

A Midtown portal into the Far East, minus fireworks and dragon boat festivals, Xing makes a new taste out of old flavors with dishes like the Peking Duck Salad with Citrus Vinaigrette ($11). A restaurant with late nights Thursday through Saturday (open until 2am), this new kid opens for lunch and sports a traditional Chinese menu that's prepared in a wok kitchen, which means the food is fired up immediately, so you might not get your General Tso's ($12) or XO Seafood ($17) in the order you placed it. But that's why they have their specialty drink "electric karma" ($10) served in a Buddha doll—relax! Or you can munch on complimentary (and addictive) fried wontons. As beats bop in the background, the atmosphere seems dominated by lively conversation. (FYI, Xing is pronounced "shing.")

XL

357 W. 16th St. (8th & 9th Aves.)
Chelsea 212.339.0214

Some nights just aren't over until the fat drag queen sings at this Chelsea gay hotspot. Each Sunday, XL, which proudly declares itself "New York's best gay lounge," hosts Jessye Normous singing live opera and entertaining the crowds with his rowdy humor. But no night is rowdier than Wednesdays, when teams battle it out for cash in a game of "Faggot Feud," during which you'll hear questions that Richard Dawson only wished he could ask on TV (for example, "What's the fastest way to make a guy come?"). Regardless of the night, though, four years after it opened, XL remains one of Chelsea's most popular bars. Two floors, hot bartenders, and a happy hour that ends at 9pm all ensure an XXXL good time.

XR Bar

128 Houston St. (@ Sullivan St.)
Greenwich Village 212.674.4080

Either XR Bar is a front for some sort of numbers racket—or else the power of some divine force has kept this place in business. XR is a small, well-maintained corner hangout, with so much light it seems truly meant to be a café (both of the street-facing walls teem with long windows that are flung open in nice weather); the problem is that no one ever seems to go in. The non-descript atmosphere and generic hip-hop, reggae, and soul music selection that's played a little too loudly here would be better suited for a larger space that encourages dancing and excessive macking. There's truly nothing memorable about this neighborhood bar, but maybe its lifeline is the locals who are sick of overcrowded West Village drinkeries. Go figure.

Xth Avenue Lounge

642 10th Ave. (45th & 46th Sts.)
Hell's Kitchen 212.245.9088

Holy moley—are there really hipsters this far uptown? The cool Sistine Chapel design over the bar is holy indeed and sprinkled between afterworkers is the occasional bed-headed kid in Pumas and a tee. From behind the stone altar of a bar comes a daily happy hour from 6pm-8pm daily. Looking for something softer? Unwind with $5 cosmos on one of the couches in the back area. This space rarely gets crowded, and the best time to come is on Tuesdays when the bar hosts an open mic night. Because of this place's proximity to Broadway, Xth often marks the spot for some rather entertaining crooning. You're more likely to hear Streisand than Hootie from the crowd that attends this event, but bad-done-well beats bad-done-badly any time.

Xunta

174 1st Ave. (10th & 11th Sts.)
East Village 212.614.0620

Sipping sangria at Xunta, you'll scan the crowd of attractive, diverse 20-somethings and wonder what it is they see in this place. Netting, blue lights, and dark wooden barrels serve as décor. In back, metal folding chairs and thick plastic tablecloths smack more of fish and chips in a basket than late-night tapas in Spain. Then it hits you. A friendly wait staff serves 54 tapas (all under $10), $2.25 Buds, and wine starting at $3.25. Tuesdays and Wednesdays feature live music, and on Thursdays you'll catch a spectacular flamenco performance that transforms those conservative cuties in the corner into clapping, hollering, dancing fools. Don't let that stop you from joining them. That said, don't you dare bring back the Macarena.

Yaffa Café

97 St. Marks Pl. (Ave. A & 1st Ave.)
East Village 212.674.9302

Xunta

Part of the fun of living in the city that never sleeps is making the rounds of the places that stay open 24 hours. An East Village mainstay, Yaffa Café has been harboring thirsty clubbers, night-crawlers, hungry punks, and drunken NYU grads looking for a little adventure for over 20 years. Maybe it's their carrot ginger dressing, the chic garage-sale décor (velvet portraits, nude table-top prints, and tiger-print wallpaper), or the complimentary Yaffa condoms that has them coming back again and again. (It's the condoms.) Yaffa recently expanded their backyard dining area to accommodate the throes of even-keeled out-of-towners and buttoned-up residents who have moved into the neighborhood—it's the perfect spot to dine on stir fry or other quick snacks on a starry night, and a nice alternative to getting your rubbers at Duane Reade.

The Yard (@ the SoHo Grand)
310 W. Broadway (Canal & Grand Sts.)
SoHo 212 965-3000

Sex and the City meets cocktailing in the country at this outdoor space adjacent to the über-fab SoHo Grand Hotel. Step into the Yard and find yourself on the dream patio you've always dreamed of, complete with full bar, chef's grill, and…an outline of actual grass. Say hello to summer as you pull up a lawn chair and settle in with the Perfect Ten—a seasonal mixture of vanilla-infused vodka, pineapple juice, and fresh lemon. The outdoor grill invites customers to design their own kebabs and Sunday brunch makes doing time in the Yard a "must." This space is also dog-friendly, so feel free to bring Fido by as a center-piece for singles-y mingling. Also bring your Amex—this is SoHo.

Ye Olde Tripple Inn
263 W. 54th St. (Broadway & 8th Ave.)
Midtown 212.245.9847

Christmas tinsel hangs from the ceiling, a blinking cardboard snowman hovers over the dartboard, and St. Patrick's Day decorations pepper the bar. And this is June. If you want to call Ye Olde Tripple Inn a "hole in the wall," go right ahead, but you'll never see a more interestingly-decorated hole, complete with old-school headshots of actors (some even autographed) all over the walls. Red-and-white-checkered tablecloths dominate the dining area in the back and upstairs, and the crowd is random enough to keep you guessing what the vibe will be on any given night. Saturday night comedy shows, live music during the week, and an atmosphere that allows you to order anything from a Bud pitcher to a glass of white zinfandel; "eclectic" doesn't do it justice.

Yello
32 Mulberry St. (@ Mosco St.)
Little Italy 212.964.3410

A swanky karaoke lounge? Surely that must be an oxymoron even for the irony-prone hipster set. Yet Yello makes it work. The trendy, mostly Asian-American crowd can be seen and heard belting out tunes from a mind-numbing catalog of American and Asian pop tunes. With Chinese, Italian, and even barbecued bites, the food here is as eclectic as the music. The upstairs portion of this two-floor lounge has enough prerequisite flat-screen televisions to put many sports bars to shame. On the topic of shame, the downstairs boasts a roomy and comfortable atmosphere in which to watch in horror as aspiring Kelly Clarksons and William Hungs butcher Top 40 tunes that initially seemed as though they couldn't have gotten any worse. During happy hour, well drinks are $4-$7 and beer is buy-one-get-one-free.

Yogi's
2156 Broadway (75th & 76th Sts.)
Upper West Side 212.579.9852

Bras, hats, balloons, flags, stirrups, and TVs showing sports all hang high at this bawdy, unrepentant American classic. It's all about Elvis, Johnny Cash, Hank Williams, and getting ripped with your buddies—whether they're your mates from college or AA. There's always lots of hooting and hollering, and empty cans, darts, and even shot glasses flying at this dive bar. The bartender yells, curses, and keeps barflies entertained with her (yes, her) crude sexual comments. She pours shots of tequila and Tabasco, proclaiming, "Some call these Prairie Farts, but I call 'em Fire in the Hole." Formerly the Bear Bar, a 15-foot wooden bear still stands guard out front, warding off the faint of heart.

Yuca Bar & Restaurant
111 Ave. A (@ 7th St.)
East Village 212.982.9533

Another day, another tapas restaurant. But for some of the best small plates and mango mojitos this side of Tijuana, yucan count on Yuca. Unfortunately, the bar portion of this place is a bit of an afterthought, which is a shame given the quality of the caipirinha and sangria, both of which are sold by the pitcher. Still, the sultry lighting and hot Latin barista will compel even the most staid individual to start catcalling. Sip margaritas while harkening back to a time when Alphabet City was a crack-infested crime scene waiting to happen—or as some refer to it—pre-gentrified.

Yujin
24 E. 12th St. (5th Ave. & University Pl.)
Greenwich Village 212.924.4283

This "modern Japanese restaurant" goes out of its way to be a flashy, upscale seafood extravaganza. The style is over-the-top and the presentation of the dishes is artful, but don't venture in if you're just looking to fill your belly. Yujin's prices are as

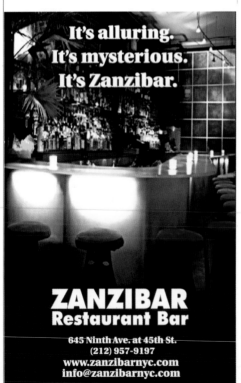

Yumcha

high-end as the interior; soon you'll realize you're paying for more than just the sushi and sake. Inside, it's an interior designer's wet dream—the glass doors, glass and gold leaf wall, and the moat must have cost a small fortune. Unfortunately, nightlife experiences are hit or miss here—you'll have to drink a lot of sake and plum wine to feel remotely buzzed.

Yumcha
29 Bedford St. (@ Downing St.)
West Village 212.524.6800

They call it Yumcha, and there's a definite emphasis on the "yum." This new restaurant doesn't have a single miss on its simple but flavorful menu, and your only frustration will be deciding what to order. Will it be the savory frog legs? The pork and shrimp spring rolls with ginger sauce? How about the sorbet-topped cold udon noodles with cashews? Do yourself a favor and make room for all of them, and wash everything down with a rosewater-infused champagne cocktail. (The teas are also highly recommended.) Like the menu, Yumcha's décor is Asian-influenced and deceptively streamlined with a few bold kicks, and don't be surprised if you see a movie star or celebrity chef at the table next to you. They're only human, after all.

Zablozki's
107 N. 6th St. (Berry St. & Wythe Ave.)
Williamsburg 718.384.1903

Dark cherry wood makes up the walls, ceiling, floor, and bar, giving this slightly hip townie bar a touch of class. Williamsburg isn't known for its after-work crowd, as most locals are "freelance," but Zablozki's draws a decent-sized crowd of 30-something Brooklynites to their happy hour where a dozen beers are on tap. It's the little things that let us know that they care: sporadically placed fresh flowers, gratis spicy pretzel mix, a flat-screen TV, and an immaculate pool table are a few of the nice touches. In fair weather, the front opens up for people-watching and cavorting with smokers.

Zablozki's

Zakuro

143 2nd Ave. (@ 9th St.)
East Village 212.505.5625

If you build it, will they come? The answer for Zakuro, the newest kid on a block of about a dozen Japanese sushi bars is sadly "No" (or at least not yet). Housed in a long-empty former Starbucks, Zakuro opened to lukewarm reception. The location is great, so what could it be? Is it the competition (longtime favorites Decibel and Soba-ya are just steps away)? Is it because with all the muted neon and plate glass, Zakuro kind of looks and feels like a fishbowl? The prices are pretty standard, and the menu intrigues...So what gives? It could be there are so many sushi joints, New York might have to claim a section called "Little Japan." Maybe Zakuro needs to bang the gong a little louder to be heard. In the meantime, enjoy the sake and not having to wait for a table.

Zanzibar

645 9th Ave. (@ 45th St.)
Hell's Kitchen 212.957.9197

Lovers of Moroccan and Middle Eastern food need not journey far in New York—just head to this exotic late-night lounge in Hell's Kitchen. Sure, there's spillover from the theater crowd, but on Thursday nights, hip locals gather around the huge circular fireplace for after-after-work drinks (or to gawk at the waitresses clad in sarongs). Small tables surrounded by suede chairs and tiny red ottomans offer comfortable seating on which to enjoy the African, Arabic, and Italian-inspired menu. Weekends tend to be crowded, so stop by during the week to rock the casbah in comfort. Now if could just convince that group of lovely ladies in the corner to join your harem.

Zebulon

258 Wythe Ave. (N. 3rd St. & Metropolitan Ave.)
Williamsburg 718.218.6934

Owned by Parisian-expat avant garde jazz enthu-

siasts, Zebulon plays host to free live jazz and blues nightly, ranging from traditional to experimental. Cool cats pair the tunes with a glass or bottle from the affordable and extensive French wine list and a cheese plate to help soak up the atmosphere. Less canned "Française" than the throngs of distressed-mirrored, faux-Balthazar imitators, Zebulon's interior feels fresh and unique with flyers from long-ago jazz gigs and the decorative album covers probably borrowed from the club's collection of rare vinyl that spins between sets. And in a neighborhood that's predominately hipster-chic, this juke joint is a smoky breath of fresh air.

Zerza Bar

304 E. 6th St. (1st & 2nd Aves.)
East Village 212.529.8250

Zerza Bar isn't much of a bar at all, really—it's a tri-level Moroccan restaurant with a small bar by the front door. But that doesn't mean you shouldn't stay for a bottle of Casablanca, stick dollar bills in a belly dancer's bikini top, and take a few puffs from a hookah ($10 bucks a blow). The upstairs space is good for small parties and the tagines and kebabs are just plain yummy. Two sexy little rooms make up the make-out-friendly lower level. The scantily clad dancer undulating to sexy Middle Eastern music has been known to wrap her scarves around patrons and teach them a move or two.

Zinc Bar

90 W. Houston St. (Thompson St. & LaGuardia Pl.)
Greenwich Village 212.477.8337

This jazz club is a dark, subterranean bar with a tiny stage smack in the middle of its long passageway. In the front, relax and enjoy the nightly entertainment (ranging from Brazilian jazz to Cuban and African tunes), but note there is a $5 cover charge. The layout of the bar is not really conducive to live music, and if you venture past the mini-musical area, you'll find the real attraction of this bar, the sultry backroom. So dark you can't see who you're swapping spit with, this candlelit cave is complete with dark walls, a low ceiling, and a marauding cat to set the mood for getting hot and heavy; but if you want to make sure you can still see through your beer goggles, bring a flashlight.

Zoë
90 Prince St. (Broadway & Mercer St.)
SoHo 212.966.6722

This elegant space provides a lovely opportunity to get all dressed up and practice your newfound maturity and sophistication while aging your credit card with $9-$15 specialty cocktails. Salt-and-pepper martinis are worth every penny, and oenophiles will have trouble choosing from the list of 250 bottles and 35 wines by the glass (which ranges from $8-$18); 3-oz. servings are also available ($4-$9). Zoë's contemporary American menu of salads, soups, and such is small, though the prices are not. Luckily the attentive wait staff will soothe the pain with a warm smile as they pass along the bill. As with everything in this area, dining is best done on off-hours to avoid the tourists, but here, the out-of-towners are hard to tell apart from the locals, and we mean that in a good way.

Zombie Hut
261 Smith St. (@ Degraw St.)
Carroll Gardens 718.855.2736

Zombie Hut knows how to work a theme. Unfortunately, in this case the theme is more Spring-Break-in-Hawaii than flesh-eating-monsters-in-a-George-Romero-film. Beaded curtains, decorative surfboards, tiki torches, and Polynesian masks all ache to bring you back to that glorious week back in college. If that doesn't work, sample their signature slushy concoction, the Frozen Zombie (rum, pineapple, and OJ), or guzzle a Mai Tai ($5). Zombie Hut's clientele is happy to help you relive those days of fun in the sun, but once your three-hour tour is over, it's out the door you go, skipper.

Zum Schneider Bavarian Beer House
107 Ave. C (@ 7th St.)
East Village 212.598.1098

Is this an indoor beer garden? *Nein*! It's a *biergarten*. With a dozen German beers on tap and a welcoming, airy atmosphere to boot, this is a fantastic stop for a stein of suds. But with Kräuterquark mit Pellkartoffeln ($11), Organischer Schweinebraten ($17), and Gegrillte Forelle ($16) on the menu, Zum Schneider will quickly have you saying, "Uhhh….I'll have the $13 three-sausage platter." Want to keep it simple? Stop by for brunch and try the $6 Eierpfannkuchen, which is pancakes stuffed with apple sauce and/or jam. Sure, the Germans are a hearty bunch, but they know a deal when they see one. The few outdoor tables provide a touch of nature, as does sitting indoors under the giant tree branches lining the ceiling.

BEAUTY
BOOK
NYC
2006

NEW!

**NYC'S ONLY A-Z GUIDE TO BEAUTY AND WELLNESS:
OVER 900 SPAS, SALONS, FITNESS LOCATIONS,
STORES & PRODUCTS**

**Shecky's
Beauty Book NYC**

NYC's new "beauty bible" offers reviews and ratings on over 600 spas, salons, fitness clubs, yoga studios, and more for beauty/health-conscious New Yorkers! The A-Z guide also features product "essentials" sections and insider tips.

Suggested Retail Price: $12.95
ISBN # 1-931449-24-4

Available Now

Top Five Reasons to Plan a Party in NYC

1) After seven years of college, you're finally graduating
2) You're moving from your parents' house to a new 100-sq-ft. apt.
3) Your boss was transferred to Fiji
4) You're turning 25 (for the 6th year in a row)
5) Your ex-boyfriend was just demoted to Assistant "French Fry" Manager at McDonald's

There are SO many reasons to have a party in NYC
but finding the perfect venue is no easy task!

Shecky's is here to help.

Whether you're looking for a cool lounge or a casual bar…a space
that holds 50 or 500…or Midtown corporate vs. Downtown chic…
the following pages suggest it all!

Have a great party!

Bar XII
206 E. 34th St.
(@ 3rd Ave.)
Murray Hill
Phone: 212.545.9912
Fax: 212.545.9812

Contact: Gabby Obermeier
Alternate Contact: Paul Molloy/Garreth Molloy
E-mail: info@bar12.com
Website: www.bar12.com
Mention Shecky's when you call or e-mail

Bar XII

Twelve can cater for any party from 1 to 250 guests. Twelve provides the party-goer with the ideal lounge vibe for a great night out. Birthday parties are provided with a complimentary champagne toast and birthday cake. Bottle service is also available in our exclusive booths. You can also choose from passed hors d'oeuvres or a custom-built carving table. Party the night away as our DJ spins a red-hot club mix.

Venue Size	:	2,400 sq. ft.
Capacity	:	300 people
Private party room available	:	Yes, Private back bar
Is food served?	:	Yes, 'til 2am
Outside catering permitted	:	No
Dance floor	:	No
Live music or DJ	:	Both
Outdoor space available	:	Yes
Video/TV monitors available	:	Many, incl. Beer Tap TV
Coat check	:	Yes

Visit www.sheckys.com/partyaid for more party planning advice!

Fuelray
68 W. 3rd St.
(LaGuardia Pl. & Thompson St.)
West Village
Phone: 212.675.9557 or
212.995.1900

Contact: Tommy
E-mail: tommy@fuelray.com
Website: www.fuelray.com

Mention Shecky's when you call or e-mail

Fuelray

This West Village hotspot has quickly gained a reputation as one of the best venues to have a party. It's not hard to see why; two separate rooms, an outdoor smoking garden, signature drinks to die for, and an award-winning bar menu geared for group sharing. As for the décor? It screams sex. The space is accented with angelic statues, 18th-century paintings, crushed velvet, and candles everywhere. The crowd is hip and attractive and the DJs mash everything from '80s and hip-hop to rock and pop. If you're expecting drama at the door…you will be disappointed; the doormen are as friendly as the rest of the staff. Fuelray has created the recipe for a great night out.

Venue Size	:	2,000 sq. ft.
Capacity	:	250 people
Private party room available	:	Yes
Is food served?	:	Yes
Outside catering permitted	:	Yes
Dance floor	:	No
Live music or DJ	:	DJ
Outdoor space available	:	Yes
Video/TV monitors available	:	Yes
Coat check	:	Yes

Iguana
240 W. 54th St.
(Broadway & 8th Ave.)
Midtown
Phone: 212.765.5454
Fax: 212.397.1219

Contact: Nino G. Brusco
E-mail: iguananewyork@aol.com
Website: www.iguananyc.com

Mention Shecky's when you call or e-mail

Iguana

This bi-level Mexican restaurant features a beautifully adorned dining room, two large mahogany bars, and an intimate fireplace/dance lounge. Iguana specializes in private functions. Whether it's a corporate gathering or family party, Iguana has what it takes to make your event a memorable one. So when it comes to your next sit-down dinner, buffet, or cocktail party, be sure to go with a proven professional establishment!

Venue Size	:	10,000 sq. ft.
Capacity	:	600 people
Private party room available	:	Yes, 2
Is food served?	:	Yes, Tex-Mex
Outside catering permitted	:	Yes, cakes & pastries only
Dance floor	:	Yes
Live music or DJ	:	Both
Outdoor space available	:	Yes, 20 seats
Video/TV monitors available	:	Yes, TV
Coat check	:	Yes, on 2 levels

Visit www.sheckys.com/partyaid for more party planning advice!

Kanvas
219 9th Ave.
(23rd & 24th Sts.)
Chelsea
Phone: 212.727.2616
Fax: 212.989.2808

Contact: Leyla Bowden
Alternative Contact: Tom Murphy
E-mail: info@kanvasnyc.com
Website: www.kanvasnyc.com
Mention Shecky's when you call or e-mail

Kanvas

Somewhere between Chelsea's vibrant galleries and constantly evolving dance club scene is the most fundamental element of any creative movement—Kanvas. Possessing that rare combination of scene-y environs and neighborhood bar sensibilities, Kanvas draws a mature, but youthful crowd that lounges amongst a backdrop of regularly rotated paintings from this neighborhood's most promising artists. Add a light appetizer menu, an endless martini list, and a private party space and voilá—instant masterpiece.

Venue Size	:	2,800 sq. ft.
Capacity	:	225 main fl., 75-100 private rm.
Private party room available	:	Yes, 1
Is food served?	:	Yes, Tapas
Outside catering permitted	:	No
Dance floor	:	Yes
Live music or DJ	:	Both
Outdoor space available	:	Yes
Video/TV monitors available	:	Yes
Coat check	:	Yes

<table>
<tr><td>

Light
125 E. 54th St.
(Lexington & Park Aves.)
Midtown
Phone: 212.583.1333
Fax: 212.583.9796

</td><td>

Contact: Christina
E-mail: christina@lightnyc.com
Website: www.lightnyc.com

Mention Shecky's when you call or e-mail

</td></tr>
</table>

Light

Light is an upscale, elegant nightclub/lounge that's perfect for any type of event, ranging from birthdays to weddings. With an excellent location on the East Side and an event-planning team that will assure you of a smooth, enjoyable time, this seductive, accommodating lounge is the perfect venue for your next event. Light's décor and Asian-inspired menu make it a one-stop-shop for parties and private events. Visit www.lightnyc.com for additional pictures and information.

Venue Size	:	4,000 sq. ft.
Capacity	:	400 people
Private party room available	:	Yes, 2
Is food served?	:	Yes, Asian
Outside catering permitted	:	Yes
Dance floor	:	Yes
Live music or DJ	:	Both
Outdoor space available	:	No
Video/TV monitors available	:	Yes
Coat check	:	Yes

PARTY AID

Odea

389 Broome St.
(@ Mulberry St.)
NoLita
Phone: 212.941.9222

Contact: Frances
Alternative Contact: Jason
E-mail: reservations@odeany.com
Website: www.odeany.com
Mention Shecky's when you call or e-mail

Odea

Odea Bar & Lounge is a super-sophisticated, upscale lounge conveniently located in the heart of hip downtown NoLita (just a short walk from Broadway). Within this sleek, warm, and comfortable lounge you will experience the pleasures of our acclaimed cuisine, the outstanding cocktails mixed by our mixologists, and relish in our ultra-stylish lounge. We specialize in accommodating parties of 15 and up; we have designed special elevated bungalows to accommodate and indulge party-goers. If you're planning an after-work get-together or a birthday celebration, then Odea Bar & Lounge is the place to be.

Venue Size	:	2,600 sq. ft.
Capacity	:	200 people
Private party room available	:	3 pods (20-25 guests each)
Is food served?	:	Yes, Eclectic Small Plates
Outside catering permitted	:	Yes
Dance floor	:	No
Live music or DJ	:	Yes
Outdoor space available	:	Yes
Video/TV monitors available	:	No
Coat check	:	Yes

Visit www.sheckys.com/partyaid for more party planning advice!

Sapa

43 W. 24th St.
(Broadway & 6th Ave.)
Chelsea/Flatiron
Phone: 212.929.1800
Fax: 212.929.7070

Contact: Celeste Pillow (celeste@sapanyc.com)
or Brian Matzkow (brian@sapanyc.com)
Website: www.sapanyc.com

Mention Shecky's when you call or e-mail

Sapa

The Scene: Airy, clean, sophisticated, and perfectly lit, the AvroKo-designed space is clever but not overly showy. Note the few peek-through windows to the kitchen, soft leather banquettes, and the "roll bar" glowing from within. A mix of fashionable expense accounters, young cocktailers, and the occasional foodie make up the crowd. The Food: The pared-down menu shows off Chef Patricia Yeo's flair with French/Southeast Asian fusion cuisine. Her signature dishes include the Cocoa and Peanut-Glazed Spareribs and the Cod Roasted in Parchment. And don't forget the roll bar, where mouth-watering rolls, such as the Lobster Roll and the Lemongrass-Cured Salmon & Avocado, come alive. Lastly, dessert, the Chocolate Chili Bombe with Citrus Salad and Lime Sorbet, hits it head-on. PLUS – Enjoy half off of Sapa's wine list on Sunday and Monday and come in for their happy hour from 5:30 to 7:30 everyday for $5 martinis and $1 oysters.

Entire Venue Capacity	:	Up to 500 people
Back Room Capacity	:	Up to 200 people
Private party room available	:	Yes, 1 semi-private
Is food served?	:	Yes, Modern French/Southeast Asian
Outside catering permitted	:	Yes
Dance floor	:	Yes
Live music or DJ	:	Available
Outdoor space available	:	60 seat café coming Spring '06
Video/TV monitors available	:	Yes
Coat check	:	Yes

PARTY AID

Ship of Fools
1590 2nd Ave.
(82nd & 83rd Sts.)
Upper East Side
Phone: 212.570.2651
Fax: 212.570.2637

Contact: Glenn Treacher
Alternative Contact: Owen Treacher
E-mail: splurt@aol.com
Website: www.shipoffoolsnyc.com
Mention Shecky's when you call or e-mail

Ship of Fools

Ship of Fools is the perfect spot for your next party. With 3 areas to choose from, we have the capacity for anything from small, intimate dinner parties to all-out bashes and everything in between. We also have 2 pool tables, 3 dartboards, Golden Tee Live, and friendly staff.

Venue Size	:	3 rooms
Capacity	:	300 people
Private party room available	:	3
Is food served?	:	Yes, American
Outside catering permitted	:	No
Dance floor	:	No
Live music or DJ	:	Internet jukebox
Outdoor space available	:	No
Video/TV monitors available	:	Yes, multiple
Coat check	:	No (Can be arranged)

Visit www.sheckys.com/partyaid for more party planning advice!

Solas

232 E. 9th St.
(2nd & 3rd Aves.)
East Village
Phone: 212.375.0297

Contact: Kevin
Contact Phone: 917.402.5217
E-mail: solasbar2000@yahoo.com
Website: www.solasbar.com

Mention Shecky's when you call or e-mail

Solas

Solas, the Gaeilge word for "light," generates a warmth and a glow worthy of its name. Long an East Village favorite, this bi-level, three-room establishment can cater to everyone. The mood-setting Red Room has crimson walls and flickering candles that cast a glow on those who want to chill from the disco inferno that's burning in the rest of the part-pub, part-club. Downstairs, honeycomb lamps and golden walls light the lively, unpretentious crowd in soothing incandescence. The lounge, Coal, can fuel any desire with its funky, low lighting and bright colors. Solas has a hip but laid-back attitude and the bartenders are always on hand to entertain as well as dish out cold beer and fruity cocktails. The DJs make sure the place never goes cold, spinning a mix everyone can agree on. Add karaoke Mondays and live music Tuesdays and you have the full package. So if you want a bit of fun, just follow the light...

Venue Size	:	5,000 sq. ft.
Capacity	:	450 people
Private party room available	:	3
Is food served?	:	Coming soon
Outside catering permitted	:	Yes
Dance floor	:	No
Live music or DJ	:	Both
Outdoor space available	:	No
Video/TV monitors available	:	TV
Coat check	:	Yes

Visit www.sheckys.com/partyaid for more party planning advice!

PARTY AID

Stir
1363 1st Ave.
(73rd & 74th Sts.)
Upper East Side
Phone: 212.744.7190
Fax: 646.383.7644

Contact: Rebecca Reith
Alt. Contact: John Lafferty
E-mail: stirnyc@hotmail.com
Website: www.stirnyc.com
Mention Shecky's when you call or e-mail

Stir

Stir, located on the Upper East Side, brings the downtown flair uptown and leaves the pretentious and attitude-driven behind. With an award-winning martini menu, sophistication, style, and great service, it's no wonder that Stir is the hottest place to be on the Upper East Side.

Venue Size	:	2,200 sq. ft.
Capacity	:	140 people
Private party room available	:	None
Is food served?	:	Yes, Tapas
Outside catering permitted	:	Yes, for special events
Dance floor	:	No
Live music or DJ	:	DJ
Outdoor space available	:	No
Video/TV monitors available	:	Yes, 2 flat-screen TVs
Coat check	:	Yes

Visit www.sheckys.com/partyaid for more party planning advice!

Tre Dici
128 W. 26th St.
(6th & 7th Aves.)
Chelsea
Phone: 212.243.8183

Contact: Steven Hall
Contact Phone: 646.638.0771
E-mail: stevenh@hallpr.com

Mention Shecky's when you call or e-mail

Tre Dici

Tre Dici is a jewel box of a restaurant on a quiet street in Chelsea. We serve contemporary Italian fare specializing in the cuisine of Puglia. Tre Dici is perfect for intimate and corporate gatherings. We offer a full bar and an extensive wine list.

Venue Size	:	1,000 sq. ft.
Capacity	:	50 people
Private party room available	:	No
Is food served?	:	Yes, Italian (Puglia Region)
Outside catering permitted	:	No
Dance floor	:	No
Live music or DJ	:	No
Outdoor space available	:	No
Video/TV monitors available	:	Yes
Coat check	:	No

Visit www.sheckys.com/partyaid for more party planning advice!

Boerum Hill

Boat
Brazen Head, The
Brooklyn Inn
Chance
Hank's Saloon
Kili

Brooklyn Heights

Eamonn's
Henry Street Ale House
Magnetic Field
Montero's Bar and Grill
Palmiras

Carroll Gardens

Angry Wade's
Apartment 138
B61 @ Alma
Bar Below
Brooklyn Social Club
Cattyshack
Gowanus Yacht Club
Quench
Robin des Bois
SoFo
Vegas
Village Speakeasy Pub
Zombie Hut

Chelsea

Amuse
Avalon
Bar Veloce Chelsea
Barracuda
B.E.D.
Bette
Billy Mark's West
Biltmore Room
Black Door
Blarney Rock
Blarney Stone
Bongo
Bottino

Brite Bar
Bungalow 8
Cabanas (@ the Maritime
  Hotel)
Caféteria
Cain
Cajun, The
Charley O's Skybox
  American Bar and Grill
Chelsea Bistro & Bar
Chelsea Brewing Company
Cotton
Crobar
Cuba Café
Diner 24
Dusk
Eagle, The
Earth NYC
East of Eighth
El Quijote
Elmo
Flight 151
Food Bar
Frank's 410
G Lounge
Glass
Glo
Groovedeck
Gstaad
Half King Bar, The
Heaven
Helen's
Hiro Lounge (@ the Maritime
  Hotel)
Home
Kanvas
La Bottega (@ the Maritime
  Hotel)
Maroon's
Marquee
Mustang Sally's
Merchants
The Molly Wee Pub
Naima
Negril
Nisos

Nooch
Opus 22
Orchid
Park, The
Passerby
Peter McManus
Porters
Q Lounge & Billiards
Quo
Rawhide
Red Cat, The
Red Rock West Saloon
Rogue
Roxy
Ruby Falls
Sandia
Serena
Shadow
Spirit
Suede
Trailer Park Lounge
Tre Dici
Triple Crown
Twins Pub
Upright Citizens Brigade
Viceroy, The
View Bar
Westside Tavern
XES
XL

Chinatown

Double Happiness
Onieal's Grand Street
Winnie's

Clinton Hill

Amarachi Lounge
Outpost Lounge
Rope

Cobble Hill

Floyd, NY
Joya
Last Exit

Lobo
Smithwicks

DUMBO
Low Bar

East Village
Ace Bar
Alphabet Lounge
Angel's Share
Anyway Café
Apocalypse Lounge
Avenue A Sushi
Bao 111
Bar Bleu @ Café Deville
Bar None
Bar on A (BOA)
Bar Veloce East Village
Baraza
Beauty Bar
Big Bar
Big Cheech, The
Black & White
Blarney Cove Inc.
Blue & Gold Tavern
Blue Mahoe, The
Boca Chica
Bouche Bar
Boxcar Lounge
Boysroom
B-Side
Bua
Buddha Lounge
Bull McCabe's
Burp Castle
Butter
Café Deville
Cantinella
Casimir
CBGB's & OMFUG
CBGB's Gallery
Cellar Bar & Café
Central Bar
Cheap Shots
Cherry Tavern

Chikalicious
Climax
Cloister Café
Clubhouse
C-Note, The
Cock, The
Company
Continental
Counter
Coyote Ugly
Cozy Café
d.b.a.
Decibel
Dempsey's Pub
Detour
Dick's Bar
Doc Holliday's
Duke's
Edge, The
Elephant, The
11th Street Bar
Esperanto
Euzkadi
Finnerty's
Fish Bar
Forbidden City
Fuzion on A
General Store
Grassroots Tavern
Gyu-Kaku
Hangar, The
Hearth
Hi Fi
Holiday Cocktail Lounge
Hop Devil Grill
Horus Café
Il Posto Accanto
In Vino
International Bar
J.P. Warde's Saloon
Japas
Joe's Bar
Joey's
Julep
Jules Café
Kabin

Karma
Kasadela
Keybar
KGB Bar
King's Head Tavern
Korova Milk Bar
La Linea
Lakeside Lounge
Lava Gina
Le Souk
The Library
Life Café
Light
Lilly Coogan's
Lit Lounge
Louis 649
Luca Lounge
Lucien
Lucky Cheng's
Ludo
Lunasa
Mama's Bar
Mancora
Manitoba's
Mars Bar
McSorley's Ale House
Mercadito
Mermaid Inn, The
Micky's Blue Room
Miracle Grill
Miss Williamsburg Portavia
Mona's
Morrisey Park
Mosto Osteria
Mundial
Nevada Smith's
Niagara/Lei Bar
Nice Guy Eddie's
Nightingale Lounge
No Malice Palace
Nowhere Bar
Nuyorican Poets Café
Odessa
O'Hanlon's
One and One
Orange Valve

Orchid Lounge
Otto's Shrunken Head
Pangea
Parlay
Phebe's Tavern & Grill
Phoenix
Plan B
Planet Rose
Pop
Porch Bar, The
Pyramid
Quhnia
Radio Perfecto
Raga
Raven, The
Remote Lounge
Resto Leon
Route 85a
Ruby Lounge
Rue B
Ryans Irish Pub
Sake Bar Satsko
San Marcos
Satelite
Scenic
Scratcher
Second Nature
Second on Second
7B
Sidewalk Café
Sin Sin
Smoked
Solas
Sophie's Bar
St. Dymphna's
St. Marks 88
St. Marks Ale House
Standings
Starfoods
Starlight Bar & Lounge
Stay
Sunburnt Cow, The
Sutra
Tasting Room, The
Telephone Bar & Grill, The
Thirsty Scholar

Three of Cups
Tribe
2A
2 by 4
Uncle Ming's
Urge Lounge
Vera
Virage
Waikiki Wally's
WCOU Radio
Webster Hall
Winebar
Xunta
Yaffa Café
Yuca Bar & Restaurant
Zakuro
Zerza Bar
Zum Schneider Bavarian
 Beer House
Croxley Ales

Financial District

Bayard's Blue Bear
Bridge Café
Beekman, The
Bullrun
Cassis
Fino
Full Shilling, The
Irish Punt, The
Jeremy's Ale House
Jim Brady's
Killarney Rose
Les Halles
MacMenamin's Irish Pub
Mercantile Grill
Nassau Bar
O'Hara's
Rise (@ the Ritz-Carlton)
Romi Restaurant & Lounge
Cabana
Harbour Lights
John Street Bar & Grill
JP Mustard
P.J. Kelly's
Pacific Grill

Remy Lounge
Ryan Maguire's Ale House
Ryan's Sports Bar & Grill
Seaport Café
Southwest NY
St. Maggie's Café
Suspenders
Ulysses
White Horse Tavern

Flatiron

Aleo Restaurant & Bar
Beppe
Bolo
Bread Bar @ Tabla
Caviar and Banana Braserio
 Restaurant
Craftbar
Cutting Room, The
Deep
Dewey's Flatiron
Discotheque
Duvet
Eugene
Flatiron Lounge
Flute
40/40 Club
Giorgio's of Gramercy
Gotham Comedy Club
Gramercy Tavern
Gstaad
Gypsy Tea
Heartland Brewery Union
 Square
Isis @ Union Bar
Justin's
Kavehaz
Lemon
Live Bait
Lucy Latin Kitchen
Luna Park
Mesa Grill
Metro Café and Wine Bar
Neogaea
No Idea
Old Town Bar & Restaurant

Ora
Park Bar
Pipa
Prey
Punch
Rock Candy
Rogue
Sapa
Satalla
Scopa
Select
17
Slate Plus
Snitch
Splash
Steak Frites
Strata
Tamarind
Taj
Tracy J's Watering Hole
Union Square Coffee Shop
Wonderland

Fort Greene

BAMcafé
Chez Oskar
Frank's Cocktail Lounge
Gardens Bar
i-Shebeen Madiba
Moe's
Pequena
Stonehome Wine Bar
Thomas Beisl

Gramercy

Angelo & Maxie's
Artisanal
Barfly
Belmont Lounge
Black Bear Lodge, The
Bolo
Boston (212) Café
Bull's Head Tavern
Candela
Cibar

Copper Door Tavern
Duke's
Galaxy Global Eatery
Giorgio's of Gramercy
Grand Saloon
Houston's
Irving Plaza
Link
Los Dos Molinos
McSwiggan's
MJ Armstrong's
New York Comedy Club
Old Town Bar & Restaurant
Olives (@ W Hotel - Union
   Sq.)
119 Bar
Park Avalon
Pete's Tavern
Proof
Quigley's
Revival
Rolf's
Shades of Green
Snitch
Still
Strata
SugarCane
Sushi Samba Park
Tracy J's Watering Hole
Underbar (@ W Hotel - Union
   Sq.)

Greenpoint

Call Box Lounge, The
Connie O's
Driftwood Inn
Enid's
Kingsland Tavern
Lyric Lounge
Mark Bar, The
Matchless
Palace Café Inc.
Pencil Factory, The
Tommy's Tavern
Warsaw, The

Greenwich Village

Agave
Alibi
Apple Restaurant & BomBar
Arté
Asylum
Back Fence, The
Baggot Inn
Bar 6
Bar 13
Barrow Street Ale House
Bitter End, The
Blue Note
Bowlmor Lanes
Café Wha?
Caliente Cab Co.
Cedar Tavern
Comedy Cellar
Comedy Village
Cornelia St. Café
Cru
Cuba
Dove, The
Dragonfly
El Cantinero
Fat Black Pussycat
French Roast
Fuelray
Good Restaurant
Gotham Bar & Grill
Greenwich Brewing
   Company
Groove
Izakaya Izu
Jane
Josie Wood's Pub
Kenny's Castaways
Kettle of Fish
Knickerbocker Bar and Grill
L' Angelo Café
Lion's Den
Lupa
Macdougal Street Ale House
Madame X
McKenna's Pub

Negril Village
Newgate Bar & Grill
Off The Wagon
Onyx
Peculier Pub
Pinch Bar & Grill, The
Piola
Pressure
Red Lion
Reservoir
Spice
Stoned Crow, The
Strip House
Sullivan Room, The
Terra Blues
Town Tavern
V Bar & Café
Village Underground, The
XR Bar
Yujin
Zine Bar

Harlem
Cherry Lounge

Hell's Kitchen
Arriba Arriba Mexican
  Restaurant
Bann
Bar 9
Barrage
Barrymore's
Broadway Bar & Terrace (@
  the Novotel Hotel)
Bull Moose Saloon
Café Andalucia
Collins Bar, The
Copacabana
Coppersmith's
Cosmo
Dave's Tavern
Deacon Brodie's
Delta Grill, The
'disiac Lounge
Distinguished Wakamba, The

D.J. Reynolds
Door Lounge, The
Druids
Eatery/Bar E
Exit
Film Center Café
Firebird
44&X
Fusion
Gaf, The
Garvey's
Gold Rush
Hallo Berlin
Holland Bar
House of Brews
Hudson Bar (@ the Hudson
  Hotel)
Irish Rogue
Jake's Saloon
Jezebel
Julian's
Kemia
Kennedy's
Kevin St. James
Kyma
Latitude
Leisure Time Bowl
Library, The
Library Bar (@ the Hudson
  Hotel)
Lincoln Park Bar & Grill
Made
Marseille
Matt's Grill
McCoy's
McHale's
Mercury Bar & Grill
Mr. Biggs
Ninth Avenue Saloon
O'Flaherty's Ale House
Perdition
Pigalle
Port 41
Posh
Private Park (@ the Hudson
  Hotel)

Robert Emmett's
Rudy's Bar and Grill
Rufus
Scruffy Duffy's
Siberia
Single Room Occupancy
Smiths
Social Bar and
  Lounge/Fusion at Social
Swing 46
TA Cocina Express
Taboon
Therapy
Triumph Room
Varjak
Vintage
Vynl
Xing
Xth Avenue Lounge
Zanzibar

Little Italy
Asia Roma
Florio's Grill & Cigar Bar
Grotta Azzurra
Il Cortile
M Bar
Mulberry Street Bar
Odea
Oniel's Grand Street
Palais Royale
Xicala
Yello

Lower East Side
Arlene's Grocery
Barramundi
Barrio Chino
Basso Est
Belly
Birdland
BLVD
bOb
Boss Tweed's Saloon
Bowery Ballroom

CakeShop
Canapa
Chibitini
Chubo
Crash Mansion
Crudo
Darkroom, The
Delancey, The
East Side Company Bar
Epstein's Bar
Essex Restaurant
1492 Foo
Freemans
Girlsroom
Good World Bar & Grill
Grotto
Happy Ending
Iggy's Keltic Lounge
Ini Ani
'inoteca
King Size
Kitchen & Cocktails
Kos
Kush
La Caverna
Laugh Lounge NYC
Libation
Living Room, The
Local 138
Lolita
Loreley
Lotus Lounge
Lucky Jack's
Magician, The
Martignetti Liquors
Max Fish
Mercury Lounge, The
Milk & Honey
Mission
Motor City
Oliva
169 Bar
One 91
Orchard Bar
Paladar
Parkside Lounge

People Lounge
Petrosino
Pianos
Pink Pony Café
Pioneer Bar and Restaurant
Punch and Judy's
Rockwood Music Hall
Rothko
Ryan's Sports Bar & Grill
Salt Bar
Sapphire Lounge
Schiller's Liquor Bar
17 Home
Sin-e
6s and 8s
SkinNY, The
Slipper Room, The
Sortie
Stanton Social, The
Suba
Taboon
Tapeo 29
Tenement
13 Little Devils
Tonic
12"
24-7 Bar & Lounge
Vasmay Lounge
Verlaine
Vice Versa
wd-50
Welcome to the Johnsons
Whiskey Ward
White Rabbit, The

Meatpacking District

aer
APT
Ara Wine Bar
Brass Monkey
Cielo
Double Seven
5 Ninth
Florent
G2
Garden of Ono, The

Gaslight Lounge
Highline
Hog Pit, The
Hogs and Heifers
Level V
Lotus
Macelleria
Markt
Meet
One
Ono
Paradou
Pastis
Plunge (@ Hotel Gansevoort)
PM
Pop Burger Lounge
Rare
Rhone
Spice Market

Midtown

Ada
Aja
Alamo
Annie Moore's
Aquavit
Atrium Lounge
AVA Lounge at Dream Hotel
Azaza
B.B. King's Blues Club & Grill
B1 Drink Club
Bar Americain
bar.vetro
Barclay Bar and Grill, The (@
    Intercontinental Barclay)
Barrymore's
Beer Bar @ Café Centro
Believe Lounge
Bice
Bill's Gay Nineties
Black Finn
Blaggard's Pub (35th St.)
Blaggard's Pub (39th St.)
Blarney Rock
Bliss Bar and Lounge
Blue Fin (@ the W Hotel-

Times Square)
Blue Lady Lounge (@
  Shelly's)
Bond 45
Branch
Brasserie
Brasserie 8 1/2
Broadway Lounge (@ the
  Marriott Marquis)
Bryant Park Grill
Bull and Bear, The
Buzz Bar @ Pershing Square
Campbell Apartment, The
Carnegie Club, The
Caroline's on Broadway
Carriage House
Casa La Femme North
Cecil's Bar (@ the Crowne
  Plaza Hotel)
Cellar Bar (@ Bryant Park
  Hotel)
Channel 4
Charlotte (@ Millenium
  Broadway Hotel)
Chemist Club, The (@ the
  Dylan Hotel)
China Club
Clancy's
Club Shelter
Coldwaters
Connolly's 45th St.
Connolly's 47th St.
D.J. Reynolds
Del Frisco's Double Eagle
  Steakhouse
Divine Bar East
Divine Bar West
Django
Docks Oyster Bar
Dream Lounge (@ the
  Dream Hotel)
ESPN Zone
Faces and Names
Fashion 40
58
5757 @ Four Seasons

Fitzer's
Flute
44 (@ the Royalton Hotel)
Front Bar, The (@ the Four
  Seasons Hotel)
Fubar
Giggles
Glady's Comedy Room
Guastavino's
Hard Rock Café
Heartland Brewery Radio
  City
Hooters
Hurley's Saloon
Iguana
Iridium
Irish Pub
J.D.'s
Jack's Restaurant and Bar
Jameson's
Jimmy Walker's
Jimmy's Corner
Journey's Lounge (@ the
  Essex Hotel)
Juniper Suite
K Lounge
Kate Kearney's Pub and Grill
Katen Sushi Bar (@ the
  Marriott Marquis)
Katwalk
King Cole Bar
Koi
Kyma
La Prima Donna
Lea
Library (@ the Paramount
  Hotel)
Living Room, The (@ W Hotel
  - Times Square)
Local Café East
Local West
LQ
Maggie's Place
Manchester Pub
Maracas
Mars 2112

McAnns Irish Pub
McFadden's Saloon
McGee's
MeBar (@ the La Quinta Inn)
Metrazur
Metro 53
Metropolitan Café
Mica 51
Mickey Mantle's
Mini-Bar in the District (@
  the Muse Hotel)
Moda
Modern, The
Monkey Bar
Morrell Wine Bar & Café
Muldoon's
Murphy's Bar and Grill
Mustang Harry's
Mustang Sally's
Nation Restaurant & Bar
Neary's
O.W.
O2 (@ the Time Hotel)
Oak Room, The (@ Algonquin
  Hotel)
Oasis Bar (@ W New York)
Old Castle Pub & Restaurant
O'Neill's
Opal Bar
Opia
O'Reilly's Pub & Restaurant
O'Reilly's Townhouse Tavern
P.J. Clarke's
Park Blue
Parnell's Pub
Patio, The
Patrick Conway's Pub
Pen-Top Bar & Terrace, The
  (@ the Peninsula Hotel)
Peter Dillon's
Pig N Whistle
Planet Hollywood
Plantain
Playwright Tavern
Prime 54 Lounge (@ Hotel
  Rihga)

Q56 Restaurant and Cocktails
Redemption
Remedy Bar & Grill
Ribot
Rooftop Bar (@ Hotel Metro)
Round Bar (@ Royalton Hotel)
Ruby Foo's Times Square
Rum House, The (@ the Edison Hotel)
Russian Samovar
Russian Vodka Room, The
Saga
Sasha's
Show
Sidecar
Smith & Wollensk
Spanky's BBQ
Stitch
Stout NYC
Sutton Place
T.G. Whitney's
Table XII (aka Etoile)
Taj
Tao
Tapas Lounge, The
Temple New York
Thady Con's
Tir Na Nog
Tonic and the Met Lounge
Town Crier
Townhouse, The
Trattoria Dopo Teatro
Trousdale
Tupelo Grill
Turtle Bay
Twist Lounge (@ The Ameritania Hotel)
Upper Deck, The
View, The (@ the Marriott Marquis)
Villard Bar & Lounge (@ the New York Palace Hotel)
Virgil's Real Barbeque
Web, The

Wheeltapper Pub, The
Whiskey Blue
Whiskey, The (@ W-Times Sq.)
Windfall Lounge and Grill
World Bar
Ye Olde Tripple Inn

Murray Hill

Artisanal
Asia de Cuba
Aubette
Bar 515
Bar XII
Black Duck (@ Park South Hotel)
Black Sheep
Blue Smoke
Bogart's
Boston (212) Café
Bread Bar @ Tabla
Caliban
Chorus Karaoke
Desmond's Tavern
Dip
Dos Caminos
Earl's
El Parador Café
El Rio Grande
Eleven Madison Park
Failte Irish Whiskey Bar
Fitzgerald's Pub
Gallery Lounge (@ the Gershwin Hotel)
Ginger Man, The
Hairy Monk, The
Hook & Ladder Pub, The
Houston's
Hudson Place
ICON (@ the W Hotel - The Court)
IXTA
Joshua Tree
Les Halles
Maker's
Maya Lounge

McCormack's
Mercury Bar
Mica 587
Morgan's Bar (@ the Morgan Hotel)
Mulligan's Pub
Paddy Reilly's
Park Avenue Country Club
Patrick Kavanagh's
PineTree Lodge
Proseccheria
PS 450
Rare View (@ the Shelbourne Murray Hill Hotel)
Red Sky
Rocky Sullivan's
Rodeo Bar
Saga
Scopa
Slate Plus
Stone Creek
Third and Long
Trio
12:31
Under the Volcano
Underground
Vapor
Vertigo Bar & Restaurant
Waterfront Ale House
Whiskey River
Wolfgang's Steakhouse

NoHo

Ace of Clubs
Acme Bar & Grill
Agozar
Aroma
B Bar (aka Bowery Bar)
Bar 288 (aka Tom & Jerry's)
Bleecker Street Bar
Bond Street Lounge
Butter
Crime Scene
Five Points
Gonzalez y Gonzalez

Great Jones Café
Hedeh
Il Buco
Indochine
Joe's Pub
Mannahatta
Marion's Continental
Sala
Serafina
Slainte
Slide, The
Swift Hibernian Lounge
Table 50
Temple Bar
VON

NoLita

BarBossa
Barmarche
Botanica
Café Gitane
Chibi's Bar
Eight Mile Creek
Falls, The
Gatsby's Bar & Lounge
Il Buco
M Bar
Mekong
Mexican Radio
Milano's
ñ
Nolita House
Peasant
Porcupine
Pravda
Public
Puck Fair
Rialto
Room 18
Savoy
Shebeen
Spring Lounge
Sui
Sweet & Vicious
Tai
Vig Bar

Park Slope

Bar 4
Bar Minnow
Bar Reis
Bar Toto
Barbes
Buttermilk
Café Ma
Carriage Inn, The
Edessa
El Poblano Sports Grill
Excelsior
Farrell's
Gate, The
Ginger's
Great Lakes
Harry Boland's Pub
Jackie's Fifth Amendment
Loki Lounge
Long Tan
Lucky 13 Saloon
Mooney's Pub
O'Connor's
Park Slope Ale House
Press 195
Puppets Jazz Bar
Southpaw
Tamari
Tea Lounge
Timboo's
Total Wine Bar
200 Fifth

Prospect Heights

Back Room
Beast
Freddy's Bar & Backroom
Half Wine Bar
Soda Bar
Tavern on Dean

Red Hook

Moonshine

SoHo

A 60 (@ 60 Thompson)
Aquagrill
Antarctica
Balthazar
Bar 89
BINY
Boom
Boutique del Vino
Café Noir
Cendrillon
Cipriani's
Circa Tabac
Cody's Bar and Grill
Cub Room
Culture Club
Cupping Room Café
Diva
Don Hill's
Dos Caminos
Ear Inn
Emerald Pub
Falls, The
Fanelli's
Fiamma Osteria
Flow
46 Grand
Gallery, The (@ The SoHo
   Grand)
Grand Bar and Lounge (@
   The SoHo Grand)
Green Room
I Tre Merli
Ideya
Jazz Gallery, The
Jerry's
Kaña
Kin Khao
La Streghe
L'Orange Bleue
Lucky Strike
Lure Fish Bar
Merc Bar
Mercer Kitchen
Milady's Bar & Restaurant
Monkey Temple

Naked Lunch
Nerveana
Peep
Penang
Puck Fair
Red Bench
Room, The
Savoy
Sly
S.O.B.'s
SoGo NY
SoHo:323
Sway
Tennessee Mountain
Thom Bar (@ 60 Thompson Hotel)
Toad Hall
203 Spring
XR Bar
Yard, The (@ The Soho Grand)
Zoe

TriBeCa

A&M Roadhouse, The
Anotheroom
Antarctica
Biddy Early's
Blaney Stone
Brady's Tavern
Brandy Library
Bubble Lounge
Buster's Garage
Canal Room
Church Lounge (@ TriBeCa Grand)
City Hall
Dakota Roadhouse
Danube
Dekk
Don Hill's
Donald Sacks
Due South
Dylan Prime
Edward's
85 West Cocktail Bar

Flor de Sol
Harrison, The
i Restaurant & Lounge
Johnney's Fish Grill
Kimono Lounge
Knitting Factory, The
Kori
La Churrascaria Plataforma Tribeca
Landmarc
Mehanata
M1-5
Monkey Temple
Nam
Nancy Whiskey Pub
Nathan Hale's
Patriot Saloon, The
Raccoon Lodge
Reade Street Pub and Kitchen
17 Murray
Shore
South's
Spaghetti Western
Sugar Bar & Lounge
UK New York
Viet-Café
Walker's

Upper East Side

Amber
American Spirits
American Trash
Archer's
Auction House
Back Page
Bailey's Corner Pub
Bait Shack
Baker Street
Banshee Pub
Bar @ Etats-Unis
Bar East
Bar Seine @ The Hôtel Plaza Athénée
Barbalùc
Bar-Coastal

Becky's
Bemelmans Bar @ The Carlyle, A Rosewood Hotel
Biddy's Pub
Big City Bar & Grill
Big Easy
Blondies
Blue Room, The
Bounce
Brady's Bar
Brandy's Piano Bar
Brother Jimmy's Bait Shack
Brother Jimmy's BBQ
Café Carlyle (@ the Carlyle)
Café Pierre (@ the Pierre Hotel)
Cantor Roof Garden, The (@ the Met)
Canyon Road
Club Macanudo
Comic Strip Live
Coogan's Parrot Bay
Dangerfield's
David Copperfield's House of Beer
Doc Watson's
Dorrian's Red Hand
DT/UT
East Side Steak & Ale
Elaine's
Finnegan's Wake
Fiona's
Frederick's Madison
Gael Pub, The
Geisha
Hacienda de Argentina
Hanratty's
Hi-Life Restaurant & Lounge
Hookah Café
Hooligan's
Hunter's American Bar & Grill
Iggy's
Kinsale Tavern
La Tour
Le Refuge
Lexington Bar & Books

Library, The (@ The
  Regency)
Mad River Bar & Grille
Manhattan Grille
Manhattan Lounge
Mark's Bar (@ the Mark
  Hotel)
Martell's
Marty O'Brien's
McKeown's
Merchants NY
Merrion Square
Mo's Caribbean Bar and
  Mexican Grille
Murphy's Law Bar &
  Restaurant
Mustang Grill
O'Flanagan's
Panorama Café
Pat O'Brien's
Pegasus
Phoenix Park
Rain
Rathbone's
Reif's Tavern
Ruby's Tap House
Ryan's Daughter
Sake Hana
Saloon
Session 73
Ship of Fools
Snapper Creek
Stir
Subway Inn
Sushi Generation
Taste
Tavern on First
Tin Lizzie's
Tool Box
Trinity Public House
Turquoise Seafood
  Restaurant
Ulrika's
Uptown Restaurant &
  Lounge
Uva

Vudu Lounge
Waterloo Tavern
Wild Spirits
Willy's Bar & Grill

Upper West Side
Acqua
AIX
All State Café
Amsterdam Billiards Club
Blondies
Boat Basin Café
Boathouse, The
Bourbon Street
Broadway Dive
Brother Jimmy's
Café del Bar
Café Luxembourg
Café Ronda
Calle Ocho
'Cesca
Cherry Lounge
Citrus Bar & Grill
City Grill, The
Cleopatra's Needle
Compass
Crossroads
Dead Poet, The
Ding Dong Lounge, The
Dive 75
Dive Bar, The
Dorian's
Eight of Clubs
Emerald Inn
Evelyn Lounge
Fez North @ Time Café
Firehouse
420 Bar and Lounge
Fujiyama Mama
Gabriel's Wine Bar &
  Restaurant
George Keeley, The
Gin Mill, The
Harrison's Tavern
Helen's
Hi-Life Bar and Grill

Jacques-imo's NYC
Jake's Dilemma
Jean-Luc
Kitchen 82
Makor
Malachy's
MOBar (@ Mandarin Oriental
  Hotel)
North West Restaurant &
  Lounge
O'Neals'
Ouest
Ouzerie @ En Plo
P & G Café
P.D. O'Hurley's
Parlour, The
Pasha
Peter's Bar & Restaurant
Prohibition
Rancho Café
Rosa Mexicano
Sambuca
Santa Fe
Senor Swanky's
Shalel Lounge
Shark Bar Restaurant, The
Stand-Up NY
Stone Rose, The
Sugar Bar
Tavern on the Green
Time Out
Triad, The
Vince & Eddie's
Westside Brewing Co.
Whiskey Park
Yogi's

West Village
Absolutely 4th
Agave
Alfama
Andavi
Art Bar
Arthur's Tavern
Automatic Slims
Barbuto

Bivio
Blind Tiger Ale House
Blue Mill Tavern, The
Boots & Saaddle
Boxer's
Caliente Cab Company
Camaje
Cabin
Conelia St. Café
Chi Chiz
Chow Bar
Chumley's
Corner Bistro
Cowgirl
Crispo
Daddy-O
Day O
Do Hwa
Down the Hatch
Dragonfly
Dublin 6
Dugout, The
Duplex, The
El Faro
El Rey Del Sol
Employees Only
Fiddlesticks
55 Bar
Figa
Fish
Flannery's Bar
Four Faced Liar
Girl from Ipanema, The
Good Restaurant
Hanger, The
Henrietta Hudson
Hudson Bar & Books
Hue
ICU Bar
'ino
Inside
Jane
Jekyll & Hyde
Julius
Junno's
Karavas Tavern

Kettle of Fish
La Cave
Lips
Little Branch
Luke & Leroy
Marie's Crisis Café
Mc Kenna's
Metropol
Miracle Bar & Grill
Mixx Lounge
Monster, The
Movida
Mr. Dennehy's
Otheroom, The
Otto Enoteca Pizzeria
Paris Commune
Pearl Oyster Bar
Philip Marie
Pieces
Place, The
Riviera Café & Sports Bar
Rose's Turn
Rubyfruit Bar & Grill
S.O.B.'s
Salon
Shag
Slane
Slaughtered Lamb, The
Small's
Spotted Pig, The
Stonewall
Sushi Samba 7
Tavern on Jane
Tortilla Flats
Turks & Frogs
2i's
Ty's
Village Tavern
Village Vanguard
Voyage
Wallse
White Horse Tavern
Wogie's
WXOU Radio Bar
Yumcha

Williamsburg

Abbey, The
Alligator Lounge
Artland
Balanza Bar
Barcade
Bembe
Black Betty
Blu Lounge
Boogaloo
Brooklyn Ale House
Brooklyn Brewery
Bushwick Country Club
Capone's
Chai Home Kitchen
Charleston, The
Clem's
Daddy's
D.O.C. Wine Bar
Daddy's
Diner
Duff's
DuMont
East River
Funhouse
Galapagos Artspace
Grand Central
Grand Press
Hurricane Hopeful
iO
Iona
Jarrod's Lounge
Laila Lounge
Larry Lawrence
Levee
Lodge
Lucky Cat, The
LuLu Lounge
M Shanghai Bistro & Den
Marlow and Sons
Metropolitan
Moto
Mugs Ale House
Northsix
Pete's Candy Store
Planet Thailand

Pourhouse, The
R Bar
Rain Lounge
Red and Black
Redd's Tavern
Relish
Rice Republic
Rock Star Bar
Rose Mary's Greenpoint
 Tavern
Royal Oak
Savalas
Sea Thai Bistro
Snacky
Southside Lounge
Spike Hill Bar & Grill
Spuyten Duyvil
Stain
Subway Bar
Supercore
Supreme Trading
Sweet Ups
Tainted Lady Lounge
Teddy's Bar & Grill
Trash
Turkey's Nest
Union Pool
Vera Cruz
Zablozki's
Zebulon

Shecky's Picks

Absolutely 4th
Ace Bar
Ada
Aer
Agave
Agozar
Amuse
Angel's Share
Antarctica
Apocalypse Lounge
Ara Wine Bar
Arté
Artisanal
Artland
Auction House
AVA Lounge (@ Dream Hotel)
B.B. King's Blues Club & Grill
B1 Drink Club
Back Page
Balthazar
Bann
Bar 288 (aka Tom & Jerry's)
Bar 6
Bar 89
Bar East
Bar Seine (@ The Hôtel
  Plaza Athénée)
Bar Toto
Bar Veloce Chelsea
Bar Veloce East Village
Bar XII
Baraza
Barbes
Barcade
Barmarche
Barracuda
Basso Est
Belly
Belmont Lounge
Bembe
Biddy Early's
Big Easy
Billy Mark's West
The Black Bear Lodge
Black Betty

Black Door
Bleecker Street Bar
Blind Tiger Ale House
Bliss Bar and Lounge
Blue Fin (@ the W Hotel-
  Times Square)
The Blue Mill Tavern
Boat
bOb
Bond Street Lounge
Boogaloo
Boss Tweed's Saloon
Bottino
Bounce
Bowlmor Lanes
Boxcar Lounge
Brandy Library
Brass Monkey
Brite Bar
Brooklyn Brewery
Brooklyn Inn
Brooklyn Social Club
Bua
The Bull and Bear
Bungalow 8
Bushwick Country Club
Buttermilk
Café Carlyle (@ the Carlyle)
Café Ronda
Cain
Calle Ocho
Canapa
Candela
Caviar and Banana Braserio
  Restaurant
Cellar Bar & Café
Cellar Bar (@ Bryant Park
  Hotel)
'Cesca
The Charleston
Chelsea Bistro & Bar
Chelsea Brewing Company
The Chemist Club
Chibi's Bar
Chibitini
Cibar

Cipriani's
Circa Tabac
The City Grill
Climax
Company
Cowgirl
Crash Mansion
Crispo
Cru
d.b.a.
D.J. Reynolds
D.O.C. Wine Bar
Daddy's
The Darkroom
The Dead Poet
Dekk
The Delancey
Diner
Diner 24
The Ding Dong Lounge
Do Hwa
Don Hill's
Dorian's
Dos Caminos
Double Happiness
The Dove
Dream Lounge (@ the
  Dream Hotel)
Druids
Duff's
The Duplex
Duvet
The Eagle
East Side Company Bar
El Parador Café
11th Street Bar
Elmo
Employees Only
Esperanto
Euzkadi
Excelsior
Fanelli's
Fiddlesticks
Fish
5 Ninth
Flatiron Lounge

Flor de Sol
Florent
Floyd, NY
Flute (Flatiron)
Flute (Midtown)
40/40 Club
Frank's 410
Freddy's Bar & Backroom
Frederick's
Frederick's Madison
Freemans
Fuelray
Funhouse
G Lounge
G2
The Gaf
The Garden of Ono
Garvey's
Gaslight Lounge
Geisha
The Ginger Man
Ginger's
Glass
Great Jones Café
Groovedeck
Grotto
Gstaad
The Hanger
Happy Ending
Helen's
Henrietta Hudson
Hi Fi
Hiro Lounge (@ the Maritime Hotel)
The Hog Pit
Holland Bar
Home
Hop Devil Grill
Horus Café
Hurley's Saloon
i Restaurant & Lounge
Ideya
'ino
'inoteca
Iona
Jean-Luc

Josie Wood's Pub
Jules Café
Juniper Suite
K Lounge
Kanvas
Kasadela
Kili
Kimono Lounge
Kush
La Bottega (@ the Maritime Hotel)
La Churrascaria Plataforma Tribeca
Lakeside Lounge
Latitude
Level V
Libation
The Library
Little Branch
Lolita
Long Tan
Los Dos Molinos
Louis 649
Luca Lounge
Lucien
The Lucky Cat
Lucky Jack's
Ludo
Luke & Leroy
Lure Fish Bar
Madame X
Magnetic Field
Mannahatta
Marion's Continental
Markt
Marlow and Sons
Marquee
Martignetti Liquors
Max Fish
McAnns Irish Pub
The Mercury Lounge
Metropol
Metropolitan
Mexican Radio
Micky's Blue Room
Milady's Bar & Restaurant

Mission
MOBar (@ Mandarin Oriental Hotel)
Moe's
Moonshine
Morrell Wine Bar & Café
Moto
Motor City
Movida
Newgate Bar & Grill
Niagara/Lei Bar
North West Restaurant & Lounge
Northsix
Nuyorican Poets Café
O'Connor's
Odea
O'Flanagan's
One
Onieal's Grand Street
Ora
Orchid Lounge
Park Bar
Park Slope Ale House
Passerby
The Pencil Factory
People Lounge
Pete's Candy Store
Pete's Tavern
Petrosino
Phoenix Park
Planet Thailand
PM
Porcupine
Punch and Judy's
Quo
Radio Perfecto
Rare View (@ the Shelbourne Murray Hill Hotel)
Red Bench
The Red Cat
Redd's Tavern
Relish
Remedy Bar & Grill
Republic

Resto Leon
Rhone
Rock Star Bar
Rodeo Bar
The Room
Rope
Rosa Mexicano
Roxy
Royal Oak
Ruby Lounge
Ruby's Tap House
Rudy's Bar and Grill
Rue B
Rufus
Russian Samovar
The Russian Vodka Room
S.O.B.'s
Sapa
Scenic
Schiller's Liquor Bar
Sea Thai Bistro
Serena
Session 73
Ship of Fools
Siberia
Small's
Snacky
Soda Bar
Southpaw
Spanky's BBQ
Spuyten Duyvil
Starlight Bar & Lounge
Stir
Stonehome Wine Bar
Strip House
Suba
Suede
Supercore
Swift Hibernian Lounge
Table 50
Tainted Lady Lounge
Taj
Tavern on First
Tavern on the Green
Tea Lounge
Temple Bar

Time Out
Tonic and the Met Lounge
Tre Dici
Triple Crown
Trousdale
Turks & Frogs
Uncle Ming's
Under the Volcano
Union Pool
V Bar & Café
Varjak
Vasmay Lounge
Verlaine
The View (@ the Marriott
  Marquis)
Villard Bar & Lounge (@ the
  New York Palace Hotel)
Voyage
The Warsaw
The Web
Whiskey Park
Winnie's
Xicala
XL
Yello
Yumcha
Zebulon

After-Work Scene

The A&M Roadhouse
Absolutely 4th
Ace Bar
Acme Bar & Grill
Acqua
Agozar
Alibi
All State Café
Alligator Lounge
American Trash
Amuse
Andavi
Angelo & Maxie's
Angel's Share
Annie Moore's
Anotheroom
Antarctica

Apple Restaurant & BomBar
Aquagrill
Ara Wine Bar
Arriba Arriba Mexican
  Restaurant
Artisanal
Aubette
Automatic Slims
B61 @ Alma
The Back Fence
Baggot Inn
Bailey's Corner Pub
Baker Street
Balanza Bar
Balthazar
Banshee Pub
Bar 288 (aka Tom & Jerry's)
Bar 4
Bar 89
Bar 9
Bar Americain
Bar Minnow
Bar Reis
Bar Seine (@ The Hôtel
  Plaza Athénée)
Bar Toto
Bar Veloce Chelsea
Bar Veloce East Village
Bar XII
Barbuto
Bar-Coastal
Barfly
Barracuda
Barrage
Barrio Chino
Barrymore's
Bayard's Blue Bar
Beast
Beauty Bar
Becky's
The Beekman
Beer Bar @ Café Centro
Belmont Lounge
Beppe
Biddy Early's
Big Bar

The Big Cheech
Big City Bar & Grill
Bill's Gay Nineties
Biltmore Room
Bivio
The Black Bear Lodge
Black Door
Black Finn
Black Sheep
Blaggard's Pub (35th St.)
Blaggard's Pub (39th St.)
Blarney Cove Inc.
Blarney Rock
Blarney Stone
Bleecker Street Bar
Blind Tiger Ale House
Bliss Bar and Lounge
Blondies
Blue & Gold Tavern
Blue Fin (@ the W Hotel-
  Times Square)
Blue Lady Lounge (@
  Shelly's)
The Blue Mill Tavern
The Blue Room
Blue Smoke
The Boathouse
Bogart's
Bolo
Bongo
Boss Tweed's Saloon
Boston (212) Café
Bottino
Bounce
Boutique del Vino
Boxer's
Brady's Bar
Brady's Tavern
Brandy Library
Brasserie 8 1/2
The Brazen Head
Bread Bar @ Tabla
Broadway Bar & Terrace (@
  the Novotel Hotel)
Broadway Dive
Brooklyn Ale House

Brooklyn Brewery
Brooklyn Inn
Brother Jimmy's
Brother Jimmy's BBQ
Bryant Park Grill
B-Side
The Bull and Bear
Bull McCabe's
Bull Moose Saloon
Bull Run
Bull's Head Tavern
Bushwick Country Club
Buzz Bar @ Pershing Square
Cabanas (@ the Maritime
  Hotel)
Café Ma
Café Pierre (@ the Pierre
  Hotel)
Café Ronda
The Cajun
Caliban
Caliente Cab Co.
The Campbell Apartment
Candela
Canyon Road
Carriage House
Cedar Tavern
Cellar Bar & Café
Cellar Bar (@ Bryant Park
  Hotel)
Central Bar
Chai Home Kitchen
Channel 4
The Charleston
Charley O's Skybox
  American Bar and Grill
Chelsea Bistro & Bar
Chelsea Brewing Company
Cherry Tavern
Chi Chiz
Chumley's
Circa Tabac
The City Grill
City Hall
Clancy's
Clem's

Cleopatra's Needle
Cloister Café
Cody's Bar and Grill
Coldwaters
The Collins Bar
Comedy Village
Company
Connolly's 45th St.
Connolly's 47th St.
Continental
Coogan's Parrot Bay
Coppersmith's
Craftbar
Crossroads
Croxley Ales
Cru
Cub Room
Cuba Café
d.b.a.
D.J. Reynolds
D.O.C. Wine Bar
Dave's Tavern
David Copperfield's House of
  Beer
Day O
Deacon Brodie's
The Dead Poet
Decibel
Del Frisco's Double Eagle
  Steakhouse
The Delta Grill
Detour
Dewey's Flatiron
Dick's Bar
The Ding Dong Lounge
Dip
'disiac Lounge
Dive 75
Divine Bar East
Divine Bar West
Django
Doc Watson's
Docks Oyster Bar
The Dove
Druids
Dublin 6

Due South	Freemans	'ino
Duff's	Front Bar, The (@ the Four	'inoteca
The Dugout	Seasons Hotel)	Inside
Duke's	Fubar	International Bar
The Duplex	Full Shilling, The	Irish Pub
Dylan Prime	Fusion	i-Shebeen Madiba
Eamonn's	G Lounge	IXTA
East of Eighth	Gabriel's Wine Bar &	J.D.'s
Eatery/Bar E	Restaurant	Jack's Restaurant and Bar
The Edge	Gaf, The	Jacques-imo's NYC
Eight Mile Creek	Garden of Ono, The	Jake's Dilemma
El Parador Café	Garvey's	Jameson's
El Quijote	Gaslight Lounge	Jane
El Rey Del Sol	Giggles	Jarrod's Lounge
El Rio Grande	The Gin Mill	Jean-Luc
The Elephant	Gold Rush	Jeremy's Ale House
11th Street Bar	Gonzalez y Gonzalez	Jerry's
Elmo	Good World Bar & Grill	Jim Brady's
Emerald Pub	Grand Press	Jimmy's Corner
The Falls	Greenwich Brewing	John Street Bar & Grill
Fanelli's	Company	Johnney's Fish Grill
Fat Black Pussycat	Grotto	Joshua Tree
Fez North @ Time Café	Gstaad	Josie Wood's Pub
Fiddlesticks	Half Wine Bar	Joya
55 Bar	Hallo Berlin	JP Mustard
Finnegan's Wake	Hank's Saloon	Julep
Finnerty's	Hanratty's	Julius
Fiona's	Harrison's Tavern	Junno's
Firehouse	Harry Boland's Pub	Justin's
Fish Bar	Hearth	K Lounge
Five Points	Heartland Brewery Union	Kabin
Flannery's Bar	Square	Karma
Flatiron Lounge	Helen's	Kasadela
Flight 151	Henrietta Hudson	Kate Kearney's Pub and Grill
Floyd, NY	Henry Street Ale House	Kavehaz
Flute	Hi-Life Restaurant & Lounge	Kettle of Fish
Food Bar	Hooters	Kevin St. James
420 Bar and Lounge	House of Brews	Kili
The Four-Faced Liar	Houston's	Killarney Rose
44 (@ the Royalton Hotel)	Hudson Bar & Books	King's Head Tavern
40/40 Club	Hunter's American Bar & Grill	Knickerbocker Bar and Grill
Frank's 410	Hurley's Saloon	Kori
Frank's Cocktail Lounge	ICON (@ the W Hotel - The	La Churrascaria Plataforma
Fraunces Tavern	Court)	Tribeca
Freddy's Bar & Backroom	Iguana	La Linea
Frederick's	Ini Ani	Lakeside Lounge

L'Angolo Café
Larry Lawrence
Lea
Leisure Time Bowl
Les Halles
Les Halles Downtown
Levee
Library (@ the Paramount Hotel)
Life Café
Light
Lincoln Park Bar & Grill
Live Bait
Local Café East
Local West
Lodge
Loki Lounge
Lolita
Long Tan
L'Orange Bleue
Loreley
Los Dos Molinos
Louis 649
Luca Lounge
Lucky 13 Saloon
Lucky Cheng's
Lucky Jack's
Lucky Strike
Luke & Leroy
Luna Park
Lupa
Lure Fish Bar
M Shanghai Bistro & Den
M1-5
MacMenamin's Irish Pub
Mad River Bar & Grille
Madame X
Maggie's Place
Mancora
Manhattan Lounge
Manitoba's
Mannahatta
Maracas
Marion's Continental
Mark's Bar (@ the Mark Hotel)

Markt
Maroon's
Mars 2112
Martell's
Matt's Grill
Maya Lounge
McAnns Irish Pub
McCoy's
McGee's
McKenna's Pub
McKeown's
MeBar (@ the La Quinta Inn)
Meet
Merc Bar
Mercadito
Mercantile Grill
Merchants NY
Mercury Bar
Mercury Bar & Grill
Merrion Square
Metrazur
Metro 53
Metro Café & Wine Bar
Metropolitan
Metropolitan Café
Mexican Radio
Mica 587
Mickey Mantle's
Micky's Blue Room
Milady's Bar & Restaurant
Milano's
Mini-Bar in the District (@ the Muse Hotel)
Miss Williamsburg Portavia
MJ Armstrong's
Moda
Monkey Bar
Monkey Temple
Montero's Bar and Grill
Mooney's Pub
Morgan's Bar (@ the Morgan Hotel)
Mo's Caribbean Bar and Mexican Grille
Mr. Biggs
Mr. Dennehy's

Mugs Ale House
Mulberry Street Bar
Mulligan's Pub
Murphy's Bar and Grill
Murphy's Law Bar & Restaurant
Mustang Grill
Naima
Nathan Hale's
Nation Restaurant & Bar
Newgate Bar & Grill
Nightingale Lounge
Ninth Avenue Saloon
No Idea
Nolita House
Nowhere Bar
O.W.
O2 (@ the Time Hotel)
Oasis Bar (@ W New York)
O'Connor's
Off The Wagon
O'Flaherty's Ale House
O'Flanagan's
O'Hanlon's
O'Hara's
Old Town Bar & Restaurant
Oldcastle Pub and Restaurant
169 Bar
One and One
O'Neill's
Onieal's Grand Street
Onyx
Opal Bar
O'Reilly's Townhouse Tavern
Otto's Shrunken Head
Ouest
P.J. Clarke's
P.J. Kelly's
Palace Café Inc. (aka Goodman's)
Paladar
Pangea
Panorama Café
Paradou
Park Bar

Park Blue
Park Slope Ale House
Pasha
Pat O'Brien's
Patrick Conway's Pub
Patrick Kavanagh's
Pearl Oyster Bar
Peculier Pub
Pegasus
Penang
People Lounge
Perdition
Peter Dillon's
Peter's Bar & Restaurant
Pete's Tavern
Petrosino
Philip Marie
Phoenix Park
Pig N Whistle
Pigalle
PineTree Lodge
Pink Pony Café
Pioneer Bar and Restaurant
Planet Hollywood
Planet Rose
Plantain
Playwright Tavern
Pop
Pop Burger Lounge
Porcupine
Port 41
Porters
Posh
Prey
Prime 54 Lounge (@ Hotel
  Rihga)
Proseccheria
Puck Fair
Punch
Punch and Judy's
Q Lounge & Billiards
Q56 Restaurant and
  Cocktails
Quench
Radio Perfecto
Raga

Rancho Café
Rare View (@ the
  Shelbourne Murray Hill
  Hotel)
Rathbone's
Rawhide
Reade Street Pub and
  Kitchen
Red Sky
Reif's Tavern
Relish
Remedy Bar & Grill
Remy Lounge
Republic
Reservoir
Revival
Rice Republic
Rise (@ the Ritz-Carlton)
Robert Emmett's
Rocky Sullivan's
Rodeo Bar
Rogue
Romi Restaurant & Lounge
Rooftop Bar (@ Hotel Metro)
Rope
Rosa Mexicano
Rose Mary's Greenpoint
  Tavern
Round Bar (@ Royalton
  Hotel)
Ruby Foo's Times Square
Rubyfruit Bar & Grill
Ruby's Tap House
Rudy's Bar and Grill
Rue B
Russian Samovar
Ryan's Daughter
Ryan's Sports Bar & Grill
Saga
Sake Hana
Saloon
San Marcos
Santa Fe
Sasha's
Scenic
Schiller's Liquor Bar

Scopa
Second on Second
17 Murray
Shag
Shebeen
Siberia
Slainte
Slane
Slate Plus
Smiths
Smithwicks
Smoked
Snacky
Social Bar and
  Lounge/Fusion at Social
Solas
SouthWest NY
Spaghetti Western
Spanky's BBQ
Spike Hill Bar & Grill
Splash
Spring Lounge
Spuyten Duyvil
St. Maggie's Café
St. Marks 88
Standings
Still
Stir
Stone Creek
Stonewall
Stout NYC
Strip House
Subway Inn
Supercore
Sushi Samba 7
Suspenders
Sutton Place
Sweet & Vicious
T.G. Whitney's
TA Cocina Express
Taj
Tamarind
Tavern on Dean
Tavern on First
Tavern on Jane
Tea Lounge

Tenement
Tennessee Mountain
Terra Blues
Thady Con's
Therapy
Third and Long
Thirsty Scholar
Thom Bar (@ 60 Thompson)
Thomas Beisl
Timboo's
Tin Lizzie's
Tir Na Nog
Tonic and the Met Lounge
Tortilla Flats
Total Wine Bar
Town Crier
The Townhouse
Tracy J's Watering Hole
Trailer Park Lounge
Trattoria Dopo Teatro
Trinity Public House
Triple Crown
Trousdale
Turkey's Nest
Turks & Frogs
Turtle Bay
Twins Pub
200 Fifth
203 Spring
Ty's
Ulysses
Under the Volcano
Union Square Coffee Shop
The Upper Deck
Uptown Restaurant &
  Lounge
Varjak
Vegas
Vera
Vera Cruz
Verlaine
The Viceroy
View Bar
Vig Bar
Village Speakeasy Pub
Vince & Eddie's

Vintage
Virage
VON
Vudu Lounge
Vynl
Walker's
Waterloo Tavern
WCOU Radio (aka Tile Bar)
Westside Brewing Co.
Westside Tavern
The Wheeltapper Pub
Whiskey Blue
Whiskey Park
Whiskey River
White Horse Tavern
White Horse Tavern
Windfall Lounge and Grill
Winnie's
World Bar
WXOU Radio Bar
Xicala
XL
XR Bar
Xth Avenue Lounge
Xunta
The Yard (@ The Soho
  Grand)
Ye Olde Tripple Inn
Yujin
Zablozki's
Zoe

Annoying Door

A60 (@ 60 Thompson)
Avalon
Branch
Bungalow 8
Cabanas (@ the Maritime
  Hotel)
Cain
Cherry Lounge
China Club
Cielo
Club Shelter
Copacabana
Crobar

Deep
The Double Seven
Duvet
58
Groovedeck
Gypsy Tea
Hiro Lounge
Home
Kos
La Cave
Level V
Light
Lot 61
Lotus
Marquee
NA
One
PM
Quo
Ruby Falls
Select
Strata
Suede
Sway
Triumph Room

Comedy

Carolines on Broadway
Comedy Cellar
Comedy Village
Comic Strip Live
Dangerfield's
Gladys' Comedy Room
Gotham Comedy Club
Laugh Lounge NYC
New York Comedy Club
Stand-Up NY
Upright Citizens Brigade

Dancing/Clubs

Aer
Alibi
Alphabet Lounge
Amarachi Lounge
APT
Asylum
Avalon
Bar Below
Bar East
Bar None
Baraza
Bembe
Black Betty
BLVD
bOb
Bogart's
Boogaloo
Boysroom
Branch
Bungalow 8
Café Wha?
Cain
Canal Room
Cattyshack
Cherry Lounge
China Club
Church Lounge (@ TriBeCa Grand)
Cielo
Club Shelter
CockThe Cock
Copacabana
Crobar
Culture Club
Deep
Discotheque
Diva
Don Hill's
Double Happiness
El Cantinero
Eugene
Exit
Flow
Galapagos Artspace
Girlsroom

Glo
Gypsy Tea
Happy Ending
Heaven
Home
Hue
iO
Jarrod's Lounge
Kaña
Kingsland Tavern
La Cave
La Caverna
Level V
Libation
Light
Lotus
LQ
Made
Mannahatta
Marquee
Maya Lounge
Mehanata
Metro 53
Metropolitan
Mission
The Monster
NA
Naked Lunch
Nerveana
Oliva
One
Opus 22
Parlay
Plan B
Plantain
Pressure
Prey
Pyramid
Quo
Rain Lounge
Red and Black
Red Lion
Remy Lounge
Rock Candy
Rock Star Bar
Rocky Sullivan's

Rothko
Roxy
Ruby Falls
S.O.B.'s
Sapphire Lounge
Satalla
Savalas
Second Nature
Select
Session 73
Shadow
Show
Sin Sin
6s and 8s
The SkinNY
The Slipper Room
Spirit
Splash
Stonewall
Strata
Suede
Sugar Bar & Lounge
The Sullivan Room
Sway
Swing 46
Table 50
Table XII (aka Etoile)
Temple New York
Therapy
13 Little Devils
Triumph Room
24-7 Bar & Lounge
200 Fifth
2i's
Uncle Ming's
The Web
Webster Hall

Date/Romantic Spots

Amuse
Angel's Share
Ara Wine Bar
Auction House
AVA Lounge (@ Dream Hotel)
Boutique del Vino

Brandy Library
Bubble Lounge
Canapa
Cantor Roof Garden, The (@ the Met)
Casa La Femme North
Casimir
Caviar and Banana Braserio Restaurant
Cellar Bar (@ Bryant Park Hotel)
Dove, The
East Side Company Bar
Fez North (@ Time Café)
Figa
5 Ninth
Five Points
Flatiron Lounge
Flute
K Lounge
Kimono Lounge
Koi
Kush
Lexington Bar & Books
Little Branch
Ludo
Marlow and Sons
Megu
Metrazur
Metropol
MOBar (@ Mandarin-Oriental Hotel)
Monkey Bar
Morgan's Bar (@ the Morgan Hotel)
Odea
Ono
Pravda
Public
Sapa
Shalel Lounge
Spice Market
Suba
Temple Bar
Underbar (@ W Hotel-Union Sq.)

Voyage
Zanzibar
Zerza Bar

Dive Bars

The A&M Roadhouse
Ace Bar
Alphabet Lounge
American Spirits
American Trash
Apocalypse Lounge
Balanza Bar
Billy Mark's West
Blarney Cove Inc.
Blarney Stone
Blarney Stone
Bleecker Street Bar
Blue & Gold Tavern
Botanica
Bourbon Street
Bowery Ballroom
Boysroom
Broadway Dive
B-Side
Bull McCabe's
Café Andalucia
The Call Box Lounge
The Carriage Inn
CBGB's & OMFUG
CBGB's Gallery
The Charleston
Cheap Shots
Cherry Tavern
The Cock
Coldwaters
Continental
Coogan's Parrot Bay
Coyote Ugly
Crime Scene
Dakota Roadhouse
Dave's Tavern
Dick's Bar
The Distinguished Wakamba
Doc Holliday's
Don Hill's
Down the Hatch

Driftwood Inn
Duff's
Duke's
The Edge
Eight of Clubs
El Rey Del Sol
Farrell's
55 Bar
Finnerty's
Frank's Cocktail Lounge
Freddy's Bar & Backroom
Fubar
Gardens Bar
The Girl from Ipanema
Grand Central
Grassroots Tavern
Hank's Saloon
Hogs and Heifers
Holiday Cocktail Lounge
Holland Bar
Hooligan's
Iggy's
Iggy's Keltic Lounge
International Bar
Jackie's Fifth Amendment
Jimmy's Corner
Joe's Bar
John Street Bar & Grill
Karavas Tavern
Korova Milk Bar
Lit Lounge
Lucky 13 Saloon
Lyric Lounge
MacDougal Street Ale House
Malachy's
Mama's Bar
Manitoba's
Mars Bar
Max Fish
McHale's
McKenna's Pub
McSorley's Ale House
Milano's
Mona's
The Monster
Montero's Bar and Grill

Mooney's Pub
Moonshine
Motor City
Mulberry Street Bar
Nancy Whiskey Pub
Nassau Bar
No Idea
Nowhere Bar
Off The Wagon
169 Bar
119 Bar
Otto's Shrunken Head
P & G Café
Palais Royale
Parkside Lounge
Pat O'Brien's
The Patriot Saloon
Peculier Pub
Peter McManus
PineTree Lodge
Port 41
Pyramid
The Raven
Red Rock West Saloon
Rock Star Bar
Rose Mary's Greenpoint
 Tavern
Rothko
Rudy's Bar and Grill
7B
Siberia
The Slide
Sophie's Bar
The Stoned Crow
Subway Bar
Subway Inn
T.G. Whitney's
Timboo's
Tin Lizzie's
Tommy's Tavern
Tonic
Tool Box
Trash
12"
2 by 4
Upright Citizens Brigade

Vasmay Lounge
Vudu Lounge
Welcome to the Johnsons
Wild Spirits
Winnie's
Ye Olde Tripple Inn
Yogi's

Food

A 60 (@ 60 Thompson)
The A&M Roadhouse
Absolutely 4th
Ace of Clubs
Acme Bar & Grill
Acqua
Ada
Aer
Agave
Agozar
AIX
Aja
Alamo
Aleo Restaurant & Bar
Alfama
All State Café
Alligator Lounge
Amarachi Lounge
Amber
Amuse
Andavi
Angelo & Maxie's
Angel's Share
Annie Moore's
Anyway Café
Apartment 138
Apple Restaurant & BomBar
APT
Aquagrill
Aquavit
Ara Wine Bar
Aroma
Arriba Arriba Mexican
 Restaurant
Art Bar
Arté
Artisanal

Asia de Cuba
Asia Roma
Atrium Lounge
Aubette
Automatic Slims
Avenue A Sushi
Azaza
B Bar (aka Bowery Bar)
B.B. King's Blues Club & Grill
B1 Drink Club
Back Page
Baker Street
Balthazar
BAMcafé
Bann
Bao 111
Bar @ Etats-Unis
Bar 515
Bar 6
Bar 89
Bar 9
Bar Americain
Bar Bleu @ Café Deville
Bar Minnow
Bar on A (BOA)
Bar Seine (@ The Hôtel
 Plaza Athénée)
Bar Toto
Bar Veloce Chelsea
Bar Veloce East Village
Bar XII
bar.vetro
Barbalùc
BarBossa
Barbuto
The Barclay Bar and Grill (@
 Intercontinental Barclay)
Bar-Coastal
Barfly
Barmarche
Barrio Chino
Barrow Street Ale House
Barrymore's
Basso Est
Bayard's Blue Bar
Beast

Becky's
The Beekman
Beer Bar @ Café Centro
Belly
Belmont Lounge
Bemelmans Bar @ The
  Carlyle, A Rosewood Hotel
Beppe
Bette
Bice
The Big Cheech
Big City Bar & Grill
Bill's Gay Nineties
Biltmore Room
BINY
Birdland
Bivio
Black Betty
Black Duck (@ Park South
  Hotel)
Black Finn
Black Sheep
Blaggard's Pub (35th St.)
Blaggard's Pub (39th St.)
Blarney Rock
Blarney Stone
Bliss Bar and Lounge
Blondies
Blu Lounge
Blue & Gold Tavern
Blue Fin (@ the W Hotel-
  Times Square)
Blue Lady Lounge (@
  Shelly's)
The Blue Mahoe
The Blue Mill Tavern
Blue Note
The Blue Room
Blue Smoke
BLVD
The Boathouse
Boca Chica
Bogart's
Bolo
Bond 45
Bond Street Lounge

Bongo
Boom
Boss Tweed's Saloon
Botanica
Bottino
Bounce
Boutique del Vino
Bowlmor Lanes
Boxer's
Brady's Tavern
Branch
Brandy Library
Brass Monkey
Brasserie
Brasserie 8 1/2
The Brazen Head
Bread Bar @ Tabla
Bridge Café
Brite Bar
Broadway Lounge (@ the
  Marriott Marquis)
Brooklyn Social Club
Brother Jimmy's
Brother Jimmy's (2nd Ave.)
Brother Jimmy's BBQ
Bryant Park Grill
Bubble Lounge
The Bull and Bear
Bull Moose Saloon
Bull Run
Buster's Garage
Butter
Buzz Bar @ Pershing Square
Cabana
Cabin
Café Andalucia
Café Carlyle (@ the Carlyle)
Café Deville
Café Gitane
Café Luxembourg
Café Ma
Café Noir
Café Pierre (@ the Pierre
  Hotel)
Café Ronda
Café Wha?

Caféteria
The Cajun
CakeShop
Caliban
Caliente Cab Co.
Caliente Cab Company
The Call Box Lounge
Calle Ocho
Camaje
Canapa
Candela
Cantinella
The Cantor Roof Garden (@
  the Met)
Canyon Road
Capone's
The Carnegie Club
Caroline's on Broadway
Carriage House
The Carriage Inn
Casa La Femme North
Casimir
Cassis
Caviar and Banana Braserio
  Restaurant
Cedar Tavern
Cellar Bar (@ Bryant Park
  Hotel)
Cendrillon
Central Bar
''Cesca
Chai Home Kitchen
Chance
Channel 4
The Charleston
Charley O's Skybox
  American Bar and Grill
Charlotte (@ Millenium
  Broadway Hotel)
Chelsea Bistro & Bar
Chelsea Brewing Company
The Chemist Club (@ the
  Dylan Hotel)
Chez Oskar
Chi Chiz
Chibi's Bar

Chibitini
Chikalicious
Chorus Karaoke
Chow Bar
Chubo
Chumley's
Church Lounge (@ TriBeCa Grand)
Cibar
Cipriani's
Circa Tabac
Citrus Bar & Grill
The City Grill
City Hall
Clancy's
Cleopatra's Needle
Cloister Café
Club Macanudo
Cody's Bar and Grill
Coldwaters
Comedy Cellar
Comedy Village
Comic Strip Live
Company
Compass
Connolly's 45th St.
Connolly's 47th St.
Coogan's Parrot Bay
Copper Door Tavern
Coppersmith's
Corner Bistro
Counter
Cowgirl
Cozy Café
Craftbar
Crash Mansion
Crispo
Crossroads
Croxley Ales
Cru
Crudo
Cub Room
Cuba
Cuba Café
Cupping Room Café
The Cutting Room

D.J. Reynolds
D.O.C. Wine Bar
Daddy-O
Daddy's
Dakota Roadhouse
Dangerfield's
Danube
David Copperfield's House of Beer
Day O
The Dead Poet
Decibel
Dekk
Del Frisco's Double Eagle Steakhouse
The Delta Grill
Desmond's Tavern
Dewey's Flatiron
Diner
Diner 24
Dip
'disiac Lounge
Diva
The Dive Bar
Divine Bar East
Divine Bar West
Django
Do Hwa
Doc Watson's
Docks Oyster Bar
The Door Lounge
Dorian's
Dorrian's Red Hand
Dos Caminos
Dos Caminos
Down the Hatch
Dragonfly
Druids
DT/UT
Dublin 6
Due South
Duff's
The Dugout
Duke's
DuMont
Duvet

Dylan Prime
Eamonn's
Ear Inn
Earl's
Earth NYC
East of Eighth
East Side Company Bar
East Side Steak & Ale
Eatery/Bar E
Edessa
Edward's
Eight Mile Creek
85 West Cocktail Bar
El Cantinero
El Faro
El Parador Café
El Poblano Sports Grill
El Quijote
El Rey Del Sol
El Rio Grande
Elaine's
The Elephant
Eleven Madison Park
Elmo
Emerald Inn
Emerald Pub
Employees Only
Enid's
Esperanto
ESPN Zone
Essex Restaurant
Euzkadi
Evelyn Lounge
Faces and Names
Failte Irish Whiskey Bar
The Falls
Fanelli's
Fashion 40
Fat Black Pussycat
Fez North @ Time Café
Fiamma Osteria
Fiddlesticks
5757 @ Four Seasons
Figa
Film Center Café
Finnegan's Wake

Fino
Fiona's
Firebird
Firehouse
Fish
Fitzer's
Fitzgerald's Pub
5 ninth
Five Points
Flight 151
Flor de Sol
Florent
Florio's Grill & Cigar Bar
Floyd, NY
Flute (Flatiron)
Flute (Midtown)
Food Bar
Forbidden City
1492 Food
44 (@ the Royalton Hotel)
44&X
40/40 Club
Frank's 410
Fraunces Tavern
Frederick's
Frederick's Madison
Freemans
French Roast
The Front Bar (@ the Four
  Seasons Hotel)
Fuelray
Fujiyama Mama
The Full Shilling
Funhouse
Fusion
Fuzion on A
Gabriel's Wine Bar &
  Restaurant
Galaxy Global Eatery
The Gallery (@ the Soho
  Grand)
The Garden of Ono
Garvey's
Gatsby's Bar & Lounge
Geisha
General Store

The George Keeley
Giggles
The Gin Mill
The Ginger Man
Giorgio's of Gramercy
The Girl from Ipanema
Gold Rush
Gonzalez y Gonzalez
Good Restaurant
Good World Bar & Grill
Gotham Bar & Grill
Gotham Comedy Club
Gowanus Yacht Club
Gramercy Tavern
Grand Bar and Lounge (@
  the Soho Grand)
Grand Saloon
Great Jones Café
Greenwich Brewing
  Company
Groove
Groovedeck
Grotta Azzurra
Grotto
Guastavino's
Gyu-Kaku
Hacienda de Argentina
The Half King Bar
Half Wine Bar
Hallo Berlin
Hank's Saloon
Hanratty's
Harbour Lights
Hard Rock Café
The Harrison
Harrison's Tavern
Hearth
Heartland Brewery Radio
  City
Heartland Brewery Union
  Square
Hedeh
Helen's
Henry Street Ale House
Highline
Hi-Life Bar and Grill

Hi-Life Restaurant & Lounge
The Hog Pit
The Hook & Ladder Pub
Hookah Café
Hooters
Hop Devil Grill
Horus Café
House of Brews
Houston's
Hudson Place
Hue
Hunter's American Bar & Grill
Hurley's Saloon
Hurricane Hopeful
i Restaurant & Lounge
I Tre Merli
ICON (@ the W Hotel - The
  Court)
Ideya
Iguana
Il Buco
Il Cortile
Il Posto Accanto
In Vino
Indochine
Ini Ani
'ino
'inoteca
Inside
iO
Iona
Iridium
The Irish Punt
Irish Rogue
i-Shebeen Madiba
Isis @ Union Bar
IXTA
Izakaya Izu
J.D.'s
Jack's Restaurant and Bar
Jacques-imo's NYC
Jake's Dilemma
Jake's Saloon
Jameson's
Jane
Jean-Luc

Jekyll & Hyde
Jeremy's Ale House
Jerry's
Jezebel
Jim Brady's
Jimmy Walker's
Joe's Pub
Joey's
John Street Bar & Grill
Johnney's Fish Grill
Joshua Tree
Joshua Tree
Josie Wood's Pub
Journey's Lounge (@ the Essex Hotel)
Joya
JP Mustard
Julep
Jules Café
Julian's
Julius
Juniper Suite
Justin's
K Lounge
Kaña
Kanvas
Karavas Tavern
Karma
Kasadela
Kate Kearney's Pub and Grill
Katen Sushi Bar (@ the Marriott Marquis)
Katwalk
Kavehaz
Kemia
Kennedy's
Kevin St. James
Kili
Killarney Rose
Kin Khao
Kingsland Tavern
Kinsale Tavern
Kitchen & Cocktails
Kitchen 82
Knickerbocker Bar and Grill
Koi

Kori
Kush
Kyma
La Bottega (@ the Maritime Hotel)
La Cave
La Caverna
La Prima Donna
La Streghe
La Tour
Landmarc
L'Angolo Café
Latitude
Lava Gina
Le Refuge
Le Souk
Lea
Leisure Time Bowl
Lemon
Les Halles
Les Halles Downtown
Levee
Level V
Libation
Life Café
Light
Light
Lincoln Park Bar & Grill
Link
Lips
Live Bait
Lobo
Local Café East
Local West
Lodge
Long Tan
L'Orange Bleue
Loreley
Los Dos Molinos
Lotus
Lotus Lounge
Low Bar
LQ
Luca Lounge
Lucien
The Lucky Cat

Lucky Cheng's
Lucky Strike
Lucy Latin Kitchen
Ludo
LuLu Lounge
Luna Park
Lunasa
Lure Fish Bar
M Shanghai Bistro & Den
Macelleria
MacMenamin's Irish Pub
Mad River Bar & Grille
Maggie's Place
Maker's
Makor
Mama's Bar
Manchester Pub
Mancora
Manhattan Grille
Mannahatta
Maracas
Marion's Continental
Mark's Bar (@ the Mark Hotel)
Markt
Marlow and Sons
Maroon's
Mars 2112
Marseille
Martell's
Matt's Grill
Maya Lounge
McAnns Irish Pub
McCormack's
McCoy's
McFadden's Saloon
McGee's
McHale's
McKenna's Pub
McKeown's
McSorley's Ale House
Meet
Mekong
Mercadito
Mercantile Grill
Mercer Kitchen

Merchants
Merchants NY
Mercury Bar
Mercury Bar & Grill
The Mermaid Inn
Merrion Square
Mesa Grill
Metrazur
Metro 53
Metro Café & Wine Bar
Metropol
Metropolitan Café
Mexican Radio
Mica 51
Mica 587
Mickey Mantle's
Milady's Bar & Restaurant
Mini-Bar in the District (@ the Muse Hotel)
Miracle Bar & Grill
Miracle Grill
Miss Williamsburg Portavia
Mission
Mixx Lounge
MJ Armstrong's
MOBar (@ Mandarin Oriental Hotel)
Moda
The Modern
Monkey Bar
Monkey Temple
Montero's Bar and Grill
Morgan's Bar (@ the Morgan Hotel)
Morrell Wine Bar & Café
Mo's Caribbean Bar and Mexican Grille
Mosto Osteria
Moto
Movida
Mr. Biggs
Mr. Dennehy's
Mugs Ale House
Muldoon's
Mulligan's Pub
Murphy's Bar and Grill

Murphy's Law Bar & Restaurant
Mustang Grill
Mustang Harry's
Mustang Sally's
ñ
Naima
Nam
Nancy Whiskey Pub
Nathan Hale's
Nation Restaurant & Bar
Neary's
Negril
Negril Village
Neogaea
New York Comedy Club
Newgate Bar & Grill
Nice Guy Eddie's
Nisos
Nolita House
Nooch
North West Restaurant & Lounge
O.W.
02 (@ the Time Hotel)
The Oak Room (@ Algonquin Hotel)
Odea
Odessa
Off The Wagon
O'Flaherty's Ale House
O'Hara's
Old Town Bar & Restaurant
Oldcastle Pub and Restaurant
Oliva
Olives (@ W Hotel - Union Sq.)
One
One 91
One and One
O'Neals'
O'Neill's
Onieal's Grand Street
Ono
Onyx

Opal Bar
Opus 22
Ora
Orange Valve
Orchid
Orchid Lounge
O'Reilly's Pub & Restaurant
O'Reilly's Townhouse Tavern
Otto Enoteca Pizzeria
Ouest
Outpost Lounge
Ouzerie @ En Plo
P.D. O'Hurley's
P.J. Clarke's
P.J. Kelly's
Pacific Grill
Palace Café Inc. (aka Goodman's)
Paladar
Palmiras
Pangea
Panorama Café
Paradou
Paris Commune
Park Avalon
Park Avenue Country Club
Park Blue
Park Slope Ale House
The Park
Parkside Lounge
The Parlour
Parnell's Pub
Pasha
Pastis
Pat O'Brien's
Patrick Conway's Pub
The Patriot Saloon
Pearl Oyster Bar
Peasant
Peep
Penang
The Pencil Factory
People Lounge
Pequena
Perdition
Peter McManus

Peter's Bar & Restaurant	Quhnia	Ryan Maguire's Ale House
Pete's Candy Store	Quigley's	Ryans Irish Pub
Pete's Tavern	Radio Perfecto	Ryan's Sports Bar & Grill
Petrosino	Raga	S.O.B.'s
Phebe's Tavern & Grill	Rain	Saga
Philip Marie	Rancho Café	Sake Bar Satsko
Phoenix Park	Rathbone's	Sake Hana
Pianos	Reade Street Pub and	Sala
Pig N Whistle	Kitchen	Salon
Pigalle	The Red Cat	Salt Bar
The Pinch Bar & Grill	Red Lion	Sambuca
Pink Pony Café	Red Sky	San Marcos
Piola	Redemption	Sandia
Pioneer Bar and Restaurant	Relish	Santa Fe
Pipa	Remedy Bar & Grill	Sapa
The Place	Remy Lounge	Sasha's
Planet Hollywood	Republic	Satalla
Planet Thailand	Reservoir	Savoy
Plantain	Resto Leon	Scenic
Playwright Tavern	Rhone	Schiller's Liquor Bar
Plunge (@ Hotel Gansevoort)	Rialto	Scopa
PM	Ribot	Scruffy Duffy's
Pop	Rice Republic	Sea Thai Bistro
Pop Burger Lounge	Rise (@ the Ritz-Carlton)	Seaport Café
Porcupine	Riviera Café & Sports Bar	Second on Second
Port 41	Robert Emmett's	Senor Swanky's
Porters	Robin des Bois (aka	Serafina
The Pourhouse	Sherwood Café)	Session 73
Pravda	Rock Star Bar	17 Murray
Press 195	Rodeo Bar	17 Home
Pressure	Rogue	Shades of Green
Prey	Rolf's	Shag
Prime 54 Lounge (@ Hotel	Romi Restaurant & Lounge	Shalel Lounge
Rihga)	Rooftop Bar (@ Hotel Metro)	The Park Bar Restaurant
Prohibition	Room 18	Ship of Fools
Proof	Rosa Mexicana	Shore
Proseccheria	Round Bar (@ Royalton	Sidecar
PS 450	Hotel)	Sidewalk Café
Public	Ruby Foo's Times Square	Slainte
Puck Fair	Ruby Lounge	Slane
Punch	Rubyfruit Bar & Grill	Slate Plus
Punch and Judy's	Ruby's Tap House	The Slaughtered Lamb
Puppets Jazz Bar	Rudy's Bar and Grill	Smith & Wollensky
Q Lounge & Billiards	Rue B	Smiths
Q56 Restaurant and	Russian Samovar	Smithwicks
Cocktails	The Russian Vodka Room	Smoked

Snacky
Snitch
Social Bar and
  Lounge/Fusion at Social
Soda Bar
SoFo
SoGo NY
Solas
Sortie
South's
SouthWest NY
Spaghetti Western
Spanky's BBQ
Spice
Spice Market
Spike Hill Bar & Grill
The Spotted Pig
Spuyten Duyvil
St. Dymphna's
St. Maggie's Café
St. Marks 88
Stain
Stand-Up NY
The Stanton Social
Starfoods
Steak Frites
Still
Stir
Stitch
Stone Creek
The Stone Rose
Stonehome Wine Bar
Stout NYC
Strata
Strip House
Suba
Sugar Bar
Sugar Bar & Lounge
SugarCane
Sui
The Sunburnt Cow
Supercore
Sushi Generation
Sushi Samba 7
Sushi Samba Park
Sutton Place

Swift Hibernian Lounge
Swing 46
T.G. Whitney's
TA Cocina Express
Table XII (aka Etoile)
Taboon
Tai
Tainted Lady Lounge
Taj
Tamari
Tamarind
Tao
The Tapas Lounge
Tapeo 29
Taste
The Tasting Room
Tavern on Dean
Tavern on Jane
Tavern on the Green
Tea Lounge
Teddy's Bar & Grill
The Telephone Bar & Grill
Temple Bar
Tenement
Tennessee Mountain
Thady Con's
Therapy
Thom Bar (@ 60 Thompson)
Thomas Beisl
Three of Cups
Timboo's
Time Out
Tin Lizzie's
Tir Na Nog
Tonic and the Met Lounge
Tortilla Flats
Total Wine Bar
Town Crier
Town Tavern
Tracy J's Watering Hole
Trailer Park Lounge
Trash
Trattoria Dopo Teatro
Tre Dici
The Triad
Trio

Triple Crown
Triumph Room
Trousdale
Tupelo Grill
Turkey's Nest
Turks & Frogs
Turquoise Seafood
  Restaurant
Turtle Bay
12:31
Twins Pub
200 Fifth
203 Spring
UK New York
Ulrika's
Ulysses
Under the Volcano
Union Square Coffee Shop
The Upper Deck
Uptown Restaurant &
  Lounge
Urge Lounge
Uva
V Bar & Café
Varjak
Vera
Vera Cruz
Verlaine
Vertigo Bar & Restaurant
The Viceroy
ViceVersa
Viet-Café
The View (@ the Marriott
  Marquis)
Village Speakeasy Pub
Villard Bar & Lounge (@ the
  New York Palace Hotel)
Vince & Eddie's
Vintage
Virage
Virgil's Real Barbeque
Voyage
Vynl
Waikiki Wally's
Walker's
Wallse

The Warsaw
Waterfront Ale House
wd-50
Westside Brewing Co.
The Wheeltapper Pub
White Horse Tavern (TriBeCa)
White Horse Tavern (West Village)
The White Rabbit
Willy's Bar & Grill
Windfall Lounge and Grill
Winebar
Winnie's
Wogie's
Wolfgang's Steakhouse
World Bar
Xicala
Xing
Xth Avenue Lounge
Xunta
Yaffa Café
The Yard (@ The Soho Grand)
Ye Olde Tripple Inn
Yello
Yuca Bar & Restaurant
Yujin
Yumcha
Zakuro
Zanzibar
Zebulon
Zerza Bar
Zoe
Zum Schneider Bavarian Beer House

Frat/College

American Spirits
Bar 515
Bar None
Bar-Coastal
Barfly
Biddy Early's
Big Easy
Black Finn
Blondies

Blondies
Blue & Gold Tavern
The Blue Room
Boss Tweed's Saloon
Bourbon Street
Brother Jimmy's
Brother Jimmy's BBQ
Bull McCabe's
Bull's Head Tavern
Comedy Village
Coppersmith's
Coyote Ugly
Croxley Ales
Dakota Roadhouse
Django
Doc Watson's
Dorrian's Red Hand
Down the Hatch
Duke's
Finnerty's
Garvey's
Gatsby's Bar & Lounge
The Gin Mill
The Hook & Ladder Pub
Hurley's Saloon
Jake's Dilemma
John Street Bar & Grill
Joshua Tree (Hell's Kitchen)
Joshua Tree (Murray Hill)
Josie Wood's Pub
Kate Kearney's Pub and Grill
Kevin St. James
Live Bait
Local 138
Loki Lounge
MacDougal Street Ale House
McGee's
McSwiggan's
Mercury Bar
Metro 53
Mica 587
MJ Armstrong's
Mo's Caribbean Bar and Mexican Grille
Naked Lunch
Nathan Hale's

No Idea
Nowhere Bar
Off The Wagon
O'Neill's
Park Avenue Country Club
Pat O'Brien's
Patrick Kavanagh's
The Patriot Saloon
Pig N Whistle
The Pinch Bar & Grill
PineTree Lodge
Proof
Q Lounge & Billiards
Rathbone's
Reservoir
Riviera Café & Sports Bar
Robert Emmett's
Ryan's Daughter
Ryan's Sports Bar & Grill
Senor Swanky's
Ship of Fools
Spring Lounge
St. Marks Ale House
Standings
The Stoned Crow
Sutton Place
T.G. Whitney's
Third and Long
Thirsty Scholar
Time Out
Town Crier
Tracy J's Watering Hole
Turtle Bay
The Upper Deck
Village Tavern
Waterloo Tavern
Whiskey River
White Horse Tavern
WXOU Radio Bar

Gay/Lesbian

Barracuda
Barrage
Boots & Saaddle
Boysroom
Brandy's Piano Bar

Cattyshack
Chi Chiz
Clubhouse
The Cock
Dick's Bar
The Dugout
The Duplex
The Eagle
East of Eighth
Eight of Clubs
Excelsior
Food Bar
G Lounge
Ginger's
Girlsroom
The Hangar
Heaven
Helen's
Henrietta Hudson
Julius
Lips
Marie's Crisis Café
Metropolitan
The Monster
Ninth Avenue Saloon
Nowhere Bar
O.W.
Pegasus
Phoenix
Pieces
Posh
Pyramid
Rawhide
Roxy
Rubyfruit Bar & Grill
The Slide
Splash
Starlight Bar & Lounge
Stonewall
Therapy
Tool Box
The Townhouse
Ty's
Urge Lounge
View Bar
The Web

XES
XL

Hotel Bars

A 60 (@ 60 Thompson)
Atrium Lounge (@ Marriott Marquis)
AVA Lounge (@ Dream Hotel)
Bar Seine (@ the Hôtel Plaza Athénée)
Barclay Bar and Grill (@ Intercontinental Barclay), The
Barna (@ Hotel Giraffe)
Bemelmans Bar (@ the Carlyle)
Black Duck (@ Park South Hotel)
Blue Fin (@ the W Hotel-Times Square)
Broadway Bar & Terrace (@ the Novotel Hotel)
Broadway Lounge (@ the Marriott Marquis)
Bull and Bear (@ Waldorf-Astoria), The
Cabanas (@ the Maritime Hotel)
Café Carlyle (@ the Carlyle)
Café Pierre (@ the Pierre Hotel)
Cecil's Bar (@ the Crowne Plaza Hotel)
Cellar Bar (@ Bryant Park Hotel)
Charlotte (@ the Millennium Broadway Hotel)
Chemist Club (@ the Dylan Hotel), The
Church Lounge (@ TriBeCa Grand)
Dream Lounge (@ Dream Hotel)
5757 (@ the Four Seasons Hotel)
44 (@ the Royalton Hotel)

Front Bar (@ the Four Seasons Hotel), The
Gallery (@ the SoHo Grand), The
Gallery Lounge (@ the Gershwin Hotel)
Grand Bar and Lounge (@ the SoHo Grand)
Hiro Lounge (@ the Maritime Hotel)
Hudson Bar (@ the Hudson Hotel)
ICON (@ W Hotel – The Court)
Journey's Lounge (@ the Essex Hotel)
Katen Sushi Bar (@ the Marriott Marquis)
Koi (@ Bryant Park Hotel)
La Bottega (@ the Maritime Hotel)
Library Bar (@ the Hudson Hotel)
Library (@ the Paramount Hotel)
Library (@ the Regency), The
Living Room (@ W Hotel – Times Square), The
Mark's Bar (@ the Mark Hotel)
MeBar (@ La Quinta Inn)
Mini-Bar in the District (@ the Muse Hotel)
MOBar (@ Mandarin Oriental Hotel)
Morgan's Bar (@ the Morgan Hotel)
Oak Room (@ the Algonquin Hotel), The
Oasis Bar (@ W New York)
Olives (@ W Hotel – Union Sq.)
O2 (@ the Time Hotel)
Pen-Top Bar & Terrace (@ the Peninsula Hotel), The
Plunge (@ Hotel Gansevoort)

Prime 54 (@ Hotel Rihga)
Private Park (@ the Hudson
  Hotel)
Q56 (@ Swissôtel)
Rare View (@ the
  Shelbourne Murray Hill
  Hotel)
Rise (@ the Ritz-Carlton)
Rooftop Bar (@ Hotel Metro)
Round Bar (@ Royalton
  Hotel)
Rum House (@ the Edison
  Hotel), The
Thom Bar (@ 60 Thompson)
12:31 (@ the Hotel
  Chandler)
Twist Lounge (@ the
  Ameritania Hotel)
Underbar (@ W Hotel –
  Union Sq.)
Villard Bar & Lounge (@ the
  New York Palace Hotel)
Wheeltapper Pub (@
  Fitzpatrick Hotel), The
Whiskey (@ W Hotel – Times
  Sq.), The
Whiskey Blue (@ W New
  York)
Yard (@ the SoHo Grand),
  The

Karaoke Bars

Asia Roma
BINY
Chorus Karaoke
Iggy's
Izakaya Izu
Japas
Lucky Cheng's
Orange Valve
Pegasus
Planet Rose
Second on Second
Winnie's
Yello

Live Music

The A&M Roadhouse
Ace of Clubs
Acme Bar & Grill
Alfama
Alphabet Lounge
Amarachi Lounge
American Spirits
American Trash
Anyway Café
Apocalypse Lounge
Arlene's Grocery
Arthur's Tavern
Artland
Atrium Lounge
B.B. King's Blues Club & Grill
The Back Fence
Baggot Inn
Balanza Bar
BAMcafé
Bao 111
Bar 4
Bar 515
Bar 9
Bar East
Bar on A (BOA)
Barbes
Bayard's Blue Bar
Becky's
The Beekman
Believe Lounge
Bembe
Bemelmans Bar @ The
  Carlyle, A Rosewood Hotel
Bill's Gay Nineties
Birdland
The Bitter End
Black Betty
Black Duck (@ Park South
  Hotel)
Blu Lounge
Blue Lady Lounge (@
  Shelly's)
Blue Note
The Blue Room
Blue Smoke

Boogaloo
Boss Tweed's Saloon
Bourbon Street
Bowery Ballroom
Brandy Library
Brandy's Piano Bar
Bull's Head Tavern
Café Carlyle (@ the Carlyle)
Café Pierre (@ the Pierre
  Hotel)
Café Wha?
The Cajun
CakeShop
Camaje
The Campbell Apartment
Canal Room
The Carnegie Club
CBGB's & OMFUG
CBGB's Gallery
The Charleston
Charley O's Skybox
  American Bar and Grill
Chibi's Bar
Church Lounge (@ TriBeCa
  Grand)
Cleopatra's Needle
Cloister Café
Club Macanudo
The C-Note
Connolly's 45th St.
Connolly's 47th St.
Continental
Coppersmith's
Cornelia St. Café
Cozy Café
Crash Mansion
Crobar
Crossroads
Cuba
Culture Club
The Cutting Room
The Delancey
The Delta Grill
Desmond's Tavern
Detour
The Ding Dong Lounge

Doc Watson's
Don Hill's
The Door Lounge
The Duplex
East River
85 West Cocktail Bar
11th Street Bar
Emerald Pub
Esperanto
Eugene
Faces and Names
58
55 Bar
Figa
Finnegan's Wake
Freddy's Bar & Backroom
Galapagos Artspace
The George Keeley
Gonzalez y Gonzalez
Good World Bar & Grill
Grand Central
Grand Press
Groove
The Half King Bar
Hank's Saloon
Harrison's Tavern
Helen's
Hiro Lounge (@ the Maritime
 Hotel)
ICU Bar
Ideya
iO
Iridium
Irving Plaza
Jacques-imo's NYC
The Jazz Gallery
Jezebel
Joe's Pub
Jules Café
Kavehaz
Kenny's Castaways
Kingsland Tavern
Knickerbocker Bar and Grill
The Knitting Factory
La Churrascaria Plataforma
 Tribeca

Laila Lounge
Lakeside Lounge
Lava Gina
Lion's Den
Lips
Lit Lounge
The Living Room
Louis 649
Low Bar
LQ
The Lucky Cat
Lucy Latin Kitchen
Lunasa
Lyric Lounge
M Shanghai Bistro & Den
Magnetic Field
Makor
Manitoba's
Maracas
Marie's Crisis Café
Marion's Continental
Maroon's
Marty O'Brien's
Matchless
Merchants NY
The Mercury Lounge
Metropolitan Café
Mica 587
Micky's Blue Room
MJ Armstrong's
Monkey Bar
The Monster
Moonshine
Moto
Mr. Dennehy's
ñ
Negril Village
Newgate Bar & Grill
Niagara/Lei Bar
Nightingale Lounge
No Malice Palace
Northsix
Nuyorican Poets Café
The Oak Room (@ Algonquin
 Hotel)
O'Flaherty's Ale House

O'Flanagan's
Oliva
One and One
Opal Bar
Orchid
Orchid Lounge
Otto's Shrunken Head
Paddy Reilly's
Parkside Lounge
The Patio
Pegasus
Perdition
Pete's Candy Store
Philip Marie
Pianos
The Pinch Bar & Grill
Porters
The Pourhouse
Pressure
Prohibition
Puppets Jazz Bar
Pyramid
Raga
Rare
Red Lion
Rock Star Bar
Rockwood Music Hall
Rocky Sullivan's
Rodeo Bar
Rose's Turn
Rothko
Rue B
The Rum House (@ the
 Edison Hotel)
Russian Samovar
The Russian Vodka Room
S.O.B.'s
Sandia
Sapa
Satalla
Satelite
Scenic
Scopa
Second on Second
Session 73
Show

Siberia
Sidewalk Café
Sin Sin
Sin-e
6s and 8s
The Slipper Room
Small's
Smiths
Smithwicks
Snitch
Southpaw
Stain
Starlight Bar & Lounge
Stir
Strata
Sugar Bar
Swing 46
Taboon
Tavern on the Green
Tea Lounge
Teddy's Bar & Grill
The Telephone Bar & Grill
Terra Blues
Thady Con's
Three of Cups
Tir Na Nog
Tommy's Tavern
Tonic
Trash
The Triad
Trio
200 Fifth
Union Pool
Varjak
Vasmay Lounge
The View (@ the Marriott
  Marquis)
Village Speakeasy Pub
The Village Underground
Village Vanguard
Vintage
The Warsaw
Webster Hall
The White Rabbit
Wild Spirits
World Bar

XL
Xth Avenue Lounge
Xunta
Ye Olde Tripple Inn
Zinc Bar

Neighborhood Spots
The Abbey
Ace of Clubs
Acme Bar & Grill
Alamo
Aleo Restaurant & Bar
All State Café
Alligator Lounge
Amber
Amsterdam Billiards Club
Angry Wade's
Annie Moore's
Anotheroom
Antarctica
Anyway Café
Apartment 138
Archer's
Arlene's Grocery
Aroma
Arriba Arriba Mexican
  Restaurant
Art Bar
Arthur's Tavern
Artland
Asia Roma
Auction House
Automatic Slims
Avenue A Sushi
B.B. King's Blues Club & Grill
B61 @ Alma
The Back Fence
Back Page
Baggot Inn
Bailey's Corner Pub
Baker Street
Banshee Pub
Bar @ Etats-Unis
Bar 288 (aka Tom & Jerry's)
Bar 4
Bar 515

Bar Bleu @ Café Deville
Bar East
Bar Minnow
Bar None
Bar on A (BOA)
Bar Reis
Bar Toto
Bar XII
Baraza
Barbes
BarBossa
Barbuto
Barcade
The Barclay Bar and Grill (@
  Intercontinental Barclay)
Bar-Coastal
Barfly
Barmarche
Barracuda
Barramundi
Barrio Chino
Barrow Street Ale House
Barrymore's
Basso Est
Beast
Beauty Bar
Becky's
The Beekman
Beer Bar @ Café Centro
Belly
Biddy Early's
Biddy's Pub
Big Bar
The Big Cheech
Big City Bar & Grill
Big Easy
Bill's Gay Nineties
The Bitter End
Black & White
The Black Bear Lodge
Black Betty
Black Finn
Black Sheep
Blaggard's Pub (35th St.)
Blaggard's Pub (39th St.)
Blarney Rock

Blind Tiger Ale House
Blondies
Blu Lounge
The Blue Mill Tavern
The Blue Room
Blue Smoke
Boat
bOb
Boca Chica
Bond 45
Bongo
Boom
Boots & Saaddle
Boss Tweed's Saloon
Boston (212) Café
Bouche Bar
Bowlmor Lanes
Boxcar Lounge
Boxer's
Brady's Bar
Brady's Tavern
Brandy's Piano Bar
Brass Monkey
The Brazen Head
Bridge Café
Broadway Bar & Terrace (@ the Novotel Hotel)
Brooklyn Ale House
Brooklyn Brewery
Brooklyn Inn
Brother Jimmy's
Brother Jimmy's (2nd Ave.)
Brother Jimmy's BBQ
Bua
Bull Moose Saloon
Bull Run
Bull's Head Tavern
Burp Castle
Bushwick Country Club
Buster's Garage
Buttermilk
Buzz Bar @ Pershing Square
Cabin
Café del Bar
Café Deville
Café Gitane

Café Luxembourg
Café Ma
Café Noir
Café Ronda
Café Wha?
The Cajun
CakeShop
Caliban
Caliente Cab Co.
Caliente Cab Company
Camaje
Cantinella
Canyon Road
Capone's
Carriage House
Casimir
Cassis
Cattyshack
Cecil's Bar (@ the Crowne Plaza Hotel)
Cedar Tavern
Cellar Bar & Café
Central Bar
Chai Home Kitchen
Channel 4
Charley O's Skybox American Bar and Grill
Chelsea Bistro & Bar
Chelsea Brewing Company
Chi Chiz
Chibi's Bar
Chibitini
Chikalicious
Chorus Karaoke
Chubo
Chumley's
Clancy's
Clem's
Cloister Café
The C-Note
Cody's Bar and Grill
The Collins Bar
Company
Connie O's
Connolly's 45th St.
Connolly's 47th St.

Copper Door Tavern
Coppersmith's
Cornelia St. Café
Corner Bistro
Counter
Cowgirl
Cozy Café
Crispo
Crossroads
Croxley Ales
Crudo
Cuba
Cuba Café
Cupping Room Café
d.b.a.
D.J. Reynolds
D.O.C. Wine Bar
Daddy-O
Daddy's
The Darkroom
David Copperfield's House of Beer
Day O
Deacon Brodie's
The Dead Poet
The Delancey
The Delta Grill
Dempsey's pub
Desmond's Tavern
Detour
Dewey's Flatiron
Diner
The Ding Dong Lounge
Dive 75
The Dive Bar
Doc Watson's
Donald Sacks
Dorian's
Dorrian's Red Hand
Druids
DT/UT
Dublin 6
Due South
The Dugout
Duke's
The Duplex

The Eagle
Eamonn's
Ear Inn
Earl's
East of Eighth
East River
East Side Steak & Ale
Eatery/Bar E
Edessa
Edward's
Eight Mile Creek
El Cantinero
El Faro
El Parador Café
El Poblano Sports Grill
El Quijote
El Rio Grande
Elaine's
The Elephant
11th Street Bar
Emerald Inn
Emerald Pub
Enid's
Epstein's Bar
Esperanto
ESPN Zone
Essex Restaurant
Euzkadi
Faces and Names
Failte Irish Whiskey Bar
The Falls
Fanelli's
Fat Black Pussycat
Fiddlesticks
Film Center Café
Finnegan's Wake
Fiona's
Firehouse
Fish
Fish Bar
Fitzer's
Fitzgerald's Pub
Five Points
Flannery's Bar
Flight 151
Florio's Grill & Cigar Bar

Floyd, NY
Food Bar
The Four-Faced Liar
Fraunces Tavern
Freemans
French Roast
The Full Shilling
Funhouse
The Gael Pub
The Gaf
Garvey's
The Gate
Gatsby's Bar & Lounge
General Store
The George Keeley
Giggles
The Gin Mill
The Ginger Man
Ginger's
Girlsroom
Glady's Comedy Room
Gold Rush
Gonzalez y Gonzalez
Good World Bar & Grill
Gowanus Yacht Club
Grand Press
Grand Saloon
Great Jones Café
Great Lakes
Greenwich Brewing
  Company
Groove
The Hairy Monk
The Half King Bar
Hallo Berlin
The Hangar
The Hanger
Hanratty's
The Harrison
Harrison's Tavern
Harry Boland's Pub
Heartland Brewery Radio
  City
Heartland Brewery Union
  Square
Henrietta Hudson

Henry Street Ale House
Hi Fi
Hi-Life Bar and Grill
Hi-Life Restaurant & Lounge
The Hog Pit
The Hook & Ladder Pub
Hookah Café
Hooters
Hop Devil Grill
Horus Café
House of Brews
Hudson Place
Hunter's American Bar & Grill
Hurley's Saloon
Hurricane Hopeful
i Restaurant & Lounge
ICU Bar
Iguana
Il Cortile
Il Posto Accanto
In Vino
'ino
'inoteca
iO
Iona
Irish Pub
The Irish Punt
Irish Rogue
Irving Plaza
i-Shebeen Madiba
Izakaya Izu
J.D.'s
J.P. Warde's Saloon
Jack's Restaurant and Bar
Jacques-imo's NYC
Jake's Dilemma
Jake's Saloon
Jameson's
Japas
Jekyll & Hyde
Jeremy's Ale House
Jerry's
Jim Brady's
Jimmy Walker's
Joey's
Joshua Tree

Joshua Tree
Josie Wood's Pub
JP Mustard
Julep
Julius
Junno's
Kabin
Kate Kearney's Pub and Grill
Kennedy's
Kenny's Castaways
Kettle of Fish
Kevin St. James
KGB Bar
Kili
Killarney Rose
Kin Khao
King Size
King's Head Tavern
Kingsland Tavern
Kinsale Tavern
Kitchen & Cocktails
The Knitting Factory
La Caverna
La Linea
Laila Lounge
Lakeside Lounge
L'Angolo Café
Larry Lawrence
Last Exit
Latitude
Leisure Time Bowl
Levee
The Library
Life Café
Light (East Village)
Lilly Coogan's
Lincoln Park Bar & Grill
Lion's Den
Live Bait
The Living Room
Lobo
Local 138
Local Café East
Local West
Lodge
Loki Lounge

Lolita
Long Tan
Loreley
Los Dos Molinos
Lotus Lounge
Louis 649
Low Bar
Lucien
The Lucky Cat
Lucky Jack's
LuLu Lounge
Luna Park
Lunasa
MacMenamin's Irish Pub
Mad River Bar & Grille
Maggie's Place
The Magician
Magnetic Field
Maker's
Makor
Manchester Pub
Mancora
Maracas
Marie's Crisis Café
The Mark Bar
Marlow and Sons
Maroon's
Martell's
Martignetti Liquors
Marty O'Brien's
Matchless
Matt's Grill
McAnns Irish Pub
McCormack's
McCoy's
McFadden's Saloon
McGee's
McKeown's
McSwiggan's
MeBar (@ the La Quinta Inn)
Mehanata
Mekong
Mercadito
Mercantile Grill
Mercury Bar
Mercury Bar & Grill

The Mercury Lounge
Merrion Square
Metro 53
Metropolitan
Metropolitan Café
Mexican Radio
Mica 587
Micky's Blue Room
Milady's Bar & Restaurant
Miracle Bar & Grill
Miracle Grill
MJ Armstrong's
Moe's
Mo's Caribbean Bar and
  Mexican Grille
Mosto Osteria
Moto
Mr. Biggs
Mr. Dennehy's
Mugs Ale House
Muldoon's
Mulligan's Pub
Mundial
Murphy's Bar and Grill
Murphy's Law Bar &
  Restaurant
Mustang Grill
Mustang Harry's
Mustang Sally's
ñ
Nathan Hale's
Neary's
Negril
Negril Village
Nevada Smith's
Newgate Bar & Grill
Niagara/Lei Bar
Nice Guy Eddie's
Ninth Avenue Saloon
Nisos
No Malice Palace
Nolita House
Northsix
Nuyorican Poets Café
O'Connor's
Odessa

O'Flaherty's Ale House
O'Flanagan's
O'Hanlon's
O'Hara's
Old Town Bar & Restaurant
Oldcastle Pub and
  Restaurant
Oliva
One and One
O'Neals'
O'Neill's
Onieal's Grand Street
Opal Bar
Orchard Bar
Orchid
O'Reilly's Pub & Restaurant
O'Reilly's Townhouse Tavern
Outpost Lounge
P.D. O'Hurley's
P.J. Clarke's
P.J. Kelly's
Paddy Reilly's
Palace Café Inc. (aka
  Goodman's)
Palmiras
Pangea
Panorama Café
Park Avenue Country Club
Park Bar
Park Slope Ale House
The Parlour
Parnell's Pub
The Patio
Patrick Conway's Pub
Patrick Kavanagh's
Pearl Oyster Bar
The Pencil Factory
Pequena
Perdition
Peter Dillon's
Peter's Bar & Restaurant
Pete's Candy Store
Pete's Tavern
Petrosino
Phebe's Tavern & Grill
Philip Marie

Phoenix
Phoenix Park
Pianos
Pieces
Pig N Whistle
The Pinch Bar & Grill
Pink Pony Café
Piola
The Place
Planet Rose
Planet Thailand
Plantain
Playwright Tavern
The Porch Bar
The Pourhouse
Press 195
Proof
Puck Fair
Puppets Jazz Bar
Q Lounge & Billiards
Quhnia
Quigley's
R Bar
Raccoon Lodge
Radio Perfecto
Rain Lounge
Rare
Rathbone's
Rawhide
Reade Street Pub and
  Kitchen
Red and Black
Red Lion
Red Sky
Redd's Tavern
Reif's Tavern
Remedy Bar & Grill
Remote Lounge
Reservoir
Resto Leon
Revival
Riviera Café & Sports Bar
Robert Emmett's
Robin des Bois (aka
  Sherwood Café)
Rockwood Music Hall

Rocky Sullivan's
Rodeo Bar
Rolf's
Rooftop Bar (@ Hotel Metro)
Rope
Rose's Turn
Route 85a
Royal Oak
Rubyfruit Bar & Grill
Ruby's Tap House
Rue B
Rufus
The Rum House (@ the
  Edison Hotel)
The Russian Vodka Room
Ryan Maguire's Ale House
Ryan's Daughter
Ryans Irish Pub
Ryan's Sports Bar & Grill
Sake Bar Satsko
Saloon
Salt Bar
San Marcos
Santa Fe
Satelite
Scenic
Scratcher
Scruffy Duffy's
Seaport Café
Second on Second
Senor Swanky's
Session 73
17 MurrayShades of Green
Ship of Fools
Shore
Sidewalk Café
Sin-e
The SkinNY
Slainte
Slane
The Slaughtered Lamb
Small's
Smiths
Smithwicks
Smoked

New Spots

Cake Shop
Chemist Club, The
Climax
Copper Chimney
Double Seven
Duff's
East Side Company Bar
El Poblano Sports Grill
Frederick's Madison
Garden of Ono
Groovedeck
Gyu-Kaku
Home
Juniper Suite
King Size
Kitchen & Cocktails
Koi
La Cave
Latitude
Light (East Village)
Little Branch
Local West
Ludo
Maya Lounge
MeBar
Movida
Naima
Opus 22
Palais Royale
Park Blue
Pinch Bar & Grill, The
Piola
Prey Bar & Lounge
PS 450
Ribot
Rock Candy
Salon
Scenic
Slane
Sly
Standings
Stanton Social, The
Stay
Stone Creek
Stout NYC
Table XII

Tapeo 29
Tre Dici
Triumph Room
Turquoise Seafood
  Restaurant
Underground
Uva
Vapor
Vertigo Bar & Restaurant
Winebar

Older Scene (Over 30 Crowd)

Acqua
Ada
Aleo Restaurant & Bar
All State Café
Amuse
Angelo & Maxie's
Aquagrill
Archer's
Arthur's Tavern
Asia de Cuba
Atrium Lounge
Auction House
B.B. King's Blues Club & Grill
Baggot Inn
Bailey's Corner Pub
Balthazar
BAMcafé
Bar Americain
Bar Bleu @ Café Deville
Bar 89
Bar Minnow
Bar Seine (@ the Hôtel Plaza
  Athénée)
Bar 288
Barbes
The Barclay Bar and Grill
Barramundi
Barrymore's Restaurant
Basso Est
Bayard's Blue Bar
The Beekman
Bemelmans Bar (@ the
  Carlyle)

Beppe
Bice
Biddy's Pub
Bill's Gay Nineties
Biltmore Room
Birdland
Black Duck
Black Sheep
Blaggard's Pub (35th St.)
Blaggard's Pub (39th St.)
Blarney Cove
Blarney Stone
Blondies
Blue Lady Lounge (@
  Shelly's)
The Blue Mahoe
Blue Note
Bolo
Bongo
Boots
Brady's Tavern
Brandy Library
Brasserie 8 1/2
The Brazen Head
Brewsky's
Bridge Café
Brite Bar
Broadway Lounge
Brooklyn Brewery
Bryant Park Grill
The Bull and Bear
Bull Run
Buzz Bar @ Pershing Square
Café Carlyle (@ the Carlyle)
Café Luxembourg
Café Pierre (@ the Pierre
  Hotel)
Canapa
Candela
Cantinella
The Carnegie Club
Caroline's
The Carriage Inn
Casimir
Cecil's Bar
Cedar Tavern

'Cesca
Channel 4
Charley O's Skybox
The Charleston
Charlotte (@ the Millennium Broadway Hotel)
Chelsea Bistro and Bar
Chelsea Brewing Company
Chikalicious
Cibar
Cipriani's
The City Grill
City Hall
Clancy's
Cleopatra's Needle
Cloister Café
Club Macanudo
Club Shelter
Cody's Bar and Grill
Coldwaters
Comedy Village
Connie O's
Connolly's 47th St.
Craftbar
Crispo
Cru
Cub Room
Cupping Room Café
d.b.a.
D.J. Reynolds
David Copperfield's House of Beer
Deacon Brodie's
The Delta Grill
Django
Docks Oyster Bar
Dorian's
Driftwood Inn
Druids
Dublin 6
Due South
The Dugout
The Duplex
Dylan Prime
Eamonn's
The Eagle

Ear Inn
East of Eighth
Eight of Clubs
El Quijote
Elaine's
Eleven Madison Park
11th Street Bar
Emerald Inn
The Emerald Pub
Farrell's Bar and Grill
Fat Black Pussycat
5757 (@ the Four Seasons)
Figa
Finnegan's Wake
Fino
Fiona's
Firebird
Firehouse
5 Ninth
Flatiron Lounge
Flute
1492 Food
40/40 Club
Frank's 410
Fraunces Tavern
French Roast
The Front Bar (@ the Four Seasons)
Gabriel's
The Gallery (@ SoHo Grand)
The Garden
The Garden of Ono
Giggles
The Girl from Ipanema
Gotham Bar & Grill
Gramercy Tavern
Grand Bar & Lounge (@ SoHo Grand)
Grand Central
Grassroots Tavern
Hacienda de Argentina
The Hangar
Hank's Saloon
Hanratty's
Harbour Lights
Hard Rock Café

Harrison's Tavern
Harry Boland's Pub
Helen's
Hi-Life Bar and Grill
Hi-Life Restaurant & Lounge
Holiday Cocktail Lounge
Hooligan's
Hudson Bar & Books
Hudson Place
Hunter's American Bar & Grill
Hurley's Saloon
Icon (@ W New York - The Court)
Iguana
'ino
'inoteca
iO
Iridium
Irish Pub
Jackie's Fifth Amendment
Jack's Restaurant and Bar
Jameson's
Jazz Gallery
Jezebel
Jimmy Walker's
Johnney's Fish Grill
Journey's Lounge
JP Warde's
Julian's
Julius
Kaña
Kasadela
Katen Sushi Bar
Kennedy's
Kettle of Fish
Kiev East
King Cole Bar (@ the St. Regis Hotel)
Kinsale Tavern
Knickerbocker
Kyma
La Belle Epoque
La Tour
Lexington Bar & Books
Library (@ the Paramount

Hotel)
The Library (@ the Regency)
Library Bar (@ the Hudson
  Hotel)
Life Café
Lips
Los Dos Molinos
LQ
Lupa
Lure Fishbar
Malachy's
Manchester Pub
Mancora
Manhattan Grille
Maracas
Marie's Crisis Café
Marion's Continental
Mark's Bar (@ the Mark
  Hotel)
Marty O'Brien's
Matt's Grill
Maya Lounge
McCarthy's Bar & Grill
McCormack's
McKenna's Pub
McSorley's Old Ale House
Merc Bar
The Mermaid Inn
Merrion Square
Mesa Grill
Metropolitan Café
Mickey Mantle's
Milady's Bar & Restaurant
Mini-Bar in the District (@
  the Muse Hotel)
Miracle Bar &Grill
MOBar (@ the Mandarin
  Oriental Hotel)
Mona's
The Monster
Montero's Bar and Grill
Mooney's Pub
Moonshine
Morrell Wine Bar & Café
Mulberry Street Bar
Mulligan's Pub

Murphy's Bar and Grill
Mustang Harry's
Mustang Sally's
Nathan Hale's
Neary's
Negril
North West Restaurant and
  Lounge
Nowhere Bar
O.W.
O'Connor's
O'Flanagan's Old Ale House
O'Hanlon's
O'Hara's
O'Reilly's Pub & Restaurant
The Oak Room
Oasis
Oldcastle Pub and
  Restaurant
Opia
The Otheroom
P & G Café
P.D. O'Hurley's
P.J. Clarke's
Paladar
Palmiras
Panorama Café
Paradou
Paris Commune
Park Blue
Park Slope Ale House
The Parlour
Parnell's Pub
Pasha
Pastis
Patrick Kavanagh's
The Patriot Saloon
Peculier Pub
Pegasus
Peter Dillon's
Peter's Restaurant and Bar
Petrosino
Pigalle
PineTree Lodge
Planet Hollywood
Plate

Playwright Tavern
Porcupine
Porters
Pravda
Prime 54 Lounge
Private Park (@ the Hudson
  Hotel)
Public
Punch
Q56 Restaurant and
  Cocktails
Quigley's
Raccoon Lodge
Raga
Rawhide
Reade Street Pub and
  Kitchen
The Red Cat
Rise (@ the Ritz-Carlton)
Robert Emmett's
Rock Star Bar
Rolf's
Romi Restaurant & Lounge
Rose Mary's Greenpoint
  Tavern
Rose's Turn
Ruby Foos
Ruby's Tap House
The Rum House
Russian Samovar
Saga
17 Home
17 Murray
Shore
Sidecar
Slane
Smith & Wollensky
Smith's Bar and Restaurant
Snapper Creek
Spike Hill Bar & Grill
The Spotted Pig
Spuyten Duyvil
St. Dymphna's
St. Maggie's Café
The Stanton Social
Stonewall

Strip House
Subway Inn
Sugar Bar
Sweet Ups
Swing 46
Tacocina
Taj
Tamarind
Tao
Taste
Tavern on First
Tavern on Jane
Tavern on the Green
Tea Lounge
Teddy's Bar & Grill
The Telephone Bar and Grill
Tennessee Mountain
Terra Blues
Thom Bar (@ 60 Thompson)
Thomas Beisl
Three of Cups
Timboo's
Tin Lizzie's
Tir Na Nog
Toad Hall
Tool Box
The Townhouse
Trattoria Dopo Teatro
Triumph Room
Tupelo Grill
Turks & Frogs
200 Fifth
Twins
Two Boots (Brooklyn)
Ty's
Vice Versa
The View
Vig Bar
Village 247
Village Pub
Village Speakeasy Pub
Village Vanguard
Villard Bar & Lounge (@ the New York Palace Hotel)
Vince & Eddie's
Waikiki Wally's

Walker's
Waterfront Ale House
WCOU Radio (aka Tile Bar)
Westside Brewing Co.
The Whiskey
Whiskey Blue
Whiskey Park
White Horse Tavern
Wild Spirits
Willy's Bar & Grill
Wine Bar
Wolfgang's Steakhouse
WXOU Radio Bar
XR Bar
Xth Avenue Lounge
Ye Olde Tripple Inn
Zabloski's
Zebulon
Zoe

Outdoor Space

A 60 (@ 60 Thompson)
Acqua
Agave
AIX
Aleo Restaurant & Bar
Andavi
Anotheroom
Apartment 138
Aquagrill
Aroma
Arriba Arriba Mexican Restaurant
Arté
AVA Lounge (@ Dream Hotel)
Avalon
B Bar (aka Bowery Bar)
B1 Drink Club
Bar Minnow
Bar Reis
Bar Toto
Bar XII
Barbuto
Barcade
Barfly
Beast

Beer Bar @ Café Centro
Belmont Lounge
Bice
Big City Bar & Grill
Black Betty
Black Duck (@ Park South Hotel)
Bliss Bar and Lounge
Blu Lounge
The Boathouse
Boogaloo
Boss Tweed's Saloon
Bottino
Bourbon Street
Boutique del Vino
Boxcar Lounge
Boxer's
Brandy Library
Brass Monkey
The Brazen Head
Bread Bar @ Tabla
Broadway Bar & Terrace (@ the Novotel Hotel)
Brooklyn Social Club
Brother Jimmy's
Bryant Park Grill
Bua
Bull McCabe's
Burp Castle
Bushwick Country Club
Buster's Garage
Cabana
Cabanas (@ the Maritime Hotel)
Café Deville
Café Gitane
Café Ronda
Caliban
Caliente Cab Co.
Caliente Cab Company
Camaje
Candela
The Cantor Roof Garden (@ the Met)
Capone's
Cattyshack

Caviar and Banana Braserio Restaurant	Eight of Clubs	Hooters
Cellar Bar & Café	El Cantinero	Horus Café
Chelsea Bistro & Bar	El Rey Del Sol	Hudson Bar & Books
Chelsea Brewing Company	Esperanto	Hudson Place
Chez Oskar	Excelsior	Hurley's Saloon
China Club	Exit	Hurricane Hopeful
Cibar	Fiddlesticks	I Tre Merli
Cielo	Finnegan's Wake	ICON (@ the W Hotel - The Court)
Cipriani's	Firehouse	ICU Bar
Citrus Bar & Grill	5 ninth	International Bar
City Hall	Five Points	iO
Cloister Café	The Four-Faced Liar	Iona
Club Shelter	1492 Food	i-Shebeen Madiba
Coogan's Parrot Bay	44&X	IXTA
Cowgirl	French Roast	Jake's Dilemma
Cozy Café	Fubar	Jake's Saloon
Crispo	Fuelray	Jekyll & Hyde
Croxley Ales	Funhouse	Jeremy's Ale House
Crudo	Fusion	Joe's Pub
d.b.a.	Fuzion on A	Joey's
D.O.C. Wine Bar	The Gallery (@ the Soho Grand)	Joshua Tree
Daddy's	The Garden of Ono	Joya
David Copperfield's House of Beer	Gardens Bar	JP Mustard
The Delancey	The Gate	Julep
Diner	The Gin Mill	Jules Café
Dip	Ginger's	Julian's
'disiac Lounge	Glass	Kanvas
Divine Bar East	Good World Bar & Grill	Kitchen & Cocktails
Divine Bar West	Gowanus Yacht Club	Kitchen 82
Django	Grand Bar and Lounge (@ the Soho Grand)	La Bottega (@ the Maritime Hotel)
Doc Watson's	Grand Central	Laila Lounge
Dos Caminos	Grand Press	Larry Lawrence
Druids	Groovedeck	Last Exit
Duff's	Grotta Azzurra	Latitude
Duke's	Grotto	Le Refuge
DuMont	Guastavino's	Les Halles
The Duplex	The Half King Bar	Life Café
The Eagle	Half Wine Bar	Lilly Coogan's
Earl's	Harbour Lights	Local Café East
East of Eighth	The Harrison	Local West
East River	Heartland Brewery Union Square	Lodge
Eatery/Bar E	Hi-Life Bar and Grill	Loki Lounge
Edward's	The Hook & Ladder Pub	Loreley
Eight Mile Creek		Luca Lounge

The Lucky Cat
Luna Park
Lunasa
Lupa
Lyric Lounge
Macelleria
MacMenamin's Irish Pub
Madame X
Mannahatta
The Mark Bar
Markt
Marlow and Sons
Marseille
Martell's
McKenna's Pub
MeBar (@ the La Quinta Inn)
Meet
Mercadito
Merchants
Merchants NY
Mercury Bar & Grill
The Mermaid Inn
Metropolitan
Metropolitan Café
Mica 587
Mickey Mantle's
Miracle Grill
Moda
Moonshine
Morrell Wine Bar & Café
Mr. Biggs
Mr. Dennehy's
Muldoon's
Mundial
Mustang Grill
Newgate Bar & Grill
No Malice Palace
North West Restaurant &
  Lounge
O.W.
O'Flaherty's Ale House
One
One 91
One and One
Ono
Outpost Lounge

Pacific Grill
Pangea
Panorama Café
Paradou
Park Slope Ale House
The Park
Parnell's Pub
Pasha
Pastis
The Patio
The Pencil Factory
The Pen-Top Bar & Terrace
  (@ the Peninsula Hotel)
Pete's Candy Store
Pete's Tavern
Philip Marie
The Place
Plunge (@ Hotel Gansevoort)
The Porch Bar
Porcupine
Porters
Posh
Press 195
Private Park (@ the Hudson
  Hotel)
Proseccheria
Public
Punch and Judy's
Quigley's
Radio Perfecto
Rain Lounge
Rancho Café
Rare View (@ the
  Shelbourne Murray Hill
  Hotel)
Rathbone's
Red and Black
Red Sky
Redd's Tavern
Redemption
Reif's Tavern
Relish
Republic
Resto Leon
Revival
Rhone

Ribot
Riviera Café & Sports Bar
Robin des Bois (aka
  Sherwood Café)
Rock Star Bar
Rooftop Bar (@ Hotel Metro)
Rope
Ruby Lounge
Rudy's Bar and Grill
Rue B
Ryans Irish Pub
Sake Bar Satsko
Salon
Sambuca
San Marcos
Savalas
Seaport Café
Senor Swanky's
17 Home
Sidewalk Café
Slate Plus
The Slaughtered Lamb
Sly
Smithwicks
Social Bar and
  Lounge/Fusion at Social
Soda Bar
SoFo
Sortie
SouthWest NY
Spuyten Duyvil
St. Dymphna's
St. Marks 88
Stain
Steak Frites
Stonehome Wine Bar
The Sunburnt Cow
Supercore
Supreme Trading
Sushi Generation
Sushi Samba 7
Sutton Place
Sweet & Vicious
T.G. Whitney's
Tavern on Dean
Tavern on First

Tavern on the Green
Teddy's Bar & Grill
Tortilla Flats
Total Wine Bar
Tupelo Grill
Underground
Union Pool
Union Square Coffee Shop
Uptown Restaurant &
  Lounge
Uva
Vera
Vera Cruz
ViceVersa
Village Speakeasy Pub
Vince & Eddie's
Vintage
Waterloo Tavern
Westside Brewing Co.
Whiskey River
White Horse Tavern
Willy's Bar & Grill
Winebar
Wogie's
Yaffa Café
The Yard (@ The Soho
  Grand)
Yuca Bar & Restaurant
Zanzibar
Zum Schneider Bavarian
  Beer House

Pick-up Spots (Singles Scene)

Agozar
Alphabet Lounge
Angelo & Maxie's
APT
Art Bar
Artland
Asia de Cuba
Atrium Lounge
Aubette
Automatic Slims
AVA Lounge (@ the Dream
  Hotel)

Avenue A Sushi
B1 Drink Club
B61 @ Alma
Banshee Pub
Bar 4
Bar 89
Bar Bleu @ Café Deville
Bar East
Bar Nine
Bar None
Bar Reis
Bar XII
Bar Veloce
Baraza
Barbuto
Barrage
Beast
Beauty Bar
Becky's
Beer Bar @ Café Centro
Believe Lounge
Belmont Lounge
Bembe
Big Easy
Big 6 Bar and Lounge
The Black Bear Lodge
Black Betty
Black Door
Blarney Cove
Blarney Stone
Blind Tiger Ale House
Bliss Bar and Lounge
Blue & Gold Tavern
BLVD
bOb
Bogart's
Boogaloo
Boots
Bottino
Bounce
Bowlmor Lanes
Boxcar Lounge
Boysroom
Branch
Brandy Library
Brite Bar

Brother Jimmy's
B-Side
Bubble Lounge
Bungalow 8
Bushwick Country Club
Buttermilk
Cabanas (@ the Maritime
  Hotel)
Cain
Canyon Road
The Cellar Bar
Charley O's Skybox
Chelsea Brewing Company
Cherry Tavern
Chi Chiz
China Club
Church Lounge
Cibar
Cielo
Circa Tabac
Cleopatra's Needle
Climax
Cloister Café
Club Macanudo
Club Shelter
Clubhouse
The Cock
The Cocktail Room
The Collins Bar
Connolly's 47th St.
Continental
Copacabana
Coppersmith's
Cosmo
Coyote Ugly
Craftbar
Crash Mansion
Crobar
The Cutting Room
d.b.a.
Daddy's
The Darkroom
The Delancey
Dewey's Flatiron
Dick's Bar
Dip

Discotheque
'disiac Lounge
Dive 75
Divine Bar East
Divine Bar West
Docks Oyster Bar
Dorrian's Red Hand
Double Down
Double Happiness
Dragonfly
Dublin 6
The Dugout
Duke's
The Duplex
Dylan Prime
The Eagle
East of Eighth
Edessa
Eight of Clubs
Elmo
Eugene
Excelsior
Fat Black Pussycat
58
Finnerty's
Flatiron Lounge
Flow
Flute Gramercy
Food Bar
420 Bar and Lounge
40/40 Club
Frank's Cocktail Lounge
Fubar
G Lounge
The Gallery (@ SoHo Grand)
The Garden of Ono
Garvey's
Gaslight Lounge
The Gate
Giggles
Gin Mill
The Ginger Man
The Girl from Ipanema
Girlsroom
Grand Bar & Lounge (@
 SoHo Grand)

Great Lakes
Groove
Gypsy Tea
The Hangar
Happy Ending
Heartland Brewery (Union
 Square)
Heaven
Henrietta Hudson
Hi-Fi
Hi-Life Restaurant & Lounge
Hiro Lounge
Home
The Hook & Ladder Pub
Hue
Iguana
Ikon
Ini Ani
iO
IXTA
Jack's Restaurant and Bar
Jane
Japas
Jean-Luc
Joshua Tree
Julee
Julius
Kaña
Kanvas
Kate Kearney's Pub and Grill
Katen Sushi Bar
Kevin St. James
King Size
King's Head Tavern
Kingsland Tavern
La Cave
La Caverna
La Churrascaria Plataforma
 (Tribeca)
La Linea
Lakeside Lounge
Larry Lawrence
Lava Gina
Les Halles
Level V
Lexington Bar & Books

Libation
The Library
Light
Lincoln Park Bar & Grill
Lion's Den
Live Bait
Local 138
Lolita
L'Orange Bleue
Lotus
LQ
Luca Lounge
Lucien
The Lucky Cat
Lucky 13 Saloon
Lucky Strike
M Bar
M Shanghai Bistro and Den
M1-5
Macelleria
Mad River
Madame X
Manitoba's
Mannahatta
Maracas
Markt
Marquee
Martell's
Maya Lounge
Meet
Merc Bar
Merchants NY
Mercury Bar
Mercury Bar & Grill
Metrazur
Metro 53
Metropolitan
Mica 587
Mica Bar & Lounge
Moe's
Monkey Temple
The Monster
Morgan's Bar
Mo's Caribbean Bar and
 Mexican Grille
Motor City

Movida	Pravda	Single Room Occupancy
Mustang Grill	Pressure	6s and 8s
NA	Prey	667 Bar Gallery Lounge
Naked Lunch	Private Park (@ the Hudson	Slate Plus
Negril Village	Hotel)	The Slide
Newgate Bar & Grill	Puck Fair	Sly
Ninth Avenue Saloon	Puppets Jazz Bar	Snitch
No Idea	Pyramid	Social Club
The No Malice Palace	Quench	Solas
Nowhere Bar	Quo	Spaghetti Western
O.W.	Raccoon Lodge	Spice Market
O'Flanagan's	Rare View	Spill
O'Hara's	Rathbone's	Splash
Off The Wagon	Rawhide	The Stanton Social
Old Town Bar & Restaurant	The Raven	Starfoods
Olives Restaurant	Red Bench	Starlight
One	Red Lion	Stay
169 Bar	Red Rock West	Still
Oneill's	Red Sky	Stir
Onieal's Grand Street	Relish	Stonewall
Onyx	Remote Lounge	Strata
Opal Bar	Remy Lounge	Suede
Opus 22	Rise (@ the Ritz-Carlton)	Sugar
Otto's Shrunken Head	Rock Candy	The Sullivan Room
The Park	Rooftop Bar (@ the Hotel	The Sunburnt Cow
Park Avalon	Metro)	Sushi Samba 7
Park Bar	The Room	Sutra
Park Blue	Rope	Sutton Place
Parlay	Rothko	Sway
Passerby	Route 85a	Sweet & Vicious
The Patriot Saloon	Roxy	T.G. Whitney's
Peculier Pub	Royal Oak	Table 50
Pegasus	Ruby Falls	Taj
People Lounge	Rue B	Tao
Perdition	Ryan's Daughter	Tavern on Dean
Peter Dillon's	Sasha's	Tea Lounge
Peter's Restaurant and Bar	Savalas	The Telephone Bar and Grill
Phoenix	Schiller's Liquor Bar	Therapy
Phoenix Park	Scopa	Third and Long
Pieces	Second Nature	The Thirsty Scholar
Planet Rose	Second on Second	13
Plunge	Select	13 Little Devils
PM	Session 73	Thom Bar (@ 60 Thompson)
Pop	Shadow	Tin Lizzie's
Pop Burger	Shalel Lounge	Tonic and the Met Lounge
Posh	Sin Sin	Tool Box

The Townhouse
Tracy J's Watering Hole
Tribe
Triumph Room
Turtle Bay
24-7 Bar & Lounge
Twist Lounge (@ the
  Ameritania Hotel)
212
200 Fifth
Ty's
Ulysses'
Uncle Ming's
Under the Volcano
Underbar
Union Pool
The Upper Deck
Uptown Lounge
Vegas
Verlaine
View Bar
Vig Bar
Village 247
Village Pub
Village Underground
Vintage
Virage
Waterloo
The Web
Webster Hall
Welcome to the Johnsons
Westside Tavern
The Whiskey
Whiskey Blue
White Rabbit
Windfall Lounge and Grill
The World Bar
Xicala
XL
Xth Avenue Lounge
Yello
Yogi's

Pool Table

The A&M Roadhouse
Abbey
Ace Bar
Alligator Lounge
American Spirits
American Trash
Amsterdam Billiards Club
Angry Wade's
Antarctica
Apartment 138
Artland
Balanza
Bar East
Bar None
Bar Reis
Barcade
Barfly
Barracuda
Barrow Street Ale House
Biddy Early's
Billy Mark's West
Blarney Stone
Bleecker Street Bar
Blue & Gold Tavern
The Blue Room
Boss Tweed's
Bourbon Street
Brady's
Brooklyn Ale House
Brooklyn Brewery
Brooklyn Inn
B-Side
B61 @ Alma
Bull McCabe's
Bull Moose Saloon
Bull's Head Tavern
The Call Box Lounge
Capone's
Carriage House
The Carriage Inn
Cherry Tavern
Connie O's
Dakota Roadhouse
Dave's Tavern
The Dead Poet

Dempsey's Pub
Dewey's Flatiron
Dick's Bar
Ding Dong Lounge
Dip
Doc Holliday's
Doc Watson's
The Dugout
Duke's
The Eagle
East River
The Edge
Eight of Clubs
Failte Irish Whiskey Bar
Fat Black Pussycat
40/40 Club
Fubar
The Garden
Gin Mill
Ginger's
The Girl from Ipanema
Gold Rush
Grand Central
The Hangar
Hank's Saloon
Henrietta Hudson
Hi-Fi
The Hog Pit
Hogs and Heifers
The Hook & Ladder Pub
Jake's Dilemma
Jarrod's Lounge
Jimmy Walker's
Joe's Bar
John Street Bar & Grill
Josie Wood's Pub
JP Warde's
Julee
Kabin
Kate Kearney's Pub and Grill
Kingsland Tavern
Kinsale Tavern
Laila
Latitude
Levee
Library Bar (@ the Hudson

Farrell's
Fiona's
Flannery's Bar
40/40 Club
Frank's Cocktail Lounge
The Gaf
The George Keeley
The Gin Mill
Grassroots Tavern
The Hairy Monk
Hard Rock Café
Harrison's Tavern
The Hook & Ladder Pub
Hooters
House of Brews
Hurley's Saloon
Irish Rogue
J.P. Warde's Saloon
Jackie's Fifth Amendment
Jake's Dilemma
Jake's Saloon
Jimmy Walker's
John Street Bar & Grill
Josie Wood's Pub
Kabin
Kate Kearney's Pub and Grill
Kennedy's
Kettle of Fish
Kevin St. James
Kingsland Tavern
Leisure Time Bowl
Lincoln Park Bar & Grill
Lucky Jack's
Lunasa
Maker's
Manchester Pub
Martell's
Matt's Grill
McCoy's
McGee's
McHale's
Mercury Bar
Mercury Bar & Grill
Merrion Square
Metro 53
Mica 587

Mickey Mantle's
MJ Armstrong's
Mooney's Pub
Mr. Biggs
Mugs Ale House
Mundial
Mustang Harry's
Mustang Sally's
Nathan Hale's
Nevada Smith's
Newgate Bar & Grill
Nice Guy Eddie's
O'Flanagan's
O'Hanlon's
O'Hara's
Old Town Bar & Restaurant
Oldcastle Pub and
 Restaurant
One and One
O'Neill's
Opal Bar
O'Reilly's Townhouse Tavern
P.D. O'Hurley's
P.J. Kelly's
Park Avenue Country Club
Park Slope Ale House
The Parlour
Pat O'Brien's
Patrick Kavanagh's
The Patriot Saloon
Perdition
Peter Dillon's
Peter's Bar & Restaurant
Phoenix Park
The Pinch Bar & Grill
Pioneer Bar and Restaurant
Planet Hollywood
Playwright Tavern
Port 41
Proof
Q Lounge & Billiards
Quigley's
Raccoon Lodge
Reservoir
Riviera Café & Sports Bar
Rose Mary's Greenpoint

Tavern
Ryan Maguire's Ale House
Ryan's Sports Bar & Grill
Scruffy Duffy's
7B
Social Bar and
 Lounge/Fusion at Social
St. Marks Ale House
Standings
Still
Stout NYC
Third and Long
Time Out
Tonic and the Met Lounge
Town Crier
Town Tavern
Tracy J's Watering Hole
Triple Crown
Turkey's Nest
Turtle Bay
200 Fifth
Underground
Village Speakeasy Pub
Village Tavern
Waterloo Tavern
Westside Brewing Co.
Whiskey River
White Horse Tavern

Swanky/Lounge
A 60 (@ 60 Thompson)
Absolutely 4th
Acqua
Ada
Aer
Agave
Agozar
AIX
Aja
Alfama
Alibi
Amarachi Lounge
Amuse
Andavi
Angelo & Maxie's
Angel's Share

Apple Restaurant & BomBar
APT
Aquagrill
Aquavit
Ara Wine Bar
Arté
Artisanal
Asia de Cuba
Asylum
Atrium Lounge
Aubette
AVA Lounge (@ Dream Hotel)
Avalon
Azaza
B Bar (aka Bowery Bar)
B1 Drink Club
Balthazar
BAMcafé
Bann
Bao 111
Bar 6
Bar 89
Bar 9
Bar Americain
Bar Below
Bar Seine (@ The Hôtel
  Plaza Athénée)
Bar Veloce Chelsea
Bar Veloce East Village
bar.vetro
Barbalùc
Barrage
Bayard's Blue Bar
Believe Lounge
Belmont Lounge
Bembe
Bemelmans Bar @ The
  Carlyle, A Rosewood Hotel
Beppe
Bette
Bice
Biltmore Room
BINY
Birdland
Bivio
Black Door

Black Duck (@ Park South
  Hotel)
Bliss Bar and Lounge
Blue Fin (@ the W Hotel-
  Times Square)
Blue Lady Lounge (@
  Shelly's)
The Blue Mahoe
Blue Note
BLVD
The Boathouse
Bogart's
Bolo
Bond Street Lounge
Boogaloo
Bottino
Bounce
Boutique del Vino
Branch
Brandy Library
Brasserie
Brasserie 8 1/2
Bread Bar @ Tabla
Brite Bar
Broadway Lounge (@ the
  Marriott Marquis)
Brooklyn Social Club
Bryant Park Grill
Bubble Lounge
Buddha Lounge
The Bull and Bear
Bungalow 8
Butter
Cabana
Cabanas (@ the Maritime
  Hotel)
Café Carlyle (@ the Carlyle)
Café Pierre (@ the Pierre
  Hotel)
Caféteria
Cain
Calle Ocho
The Campbell Apartment
Canal Room
Canapa
Candela

The Cantor Roof Garden (@
  the Met)
The Carnegie Club
Casa La Femme North
Caviar and Banana Braserio
  Restaurant
Cellar Bar (@ Bryant Park
  Hotel)
Cendrillon
''Cesca
Chance
Channel 4
Charlotte (@ Millenium
  Broadway Hotel)
The Chemist Club (@ the
  Dylan Hotel)
Cherry Lounge
Chez Oskar
China Club
Chow Bar
Church Lounge (@ TriBeCa
  Grand)
Cibar
Cielo
Cipriani's
Circa Tabac
Citrus Bar & Grill
The City Grill
City Hall
Cleopatra's Needle
Climax
Club Macanudo
Club Shelter
Clubhouse
Compass
Copacabana
Cosmo
Cotton
Craftbar
Crash Mansion
Crobar
Cru
Cub Room
Culture Club
The Cutting Room
Danube

Decibel
Deep
Dekk
Del Frisco's Double Eagle
  Steakhouse
Diner 24
Dip
Discotheque
'disiac Lounge
Diva
Divine Bar East
Divine Bar West
Django
Do Hwa
Docks Oyster Bar
The Door Lounge
Dos Caminos
Dos Caminos
Double Happiness
Double Seven
The Dove
Dragonfly
Dream Lounge (@ the
  Dream Hotel)
DuMont
Dusk
Duvet
Dylan Prime
Earth NYC
East Side Company Bar
85 West Cocktail Bar
Eleven Madison Park
Elmo
Employees Only
Eugene
Evelyn Lounge
Excelsior
Exit
Fashion 40
Fez North @ Time Café
Fiamma Osteria
58
5757 @ Four Seasons
Figa
Fino
Firebird

5 ninth
Flatiron Lounge
Flor de Sol
Florent
Flow
Flute (Flatiron)
Flute (Midtown)
Forbidden City
420 Bar and Lounge
1492 Food
44 (@ the Royalton Hotel)
44&X
40/40 Club
fourty six grand (46 Grand)
Frank's 410
Frederick's
Frederick's Madison
The Front Bar (@ the Four
  Seasons Hotel)
Fuelray
Fujiyama Mama
Fusion
Fuzion on A
G Lounge
G2
Gabriel's Wine Bar &
  Restaurant
Galapagos Artspace
Galaxy Global Eatery
Gallery Lounge (@ the
  Gershwin Hotel)
The Gallery (@ the Soho
  Grand)
The Garden of Ono
Gaslight Lounge
Geisha
Giorgio's of Gramercy
Glass
Glo
Good Restaurant
Gotham Bar & Grill
Gramercy Tavern
Grand Bar and Lounge (@
  the Soho Grand)
Green Room
Groovedeck

Grotta Azzurra
Grotto
Gstaad
Guastavino's
Gypsy Tea
Gyu-Kaku
Hacienda de Argentina
Half Wine Bar
Happy Ending
Harbour Lights
Hearth
Heaven
Hedeh
Helen's
Highline
Hiro Lounge (@ the Maritime
  Hotel)
Home
Houston's
Hudson Bar & Books
Hudson Bar (@ the Hudson
  Hotel)
Hue
I Tre Merli
ICON (@ the W Hotel - The
  Court)
Ideya
Il Buco
Indochine
Ini Ani
Inside
Iridium
Isis @ Union Bar
IXTA
Jane
Jarrod's Lounge
The Jazz Gallery
Jean-Luc
Jezebel
Joe's Pub
Johnney's Fish Grill
Journey's Lounge (@ the
  Essex Hotel)
Joya
Jules Café
Julian's

Juniper Suite
Justin's
K Lounge
Kaña
Kanvas
Karma
Kasadela
Katen Sushi Bar (@ the Marriott Marquis)
Katwalk
Kavehaz
Kemia
Keybar
Kimono Lounge
King Cole Bar
Kitchen 82
Knickerbocker Bar and Grill
Koi
Kori
Kos
Kush
Kyma
La Bottega (@ the Maritime Hotel)
La Cave
La Churrascaria Plataforma Tribeca
La Prima Donna
La Streghe
La Tour
Landmarc
Laugh Lounge NYC
Lava Gina
Le Refuge
Le Souk
Lea
Lemon
Les Halles
Les Halles Downtown
Level V
Lexington Bar & Books
Libation
Library (@ the Paramount Hotel)
Library Bar (@ the Hudson Hotel)

Light
Link
Lips
Little Branch
The Living Room(@ W Hotel - Times Square)
L'Orange Bleue
Lotus
LQ
Luca Lounge
Lucky Cheng's
Lucky Strike
Lucy Latin Kitchen
Ludo
Luke & Leroy
Lupa
Lure Fish Bar
M Bar
M Shanghai Bistro & Den
M1-5
Macelleria
Madame X
Made
Manhattan Grille
Manhattan Lounge
Mannahatta
Marion's Continental
Mark's Bar (@ the Mark Hotel)
Markt
Marquee
Marseille
Maya Lounge
Meet
Merc Bar
Mercer Kitchen
Merchants
Merchants NY
The Mermaid Inn
Mesa Grill
Metrazur
Metro Café & Wine Bar
Metropol
Mica 51
Milk & Honey
Mini-Bar in the District (@

the Muse Hotel)
Miss Williamsburg Portavia
Mission
Mixx Lounge
MOBar (@ Mandarin Oriental Hotel)
Moda
The Modern
Monkey Bar
Monkey Temple
Morgan's Bar (@ the Morgan Hotel)
Morrell Wine Bar & Café
Morrisey Park
Movida
NA
Naima
Naked Lunch
Nam
Nation Restaurant & Bar
Neogaea
Nerveana
Nightingale Lounge
Nooch
North West Restaurant & Lounge
O.W.
02 (@ the Time Hotel)
The Oak Room (@ Algonquin Hotel)
Oasis Bar (@ W New York)
Odea
Olives (@ W Hotel - Union Sq.)
One
One 91
Ono
Onyx
Opia
Opus 22
Ora
Orange Valve
Orchid Lounge
The Otheroom
Otto Enoteca Pizzeria
Ouest

Ouzerie @ En Plo
Pacific Grill
Paladar
Paradou
Paris Commune
Park Avalon
Park Blue
The Park
Parlay
Pasha
Passerby
Pastis
Peasant
Peep
Pegasus
Penang
The Pen-Top Bar & Terrace
  (@ the Peninsula Hotel)
People Lounge
Pigalle
Pioneer Bar and Restaurant
Pipa
Plan B
Plunge (@ Hotel Gansevoort)
PM
Pop
Pop Burger Lounge
Porcupine
Porters
Posh
Pravda
Pressure
Prey
Prime 54 Lounge (@ Hotel
  Rihga)
Private Park (@ the Hudson
  Hotel)
Prohibition
Proseccheria
PS 450
Public
Punch
Punch and Judy's
Q56 Restaurant and
  Cocktails
Quench

Quo
Raga
Rain
Rancho Café
Rare View (@ the
  Shelbourne Murray Hill
  Hotel)
Red Bench
The Red Cat
Redemption
Relish
Remy Lounge
Republic
Rhone
Rialto
Ribot
Rice Republic
Rise (@ the Ritz-Carlton)
Rock Candy
Rogue
Romi Restaurant & Lounge
Room 18
The Room
Rosa Mexicano
Round Bar (@ Royalton
  Hotel)
Roxy
Ruby Falls
Ruby Foo's Times Square
Ruby Lounge
Russian Samovar
S.O.B.'s
Saga
Sake Hana
Sala
Salon
Sambuca
Sandia
Sapa
Sapphire Lounge
Sasha's
Satalla
Savalas
Savoy
Schiller's Liquor Bar
Scopa

Sea Thai Bistro
Second Nature
Select
Serafina
Serena
17 Home
Shadow
Shag
Shalel Lounge
Shebeen
Show
Sidecar
Sin Sin
Single Room Occupancy
6s and 8s
Slate Plus
The Slipper Room
Sly
Smith & Wollensky
Snitch
SoGo NY
SoHo:323
Sortie
Spice
Spice Market
Spirit
Splash
St. Maggie's Café
St. Marks 88
The Stanton Social
Stay
Steak Frites
Stir
Stone Creek
The Stone Rose
Strata
Strip House
Suba
Suede
Sugar Bar
Sugar Bar & Lounge
SugarCane
Sui
The Sullivan Room
Supercore
Sushi Samba 7

Sushi Samba Park
Sutra
Sway
Swing 46
Table 50
Table XII (aka Etoile)
Taboon
Tai
Taj
Tamari
Tamarind
Tao
The Tapas Lounge
Tapeo 29
Taste
Tavern on the Green
Temple Bar
Temple New York
Tenement
Therapy
Thom Bar (@ 60 Thompson)
Trattoria Dopo Teatro
Tre Dici
Tribe
Trio
Triumph Room
Trousdale
Tupelo Grill
Turks & Frogs
Turquoise Seafood
 Restaurant
12:31
24-7 Bar & Lounge
Twist Lounge (@ The
 Ameritania Hotel)
2i's
203 Spring
Ulrika's
Uncle Ming's
Underbar (@ W Hotel - Union
 Sq.)
Uptown Restaurant &
 Lounge
Uva
Vapor
Verlaine

ViceVersa
Viet-Café
The View (@ the Marriott
 Marquis)
Vig Bar
Villard Bar & Lounge (@ the
 New York Palace Hotel)
Vintage
Voyage
Vudu Lounge
Wallse
wd-50
The Web
Webster Hall
Whiskey Blue
Whiskey Park
The Whiskey (@ W-Times
 Sq.)
The White Rabbit
Winebar
Wolfgang's Steakhouse
Wonderland
World Bar
XES
Xicala
XL
Xth Avenue Lounge
The Yard (@ The Soho
 Grand)
Yello
Yujin
Yumcha
Zakuro
Zanzibar
Zebulon
Zinc Bar
Zoe

Top Beer/Wine

AIX
Ara Wine Bar
Aroma
Artisanal
Balthazar
Bar 515
Bar on A (BOA)
Bar 6
Bar Veloce Chelsea
Bar Veloce East Village
Barbaluc
Barbuto
Barcade
Bayard's Blue Bar
Beekman, The
Black Sheep, The
Blind Tiger Ale House
Bolo
Boutique del Vino
Brass Moneky
Brazen Head, The
Brooklyn Brewery
Bubble Lounge
Burp Castle
Café Carlyle (@ the Carlyle)
Camaje
Canapa
Candela
Cassis
'Cesca
Chelsea Brewing Company
Cipriani's
Cloister Café
Compass
Connolly's
Crispo
Croxley Ales
Cru
David Copperfield's House of
 Beer
d.b.a.
Dekk
Dewey's Flatiron
Dive 75
Divine Bar East

Photos by Ginelle Ligon:

Apocalypse Lounge, Bar 89, Barbes, Bar-Coastal, Belmont Lounge, Big Easy, bOb, Brite Bar, Brother Jimmy's, Cellar Bar, Cody's Bar & Grill, Company, Croxley Ales, The Dead Poet, Earl's, El Poblano Sports Grill, 40/40 Club, 46 Grand, Fuelray, Gaslight Lounge, The Gate, Gatsby's Bar & Lounge, The George Keeley, G2, Laugh Lounge NYC, The Living Room, Madame X, Mannahatta, McSorley's, Mission, Peep, Red Sky, Riviera Café, Rockwood Music Hall, Ruby Falls, Ship of Fools, South's, Suede, Uncle Ming's, Uptown Restaurant & Lounge

Photos by Alecia Reddick:

Amber, Arlene's Grocery, AVA Lounge, Bao 111, Bar 288, Beast, Believe Lounge, Bleecker Street Bar, Blu Lounge, B1 Drink Club, Bourbon Street, Bubble Lounge, Cake Shop, Channel 4, Chibi's Bar, Circa Tabac, Cupping Room Café, Daddy's, Dekk, The Delancey, Don Hill's, Duff's, The Eagle, The Elephant, Fish Bar, Floyd NY, Frank's 410, The Ginger Man, Great Jones Café, Groove, Hop Devil Grill, House of Brews, Josie Wood's Pub, Julep, Kenny's Castaways, King Size, Korova Milk Bar, Kush, Lava Gina, Little Branch, Loreley, Lure Fish Bar, Marion's Continental, Mugs Ale House, Nancy Whiskey Pub, Nice Guy Eddie's, Northsix, Odea, Off the Wagon, One 91, Otto Enoteca Pizzeria, Peasant, Pianos, Royal Oak, Sake Bar Satsko, Savalas, The SkinNY, Sophie's Bar, Stir, Stone Creek, Swift Hibernian Lounge, Table XII, Tapeo 29, Trash, 12", Vudu Lounge, Waikiki Wally's, Welcome to the Johnsons, Winebar, Xicala, Xunta, Zablozki's

Photos by Patrik Rytikangas:

Absolutely 4th, Amuse, Bar Americain, Biltmore Room, Black Door, Blue Mill Tavern, Brass Monkey, Caliente Cab Co., Cedar Tavern, Coppersmith's, Cuba Café, Fat Black Pussycat, Freemans, G Lounge, Glo, Hogs and Heifers, Holland Bar, i Restaurant & Lounge, Jacques-imo's NYC, Kemia, Level V, Lips, Live Bait, The Park, Park Bar, The Place, Porters, Quo, Rare, Reservoir, Rogue, Schiller's Liquor Bar, Scruffy Duffy's, Select, 17, Trailer Park Lounge, The Viceroy

Photos by Supong Aroonpattanachai:

King's Head Tavern, Otto's Shrunken Head, The Phoenix

Photos by Ken Derry:

O'Hanlon's

Photos by Christina Preston:

Motor City

Courtesy Photos:

A60, Ace of Clubs, APT, Aquavit, Aroma, Asia de Cuba, Balthazar, Bar 6, Bar Seine, Bar XII, B.E.D. New York, Bogart's, Bowlmor Lanes, Brandy Library, Brooklyn Brewery, Cabanas, Capone's, Caviar and Banana Braserio, Continental, Danube, Dos Caminos, Dream Lounge, Duvet, El Faro, Galapagos Art Space, The Garden of Ono, Grand Bar and Lounge, Grotta Azzura, The Harrison, Hiro, Indochine, Katwalk, Keybar, Kitchen & Cocktails, Latitude, M Bar, Marquee, Maya Lounge, Metropol, MJ Armstrong's, Movida, One, Peter McManus, Piola, Prey, Ribot, Rock Candy, Sandia, Sapa, Sly, Smoked, Stain, Stout NYC, Temple Bar, Therapy, Thom Bar, Turquoise Seafood Restaurant, UK New York, Whiskey Blue, Yumcha

For photo credits please contact the venue directly.